PHP
Professional Projects

PHP
Professional Projects

Ashish Daniel Wilfred
Meeta Gupta
Kartik Bhatnagar

WITH

NIIT

Premier
Press

Premier

Press

The Premier Press logo, top edge printing, and related trade dress are trademarks of Premier Press, Inc. and may not be used without written permission. All other trademarks are the property of their respective owners.

Important: Premier Press cannot provide software support. Please contact the appropriate software manufacturer's technical support line or Web site for assistance.

Premier Press and the author have attempted throughout this book to distinguish proprietary trademarks from descriptive terms by following the capitalization style used by the manufacturer.

Information contained in this book has been obtained by Premier Press from sources believed to be reliable. However, because of the possibility of human or mechanical error by our sources, Premier Press, or others, the Publisher does not guarantee the accuracy, adequacy, or completeness of any information and is not responsible for any errors or omissions or the results obtained from use of such information. Readers should be particularly aware of the fact that the Internet is an ever-changing entity. Some facts may have changed since this book went to press.

ISBN: 1-931841-53-5

Library of Congress Catalog Card Number: 2001097644

Printed in the United States of America

02 03 04 05 06 RI 10 9 8 7 6 5 4 3 2 1

Publisher:
Stacy L. Hiquet

Marketing Manager:
Heather Buzzingham

Managing Editor:
Sandy Doell

Editorial Assistant:
Margaret Bauer

Book Production Services:
Argosy

Cover Design:
Mike Tanamachi

About NIIT

NIIT is a global IT solutions corporation with a presence in 38 countries. With its unique business model and technology-creation capabilities, NIIT delivers software and learning solutions to more than 1,000 clients across the world.

The success of NIIT's training solutions lies in its unique approach to education. NIIT's Knowledge Solutions Business conceives, researches, and develops all of its course material. A rigorous instructional design methodology is followed to create engaging and compelling course content.

NIIT trains over 200,000 executives and learners each year in information technology areas using stand-up training, video-aided instruction, computer-based training (CBT), and Internet-based training (IBT). NIIT has been featured in the Guinness Book of World Records for the largest number of learners trained in one year!

NIIT has developed over 10,000 hours of instructor-led training (ILT) and over 3,000 hours of Internet-based training and computer-based training. IDC ranked NIIT among the Top 15 IT training providers globally for the year 2000. Through the innovative use of training methods and its commitment to research and development, NIIT has been in the forefront of computer education and training for the past 20 years.

Quality has been the prime focus at NIIT. Most of the processes are ISO-9001 certified. It was the 12th company in the world to be assessed at Level 5 of SEI-CMM. NIIT's Content (Learning Material) Development facility is the first in the world to be assessed at this highest maturity level. NIIT has strategic partnerships with companies such as Computer Associates, IBM, Microsoft, Oracle, and Sun Microsystems.

About the Authors

Ashish Daniel Wilfred is Microsoft Certified in Visual Basic 6.0, Visual C++, Windows NT 4.0 Server, and Windows NT Workstation 4. He has worked for the past three years at NIIT Ltd. For the past two years, he has been working as a development executive in the Knowledge Solutions Business (KSB) division of NIIT. During his tenure at KSB, Ashish has had the opportunity to work on varied technical assignments. His work involves designing, developing, testing, and implementing of instructor-led training courses. He has developed learning materials for audiences with profiles ranging from network administrators to programmers. He developed learning materials on a wide range of technologies such as Windows 2000, Windows XP, SQL, Cisco, and Office XP. The learning materials were developed on different media such as ILTs, CBTs, WBTs, and books for various NIIT clients such as Microsoft, Course Technology, and Premier Press. Ashish also possesses experience in networking at NIIT Ltd. Before joining KSB, he was the network administrator at the School for Employee Education and Development (SEED), a division of NIIT.

Meeta Gupta has a masters degree in computer engineering. At NIIT Ltd., she designs, develops, and authors books on a variety of subjects. She has co-authored books on TCP/IP, A+ Certification, Visual C#, ASP.NET, and Storage Area Networks (SANs). She also has extensive experience in designing and developing ILTs. Besides writing, Meeta has two years of experience in training and instruction. She was involved with the CEG division of NIIT Ltd, which is a premier institute for providing computer-related knowledge to a wide range of clients—from students to corporations.

Kartik Bhatnagar is a Microsoft Certified Professional (MCP) with an MBA in systems and is currently employed as a development executive with NIIT. His work involves design, development, testing, and implementation of instructor-led training courses and textbooks. Kartik has developed several instructor-led training courses on Macintosh OS 9.0, Cisco Security, and Windows 2000 Server. He has done extensive research and implementation of Cisco Security, Windows 2000 Security, and Oracle Applications. He has authored a book on Public Key Infrastructure (PKI).

Contents at a Glance

Contents

Introduction

Goal of the Book

This book provides a hands-on approach to learning PHP: Hypertext Preprocessor, which is a server-side scripting language. The book is aimed at both novice as well as advance level readers. Readers might only have the basic knowledge of HTML or might already know Web-based programming. The readers will use the PHP concepts that they learn in the book to create professional projects.

The book starts with a few overview chapters that cover the key concepts of Web-based programming. These chapters act as an information store for programmers who may need to brush up their prior programming knowledge. A major part of the book revolves around professional projects. These projects enable programmers to learn about various tasks by following a simple to complex approach. Each project covers a specific subject area and guides the readers by using practical scenarios. The projects range from a simple project that involves creating plain data entry Web pages using HTML and saving the information in a text file. Then the books moves to complex projects that involve creating Web pages containing PHP scripts and storing information in MySQL databases. These projects help programmers to accomplish their goals by understanding the practical and real-life application of PHP in Web page designing. Each project in the book is a guide for the reader to create a part of a large Web site.

Apart from the overview chapters and the professional projects, this book also includes two additional sections, Beyond the Lab and Appendices. The Beyond the Lab section serves as both a summary of what the reader has learned throughout the projects and as a road map for where the reader can go to expand on this knowledge. This section also covers the future direction of the programming language. The Appendices act as a quick reference for PHP functions and certain concepts that a reader might want to explore further.

Why PHP?

Customers on the Web no longer want to view static Web pages. Nowadays, more and more customers seek dynamic Web pages that provide up-to-date information. Dynamic Web pages involve the use of Web databases. The use of Web based databases in Web page development requires developers to have an in-depth knowledge of both, databases and the Web, since Web database application development is a synthesis of the two technologies.

The increased demand for Web-based databases is fundamentally due to increasing popularity of the Client/Server technology in business applications. This technology is used by e-Markets to provide all their customers latest information about their products on the Web site. This has also introduced the concept of online shopping in which a purchase made by one customer is automatically updated in a central database. This information then reflects on the number of goods available for the rest of the users.

This book provides an in-depth look at basic programming concepts, database concepts, file handling concepts, and creating dynamic Web pages using PHP. Using PHP is an excellent choice if you want to use a language that is fast, flexible, and simple to use.

A basic Web database application requires a database server, a Web server, and a Web browser to function. The Web server and the database server perform the server-side processing while the Web browser forms the client side. The database server stores and displays information on the Web, and the Web server processes the PHP codes. The Web browser transfers information between a client and the Web server.

Technology Required

There are certain software requirements that you need to fulfill before you can create server-side scripts. The first requirement is a Web server that you should install on your machine. For a Windows operating system you might use IIS, while for a Linux system you may use an Apache Web server. For the purpose of this book, I have used Linux as the operating system and an Apache server as the Web server. Apache controls a large percentage of the Web server market. Another software that you need to install on the server is the PHP language interpretator. This is a freely downloadable component that can be downloaded from the location `http://www.php.net`. The documentation for PHP is also available on the same site. You will also learn about installing and configuring PHP in chapter 2 of the book.

You also require the use of a relational database to run the codes provided in the book. We have used the relational database MySQL to run the codes in the books. Although you have the choice of other databases, the justification of using MySQL will be explained later in the book. For writing the actual code, you only require the use of a simple test editor such as Notepad, Editpad, or gnotepad.

PHP scripts are saved with a .php extension and are referred to in the HTML Web page. On the client side, you have the choice of using either Netscape Communicator or Internet Explorer.

Focus of This Book

PHP is freely available and downloadable. Developers can modify the code based on their requirements. This book aims at introducing you to all the basic concepts that you need to know to create an effective Web page that has dynamic content. After you have mastered the basic concepts, you can experiment with the language to create new features. Some of the fundamental concepts you will be introduced to are:

◆ The use of variable, constants, and operators in server-side scripts

◆ The use of control structures, arrays, and functions in server-side scripts

◆ Introduction to basic HTML elements and using them to create a Web page

◆ Reading and Writing to text file by using a Web page

◆ Introduction to database concepts and data handling using MySQL

◆ Creating an e-commence site

◆ Introduction to advanced concepts such as PEAR and PHP-NUKE

How to Use This Book

This book has been organized to facilitate a better grasp of content covered in the book. The various conventions used in the book include the following:

◆ **Analysis.** The book incorporates an analysis of code, explaining what it did and why, line-by-line.

◆ **Tips.** Tips have been used to provide special advice or unusual shortcuts with the product.

◆ **Notes.** Notes give additional information that may be of interest to the reader, but it is not essential to performing the task at hand.

◆ **Cautions.** Cautions are used to warn users of possible disastrous results if they perform a task incorrectly.

◆ **New term definitions.** All new terms have been italicized and then defined as a part of the text.

PART I

PHP Overview

Chapter 1

PHP Introduction

PHP Basics

Surfing the Web for information can be a boring or a pleasant experience depending on the user friendliness, visual appeal, and interactivity of the Web page. If you have been surfing the Web for quite some time now, you might have noticed that the appearance and functionality of Web pages have undergone a sea change. Gone are the days when a Web page comprised just a few static graphics and some textual information. Today, Web pages have a lot more to offer than just displaying information in a jazzy or eye-catching way. It is the level of interactivity and dynamism that distinguishes one Web page from another and thus affects pages' popularity.

Interactivity and dynamism, in the present-day scenario, are considered the most fundamental features of any Web page besides the obvious visual appeal. To incorporate these features in Web pages, scripting languages today are focusing more on Web-based applications.

 NOTE

Scripting languages have been in existence since the 1960s. The first most widely used scripting language was Job Control Language (JCL), which was used in the 1960s to control and arrange data flow in card decks for OS/360. Since then, as a result of technological advancements and ever-changing customer requirements, scripting languages have improved immensely, in terms of both their power and their functionality.

Some of the most common scripting languages that are used today for the Web are Perl, Tcl, Python, and JavaScript. However, one name that stands out among all these scripting languages is PHP. It is a relatively simple language and a much younger one than others of the same class. In this chapter you will learn how PHP scores over other languages and get to know some of the features of PHP that have made PHP the choice of millions of Web developers. PHP has gained widespread popularity and acceptance in the Web-developing community because of its powerful functionality and ease of use.

PHP Primer

PHP stands for Hypertext Pre-Processor. As is suggested by the name, PHP is a pre-processor for hypertext. Being a pre-processor, PHP runs on a remote Web server to process a Web page before it is loaded in a browser. Despite its powerful features, PHP is quite a simple language that has been designed specifically for developing and working with Web pages. Its syntax is similar to that of C and Perl. However, knowledge of both of these languages is not a prerequisite for getting started with PHP, so you can rest easy. It is an open-source software and can be downloaded for free.

One of the foremost reasons for the success of PHP, in addition to other factors such as simplicity and powerful features, is its low entry barrier. Even non-programmers or starters can create their Web sites with ease by using PHP. This probably explains the existence of over five million PHP-based Web sites on the Internet.

I have said much about the popularity of PHP, without discussing some of the fundamental features of PHP that have contributed to this popularity. These features are discussed next.

Fundamental Features of PHP

PHP includes the strengths of relatively older languages, such as Perl and Tcl, and does away with their weaknesses. Although it is known for its advanced features, its fundamental features should be considered first. The advanced features of PHP will be discussed later in the chapter under the topic "PHP 4: The Latest Version."

- ◆ It is an open source, server-side scripting language.
- ◆ It is operating-system independent and thus can be used on any operating system, including Microsoft Windows, Mac OS, Linux, HP-UX, and Solaris, to name a few.
- ◆ It supports a wide range of Web servers, such as Apache, Microsoft Internet Information Server, Netscape, and iPlanet.
- ◆ It supports a large number of databases, such as MySQL, Ingres, Sybase, Oracle, Base, Informix, FrontBase, and Unix dbm. One of the distinctive

features of PHP is that it provides support to database-driven e-commerce Web sites.

◆ It is simpler to write codes in PHP than in other scripting languages.

◆ It can be used for creating images, reading/writing files, and sending e-mail. To provide these services, PHP communicates with many protocols, such as HTTP, POP3, SNMP, LDAP, and IMAP.

Now that you're acquainted with the fundamental features of PHP, you will learn about the evolution of PHP.

Evolution of PHP

Rasmus Lerdorf developed PHP in the year 1994. He incorporated this unreleased version of PHP into his home page. He used this version to monitor the number of users who accessed his online resume. No one knew about the existence of PHP until early 1995, when the first version of PHP was released. It was then known as Personal Home Page Tools.

Personal Home Page: PHP's First Released Version

When PHP was first released for developers in early 1995, it was known as Personal Home Page Tools. This version of PHP comprised a *parser* engine that supported a few special macros and some utilities that were commonly used in home pages. This made PHP a popular choice among developers for creating and enhancing their home pages. PHP allowed developers to add some common functionality, such as guest books and counters, to their Web pages.

 NOTE

A parser is a program that breaks the source code into an object code. A parser is usually a part of the compiler and it receives input in the form of source program code, markup tags, or online commands. The parser breaks this input to yield objects and methods. These objects and methods can then be managed by other components of the compiler. A compiler is a program that converts programming language into machine language.

PHP/FI: PHP's Second Version

In mid-1995, Rasmus wrote the parser again and renamed it PHP/FI Version 2. The FI in PHP/FI stands for Form Interpreter. This FI was a part of the package developed by Rasmus that could interpret HTML form data. However, PHP/FI did not contain only the Personal Home Page tools scripts and FI. In addition, it included support for mSQL. Thus, the combination of Personal Home Page tools scripts, Form Interpreter, and mSQL resulted in the second version of PHP, or PHP/FI.

Because of its powerful features and built-in database support, PHP/FI did not take long to get noticed, and soon people started working on it to find ways to improve it and add more functionality to it. Such was the popularity of PHP/FI that people even started to contribute their code to it. The rise in popularity of PHP/FI can be gauged from the fact that in late 1996 an estimated 15,000 Web sites used PHP/FI and by mid-1997 this number had swelled to more than 50,000 Web sites.

After PHP/FI came PHP 3, with more powerful and enhanced features.

PHP 3: PHP's Third Version

Until mid-1997, PHP was limited to only a few people who had contributed their code to it—and, of course, to Rasmus, who had conceived it. However, given the speed with which PHP/FI gained recognition and popularity, it soon became the effort of a much bigger, well-coordinated, and systematic team. The parser was completely rewritten from scratch. This new parser, written by Zeev Suraski and Andi Gutmans, formed the very core of the third version of PHP, known as PHP 3. PHP 3 contained a considerable number of new features, and within no time people started using it for developing Web applications.

The combination of PHP 3, Apache, and MySQL soon became an instant hit and was considered the choice for developing Web pages. In addition to improved performance and other features, one more factor that made this combination an ideal one was that all three technologies were open-source technologies and were freely available. Thus, the problems of obtaining licenses and other hassles were completely eliminated.

Although Apache and MySQL are considered ideal and are the preferred software for use with PHP, this does not mean that PHP is not compatible with other software. It provides an equal degree of support to a variety of Web servers, such as Microsoft Internet Information Server (IIS), Personal Web Server (PWS), iPlanet servers, Oreilly Website Pro server, and Caudium. PHP provides support to a large number of databases. In fact, PHP's support for such a large number of databases is one of its strongest and most significant features. The databases supported by PHP include Adabas, Oracle, Ingres, interBase, FrontBase, Empress, Ovrimos, PostgreSQL, FilePro (read-only), mSQL, Solid, Hyperwave, Direct MS-SQL, Sybase, IBM DB2, Unix dbm, Informix, and Velocis.

The latest version of PHP is PHP 4. This version was introduced in a more complex environment where Web development was not just about writing hard-coded HTML pages. Web applications were needed to be dynamic and interactive, and to provide support for database interactivity. Web applications were developed in such a manner that multiple users could send and retrieve data at the same time. In addition, the time to retrieve data or even load a page was also under consideration. According to a survey based on traditional human factors guidelines, 10 seconds is the maximum response time that the users can wait patiently for a Web page to load; beyond this they tend to lose interest. In addition, if even a single JavaScript error is detected on a Web page, a user is most likely to leave the Web page immediately.

Now you will learn about PHP 4 in detail.

PHP 4: The Latest Version

PHP 4, the latest version of PHP, has a lot of new features that allow it to deliver higher performance and to provide support to an ever-larger range of extensions and libraries. PHP 4 is fast becoming a de facto industry standard for developing Web pages. According to a recent survey conducted by Security Space (www.securityspace.com), PHP has emerged as the most popular and widely used scripting language. In October 2001, there were an estimated 1,107,914 PHP users as against 328,856 Perl users, 473,053 Open SSL users, and 1,873 mod_python users. Some of the most common and yet important factors that contributed to the success and rise of PHP are:

◆ PHP 4 is available for free download from PHP's official Web site. In addition, most software that is used with PHP, such as Apache and MySQL, is also available free of cost.

◆ PHP is an open-source software. When I say that PHP is open-source software, I do not want to imply that there is any lack of support available for developers who choose PHP for Web development. The advice of several developers who have tried and tested applications using PHP is available free of cost on the Internet.

◆ A lot of PHP support documents are available free of cost on the Internet.

◆ Given the enormous number of users who are using PHP, there are numerous mailing lists that you can join. You can then post your problems or take part in discussion forums to solve the problems you are facing.

◆ There is a dedicated team of volunteer experts who immediately rectify any bugs that are reported or detected in PHP. These experts are the people who are involved with the development of PHP language. They are not affiliated with any organization. If you encounter any bugs in PHP, you can report these bugs at the official site of PHP, **www.php.net/**. This site provides you with all the help you'll need for reporting a bug and contacting the experts.

◆ In terms of its performance, you can compare PHP with Active Server Pages (ASP). PHP is popular on Linux platforms, as ASP is popular on Windows. However, cross-platform support provided by PHP makes it score over ASP. PHP can be used as effectively on Windows platforms as on any other platform.

◆ Unlike many other scripting languages, such as ASP, PHP comes with a built-in compiler that compiles PHP code and can detect errors in it. You can rectify the mistakes in your PHP code based on the mistakes pointed out by the compiler. No such compiler that compiles ASP code is available with ASP.

◆ Another significant feature of PHP is its portability. PHP is compatible with any combination of software, and this is what makes it portable. It can work with almost any combination of operating system, Web server, and database server.

Now that you're familiar with the success factors of PHP, it's time to review the new and advanced features that have been added in PHP 4.

- Support for Boolean datatype.

- Support for Java and XML.

- Support for COM/DCOM. This support is available only for Windows.

- Support for FTP.

- The "= = =" operator. In addition to checking whether or not the two values are equal, this operator also checks whether the datatypes of these values are the same or not.

- The ability to call a function even before it is declared. This is accomplished by using the runtime binding of functions in PHP 4.

- The PHP highlighter. This feature enables you to view the source code instead of the complete script. This feature helps you to have a faster and better look at the source code.

- Support for variable assignment by reference. This helps you to link two variables so that the value of one variable is dependent on the value of the other variable. Thus, the value of the variable is updated automatically whenever a value is assigned to another variable.

- Server API (SAPI). This feature further enhances the support for Web servers.

- Support for many algorithms, namely Triple DES, MD5, Blowfish, and SHA1. Through the mcrypt library, PHP 4 supports full encryption.

- The ability to reference variables in PHP 4 by using quotes. Additionally, variable expansion is supported using double quotes.

Additional improvements to PHP 4 include:

- In PHP 4, all syntax limitations that existed in PHP 3 have been overcome.

- GET, POST methods in PHP 4 support multi-dimensional arrays.

- In PHP 4, the php.ini file is simple to understand and configure.

- In PHP 4, better ways of creating classes and objects have been introduced.

Introduction to PHP Programming

As discussed earlier, PHP is an open-source, server-side scripting language. What I didn't mention, on purpose, was the fact that it is also an embedded CGI language. This certainly will raise some eyebrows! Now, PHP is an embedded language in the sense that it is enclosed within tags and you can easily switch between PHP and HTML without having to use large amounts of code to output HTML. Common Gateway Interface (CGI) allows you to write computer programs, which can generate HTML and can dynamically process data from Web pages. Before the advent of CGI, you had no option but to create static HTML pages and to keep updating them. Since PHP is a server-side language, you do not need any special browser plug-in or program to run a PHP-enabled Web page. PHP supports all major Web browsers and provides you with tools to build dynamic Web pages.

PHP might be classified as a CGI; however, it imbibes in itself all the characteristics of a complete programming language, such as loop structures, control structures, repetitive tasks, variables, and conditional statements. I will, of course, be dealing with all these features and much more in later chapters.

The three areas where PHP is used are:

- ◆ **Server-side scripting:** PHP is most commonly used as a server-side scripting language. To make PHP work as a server-side scripting language, all you need is a PHP parser, a Web server, and a Web browser. However, the Web server has to have a connected PHP installation.

- ◆ **Building client-side GUI applications:** Although this is not a preferred use of PHP, with a very good working knowledge of PHP you can build your own client-side GUI applications. You can use PHP-GTK, an extension of PHP, which provides an object-oriented interface for building client-side GUI applications.

- ◆ **Command-line scripting:** Your PHP script can run without any browser or server. In this way, it can be used as a simple and easy-to-use scripting language for tasks such as managing databases and messaging files.

After having read so much about the features of PHP, you must by now be quite eager to actually get started with PHP scripting. Without more ado, you may begin. You'll use the customary "Hello World" example. (Isn't the popularity of this example amazing? This single example has been to software developers what "Twinkle Twinkle, Little Star" has been to all children.)

The simplest HTML code that you might be aware of goes like this:

```
1.          <html>
2.          <head>
3.          <title> Hello World</title>
4.          </head>
5.          <body>
6.          Hello World
7.          </body>
8.          </html>
```

It can't get any simpler than this!

Now see how PHP can be embedded into this HTML code:

```
1.          <html>
2.          <head>
3.          <title> Hello World</title>
4,          </head>
5.          <body>
6.          <?php
7.          echo "Hello, World";
8.          ?>
9.          Hello World
10.         </body>
11.         </html>
```

Most of the preceding code is quite similar to the first example discussed, except for the piece of code that is written between line numbers 6 and 8. This piece of code is the actual PHP code.

 TIP

You can also use just <? and ?> to start and end the code.

Hence, the basic PHP code can be written as:

```php
<?php
echo "Hello, World";
?>
```

This produces the output:

```
Hello, World
```

Notice here that instead of writing enormous amounts of code to output HTML, writing only a few PHP commands—just three in the preceding example—does the job.

Summary

In this chapter, you were introduced to PHP. You learned that PHP is an open-source, embedded server-side scripting language. You learned that because of its powerful, flexible, and simple features, PHP is fast becoming the choice of Web developers today. You learned about the evolution of PHP. Finally, you learned the basics of PHP programming.

Chapter 2

Installing and Configuring PHP

In the previous chapter I introduced you to PHP. You learned that PHP is an open-source, server-side scripting language. You also learned that it is independent of various operating systems and therefore can be used on any operating system, including Microsoft Windows, Mac OS, Linux, HP-UX, and Solaris. In addition, you can run PHP in any software combination.

In this chapter you will learn to install and configure PHP on two popular platforms, Windows and Linux.

Let me first tell you how to install and configure PHP on the Windows platform.

Installing PHP on Windows 2000

When you install PHP on a Windows platform, you can choose from a number of options, such as using Apache and MySQL with Windows or using a combination of Microsoft SQL Server 2000 and IIS. This section details the steps that you need to perform to configure PHP on Windows 2000 Server. These steps will also include the configuration of IIS Web Server. This is important because configuring IIS Web Server for PHP allows you to open PHP files in the native browser of Windows, Internet Explorer.

To install PHP on Windows, you need to perform the following steps:

1. From the URL **www.php.net**, download PHP 4.1.0 installer.exe. You will use this installer file to install PHP on Windows.

 NOTE

You should choose the latest version of the installer file available at the time you read this book.

2. Navigate to the location on your system where you have downloaded the file, and then double-click on the installer file to start the installation of

PHP. The name of the file will appear as php410-installer. The PHP installer wizard starts and the Welcome screen appears, as shown in Figure 2-1.

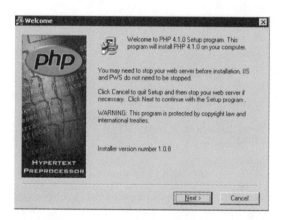

FIGURE 2-1 *PHP installer wizard Welcome screen*

3. Click on Next. The License Agreement screen appears, as shown in Figure 2-2. Read the PHP License Agreement.

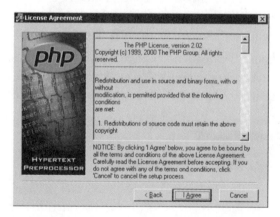

FIGURE 2-2 *The License Agreement screen*

4. Click on I Agree if you concur with the terms and conditions of the License Agreement. The Installation Type screen appears, as shown in Figure 2-3.

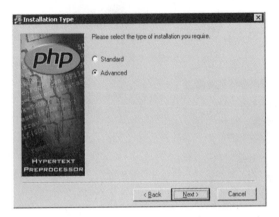

FIGURE 2-3 *The Installation Type screen*

By default, Standard is selected as the installation type. Choose the Advanced installation type option. When you choose Advanced, the wizard gives you the option to create backups of the files that are replaced during the installation. Choose a directory that can be used as a temporary directory for uploading files. Then choose a session-save directory for storing session data, and choose an appropriate error-displaying level. You'll also need to choose an appropriate file extension that you want PHP to interpret. However, remember that these options will not be available if you choose Standard as the installation type.

5. Click on Next. The Choose Destination Location screen appears, as shown in Figure 2-4. In this screen you can either select a destination folder where you want to install PHP 4.1.0 or install PHP at the default location.

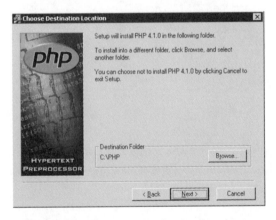

FIGURE 2-4 *The Choose Destination Location screen*

6. Click on Next to install PHP at the default location. The Backup
   Replaced Files screen appears, as shown in Figure 2-5. When you install
   PHP, some of your files may be replaced. To keep these replaced files,
   choose the option of making a backup and select a location for storing
   the backup.

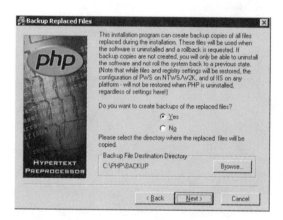

FIGURE 2-5 *The Backup Replaced Files screen*

7. Click on Next to retain the default location of the Backup File directory.
   The Choose Upload Temporary Directory screen appears, as shown in
   Figure 2-6. In this screen you can choose a directory to be used as a
   temporary directory for uploading your files.

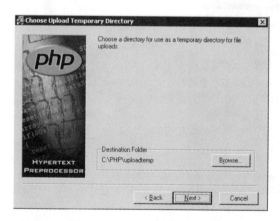

FIGURE 2-6 *The Choose Upload Temporary Directory screen*

8. Click on Next to retain the default location of the temporary directory for file uploads. The Choose Session Save Directory screen appears, as shown in Figure 2-7. In this screen you can choose a directory for storing data for a session.

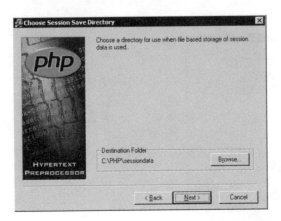

FIGURE 2-7 *The Choose Session Save Directory screen*

9. Click on Next to retain the default location of the Session Save Directory. The Mail Configuration screen appears, as shown in Figure 2-8. In this screen you can specify your SMTP server address to configure mail on PHP.

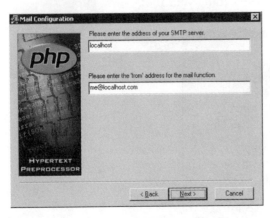

FIGURE 2-8 *The Mail Configuration screen*

10. Click on Next. The Error Reporting Level screen appears, as shown in Figure 2-9. In this screen you have different options for choosing the level of error reporting. Select the first option. The first option is "Display all error warnings and notices." If you choose the second option, which is "Display all errors and warnings," PHP will issue only error and warning messages, but no notices. On the other hand, if you choose the last option, which is "Display all errors," you will not get any warning messages or notices, but only error messages. As you observed in the screen, PHP recommends that you select the first option while developing Web pages.

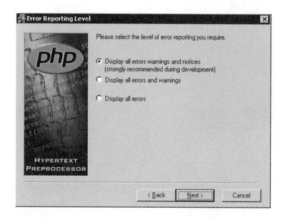

FIGURE 2-9 *The Error Reporting Level screen*

11. Click on Next. The Server Type screen appears, as shown in Figure 2-10. By default, "Microsoft IIS 4 or higher" is selected.

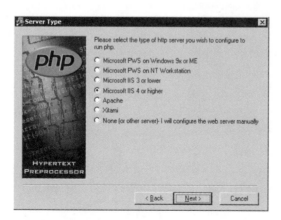

FIGURE 2-10 *The Server Type screen*

12. Click on Next to retain Microsoft IIS 4 as the HTTP server. The File Extensions screen appears, as shown in Figure 2-11. You can choose the type of file extension that you want your PHP to interpret. You can choose either .php, .phtml(deprecated), or .php3(deprecated). By default, .php is selected.

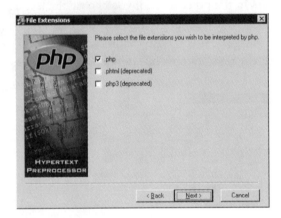

FIGURE 2-11 *The File Extensions screen*

13. Click on Next to retain the default file extension type. The Start Installation screen appears, as shown in Figure 2-12.

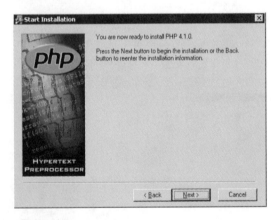

FIGURE 2-12 *The Start Installation screen*

14. Click on Next to install PHP.

15. If your computer already has an earlier version of PHP running, you may be prompted to retain the earlier version of the php.ini file. Click on No to proceed.

16. While PHP is being installed, the IIS ScriptMap Node Selection screen appears, as shown in Figure 2-13. The screen prompts you to choose a scriptmap mode to which your PHP file extensions will be mapped. Select WWW Service Master Properties.

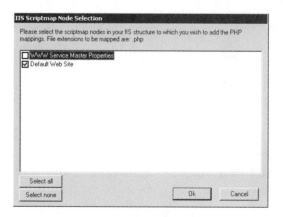

FIGURE 2-13 *The IIS ScriptMap Node Selection screen*

17. Click on OK. The Installation complete dialog box appears, as shown in Figure 2-14. The dialog box indicates that PHP 4.1.0 has been successfully installed.

FIGURE 2-14 *The Installation complete dialog box*

18. Click on OK to exit the PHP installation wizard.

After you perform these steps, you need to verify that PHP has been successfully installed. You can do so by verifying that IIS is functioning properly and that the PHP code is being executed.

Verifying PHP Installation

You need to perform the following steps to verify successful configuration of IIS for PHP and execution of the PHP code.

1. Create a .php file—for instance, test.php. This file should contain the PHP code:

   ```
   <?
   phpinfo();
   ?>
   ```

2. After you have created the .php file, you need to save the file in C:\Inetpub\wwwroot.

3. Open Internet Explorer. In the Address box, specify the address of the file as http://localhost/test.php.

Output of the test.php file is illustrated in Figure 2-15.

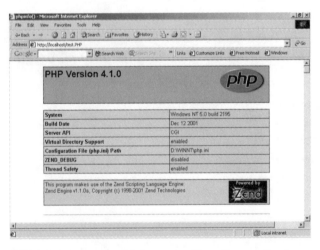

FIGURE 2-15 *Output of the test.php file on Internet Explorer*

If you want to install an earlier version of PHP (that is, one of the versions that were released before the current version of PHP—which is version 4.1.0 as of this writing) you will have to configure IIS for PHP. Without configuring IIS for PHP, you will not be able to get the output of the PHP programs in the browser window.

Let me now tell you how to configure IIS 4.0 for PHP.

Configuring IIS 4.0 for PHP

To configure IIS 4.0 for PHP, you need to perform the following steps:

1. Choose Start, Programs, Administrative Tools, and Internet Services Manager to open the Internet Information Services window, as shown in Figure 2-16.

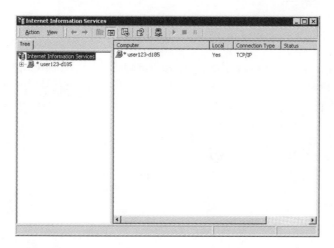

FIGURE 2-16 *Internet Information Services window*

2. In the left pane of the Internet Information Services window, under Internet Information Services, expand the computer name, as shown in Figure 2-17, to display the available Internet Information Services on your computer.

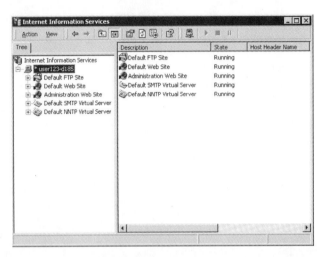

FIGURE 2-17 *Available Internet Information Services on your computer*

3. Under the computer name, right-click on the Default Web Site option and choose Properties from the shortcut menu. The Default Web Site Properties dialog box appears, as shown in Figure 2-18. You will now set properties to configure IIS for PHP.

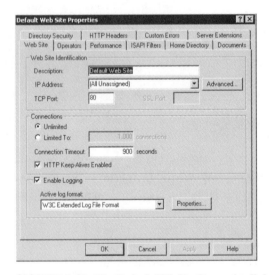

FIGURE 2-18 *The Default Web Site Properties dialog box*

4. In the Default Web Site Properties dialog box, activate the ISAPI Filters tab, as shown in Figure 2-19.

FIGURE 2-19 *The ISAPI Filters tab*

5. Click on Add to open the Filter Properties dialog box, as shown in Figure 2-20. In the Filter Name text box, specify the filter name as php. In the Executable text box, specify the path for the php4isapi.dll file by clicking on Browse, navigating to C:\PHP\sapi, and clicking on Open.

FIGURE 2-20 *The Filter Properties dialog box*

6. Click on OK to close the Filter Properties dialog box.

7. Activate the Home Directory tab, as shown in Figure 2-21.

FIGURE 2-21 *The Home Directory tab*

8. Under Application Settings, click on Configuration to open the Application Configuration dialog box, as shown in Figure 2-22. Verify that the App Mappings tab is active.

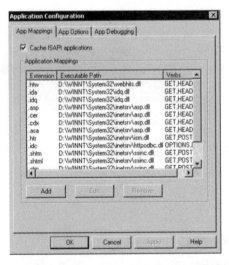

FIGURE 2-22 *The Application Configuration dialog box*

9. Click on Add to open the Add/Edit Application Extension Mapping dialog box, as shown in Figure 2-23. Click on Browse and navigate to

the php4isapi.dll file. Click on Open to specify the complete file path. In the Extension box, specify the extension for the .php files. Verify that the Script engine option is selected. Click on OK to close the Add/Edit Application Extension Mapping dialog box.

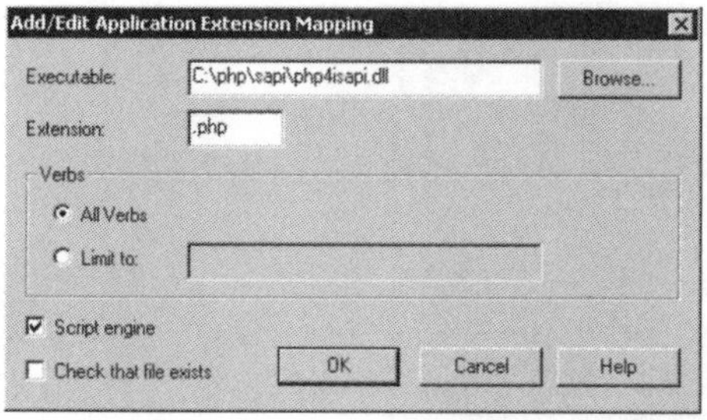

FIGURE 2-23 *The Add/Edit Application Extension Mapping dialog box*

10. Click on OK to close the Application Configuration dialog box.

11. Click on OK to close the Default Web Site Properties dialog box.

12. Close the Internet Information Services dialog box.

13. Choose Start, Run to open the Run dialog box. At the command prompt, type cmd to open the Command Prompt window.

14. At the command prompt, type net stop iisadmin to stop all IIS-related services. A message appears, as shown in Figure 2-24, giving a list of services that will also be stopped when IIS Admin Service service is stopped.

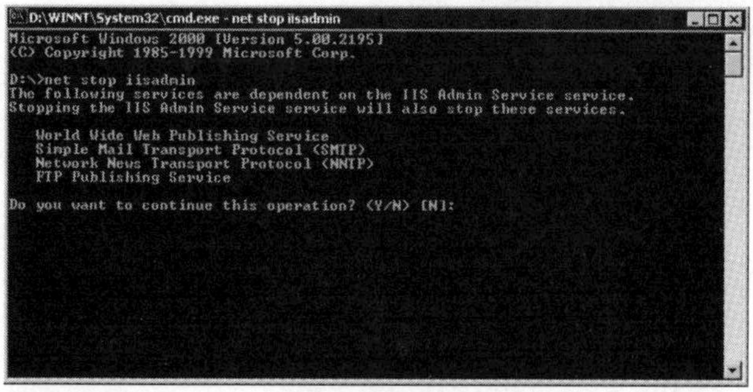

FIGURE 2-24 *Stopping the IIS Admin Service service*

15. Type y to stop the IIS Admin Service service. When all IIS-related services and IIS Admin Service services are stopped, you will receive the message that the IIS Admin Service service was stopped successfully, as is shown in Figure 2-25.

FIGURE 2-25 *Successful stoppage of IIS Admin Service service*

16. To restart the IIS Admin Service service, type net start iisadmin in the Command Prompt window. A message appears stating that the IIS Admin Service service was successfully started.

17. To start the World Wide Web Publishing service, in the Command Prompt window type net start w3svc, as shown in Figure 2-26.

FIGURE 2-26 *Restarting the World Wide Web Publishing service*

18. Type exit to close the Command Prompt window.

This completes the process of PHP installation on the Windows platform.

In the next section, you will learn how to configure PHP on the Linux platform.

Installing PHP on the Linux Platform

I have already talked about the compatibility of PHP and its multi-platform support in the previous chapter. However, the most widely used, and inarguably the best, software combination for PHP is using Apache and MySQL on a Linux platform. In this section, I will discuss the steps that are required to configure PHP to work with Apache and MySQL in Linux.

 NOTE

When you install Red Hat Linux, you are provided with various choices for the type of installation that you want. The Custom (everything) installation of Linux is a convenient method to install Linux, as it also installs Apache, MySQL, and PHP by default. You can straightaway get down to the business of PHP programming after using the Custom (everything) installation. However, there are a couple of things that you need to keep in mind: first, the amount of disk space required by a Custom (everything) installation is 2.4 GB; second, your computer should be running the httpd service. If the httpd service is not running, you need to enable the service by giving the ntsys command. After enabling the service, you need to start the service with the following command:

```
#/etc/rc.d/init.d/httpd start.
```

If you have not performed the Custom (everything) installation on Linux, you need to install PHP separately. You can install PHP in either of two ways:

- ◆ Using Red Hat Package Manager (RPM)
- ◆ Compiling PHP from source

In the following section, I will tell you about each of these installation options in detail.

Installing PHP by Using Red Hat Package Manager (RPM)

Installing PHP by using RPM is the easiest and simplest method. This method is generally recommended for users who do not have much experience in complicated installations that involve compiling.

To start installation, you need to first download the .rpm files for the latest packages from the Web site, **www.rpmfind.com**. Alternatively, you can find these .rpm files in the Red Hat Linux CD.

After obtaining the rpm file, all you need to do to install PHP is type the following command:

```
$rpm -ivh php-4.0.6-7.i386.rpm
```

This command installs PHP on its own. Nice!

However, installing PHP by using RPM has some disadvantages. These include the following:

◆ RPM has precompiled binaries; it does not allow you to specify any compile options while installing PHP.

◆ After the RPM installation of PHP, you cannot have any kind of post-installation configurations.

In the next section, I will discuss the compilation of PHP from source.

Compiling PHP from Source

As mentioned earlier, you can also configure PHP by compiling it from source as an Apache module. To do so, you need to perform the following steps:

1. For configuring PHP by compiling it from source as an Apache module, you require two distributions, namely:

   ◆ **The apache distribution, apache _1.3.x.tar.gz.** You can download this distribution from **www.apache.org**. You use this distribution to update Apache in case it is installed using source.

   ◆ **The PHP distribution, php-4.x.y.tar.gz.** You can download this distribution from **www.php.net**. You use this distribution to install PHP.

2. After you have downloaded these two files, you need to copy the files into a directory and then navigate to that directory. Preferably, copy these files to the directory where you had earlier copied (or downloaded) files related to installation of PHP. You might save yourself some effort if you need to search for these files later.

3. Uncompress these distributions by using the following commands:

```
$tar xvfz apache_1.3.x.tar.gz
$tar xvfz php_4.x.y.tar.gz
```

Uncompressing these two files creates two directories, apache_1.3.x.y and php_4.x.y.

4. By using the command `chdir apache_1.3.x.y`, change to the newly created apache directory, which is apache_1.3.x.y.

5. (If Apache is not installed using the source distribution, you can skip this step.) Run the `./configure` script and mention all the options that are used to install Apache.

```
$ ./configure –configuration-options-for-apache
```

6. Change to the PHP directory by using the command `chdir ../php_4.x.y`.

7. Configure PHP to be used with Apache (and the basic module MySQL) by using the following command:

```
$ ./configure —with-apache=../apache_1.3.x —with
mySQL.
```

The `—with-apache` option tells PHP about the location of the Apache distributions. This option informs PHP that it will be a module for Apache.

 NOTE

If Apache is installed by using RPM, you need to execute the following command:

```
# ./configure –with-mysql –with-apxs
```

---

8. Type the following command to compile PHP distribution files:

```
$make
```

9. Install the PHP compiled files by typing the following command:

```
$ make install.
```

The above command also creates a library called src/modules/ php4/libphp4.a, which is used to configure the Apache distribution module.

 NOTE

To execute the preceding commands, you require root user privileges.

If you have installed Apache by using RPM, you can skip steps 10, 11, and 12.

10. After compiling PHP distribution files, you need to compile the Apache distribution files. Change to the Apache directory again by using the following command:

   ```
   chdir apache_1.3.x.y
   ```

   Now type the following command to obtain the necessary files from the library source module. These files are used for compiling the Apache distribution:

   ```
   $ ./configure –activate-module=src/modules/php4/
   libphp4.a –other-apache-options
   ```

11. To compile the Apache distribution, type the following command:

   ```
   $make
   ```

12. After compiling the Apache distribution, you need to install Apache (with the PHP module). Do so by typing the following command:

   ```
   $ make install
   ```

13. Start the new Apache server:

   ```
   $ /usr/local/apache/bin/apacheect1 start
   ```

14. Verify that the location of the files, namely:

   ◆ LoadModule php4_module libexec/libphp4.so

   ◆ AddModule mod_php4.c

   ◆ AddType application/x-httpd-php .php

   is set to etc/httpd/config/httpd.conf.

NOTE

You may already have the Apache server running on your computer. (This may be as a result of Linux installation). In this case, you need to stop the Apache server first. You can do so by giving the following command:

```
$ /usr/local/apache/bin/apacheect1 stop
```

If your computer does not support the above command, you can kill Apache by using the following command:

```
$ killall -9 apache
```

15. Copy the file php.ini-dist to the directory /usr/local/lib by executing the following command:

```
$ cp php.ini-dist /usr/local/lib/php/php.ini
```

16. After copying the php.ini-dist file to the desired location, you need to restart the httpd service. You can do so by specifying the following command:

```
#/etc/rc.d/init.d/httpd restart
```

To verify that PHP was configured properly, you may need to perform the following two steps:

1. In the /var/www/html directory of the root user, create a file called test.php.

2. In test.php, type the following code:

```
<?
phpinfo();
?>
```

3. Open Netscape Navigator or any other Web browser of your choice and specify the following address:

```
http://localhost/test.php
```

The following output should appear, as shown in Figure 2-27.

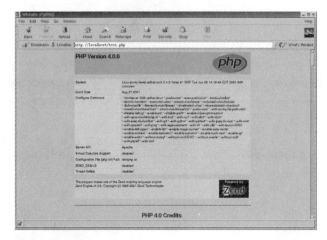

FIGURE 2-27 *The output of test.php in the Web browser window*

This completes the entire process of installation and configuration of PHP on Linux.

Summary

In this chapter you learned how to install and configure PHP on two of the most popular and commonly used platforms, Microsoft Windows and Linux. Then you learned how to configure IIS for working with PHP in the Windows environment. In addition you learned to install PHP in the Linux environment in two ways, using RPM and compiling PHP from source.

Chapter 3

Do you remember how your teachers introduced you to the concept of arithmetic in elementary class? If not, let me refresh your memory a little. Your teacher might have given you a simple example of a basket containing six tomatoes. She might have asked you to put a few more tomatoes in the basket. Then you had to calculate the total number of tomatoes added to the basket, if the final number of tomatoes was eight. For our purposes, you might equate a variable with the basket and an operator with the process of calculating the total number of tomatoes kept in the basket.

In the previous chapters you learned the basics of PHP along with installation and configuration of PHP. In this chapter you will learn about variables, operators, and constants, which are the building blocks of any programming language. The first thing you'll look at will be *variables*. Variables are an important part of writing any code, and you need to understand their use before you begin writing the code. Next you will learn about the different types of *operators* available in PHP and their use. Operators are used by variables or elements to perform calculations and to compare expressions. Finally, you will learn about *constants* and how you can use them effectively while writing your code.

Introduction to Variables

In the previous section I tried to explain the concept of variables by using an example of a vegetable basket. Let me generalize what variables actually are. *Variables* are entities that can hold different values over different periods of time.

Every programming language follows certain rules based on which variables are declared. These rules include the acceptable length of the variables, whether they can contain numeric or alphanumeric characters, whether the name of the variable can include special characters, and whether they can begin with a number. You will now look at the rules that should be followed while naming variables in PHP.

Rules for Naming Variables

In PHP, unlike some other programming languages, there is no restriction on the size of a variable name. In addition, you are free to use both numeric and alphanumeric characters in a variable name. However, there are certain rules that you need to follow. These include:

◆ Variable names should begin with a dollar ($) symbol.

◆ Variable names can begin with an underscore.

◆ Variable names cannot begin with a numeric character.

◆ Variable names must be relevant and self-explanatory.

Names like $a or $temporary might be understood and remembered while programming in the short run. However, it would be difficult to find out what they referred to later, when you or other developers look at the code after a long time.

Some examples and non-examples of variable names are:

Examples:

◆ $prod_desc

◆ $Intvar

◆ $_Salesamt

Non-examples:

◆ $9OctSales

◆ $Sales123

◆ $asgs

Now that you have learned about the rules that need to be followed while naming variables, let me explain how to declare variables in PHP.

Declaring and Initializing Variables

Declaring variables implies specifying all the variables that you plan to use within the program. In programming languages like C and C++, these variables have to be declared explicitly along with their datatypes—for example:

```
int Number=10;
```

However, in PHP you do not need to declare the datatype of the variable. You can declare a variable the first time you use it. This is because PHP does not force variables to belong to a specific datatype. The datatype of variables changes based on their content.

Initialization involves assigning values to variables. These values can belong to different datatypes. Datatypes in PHP can be divided into two types, *scalar* and *compound*. Scalar datatypes are simple datatypes that are found in most of the programming languages. These datatypes form the building blocks of a program written in any programming language. Scalar datatypes contain:

◆ string

◆ integer

◆ boolean

◆ float

On the other hand, combining multiple simple datatypes together and storing them under one name creates complex datatypes. These datatypes are known as compound datatypes, and are used to store data belonging to different datatypes and to manipulate them. Compound datatypes can contain an:

◆ array

◆ object

Let me explain these datatypes individually.

◆ **Integer.** An integer datatype can only contain whole numbers. These numbers can be either positive or negative. You use the '-' symbol before the number to represent negative integers.

◆ **String.** A string datatype is used to store a series of characters. A character is equal to a single byte of data. You can store 265 different types of characters in a string. However, in PHP there is no restriction on the size of a string.

◆ **Boolean.** A boolean datatype can only contain either True or False. If you need to refer to the numeric value of a boolean value, True is represented by 1 and False by 0. This datatype is available only in PHP4.

◆ **Float.** The float datatype is also used to store numbers. However, float values can also contain decimal numbers. You use the integer datatype to store non-decimal numbers.

◆ **Array.** An array is used to store multiple values belonging to the same datatype. You can specify the length of an array while declaring it explicitly or at runtime. Each value stored in an array is called an *element*. You reference an element of an array and access its content by referring to its position within the array. You will learn in detail about arrays in Chapter 5, "Arrays."

◆ **Objects.** Objects are the integral part of any programming language. They contain not only data but also its functionality or what needs to be done with the data.

Following are some examples of assigning values to variables:

```
                $Mystrval = "This is an example of a string value";
                $Myintval = 145665;
// An integer value
                $Myboolval = True;
// A boolean value can either be True or False
                $Myarrval[0] = "My";
//A array containing three elements
                $Myfloatval=2346.45
// A float value


                $Myarrval[1] = "First";
//All three elements are referred to by the same
                $Myarrval[2] = "Array";

// variable name.
```

In the above examples, you are directly assigning values to the variables. You can also assign values to variables by reference. Let me explain in detail about assigning values by reference.

Assigning Values to Variables by Reference

By default, each variable has its own unique value. This means that each variable has an area assigned to it in local memory that it uses to store its current value. Consider, for example, $empname=Timothy. Here the system assigns a memory location to the variable $empname, where the variable stores the value Timothy. If another variable needs to use this value, you need to assign the data explicitly. Therefore, the system needs to maintain multiple copies of the same data, which leads to data redundancy. You can avoid this by assigning value by reference. In this case, the system maintains only a single copy of the data, which is referenced by all variables that require the value. Therefore, all the variables access the same area in the memory.

You can assign a value by reference by putting an ampersand (&) symbol in front of the variable name. This assigns the memory location of the data to the variable instead of creating another copy of the data.

Now that you know the rules that should be followed while specifying a variable name, consider the different scopes of variables. The *scope* of a variable in a program is the area where you can reference the variable directly.

Scope of Variables

The scope of a variable in a program determines whether other programs can access the variable from outside the parent program or whether parts of the same program can access the variable. The parent program is the program in which the variable is defined and initialized. The scope of a variable also determines when the system creates the variable in the memory and when it destroys it.

If you declare a variable inside a function or as an argument to a function, the scope of the variable is limited to *local* scope. This means that the variable can only be assigned a value or used inside the function in which it is declared. However, if you declare the variable outside the function, the scope of the variable is *global*. This means that you can use the variable or manipulate its value in any function.

 NOTE

You use a *function* to store a piece of code together and under one name. This provides easy reusability since you only need to specify the function name whenever you need to reuse code. Using functions also helps in debugging the code, as you only need to make a change in one place. Any change made to the code is cascaded across all references of the function. This makes the code easy to follow and understand. You will learn more about functions in Chapter 6, "Functions."

In PHP, you can have either local or global variables. The scope of any variable declared within a function is by default limited to local. In PHP, a variable can be global by declaration, but it is still limited to local scope if you do not assign a value to it outside the function. In PHP, you need to declare variables as global and initialize them inside the function where they are used. This is unlike C, where a variable once defined as global is accessible within all functions. A function can contain an unlimited number of global variables. You will learn more about the variables in Chapter 6, in the section "Variable Functions and Variable Argument Functions."

Environment Variables

You might already know that most scripts or certain types of program codes execute on the client browser. However, certain types of scripts execute on a Web server; these scripts are known as *server-side scripts*. These server-side scripts use *environment variables* to pass information stored on a Web server to external programs requesting the information. These variables store information regarding the server, such as access and logon information. Although these variables are called environment variables, they are not related to the variables managed by the operating system. These variables manipulate information on the Web server. The only time these variables are used by the operating system is while passing information back to the program that had requested the information.

You can also set values for environment variables. Some of the common environment variables available in PHP and their functions are shown in Table 3-1.

Table 3-1 PHP Environment Variables and Their Functions

Variable name	Function
$argv	Contains all the arguments passed to a script from the command table text.
$argc	Contains a count of the number of arguments passed to a script from the command line.
$PHP_SELF	Contains the name of the currently executing script. However, it is not available if PHP is run from the command line.
$HTTP_GET_VARS	Contains an array of variables retrieved by using the HTTP GET method and is stored in the current script.

continues

Table 3-1 *(continued)*

Variable name	Function
$HTTP_POST_VARS	Contains an array of variables retrieved by using the HTTP POST method and is stored in the current script.
$HTTP_COOKIE_VARS	Contains an array of variables retrieved by using HTTP cookies and is stored in the current script.
$HTTP_ENV_VARS	Contains an array of variables stored in the current script by using the parent environment.
$HTTP_POST_FILES	Contains an array of variables that have information regarding uploaded files. By using the HTTP POST method, you can upload these files.
$HTTP_SERVER_VARS	Contains an array of variables passed to the current script by the HTTP server.

Now that you know about variables, let me tell you how you can further manipulate these variables. Manipulating variables involves performing mathematical, assignment, comparison, and concatenation operations on them. In order to manipulate variables, you need to use operators to perform these operations. PHP provides different types of operators to perform different tasks. The following section discusses these operators in detail.

Operators

An *operator* is a part of code that is used by one or more variables or elements to perform calculation and to compare expressions. You can use an operator to perform arithmetic, concatenation, comparison, and logical operations.

PHP provides the following operators as shown in Table 3-2:

Table 3-2 Operators Available in PHP

Operator	Used for
Arithmetic operators	Are used for mathematical calculations.
Assignment operators	Are used for assignment operations.
Comparison operators	Are used for comparisons.

Operator	Used for
Execution operators	Are used for executing the stored code as a shell command and assigning the output to a variable.
Increment/decrement operators	Are used for incrementing and decrementing values.
String operators	Are used for concatenating two expressions.
Concatenation operators	Are used for combining strings.

Now you'll learn about these operators in detail.

Arithmetic Operators

As you might have guessed from the name, you use arithmetic operators to perform mathematical calculations. Table 3-3 lists the arithmetic operators available in PHP.

Table 3-3 Arithmetic Operators Available in PHP

Operator	Name	Purpose
+	(Addition)	Calculates sum of two integers or concatenates two strings.
-	(Subtraction)	Calculates the difference between two integers.
*	(Multiplication)	Calculates the product of two integers.
/	(Division)	Calculates the quotient of two integers.
%	(Modulus)	Calculates the remainder obtained by dividing two integers.

Consider the following examples of arithmetic operators:

```
$Num1 = 9;
$Num2 = 3;
$Result = $Num1 + $Num2;        // Output $Result == 12
$Result = $Num1 - $Num2;        // Output $Result == 6
$Result = $Num1 * $Num2;        // Output $Result == 27
$Result = $Num1 / $Num2;        // Output $Result == 3
$Result = $Num1 % $Num2;        // Output $Result == 0
```

In the above example, variables $Num1 and $Num2 are assigned values and arithmetic operators are used to add, subtract, multiply, and divide these variables. For example, in the first case the value stored in the variable $Num1 is added to the value stored in the variable $Num2 and the output is stored in a variable $Result.

The Multiplication (*) Operator

The multiplication operator is used to calculate the product of two numbers. The syntax for the multiplication operator is given below:

```
$Result=$Num1*$Num2;
```

In the above syntax, PHP considers the datatype of $Num1 and $Num2 as numeric. The multiplication operator calculates the product of $Num1 and $Num2.

In the following examples, the multiplication operator is used to calculate the product of two integer values:

```
$Result=3*5; // Returns a value of 15
$Result=556.26*262.34; //Returns a value of 145929.2484
```

The Division (/) Operator

You use the division operator to divide two numbers. The operator returns the result as a float. The syntax for the division operator is given below:

```
$Result=$Num1/$Num2;
```

In the above syntax, $Num1 and $Num2 are numeric variables. The / operator returns the quotient of $Num1 divided by $Num2 as a float number.

The following examples show the use of the / operator to divide two numbers.

```
$Result=19/3;                          //Returns a value
of 6.3
$Result=26/3;                          //Returns a value
of 8.66667
```

In the above examples, the first integer value is divided with the second integer value and the result is stored in the variable $Result.

The Modulus (%) Operator

You use the modulus operator to divide two numbers and retrieve the remainder. Following is the syntax of the modulus operator:

```
$Result=$Num1%$Num2;
```

In the syntax, $Num1 and $Num2 are two integer values. The modulus operator returns the remainder left after dividing $Num1 and $Num2.

Following are a few examples in which the % operator is used:

```
$Result=24%8;                                    //Returns
0
$Result=18%8;                                    //Returns
2
$Result=12%4.3;                                  //Returns
3.4
$Result=47.9%9.35;                               //Returns
1.15
```

 NOTE

If you use float variables as operands along with the modulus operator, then the remainder will also be a float variable.

The Addition (+) Operator

You use the addition operator to concatenate two strings or to add two numbers. Following is the syntax for the addition operator:

```
$Result=$Variable1+$Variable2;
```

The variables used in the expression can be either integers or strings. If you use integer values, the addition operator returns the sum of $Variable1 and $Variable2. However, if the variables are strings then the result is a concatenated string.

CAUTION

While using the addition operator, you must ensure that both variables are of the same datatype.

Consider the following examples:

```
            $IntValue=8+6;
//Returns 14
            $IntValue=348.45+5468;
//Returns 5816.45
            $StrValue="Hello"+ "World";
//Returns Hello World
```

If the operands are integers or floats, as is the case of the above two examples, operators add the numbers to each other and return an integer or float value respectively. In cases where the operands are strings, the operator concatenates both the strings to each other.

The Subtraction (-) Operator

You can calculate the difference between two numbers by using the subtraction operator. The syntax of the subtraction operator is as follows:

```
            $Result=$Num1-$Num2;
```

In the above syntax, $Num1 and $Num2 are two integer values. Consider the following examples:

```
            $IntResult=15-4;
//Returns 11
            $IntResult=756.45-325.26;
//Returns 431.19
```

Assignment Operators

The moment you see the = operator you probably associate it with "equal to." Though this might be true in the case of other languages, in the case of PHP it is an *assignment* operator and you use it to assign a value to a variable.

For example:

```
            $Myvar=12;                                    //$Myvar
becomes an integer type
```

```
variable and contains the value 12.
            $Myvar="World";                               //$Myvar
becomes a string type variable
```

```
and now contains the value 'World'.
```

PHP also allows the use of more that one assignment operator in a single statement. For example:

```
            $Result=($Num1=3)+($Num2=1);                  //$Result,$Num1, and
$Num2 are integer datatype
```

```
variables and hold the value 4,3,and 1, respectively.
```

In the above example, first $Num1 and $Num2 are assigned values, then their sum is calculated, and finally the result is stored in $Result.

PHP also supports the combined arithmetic operators += and .=. These operators not only initialize a value to an expression but also store the result obtained from executing the expression. The += operator is used for numeric type data while the .= operator is used for string type data.

For example:

```
            $Num=4;
            $Num+=1;                                //Increments the value
of $Num by 1
            echo $Num;                              //Result 5
```

Note that you can also write the expression $Num+=4 as $Num= $Num + 4. In the above example, the variable $Num is assigned a value and in the next step 1 is added to the current value of $Num and the result is assigned back to the variable.

```
            $Myvar="Add";
            $Myvar .=" Something";
//$Myvar=="Add Something"
```

The above expression can also be written as $Myvar = "Add". "Something" or even as $Myvar = "Add Something". The .= operator appends the new value with the current value of $Myvar.

Comparison Operators

You use the *comparison* operators to compare expressions. You can compare whether the values of two expressions are either more than, less than, or equal to one another. Table 3-4 lists the comparison operators used in PHP.

Table 3-4 Comparison Operators Available in PHP

Name	Symbol	Purpose
Equal	==	Returns True if the value of one variable is equal to another.
Identical	===	Returns True if the value of one variable is equal to another and both are of the same datatype.
Not equal	!=	Returns True if the value of one variable is not equal to the other.
Less than	<	Returns True if the value of one variable is less.
Greater than	>	Returns True if the value of one variable is more.
Less than or equal to	<=	Returns True if the value of one variable is less than or equal to the other.
Greater than or equal to	>=	Returns True if the value of one variable is more than or equal to the other.

The ternary operator ? is another conditional operator that is available in PHP. You might have used this operator in C and many other languages to compare two expressions and display a third expression if both the expressions match. The syntax of the ternary operator is shown below:

```
(expr1)?(expr2):(expr3);
```

In the above example, two variables $Num1 and $Num2 are compared and checked if they are equal to each other. The datatypes of the variables are also checked by using the comparison operators (==, ===, !=, <, >, <=, >=). The expressions return the boolean value True or False based on their result.

```php
<?php
    $Num1 = 13;
    $Num2 = 12;
    echo $Num1," == ", $Num2, " = ", $Num1 == $Num2, "<br>\n";//
Returns False


    $Num1 = 12.0;
    $Num2 = 12;
    echo $Num1," == ",  $Num2, " = ", $Num1 ==  $Num2, "<br>\n";
    // Returns True because == does not compare the datatypes, only
compares the values


    $Num1 = 12;
    $Num2 = 12;
    echo $Num1," == ",  $Num2, " = ", $Num1 ==  $Num2, "<br>\n";//
Returns True
?>
```

The output of the above code is shown in Figure 3-1.

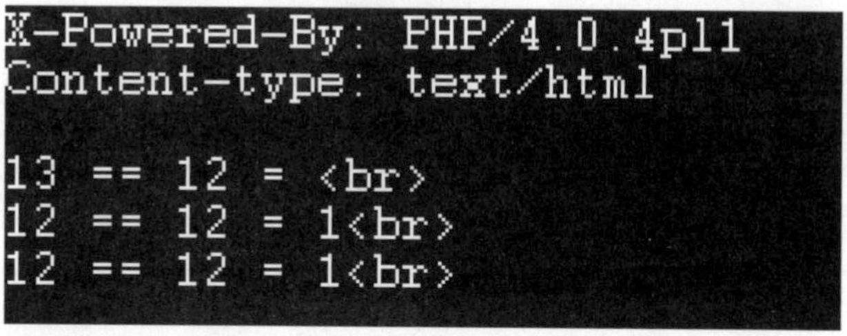

```
X-Powered-By: PHP/4.0.4pl1
Content-type: text/html

13 == 12 = <br>
12 == 12 = 1<br>
12 == 12 = 1<br>
```

FIGURE 3-1 *Output of comparison operators*

In the above examples, the values of $Num1 and $Num2 are compared to each other by using the == operator. In the first case, since the value of $Num1 is not equal to the value of $Num2, the expression returns False. In the second case, the expression returns True because the values of both the expressions match even though their datatypes differ. Similarly, the third expression also returns True.

Consider another example.

```
<?php
            $Num1 = 13;
            $Num2 = 12;
            echo $Num1," == ", $Num2, " = ", $Num1 == $Num2, "<br>\n";//
Returns False

            $Num1 = 12.0;
            $Num2 = 12;
            echo $Num1," == ",  $Num2, " = ", $Num1 ==  $Num2, "<br>\n";
            // Returns True because == does not compare the datatypes, only
compares the values

            $Num1 = 12;
            $Num2 = 12;
            echo $Num1," == ",  $Num2, " = ", $Num1 ==  $Num2, "<br>\n";//
Returns True
        ?>
```

The output of the above code is shown in Figure 3-2.

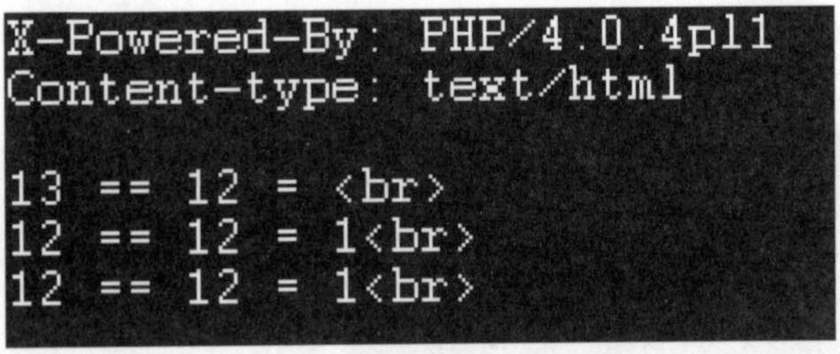

FIGURE 3-2 *Another program using comparison operators*

In the above examples, the values of $Num1 and $Num2 are compared to each other by using the === operator. The === operator not only compares the values of variables but also their datatypes. In the first case, even though the value of $Num1 and $Num2 are the same, their datatypes are different. Therefore, the expression returns False. Similarly, the second expression also returns False since one variable is a string datatype and the other an integer. The third expression returns True because the values and the datatypes of both the variables are the same.

```
<?php
        $Num1 = 12;
        $Num2 = 12.0;
        echo $Num1," != ",  $Num2, " = ", $Num1 != $Num2, "\n";//
Returns 12 != 12 False

        $Num1 = 12;
        $Num2 = 13;
        echo $Num1," != ",  $Num2, " = ", $Num1 != $Num2, "\n";//
Returns 12 !=13 True
        echo $Num1," < ",   $Num2, " = ", $Num1 <  $Num2, "\n";//
Returns 12<13 True
        echo $Num1," > ",   $Num2, " = ", $Num1 >  $Num2, "\n";//
Returns 12 > 13 False
        echo $Num1," <= ",  $Num2, " = ", $Num1 <= $Num2, "\n";//
Returns 12<=13 True
        echo $Num1," >= ",  $Num2, " = ", $Num1 >= $Num2, "\n";//
Returns 12 >=13 False
    ?>
```

In the above examples, the values of the variables $Num1 and $Num2 are evaluated by using the comparison operators and their result is displayed.

In the next section, you'll learn about the third type of operator—the execution operator.

Execution Operator (` `)

In PHP, only one type of execution operator is available, the backticks (` `) operator. You use the execution operator to implement the code stored in the backticks as a shell script and assign the output to a variable. Shell scripts are similar to programs and are used to execute multiple commands together. The variable, in which the output is stored, is used to manipulate the data since the output is not dumped on the HTML page. You can manipulate the output and display it in the format you want.

For example,

```
$allfiles=`ls`;
echo"<pre>$allfiles</pre>"                  //Pre is the html tag for
pre formatted output.
```

In the above output, the LINUX command ls is executed and its result is stored in the variable $allfiles. You can now manipulate the content of the variable $allfiles and display specific files based on certain conditions.

Increment and Decrement Operators

In the previous section, you learned how to increment the value of variables by using the arithmetic operators. Though this is the conventional method, it is better suited to cases of two different operands. In the case of a single operand, the expression is unnecessarily longer since the same variable is repeated twice—for example, $Num=$Num+1 or $Num=$Num-1. Instead of the arithmetic operators, you can use the ++ and -- operators, also known as the *unary operators*. In the case of unary operators, the variable is incremented and the incremented value is then reassigned back to the variable.

You can use the unary operators in two ways. You can either increment the value of a variable or decrement it. The assigned incremented/decremented value of the variable depends on whether you write the operator at the beginning or the end of the variable. When the -- operator is at the beginning of the variable, the variable is first decremented and then the decremented value is reassigned to the variable. Otherwise, if the -- operator is at the end of the variable, the current value is returned and then the variable is incremented. Table 3-5 lists the various increment and decrement operators.

Table 3-5 Increment and Decrement Operators

Name	Operator	Purpose
Pre-increment	++$myvar	Increments the current value of $myvar by 1, then returns the new value of $myvar.
Post-increment	$myvar++	Returns the current value of $myvar, and then increments the current value of $myvar by 1.
Pre-decrement	--$myvar	Decrements the current value of $myvar by 1, then returns the new value of $myvar.
Post-decrement	$myvar--	Returns the current value of $myvar, then decrements the value of $myvar by 1.

For example:

```php
<?php
        $Num = 17;
        echo "Num++: " . $Num++ . "<br>\n";
// Current value 17 (Post Increment)
        echo " Num1: " . $Num . "<br>\n";
// Current value 18
        $Num = 17;
        echo "++Num: " . ++$Num . "<br>\n";
// Current value 18 (Pre Increment)
        echo " Num: " . $Num . "<br>\n";
// Current value 18
        $Num = 17;
        echo "Num--: " . $Num-- . "<br>\n";
// Current value 17 (Post Decrement)
        echo " Num: " . $Num . "<br>\n";
// Current value 16
        $Num = 17;
        echo "--Num: " . --$Num . "<br>\n";
// Current value 16 (Pre Decrement)
        echo "  Num: " . $Num . "<br>\n";
// Current value 16
?>
```

The output of the above code is shown in Figure 3-3.

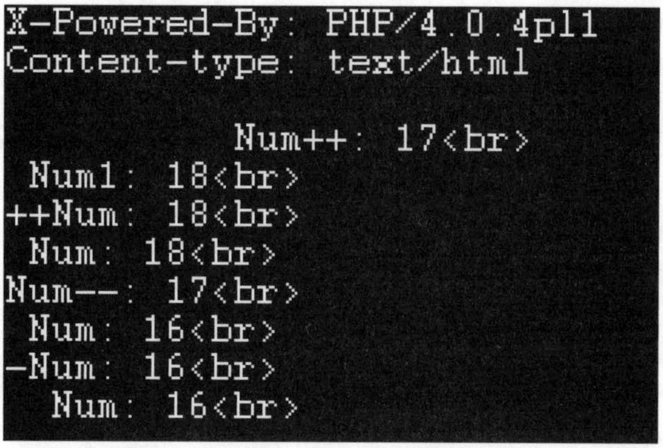

```
X-Powered-By: PHP/4.0.4pl1
Content-type: text/html

        Num++: 17<br>
 Num1: 18<br>
++Num: 18<br>
 Num: 18<br>
Num--: 17<br>
 Num: 16<br>
-Num: 16<br>
  Num: 16<br>
```

FIGURE 3-3 *Output of the increment/decrement operators*

In the preceding example, the value of variable $Num is first incremented and then decremented by using the pre- and post-incremental and decremental operators. As you might have noticed, when you use the post-incremental operator, the current value of $Num, which was 17, is first displayed and then incremented. The current value of $Num is now 18. However, when you use the pre-incremental operator, the current value of variable $Num is first incremented and then the value is assigned back to the variable. Therefore, the value 18 is displayed twice. Similarly, when you use the pre-decremental operator, the current value of the variable, which was 17, is first displayed and then the value is decremented. The current value of the variable is now 16. Finally, in the case of post-decremental operator, the value of $Num is first decremented and then the old value is assigned to the variable. Therefore, in both cases the value 16 is displayed.

String Operators (.)

There are two types of *string operators* available in PHP. The ., or *concatenation operator*, concatenates two expressions and forms a new string. The other is the .=, or *concatenation assignment operator*, which concatenates the expression specified on the right side with the one on the left.

See, for example:

```php
<?php
    $Myvar1 = "some";
    $Myvar2 ="thing";
    $concat = $Myvar1 . $Myvar2;
    echo $concat ,"\n";                    // $concat1=="something"

    $Myvar1 = "some";
    $Myvar1 .= "thing";
    echo $Myvar1,"\n";                     // $Myvar1=="something"

    $Myvar1 = "24 cats" +5;
    echo $Myvar1 ,"\n";                         //Returns 29

    $Myvar1 = "24cats" + 5;
    echo $Myvar1 ,"\n";                         //Returns 29
```

```
$Myvar1 = "cats 24" + 5;
echo $Myvar1 ,"\n";                        //Returns 5

$Myvar1 = "24 cats" . 5;
echo $Myvar1 ,"\n";                        //Returns 24 cats5

$Myvar1 = "24cats" . 5;
echo $Myvar1 ,"\n";                        //Returns 24cats5

?>
```

The output of the above code is shown in Figure 3-4.

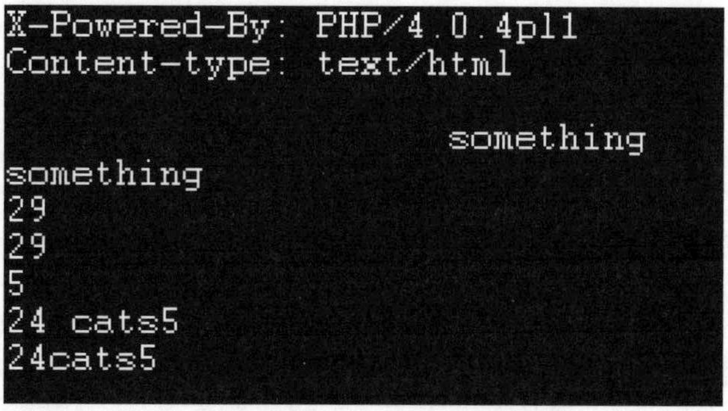

FIGURE 3-4 *String manipulation by using the string operator*

In the above example, the string operators are used to concatenate strings and integer values. As you might have noticed, the two strings (some and thing) are combined together to form a single string (something). However, in cases of concatenating a string and an integer, if the string begins with numeric characters, the result is the sum of the integer values. If the numeric characters are in the middle of the string, only the numeric variable is displayed. If you use the . operator, the integer variable is also treated as a string and both the string and the integer are concatenated.

Now that you have learned about operators and how they are used to work with variables, you'll next learn how you can manipulate string. In the next section, you'll also look at changing the datatype of variables.

String Manipulation

You need to know how to manipulate strings in order to work effectively with any scripting language. You manipulate strings to extract information from HTML pages. For example, you can dynamically create unique user IDs by extracting the user's name from the details form and create a user ID with it. PHP provides certain functions to help in string manipulation. Let me now describe these functions and their use in detail.

The substr *Function*

The substr function extracts a part of a string. It uses three parameters—the string, the start position, and the number of characters to retrieve. The start position starts at zero and the length parameter is optional. The syntax of the substr function is given below.

```
string substr(string string, int start [, int length])
```

If the value of the start position is positive, the extraction starts from the first character in the string. However, if the start position is negative, the starting point of extraction is calculated from the end of the string.

For example:

```
$extract = substr("Hello",1);
// Returns "ello"
$extract = substr("Hello",1,2);
// Returns "el"
$extract = substr("Hello",-2);
// Returns "lo"
$extract = substr("Hello",-3,2);
// Returns "ll"
```

If the length parameter is available and is a positive value, the specified number of characters is retrieved. However, if the length is negative, then the extracted string contains the specified number of characters until the end of the string—for example:

```
$extract = substr("Hello",1,-1);
// Returns "ell"
$extract = substr("Hello",2,-2);
// Returns "l"
```

The substr Function

The substr function finds the first occurrence of a search string in a given string. The function returns the value False if the string is not found.

The function is case sensitive and its syntax is as follows:

```
string strstr(string search_string, string base_string)
```

For example:

```
$content="Motherboard";
$base=strstr($content, 'b');
echo $base;
```
// Returns 'board'

In the above example, the string $content is searched for the character 'b' and when the character is found, the rest of the string from the character to the end of the string is extracted.

The str_replace Function

The str_replace function searches in a base string for all instances of a search string and then replaces it with another string. In cases where the size of the replace string is smaller than the search string, spaces are appended at the end of the replacement string. The function's syntax is as follows.

```
mixed str_replace(mixed search_string, mixed replace_string,
mixed base_string)
```

For example:

```
$story = "This is an excellent example of a horror story.";
$retstring = str_replace("excellent", "exceptional", $story);
```

In the above example, the string "excellent" is searched for in the text stored in the variable $story and if it is found, it is replaced by the string "exceptional". All instances of the search string are found and replaced. The final content of the variable $story is "This is an exceptional example of a horror story."

In the next section, you'll learn about type juggling and how it helps you to program in PHP.

Type Juggling

You do not need to declare variables in PHP to belong a specific datatype; their datatype changes based on their content. For example, a variable called `$Test_item` can initially contain a user's name, which is of string type, then it can store the user's age, which is an integer type, and finally it can also store the user's salary, which is of float type. Therefore, in PHP, a variable can store any kind of data without it being explicitly declared of the specific datatype. You can also store a numeric value as string, if you assign it within a pair of quotes.

Following are some examples of type juggling.

```
$Myval = "1500";              //Stores the value as a string
$Myval=1500;            //Stores the value as an integer
$Myval="14567.57";          //Stores the value as a string
$Myval=14567.57;            //Stores the value as a float
```

In the above example, the datatype of `$Myval` changes based on the value you assign to the variable.

Besides changing the datatypes of variables based on their content, you can also explicitly assign a datatype to a variable by using type casting.

Type Casting

PHP also handles the functionality of type casting in the same way that languages such as C handled it. In type casting, you explicitly change the datatype of a variable from one type to another. In PHP, you can implement the following types of type casting, as shown in Table 3-6.

Table 3-6 Categories of Type Casting

Purpose	Datatype
To convert a value to boolean	(bool), (boolean)
To convert a value to integer	(int), (integer)
To convert a value to float	(float), (double), (real)
To convert a value to array	(array)
To convert a value to object	(object)

You can also convert a variable to a string by enclosing it within double quotes. When you cast an array to a string, the result is the string "Array". However, if you cast an object to a string, the result is the string "Object". On the other hand, if a string is converted to an array, the string forms the first element of the array. In a case where you convert a string to an object type, the result is an attribute called 'scalar', with the variable as its attribute.

For example:

```
$Val = 'Hello';
$Greet = (array) $Val;
echo $Greet [0];
```
//Result 'Hello'

```
$Val = 'Hello';
$obj = (object) $Val;
echo $obj->scalar;
```
//Result 'Hello'

In the above examples, the variable $Val contains the value Hello. In the first example, the variable $Val is type casted into an array variable named $Greet. This variable stores each character of the word as separate elements of the array. In the second example, the same variable $Val is type casted into an object variable named $obj. You can also use this object to display the value.

You can convert the datatype of any variable to either boolean, integer, or string. However, you need to follow certain rules while converting a variable from one datatype to another. The following sections discuss the conversion of variables to boolean, integer, and string datatypes.

Boolean Conversion

PHP 4 provides the functionality to convert a value of a different datatype to boolean. A boolean value is derived from an expression and can be either True or False.

You can use either of the (bool) or (boolean) typecasts to convert a variable datatype to boolean datatype. However, implicit conversion of the value to boolean datatype is more common in PHP if the operator or the function needs a boolean argument.

While converting a value to boolean datatype, in the following conditions the boolean value will be False:

- ◆ String variable contains 0 or is empty.
- ◆ Integer variable is 0.
- ◆ Variable contains the value NULL.
- ◆ Array contains 0 elements.
- ◆ Object contains 0 elements.

In all other cases, the boolean value is True.

 NOTE

Here it is important to note that even -1 is converted to False since it is a non-zero value.

Integer Conversion

You use the typecasts (int) or (integer) to convert a value to an integer datatype. However, automatic type conversion is more common. If you try to convert a float value to an integer, the value is rounded off to the closest value near zero. If you convert a boolean value to an integer, a True value is converted to 1 and a False is converted to 0. As you will see in cases of string conversion, in string variables the initial part of the string is taken into consideration while determining how it will be converted.

String Conversion

A string that contains a numeric value can easily be converted to an integer. However, if the string contains the characters ., e, or E, it is converted into a float value. The initial section of the string is taken into consideration when determining the datatype of the converted string. For example, if the string begins with a numeric value, the converted value is numeric, and if the string ends with a numeric value, the converted value is 0. An exception to this rule is in cases where the string contains both alphabets as well as numeric values but with a space between them. In this case, the converted value will only be the numeric part.

For example,

```
$SalesItem = "15 boxes grain" + 2;                          //Result is
17
$SalesItem = "15units" + 2;
//Result is 15
$SalesItem = "12.4" + 2;
//Result is 14.4
$SalesItem = "-12.4kg" + 2;                                 //Result
is -14.4
```

In the above examples, the addition operator is used to add two types of values; one is a string and the other an integer. As you might have noticed, if the string value contains numeric characters, the characters are extracted and added to the numeric value.

In the following section, you'll learn about a unique concept in PHP, known as variable variables.

Variable Variables

A *variable variable* creates a new variable and assigns the current value of a variable as its name. Though this may sound a little confusing, what it means is that the current value stored in variable $greet is used to create another variable. This is explained in the following example.

```
                    $greet= "greeting";
                    $$newgreet= "hello!";
//This is the same as writing $greeting="hello!";
```

In the above example the variable $greet contains the value greeting. Instead of creating another variable called $greeting and assigning a value to it, you can use $$newgreet. This creates a new variable based on the current value of $greet and assigns the value hello to it. In this way, you can create dynamic variables and assign values to them.

Similarly, any data stored in a variable can also become a function name. In the example shown below, the value greeting is assigned to the variable $func. Since greeting is an already defined function, writing $func( ) in your code is the same as referencing the function greeting(). You'll learn more about variable variables in Chapter 6, "Functions."

As discussed before, variables in PHP are declared only when they are used and do not need to be defined as being of a specific datatype. However, sometimes you might need to assign a datatype to a variable. This is common in cases where you want to force the variable to store data of only a specific datatype. In such cases, you need to explicitly set the variable to belong to a specific datatype. PHP provides two functions, settype() and gettype(), to do this. The gettype() function retrieves the current datatype of a variable and the settype() function assigns the variable to a specific datatype. Now I will explain these functions in detail.

Functions for Determining and Setting Variable Types

Although in PHP you usually do not need to declare the datatypes for variables, in certain cases it becomes necessary to do so. For example, you might need to dynamically set the datatype of a variable based on some output. To do so, you first need to find out its current datatype and set a new datatype. PHP provides two functions for determining and setting the datatypes of variables.

The settype() Function

This function forcibly converts the datatype of a variable to another. The syntax of settype() is as follows:

```
boolean settype (mixed $myvariable, string set-
datatype)
```

The settype() function converts the datatype of $myvariable to the value of setdatatype. The return type is boolean and returns the value True if the conversion is successful. If it is not successful, the value False is returned.

The value setdatatype can belong to any of the following datatypes: integer, string, boolean, float, null, array, and object.

For example:

```
                              $Mystrval = "Container 72";
//String value
                              $Myboolval=False;
//Boolean value
                              settype($Myboolval, "string");
//Returns 0
                              settype($Mystrval, "integer");
//Returns 72
                              settype($Myboolval, "integer");
//Returns 0
```

In the above example, the variables $Myboolval and $Mystrval contain boolean and string values, respectively. You use the settype() function to explicitly convert the datatype of $Myboolval to string or integer datatypes and the value of $Mystrval to an integer datatype.

The gettype() Function

The gettype() function retrieves the datatype of a variable. The syntax is as follows:

```
                    String gettype (mixed $mixedvar)
```

The datatype of the variable $mixedvar is retrieved and returned as a string. The string can be any of the following datatypes: integer, string, boolean, double, null, array, object, or resource.

For example:

```
                    <?php
                    $Myval = "10 pigs" +2;
                    echo $Myval;
//Returns 12
                    echo gettype($Myval),"\n";
//Returns integer
                    settype($Myval,"double");
                    echo $Myval ;
//Returns 12
                    echo gettype($Myval),"\n";
//Returns double
```

```
                              $Myval = "10pigs" + 2;
                              echo $Myval ;
//Returns 12
                              echo gettype($Myval),"\n";
//Returns integer
                              $Myval = "10 pigs" . 2;
                              echo $Myval ;
//Returns 10 pigs2
                              echo gettype($Myval),"\n";
//Returns string


                              settype($Myval,"integer");
                              echo $Myval ;
//Returns 10
                              echo gettype($Myval),"\n";
//Returns integer


                              $a = "10pigs" . 2;
                              echo $Myval ;
//Returns 10pigs2
                              echo gettype($Myval),"\n";
//Returns string


                              settype($Myval,"integer");
                              echo $Myval ;
//Returns 10
                              echo gettype($Myval),"\n";
//Returns integer


                              settype($Myval,"boolean");
                              echo $Myval ;
//Returns (1/true)
                              echo gettype($Myval),"\n";
//Returns boolean


                              $Myval ="";
                              settype($Myval,"boolean");
                              echo $Myval ;
```

```
//Returns (blank/NULL/FALSE)
                        echo gettype($Myval),"\n";
//Returns boolean
                ?>
```

In the above examples, the datatypes of the variables are retrieved and displayed. You can also explicitly set the datatype of the variables by using the set-datatype() function and display the datatype by using the getdatatype() function.

Constants

Suppose you need to use a particular value throughout an application. For example, say you need an application that calculates and displays the highest marks attained by individual students on a test. To calculate this, the application needs to store the highest marks at a single location, since it needs to be accessed repeatedly. In such a case, instead of creating multiple instances of the same data every time, you can use *constants*. A constant is a space in the memory where you can store values that do not change during the execution of a program.

Defining Constants

A constant has the following properties:

- ◆ It is case sensitive and can be in either uppercase or lowercase.
- ◆ It follows the same naming convention as a variable.
- ◆ It can only begin with an alphabet or an underscore followed by any number of alphanumeric characters.
- ◆ It, by default, has global scope.

To define a constant you use the define() function. Once a constant is defined, it cannot be changed. A constant can have four types of values: string, boolean, double, or integer.

Unlike a variable, you can directly access a constant by its name instead of appending a $ symbol before it. You can use the constant() function in case you need to dynamically retrieve a constant's value in a program. You use the get_defined_constants() function to retrieve a list of all the currently defined constants.

Consider the following statement:

```
<?php
define ("CONSTANT", "This cannot be changed");
echo $CONSTANT;                                         // Returns This
cannot be changed
echo $Constant;                                         // Returns
Constant
echo "CONSTANT";                                        //Returns CON-
STANT
echo 'CONSTANT';                                        // Returns CON-
STANT
?>
```

In the above example, you created a constant variable and named it CONSTANT. You also stored the value "This cannot be changed" in it. Since constants are case sensitive by default, the name CONSTANT is different from Constant. Therefore, after the execution of the second echo statement, the compiler first searches for a value in the *predefined constants*. Since it does not find the value, it then searches for the value in the *user-defined constants*. As it still does not find the value, it just prints the value. However, PHP will produce a notice for such an operation. PHP assumes all values outside double quotes and without a dollar sign are constants and prints the value. In other words, you cannot print constants within quotes.

Although constants are by default case sensitive, you can use the define function to make them case insensitive. Observe the example given below.

```
define("CONSTANT", "This cannot be changed.");         //Creates a
case-sensitive constant.

define("CONSTANT", "This cannot be changed.", 1);      //Creates a
case-insensitive constant.
```

In the above example, when you add the third parameter 1 to the define() function, the variable CONSTANT becomes case insensitive. Now you'll consider some of the predefined constants available in PHP.

Predefined Constants

Just as you have predefined variables, you also have predefined constants in PHP. You can use these constants to retrieve information regarding the PHP. These constants are listed in Table 3-7.

Table 3-7 Predefined Constants Available in PHP

Constant name	Function
PHP_VERSION	Retrieves the version of PHP currently in use.
__FILE__	Retrieves the name of the file currently being parsed. If the constant is used within an included file, then the file name is retrieved and not the name of its parent file.
__LINE__	Retrieves the total number of lines in the current parsed file. If the constant is used within an included file, then the number of lines in the included file is given.
E_ERROR	Indicates errors except for parsing errors from which it is not possible to recover.
E_PARSE	Indicates that the parser was stuck in a syntax error in the script and recovery is not possible.
E_WARNING	Indicates that a warning is generated about an error encountered by PHP but the program can still work.
E_ALL	Stands for all the E_* constants combined.
E_NOTICE	Indicates something that you should notice that is not an error.
TRUE	Indicates a TRUE value.
FALSE	Indicate a FALSE value.
NULL	Indicates a NULL value.

Alternative Syntax for HTML-Embedded PHP Code

This syntax is not very popular, but you still need to use it when you require static HTML content along with the dynamic PHP content. This syntax is common for all control structures. The opening braces of the control structure change to a colon (:) and the closing braces are replaced by `endfor`, `endwhile`, `endif`, `end-foreach`, and `endcase`, 4 based on the control structure used.

For example:

```php
<?php if ($Intval >= 20 &&  $Intval < 26): ?>
This text will only be displayed if the value of $Intval is more than or equal to
20 and less than 26.
<?php endif; ?>
```

In the above example, the `if` statement is written using the alternative syntax and the HTML text is contained within it. The text would be displayed only if `$Intval` is more than or equal to 20 and less than 26. You can use the syntax to similarly work with the other control structures and loops.

Summary

In this chapter you learned about variables, operators, and constants. You learned that a variable is a memory location used to store the data. You also learned that in PHP you do not need to declare a variable before you can use it. PHP allows initialization of the variable in the same line where it is declared. The scope of the variable refers to its accessibility, and it can be global or local. Then you learned that PHP allows type juggling, type casting, and constants. You also learned about the different operators that you can use in PHP to perform operations on variables such as arithmetic operators (for mathematical calculations), assignment operators (for assignment operations), comparison operators (for comparisons), execution operators (for executing code), and increment/decrement operators (for incrementing/decrementing values). Then, under string operators, you learned about the concatenation operator (for combining strings) and the concatenation assignment operator. You also learned about the alternative syntax for control structures available in PHP. Finally you learned about constants. You learned that a constant is a space in the memory where you can store values that do not change during the execution of a program. You learned that PHP provides a number of predefined constants.

Chapter 4

Most of you have written programs at some time or another. The basic logic that you follow while writing a program, irrespective of the programming language,
is to:

◆ Initialize variables.

◆ Evaluate a condition or make decisions.

◆ Print the output.

You already learned about declaring and initializing variables in Chapter 3. In this chapter, you will learn about evaluating conditions or making decisions. *Control structures* are the decision-making mechanisms of any programming language and are used for evaluating conditions. In any programming language, including PHP, control structures are of two types:

◆ **Conditional statements.** These statements execute a code if a condition is either True or False.

◆ **Conditional loops.** These loops run a set of instructions once or multiple times until a condition returns True or False.

By now you are familiar with the basics of PHP—variables, operators, and constants. In this chapter you will look at the various types of control structures that you can use in PHP. Control structures govern the flow of control in PHP scripts. Before you look at control statements and loops in detail, first look at what conditional expressions are.

Conditional Expressions

Decision making plays a major role in your life. You make decisions from the time you wake up to the time you go back to sleep! You perform actions based on the decisions that you make. Each decision involves evaluating a condition. If the condition evaluates to True, you perform certain actions; you perform another set of actions if the condition evaluates to False. For example, when you go shopping you might see a lovely vase that you always wanted to buy (I can definitely relate to this). The dilemma that you face or the decision that you need to make is, do you have money to buy the vase? If the answer is yes, then you can buy the vase. However, if the answer is no (oops!), then you cannot buy it. Similarly, *conditional expressions* are used in programming languages to evaluate conditions.

Conditional expressions consist of three components:

◆ **Operands.** These can be numeric, alphanumeric, and plain text. Plain text needs to be enclosed in double quotes ("") before being evaluated.

◆ **Logical connectors.** These determine if all or only one of the conditions should return True for the code to execute.

◆ **Operators.** These are used to perform calculations and to compare expressions.

 NOTE

To learn more about operators, refer to Chapter 3, "Variables, Operators, and Constants."

Now look at some of the popularly used conditional statements available in PHP.

Conditional Statements

Sometimes you need to test a condition, and based on the result returned by this condition, you will perform certain actions. You can use conditional statements to do this. In a conditional statement, an expression is evaluated and, based on whether the condition returns True or False, the code is executed. In PHP, some of the commonly used conditional statements are:

◆ `if ... else ... else if`

◆ `switch ... case`

Both of these are covered in detail below.

The if Statement

The `if` statement is used to evaluate an expression and returns a Boolean value. The Boolean value can be either True or False. If the condition returns True, the set of statements following the `if` condition are executed. Otherwise the control is transferred to the statements at the end of the if block. Following is the syntax of the if statement:

```
if (expression)
    statement1;
```

In the above example, the condition is first evaluated and, provided the condition returns True, statement1 is executed. Otherwise, nothing happens. However, you can also write the above example as:

```
if (expression)
    {
            statement1;
    }
```

 NOTE

You might notice that the only difference between the first and second examples are the delimiters, or the curly braces ({}), as they are commonly known. By using delimiters, you can group together multiple statements and execute all of them together.

An example of the if statement is shown below:

```
<?php
 $Myvalue=5;
 if ($Myvalue ==5)
     {
             echo "I made a variable that contains the value 5";
             //The statement will execute only if $Myvalue is
equal to 5.
     }
 ?>
```

The above program assigns the value 5 to the variable $Myvalue and then checks to find if $Myvalue is equal to 5. Since the condition returns True, the text is displayed on the screen.

```
<?php
 $Myvalue=5;
```

```
if (!($Myvalue==4))
    {
            echo "See ! I told you 'Myvalue' cannot be 4!";
            //This statement will always execute except when
$Myvalue is equal to 4.
    }
?>
```

In the above program, the value 5 is assigned to the variable $Myvalue and the text is displayed on the screen if $Myvalue is not equal to 4. You can use the not (!) operator to specify that the statements should be executed only if the condition returns True. In the case of the (!) operator, if the expression returns True, then the result is False; if the expression is False, then the result is True. Consider another example:

```
<?php
if (TRUE)
    {
            echo " I will always run."; //This statement will
always execute.
    }
?>
```

You can evaluate multiple conditions in the same if construct by using operators. Based on the operator used, you can execute a set of statements if all or one of the conditions is fulfilled. Following are some examples that use operators to evaluate multiple conditions. For detailed information on operators, refer to Chapter 3, "Variables, Operators, and Constants."

```
<?php
$VarA=5;
$VarB=6;
if (($VarA==5) && ($VarB==6))
    {
            echo "The text is shown only when the value of variable
'VarA' is 5 and variable 'VarB' is 6";
    }
?>
```

In the preceding code, variables $VarA and $VarB are assigned values 5 and 6, respectively. The condition is checked, and only if the condition returns True will the text be displayed on the screen. Here is another example where multiple conditions are evaluated simultaneously:

```php
<?php
  $Num1=5;
  $Num2=6;
  $Num3=7;
  $Num4=10;
  $Num5=12;
  $Num6=14;
  if ( ( (($Num1+$Num2)==11) && (($Num3+$Num4)==17)) ||
(($Num5+$Num6) < 50))
          {
                  echo " OK!\n If this text is displayed, it means
that either sum of variable ' Num1' and ' Num2' is 11 and sum of variable ' Num3'
and ' Num4' is 17 \n";
                  echo " OR,\n the sum of variable 'Num5' and 'Num6'
is less than 50.";
          }
      ?>
```

In the above example, two main conditions are evaluated. The first condition contains two more subconditions. The first condition will return True if both of the subconditions return True. This means that the sum of $Num1 and $Num2 should be equal to 11 and the sum of $Num3 and $Num4 should be equal to 17. The second condition will return True if the sum of $Num5 and $Num6 is less than 50. If either of the two main conditions returns True, the statement contained in the if loop is executed.

 NOTE

You can also nest one if statement within another to evaluate multiple conditions. This topic is covered later in the chapter.

Now consider how to enhance the use of the if statement by adding the else statement to it.

The *else* Statement

Consider a scenario where you want to execute a particular code segment when the condition evaluates to True. If the same condition (based on the if statement) evaluates to False, another set of statements must be executed. This is where the else statement proves to be useful. Certain points that you need to remember about the else statement are:

- The else statement can only be used along with the if statement and not separately.
- The code after the else statement will be executed only when the if statement returns False.
- You can have only a single else statement and it should always be the last set of code in the block.

The following example shows the use of the else statement together with the if statement.

```php
<?php
  $age=19;
  if ($age < 18)
      {
              echo " You are not an adult since your age is less
than 18 ";
              //This statement will not be printed.
      }
  else
      {
              echo " You are an adult since your age is more than
18";
              //This statement will be printed.
      }
  ?>
```

In the above code, the value 18 is assigned to the variable $age and the program checks whether the value is less than 18. Since the condition returns False, the code after the else statement is executed. This statement displays the text "You are an adult since your age is more than 18".

CAUTION

You cannot specify a condition along with the else statement. You can use the else if statement (covered below) to evaluate any additional conditions.

In an if conditional statement you can also evaluate other conditions, provided that the if condition returns False. To do so, you can use the else if statement.

The *else if* Statement

The else if statement is used along with the if and else statements. You can have multiple else if statements in a single if construct; however, there can be only a single else statement. An else if statement is executed only when the if condition and all the other else if statements return False.

NOTE

You can use the words elseif and else if interchangeably because in PHP both mean the same thing and return the same value.

All the else if statements should be declared after declaring the if statement and before declaring the else statement in the same structure.

For example:

```php
<?php
    $Num=50;
    if (($Num>9) && ($Num<100))
        {
                echo $Num, " is a 2 digit number";
        }
    elseif ($Num>=100)
        {
                echo $Num, " has 3 digits or more !";
```

```
                    }
              else
                    {
                            echo $Num, " is a single digit number";
                    }
        ?>
```

In the above code, $Num is assigned the value 50 and is checked against various conditions. If the value of $Num is between 9 and 100, a message "$Num is a 2 digit number" is displayed. If the value is more than 100, the message states "$Num has 3 digits or more". Otherwise the message reads "$Num is a single digit number".

As stated earlier, you can have only a single else statement in an if structure. However, you can have multiple else if statements in the same if structure. This is illustrated in the following example.

```
<?php
  $Num=50;
  if (($Num>9) && ($Num<100))
        {
                echo  $ Num, " is a 2 digit number";
        }
  elseif (($Num>99) && ($Num<1000))
        {
                echo $ Num, " is a 3 digit number";
        }
  elseif (($Num>999) && ($Num<10000))
        {
                echo $ Num, " is a 4 digit number";
        }
  elseif ($Num>=10000)
        {
                echo $ Num, " is a 5 digit number or more";
        }
  else
        {
                echo $ Num, " is a single digit number";
        }
  ?>
```

The preceding example is similar to the one explained previously, except that two additional else if conditions are also evaluated. If the value of $Num is between 999 and 10000, the message "$Num is a 4 digit number" is displayed. If the value is more than 10000, the message states "$Num is a 5 digit number or more". Otherwise the message states "$Num is a single digit number".

Therefore, in case the if condition returns a False value, the variable is evaluated against each of the else if conditions. The moment one of the else if conditions returns True, the corresponding text is displayed and the control leaves the if structure.

The break *and* continue *Statements*

The break and continue statements are used in all the looping constructs. You use the break statement to end the execution of the current loop and return the control to the next statement immediately after the loop.

The continue statement does not move the control out of the loop; however, the rest of the statements in the loop after the continue statement are skipped and the loop is restarted.

 NOTE

You can also specify a numeric value along with the break statement, though this is optional. The specified number represents the number of loops that need to be skipped or ended. Just as in the break statement, you can also specify a numeric value along with the continue statement; this is also optional.

You have just learned about the if control structure, where a condition is first evaluated and code is executed based on the result. Now look at how you can evaluate a condition and execute a code if the result matches one of the predefined values.

The switch *Statement*

In the case of the if construct, the condition is either evaluated by using the if statement or the else if statements. However, in the case of the switch construct, the condition is evaluated only once and then the value is compared against a list of predefined values. Each value is stored in a case statement and refers to the same variable. When a matching value is found, the control shifts to the specific case statement and all the statements under it are executed sequentially. If no matching value is found, then the statements stored under the default label are executed until the end of the block is reached or you come across a break statement. In case neither a matching value is found nor a default label exists, the control shifts to the statements outside the switch block.

Following is the syntax of the switch statement.

```
switch (variable)
    {
        case value1:

                        statement;
                        statement;
        case value2:

                        statement;
                        statement;

            ...
        default:

                        statement;
                        statement;

    }
```

 NOTE

Not every case statement needs to contain a value. You can leave a case statement empty. This means that you can omit adding statements in the body of the case structure. This is helpful in cases where you do not want the program to perform any action if the variable matches a certain case.

Expressions specified in a case statement can only belong to the integer, string, or float datatype. You cannot use arrays or object values as case expressions.

Following are some examples of the switch statement.

```
?php
  $val="first";
  switch ($val)
  {
          case "first":
              echo "You have encountered the first case.", "\n";
          case "second":
              echo "You have encountered the second case.", "\n";
          case "third":
              echo "You have encountered the third case.", "\n";
          case "fourth":
              echo "You have encountered the fourth case.", "\n";
              break;

  }
?>
```

The output of the above code is shown in Figure 4-1.

```
X-Powered-By: PHP/4.0.4pl1
Content-type: text/html

You have encountered the first case.
You have encountered the second case.
You have encountered the third case.
You have encountered the fourth case.
```

FIGURE 4-1 *The* switch case *construct without* break *in each statement*

In the above example, if the value of the variable $val is fourth, the last statement will be executed. However, if the value is first, then all the statements in each of the case statements are displayed. To avoid this, you should insert a break statement at the end of each case statement. The break statement forces the control out of the switch construct to the next statement immediately after the loop. You can rewrite the above code as follows.

```
?php
  $val="first";
  switch ($val)
  {
          case "first":
```

```
                echo "You have encountered the first case.", "\n";
                break;
            case "second":
                echo "You have encountered the second case.", "\n";
                break;
            case "third":
                echo "You have encountered the third case.", "\n";
                break;
            case "fourth":
                echo "You have encountered the fourth case.", "\n";
                break;
        }
    ?>
```

The output of the above code is shown in Figure 4-2.

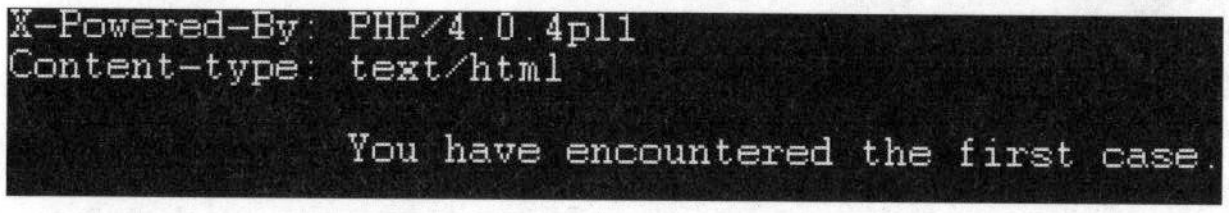

FIGURE 4-2 *The* switch case *construct with* break *in each statement*

Now that you know about control statements, it's time to look at the various looping constructs that are available in PHP.

Conditional Loops

You use conditional loops to execute a set of statements until a condition remains True. To ensure that the loop performs correctly, the value that is evaluated in the condition should be modified every time the loop is executed.

Some of the common conditional loops that are available in PHP are

◆ for

◆ while

◆ while ... endwhile

◆ do ... while

◆ foreach

Each of these conditional loops will be discussed in detail below. The first looping construct that you will look at is the for loop.

The for *Loop*

For loops are loops in which the number of times the loop will be executed is fixed and the information is included in the statement itself. A for loop evaluates three different expressions, which are also the various stages of the loop.

◆ **Initialization of variables.** You assign a value to the variable in expr1. The assigned value is generally the starting point of the loop.

◆ **Evaluation of the condition.** The conditional expression (expr2) is evaluated at the beginning of each loop. If the condition evaluates to True, the loop continues and the statements inside the loop are executed. However, if the condition evaluates to False, the execution of the loop ends and the program exits the loop.

◆ **Reinitialization of the variables once the code executes.** At the end of each loop, expr3 is evaluated, or rather executed. Mostly, expr3 is not a conditional expression and mainly involves incrementing the value of the variables used in the code.

The syntax of the for loop is as follows:

```
for (expr1;expr2;expr3) statement;
```

Since all the instructions are in the same line of code, it is easier to follow the flow of control and understand the execution of the code in the loop.

You can have a single statement inside a for loop. However, it is preferable to have the statement on a separate line. This makes the code more flexible. You can also write the above for loop as shown below.

```
for(expr1;expr2;expr3)
    {
    statement1;
    statement2;
    }
```

The second syntax is preferable because it is more flexible and you can execute multiple statements at one go. When the code is executed, all the statements written between the braces are performed before incrementing the variable and reevaluating the condition. Consider a few examples of the for loop.

```php
<?php
for ($Myval = 1; $Myval <= 10; $Myval++)
        {
                echo $Myval , "\n";
        }
?>
```

It is not mandatory to have values in all the expressions in the for loop. You can leave any, or all, of the expressions in a for loop blank. This makes the for statement very flexible and one of the most popular looping constructs in PHP.

For example:

```php
<?php
echo " LOOP 1 \n";
$Myval=1;
for ( ;$Myval <= 10; $Myval ++)
        {
                echo $Myval;
        }
echo "\ n              LOOP 2 \n";
$Myval=1;
for ( ;$Myval <= 10;)
        {
                echo $Myval;
                $Myval ++;
        }
echo "\n              LOOP 3 \n";
$Myval =1;
for (;;)
        {
            if ($Myval >10) {break;}
                echo $Myval;
                $Myval ++;
        }
echo "\n";
?>
```

The output of the preceding code is shown in Figure 4-3.

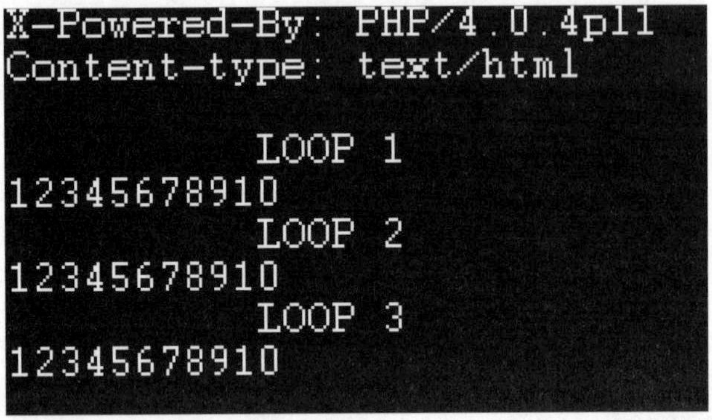

```
X-Powered-By: PHP/4.0.4pl1
Content-type: text/html

          LOOP 1
12345678910
          LOOP 2
12345678910
          LOOP 3
12345678910
```

FIGURE 4-3 *Three* for *loops with and without parameters*

As you might have already noticed, the first loop has only two parameters, the second loop has only one, and the final loop does not have any parameters. Despite this, all three loops will produce the same output. Every programmer can modify the loops based on their requirements.

The for loop executes a code for a predefined number of instances. Suppose that you do not know how many times the code would be executed or whether you need to execute a code until a condition return False. In such cases, you can use the while loop.

The while *Loop*

You use the while loop to check whether an expression is True or False. All the statements inside the while loop will execute repeatedly, as long as the expression remains True. On the other hand, the loop might not execute at all. This is because the while loop checks the expression before entering the loop. This means that if the condition is False, the compiler will not enter the while loop even once. The syntax of the while loop is as follows:

```
while (exprn) statement;
              or
while (exprn)
   {
          statement1;
```

```
            statement2;
    }
```

Following are a few examples of the while loop.

```
<?php
$Num=5;
while ($Num)
    {
            echo "I will print infinitely. Press Ctrl + C to
stop me. \n";
                    //This is because as long as $Num returns the
value 5 the loop will go on.
    }
?>
<?php
  $Num=5;
  while ($Num<10)
    {
            echo "I will also print infinitely. Press Ctrl + C
to stop me.\n";
                //This is because $Num will always return 5
    }
?>
<?php
  $Num=5;
  while ($Num<10)
    {
        echo "I will print till variable 'Num' is less than 10. Right
now the value of Num is ", $Num, "\n";
                ++$Num;
    }
            echo " OK! We are out of the loop and the current
value of the variable 'Num' is ", $Num;
    ?>
```

The while loop also supports all valid expressions, including those with operators. You use the && (And) or the ¦¦ (Or) operators to check for two conditions. In the case of the && operator, both the conditions should return True. The loop will end if either of the conditions returns False. In the case of the ¦¦ operator, the code is executed if either of the conditions returns True.

For example:

```php
<?php
    $Num1=1;
    $Num2=35;
    echo "The loop stops executing if variable 'Num1' is 15 or
greater and if variable 'Num2' is 18 or
    lesser";
    while (($Num1<15) && ($Num2>18))
        {
                ++$Num1;
                --$Num2;
                echo " Variable 'Num1' = ", $Num1," and variable
'Num2'= ", $Num2 ,"\n";
                //The loop will end even if one of the two sub-
expressions returns False.
        }
        echo " We are out of the loop and, 'Num1' = ", $Num1," and
'Num2'= ", $Num2 ,"\n";
    ?>
```

In the above example, the while loop continues until either $Num1 becomes more than or equal to 15 or $Num2 becomes less than or equal to 18. Now that you know about the while loop, take a look at another kind of looping construct, the while ... end while loop.

The while ... end while *Loop*

The while ... endwhile loop is very similar to the while loop. The only difference is that in the while loop you use delimiters to mark the loop segment. However, in the while ... endwhile loop, all statements after the while (expr) statement and before the endwhile statement are considered inside the loop and executed sequentially. The syntax of the while ... endwhile loop is as shown below.

```php
while (expr):
        statement1;
```

```
                statement2;
        endwhile;
```

For example:

```
<?php
  $Num = 1;
   while ($Num <= 10):
                echo $Num;
                $Num++;
        endwhile;
  ?>
```

The output of the above code will appear as shown in Figure 4-4.

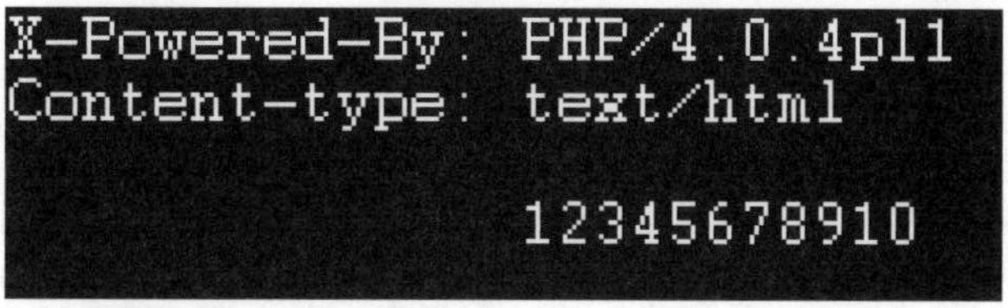

FIGURE 4-4 *The while loop*

In the above example, the while loop will execute as long as the value of $Num is less than or equal to 10. The moment the value becomes greater than 10, the control exits the loop and is transferred to the statements immediately after the end of the while loop. The third loop in the while loop series is the do ... while loop, in which the code is executed at least once.

The do ... while Loop

The do ... while loop is also similar to the while loop. However, in the case of the do ... while loop, the code executes once before the condition is evaluated. All the statements after do and before while (expr) are considered as a part of the loop, and you need to enclose all the statements in delimiters. The syntax of the do ... while loop is as shown below.

```
do
    {
        statement1;
        statement2;
```

```
    }
while (expr)
```

As you might have noticed by now, in the do ... while loop the expression is evaluated at the end of the loop. This means that even if the condition is False the code in the loop is still executed at least once.

For example:

```
<?php
  $Num=1;
  do
      {
          echo " Let us increase the value of variable 'Num' to get
out of this loop! variable is $Num \n";
                ++$Num;
      }
  while ($Num <20);
  echo "Hurray ! I am out of the trap! Variable 'Num' =", $Num;
?>
```

The above code will run 20 times, since the initial value of $Num is 1. However, if you initialized $Num with the value 21, the code would still be executed once, even though the condition is False. This is because the code is executed in the beginning of the loop and the condition is only evaluated at the end of the loop.

 NOTE

Some of the common syntax errors found in loops can be avoided by remembering to put the semicolon in the while and the do ... while statements.

The while and do ... while loops execute a code if a condition evaluates to True, but suppose you need to execute a single code for each element of an array or a group of objects. You can do this by using the foreach loop.

The foreach Loop

In the case of the foreach loop, a set of code is executed against a set of elements of an array or object. Each element of the array is evaluated independently and the control leaves the loop only after all the elements of the array have been evaluated. The control passes to the next statement after the end of the `foreach` loop. The syntax of the `foreach` loop is as follows:

```
foreach(arrexpression as $currval) statement
```

or

```
foreach(arrexpression as $sourceval => $currval) statement
```

In the first syntax, all elements in the array are traversed and the variable is incremented before the next loop begins. In the second syntax, the current value of the variable is first stored in another variable $sourceval before incrementing $currval.

You can also use the `for` loop to find out the number of elements in an array or the number of objects in a collection.

 NOTE

You use the `break` and `continue` statements to exit the loop or to skip statements in the loops.

Consider some examples of the `foreach` loop.

Example 1:

```
<?php
$arrayval = array (12, 22, 32, 72);
foreach ($arrayval as $currval)
    {
            echo "The current value stored in the array \$
arrayval: $currval \n";
    }
?>
```

Figure 4-5 shows the output of the above code.

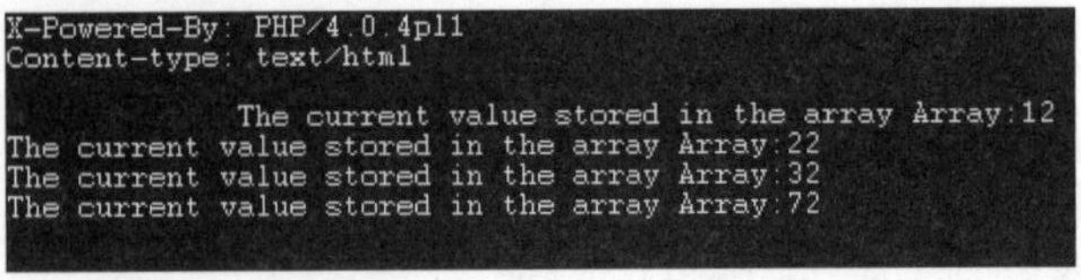

```
X-Powered-By: PHP/4.0.4pl1
Content-type: text/html

                The current value stored in the array Array:12
The current value stored in the array Array:22
The current value stored in the array Array:32
The current value stored in the array Array:72
```

FIGURE 4-5 *The foreach loop displaying each value of an array*

Example 2:

```php
<?php
$arrayval = array (Jack, Tom, Mary, James);
$count = 0;
foreach($arrayval as $currval)
    {
                echo "\n $arrayval [$count] => $currval.\n";
    }
?>
```

Figure 4-6 shows the output of the above code.

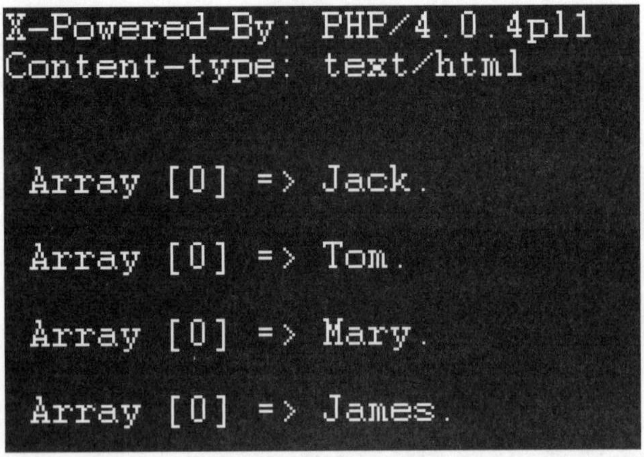

```
X-Powered-By: PHP/4.0.4pl1
Content-type: text/html


Array [0] => Jack.

Array [0] => Tom.

Array [0] => Mary.

Array [0] => James.
```

FIGURE 4-6 *The foreach loop displaying each value of an array*

Example 3:

```php
<?php
    $arrayval = array (
                "Sunday            "    => 1,
                "Monday            "    => 2,
                "Tuesday           "    => 3,
```

```
                        "Wednesday    "    => 4,
                        "Thursday      "    => 5,
                        "Friday         "    => 6,
                        "Saturday       "    => 7
            );
            foreach($arrayval as $tempval => $currval)
            {
                        echo "\$arrayval[$tempval] => $currval.\n";
            }
    ?>
```

Figure 4-7 shows the output of the above code.

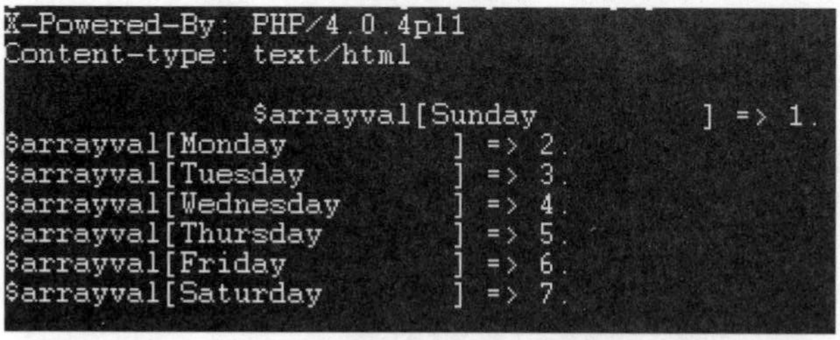

FIGURE 4-7 *The* foreach *loop displaying each value of an array*

In all the three examples, each element of the $arrayval array is displayed separately. Once the current value is displayed, the value of the counter is incremented and the next element is displayed.

Until now you have only worked with a single level of control structure, but you can also have multiple levels of control structures.

Nested Control Structures

You have already learned how to use each control structure separately. You can also insert or nest one control structure inside another. For example, in a for loop you can evaluate one condition and run another for loop inside the first loop to evaluate another condition. These are known as *nested control structures*.

You can nest control structures to as many levels as you require. As good programming practice, you should indent each level of the structure for better readability and understanding.

For example:

Example 1:

```php
<?php
  for ($Num1=1;$Num1<5;$Num1++)
      {
              for ($Num2=1;$Num2<5;$Num2++)
                  {
                              echo" I will be printed 25 times
total \n";
                  }
      }
  ?>
```

Figure 4-8 shows the output of the above code.

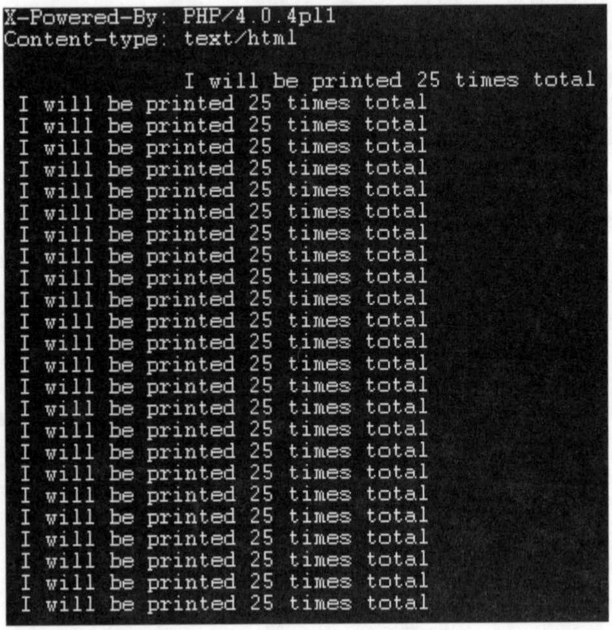

FIGURE 4-8 *Nested control structure using* for *loops*

In the above code the outer for loop is first evaluated and is executed until $Num1 is less than 5. For each instance of the outer loop, the inner for loop runs five times. Therefore, in total the text is displayed 25 times. See Figure 4-8.

Example 2:

```php
<?php
$arrayval [0][0] = "2";
$arrayval [0][1] = "6";
$arrayval [1][0] = "8";
$arrayval [1][1] = "12";
   foreach($arrayval as $currval1)
     {
        foreach ($currval1 as $currval2)
           {
                echo "$currval2 \n";
           }
     }
?>
```

In the above code, the inner loop is executed for a specific number of instances depending upon the number of elements in the array. For each instance, the current value of $currval2 is displayed and the counter incremented.

Summary

In this chapter, you learned about control structures. First you learned about conditional expressions. Then you learned that control structures are of two types, the conditional statements and the conditional loops. The conditional statements contain the if ... else ... else if and the switch case statements. The conditional loops contain the for, while, do ... while, and while ... endwhile loops. In this chapter, you also learned about the use of break and continue statements, which help you in breaking out of a conditional block or omitting statements in a conditional statement. Then you learned about each one of the loops and statements in detail. Finally you learned about nested control structures.

Chapter 5

Consider that you need to store 100 values. To do so you must define 100 variables and assign a value to each variable. However, the task of defining 100 variables is time-consuming and tedious. Moreover, it is difficult to juggle so many variables at the same time. To solve the difficulties that arise due to handling many variables, you can define an array that can store 100 values. Besides storing one or more values simultaneously, an array is also flexible and comparatively easy to handle. You'll find that the manipulation of arrays and their elements is much simpler and faster than manipulation of many variables at any given time.

In the previous chapter you learned about variables and constants, the building blocks of the PHP language. In this chapter you will learn to work with arrays, a fixture in most of the programming languages. You will learn about the different types of arrays that are available in PHP. You will also learn to create and manipulate these arrays.

Introduction to Arrays

You already know that a variable is a container for a single value. An array, on the other hand, is a container for multiple values. An array can also contain multiple elements having different values. PHP also allows an array to contain elements of different data types. Elements in an array are referred or manipulated on the basis of their *index*. The index of an element in an array is normally an integer.

 NOTE

Indices in PHP are also referred to as *keys*.

There are many types of arrays available to you in PHP. Consider the following types of arrays in detail.

Types of Arrays

Arrays can be classified on the basis of indices and array elements. The different types of arrays include:

- ◆ Enumerated arrays
- ◆ Associative arrays
- ◆ Multidimensional arrays

Enumerated Arrays

Arrays that have integer indices are known as *enumerated* or *numerically indexed* arrays. These arrays are used to store values. For example, you can have an array named Students, where each element of the array stores the name of a student.

In the above array, each individual element can be referred to by its index number. For example, the name James can be referred to by the index 0. To display the array element at index 2, you can use the following statement:

```
echo "$Student[2]";
```

 NOTE

By default, the index number of an array element starts with zero and increases sequentially. Therefore, the index of the last element in an array is always one less than the total number of elements in that array.

Associative Arrays

If you need to access elements in an array by name, then you should use strings as an index of the array. You can use a string as an index of an array element to store both values and names. The arrays that use strings, as indices, are referred to as *associative arrays*.

To ACCESS AN ARRAY

You can use the command Print "Student [x]" instead of the echo("Student [x]") command to access the value of the array elements according to their index numbers. Here *x* refers to the index number of the element in the array named Student.

You will find one subtle difference while working with numerically indexed (enumerated) arrays and string indexed (associative) arrays. With associative arrays having strings as an index, you will not be able to compute the next valid index in the array. However, indices can be assigned to the Student array discussed earlier using the array identifier. You can create an associative array Student_Name by assigning a value to the index.

```
$Student_Name["name1"] = "James Patt";
$Student_Name["name2"] = "John Smith";
$Student_Name["name3"] = "Susan Carter";
```

You can also convert an existing enumerated array into an associative array. To convert the existing Student array into an associative array:

```
$Student = array ( "name1" =>"James Patt", "name2" =>"John Smith", "name3" =>"Susan
Carter");
```

After you have converted an enumerated array into an associative array, you can use the echo command to access the elements of the given array.

```
echo "$Student[name3]";
```

You will get the output as Susan Carter.

You can also use list() and each() functions to access the elements in string indexed arrays. The list() function is used to assign the values of array elements to variables. On the other hand, the each() function takes an array as the argument and returns the index and value of each element of the array.

 NOTE

You'll learn about functions in detail in Chapter 6, "Functions."

For example:

```
$Student = array ("name1" =>"James Patt", "name2" =>"John Smith", "name3" =>"Susan
Carter");
list($key_name, $val) = each($Student);
echo("$key_name");
echo("$val");
```

The preceding code snippet sets $key_name equal to the index of the element and $value equal to the value of the element for each element of the array. Next you display the value of $key_name and $val using the echo() command. Therefore, the indices will be name1, name2, and name3. The corresponding values would be James Patt, John Smith, and Susan Carter.

Multidimensional Arrays

You can store different variables as well as complete arrays in another array. An array that stores arrays as its elements is known as a *multidimensional array*. Again, if the array elements in the two-dimensional array contain arrays, you have a three-dimensional array, and so on. Although these arrays can be three-dimensional, four-dimensional, etc., two-dimensional arrays are the most popular. An illustration of a multidimensional array is given below.

```
Roll No    1            2            3

Name       James Patt   John Smith   Susan Carter
```

The array illustrated above is an example of two-dimensional arrays. Here the Student array contains another array called Roll No within it.

Consider that the Student array contains arrays as elements. Therefore, if you want to access the second sub-element of the first element of the Student array, you have to use two indices as shown below:

```
$Student[0][1]
```

You can also think of an image as an example of an array. For instance, you need to trap the coordinates of an image as you move the mouse cursor over it. In this case, you need to use a multidimensional array to trap the x and y coordinates as shown below:

```
Coordinates[x][y]
```

There is no limit on the number of dimensions that you can have for the arrays. There can also be a combination of dimensions. For example, you can have the first dimension in your array indexed by integers, the second dimension indexed by strings, the third dimension indexed by integers, etc. Multidimensional arrays are very useful in representing complex statistical data.

```
<html>
<body>
<?php
$Student = array (
                    "0"=> array ("name"=>"James", "sex"=>"Male", "age"=>"28"),
                    "1"=> array ("name"=>"John", "sex"=>"Male", "age"=>"25"),
                    "2"=> array ("name"=>"Susan", "sex"=>"Female", "age"=>"24")
                    );
Print $Student [2][age];
?>
</body>
</html>
```

The output of the code is 24.

Now that you have learned to identify an array, you will next learn to create and initialize an array in PHP.

Initializing Arrays

An array can be initialized in two ways. You can initialize an array using:

◆ An array identifier

◆ The array() function

Using the Array Identifier

The *array identifier* is an empty set of square brackets. You can use an array identifier to initialize the Student array as shown below:

```
$Student[] = "James";
$Student[] = "John";
```

Here you assigned values "James" and "John" to the Student array. Note that you have not specified the indices for the array. Therefore, indices 0 and 1 have been assigned respectively to James and John.

You can also specify the indices for an array explicitly. For example:

```
$Student[0] = " James";
$Student[1] = " John";
```

Normally, indices are assigned sequentially in arrays. But you can also assign indices to array elements randomly. For example:

```
$Student[10] = " James";
$Student[3] = " John";
```

In the above example, you assigned indices to arrays in a nonsequential manner. If you need to assign indices to the elements of the array, the next index value will begin after the highest-indexed element in the array. Consider that you want to assign an index to the array element containing the name Sarah. Here the highest index among the elements is 10. Therefore, the element containing the name Sarah will have an index 11.

Using the `array()` Function

A simpler way to initialize an array is by using the array() function. This is simpler because, by using the array() function, you can assign multiple values to an array simultaneously. You can use the array() function to define the array Student in the following manner:

```
$Student = array("James", "John", "Susan");
```

 NOTE

You normally use the default indices while working with arrays. This implies that the indexing of an array would normally start with 0. However, you can also override the default indices using the => operator. In the above example, the Student array has three elements with indices 0, 1, and 2. However, you can specify the indices to start from 1. To do so, you can write the following code:

```
$Student = array (1 => "James", "John", "Susan");
```

Now if you use the Print "Student [1]" command, you will get the output as James.

You can also use the => operator in the following manner:

```
$Student = array ("James", 5 => "John", "Susan");
```

In the preceding example, you have assigned an index of 0 to James, 5 to John, and 6 to Susan.

So far, you have learned to identify the different types of arrays. You have also learned to initialize arrays in your PHP codes. Next you will learn to manipulate the arrays using different functions that are supported by PHP.

Working with Arrays

Using the built-in functions, you can perform the following tasks:

- ◆ Modify the size of an array.
- ◆ Loop through the array.
- ◆ Find elements in the array.
- ◆ Reverse an array.
- ◆ Sort an array.

The following sections will discuss the functions in detail.

Modifying the Size of an Array

You can modify the size of an array by using the different functions supported by PHP. By using these functions, you can:

- ◆ **Determine the size or number of elements of an array.** You can access an element of an array using the index. However, to calculate the number of elements contained in an array, you need to use the count() function. You can also calculate the index number of the last element of the array. To understand the count() function better, look at the following code snippet.

```
$Student = array ( "Susan", "Betty", "Reggie" );
$Number = count ($Student);
Print $Number;
```

The above code initializes the array Student with three elements. The count() function returns a count of the number of elements in this array. This count is stored in a variable called Number. When you display the value of this variable, the output is 3. To find out the index number of the last element in the array, you need to subtract 1 from the variable Number. For example:

```
Print "$Student[count($Student) -1]";
```

◆ **Change the size of an array.** You can decrease or increase the length of an array using different functions in PHP. Changing the size of an array involves:

   ◆ **Reducing the size of an array.** To reduce the size of an array, you use the array_slice() function. The array_slice function accepts an array, a starting position, and length as the parameters. For example, you have an array that consists of seven elements. To reduce the number of elements from seven to four, use the array_slice function.

   ```
   $Student = array( "ab", "bc", "cd", "de", "ef", "fg", "gh");
   array_slice($Student, 4)
   ```

   The array_slice() function reduces the number of elements from seven to four.

   You have learned to reduce the length of an array. However, this reduction in the number of elements of an array takes place from the end. If you wish to remove the first element of an array, you will need to use the function array_shift().

   The array_shift() function removes the first element of an array. The elements are passed to the array as arguments. For example, you initialize:

   ```
   $Student = array("James", "Susan", "John");
   ```

   Now, you can use the array_shift() function and store the output in a variable called New as:

   ```
   $New = array_shift($Student);
   ```

   The first element of the Student array "James" would be automatically removed by the array_shift() function.

NOTE

You can also delete an element from an associative array permanently by using the `unset()` function. The `unset()` function is a built-in function in PHP. Using the `unset()` function, you can destroy more than one variable at a time. You can also delete index values from an associative array.

♦ **Increasing the length of an array.** Assume that you need to insert some elements to the Student array mentioned earlier. You can do so by using the `array_push()` function. The `array_push()` function accepts an array as a parameter. The `array_push()` function returns the total number of elements in the array. Consider the following code snippet:

```
$Student = array("Susan", "James", "John");
$Insert = array_push($Student, a, b, c);
```

Here you have taken the Student array and added elements a, b, and c to it. You then store the total number of elements into another array called Insert. Therefore, the Insert array has six elements.

 NOTE

If you want to add a new element into an associative array, you need to specify the index and value for the array and add it. For example,

```
$Array_1 =array("a" =>"1", "b" =>"2", "c" =>"3");
$Array_1 =array("d" => "4");
```

In the above code, you have added a new element to Array_1.

Now suppose that you want to add all the elements of an array to another array. In that case, you should add arrays instead of adding individual elements because it is faster and easier. You will not be able to add one array to another with the `array_push()` function. In PHP, there is a function called `array_merge()` that allows you to merge one or more arrays.

The `array_merge()` function merges two or more arrays and returns a combined array.

For example, consider the following:

```
$Student= array("John", "James", "Susan");
$Class = array("4","5","6");
$Combine = $Student + $Class;
```

The `Combine` array contains the copies of all the elements of both `Student` and `Class` arrays. Therefore, the `Combine` array will contain the following values:

```
"John", "James", "Susan", "4", "5", "6"
```

Now suppose that the arrays `Student` and `Class` contain some common elements between them. For example:

```
$Student= array("John", "James", "5");
$Class = array("4","5","6");
```

Now when you merge the two arrays, the common element is copied only once into the merged array. However, if you don't want to lose the common element in the two arrays, you can use the `array_merge_recursive()` function. You can also use this function to avoid losing indices when merging arrays. The `array_merge_recursive()` function copies all the elements that are in the arrays.

◆ **Computing intersection or union of arrays.** Sometimes you might need to determine the intersection of two arrays. In that case, you should use the `array_intersect()` function. For example, look at the following snippet:

```
$old = array ("a", "b", "c");
$new = array ("c", "d", "e");
$Intersection = array_intersect ($old, $new);
```

In the preceding code snippet, first you initialize two arrays—old and new. Then you find the intersection of the two arrays and store the result in another array.

 NOTE

If you wish to find similarities between two arrays, first you should use this function to find the intersection. Then you should use the count() function to count the number of elements. The count() function takes the following form.

```
$Count_intersection = count($Intersection);
```

In the above statement, Count_intersection is the variable used to store the number of elements after intersection.

If you wish to determine all the elements of both arrays, use the union function. The union function takes the following syntax:

```
Union = (array);
```

◆ **Extracting unique elements from an array.** In order to extract a unique element from an array, you need to use the array_unique() function. This is a built-in function in PHP. The array_unique() function passes the array as argument, removes the duplicate elements, and returns a new array. You can use this function on both numerically indexed and associative arrays. You use the array_unique() function in the following manner:

```
$unique = array_unique ($old);
```

You learned to modify the size of an array, find the intersection and union of two arrays, and determine unique elements within an array. Now you will see how to navigate through arrays.

Looping through an Array

To perform operations on the elements of arrays repeatedly, you need to navigate through the arrays in a continuous manner. There are different ways of looping through each element of an array. However, the most powerful method is using the foreach statement of PHP. Consider an example.

You have a numerically indexed array called `Student` that contains `"John"`, `"James"`, and `"Susan"` as array elements. Now you use the `foreach` statement to access each element at a time and store each element temporarily in a variable called `new`. The syntax of the command is as below:

```
$Student = array("John", "James", "Susan");
foreach ($Student as $new)
            {
              print "$new";
              }
```

The above-mentioned code snippet will display all the array elements. You used the `foreach` statement to loop through a numerically indexed array. To loop through an associative array and access its indices and values, you need to modify the `foreach` statement in the following manner:

```
foreach($Student as key_name=>$new)
            {                    //
            }
```

Here `key_name` is the variable that stores the index and `new` is the variable that stores each value temporarily.

 NOTE

To loop through sequentially indexed arrays, you can use the `count()` function to find out the number of elements in the array and then use a `for()` loop.

Again, to loop through nonsequentially indexed arrays, you can use the `current()` function and the `key()` function. The `current()` function is used to determine the value of the current element in the array and the `key()` function is used to determine the index of the current element.

You learned to navigate through an array using the `foreach` statement. You also learned to use the `count()` and `current()` functions. You can use two other functions to navigate through arrays in PHP. These two functions are the `next()` and the `prev()` functions.

The next() function takes an array as its argument. This function traverses from the left to right of an array. The next() function returns the value of the next element. Whenever it reaches the last element, it returns a value of False. The prev() function also takes an array as its argument and traverses from the end to the beginning of the array.

NOTE

Assume that you have written a function f1() that displays a text. You want this function to be executed automatically whenever you access any element of the Student array. For it to do so, you have to navigate through the array and apply the f1() function to all the elements of the array. You can use the array_walk() function for this purpose. The array_walk() function takes two arguments. The first argument is the array and the second argument is the name of the function to be applied. The array_walk() function takes the following form:

```
array_walk ($Student, f1);
```

You have learned to navigate through arrays. Now you will learn to find elements in arrays.

Finding Elements in an Array

PHP provides some functions to find elements from arrays. In PHP, you will be able to:

◆ **Find elements that match a certain criteria.** Consider that you need to store those elements from an array that match a certain criteria. You can find these elements in two ways. You can use the foreach() construct to navigate through the array and test the value of each element in the array. You can also use the preg_grep() function to perform the same task. The preg_grep() function searches the array for the given criteria and returns the elements matching the criteria as an array.

Consider that you need to search the Student array and list all the students having Smith as their surname. The usage of the preg_grep() function is shown as follows:

```
$Student = array ("James Patt", "John Smith"," Susan Carter", "Joe Smith",
"Janet Jones");
$array_Smith = preg_grep ("/^Smith", $Student);
```

In the code snippet written above, you have searched the array Student with the preg_grep() function for the string Smith. The above code will give John Smith and Joe Smith as the output.

NOTE

You use the preg_grep() function along with the array_shift() method to find the first element in an array that matches a given criteria. You can also use the while loop to find the first relevant match. The preg_grep() function is very useful in searching short arrays efficiently. However, if the array is large, using the preg_grep() function will result in very slow processing.

◆ **Find elements in one array but not another.** Till now, you have determined unique elements in an array. Now suppose you need to determine those elements in an array that are not present in another array. You can use the array_diff() function to find the difference between the two arrays. The array_diff() function takes the following form:

```
array_diff ($Array_1, $Array_2);
```

In the above example, you have used the array_diff() function to determine the elements present in Array_1 and not in Array_2. You can use this function to search more than one array. You use commas to specify more than two arrays. This function usually allows duplicate elements. To eliminate the duplicate elements, you need to use the array_unique() function.

Now that you have learned to find the difference between two arrays, it's time to move on to reversing arrays.

Reversing an Array

Consider that you need to process an array in the reverse order. If the array is short, you can use the array_reverse() function provided by PHP. The array_reverse() function takes one argument, the array. The array_reverse() function takes the following form:

```
$array2 = array_reverse ($array1);
```

If you have an array that is large, the array_reverse() function will prove to be time-consuming. To reverse an array that is big in size, you can use a for() loop to process the array backward. For example, you can reverse the Rate array (discussed earlier) using the for() loop as shown below:

```
for (x = count ($Rate) -1; Rate >=0; x--)
{
//code
}
```

Here you first find out the total number of elements by using the count() function. Next you move to the index of the last element of the array. Finally, you navigate through the array in the reverse order.

You have learned to add or remove elements from an array. You also have learned to find elements from arrays. Now you will learn to sort the arrays with some functions provided by PHP.

Sorting and Unsorting Arrays

The sort() function is a simple function used for sorting arrays.

The sort() Function

You can use the sort() function to sort arrays according to the numeric and alphabetical order. This function also changes the indices of the arrays according to the sorted order. For example:

```
$Student = array ("John", "James", "Susan");
Sort ($Student);
```

When you display the index number and the value of the array elements, you get the output as:

```
0          James

1          John
```

```
2              Susan
```

Note that the indices have also changed after sorting the array.

Now assume that you have an associative array. For example:

```
$Student = array ("JS" -=> "John Smith",
                        ("JP" -=> "James Patt","
                        ("SC" -=> Susan Carter");
```

If you sort the array using the sort() function and then display the index number and value of the array element, you get the output:

```
0              James
```

```
1              John
```

```
2              Susan
```

Note that the string indices of the associative array have been changed to numeric indices. This is the problem when you sort an array using the sort() function. This problem can be avoided if you sort the arrays using the asort() function. The asort() function will be discussed next.

There are other functions that help you to sort associative and numerically indexed arrays. These are:

♦ **asort():** The asort() function is used to sort arrays without changing the indices. If you sort the Student array mentioned earlier using the asort() function, you will get the following output:

```
JP             James Patt
```

```
JS             John Smith
```

```
SC             Susan Carter
```

♦ **rsort():** The rsort() function is similar to the sort() function. The only difference is that it sorts the arrays in the reverse order. Consider the following code:

```
$Student = array ("John", "James", "Susan");
rsort ($Student);
```

When you display the index number and the value of the array elements after sorting the array using the rsort() function, you get the following output:

```
0              Susan
```

```
1           John

2           James
```

◆ **arsort():** The arsort() function is similar to the asort() function. The only difference is that it sorts the arrays in the reverse order. Assume that you need to sort the Student array in reverse order such that the indices are not modified. To sort an array in the reverse order without modifying the indices, you need to use the arsort() function.

Using the arsort() function to sort the Student array, you would get the following output:

```
SC          Susan Carter

JS          John Smith

JP          James Patt
```

◆ **ksort():** To sort the indices of an associative array, you need to use the ksort() function. Assume that you have an array Student and you need to sort according to the indices.

```
$Student = array ("b" =>"Susan", "d" =>"Andrew", "a" =>"John", "c"
=>"James");
```

Sorting the Student array using the ksort() function will provide the following output:

```
a           John

b           Susan

c           James

d           Andrew
```

Therefore, the Student array has been sorted according to the indices.

◆ **krsort():** The krsort() function is similar to the ksort() function. The only difference is that this function sorts the arrays in reverse order. Therefore, if you use krsort() in the example of the Student array mentioned above, you will notice the following output:

```
d           Andrew

c           James
```

b	Susan
a	John

◆ **usort()**: The regular sorting functions of PHP do not support sorting multidimensional arrays. To sort multidimensional arrays, you need to use the usort() function. You can also use the usort() function to specify a user-defined function for sorting the array. The usort() function takes an array and a function as the arguments. PHP provides two functions to sort associative arrays using user-defined functions. You can use the uasort() function to sort an associative array. You can also use the uksort() function to sort an array by the indices.

You have learned to sort the arrays. Now you will learn to randomize an array. You can randomize an array using the shuffle() function.

shuffle()

You use the shuffle() function to randomize or unsort arrays. The shuffle() function changes the order of the elements in the array. The shuffle() function takes the following form:

```
$Array_shuffle = range(1,100);
shuffle($Array_shuffle);
```

Here you use another function, known as the range() function. The range() function takes two integer parameters, the start and the end point. This function returns an array of all the integers between 1 and 100. The shuffle() function then randomizes the integers from 1 to 100 and stores them in the array called Array_shuffle.

Summary

In this chapter, you identified an array as a variable containing multiple elements having different values. You learned that an array in PHP can contain elements of different data types and that the elements in an array can be referred to by their index or key. You also learned about the different types of arrays. These include enumerated, associative, and multidimensional arrays. Next you learned to initialize an array by using the array identifier or using the array() function. You learned that PHP supports a number of functions that can be used to manipulate arrays. Using those functions, you can create, sort, find, delete, print, and process arrays.

Chapter 6

Suppose that during the festive season an online bookstore is offering a 10 percent discount on every purchase that costs $90 or less. For any purchase priced above $90, the discount rate is 12 percent. So every time a book is sold, the discount needs to be calculated on the basis of the total purchase. The discount is then deducted from the net price to be paid by the customer. Now suppose that on a particular day 23 customers placed orders of different amounts. How would the PHP script deal with a situation like this?

With your previous programming knowledge, you might recall that the PHP script, in this case, need not execute 23 times. The script will simply call a function that will calculate the discount for each book and return the cumulative result to the main program. Therefore, even if a customer buys 10 books the script doesn't look bulky and works as efficiently as ever.

In this chapter, you will learn about functions. You will learn how to declare and create your own custom functions and make them work for you.

Introduction to Functions

A *function* is a self-contained and independent block of code that accomplishes a specific task. Generally, this task might need to be repeated several times over. As a function is a self-contained chunk of code that can operate independently, it is not necessary that it be a part of a given script. This means that a function may be an integral part of a script or may be a part of an external library. If a function is a part of a given script, the code within a function is ignored until the function is called.

The major advantages of using functions while scripting in PHP (or in any other programming language, as a matter of fact) are:

◆ **Simplification of code**. Functions make the code very easy on the eye and therefore very easy to understand. Instead of writing the repetitive code as and where required in the script, you write the code once as a function and call it whenever you need to perform the task. As a result, functions also save your script from being needlessly bulky.

◆ **Reusability of code**. Once written, the function can be called not only from the script that contains the function but also from other scripts. This reduces the onus on you as a programmer to repeat the same functionality in different scripts.

◆ **Modularity of code**. To understand how functions also offer modularity, consider the example cited in the beginning of the chapter. Suppose that after some months the discount being offered on the books is 5 percent, regardless of the total purchase. In this case, you only need to change the code of the function instead of changing the code in many places.

So how does a function work? It's simple! Though you could code a function to behave differently, generally a function will:

1. Accept a value from the script that called it.
2. Process the result on the basis of code specified within it.
3. Return the result and the control to the caller script.

You should be aware of the main features of built-in PHP functions.

◆ The latest and the best feature of PHP 4 is that you don't need to define a function before you reference it. In simpler words, you can call (or reference) a function much earlier in the script and define it much later.

◆ If you have declared a function, you cannot redefine or undefine it. This is because PHP does not support function overloading. Therefore, you have to define each function with a unique name.

NOTE

Function overloading is a feature of functions in other programming languages, such as C and C++, that allows the creation of multiple functions with the same name.

◆ PHP 4 does not allow functions to support a variable number of arguments.

◆ PHP 4 supports default arguments.

You'll get familiar with all of these features as you progress with the chapter.

Next you'll look at the types of functions PHP has to offer you.

Types of Functions

PHP offers two types of functions. These are categorized as:

- ◆ Built-in functions
- ◆ User-defined functions

A close look at these functions follows.

> **NOTE**
>
> Some experts also refer to a third category of functions, namely variable functions. You'll learn about these functions later in this chapter.

Built-in Functions

Built-in functions are predefined functions that are available with PHP and behave in a predetermined manner for which they were created. There are hundreds of built-in functions that you can use. Some of the most commonly used built-in PHP functions that you are already familiar with from the previous chapters include count(), echo(), array_diff(), array_reverse(), etc.

In contrast to the built-in functions provided by PHP are the user-defined functions that are entirely dependent on the programmer's discretion.

User-Defined Functions

Also referred to as custom functions, *user-defined functions* are not provided by PHP. Rather, they are created by the programmer—that is, you. Since you create them, you have complete control of these functions. As a result, you can make a function behave exactly the way you want it to. For this reason, user-defined functions are quite popular in the programmer community.

How can you create your own functions in PHP?

Declaring a Function

The syntax that you would use in PHP is much the same as in other programming languages. Following is the syntax you would use to declare a function in PHP:

```
function function_name ($argument 1, $argument 2, $argument
... ... .., $argument n)
        {
                //code
        }
```

In the above syntax:

- **Function** is the keyword used to declare a user-defined function.

- **Function_Name** is the name of the function that you want to create. This would be the name by which you'll later reference (or call) the function. The function name should be unique because PHP doesn't support function overloading. When naming a function, you need to follow the same rules as in variable-naming conventions. However, the function name cannot start with the $ character, as variables do.

- **Argument(s)** is the value that you pass to the function. As you can see from the above syntax, a function can have multiple arguments, separated by commas. However, arguments are optional. You can choose not to pass an argument while calling a function.

CAUTION

Remember that an argument is always enclosed within parentheses (). Even if you declare a function that takes no arguments when it is called, you still would need to use the parentheses, as in `Function_Name()`.

- **Code** is the set of statements that are executed when the function is called by the main program. The output of the function is the result of this code. If the number of statements is two or more, the code must be included within curly braces ({}). However, you don't need to use these curly braces if the code part of the function contains only one statement.

On the basis of the syntax specified above, you will now learn to create simple argument-less functions.

Argument-less Functions

Following is the example of a simple "argument-less" function.

```php
<?php
  function no_arg() //Declaring the function called no_arg
  {
        echo "Hello World! This is the output of the function.",
"\n"; //Function code
  }
    echo "The function has not been called yet.", "\n";
    no_arg(); //Calling the function from the main script
    echo "The function has been called!", "\n";
  ?>
```

In the above example, a function no_arg has been declared. Since no arguments have been specified in the parentheses following the function name, no_arg is an argument-less function. When the function is called with the help of the statement no_arg();, it displays the message Hello World! This is the output of the function. on the screen. The output of the function is given in Figure 6-1.

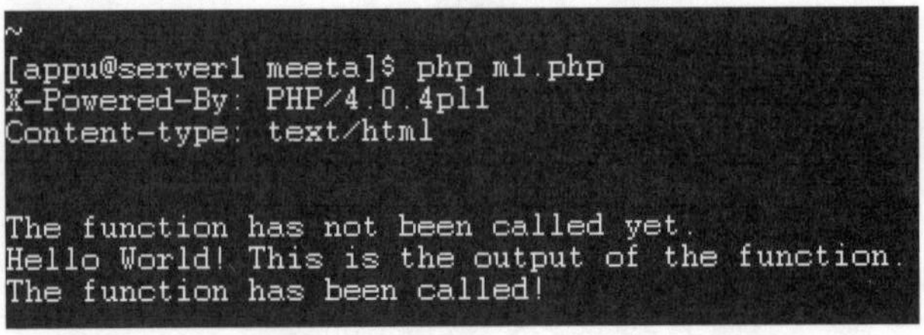

FIGURE 6-1 *Output of an argument-less function*

Now look at how to declare a function with arguments. In this section, you'll also look at what it means to pass parameters to a function and implement the knowledge in your custom functions.

Passing Arguments to Functions

Arguments can be passed to functions in PHP in the following three ways:

◆ Passing default argument values
◆ Passing arguments by values

◆ Passing arguments by reference

You'll focus in detail on each of these argument-passing methods in the following sections.

Passing Default Argument Values

In this method, the function must take an argument when it is called. However, if no value is passed when the function is referenced from the main script, a default value is assigned to the function argument. Following is the example of a function that takes default arguments:

```php
<?php
    function counter( $number = 6) //Declaring a function called
"counter"
    {
        for (; $number < 10; $number++)
        {
            echo $number, "\n";
        }
    }
    echo "The function has not been called yet.", "\n";
    counter(8); //Calling the function and passing the value "8"
to the argument of the function
    counter(); //Calling the function and passing the default
value (6) to the argument of the function
    echo "The function has been called!", "\n";
?>
```

In the above code, the counter function takes the argument number, which has been assigned a value of 6. When the function is called and is passed a value of 8 (counter(8)), the default value of the argument is overridden and is substituted by 8. The function is then executed accordingly. On the other hand, when the function is called and passed no value (counter()), the function takes the default value of the argument and is executed accordingly. The output of the above code is shown in Figure 6-2:

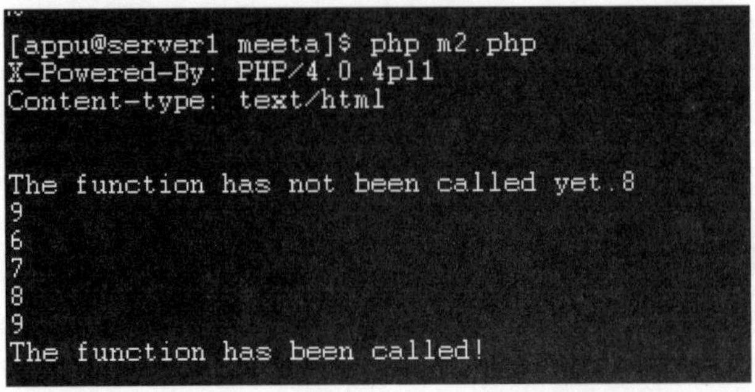

```
[appu@server1 meeta]$ php m2.php
X-Powered-By: PHP/4.0.4pl1
Content-type: text/html


The function has not been called yet.8
9
6
7
8
9
The function has been called!
```

FIGURE 6-2 *Passing default argument values*

Now consider the second method of passing parameters to functions in PHP.

Passing Arguments by Values

This is the default method of passing values to functions in PHP. In this method, a value (or parameter) must be passed to the function when it is called from the main program. Following is the example of a function that takes arguments when it is called:

```php
<?php
    function counter( $number) //Declaring a function called
"counter" that requires a value to be passed to the argument called "number"
    {
        for (; $number < 10; $number++)
        {
            echo $number, "\n";
        }
    }
    echo "The function has not been called yet.", "\n";
    counter(3); //Calling the function and passing the value "3"
to the argument of the function
    echo "The function has been called!", "\n";
?>
```

In the above example, a function called counter has been declared, which takes an argument called number. When you call this function, you must pass a value to the argument of the function. Otherwise, PHP displays an error message. When the counter function is referenced from the main script (counter(3)), the value 3 is passed to its argument number. Each time the for loop runs, it increments the value of number by 1 and prints the result. The output of the above example is shown below in Figure 6-3.

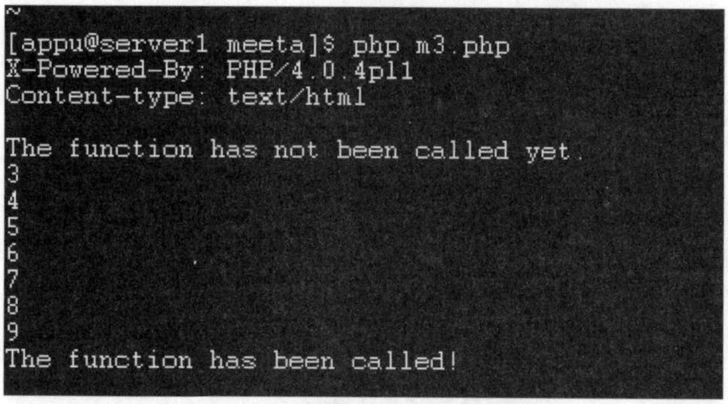

FIGURE 6-3 *Passing argument by values*

The next section discusses the third method of passing values to a function when it is referenced from the main script.

Passing Arguments by Reference

While passing arguments by value, only copies of arguments are passed to the called function. As a result, any modifications done to these values within the called function do not affect the original value in the calling function. Consider the example below:

```php
<?php
  $num = 10;
  function called_function( $number) //Declaring a function that
requires a value to be passed to the argument called "number"
  {
        $number = $number+1;
        echo $number, "\n";
  }
  called_function($num); //Calling the function and passing the
argument "num" to the function
        echo $num, "\n";
?>
```

In this example, the value of the variable num is passed to the `called_function` and is stored in the local variable of `called_function`, which is `number`. The original value passed to the function is incremented by 1 and is displayed. When the control returns to the caller (the main script, here), the original value of num is displayed. This shows that although num was passed to another function, its value remained unchanged in the main script. The output of the above code is shown below in Figure 6-4.

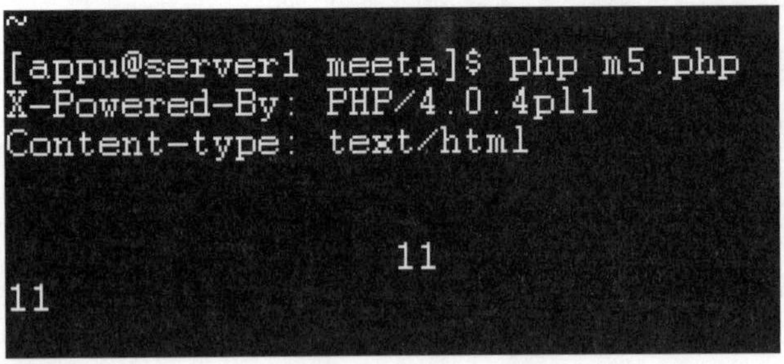

```
~
[appu@server1 meeta]$ php m5.php
X-Powered-By: PHP/4.0.4pl1
Content-type: text/html


                       11
11
```

FIGURE 6-4 *Not passing argument by reference*

Sometimes, such as in a script used for complex mathematical computations, you might want a parameter to be passed to a function and its new value, instead of the older value, to be returned to the calling program or the main script. As you saw in the above example, this is not possible if you pass the argument by its value. However, by passing arguments by reference, you can allow the called function to modify the value of an argument passed to it and return the modified value to the calling function. Arguments are passed by reference by using the sign & before the argument. Consider the following example. It is almost the same as the above example. However, you'll be passing the argument by reference instead of value.

```php
<?php
   $num = 10;
   function called_function( $number) //Declaring a function that
requires a value to be passed to the argument called "number"
      {
              $number = $number+1;
              echo $number, "\n";
      }
   called_function(&$num); //Calling the function and passing the
argument "&num" to the function
```

```
        echo $num, "\n";
    ?>
```

In the preceding example, the argument num is passed by reference. Therefore, instead of a copy of the argument, a reference to the memory location of the argument is passed. As a result, num is modified by called_function. The output of the above code is shown below in Figure 6-5.

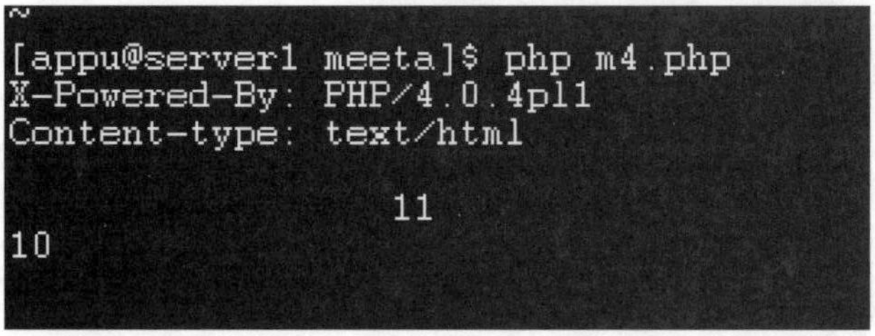

FIGURE 6-5 *Passing argument by reference*

Returning Values from Functions

Functions are also capable of returning a value to the calling function or the main script. In PHP, as in most other programming languages (such as C++), the return statement is used to return the value of a variable to the main script or the calling function. Consider the following example:

```
<?php
  function sum( $num1, $num2) //Declaring a function called sum
  {
          $result = $num1 + $num2;
          return $result;
  }
  echo sum(233, 19), "\n";
?>
```

In the above code, the function named sum has been declared. This function, as the name suggests, is used to calculate the sum of two numbers supplied by the main script. The variable result within the function is used to store the sum of the two numbers that are passed to the function, when the function is called. With the help of the return statement, the result of the computation is returned to the main script, which in turn is displayed on the screen. The output of the above code is shown below in Figure 6-6.

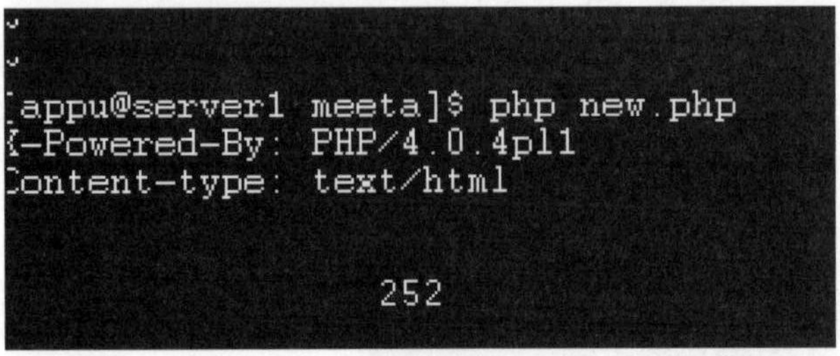

FIGURE 6-6 *Returning values to functions*

Understanding the Scope of a Variable within a Function

Because of your previous programming experience, you have probably come across the term *scope*. If this term doesn't seem familiar, a little discussion might refresh your memory. The term scope refers to the accessibility of a variable that is specified inside a function. In other words, the parts of the PHP script that are outside the function cannot use a variable declared within a function.

Consider an example to understand this well.

```php
<?php
  function sum() //Declaring a function called sum
  {
        $result = 117 + 28;
  }
  echo $result, "\n";
?>
```

In the above example, the output would be blank! Can you guess why? This will make it clearer: The variable result is declared with the function sum. Therefore, its scope is limited to the function. In simpler words, it can only be used within the function and remains inaccessible to the rest of the script that is not a part of the function. When the variable result is used outside the function, it is treated as a new variable whose value has not yet been specified.

Although the scope of a variable limits its accessibility outside the specified function, you can still access a variable specified within a function from outside to make your script more flexible and dynamic. PHP allows the use of two keywords—global and static—to do so.

The global Statement

The global statement allows you to access a variable defined within a function from anywhere in the script. For this, when the variable is declared, it must be preceded by the global statement as follows:

```
global $variable 1;
```

TIP

You can declare more than one variable as global in a single statement. The syntax to do so is: global $variable 1, variable 2, ...;

A modification to the example used earlier to illustrate the concept of scope will show how you can access the variable result from the main script.

```php
<?php
  function sum() //Declaring a function called sum
  {
          global $result;
          echo $result, "\n";
  }
  $result = 0;
  echo $result, "\n";
?>
```

In this example, the output of the code wouldn't be blank. Both results of the echo commands would display 0 and 0 because now the variable result is a global variable and can be accessed from anywhere outside the function, even if it has been initialized outside the function sum. The output of the code is shown in Figure 6-7.

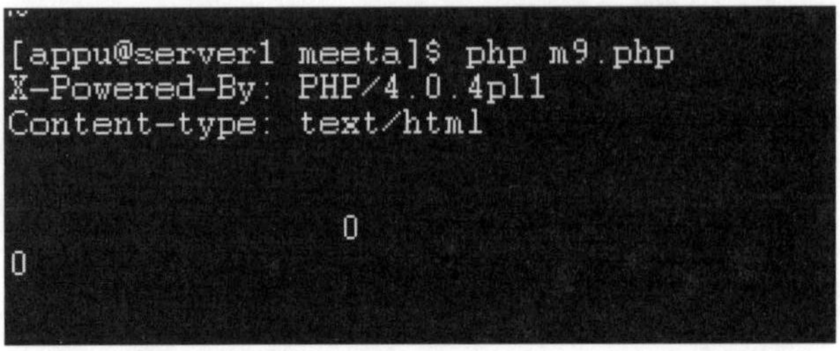

```
[appu@server1 meeta]$ php m9.php
X-Powered-By: PHP/4.0.4pl1
Content-type: text/html

                          0
0
```

FIGURE 6-7 *Using the* global *statement*

The static keyword, although it increases the life span of a variable, functions a little differently from the global keyword. Here's how.

The static Statement

The scope of a variable that has been declared within a function is very short-lived. This means that a variable within a PHP function is initialized when the function is called and is de-initialized when the execution of the function is over and the control is transferred back to the main script or the calling program. By the use of the static keyword, you can effectively increase the life span of a variable within a function.

 CAUTION

Do not confuse static and global variables! A static variable is very different from a global variable. The global variable is, as you already know, accessible from anywhere in the entire script. On the other hand, a static variable remains local to the function. However, unlike normal variables, it doesn't lose its last value once the execution of the function is over.

To understand the concept of the static keyword, consider the following simple example:

```php
<?php
  function sum() //Declaring a function called sum
  {
        $result = 1;
        echo $result, "\n";
```

```
            $result++;
    }
    sum();
    sum();
?>
```

In this example, the function sum is called twice by the main script. Can you predict the result of the above code? Cross-check your answer with what PHP has to display. Refer to Figure 6-8.

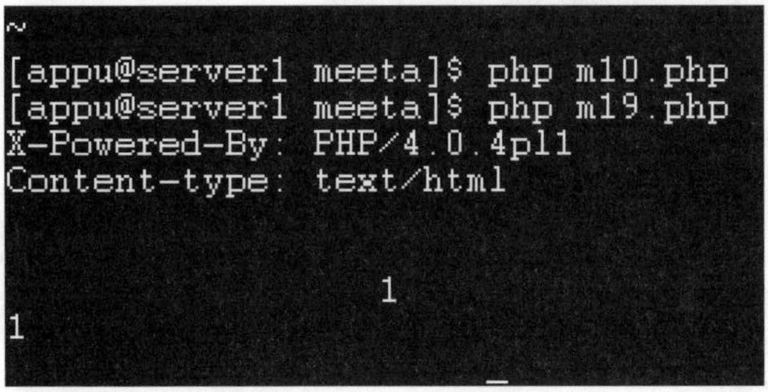

```
~
[appu@server1 meeta]$ php m10.php
[appu@server1 meeta]$ php m19.php
X-Powered-By: PHP/4.0.4pl1
Content-type: text/html


                    1
1
```

FIGURE 6-8 *Not using the* static *statement*

Wondering why? This is because each time you call the function, the variable result is initialized anew and the result of increment statement is lost. This is what is meant by the short life span of a variable. What if you wanted an output that should first display 1 and then, when the function is called next time, display 2? You can make a slight addition to the above code to make it behave the way you want. Precede the declaration of the variable result with the static keyword. Now consider the code below:

```
<?php
  function sum() //Declaring a function called sum
  {
          static $result = 1;
          echo $result, "\n";
          $result++;
  }
  sum();
  sum();
?>
```

When the preceding code is executed, it would display 1 followed by 2 in the next line, as shown in Figure 6-9. All because you made the variable result a `static` variable and forced it to remember its changed value even after the function execution was over.

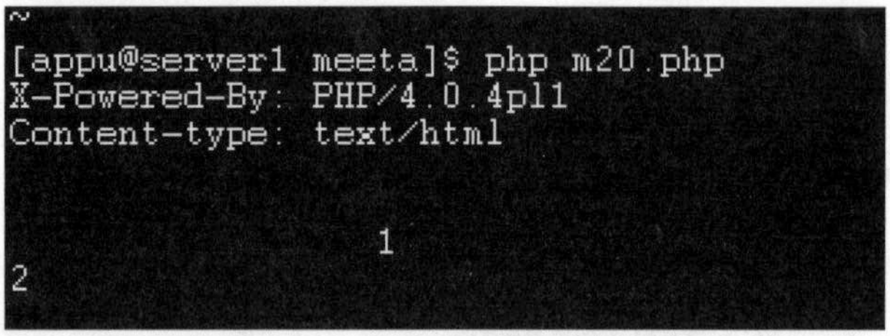

```
[appu@server1 meeta]$ php m20.php
X-Powered-By: PHP/4.0.4pl1
Content-type: text/html


                        1
2
```

FIGURE 6-9 *Using the* static *statement*

PHP supports the concept of *variable functions* and *variable argument functions*. Next you'll learn what variable functions and variable argument functions are and how can you use them.

Variable Functions and Variable Argument Functions

Variable functions are one of the best features used in PHP. If you append parentheses to a variable name, PHP attempts to locate a function with the same name and attempts to execute it. Confused? Then consider the example given below:

```php
<?php
  function amanda()
  {
          echo "My name Is Amanda, \n";
  }
  function noname($name) //Function that accepts an argument as
an Input
  {
          echo "My name Is $name, \n";
  }
  $show = 'amanda';
  $show(); //This Is same as writing amanda();
```

```
$show = 'noname';
$show(Harry);//This Is same as writing noname('Harry');
?>
```

In the above example, there are two functions—amanda and noname. The function noname accepts the name Harry as a parameter, when it is called. In the main script, a variable show has been declared. As you can see, function names have been assigned as a value to this variable. Therefore, it is referred to as a *variable function*.

The output of the above code is shown below in Figure 6-10:

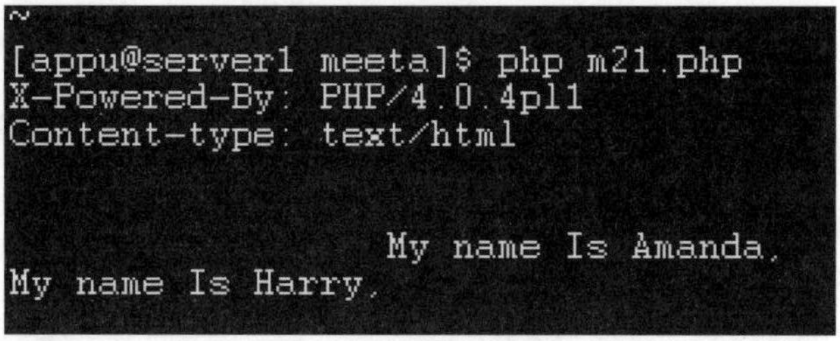

```
[appu@server1 meeta]$ php m21.php
X-Powered-By: PHP/4.0.4pl1
Content-type: text/html


                    My name Is Amanda,
My name Is Harry,
```

FIGURE 6-10 *Using variable functions*

TIP

Variable functions, as you will see later in the projects section of the book, prove to be very useful when the value of the variable is supplied by HTML drop-down lists.

PHP also supports the variable argument functions. A variable argument function is one where the number of arguments passed to the function is not fixed. For example:

```
<?php
showtitles($Itemcode 1);
showtitles($Itemcode 1, $Itemcode 2);
showtitles($Itemcode 1, $Itemcode 2, $Itemcode 3);
?>
```

PHP also provides three other functions to support variable argument functions. These include:

◆ **func_num_args()**: Returns the number of arguments passed to a variable argument function.

NOTE

The index of the argument within a function goes from 0 through *n*, where *n* represents the last argument of the function.

◆ **func_get_arg()**: Returns the value of a particular argument. For example, to return the value of the first argument of a variable argument function, you can state $arg1 = func_get_arg(0).

◆ **func_get_args()**: Returns all arguments passed to the function in the form of an array.

CAUTION

Remember that all of these three functions can only be used with variable argument functions. If you use them with other functions, the results may get interesting!

Summary

In this chapter, you became familiar with functions. You learned what functions are and how they can prove to be useful to you as a PHP programmer. You learned about the various types of functions that are available in PHP—built-in and user-defined. You learned to pass arguments to a function in PHP in three ways, depending on the need of your script: passing default argument values, passing arguments by value, and passing arguments by reference. Next you learned about the scope of a function variable and how it limits the accessibility of these variables outside a function. You also learned how to increase the scope of function variables by using the global statement as well as increase the life span of a function variable after the function execution is over. Finally, you learned about the third type of functions, known as variable functions, which allow you a high degree of flexibility in programming PHP scripts.

Chapter 7

You hear a lot about object-oriented programming. What is it? And most importantly, why do you have to talk about it at all, if you are learning to write scripts in PHP? Well, here I will not go into the depths of object-oriented programming (which is very deep indeed!), but you need to have some idea about object-oriented programming. Although PHP is not a true object-oriented language, many aspects of object-oriented programming have been incorporated into it, more so in PHP 4.

The basic concept of object-oriented programming is that programs should be modeled on real life. In simple words, your PHP scripts must reflect the real world, which they are meant to serve. In the real world, you deal with objects. But look at the world around you. It is full of objects of different shapes, sizes, and colors; objects stationary and mobile; objects that exist in this world for different purposes. If you were to deal with this vast number and variety of objects simultaneously, you would be at a loss. So you can only do what the zoologists do—classify them on the basis of their attributes. Similarly, the millions of objects that you see in this world can be classified into various groups on the basis of common attributes that they possess. These groups are known as *classes*.

In this chapter, you will learn about the concept of classes and the role they have to play in making your PHP scripts survive in the real world. You'll learn how classes are created and how classes inherit functionality from other classes.

Classes

In object-oriented terminology, a *class* is defined as a set of objects that share the same characteristics and display common behavior. Along the same lines, an *object* is defined as an entity that belongs to a class, can be uniquely identified, and exhibits certain behavior that is common to the entire class.

To understand and relate the concept of classes and objects to the real world, consider a simple example from the animal kingdom. The peacock, the sparrow, and the kingfisher are all called birds. Why? Because all of these share some common characteristics. All of them lay eggs and hatch their young ones; all of them are covered with feathers, have hollow bone structures, and have the ability to fly. Thus, you may say that the peacock, the sparrow, and the kingfisher all represent unique objects that share structural and behavioral similarities and belong to the class called birds.

In PHP, a class is a collection of variables and functions. The class variables contain the data that is required for the functionality of the class. Class functions, on the other hand, operate on these class variables and implement the functionality of the given class. An object is an instance of a class that is used to initialize the class.

 NOTE

In PHP literature, class variables are also commonly referred to as *member variables* or *properties*. Similarly, class functions are also known as *methods*.

In the following section, you will learn how to create a class and its objects in the PHP scripting language.

Creating a Class

In PHP, you can define (or create) a class using the following syntax:

```
class class_name //Declaring a class
{
var $variable_name; //Declaring a class variable
function function_name($argument 1, [...][...], $argument n) //Declaring a class
function
{
        //function code
} //The class function ends here
} //The class ends here
```

You'll now create a simple class, using the syntax specified above.

```php
<?php
class PrintName
{
    var $name;

    function show_name()
    {
        echo "\n";
        echo "The name passed to this method is $name.",
"\n";
        echo "Hi $name! How are you doing?", "\n", "\n";
    }
}
?>
```

In the above example, a class called PrintName has been created. This class consists of one member variable (or attribute) called name. The class also consists of a method show_name. This method, when called—as you'll see later—displays two messages with the value that the name variable receives during execution.

Note the keyword var before the member variable, name. Member variables of a class are always declared with the keyword var. This is because var declares the variables as a part (member) of a given class and hence allows member variables to be accessed from outside the class. If you forget to declare member variables of a class without the var keyword, you will end up with a parse error.

Now that you've learned to create a class in PHP, how do you work with it? Bear in mind that, as in other object-oriented programming languages, the data residing in a class (in the form of class variables) and class functions cannot be accessed from outside the class! If you remember your basic concepts in object-oriented programming, this feature is known to programmers as *encapsulation*. Encapsulation entitles the prevention of access to nonessential details within a class.

The member variables and methods are well hidden within the class and are inaccessible. So how will you access these attributes and methods from outside the class? You'll need to instantiate the class to do so. The next section throws light on the instantiation of a class.

NOTE

Note that nonessential does not mean unimportant! Nonessential, here, refers to information that is not required in a given case, but might be highly important in another circumstance.

Instantiating a Class—Making Use of Objects

A class is simply a blueprint. Therefore, it does not exist until you create at least one instance of it. In the terminology of object-oriented languages, this instance of the class is referred to as an *object*. After you've created an object of a class, you can access the member variables as well as the methods hidden within the class to which the object belongs. Consider the following example to understand how you can use the name variable and the show_name() method of the PrintName class that was designed in the preceding example.

```php
<?php
class PrintName
{
        var $name;

        function show_name()
        {
            echo "\n";
            echo "The name passed to this method is $name.",
"\n";

            echo "Hi $name! How are you doing?", "\n", "\n";
        }
}
        $obj1 = new PrintName;    //Instantiating the class called
"PrintName" with the object "obj1".
        $obj1 -> name = "George";    //Setting the value of the class
variable "name" to "George".
        $obj1 -> show_name();   //Calling the method "show_name()".
        ?>
```

In the above example, an object—obj1—of the PrintName class is created. This object instantiates the PrintName class. This means that the class is now allocated

memory and you can now access the variables and methods hidden within it with
the help of the obj1 object. Obj1 uses the -> operator to access the name variable
and show_name() method within the class. Obj1 sets the value of the name variable
to George with the help of the statement $obj1 -> name = "George", and then
calls the show_name() method, which displays the messages The name passed to
this method is George. and Hi George! How are you doing?

NOTE

If you would have tried to set the value of the name variable to George and call the
show_name() method without the object obj1 of the PrintName class, PHP would
have displayed an error.

Figure 7-1 shows the output of the preceding example.

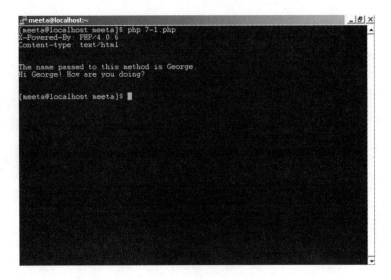

FIGURE 7-1 *Output of the instantiation of a class*

You have learned how to access member methods of a class by using objects. Let
me tell you how you can access these hidden methods without using an object at
all!

Accessing Class Methods without an Object

You can access methods hidden within a class without using an object, with the help of :: notation. Consider the following example to understand how you can do so.

```php
<?php
class area
{
        function calculate_area($length, $breadth)
        {
                return $length * $breadth;
        }
}
$result = area::calculate_area(225, 56);
 echo "The area Is: $result.";
?>
```

In the above code, the use of :: notation provides direct access to the calcu-late_area() method of the area class. The result is calculated on the basis of values supplied at the time the method is called and is returned to the result variable. The output of the above code is The area is 12600.

You've just seen how to access class variables and methods from outside the class in two ways. But how would you access a class variable or method from within the class? Unlike C and C++, PHP doesn't allow you to access class variables and methods by simply using their names even in the class where they were created (or declared). The next section shows you how to get around this problem.

The *$this* Variable

PHP uses a special variable called $this to access a class variable (declared with the help of the var keyword) from within a given class. The use of the $this variable in PHP is the same as creating an instance of the class within the class. It is unlike an object that creates an instance of a class outside a class. The preceding example has been changed a little to demonstrate the use of $this.

```php
<?php
class PrintName
{
        var $name = "George";
```

```
                    function show_name()
                    {
                            echo "Hi $this->name! How are you doing?", "\n",
"\n";
                    }
            }
            $obj1 = new PrintName;
            $obj1 -> show_name();
            ?>
```

In the above example, the `name` variable has been referenced directly within the
`PrintName` class by using the `$this` variable. The output of the above code will be
`Hi George! How are you doing?`

NOTE

In some literature, if you come across the `$this` variable as being referred to as an
"object," do not be alarmed. The terms "special variable" and "object" mean the same
in reference to `$this`.

You can also change the value of a member variable within a member method, as
is demonstrated in the following example.

```
            <?php
            class PrintName
            {
                    var $name = "George";

                    function show_name()
                    {
                            echo "\n", "\n";
                            echo "Hi $this->name! How are you doing?", "\n",
"\n";
                    }
                    function change_name($somename)
                    {
```

```
                              $this->name = $somename;    //Changing the value of
the "name" variable from "George" to

//the new name supplied to the function.
                    }
              }
              $obj1 = new PrintName;
              $obj1 -> show_name();
              $obj1 -> change_name("Amanda");
              $obj1 -> show_name();
              ?>
```

In the above example, first `Hi George! How are you doing?` will be displayed because the `show_name()` method is being called by `obj1` and `George` is the default value of the name variable. The statement `$obj1 -> change_name("Amanda");` causes the `change_name()` method to be called, which resets the value of `name` to `Amanda`. The `show_name()` method is then called, which in turn displays `Hi Amanda! How are you doing?`, as is shown in Figure 7-2.

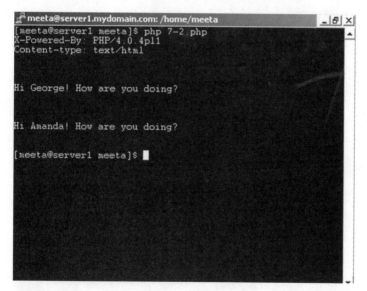

FIGURE 7-2 *Changing the value of a member variable within a member method*

As you might have realized, a member method of a class, like normal functions, is not called until an object accesses it explicitly. It means that until you write the

`$obj1 -> show_name()` statement in your code, the `show_name()` method will not be executed. In the next section, you'll learn about class methods that are executed automatically the moment you instantiate a class (that is, create an object of the class).

Constructors

A *constructor* is a special member method of a class, which is executed automatically when you create an object of the corresponding class. The constructor, by rule, must always have the same name as the class. Therefore, you can have only one constructor within a class. The following example demonstrates the working of a constructor.

```php
<?php
class PrintName
{
        var $name;

        function PrintName()
        {
                $this->name = "Angelica";
                echo "\n", "\n";
                echo "Hi $this->name! How are you doing?", "\n",
"\n";

        }
        function show_name()
        {
                echo "Hi $this->name! How are you doing?", "\n",
"\n";

        }
}
$obj1 = new PrintName;
$obj2 = new PrintName;
?>
```

As shown in Figure 7-3, the output of the above code would be `Hi Angelica! How are you doing?` twice. This is because the `PrintName` method is executed each time you create an object of the `PrintName` class.

CAUTION

Remember that the name of a constructor is case-sensitive. In the preceding example, a method called `printname` or even `Printname` would not be treated as a constructor by PHP.

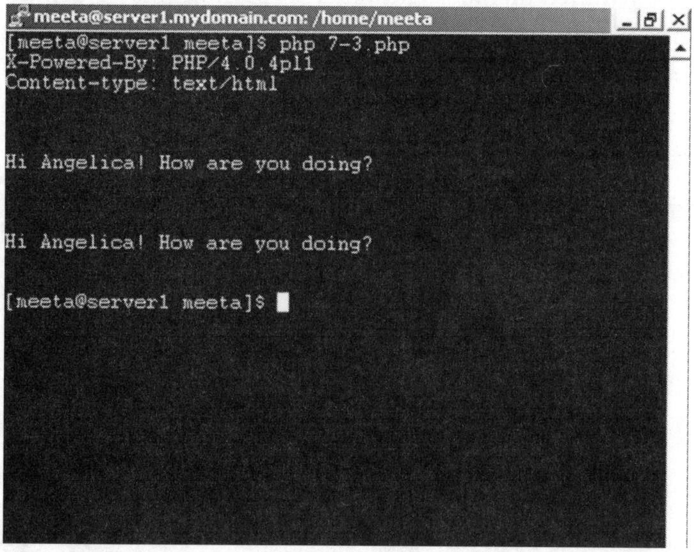

```
meeta@server1.mydomain.com: /home/meeta                    _ 8 X
[meeta@server1 meeta]$ php 7-3.php
X-Powered-By: PHP/4.0.4pl1
Content-type: text/html


Hi Angelica! How are you doing?


Hi Angelica! How are you doing?

[meeta@server1 meeta]$
```

FIGURE 7-3 *Working of a constructor*

In your previous forays with other object-oriented programming languages, you must have come across the concept of *destructors*. A destructor is a special method that is automatically called to free memory space when an object of a class is destroyed. For example, an object might be destroyed if it goes out of scope. However, PHP does not support explicit destructors. You can use the `register_shutdown_function()` to call your own customized function, where the code to free objects is written.

In the next section, you'll learn about an important aspect of classes—inheritance.

Extending a Class—Class Inheritance

The best feature of creating and using classes is the ability to use them time and again. You can create a class once and reuse it in your other programs as well. This helps you to save a lot of time. PHP, like other object-oriented programming languages, facilitates the reusability of classes by implementation of *inheritance*. Inheritance allows you to derive new classes from existing classes. This strategy allows you to reuse required methods and variables in the child (or derived) class and, at the same time, add extra functionality in the derived class, thus having to write less code. The class whose code you reuse is known as the *parent class*.

 NOTE

The parent class is also referred to as the *base class* and the derived class is frequently referred to as the *child class*.

You need to use the keyword `extends` to declare a class that has been derived from an existing class. The syntax to implement inheritance is:

```
Base_class_name extends parent_class_name
```

Inheritance is implemented from the parent class to the derived class. This implies that although an object of a child class can access member variables and methods of the parent class, the same doesn't apply to the object of a parent class. In other words, the object of the parent class cannot access the member variables and methods of the child class. Following is a simple example of inheritance in PHP.

```php
<?php
class ParentClass
{
        function show_message()
        {
            echo "\n", "\n";
            echo "Hi! This comes from the parent class.", "\n",
"\n";
        }
}
class ChildClass extends ParentClass    //Inheriting "ChildClass" from "Parent
```

```
                {
                        function show()
                        {
                                echo "\n", "\n";
                                echo "Hi! This comes from the child class.", "\n",
"\n";
                        }
                }
                $obj1 = new ParentClass;    //Object of "ParentClass".
                $obj1 -> show_message();    //This will work because "obj1" is an
object of "ParentClass" and is
                                                        //accessing the
method of the same class.
                $obj2 = new ChildClass;    //Object of "ChildClass".
                $obj2 -> show();    //This will work because object of
"ChildClass" is accessing a method in the
                                                        //same class.
                $obj2 -> show_message();    //This will work because an object of
"ChildClass" is accessing a
                                                        //method in the
"ParentClass".
                $obj1 -> show();    //This will not work because an object of
"ParentClass" is accessing a
                                                        //method in "ChildClass".
                ?>
```

In the above example, two classes—ParentClass and ChildClass—have been declared. As the name suggests, ChildClass has been derived from ParentClass with the help of the keyword extends. obj1 is the object of class ParentClass and obj2 belongs to ChildClass. When obj2 accesses the show_message() method of ParentClass, the message Hi! This comes from the parent class. is displayed. This is because ChildClass has been derived from ParentClass and has access to its hidden properties. On the other hand, when obj1 accesses the method show() of the derived class, ChildClass, PHP displays an error message. This is because the methods and member variables of the derived class are inaccessible to ParentClass.

The output of the above code is depicted in Figure 7-4.

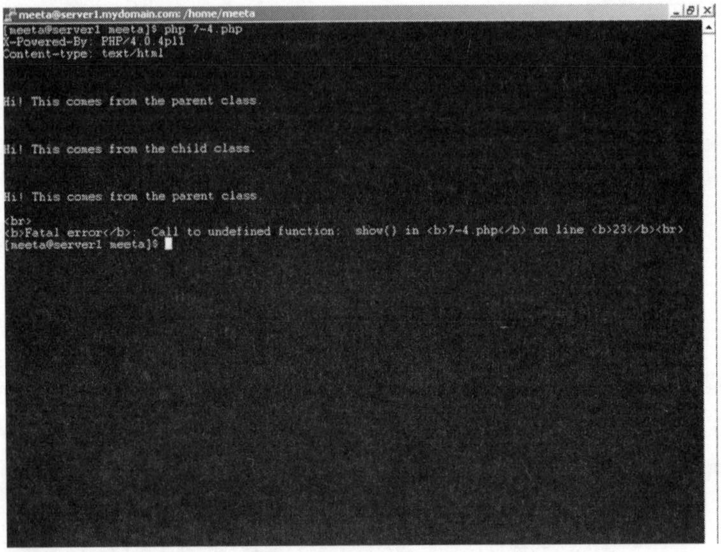

FIGURE 7-4 *Output of simple class inheritance*

If you derive a child class from the base class, the child class will inherit all the variables as well as functions of the parent class. But if you would like to redefine a function of the parent class, this would not be possible. This is because you cannot change the method's functionality in the parent class as some other program might also be using the current parent class. In such cases, PHP allows you to redefine a member method of the parent class by overriding the methods that belong to the parent class in the child class. The following section discusses the concept of method overriding in PHP.

Overriding Methods

Overriding a method means redefining a method inherited from the parent class in the child class. This feature of PHP (and any other object-oriented language) helps you avoid the rigidity while implementing the parent class and helps you make your PHP scripts flexible.

You can override methods defined in a parent class in the child class by defining a method of the same name in the child class. In this method, you can implement the desirable functionality. The following example will help you understand this.

```php
<?php
class ParentClass
```

```
        {
                function show_message()
                {
                        echo "\n", "\n";
                        echo "Hi! This comes from the parent class.", "\n",
"\n";
                }
        }
        class ChildClass extends ParentClass
        {
                function show_message()    //Overriding the "show_mes-
sage()" function In "ParentClass".
                {
                        echo "\n", "\n";
                        echo "Hi! This comes from the child class.", "\n",
"\n";

                        echo "This is how you override functions.", "\n",
"\n";
                }
        }
        $obj2 = new ChildClass;    //Object of "ChildClass".
        $obj2 -> show_message();    //This will display the message
defined In the "show_message()

                                                //method of the
child class.
        ?>
```

In the above example, ChildClass inherits the show_message() method from ParentClass. However, this method has been redefined in the child class with the same name. As a result, when the statement obj2 -> show_message(); is executed, the messages Hi! This comes from the child class. and This is how you override functions. are displayed instead of the message Hi! This comes from the parent class.

Figure 7-5 displays the output of the above code.

In the next section, you'll learn to access a method of the parent class indirectly from the child class.

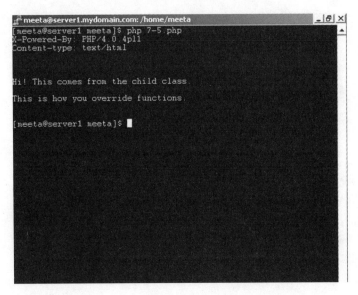

FIGURE 7-5 *Overriding methods inherited from parent class*

Indirectly Accessing Methods of Parent Class

You can once again use the :: notation to indirectly access the methods of a parent class from a child class. This feature proves to be useful when you have overridden a particular function in the child class, but would like to reuse the overridden function in the child class. The syntax to do so is:

```
parent::method_name();
```

Confused? Consider the following example.

```php
<?php
class ParentClass
{
        function show_message()
        {
            echo "\n", "\n";
            echo "Hi! This comes from the parent class.", "\n",
"\n";
        }
```

```
            }
            class ChildClass extends ParentClass
            {
                    function show_message()    //Overriding the "show_mes-
sage()" function In "ParentClass".
                    {
                            echo "\n", "\n";
                            echo "Hi! This comes from the child class.", "\n",
"\n";
                            echo "This is how you override functions.", "\n",
"\n";
                    }
                    function show()    //Overriding the "show_message()" func-
tion In "ParentClass".
                    {
                            parent::show_message();
                    }
            }
            $obj2 = new ChildClass;    //Object of "ChildClass".
            $obj2 -> show();    //This will display the message defined In
the "show_message()
                                            //method of the parent class.
            ?>
```

In the above example, when the object, obj2, of the child class calls the show()
method in the same class, the message Hi! This comes from the parent class.
is displayed. The output is shown in Figure 7-6.

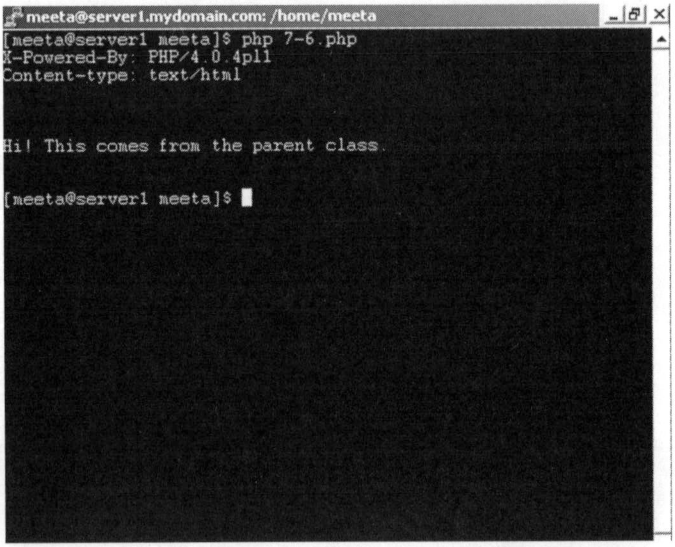

FIGURE 7-6 *Accessing the methods of the parent class indirectly*

Summary

In this chapter, you learned the basics of object-oriented programming that you can implement by using classes. First you learned to create classes in PHP. You learned that just creating a class is not enough for you to be able to use it. You learned the role an object has to play in allocating memory space to a class and facilitating access to the variables and methods hidden within the class. You also learned to access the member methods of a class without making use of an object. Then you learned about the special variable $this, which helps you to make use of member methods and variables within the class itself. You learned about the constructor functions and how they can help you to initialize a required variable automatically. Finally, you learned about another real-life aspect of classes—inheritance. You learned to create child classes that inherit complete functionality from the parent class. Here you also learned to override a method inherited from the parent class, thus making your code highly flexible.

Chapter 8

So far you have learned quite a lot about PHP. However, this learning has only been theoretical. Let me now enhance your knowledge of PHP further and put all that you have learned so far into practice. From this point on you will be creating a complete online shopping site for a book store, which will be built using PHP.

In this chapter, I'll give you an overview of the complete Web site and different features of this Web site. All of the projects in this chapter and the following chapters will be based on a fictitious book store, Bukbuz, Inc.

About Bukbuz, Inc.

Bukbuz, Inc. is a locally owned book store located in New York City, USA. Currently Bukbuz, Inc. has more than 50,000 ready-to-ship books. It covers an area of about 10,000 square feet and two floors. It also hosts at least five author appearances per month and has had the distinction of receiving the prestigious "Best Book Store in New York" five times in a row.

Of late, Bukbuz, Inc. has been experiencing a fall in its sales. Bukbuz, Inc. conducted a survey to find out the potential causes of a dip in sales. The results of the survey reflected a spurt of new competitive book stores and the growing popularity of e-commerce as the two most potential reasons for the dip in sales. As a result, Bukbuz, Inc. can no longer afford to rely only on its loyal customer base. It needs to explore new markets and also tap potential new customers.

Opening up more book stores does not seem to be a feasible solution, as it involves a lot of investment in terms of both cost and time. Hence, realizing the gravity of the situation and after studying the latest trends, the management at Bukbuz, Inc. has decided to plunge into the world of Internet commerce.

The task of putting Bukbuz, Inc. on the Internet has been assigned to Paul Solomon, who currently heads the technical books division at Bukbuz, Inc. Paul Solomon holds a masters degree in Computer Science and is considered the most tech-savvy guy at Bukbuz, Inc. Paul has been constantly upgrading his knowledge about the latest trends in IT and has done much research on the major software solution providers. As the result of his research and knowledge, Paul has decided to approach Solution@net, Inc. to get a Web site created for Bukbuz, Inc.

The Bukbuz, Inc. Web Site

As discussed, Paul has approached Solution@net, Inc. to create a Web site for Bukbuz, Inc. Solution@net, Inc. is a well-regarded Web solutions provider organization with many famous Web sites to its credit. Solution@net, Inc. has assigned the task of creating the Web site for Bukbuz, Inc. to Chris Newman. Chris is a senior Web developer at Solution@net, Inc. and has been involved in developing several online shopping sites.

After much research and groundwork, Paul has prepared a functional specifications document which details the features that the Bukbuz, Inc. Web site will have. Paul has handed over this document to Chris. A copy of this document is shown in Figure 8-1.

Bukbuz, Inc.   450 East 55th Street
                                                  New York, NY 10019
                                                  Tel: (212) 548-1221

Solutions@net, Inc
1664 Bedford Road
Pleasantville, NY 10570

Functional Specifications Document for the Bukbuz, Inc. Web site

- The first Web page of the Web site should be the Home page, which contains links to information such as "About Bukbuz, Inc.", how to contact us, an overview of the categories of books that are available in the store, and links to the other Web pages on the site. Existing users should be able to log in and new users should be able to get themselves registered.
- The Web site should also support security features such as user authentication and password encryption.
- A user registration form should be provided for new users to get registered.
- The Web site should have a database that stores each and every category of information about books, such as the author, price, publication, and some description. In addition, the database should also contain information about registered users and the details of their transactions, such as the books they bought, the price they paid, the date on which they bought the books, and a mode of payment.
- There should be a product catalog that displays information about all the books that are available.
- Users should be able to create, add items to, and modify their shopping carts.

Paul Solomon
Bukbuz, Inc.

FIGURE 8-1 *The Functional Specifications Document for the Bukbuz, Inc. Web site*

After going through the document, Chris starts developing the project. Every project has a definite project life cycle. Following are the various stages of a project life cycle.

Project Life Cycle

The project life cycle includes various development phases that occur in the life of a project starting right from the inception of the project to its final deployment at the client's end. The three development phases in a project life cycle are:

- Project initiation
- Project execution
- Project deployment

The project initiation phase is the first phase of a project life cycle. This phase involves creating a complete plan for the project, specifying various activities that will be performed, and assigning responsibilities to team members on the basis of their skill sets.

After the project plan is made and the responsibilities assigned, the actual development of the project starts. The phase in which the actual development of the project takes place is known as the project execution phase. This is the most crucial phase of any project and is subdivided into the following phases:

- Requirements analysis
- High-level design
- Low-level design
- Construction
- Integration and testing
- User acceptance test

After the project execution phase, the final phase of a project life cycle is the project deployment phase. In this phase, the project is deployed at the client side. This phase also involves providing customer support to the client for some specified period of time.

As just discussed, the project execution phase is the most crucial phase of the project life cycle. You will now learn in detail about the various phases that are included in the project execution phase.

Requirements Analysis

Accurate requirements analysis is the most basic and imperative step that determines the success or failure of any project. If the requirements are not analyzed appropriately the project loses its complete meaning and value. In case of the Bukbuz, Inc. Web site, the functional specifications document provided by Paul to Chris sets out the basic requirements that the application developed by Solution@net, Inc. should accomplish.

According to the Bukbuz, Inc.'s functional specifications document, the application should:

◆ Allow users to view categories of books available at Bukbuz, Inc.

◆ Support security features for authenticating users.

◆ Allow customers to register themselves at the Bukbuz, Inc. Web site.

◆ Allow customers to browse through the product catalog, the same way as they would do when visiting the Bukbuz, Inc. book store.

◆ Allow customers to create and modify their shopping carts.

However, these requirements are far too generic to be used as a basis for developing a complete Web site. They leave much to be desired in terms of who would be the end user of the application, what kind of visual appeal is wanted, and much more. As a result, Chris now needs to put all his experience into practice and develop such an application that adequately answers all questions and satisfies his clients.

After thoroughly analyzing the customer's requirements, Chris has decided that the Bukbuz, Inc. Web site will consist of two types of components:

◆ The customer interface component

◆ The administrator component

The customer interface component will provide a platform for customers of Bukbuz, Inc. to interact online with Bukbuz, Inc. and buy books. The administrator component will help the system administrator at Bukbuz, Inc. add new categories or products to the product catalog and keep a check on the billing and resolve security issues.

Customers visiting the Bukbuz, Inc. Web site will use the customer interface component to:

- Get themselves registered at the Bukbuz, Inc. Web site.
- Contact Bukbuz, Inc. for any specific query, comments, or feedback.
- Browse through different books and categories that are available at the Bukbuz, Inc. book store.
- Search for any particular book or author.
- Order books that they wish to buy.
- View some information about different books.
- Choose the mode of payment when they are ordering books.
- Get the books delivered on their doorsteps.

The system administrator at Bukbuz, Inc. will use the administrator component to:

- Update the database from time to time.
- Validate and authenticate billing information.
- Add new products and categories to the product catalog.

After the requirement analysis phase is over and some basic framework is ready, the project progresses into the high-level design phase.

High-Level Design

In the high-level design phase, the functionality of the application is finalized. This phase involves:

- Discussing the complete flow of information within the application.
- Finalizing the data input and output interfaces.
- Designing the database.
- Specifying the operational requirements including hardware and software requirements.
- Discussing user interfaces with the client and getting their approval.

Figure 8-2 illustrates the complete information flow in the instance of the Bukbuz, Inc. Web site.

As shown in the figure, the first screen that appears when a customer visits the Bukbuz, Inc. Web site is the home page. Figure 8-3 displays the home page of the

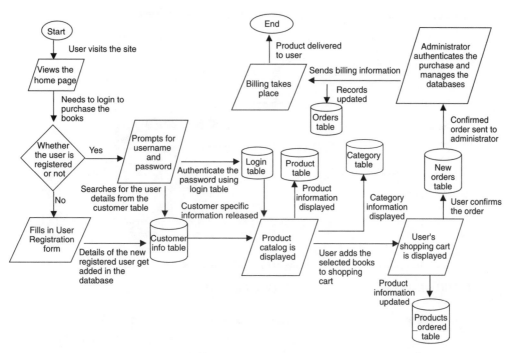

FIGURE 8-2 *The Bukbuz, Inc. Web site Data Flow Diagram*

Bukbuz, Inc. Web site. The home page contains options for registered customers as well as new customers. The home page also contains links that provide information about Bukbuz, Inc. and for contacting Bukbuz, Inc. with any queries or feedback. In addition, the home page displays information about the different categories of books that are available in Bukbuz, Inc.

Notice that the home page contains two links, which are "About us" and "Feedback". When a customer clicks on the "About us" link, a new window opens and displays information about Bukbuz, Inc. Figure 8-4 shows the "About us" window.

When a customer clicks on the "Feedback" link a new window opens, which contains a form. The customer can fill in this form and contact Bukbuz, Inc. for any feedback or suggestions. Figure 8-5 displays the "Feedback" window.

Users who are not registered with the Bukbuz, Inc. Web site cannot place an order for any books on the Web site. Therefore, users need to first register themselves with Bukbuz, Inc. to buy a book. The process of registration at Bukbuz, Inc. is very simple. When a user clicks on the link for new user in the Bukbuz, Inc. home page, a user registration form appears, as shown in Figure 8-6.

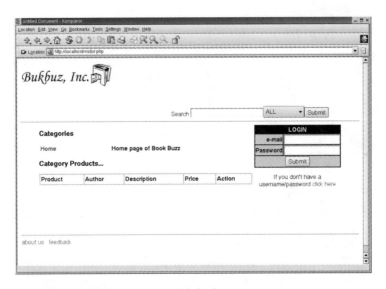

FIGURE 8-3 *The Bukbuz, Inc. Web site home page*

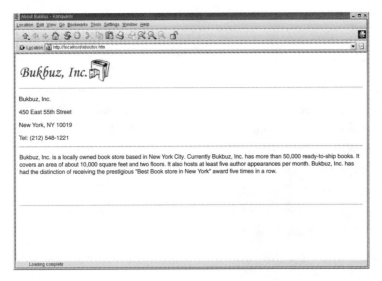

FIGURE 8-4 *The Bukbuz, Inc. "About us" information page*

After getting registered, a user can order books through the Bukbuz, Inc. online product catalog and create their own shopping cart. All details entered by a user are stored in the Bukbuz, Inc. database. I'll discuss the Bukbuz, Inc. database later in the chapter, under the topic "Database Design for the Bukbuz, Inc. Web Site."

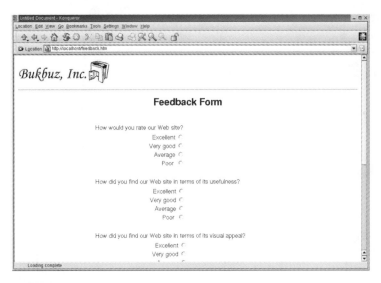

FIGURE 8-5 *The Bukbuz, Inc. "Feedback" page*

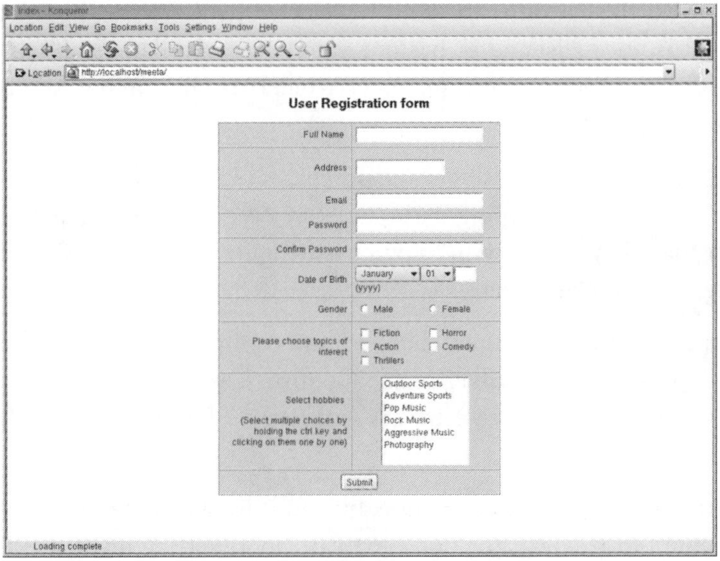

FIGURE 8-6 *The User Registration form*

Figure 8-7 displays the Bukbuz, Inc. online product catalog.

Using the product catalog, a customer can search for books of their choice. The product catalog also allows the customer to select books of their choice. After

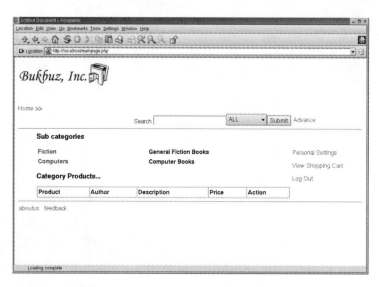

FIGURE 8-7 *The Bukbuz, Inc. online product catalog*

selecting the books the customer can add the selected books to the shopping cart. If the customer is not registered or has not entered a login name and password, then they are directed back to the login screen when they click on the Add to Cart link.

The shopping cart shows details about the purchases made by the customer. Customers can modify their shopping carts and can even remove books from the shopping cart that they do not wish to purchase. Figure 8-8 displays the Bukbuz, Inc. shopping cart for a customer.

To confirm the order, the customer clicks on the confirm order link. When the link is clicked, it takes the customer to the Confirm Order Web page. After the customer has confirmed the order, e-mail is sent to the administrator and the customer confirming the order.

This complete information flow, functionality, and design of the interfaces and forms is presented to Bukbuz, Inc. for approval. Upon getting an approval from Bukbuz, Inc., the project then moves on to its next stage, which is the low-level design phase.

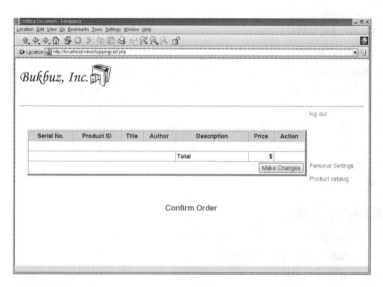

FIGURE 8-8 *The Bukbuz, Inc. shopping cart for a customer*

Low-Level Design

The low-level design phase involves preparing a comprehensive design of the various software modules based on the high-level design. In addition, it involves specifying standards, laying down processes, and documenting all the standards. Documenting the standards helps to maintain consistency across the various modules of an application. Chris and his team have also documented the various standards that they will be using in the construction phase. Some of these standards include naming conventions for variables, controls, and different file names.

Construction

The construction phase involves coding for various components of the application. This phase makes use of the various standards and specifications that are decided in the low-level design phase. The Bukbuz, Inc. Web site project will be built by using PHP. Chris has already created the home page for the Bukbuz, Inc. Web site.

 NOTE

For your reference, the code that Chris has used for creating the home page for the Bukbuz, Inc. Web site is given at the end of this chapter.

Integration and Testing

The integration and testing phase, as is evident from the name itself, involves validating the code for each component. After all code has been validated and tested, the various components are integrated. Finally, after the complete integration of all the components, a check is run to look for any malfunctions or discrepancies from the planned application. For the complete Bukbuz, Inc. Web site to function, all the user interfaces, such as user registration form, product catalog page, and shopping cart, need to be integrated.

User Acceptance Test

This is the final stage of the project execution phase. It involves testing the complete application based on acceptance criteria as defined by the client. The application is also tested in the actual deployment environment. All the issues and bugs, if reported, are fixed. In case of Bukbuz, Inc., Chris can ask Paul and a few others to first use the application and give him the feedback.

Next you'll learn how the Bukbuz, Inc. Web site stores and manages all the data.

Database Design for the Bukbuz, Inc. Web Site

Chris has decided to use MySQL database for the Bukbuz, Inc. Web site. MySQL is the most common and comprehensive database and is used by a majority of PHP applications. The Bukbuz, Inc. Web site database is named "books". It consists of the following tables that store the customer and product information:

◆ customerinfo table
◆ category table
◆ products table
◆ orders table
◆ products_ordered table
◆ neworder table
◆ login table

Let me now discuss each of these tables in detail.

The Customerinfo Table

The customerinfo table stores details of all the registered customers of Bukbuz, Inc. The fields of this table are listed in Table 8-1.

Table 8-1 Fields in the Customerinfo Table

Field	Description
customerid	This is the primary key of the customerinfo table. Every customer is assigned a unique customer ID.
name	The name field stores the full name of the customers.
address	The address field stores the address as entered by the customer. It is the value of this field that is used as a destination for delivering the books.
dob	The dob field stores the date of birth values entered by the customer.
gender	The gender field stores the gender value that is selected by the customer in the user registration field.

The customerinfo table receives its values from the user registration form.

The Category Table

The category table stores the values of different categories of books that are available at Bukbuz, Inc. The fields of this table are listed in Table 8-2.

Table 8-2 Fields in the Category Table

Field	Description
categoryid	Every category is assigned a category ID, which is unique to each category. The categoryid field is the primary key of the category table.
parentcategoryid	There are different categories of books at Bukbuz, Inc. book store. However, there are certain parent categories and certain subcategories. Each parent category has a unique ID that is stored in the parentcategoryid field.

continues

Table 8-2 *(continued)*

Field	Description
name	The name field stores the category name, such as fiction, comedy, and sports.
description	The description field contains brief information about the categories under which the books are categorized.

Only the system administrator can update the category table. These updates might include adding a category, deleting a category, or modifying the details of a category.

The Products Table

The products table stores details about all the books that are available in the Bukbuz, Inc. book store. The fields of this table are listed in Table 8-3

Table 8-3 Fields in the Products Table

Field	Description
productid	This is the primary key of the products table. Each book in the Bukbuz, Inc. database has a unique product ID.
name	The name field stores the name of each book in the products table.
author	The author field stores the name of the author of each book.
description	Just like the description field in the category table, the description field of the products table also contains brief information about each book.
price	The price field contains the price (in dollars) for each book.
category	The category field contains the name of the category under which the book is categorized.

The Orders Table

The orders table contains details about different orders that have been placed by customers. The fields of this table are listed in Table 8-4.

Table 8-4 Fields in the Orders Table

Field	Description
ordered	This is the primary key of the orders table. Every order is assigned a unique order ID.
orderdate	The orderdate field contains the date when the customer placed the order.
price	The price field gives the total price that the customer has to pay for the books that they have ordered.
status	The status field indicates whether the order is still pending or has been delivered to the customer.

The Products_ordered Table

The products_ordered table stores information about which book has been ordered and the order ID. The fields of this table are listed in Table 8-5.

Table 8-5 Fields in the Products_ordered Table

Field	Description
id	This is the primary key of the products_ordered table. The id field is an auto increment field.
productid	The productid field stores the product ID value of the book that has been ordered.
orderid	The orderid field contains the order ID value of the order under which the book has been ordered.

The Neworder Table

The neworder table stores all products that have been selected by different customers. The fields of this table are listed in Table 8-6.

Table 8-6 Fields in the Neworder Table

Field	Description
id	This is the primary key of the neworder table. The id field is an auto increment field.
customerid	Each customer is assigned a unique customer ID, which uniquely identifies a customer in the customerinfo table. However, in the neworder table the value of the customerid field is not unique, as a customer can buy more than one product. As a result customerid will appear as many times in this table as the number of products in a customer's cart.
productid	Each product is assigned a unique product ID, which uniquely identifies a product in the products table. Just like the customerid field, the productid field can also appear more than once in the neworder table, since more than one customer can order the same product.

The Login Table

The login table stores the username and password values of the registered customers. The fields of this table are listed in Table 8-7.

Table 8-7 Fields in the Login Table

Field	Description
customerid	The customerid field stores the customer login name.
password	The password field stores the value of the password entered by the customer. Passwords act as a measure of security so that an unregistered person is not able to order books by impersonating a registered user.
category	The category field contains the name of the category under which the book is categorized.

There are many more tables that will be used while developing the application.

Code for Bukbuz, Inc. Web Site Home Page

After having learned about the information flow and getting an overview of the case study, you will next get down to developing the application. As mentioned earlier in the chapter, following is the code used by Chris for developing the Bukbuz, Inc. home page.

```html
<html>
<head>
<title>Untitled Document</title>
<meta http-equiv="Content-Type" content="text/html; charset=iso-8859-1">
</head>
<body bgcolor="#FFFFFF" text="#000000">
<p> </p>

<?php
        $host="";
        $dbusername="root";
        $dbpassword="";
        $database="books";
        $x=mysql_connect($host,$dbusername,$dbpassword);
        $x2=mysql_select_db($database);

        if (empty($category))
        {
        $category=1;
        }

        $childval=$category;
         $query = "select categoryid, name from category where cate-
goryid=\"" . $childval ."\"";
        $result=mysql_query($query);
        if ($row=mysql_fetch_array($result))
        {
```

```php
$catid[1]=$row["categoryid"];
$catname[1]=$row["name"];
}

while (!($childval==0))
{
$query="select parentcategoryid from category where catego-
ryid=\"".$childval."\"";
$result=mysql_query($query);
if ($row=mysql_fetch_array($result))
{
$childval= $row["parentcategoryid"];
$query = "select categoryid,name from category where catego-
ryid=\"" . $childval ."\"";
$result=mysql_query($query);
if ($row=mysql_fetch_array($result))
{
$catid[]=$row["categoryid"];
$catname[]=$row["name"];
}
}
}

for ($i=count($catname); $i>0;$i—)
{
echo "<A href=visitor.php?category=".$catid[$i].">".$cat-
name[$i] . "</a> >> ";
}
?>

<table width="900" border="0" cellpadding="3" cellspacing="1">
<tr>
<td> </td>
<td> </td>
<td> </td>
<td>

<form name="form1" method="post" action="search.php">
```

```
<div align="right">Search
<input type="text" name="search" size="20">
<select name="searchfor">
<option value="ALL">ALL</option>
<option value="titles">Book Titles</option>
<option value="author">Authors</option>
</select>

<?php
echo "<input type=\"hidden\" name=\"category\" value=\"".$cat-
egory."\">
";
?>

<input type="submit" name="Submit" value="Submit">
</div>
</form>
</td>
<td>
</td>
</tr>
</table>
<hr>
<table width="90%" border="0" align="center" cellspacing="1"
cellpadding="3">

<tr>
<td height="121">
<h2> Sub categories </h2>
<table width="100%" border="0"  cellspacing="1" cell-
padding="3">
<?

$query="select categoryid,name,description from category where
parentcategoryid=\"".$category."\"";
$result=mysql_query($query);
while ($row = mysql_fetch_array($result))
{
echo "
```

```
                        <tr>
                        ";
                        echo "    <td  height=\"5\">
                        ";
                        echo "         <p><b><a href=\"visitor.php?category=".$row["cate-
goryid"]."\">".$row["name"]."</a></b></p>
                        ";
                        echo "
                        </td>
                        ";
                        echo "    <td width=\"400\"  height=\"5\">
                        ";
                        echo "         <p><b>". $row["description"]."</b></p>
                        ";
                        echo "   </td>
                        ";
                        echo "  </tr>
                        ";
                        }

            ?>

                        </table>
                        <h2>Category Products...</h2>
                        <table width="100%" border="1" align="center" cellspacing="1"
            cellpadding="3">

                        <tr>
                        <td><b> Product </b>
                        </td>

                        <td><b> Author   </b>
                        </td>
                        <td><b> Description </b>
                        </td>

                        <td><b> Price </b>
                        </td>
                        <td colspan=2><b> Action </b>
                        </td>
```

```
        </tr>

    <?

        $query="select productid,name, author, description,price from
products where category=\"".$category."\"";
        $result=mysql_query($query);
        while ($row = mysql_fetch_array($result))
        {
        echo "
        <tr>
        ";
        echo "   <td>
        ";
        echo "      <p><b>".$row["name"]."</b></p>
        ";
        echo "   </td>";
        echo "   <td>
        ";
        echo "      <p><b>".$row["author"]."</b></p>
        ";
        echo "
        </td>
        ";
        echo "
        <td>
        ";
        echo "
        <p>". $row["description"]."
        </p>
        ";
        echo "
        </td>
        ";
        echo "
        <td>
        ";
        echo "
        <p>". $row["price"]."
```

```
        </p>
        ";
        echo "
        </td>


        ";
        echo "
        <td width=\"120\">
        ";
        echo "
        <A href=\"login.htm\" >Add to cart</a>
        ";
        echo "
        </td>


        ";
        echo "
        <td width=\"120\">
        ";
        echo "
        <A href=\"login.htm\">Remove from cart</a>
        ";
        echo "
        </td>
        ";
        echo "
        </tr>
        ";
        }
    ?>
        </table>
        </td>


        <td width="200" height="121">
        <form name="form1" method="post" action="login.php">
        <table width="200" border="1" align="center" cellspacing="0"
cellpadding="1" bordercolor="#000000">
        <tr>
```

```
<td colspan="2" bgcolor="#000000">
<div align="center"><font
color="#FFFFFF"><b>LOGIN</b></font></div>
</td>
</tr>

<tr bgcolor="#CCCCCC">
<td>
<div align="right"><b>e-mail</b></div>
</td>

<td>
<div align="center">
<input type="text" name="email" size="15" maxlength="100">
</div>
</td>
</tr>

<tr bgcolor="#CCCCCC">
<td>
<div align="right"><b>Password </b></div>
</td>

<td>
<div align="center">
<input type="password" name="password" maxlength="15"
size="15">
</div>
</td>
</tr>

<tr bgcolor="#CCCCCC">
<td colspan="2">
<center>
<input type="submit" name="Submit2" value="Submit">
</center>
</td>
</tr>
```

```
                              </table>
                              </form>
<p align="center">If you don't have a username/password <a
href="add_customer.htm">click
                              here</a></p>
                              </td>
                              </tr>
                              </table>

                              <p> 
                              </p>
                              <p> 
                              </p>
                              <p> 
                              </p>
                              <hr>
                              <table align=\"center\">
                              <tr>
                              <td><a href="aboutus.htm"   target="_blank">  about us </a>
                              </td>
                              <td><a href="feedback.htm"  target="_blank"> feedback </a>
                              </td>
                              </tr>
                              </table>

                              <p> 
                              </p>
                              <p> 
                              </p>
                              </body>
                              </html>
```

Summary

In this chapter, you learned about the Bukbuz, Inc. book store. Due to a dip in sales the management of Bukbuz, Inc. has decided to explore the Internet world and launch a Web site. For this purpose they have hired the services of Solution@net, Inc. which is a software solution provider company. Based on the functional specifications document received from Bukbuz, Inc., Solution@net, Inc. has devised a completed solution for Bukbuz, Inc.

Then you learned about the project life cycle and its different phases. You got a feel for the various user interfaces and screens that you would be developing using PHP. Finally, you learned about the database design of the Bukbuz, Inc. Web site.

PART II

Professional Project 1

Project 1

**Creating a User
Registration Form
for an Online
Shopping Site**

Project 1 Overview

In this project, I'll teach you how to create a complete Web page using HTML. You will begin by learning about the different features and elements of HTML.

In Chapter 9 you'll learn about the basic concepts of HTML. You'll learn about tags and how you can use them to create Web pages. You'll also learn about the different categories of HTML tags. Some of the tags that you will learn about are:

◆ `Html, head,` and `body` tags and their attributes

◆ Formatting tags such as `heading, paragraph, comment, font,` and `boldface` tags

◆ Form tags that are used to accept information from users and customers

◆ Table elements that are used to arrange elements in a Web page in a systematic manner

Then you'll use some of these tags to create a user registration form. This form will accept personal information from the user, such as name, street address, e-mail address, date of birth, gender, interests, and hobbies.

In Chapter 10 you'll learn about how information is read from an HTML Web page and checked based on certain conditions. You'll learn how to retrieve information from text boxes, check boxes, radio buttons, and multiple selection lists. You'll check if the user has entered a value and if the entered information is of acceptable length. You'll also learn how to determine if the information has been entered in a specific format. For example, a valid e-mail address requires an @ symbol in the address. You'll also learn how to work with hidden files. I will explain all these concepts in detail later in the chapter. So let's begin with learning about HTML.

Chapter 9

Before you begin to learn PHP scripting, it is important to get a grip on basic HTML techniques, since PHP is embedded within HTML. Knowing the fundamental structure of HTML helps you avoid potential problems with the output of your script. Sometimes the script generates the HTML text. For example, if your PHP script generates a table layout, and that table does not appear on screen, don't jump to the assumption that there's a problem with your PHP code. Most likely, the problem is a missing table tag!

Most of you have probably surfed the Web. If you have, you are likely to be familiar with Web pages. Have you ever wondered how you could create a Web page? It is quite easy! All Web pages are written in a language called HTML. HTML stands for *Hypertext Markup Language* and is the universal language of the Internet.

You can create all kinds of Web pages by using HTML, from simple Web pages containing only text to complicated ones that include complex animations. However, you do not need to use complex applications to write these programs. To create a Web page, all you need is a simple text editor, such as Notepad, WordPad, or Word. To save a document as a Web page, you need to save the document with an .html (or .htm) extension. Figure 9-1 shows a simple HTML Web page.

All items that appear on a Web page are called *tags* or *elements*. These tags indicate what the code will do. Tags are used to arrange text in HTML pages. Most tags come in pairs; however, some do not. I will discuss the difference between both types of tags in the next section.

An opening tag marks the beginning of the HTML code and a closing tag marks the end of the code. The opening tag contains the tag name in between the two angular brackets (<>). The closing tag is similar to the opening tag. The only difference between the two tags is that in the closing tag you add a forward slash (/) to the tag name. All of the code within the tags is acted upon. Deciphering most tags is easy because the tags closely resemble the abbreviations of their names. For example, <p> stands for the Paragraph tag and <b> stands for the boldface tag. The following is part of the code that is used to create the HTML document shown in Figure 9-1.

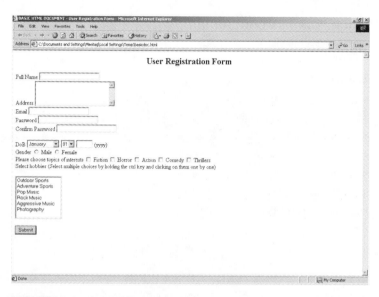

FIGURE 9-1 *An HTML Web page*

```
<html>
<head>
            <title>BASIC HTML DOCUMENT - User Registration Form</title>
</head>
<body>
            <h2 align="center">User Registration Form</h2>
            Full Name
            <input type="text" name="name" size="25" maxlength="25"><br>
            Address
            <textarea name="address" cols="26" rows="4"></textarea><br>
            Email
            <input type="text" name="email" size="25" maxlength="50"><br>
            Password
            <input type="password" name="password" size="25" maxlength="15"><br>
            Confirm password
            <input type="password" name="password" size="25"
maxlength="15"><br><br>
            Date of Birth
            <select name=birth_month>
            <option selected
            value=1>January
```

```
          <option value=2>February
          <option value=3>March
          <option value=4>April
          <option value=5>May
          <option value=6>June
          <option value=7>July
          <option value=8>August
          <option value=9>September
          <option value=10>October
          <option value=11>November
          <option value=12>December</option>
          </select>
...   ...   ...   ...   ...   ...   ...   ... <! Rest of the code -->
</body>
</html>
```

There are numerous elements available in HTML. In the following section, the various HTML elements that you can use to create an HTML page will be discussed.

HTML Elements

As stated earlier, you use tags to declare all the items and text that appear on the Web page. Each tag is declared between angular braces (<>).

HTML elements can be divided into two types:

◆ **Container tags.** As mentioned earlier, most of the HTML code contains opening and closing tags. These tags are known as _container tags_. You need to remember that for every opening container tag there should be a corresponding closing container tag. The code must be added between both the tags.

◆ **Empty tags.** You can also have single tags known as _empty tags_. This is because they do not have any code attached within them. The result of these tags is implemented until the next tag is encountered.

I will elaborate on each of these tags when I discuss specific tags later in the chapter.

In the following section, you will look at the three HTML elements that provide the basic structure to an HTML Web page.

Basic Structure of an HTML Page

Consider the html tag of the Web page you viewed earlier.

```
<html>
<head>
               <title>BASIC HTML DOCUMENT - User Registration Form</title>
</head>
<body>
//Contains all the elements placed on the HTML form
</body>
</html>
```

Essentially, an HTML page must contain at least three tags. These tags are referred to as the html, head, and body tags. Now you will consider each one of them separately.

 NOTE

HTML is not case sensitive. For example, you can use <HTML> instead of <html>, and the code will still execute without any error.

The html *Tag*

When you open the code of an HTML document, the first tag that you see is the html tag. This tag is compulsory in all HTML pages and signifies that the Web page is written in HTML. If you forget to use this tag, nothing is displayed on the Web page. This is because the browser does not recognize the content as HTML. The html tag contains the other two tags, head and body, within it.

The head *Tag*

The head tag is contained between the opening and the closing html tags and contains information about the Web page. For example, in the code mentioned earlier, the title of the Web page appears as BASIC HTML DOCUMENT - User Registration Form. The head tag contains the name of the Web page and other information about the Web page. The head tag may contain many other tags, such as the base, link, title, and meta tags.

Now I will explain these tags in detail.

- ◆ **The title tag.** As you may have noticed, the title for the Web page has been assigned by using the title tag. The title of a Web page provides information about the content of the Web page. It is important to have a meaningful title for a Web page. Otherwise the user will have to read the entire Web page to identify its content. This will be meaningless if the user is not interested in the content.

- ◆ **The base tag.** The base tag contains the address of the location where the Web page is stored. This address is referred to as the base address. All addresses mentioned in the Web page are checked against the addresses mentioned in the base tag. For example, if the base address is specified as http://microsoft.com/, the page called Products.html will be searched at the location http://microsoft.com/Products.html. Therefore, if the location of the Web page changes, you need to modify the address mentioned in the base tag to reflect the change.

- ◆ **The link tag.** The link tag provides a connection to other Web pages. You can assign a certain keyword to connect or open another Web page when the link is clicked. These links are called *hyperlinks* in HTML. A hyperlink is a predefined link between one Web page and another. Hyperlinks can also be created to link different parts of the same Web page to each other. These hyperlinks appear as either text or icons.

- ◆ **The meta tag.** Meta tags are special tags that are mostly used by Web page developers to identify the author of a Web page. This tag may also contain a brief description of the Web page.

 NOTE

The use of all the above elements is optional in the head tag, except for the title tag.

The body *Tag*

The third tag that forms the basic structure of an HTML page is the body tag. The body tag contains all the other tags on the Web page except the html tag. As the name suggests, it contains the body of the Web page. You use the body tag to contain all the elements that should appear on the Web page. One of the commonly used attributes, which you assign along with the body tag, is background. Other attributes that you can use along with the body tag are the bgcolor, text, bgproperties, leftmargin, and margin tags. All the attributes of the body tag are specified within the opening body tag. I will now discuss each of these attributes in detail.

 NOTE

To display text in a specific format, you need to pass certain information to the tags as parameters. Therefore, attributes are characteristics of a Web page that you can change or assign. For example, you can change the font style of text in a Web page from normal to boldface or change the font type from Times New Roman to Arial. Remember that in the case of container tags, attributes can only be specified in the opening tag.

The first attribute of the body tag that I will discuss is the background attribute.

◆ **The Background attribute.** You may have seen different types of backgrounds used in Web pages. These backgrounds either can be plain or can contain an image. To assign an image file as the background of an HTML page, you need to specify its path in the background attribute. You can do so by specifying the path name or the URL pointing to the location where the image file is stored. For example,

```
<body background=C:\images\defaultbkgnd.gif >
</body>
```

NOTE

You do not need to provide the complete path to an image file or other linked files, if the image file and the HTML Web page exist in the same directory.

◆ **The bgcolor attribute.** The background image is stored on the Web server and is copied to the client machine when the Web page is opened. During the time when the image is being downloaded, the Web page appears as blank. If you do not want this to happen, you can assign a color as the background until the image is downloaded. The bgcolor attribute can be used to assign a background color to an HTML page. It is always preferable to assign a color that matches the color of your background image. This is done to maintain consistency. For example, if the base color of your background image is yellow, then the background color of the Web page should also be yellow. You can rewrite the previously written code to add background color as shown below.

```
<body bgcolor = "Yellow",
background=C:\images\defaultbkgnd.gif >
                                <! You will add the rest of the
tags here. -->
            </body>
```

◆ **The bgproperties attribute.** Assume that you have a large number of elements on a Web page. You will notice that the background of the Web page moves up as you move down the page to see the rest of the elements. You can avoid this by fixing the background. You use the bgproperties attribute to do this. The syntax of the bgproperties attribute is as follows:

```
<body bgcolor = "Yellow",
background=C:\images\defaultbkgnd.gif,
                        bgproperties = "fixed" >
                            <! You will add the rest of the
tags here. -->
            </body>
```

CAUTION

You need to remember that the `bgproperties` attribute is specific to Microsoft Internet Explorer only.

◆ **The text attribute.** You use this attribute to change the color of the text in an HTML page. For example, in the code written below, you are assigning green as Text Color. As a result, all the text in the Web page will appear in green.

```
                        <body bgcolor = "Yellow",
background=C:\images\defaultbkgnd.gif,
                                bgproperties = "fixed", text = "green">
                                        You will add the rest of the tags
here.
                        </body>
```

◆ **The leftmargin attribute.** Just as you can align text in a Word document, you can also align text in a Web page to the left of the screen by using the leftmargin attribute. The text is aligned after leaving a specified number of spaces. For example, the code given below will align the text after leaving 45 pixels from the left of the screen.

```
                        <body bgcolor = "Yellow",
background=C:\images\defaultbkgnd.gif,
                                bgproperties = "fixed", text = "green",
leftmargin = "45">
                                        <! You will add the rest of the
tags here. -->
                        </body>
```

NOTE

Pixels are a basic unit of measurement and are used in computers to calculate the quality of an image or display. However, you need to remember that a pixel is a logical unit of measurement and not a physical one. This means that you cannot actually count the number of pixels in an image. (If you try to do that, you are sure to need an appointment with the doctor to get your eyesight checked!)

♦ **The topmargin attribute.** This attribute is similar to the leftmargin attribute. The only difference is that this attribute aligns the inserted text a specific number of pixels from the top of the screen.

You have now looked at the basic elements used to create the basic structure of a Web page, along with their attributes. For example, you learned how to specify the title of your Web page and set the background for the Web page. You will now learn how to format the other elements of the Web page.

Formatting the Elements of an HTML Page

You may have wondered why you should change the font of the text on your Web page, or even highlight text. The answer is simple: to beautify the Web page and to make important text appear more prominent. Highlighted text immediately catches the user's attention and helps present information in an easily understandable format. You can use bulleted lists for a similar purpose. Not only are bulleted points easy to read, but the concept explained in each point can be easily remembered. This is because each point is clearly separated from the others. You can also use text of different colors, fonts, and styles to differentiate between different content.

In the following sections, I will discuss each one of the tags in HTML that you can use to format elements in an HTML page. I will begin with how you can format text in an HTML page, as text is a major part of the content in a Web page. Table 9-1 contains a list of the various formatting tags available in HTML and a brief description of their purpose.

Table 9-1 HTML Tags

Name	Tag	Description
Heading tag	\<h\>	Is used to format text headings
Break Line tag	\<br\>	Is used to insert lines between text
Paragraph tag	\<p\> ... \</p\>	Is used to insert lines amid paragraphs
Comment tag	\<!-- ... --\>	Is used to insert comments along with the code

Name	Tag	Description
Font tag	<font> ... </font>	Is used to specify the fonts for text
Boldface tag	<b> ... </b>	Is used to make text bold
Italics tag	<I> ... </I>	Is used to italicize text
Subscript tag	_{...}	Is used to change the font of text to subscript
Superscript tag	^{...}	Is used to change the font of text to superscript
Underline tag	<u> ... </u>	Is used to underline text
Code tag	<code> ... </code>	Is used to display code along with plain text

The heading tag should be considered first while formatting text in a Web page.

The *heading* Tag

You must have noticed that headings in Web pages are formatted differently than normal text. Generally, headings appear in a font that is larger and bolder than the font in which the normal text appears. This strategy ensures that you can differentiate between where the concept begins and where it ends. Even in headings, there are different levels. For example, you may have a main heading and many subheadings under it. This ensures that text is arranged in an easily readable manner in the Web page.

However, it is important to remember that there is a major difference between a heading and a title. There is a single title for the whole Web page, but you will have separate headings for different concepts in your document. Headings can appear in different formats because HTML supports six different levels of headings. The levels range from 1 to 6, with 1 being the largest. Given below is the syntax used to define a heading tag.

```
<hi> Text to be displayed <hi>
```

Don't be alarmed! <hi> is not a heading tag. Here, i stands for the number (1-6) that indicates the level of the heading.

NOTE

An important point to remember is that you should not omit levels while specifying headings in the content of a Web page. For example, if you give your first concept a level 1 heading (<h1>), you should not use a level 3 heading (<h3>) for the next concept. This could confuse the readers by making the text difficult to follow.

Figure 9-2 shows the output of the effect of the different levels of headings used in a Web page.

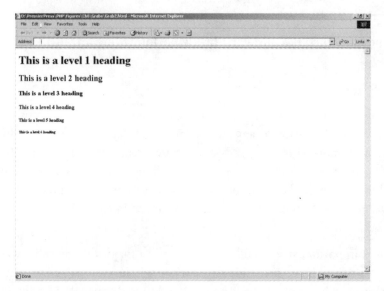

FIGURE 9-2 *Levels of headings used in an HTML Web page*

You can use the `align` attribute to align the heading differently on the Web page. You can align the heading to the left, right, or center of the screen. By default, all headings are aligned to the left. The following code aligns the text to the center of the Web page.

```
<body>

        <h1 align="Center"> This is the first level
heading </h1>

        </body>
```

Now that you know how to create headings, let me explain to you how you can insert lines between the content in your Web page.

The *break line* Tags

Suppose you simply dumped all your text onto the Web page. Wouldn't that result in an absolute mess? You would not know where one section ended and the next began. To avoid this confusion, you can insert blank lines between each section of text. This helps to separate each piece of text and provides better visibility.

You may think that pressing the Enter key would solve your problem, since you normally use the Enter key to insert a blank line. However, in HTML programming this is not so. You have to use the break line tag to insert a line break in between the text in an HTML page. The break line tag is defined by using the <br> tag and is an empty tag. Remember the empty tags I mentioned earlier? Empty tags only contain a single tag and do not have any code associated with them.

Consider the following example where the <br> tag is used.

```
<html>
<head>
                            <title>My Basic HTML Web Page</title>
</head>
<body bgcolor = "Yellow", background=C:\images\defaultbkgnd.gif,
                                bgproperties = "fixed" >
                        <h1 align="center">Leadership Styles</h1>
                        "The key to successful leadership today is influence,
not authority.[--]Kenneth Blanchard"
                        <br><br>
                        People are not necessarily born leaders, they can be
made into good leaders. Leadership
                        is a skill that needs to be cultivated. Earlier, the
moment someone mentioned a leader, the
                        image that conjured up in our minds was an individual
who was authoritative, controlling,
                        commanding, and directing. A leader was expected to
take decisions for the entire
```

```
                        organization. The entire organization was expected to
follow the strategies laid down by
                        these individuals, without any question. These leaders
were known as Autocratic leaders.
                        <br><br>
                        Autocratic leaders did not believe in recognizing an
individual's potential. Instead, they
                        believed in suppressing an individual's opinion.
Employees who took initiative or used their
                        inherent capabilities were frowned upon. Everyone was
expected to follow the path laid
                        down by the leader.
</body>
</html>
```

The output of the code given above is displayed in Figure 9-3.

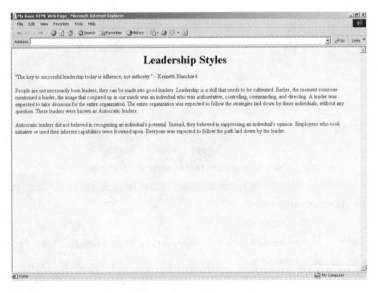

FIGURE 9-3 *Using break lines in an HTML Web page*

You have just learned how you can use the <br> tag to insert lines between continuous texts. However, HTML also allows you to format text in Web pages in the form of paragraphs. This is discussed in detail in the next section.

The *paragraph* Tag

You must have created paragraphs while writing a document. You can similarly create paragraphs in Web pages by enclosing the text between the <p> and </p> tags. Each piece of text enclosed between a pair of paragraph tags (<p> and </p>) forms a new paragraph. You may wonder why, if the break line tag separates text into different sections, you would need the paragraph tag to complicate life even more! There is a good reason why you need both. The break line tag and the paragraph tag serve separate purposes. The break line tag only shifts the rest of the content to the next line on the Web page. However, in the case of the para-graph <p>tag, the text is not only placed on the next line, but a blank line is also inserted between the two paragraphs. The <p> and the </p> tags are used to define the paragraph tags. As you may have noticed, the paragraph tag comes in pairs. Therefore, the paragraph tag is a type of container tag.

In the previous section, you learned how to use the break line tag to separate text on a Web page into separate sections. Now you'll rewrite the code that you wrote earlier using the <br> tag.

```
<html>
<head>
                        <title>My Basic HTML Web Page</title>
</head>
<body bgcolor = "Yellow", background=C:\images\defaultbkgnd.gif, bgproperties =
"fixed" >
                        <h1 align="center">This is my title</h1>
                        <h1 align="center">Leadership Styles</h1>
                        "The key to successful leadership today is influence,
not authority."[--]Kenneth Blanchard
                        <br>
                <p>People are not necessarily born leaders, they can be made
into good leaders. Leadership is
                        a skill that needs to be cultivated. Earlier, the
moment someone mentioned a leader, the
                        image that conjured up in our minds was an individual
who was authoritative, controlling,
                        commanding, and directing. A leader was expected to
take decisions for the entire
```

```
                        organization. The entire organization was expected to
follow the strategies laid down by
                        these individuals, without any question. These leaders
were known as Autocratic
                        leaders.</p>
                        <br>
                    <p>Autocratic leaders did not believe in recognizing an
individual's potential. Instead, they
                        believed in suppressing an individual's opinion.
Employees who took initiative or used their
                        inherent capabilities were frowned upon. Everyone was
expected to follow the path laid
                        down by the leader.</p>
</body>
</html>
```

If you execute the above code you will notice that the blocs of text enclosed in paragraph tags are separated from each other with a single line.

Just as you align headings, you can also align text in Web pages by using the `align` attribute with the <p> tag. The text can be left, right, or center aligned. By default, all text is left aligned.

You have learned to add headings and text to a Web page. However, you may want to add certain comments to your HTML program. You will learn how you can do this in the next section.

The *comment* Tag

You can insert comments in your HTML program in places where you want to explain how a particular piece of code works or want to include certain notes for reference. HTML uses the <!-- ... --> tags to comment on the specified text. Any text inserted between the <!-- ... --> tags is not displayed with the final output of the code. Consider the following piece of code where certain comments have been added.

```
        <body>
                        <! This is the first comment -->
                        <h1 align="Center"> This is the first level heading
        </h1>
```

```
                    <! This is a two line
                    comment      ...  ...  ...  ...  ...  ...  -->
      </body>
```

Now that you know how to add text to a Web page, let me explain how you can format individual pieces of text in a Web page.

The *font* Tag

As I explained earlier, you can change the font of the text in your Web page to make the page more attractive. HTML provides the font tag to change the font of text used in the Web page. You can also use the font tag to change the size and font type of the text. Observe Figure 9-4. Notice how the font of the first paragraph differs from that of the second. You will also notice that the color of the text in the first paragraph is different from the color of the text in the second paragraph. The difference in font and color sets the paragraphs apart.

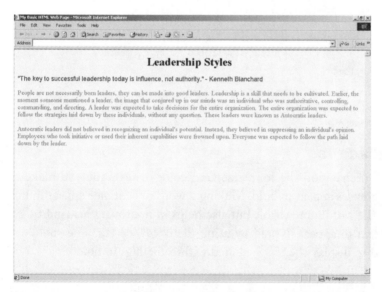

FIGURE 9-4 *A Web page using the* font *tag*

You use the <font> and the </font> tags to specify different fonts for different text. All the text enclosed between the tags is changed based on the attributes specified with the tags. The font tag supports three different attributes to further manipulate the text. You can use the color, size, and face attributes to change the color, size, and font of the specified text.

- **The color attribute.** You can use this attribute to change the color of the text placed between the start and end font tags.

- **The size attribute.** You use this attribute to change the font size of the rest of the text based on the current font size. For example, if the size of the text you are currently working on is 5, then you can set the font size as more than or less than the current font.

- **The face attribute.** You use this attribute to change the font type of the text. For example, all the text in your Web page may be in Arial. However, you may want certain text to appear in Times New Roman. You can use this attribute to change the font type of the specific text.

The example given below shows the use of all the three attributes along with the font tag.

```
<body>
        ...
        <font color="blue", size="4", face = "Arial">
                 Content that needs to be formatted.
        </font>
        ...
</body>
```

The boldface *Tag*

In addition to changing the font, size, and color of text, you can make certain words or sentences appear in bold. Making a word or sentence appear in bold not only makes the word more visible but also helps in improving readability. You can format the text to appear in bold by using the boldface tag. The <b> ... </b> tags are used to display the text included within the tags in bold.

 NOTE

However, you must remember that marking words or sentences in bold should be restricted to only important words or sentences. A large amount of bold text reduces the effectiveness of the text.

The italics *Tag*

You have probably used the italic effect while creating Word documents. Italicized text appears in a different style than normal text and is tilted forward. Generally, you italicize text to make it stand out from normal text. For example, you may italicize key words in a document. Another area where you may italicize text is while using foreign words in an English text. For example, you may italicize French or German words in the content of your Web page. You use the <i> ... </i> tags to italicize text.

The subscript *Tag*

Sometimes you may need to change the font of certain text so that the text appears slightly below the rest of the content and in a font that is slightly smaller than the normal font. You use the subscript tag to apply the subscript effect to the specified text. The effect is applied by using the _{...} tags; all the text placed between the tags appears smaller and slightly below the rest of the text.

The superscript *Tag*

Just as you use the subscript tag to make certain text appear slightly below the rest of the content, you use the superscript tag to make the text appear slightly above the rest of the content. The effect is implemented by using the ^{...} tags.

Mostly, you'll use the subscript and superscript tags in mathematical formulae and in science equations. For example, you may want to add a fraction or a chemistry equation in your Web page.

The underline *Tag*

You have learned how to format text in bold and to italicize text in your Web page. You can similarly underline text in your Web page. You can underline text by using the underline tag, which includes the <u> and </u> tags.

The code *Tag*

Just as you display text in a Web page, sometimes you may also need to display certain code in the Web page. HTML provides a separate tag to display code in the Web page. This tag is appropriately called the code tag and is displayed using the <code> and </code> tags. You generally use this tag when you are creating Web pages that contain content from a programming language or teach a programming language. For example, the code displayed below will show a sample code written in PHP.

```
<html>
<body>
                          A Sample code written in PHP   :<p>
          <code>
                 <'?php
<br>
                 $a = "10 pigs" +2;                        <br>
                 echo $a ,"\n";
<br>


<br>
                 $a = "10pigs" + 2;                        <br>
                 echo $a ,"\n";
<br>


<br>
                 $a = "pigs 10" + 2;                       <br>
                 echo $a ,"\n";
<br>


<br>
                 $a = "10 pigs" . 2;
<br>
                 echo $a ,"\n";
<br>


<br>
                 $a = "10pigs" . 2;                        <br>
                 echo $a ,"\n";
<br>
                 ?>
<br>
```

```
        </code>
</body>
</html>
```

Figure 9-5 displays a sample code written in PHP.

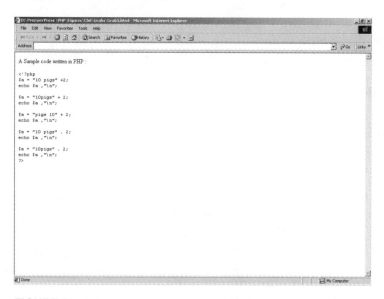

FIGURE 9-5 *Displaying code in an HTML Web page*

By now you know how to add text to a Web page and format the text. In the next section, I will teach you how to create a form by using HTML. An HTML form contains different types of elements, which will also be discussed.

Creating Forms by Using HTML

While surfing the Net, you may have visited e-commerce shopping marts or bought goods online. If you have, you will be familiar with the concept of forms in Web pages.

You can divide Web pages into two categories: pages that only provide information and pages that also accept information. In the previous section, you learned about the first category when you formatted and displayed plain text in an HTML format. *Forms* are the second type of Web pages. Forms are mostly used to accept user information. The categories of HTML forms are:

◆ Customer information forms

◆ Online order forms

◆ Customer feedback forms

◆ User registration forms

After receiving information from the user, the forms then process the information. So how does a form work?

Working of a Form

Before you learn how to create a form, you need to know the mechanism that is followed in a form. Only if the mechanism of how a form works is clear to you will you be able to design an efficient form.

Generally, all forms contain certain elements that prompt a user for information. These elements include text boxes, check boxes, radio buttons, list boxes, and combo boxes. The user enters the necessary information and then clicks on a button. By clicking on the button, the user sends the entered text to a computer known as the Web server. The Web server either stores the information or processes the information to generate a result. This result is then sent back to the browser, which displays it to the user.

It might appear to you that the Web server handles the job of storing or processing the information. Well, this is not exactly true. The information that the browser sends to the Web server also contains a reference to a script known as a *CGI script*. CGI stands for Common Gateway Interface and is a standard for linking programs on the Internet with servers, such as Web servers or HTTP servers. The server then passes the information to the CGI script, which saves it or processes it further. The result is then sent back to the Web server. The Web server in turn formats the processed information into HTML format and sends back the information to the Web browser that had earlier requested the information. Finally, the browser displays the information to the user.

Figure 9-6 shows the entire process that is followed when information is directed from the Web browser to the Web server.

Although forms have different styles, all forms contain certain common elements that are used to create them. These elements include:

NOTE

A Web browser is a program that acts like an interface between the user and the part of the Internet also known as the World Wide Web (WWW). To access information from the Web or to open a Web page, you need to type the address of the page in the address field of the browser. The address is in the form of a *URL*, Uniform Resource Locator. A URL helps in identifying resources on the Internet, such as documents, images, and files for download—for example, **http://office.microsoft.com/ downloads/2002/oxpsp1.aspx** or **http://microsoft.com/ms.htm**. Some of the most commonly used Web browsers are Microsoft Internet Explorer and Netscape Navigator.

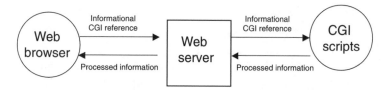

FIGURE 9-6 *Processing a form*

◆ The form element
◆ The input element
◆ The select element

The form tag is used to specify that you are creating a form. The input element, as the name rightly suggests, is used to accept text in the Web page. The select element is used to specify options. All three elements contain tags that you can use to accept different information. I will now explain each of these elements and their associated tags in detail.

The *form* Element

You have learned that you use the html tag to define that the page is created in HTML. Similarly, you use the form tag to specify that the Web page is a form. You create a form by specifying the content between the <font> and </font> tags.

As such, the form tag only specifies that you are creating a form. However, HTML also provides three other attributes that you can use along with the form tag: action, enctype, and method. I will now explain the use of each of these attributes.

- ◆ **The action attribute.** The action attribute contains the URL of the script that will handle the processing of information submitted through the form. Submitting information means sending the information entered by the user to the Web server for processing. Mostly, these scripts are CGI scripts. If the URL is not provided, the browser searches for the code required to process the information within the Web page.

- ◆ **The enctype attribute.** Sometimes certain protocols require information to be presented in a specified format so that the protocols can transfer the information to the Web server. You can specify the formatting of information by using the enctype attribute.

- ◆ **The method attribute.** This attribute specifies whether you need to get the information from the Web server or send the information to the Web server. The attribute takes either of two values, get or post. When the get value is used, the URL is sent along with the user-entered information. However, when the post value is used, the user information is sent separately as a package and not with the URL. The default value is get.

The following fragment of code displays the use of these attributes.

```
<body>
            <form name="registration" method="post" action="confirm.php" enc-
type="multipart/form-data">
Rest of the code.
            </form>
</body>
```

NOTE

A protocol is a set of rules that govern the transmission and reception of data over the network. Internet protocols facilitate the transfer of data over the Internet. There are different types of Internet protocols in use. These include Transmission Control Protocol/Internet Protocol (TCP/IP), Hypertext Transfer Protocol (HTTP), and File Transfer Protocol (FTP).

The *input* Element

HTML provides different types of input elements that you can use to accept information from a user. For example, you can ask a user to type information in a box, click on a radio button to make a choice, or click on a push button to submit the information. You use the `<input>` and `</input>` tags to specify input elements. However, the closing tag is optional in the use of the `input` tag.

Table 9-2 contains a list of commonly used input tags.

Table 9-2 Input Elements in HTML

Element Name	Description
text	Is used to accept a single line of information from users
textarea	Is used to accept multiple lines of information from users
password	Is used to accept a single line of text, which appears as *
checkbox	Is used to accept a single option or multiple options from a group of options
radio button	Is used to accept a single option from a group of options
submit	Is used to submit information entered on the form
reset	Is used to reset information entered on the form
hidden	Is used to submit hidden information to the Web server

Before I discuss these elements, let me tell you about the attributes that you can use along with these elements. HTML offers three types of attributes that you can use: `type`, `name`, and `value`.

◆ **The `type` attribute.** This attribute assigns the type of element that is being used to accept the user input. This contains the name of the element—for example, `text`, `radio`, `button`, `check`, and `submit`.

◆ **The `name` attribute.** You can also specify a name for the element. This name can then be used to reference the element anywhere in the code.

◆ **The `value` attribute.** You use this attribute to assign a default value to the element. This value will appear by default when the element is displayed.

Now I will discuss each of the elements in detail.

The text *Element*

The text element is used for accepting a single line of text from the user. This element is used along with the size attribute and maxlength attribute. The size attribute fixes the length of the text box, and the maxlength attribute assigns the maximum number of characters you can enter in the text box. The syntax is given below.

```
                                    <input type="text" name="name"
size="25" maxlength="25">
```

The textarea *Element*

Suppose you need to enter multiple lines in the text box while entering an address. For this purpose, you can use the textarea element. The size attribute and maxlength attribute are also available along with this element. The syntax is given below.

```
                                    <input type="textarea" name="address"
cols="26" rows="4"></textarea>
```

The password *Element*

The password element is similar to the text element. The only difference is that here the entered text is not displayed. As you enter the text, each character is replaced by the * symbol. The syntax is given below.

```
                                    <input type="password" name="password"
size="25" maxlength="15">
```

The checkbox *Element*

The checkbox element is used in cases where you need to choose multiple items simultaneously. There is a separate check box and name for each choice. Each choice returns a separate set of name and value. The syntax of the checkbox element is given below.

```
                            <p>Please choose topics of interests</p>
                                        Fiction <input type="check-
box" name="fiction" value="1"> <br>
```

Horror <input type="checkbox" name="horror" value="1">

Action<input type="check-
box" name="action" value="1">

Comedy <input type="checkbox" name="comedy" value="1">

The radio button *Element*

The radio button is used to select a single choice from a set of choices. You need to group all the choices together by classifying them under the same name. The user can only select a single choice from the whole set of choices. The moment the user selects another choice the first choice is automatically deselected. Only the selected choice can return the name and the value when the information is submitted. The syntax of a radio button is given below.

```
<br>
Gender<br>
                                        <input type="radio"
name="gender" value="Male">
            Male
                                        <input type="radio"
name="gender" value="Female">
            Female
```

The submit *Element*

You use the submit element to create a button to submit the information to the Web server. You use the value attribute to specify a label that appears on the top of the button. The name attribute is used to specify a name for the button. The name can then be used anywhere in the code to reference the button. When the button is clicked on, the name and value information are passed along with the submitted information. The syntax of the submit element is given below.

```
<input type="submit" value="Submit">
```

The reset *Element*

The reset element is used to reset the values of all the elements in the Web page to their initial values. You can assign a name and the value attribute in a way that is similar to the way you assign attributes to the submit button. The syntax of the reset element is given below.

```
<input type="reset" value="Reset">
```

The hidden *Element*

You can also pass certain text along with the information entered in the form. Although this information may not appear on the Web page, it will still be passed to the Web server with the rest of the entered information. This information is mostly static in nature and does not require any user intervention. You will learn more about this element in Chapter 9, where you will learn how to send information to the Web server by using PHP.

You have just learned how to create elements to accept plain text from the user. In the next section, you will learn how to get users to select a single option or multiple options from a list.

The *select* Element

The select element allows you to select an option from a whole list of options. You may have noticed lists boxes and combo boxes on Web sites. You use list boxes and combo boxes to select a single option or multiple options from the list. The select element is implemented by using the <select> and </select> container tags. You specify options in the list by using the options element. Just as the input element has attributes, similarly the select element also has certain attributes. These attributes are given below.

- ◆ **The multiple attribute.** The multiple attribute is used to specify that a user make multiple selections from the list of options.
- ◆ **The name attribute.** You can also specify a name for the element. This name can then be used to reference the element anywhere in the code.
- ◆ **The value attribute.** You use this attribute to assign a value that should be returned if the option is selected.
- ◆ **The selected attribute.** You use this attribute to assign the default option that should appear selected when the Web page is displayed.

There are two types of select elements, the combo box and the list box. They are covered in detail next.

The combo box *Element*

The combo box is a pull-down or a pop-up list that you can used to accept a value from the user. The user can only select one value from the list. You can use the name attribute to specify a name for the combo box and the selected attribute to specify the option that should appear selected by default. If no option is specified as selected, the first item in the list appears as the default selected option. The syntax for defining a combo box is given below.

```
                    Select your date of birth:
                        <select name=birth_month>
                                    <option selected
value=1>January

                                    <option value=2>February
                                    <option value=3>March
                                    <option value=4>April
                                    <option value=5>May
                                    <option value=6>June
                                    <option value=7>July
                                    <option value=8>August
                                    <option value=9>September
                                    <option value=10>October
                                    <option value=11>November
                                    <option
value=12>December</option>
```

In the code given above, the first option will appear selected by default.

In the combo box, you can only select one option. However, you can use a list box to make multiple selections.

The list box *Element*

The list box works in the same way as a combo box. The only difference is that you can make multiple selections in a list box. To allow multiple selections, you need to use the multiple attribute. By using this attribute, you can create a list box as follows.

```
                    <p>Select hobbies </p>
                    <p>(Select multiple choices by holding the
ctrl key and
```

```
                                        clicking on them one by one)</p>
                                          <select name="hobbies[]" size="7"
multiple>
                                            <option value="Outdoor
Sports">Outdoor Sports</option>
                                            <option value="Adventure
Sports">Adventure Sports</option>
                                            <option value="Pop
Music">Pop Music</option>
                                            <option value="Rock
Music">Rock Music</option>
                                            <option value="Aggressive
Music">Aggressive Music</option>
                                            <option
value="Photography">Photography</option>
                                          </select>
```

The *table* Element

Now that you have coded for all the elements that you require to create a form, you will notice that all the elements appear left aligned on the screen. You can structure your Web page by displaying all the elements in a tabular format. This not only makes the data appear visually appealing, it also provides better readability for the user. In HTML, you use the <table> and </table> container elements to define a table in your code. All the elements that appear on the page need to be included between these tags.

A table also contains a specific number of attributes that you can use to format the way a table will appear in the Web page. Some of these attributes are discussed in the following sections.

The border *Attribute*

You may have worked with borders while creating tables in a Word document. A border is a rectangular box that you place to outline a table in a document. Similarly, you have a border in a Web page that places a margin around the entire table in the Web page. A border can contain lines or just empty space. The size of the table is not affected by whether you create or do not create a border for the table.

You can set the thickness of a border by assigning a value to the border attribute. The thickness of a border is calculated based on pixels. You can set the border for a table as shown below.

```
border=value
```

 NOTE

By default, a table does not contain a border.

The cellspacing *Attribute*

You can also set the cells of a table to appear after leaving a specific amount of spaces between them. You use the cellspacing attribute along with the table tag to do this. The amount of space to be left is also calculated based on pixels.

The cellpadding *Attribute*

Similarly, you use the cellpadding attribute to set the amount of space that should appear between the data in the cells and the cell walls in the table. Generally, the cellpadding and the cellpadding attributes are specified together in the code. For example, in the code given below, the border of the table is 1 pixel thick and there is no space between the cells. There is also a space of 5 pixel spaces between the data and the cell walls.

```
<table border="1" cellpadding="5" cellspacing="0"
```

The width *and* height *Attributes*

You can also set the width and the height for a table. The height attribute and width attribute can be set either as absolutes or as percentages. If the attributes are set as absolutes, they are calculated in pixels. However, if the attributes are calculated as percentages, their values are percentages of the height and width of the entire document. The disadvantage of setting the height and width as absolutes is that if you maximize or minimize the Web page or change its size in any way, the size of the table remains the same. In the code given below, the width of the table is set to 400.

```
                              <table width="400" border="1" cellpadding="5"
cellspacing="0">
```

The align *and* valign *Attributes*

Just as you can align text to the center, right, or left of the Web page, similarly you can align the table in the Web page by using the `align` attribute. You can use the `valign` attribute, which is also known as the vertical align attribute, to align the table to either the top or bottom of the Web page. By default, a table is aligned in the center of the Web page. The following code aligns the table to the left of the Web page.

```
                              <table width="400" border="1" align="left" cell-
padding="5" cellspacing="0"
```

The bgcolor *Attribute*

You can change the appearance of your Web page by adding a color as its background. You can set the value for the `bgcolor` attribute either to fixed colors, such as red, green, blue, or yellow, or to hexadecimal values provided in the `rrggbb` format. In the following code, the color of the Web page is assigned a hexadecimal value.

```
                              <table width="400" border="1" align="center" cell-
padding="5" cellspacing="0"

                              bgcolor="#CCCCCC">
```

The bordercolor *Attribute*

Just as you learned how to set the background color for the table, you can similarly set a color for the border by using the `bordercolor` attribute. You can set the color of the border to either a fixed color or a hexadecimal value.

```
                              <table width="400" border="1" align="center" cell-
padding="5" cellspacing="0"

                              bgcolor="#CCCCCC" bordercolor=red>
```

The <tr> ... </tr> Element

You use the `<tr>` element to create rows in a table. Each new row in the table requires a separate `<tr>` tag, irrespective of the number of cells that will be

CAUTION

You need to remember that you can use this attribute only if you have previously used the border attribute.

included in a row. All the content that you need to place in a row should be included between the <tr> and </tr> tags. The <tr> element also contains a certain number of attributes that you can use to arrange text within the cells of the table. These attributes are listed below.

◆ **The align attribute.** You use the align attribute to place text to the left, right, or center of a cell in the table—for example, <tr align=center> ... </tr>.

◆ **The vertical align attribute.** The valign attribute aligns the text to the top, bottom, or center of the cells in the table. This attribute also aligns the bases of all the cells that are in the same row in one line. You can set the valign attribute either as top, bottom, middle, or baseline.

◆ **The bgcolor attribute.** Just as you set the background color for the table, you can set the background color for an individual row by assigning the bgcolor property with the <tr> tag. You can set the background color to either a fixed color or a hexadecimal value (rrggbb). For example, the code <tr bgcolor=blue> ... </tr> will set the background color of the row to blue.

The <td> ... </td> Element

Now that you know how to add rows to a table in your Web page, you need to learn how to format the table data. You use the <td> ... </td> element to format the data you want to store in the table. You can only use this element between the <tr> and </tr> tags that you learned in the previous section. A cell in a table can contain any element that you may put directly in an HTML page. You might not put the same number of cells in all rows of a table. The row that has fewer cells will be filled with empty cells.

You can also align the data in a cell. The data can either be left aligned or right aligned by using the align attribute. However, if the same attribute is set in the <tr> elements, the value assigned in the <td> elements is overwritten. You can

also ensure that the text inserted in a cell fills the cell completely by using the jus-
tify attribute with the align tag. Similarly, you can also avoid any line breaks in
the cell by using the nowrap attribute.

You learned about the align and valign attributes when I explained the <tr> element. These attributes are also available in the <td> element. There are other
attributes that can be used with the <td> elements; these attributes are discussed
below.

◆ **The width attribute.** The width attribute is used to set the required
   width of the cell. You can set the width of the cell either as an absolute
   (measured in pixels) or as a percentage of the table's width. If this
   attribute is not set, the size of the table depends on the browser's display
   settings.

◆ **The height attribute.** The height attribute is used to assign the height
   of the cell. This is also set as an absolute value (measured in pixels) or as
   a percentage of the height of the table.

◆ **The valign attribute.** The valign attribute aligns the text to the top,
   bottom, or center of the cells in the table. This attribute also aligns all
   the cells created in the row. You can set the valign attribute to top, bottom, middle, or baseline.

◆ **The rowspan attribute.** The rowspan attributes specifies the number of
   rows a cell will occupy. The default value of this attribute is 1.

◆ **The colspan attribute.** You can set the number of columns that a cell
   will occupy in a table by using this attribute. By default, the number of
   columns that a cell occupies is set to 1.

The following code uses the attributes of the <tr> and <td> elements to create the
table shown in Figure 9-7.

```
<table width="400" border="1" align="center" cell-
padding="5" cellspacing="0"
                bgcolor="#CCCCCC">
            <tr>
              <td width="47%">
                Full Name
              </td>
              <td colspan="2">
                <input type="text" name="name"
```

```
size="25" maxlength="25">
                                                        </td>
                                                    </tr>
                                                    <tr>
                                                      <td width="47%" height="57">
                                                        Address
                                                      </td>
                                                      <td height="57" colspan="2">
                                                        <textarea name="address" cols="26"
rows="4"></textarea>

                                                      </td>
                                                    </tr>
                                                    <tr>
                                                      <td width="47%">
                                                        Email
                                                      </td>
                                                      <td height="2" colspan="2">
                                                        <input type="text" name="email"
size="25" maxlength="50">

                                                      </td>
                                                    </tr>
                                                    <tr>
                                                      <td width="47%">
                                                          Password
                                                      </td>
                                                      <td height="2" >
                                                        <input type="password" name="pass-
word" size="25" maxlength="15">

                                                      </td>
                                                    </tr>
```

The <th> ... </th> Element

You may have noticed that the tables in a Web page contain a separate line for the heading. The heading will contain a title for the table and will appear in a separate font and size. You use the <th> ... </th> element to specify a heading for a table. The text contained in a header will appear in bold and is center aligned by default. The <th> element contains the following attributes: align, valign, width,

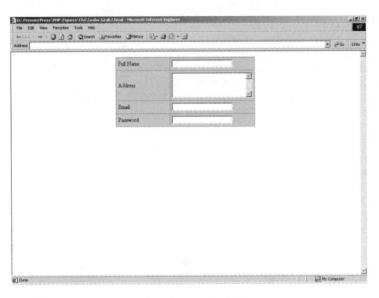

FIGURE 9-7 *Table containing elements in a Web page*

height, rowspan, colspan, bgcolor, nowrap, and bordercolor. In previous sections of this chapter, I have discussed these attributes in detail.

The <caption> ... </caption> Element

The <caption> element is used to assign a title for the entire table. The element should be specified after the <table> element and before adding any other elements in the table. You can include any type of element in the caption of the table. By default, the text specified in the <caption> element appears at the top of the table and is center aligned.

Creating the HTML Form

By now you have learned all the elements and attributes you need to create an HTML form. The following code will create a form to accept user information. Generally, you use a form to collect the following type of user information:

◆ User name
◆ Address
◆ E-mail address

◆ Password

◆ Confirm password

◆ Date of birth

◆ Gender

◆ Interests

◆ Hobbies

When you submit the information by clicking on the submit button, a PHP script processes the information. This concept will be covered in Chapter 10, "Form Parsing in PHP."

Let's create an HTML Web page that will accept user information and submit it to the PHP script for further processing.

```html
<html>
<head>
<title>Index</title>

</head>

<body>
<h2 align="center">User Registration form</h2>
<form name="registration" method="post" action="confirm.php"
enctype="multipart/form-data">
        <table width="400" border="1" align="center" cellpadding="5" cellspacing="0"
bgcolor="#CCCCCC">
                                <tr>
                                  <td width="47%">
                                    Full Name
                                  </td>
                                  <td colspan="2">
                                      <input type="text" name="name" size="25"
maxlength="25">
                                  </td>
                                </tr>
                                <tr>
                                  <td width="47%" height="57">
                                    Address
```

```
                                                </td>
                                                <td height="17" colspan="2">
                                                  <textarea name="address" cols="26"
rows="4"></textarea>
                                                </td>
                                              </tr>
                                              <tr>
                                                <td width="47%">
                                                  Email
                                                </td>
                                                <td height="2" colspan="2">
                                                  <input type="text" name="email" size="25"
maxlength="50">
                                                </td>
                                              </tr>
                                              <tr>
                                                <td width="47%">
                                                  Password
                                                </td>
                                                <td height="2" >
                                                  <input type="password" name="password"
size="25" maxlength="15">
                                                </td>
                                              </tr>
                                              <tr>
                                                <td width="47%">
                                                  Confirm Password

                                                </td>
                                                <td height="2" >
                                                  <input type="password" name="password"
size="25" maxlength="15">
                                                </td>
                                              </tr>
                                              <tr>
                                                <td width="47%">
                                                  Date of Birth
```

```
</td>
<td height="2" >
  <select name=birth_month>
    <option selected
        value=1>January
    <option value=2>February
    <option value=3>March
    <option value=4>April
    <option value=5>May
    <option value=6>June
    <option value=7>July
    <option value=8>August
    <option value=9>September
    <option value=10>October
    <option value=11>November
    <option value=12>December</option>
  </select>
  <select name=birth_day>
    <option selected value=1>01
    <option value=2>02
    <option value=3>03
    <option value=4>04
    <option value=5>05
    <option value=6>06
    <option value=7>07
    <option value=8>08
    <option value=9>09
    <option value=10>10
    <option value=11>11
    <option value=12>12
    <option value=13>13
    <option value=14>14
    <option value=15>15
    <option value=16>16
    <option value=17>17
    <option value=18>18
    <option value=19>19
    <option value=20>20
```

```
                                        <option value=21>21
                                        <option value=22>22
                                        <option value=23>23
                                        <option value=24>24
                                        <option value=25>25
                                        <option value=26>26
                                        <option value=27>27
                                        <option value=28>28
                                        <option value=29>29
                                        <option value=30>30
                                        <option value=31>31</option>
                                    </select>
                                    <input maxlength=4 name=birth_year size=4>
                                    (yyyy) </td>
                                </tr>
                                <tr>
                                    <td width="47%">
                                    Gender
                                    </td>
                            <td>
                                <table border=0>
                                <tr>
                                    <td height="2" width="26%">
                                    <input type="radio" name="gender"
        value="Male">

                                        Male </td>
                                    <td height="2" width="27%">
                                    <input type="radio" name="gender"
        value="Female">

                                        Female</td>
                                </tr>
                                </table>
                            </td>
                            </tr>
                            <tr>
                                <td width="47%">
                                Please choose topics of interest
```

```
        </td>
        <td height="2" >
          <table width="100%" border="0">
            <tr>
              <td>
                <input type="checkbox" name="fic-
tion" value="1">

                Fiction</td>
              <td>
                <input type="checkbox" name="hor-
ror" value="1">

                Horror</td>
            </tr>
            <tr>
              <td>
                <input type="checkbox"
name="action" value="1">

                Action </td>
              <td>
                <input type="checkbox" name="come-
dy" value="1">

                Comedy</td>
            </tr>
              <td>
              <tr>
              <td>
                <input type="checkbox"
name="thriller" value="1">

                Thriller </td>
            </tr>
             </td>
            </tr>
          </table>

        </td>
      </tr>
      <tr>
        <td width="47%" height="47">
```

```
                                            <p align="right">Select hobbies </p>
                                            <p align="right">(Select multiple choices
by holding the ctrl key and

                                                clicking on them one by one)</p>
                                    </td>
                                    <td  height="47">
                                      <p align="center">
                                        <select name="hobbies[]" size="7" multi-
ple>

                                            <option value="Outdoor Sports">Outdoor
Sports</option>

                                            <option value="Adventure
Sports">Adventure Sports</option>

                                            <option value="Pop Music">Pop
Music</option>

                                            <option value="Rock Music">Rock
Music</option>

                                            <option value="Aggressive
Music">Aggressive Music</option>

                                            <option
value="Photography">Photography</option>

                                            </select>
                                        </p>
                                    </td>
                                </tr>
                                <tr>
                                    <td colspan="3">
                                        <input type="submit" name="Submit"
value="Submit">

                                    </td>
                                </tr>
                    </table>
            </form>
            </body>
            </html>
```

Figure 9-8 displays the output obtained by executing the above code.

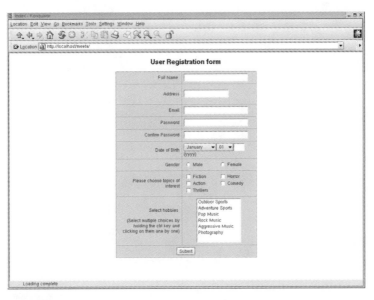

FIGURE 9-8 *Output of a Web page created to accept user information*

Summary

In this chapter, you learned about HTML. You learned that HTML is the fundamental language used on the Web to create Web pages. You also learned about tags and how they are used to create Web pages. You learned that HTML tags can be divided into two categories, container tags and empty tags. In addition, you learned about the html, head, and body tags. You also learned about each of their attributes. Next you learned about the tags used in HTML to format text. You learned about the heading tag, paragraph tag, comment tag, font tag, and boldface tag, to name a few formatting tags. Next you learned how you can create forms by using HTML. In addition, you learned how to accept different types of information from the user. Lastly you used some of the tags that you learned in the chapter to create a user registration form. You used this form to accept information from the user.

Chapter 10

**Form Parsing
in PHP**

In the previous chapter, you added to your knowledge of HTML. You created a form by using HTML and submitted information through this form for processing. At this point, the job of HTML ends and PHP takes over. The information that you submit is processed using PHP. PHP provides the easiest and the simplest means of parsing (that is, obtaining information from) an HTML form. One of the most striking features of parsing HTML forms by using PHP is that PHP does not distinguish between the GET method and the POST method. Irrespective of whether the information is submitted using the GET method or the POST method, PHP treats the information the same way.

In this chapter, I will introduce you to the concept of form parsing and tell you how it is even easier than you would think.

Parsing HTML Posted Values in PHP

As you already know, there are different types of form elements. The different types of form elements are:

◆ Text box
◆ Check box
◆ Radio button
◆ Multiple selection lists

Needless to say, you use these form elements to enter information into Web pages. In addition, these elements help you customize your Web content and make it more interactive. However, you cannot make complete use of these elements if you do not know how to extract or output information from these elements. This is where PHP figures in.

To put it simply, PHP accepts the information that you submit through an HTML form element and assigns a variable to it. Thus the variable name in PHP is the same as the Name attribute of any HTML form element. Consider an example. In an HTML form, the Name attribute of a text box is "Txtbox". In PHP, the value of this text box is automatically assigned to a variable $Txtbox. As a result, you can access Txtbox as a variable, $Txtbox, by using PHP.

NOTE

All values that are returned by various HTML form controls are accepted in PHP as string values.

Now consider how PHP parses the value of each form element. The text box will be discussed first because it is the simplest of all the form elements.

Parsing Text Box Form Elements

You use text box form elements to enter text data such as name and address. This data can be either string data or numeric data. However, in PHP, datatypes of variables are not rigid. Consider the following example. As discussed earlier, the HTML syntax for a text box form element is:

```
<input type="text" name="name" size="25" maxlength="25">
```

In the preceding code, the Name attribute of the text box control in HTML is "name". This Name attribute of HTML is assigned to the variable $name in PHP. Therefore, you can access the text field of the HTML form by using the variable $name.

To check the datatype of this variable, run the following code:

```
<?php
 echo gettype($name);
?>
```

In the preceding code, the datatype of the variable is returned as string. Similarly, you can check the datatypes of all the values entered.

Parsing Radio Button Form Controls

You use radio buttons to select one choice out of a number of choices. When you use radio buttons, PHP takes the Name attribute of the radio button and assigns the same variable name to it, as it does in the case of a text box. Consider the following example to see how PHP parses the values of a radio button control. As discussed in the previous chapter, the HTML code for a radio button form element is:

```
<input type="radio" name="gender" value="Male">
<input type="radio" name="gender" value="Female">
```

In the preceding code, the Name attribute of the radio button is `"gender"`. There-fore, in PHP, the value of the radio button is assigned to the variable $gender. In addition, note that the names of both the radio buttons are the same. This is because radio buttons are grouped together. When you select a particular option—say, Male—$gender is assigned the value Male.

Parsing Check Box Form Control

You use a check box control to select more than one choice out of a list of choices. While the Name attribute of all the radio buttons is the same, the Name attrib-utes of the check boxes are different. Consider the code snippets given below:

```
<input type="checkbox" name="fiction" value="fiction">
<input type="checkbox" name="horror" value="horror">
<input type="checkbox" name="action" value="action">
<input type="checkbox" name="comedy" value="comedy">
```

In this code, the Name attributes of all the check boxes—`"fiction"`, `"horror"`, `"action"`, and `"comedy"`—are different. As a result, PHP assigns the variables names corresponding to their Name attributes irrespective of the choice you select. For example, if you select fiction and horror, PHP assigns the variables $fiction and $horror. The remaining unselected values do not exist as variables. Therefore, when you execute the command

```
If (empty( $comedy))
```

the command returns True.

Parsing Values From Multiple Selection Lists

You use multiple selection lists to select more than one choice from the list of val-ues. A multiple selection list has only one Name attribute. This means that PHP assigns only one variable to the Name attribute. Now, if only one variable and multiple values exist, how does PHP assign values to this variable? This is where the concept of arrays comes in. When you choose multiple values from a multiple selection list, PHP assigns all the selected values as arrays to the variable. Con-sider the following code:

```
<select name="hobbies[]" size="7" multiple>
<option value="Outdoor Sports">Outdoor Sports</option>
<option value="Adventure Sports">Adventure Sports</option>
<option value="Pop Music">Pop Music</option>
<option value="Rock Music">Rock Music</option>
<option value="Aggressive Music">Aggressive Music</option>
<option value="Photography">Photography</option>
```

In the preceding code, the Name attribute of the multiple selection list is `"hobbies"`. Therefore, PHP assigns a variable, $hobbies, to this multiple selection list. However, you can select any number of values ranging from `"Outdoor Sports"` to `"Photography"`. These values are assigned to the variable as arrays. Suppose you select `"Adventure Sports"`, `"Rock Music"`, and `"Photography"`. In that case, the variable $hobbies will look like

```
$hobbies = array ("Adventure Sports", "Rock Music", "Photography");
```

Now you will learn how you can create input validators in PHP.

Form Validation

One of the most important aspects of using forms is validating user input. Consider the following code snippet, which has been taken from the previous chapter:

```
<form name="registration" method="post" action="confirm.php"
enctype="multipart/form-data">
```

In the preceding code, you submit all the information to the PHP form confirm.php. When you submit some information, PHP needs to first validate this information. Validations in PHP are performed when you click on the Submit button to send the information to the server for processing. Now you will learn how you can create different form validations in PHP.

Validating the Value of the Name Text Box

Usually the first field that you come across when filling in any form is the name field. In this case, the Full Name field is the first input field in which a user enters a value. As a result, the process of form validation starts with the value that a user enters in the name text box. Consider the code given below. This code validates the name field of your form.

```php
<?php
    if(empty($name))
    {
    die(" No Name submitted");
    }
    elseif ( (strlen($name) < 5) || (strlen($name) > 20))
    {
    die("Invalid name");
    }
    else
    {
    echo $name;
    }
?>
```

In the preceding code, the if ... ... elseif ... ... else conditional statement is used to validate the form input. Notice the code snippet given below. This code snippet has been taken from the preceding code:

```php
if(empty($name))
{
die(" No Name submitted");
}
```

According to the preceding code, if you do not enter a name, the form processing will not proceed any further and a message telling you that no name was submitted will appear. However, after you enter a name, the code checks for the length of the name. Consider the code snippet given below:

```php
elseif ( (strlen($name) < 5) || (strlen($name) > 50))
{
die("Invalid name");
}
```

In the preceding code, the name should have at least 5 characters and not more than 50 characters. If this condition is not satisfied, then you will receive the message "Invalid name".

Validating Value in the Address Text Field

The next field in your form is the Address field. Consider the code given below. This code validates the address field in the form.

```php
<?php
        if(empty($address))
        {
        die(" No address submitted");
        }
        elseif ( (strlen($address) < 5) || (strlen($address) > 50))
        {
        die("Invalid address");
        }
        else
        {
        echo $address;
?>
```

The preceding code is similar to the code that is used for validating the values in the name text field. Here the code checks whether you have filled the address field. It also checks whether the value of the address field is more than 5 characters and less than 50 characters.

Validating E-mail Address

The most common validation that you can perform for an e-mail address is checking for the existence of the "@" character in the address. Consider the code given below. This code validates the e-mail addresses in your form.

```php
<?php
         if(empty($email))
        {
        die(" No e-mail address submitted");
        }
        elseif ( (strlen($email) < 5) || (strlen($email) > 20))
        {
         die("Invalid e-mail address, e-mail address too long or too
short.");
        }
```

```
elseif(!ereg("@",$email))
 {
die("Invalid e-mail address, no @ symbol found");
}
else
{
echo $email;
 }
?>
```

Just like the previous two form validations, here also the code first checks whether you have entered the e-mail address. If e-mail values are not entered, then you receive a message stating "No e-mail address submitted". After checking for the existence of the value in the e-mail field, the code checks for the length of the field, which should be between 5 characters and 20 characters. After these two validations, the code checks whether the value contains an @ symbol. The code snippet given below does this validation for the @ symbol:

```
elseif(!ereg("@",$email))
 {
die("Invalid e-mail address, no @ symbol found");
 }
```

In the preceding code, the first line checks for the presence of the @ symbol in the e-mail address. If the @ symbol is not found, then you get a message that states "Invalid e-mail address, no @ symbol found".

Validating Passwords

User names and passwords are the most basic security features used for authenticating users. Passwords ensure confidentiality and integrity of the information that a user provides. Consider the following code that validates passwords. In addition, this code ensures that as you type your password, the actual characters remain hidden and you view only the *.

```
<?php
if(empty($password) || empty($cpassword))
{
die(" No password submitted");
}
```

```
                    elseif ( ((strlen($password) < 5) || (strlen($password) >
15))))

                    {
                    die("Invalid password length address");
                    }
                    elseif ( !(strlen($password) == strlen($cpassword)) )
                    {
                    die(" Passwords do not match ! ");
                    }
                    elseif( !($password === $cpassword))
                    //compares values and datatypes
                    {
                     die(" Passwords do not match ! ");
                    }
                    else
                    {
                     for ($i=0;$i<strlen($password);$i++)
                    {
                    echo "*";
                     }
                    }
         ?>
```

The preceding code first checks for an empty password field and then for the length of the password. After performing these validations, the code then compares the values entered in the Password field and the Confirm Password field. This comparison involves matching the lengths of the input values of the two fields and matching the values and datatypes of the two fields.

Validating the Date of Birth Fields

Validating the input value for the date of birth fields in the form involves validating three different values, the birth month, the birth day, and the birth year. Consider the following code:

```
        <?php
                    if (empty($birth_month) || empty($birth_day) ||
empty($birth_year) )
                    {
```

```php
        die(" Date of birth not submitted or incomplete.");
    }
    switch($birth_month)
    {
    case 1: print "January "; break;
    case 2: print "February "; break;
    case 3: print "March ";break;
    case 4: print "April ";break;
    case 5: print "May "; break;
    case 6: print "June "; break;
    case 7: print "July "; break;
    case 8: print "August "; break;
    case 9: print "September "; break;
    case 10: print "October "; break;
    case 11: print "November "; break;
    case 12: print "December "; break;
    default: die("Invalid birth month !!");
    }
    if (($birth_day < 1) || ($birth_day > 31))
    {
    die(" Invalid date !");
    }
    else
    {
    echo $birth_day, " ";
    }
    if (($birth_year < 1900) || ($birth_year >2000))
    {
    die("Invalid birth year");
    }
    else
    {
    echo $birth_year;
    }
?>
```

After checking for empty fields in the preceding code, the code validates the birth day fields. The days in the birth day fields should be between 1 and 31.

If this condition is not met, then an error message stating "Invalid date!" appears. After validating the days, the code checks for the year of birth. According to the birth year validation check, only users who are born between 1900 and 2000 can enter values in the form.

After you have performed all the validations in the form, you display the input values in the output form.

Printing the Confirmation Page

In the previous topic, you learned how to validate the user input. Now you will see how you can display these values. Suppose in the Full Name field you enter a value, "Ashley Norman". This value will be assigned to the variable $name in PHP. To print this value in the output form, you use the echo command. Consider the code given below. This code prints the input values.

```php
<?php
        if(empty($name))
        {
        die(" No Name submitted");
        }
        elseif ( (strlen($name) < 5) ¦¦ (strlen($name) > 50))
        {
        die("Invalid name");
        }
        else
        {
        echo $name;
        }
    ?>
```

As already discussed in the previous topic, the code first validates the input values. After validating the input, the code prints these values in an output form. However, before these values are printed, they are assigned to the hidden fields. You'll now learn how hidden fields are used in PHP.

Printing Hidden Fields

You use hidden fields to store information in dynamic Web pages. Hidden fields store names and values that remain fixed irrespective of user input. These names and values are then sent to the server. Consider the code given below. This code assigns the values to hidden fields and then prints these values in the output form.

```php
<?php
        echo "<input type=hidden name=\"name\" value=\"".$name."\"
>\n";
        echo "<input type=hidden name=\"address\"
value=\"".$address."\" >\n";
        echo "<input type=hidden name=\"email\" value=\"".$email."\"
>\n";
        echo "<input type=hidden name=\"birth_month\"
value=\"".$birth_month."\" >\n";
        echo "<input type=hidden name=\"birth_day\"
value=\"".$birth_day."\" >\n";
        echo "<input type=hidden name=\"birth_year\"
value=\"".$birth_year."\" >\n";
        echo "<input type=hidden name=\"interests\" value=\"".$inter-
ests."\" >\n";
        for ($i=0;$i<count($hobbies);$i++)
        {
         echo "<input type=hidden name=\"hobbies[]\" value=\"".$hob-
bies[$i]."\" >\n";
        }
        if ($fiction)
        {
         echo "<input type=hidden name=\"fiction\" value=\"".$fic-
tion."\" >\n";
        }
        if ($action)
        {
        echo "<input type=hidden name=\"action\" value=\"".$action."\"
>\n";
        }
        if ($horror)
```

```
                              {
                                echo "<input type=hidden name=\"horror\" value=\"".$hor-
ror."\" >\n";
                              }
                              if ($comedy)
                              {
                                echo "<input type=hidden name=\"comedy\" value=\"".$come-
dy."\" >\n";
                              }
                              if ($thrillers)
                              {
                                echo "<input type=hidden name=\"thrillers\"
value=\"".$thrillers."\" >\n";
                              }
                ?>
```

The preceding code assigns the names and values to hidden fields. Notice that hidden fields consist of three components:

- ◆ Input type
- ◆ Name
- ◆ Value

As can be observed in the preceding code, the value of the input type is hidden. The value of the name component is the name of the fields such as Name, Address, and Age.

You can now put into practice all that you have learned so far in this chapter. In the next section, you will integrate all the code snippets to create a sample project.

Putting Theory into Practice

In the previous chapter, you created a registration form (index.htm) that accepted input from the new user. You will now validate the input values. To input values and validate these input values, you need to perform the following steps:

1. To input values, open the browser window and display index.htm.
2. Enter the information as shown in Figure 10-1.

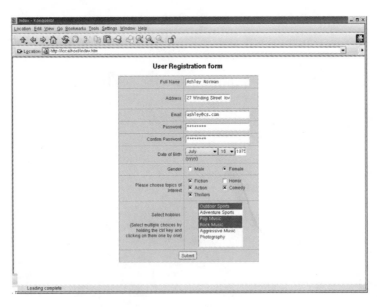

FIGURE 10-1 *The User Registration form index.htm with information filled in*

3. Click on the Submit button to submit these values to the confirm.php form, as shown in Figure 10-2. (Recall that in the code for index.htm, the information is posted to confirm.php.)

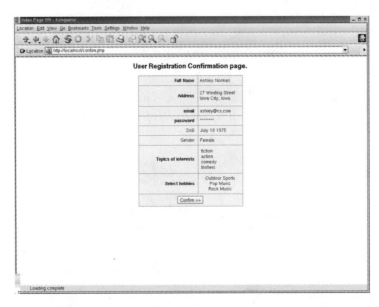

FIGURE 10-2 *User input values in confirm.php*

Here is the complete code for confirm.php.

```
<html>
        <head>
        <title>Index</title>
        </head>
        <body>
        <h2 align="center">User Registration Confirmation page.</h2>
        <form name="registration" method="post" action="output.php"
enctype="multipart/form-data">
        <table width="300" border="1" align="center" cellpadding="5"
cellspacing="0" bgcolor="#EEEEFF">
        <tr>
        <td width="47%" align="right"> <B> Full Name </B> </td>
        <td >
//--- Validating the name Input value.
<?php
        if(empty($name))
        {
        die(" No Name submitted");
        }
//--- Validating whether the length of the name Input value Is between 5
to 50 characters.
        elseif ( (strlen($name) < 5) || (strlen($name) > 50))
        {
        die("Invalid name");
        }
        else
        {
//--- Printing the name Input value.
         echo $name;
        }
        ?>
        </td>
        </tr>
        <tr>
        <td width="47%" height="57" align="right"><B> Address
</B></td>
        <td height="57">
```

```
//--- Validating Value in the Address Text field
<?php
        if(empty($address))
        {
        die(" No address submitted");
        }
        elseif ( (strlen($address) < 5) || (strlen($address) > 50))
        {
        die("Invalid address");
        }
        else
        {
        echo $address;
        }
?>
//--- Validating Value in the e-mail text field
        </td>
        </tr>
        <tr>
        <td width="47%" align="right"> <B>email</B> </td>
        <td height="2">
<?php
        if(empty($email))
        {
        die(" No e-mail address submitted");
        }
        elseif ( (strlen($email) < 5) || (strlen($email) > 50))
        {
        die("Invalid e-mail address, e-mail address too long or too
short.");
        }
        elseif(!ereg("@",$email)) //refer to php manual 4 ereg expln.
        {
        die("Invalid e-mail address, no @ symbol found");
        }
        else
        {
        echo $email;
```

```
                }
        ?>
                </td>
                </tr>
                <tr>
                <td width="47%" align="right"> <B>password </B></td>
                <td height="2">
        //--- Validating Value in the Password Text field
        <?php
                if(empty($password) || empty($cpassword))
                {
                die(" No password submitted");
                }
                elseif ( ((strlen($password) < 5) || (strlen($password) >
15))))

                {
                die("Invalid password length address");
                }
        //--- Comparing values of the Password and Confirm Password fields.
                elseif ( !(strlen($password) == strlen($cpassword)) )
                {
                 die(" Passwords do not match ! ");
                }
                elseif( !($password === $cpassword)) //compares values and
datatypes

                {
                 die(" Passwords do not match ! ");
                }
                else
                {
                for ($i=0;$i<strlen($password);$i++)
                {
                echo "*";
                }
                }
        ?>
                </td>
                </tr>
```

```
                <tr>
                <td width="47%" align="right"> DoB </B></td>
                <td height="2">
         //--- Validating Input values of the birthday fields

        <?php
                if (empty($birth_month) || empty($birth_day) ||
   empty($birth_year) )
                {
                die(" Date of birth not submitted or incomplete.");
                 }
                switch($birth_month)
                {
                case 1: print "January "; break;
                case 2: print "February "; break;
                case 3: print "March ";break;
                case 4: print "April ";break;
                case 5: print "May "; break;
                case 6: print "June "; break;
                case 7: print "July "; break;
                case 8: print "August "; break;
                case 9: print "September "; break;
                case 10: print "October "; break;
                case 11: print "November "; break;
                case 12: print "December "; break;
                default: die("Invalid birth month !!");
        }
                if (($birth_day < 1) || ($birth_day > 31))
                {
                die(" Invalid date !");
                }
                else
                {
                echo $birth_day, " ";
                }
                if (($birth_year < 1900) || ($birth_year >2000))
                {
```

```
            die("Invalid birth year");
            }
            else
            {
            echo $birth_year;
            }
?>

            </td>
            </tr>
            <tr>
            <td width="47%" align="right">
            Gender
            </td>
            <td height="2" width="26%">
//--- Validating the value of a Radio button control
<?php
            if (empty($gender))
            {
             die(" Gender not specified");
            }
            elseif (!(($gender=="Male") || ($gender=="Female")))
            {
            die("Invalid value for gender");
            }
            else
            {
            echo $gender;
            }
?>

            </td>
            </tr>
            <tr>
            <td width="47%" align="right">
            <B>    Topics of interests</B>
            </td>
            <td height="2" colspan="2">
            <table width="100%" border="0">
            <tr>
```

```
          <td>
//--- Validating Value of a check box form control

<?php
          if ($fiction)
          {
          echo "fiction <br>";
          }
          if ($horror)
          {
          echo "horror <br>";
          }
          if ($action)
          {
          echo "action <br>";
          }
          if ($comedy)
          {
          echo "comedy <br>";
          }
          if ($thrillers)
          {
          echo "thrillers <br>";
          }
?>
          </td>
          </tr>
          </table>
          </td>
          </tr>
          <tr>
          <td width="47%" height="47" align="right">
          <B>          Select hobbies</B>
          </td>
          <td colspan="2" height="47">
          <p align="center">
<?php
          for ($i=0; $i<count($hobbies);$i++)
```

```
                            {
                            echo $hobbies[$i] . "<br>";
                            }
                ?>
                            </td>
                            </tr>
                            <tr>
                            <td colspan="3">
                            <FORM Name=confirm action="output.php">
                //--- Printing Hidden field values
                <?php
                            echo "<input type=hidden name=\"name\" value=\"".$name."\"
>\n";
                            echo "<input type=hidden name=\"address\"
value=\"".$address."\" >\n";
                            echo "<input type=hidden name=\"email\" value=\"".$email."\"
>\n";
                            echo "<input type=hidden name=\"birth_month\"
value=\"".$birth_month."\" >\n";
                            echo "<input type=hidden name=\"birth_day\"
value=\"".$birth_day."\" >\n";
                            echo "<input type=hidden name=\"birth_year\"
value=\"".$birth_year."\" >\n";
                            echo "<input type=hidden name=\"interests\" value=\"".$inter-
ests."\" >\n";
                            for ($i=0;$i<count($hobbies);$i++)
                            {
                            echo "<input type=hidden name=\"hobbies[]\" value=\"".$hob-
bies[$i]."\" >\n";
                            }
                            if ($fiction)
                            {
                            echo "<input type=hidden name=\"fiction\" value=\"".$fic-
tion."\" >\n";
                            }
                            if ($action)
                            {
                            echo "<input type=hidden name=\"action\" value=\"".$action."\"
>\n";
```

```
                }
                if ($horror)
                {
                echo "<input type=hidden name=\"horror\" value=\"".$horror."\"
>\n";

                }
                if ($comedy)
                {
                echo "<input type=hidden name=\"comedy\" value=\"".$comedy."\"
>\n";

                }
                if ($thrillers)
                {
                echo "<input type=hidden name=\"thrillers\"
value=\"".$thrillers."\" >\n";
                }
        ?>
                <center>         <input type="submit" name="Submit"
value="Confirm >>">
                </center>
                </form>
                </td>
                </tr>
                </table>
                </form>
                </body>
        </html>
```

After validating the values, this information is printed in the output.php form as shown in Figure 10-3.

The complete code for the output.php form is

```
            <html>
            <head>
            <title>Display Output </title>
            </head>
            <body>
```

FIGURE 10-3 *User input values in output.php*

```
<br><br><br>
<center>
<h2> The following information was entered and accepted.</h2>
</center>
<table width="300" border="1" bgcolor="#EEFFEE" align="center"
cellspacing=2 cellpadding=5>
<tr>
<td>Full Name </td>
<td>
//--- Prints the value of the name field
<h3><?php echo $name; ?> </h3>
</td>
</tr>
<tr>
<td>e-mail </td>
<td>
//--- Prints the value of the e-mail field
<h3><?php echo $email; ?> </h3>
</td>
</tr>
```

```
            <tr>
            <td>Address </td>
            <td>
//--- Prints the value of the address field
            <h3><?php echo $address; ?> </h3>
            </td>
            </tr>
            <tr>
            <td>Date of Birth</td>
            <td>
//--- Prints the value of the Date of Birth field
            <h3> <?php echo $birth_month," ",$birth_day,"   ",$birth_year;
    ?> </h3>
            </td>
            </tr>
            <tr>
            <td>
            You prefer these books
            </td>
            <td>
            <h3>
    <?php
            if ($fiction)
            {
            echo "fiction <br>";
            }
            if ($action)
            {
            echo "action <br>";
            }
            if ($thrillers)
            {
            echo "thrillers <br>";
            }
            if ($horror)
            {
            echo "horror <br>";
            }
```

```
            if ($comedy)
            {
            echo "comedy ";
            }
            ?>
            </h3>
            </td>
            </tr>
            <tr>
            <td height="21">You like :
               </td>
            <td>
            <h3>
<?php
             for ($i=0;$i<count($hobbies);$i++)
            {
            echo $hobbies[$i], "<br>";
            }
?>
            </h3>
            </td>
</tr>
</table>
</body>
</html>
```

The preceding code prints the input values in the output.php form.

Summary

In this chapter you learned the basics of parsing an HTML form. You learned about parsing HTML posted values in PHP. Then you learned about validating input values. Next you learned about printing the confirmation page. You also learned about hidden fields in PHP. Finally, you created two scripts that validated user input values and printed the output.

PART III

Professional Project 2

Project 2

Storing and Retrieving Information from Files

Project 2 Overview

Everyone likes a well-designed Web site, but nobody likes to read outdated information, especially on a Web site. Up-to-date information is very critical for the success of Web sites dealing with promotion or with e-commerce. Imagine ordering a product and getting an e-mail a few minutes later informing you that the product is out of stock. Absolutely frustrating, isn't it? If you have taken troubles to put up a Web site for the world to see, you might as well make a little more effort to keep the site updated!

You can permanently store data from a Web page either in a file or in a database. In Chapter 11, you'll learn the basics of file handling and put this knowledge into practice. First you'll learn to test the existence of a file and then open the file. Next you'll learn to read from and write to the file. You'll also learn how to determine the file size and the End Of File (EOF) of the file. Next you'll learn how to manipulate the placement of the file pointer and to write data to a file. You'll also learn how to format a string in a specified format and unpack the formatted data as per another format into an associative array.

Chapter 11

A well-designed Web site is a sight for sore eyes. However, the same Web site might lose its attractiveness if it was not up-to-date. If you have taken the trouble to put up a Web site, make a little more effort and keep the site updated! This holds especially true for the promotional or e-commerce sites. For example, new products are added to a vendor's inventory year round. Similarly, the rates and seasonal discounts are also subject to change frequently. However, if you make these changes to the embedded HTML code of the site, you are giving yourself a lot of unnecessary extra work. The simple remedy for this situation is to store frequently changing data in an external file and retrieve it from the same file. Then, instead of updating a changed discount rate manually in countless places, you can update it once in this related file. Your life is simpler! In addition, more often than not, this persistent data might prove to be important for later reference.

Data from a Web page can be permanently stored in two ways. You can either store the data in a file or store it in a database. In fact, a database is actually an advanced and more structured form of a file.

This chapter introduces you to the basics of handling files in PHP. You will learn about various file-related functions that allow you to access data from a PHP-based Web page, store data generated by a PHP page into a text file, or simply manipulate files while reading or writing to the file. You'll learn about storing data in a database in detail in Chapters 11 and 12.

Working with Files

If you have previous experience of working with other programming languages, such as C or C++, you might remember that working with a file can be broken down into the following stages:

- ◆ **Opening a file.** The specified file is opened. If the file doesn't exist, the file is created.

- ◆ **Manipulating the file.** After the file has been accessed, it is ready for manipulation. You can read from the file if it already consists of data, write to the file anew, or append data to the preexisting data in the file.

♦ **Closing the file.** After you have finished working with the file, you then need to close the file.

PHP offers you several file-related functions that you can use to save the data from a Web page to a file, retrieve the data from a file to a Web page, or simply change or append new data to an existing file. Some of the most frequently used file operations include the following:

♦ Checking for the existence of a file

♦ Opening a file

♦ Reading from a file

♦ Writing to a file

The next sections discuss these file operations in detail.

Checking whether a File Exists

Before you perform a file-related operation with the specified file, you might want to check whether the file already exists or not. You can use the `file_exists()` function to do so. The `file_exists()` function returns True (or 1) if the specified file exists and False (or 0) if it does not. The syntax of the `file_exists()` function is given below:

```
bool file_exists(string file_name);
```

As indicated in the above syntax, the `file_exists()` function takes only one argument—file_name, which specifies the name of the file whose existence is being tested.

Consider the following code to understand the `file_exists()` function.

```php
<?php

if (!(file_exists("data.dat")))
{
 echo "The file exists.";
}
else
{
 echo "The file  does not exist.";
}
```

In the above code, the existence of the file `data.dat` is being verified with the help of the statement `if (file_exists("data.dat"))`. As you learned in Chapter 3, "Variables, Operators, and Constants", the `!` operator negates the result of the `if (file_exists("data.dat"))` statement.

Opening a File

You need to use the `fopen()` function to open a file in PHP. This function can open either a file or a URL. As a result, the file can be either a local file or a remote file. The `fopen()` function requires at least two parameters. The syntax for the `fopen()` function is given below:

```
int fopen(string file_name, string mode, int include_path);
```

In the above syntax, the argument `file_name` specifies the name of the file to be opened. If the value of the `file_name` argument begins with `http://`, it implies that the file is located on a remote Web server and an HTTP 1.0 session needs to be established with the specified server to open the file. Similarly, if the value of the `file_name` argument begins with `ftp://`, the specified file needs to be retrieved from an FTP server after an FTP session is established with the specified server. If the value of the `file_name` argument starts with `php://stdin`, `php://stdout`, or `php://stderr`, the corresponding standard Input/Output stream is opened. However, if the value of this argument begins with none of the aforementioned prefixes, the specified file is considered local and PHP searches for it on the local hard disk.

 NOTE

If the specified file needs to be retrieved from a remote HTTP server, remember that it can be opened only for reading. This effectively stops people from messing around with others' Web pages. Similarly, if the specified file needs to be retrieved from an FTP server, you must remember that you can open files for either writing or reading, but not both simultaneously.

The second argument—mode—indicates whether the file was opened for reading, writing, or appending. The `mode` argument can take one of the values indicated in Table 11-1.

Table 11-1 Values of the mode Argument

Mode	Description
r	Opens the file for reading only.
r+	Opens the file for reading and writing and places the file pointer at the beginning of the file.
w	Opens the file for writing only. If the file consists of any data, the data will be lost. If the file does not exist, creates the file.
w+	Opens the file for reading as well as writing. If the file consists of any data, the data will be lost. If the file does not exist, creates the file.
a	Opens the file for appending data after the preexisting data. If the file does not exist, creates the file.
a+	Opens the file for reading as well as appending. If the file consists of any data, the data will be written to the end of file. If the file does not exist, creates the file.

 NOTE

You might come across the mode b in few cases. This mode works only for platforms, such as Windows, that can differentiate between the text and binary formats. This mode is useless on platforms such as Unix.

The third argument—include_path—is optional and is used if you want to search in the path specified by this argument.

The following code demonstrates the use of the fopen() function.

```
if (!(file_exists("data.dat")))
   {
    $fp = fopen("data.dat","w+");
   }
   else
   {
//-----------If file exists, then open it in the append mode----
```

```
    $fp = fopen("data.dat","a");
}
```

The above code first checks to see if the file `data.dat` exists. If the file doesn't exist, a new file called `data.dat` is created with the w+ mode. This implies that the file is ready to be read from as well as written to. On the other hand, if the statement `if (file_exists("data.dat"))` returns True—that is, if `data.dat` already exists—the file is opened in `write` mode, allowing you to add data to the file.

 CAUTION

Be very careful when inputting backslashes (\) in the local file path and forward slashes (/)in the path to a remote file (http:// or ftp://) if you are working on the Windows platform. If you mix up the slashes, you might end up with a warning from PHP to the effect that the specified file path was not found!

You can use @ in front of the `fopen()` function or any other system function in PHP—for example, `@fopen("data.dat","w+");`. The use of @ in the beginning of any system function would help you to suppress standard compiler warnings in PHP. However, you must take care to provide custom error messages, in case the specified user-defined functions fail.

Now that you have learned to open a file, the next section tells you how to close the file.

Closing a File

In order to close a file, you need to use the `fclose()` function. If the `fclose()` function closes a file successfully, it returns True. If it encounters a failure in the file close operation, the `fclose()` function returns False.

The syntax of the `fclose()` function is:

```
bool fclose(int file_pointer);
```

The `fclose()` function takes a single argument in the form of the file pointer, `file_pointer`, which references the file that needs to be closed. For the function to execute successfully, it is important that the `file_pointer` argument be valid and references a file that was opened by using the `fopen()` function.

Now that you have learned to close a file, the next section discusses how to read from a file.

Reading from a File

You need to use the `fread()` function to read from an external file in PHP. The syntax for the `fread()` function is:

```
string fread(int file_pointer, int length);
```

As you can see, the `fread()` function takes two arguments—`file_pointer` and `length`. The `file_pointer` argument references the specific location in a file that has to be read. The `length` argument specifies the number of characters that have to be read from the specified location. The read operation continues until all the characters specified by the `length` argument are read. If the end of file (EOF) is reached before the specified length, the read characters would be returned before the read operation is terminated.

Consider the following code:

```
            $fo = @fopen("C:\PHP\Myfiles\data1.dat", r) or die("Could
not locate the specified file!");
            //-----The first 124 characters of the file, data1.dat, are
read
            $fr = fread($fo, 124);
        }
```

In the above code, a file `data1.dat` is opened for reading with the help of the `fread()` function. The `or die ("Could not locate the specified file!")` statement is used to print a custom message if the `fopen()` operation fails. The result—1 or 0—of the `fopen()` function is stored in the variable, `$fo`. This variable is then supplied to the `fread()` function as the reference to the file to be read. The value 124 in the `fread()` function specifies that the first 124 characters of data1.dat will be read.

PHP provides a wide range of file functions besides `fread()`. The `fgets()`, `fgetc()`, and `feof()` functions are the most commonly used. The next section gives you more information about these functions. You'll first learn about the `filesize()` function in PHP.

The filesize() *Function*

The `filesize()` function returns the total size of the specified file. However, if the specified file doesn't exist, False (or 0) is returned. The syntax of the function is given below:

```
int filesize(string file_name);
```

As shown in the above syntax, the `filesize()` function takes a single argument— the name of the file whose size is to be determined.

NOTE

Note that the `filesize()` function works only with local files.

The feof() *Function*

You can use the `feof()` function to determine if the entire content of the specified file has been traversed and the file pointer has reached the end of file (EOF) position of the file. This function returns True if the file pointer is currently at EOF of the file; otherwise, it returns False. However, if an error occurs, the `feof()` function returns True.

The `feof()` function takes a single argument in the form of the file pointer, as shown in the syntax of the function below:

```
Int feof(int file_pointer);
```

NOTE

Note that the file pointer must point to a file that was successfully opened by the `fopen()` function.

The fgetc() *and* fgets() *Functions*

The `fread()` function returns a string of specified length from the specific location in a file. What if you would like to read a single character? You can easily manipulate the `fread()` function to read the specified character by placing the pointer at the desired location and specifying the length argument as 1. However, PHP gives you a much simpler way to do this than manipulating file pointers and string lengths! It offers the `fgetc()` function to do so. This function gets a single character from the position where the file pointer is located. The syntax of the `fgetc()` function is:

```
string fgetc(int file_pointer);
```

 NOTE

If it encounters EOF, `fgetc()` returns False. Also, the file pointer must point to a file that was successfully opened by the `fopen()` function.

The `fgets()` function returns a line (string) from the location specified by the file pointer. However, unlike the `fread()` function, the length of the string returned by `fgets()` is one less than the length specified by the `length` argument. The syntax of the `fgets()` function is:

```
string fgets(int file_pointer, int length);
```

The read operation is terminated if any of the following conditions is met:

◆ `length-1` bytes have been read

◆ Newline character, \n, is encountered

◆ End of the file, `EOF`, is encountered

Consider the following code, which rounds up all the information you have gathered about `filesize()`, `feof()`, `fgetc()`, and `fgets()`functions until now.

```php
<?php
$file = "data1.dat";
//-----Opening the file data1.dat.
//-----Is displayed.
$fo =@fopen($file, "r") or die("Could not locate the specified
file! Please check If the file is valid.");
//-----Calculating the total size of the file - data1.dat.
$file_length = filesize($file);
echo "The total size of the file is: $file_length", "\n";
```

```
            //---Reading the entire file row-wise. Each time a line ends,
newline character is met, the variable
            //---$total_rows Is Incremented by 1.
              while(!(feof($fo)))
              {
                    $tr = fgets($fo, $file_length);
                    $total_rows = $total_rows + 1;
              }
            echo "Total number of lines in this file is: $total_rows ",
"\n";
            //---Closing data1.dat for the next loop to execute successfully.
              fclose($fo);
            //---Opening data1.dat again, so that the file pointer is at the
beginning of the file.
              $fo1 = @fopen($file, "r");
            //---Reading the entire file character-wise. Each time a
character is read, the variable
            //---$total_chars is Incremented by 1.
              while(!(feof($fo1)))
              {
                    $tc = fgetc($fo1);
                    $total_chars = $total_chars + 1;
              }
            echo "Total number of characters in this file is: $total_chars
", "\n";
              ?>
```

In the above code, the file, data1.dat is opened. If the open operation is not successful (if the file is not found in the specified location), the corresponding message Could not locate the specified file! Please check if the file is valid. is displayed. On the other hand, if the file-open operation is successful, the total size of the file is calculated using the filesize() function. The total size of the file is stored in the $file_length variable. Next, the entire file is read line-wise (until the newline character) with the help of the fgets() function. The variable $total_rows is incremented for every new line that is read. When the file pointer, $fo, reaches the EOF of data1.dat, the condition while(!(feof($fo))) returns False and the loop is terminated. A message, Total number of lines in this file is: 3, is displayed. The file is then closed. You need to close the file at this point because due to the previous loop, the file pointer has already reached the EOF! For the next loop (which counts the total number of characters in data1.dat) to execute successfully, the file pointer must not be at EOF. After the file is closed, it is opened again, which places the pointer in the beginning of the file. The next loop is executed and the total number of characters in the file is calculated with the help of function fgetc(). After each character, the variable—$total_chars—is incremented. When the EOF of the file is reached, the loop condition returns False and the loop is terminated. A message Total number of characters in this file is: 54 is displayed.

Figure 11-1 displays the output of the preceding code.

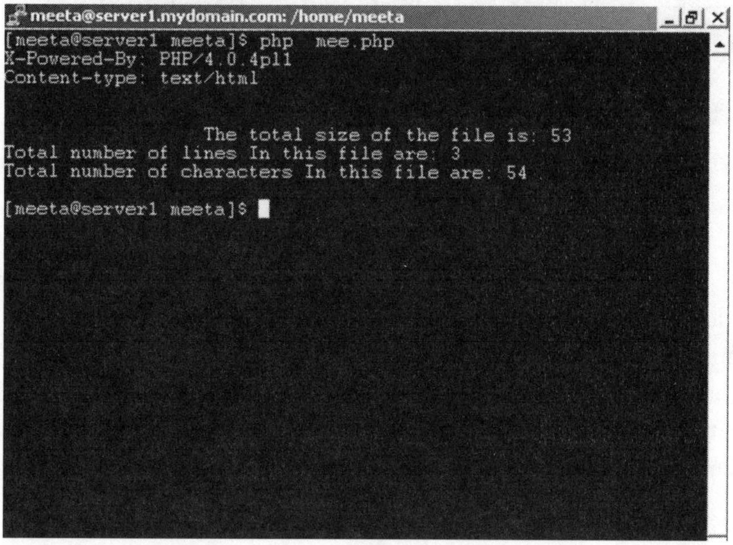

FIGURE 11-1 *Output of the file functions*

Figure 11-2 displays the content of the data1.dat file used in the preceding code.

In the next section, you'll learn about another function related to file-read operations, fseek().

The fseek() *Function*

You can use the fseek() function to set the file pointer to a specific location with respect to the current position of the pointer. The syntax of the fseek() function is:

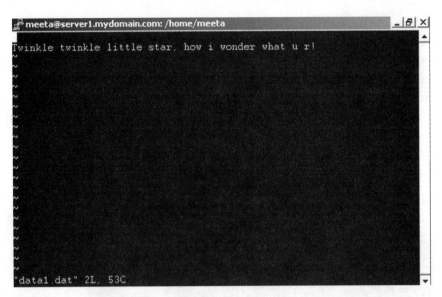

FIGURE 11-2 *Content of the* data1.dat *file*

```
int fseek(int file_pointer, int offset, int whence);
```

In the above syntax, the first argument is file pointer, file_pointer, which references the file where the desired operation is to be carried. The next argument, offset, is an integer that defines the starting point of the read operation in relation to the beginning of the specified file. The third argument, whence, specifies the end position in the file, which indicates where to stop reading the data. Both offset and whence are measured in bytes.

The whence argument has the following three standard values:

◆ **SEEK_SET.** Sets the file pointer at a position equal to the offset bytes.

◆ **SEEK_CUR.** Sets the file pointer at a position that is equal to the sum of the current location (byte) and the offset.

◆ **SEEK_END.** Sets the file pointer at a position that is obtained by the sum of EOF and offset.

 NOTE

SEEK_SET is the default value of the whence argument. So if the whence argument is not specified, the value of whence is assumed by PHP to be SEEK_SET.

To understand the fseek() function, consider the following code.

```php
<?php
$file = "data1.dat";
//---Opening the file "data1.dat, else displaying a message
$fo =@fopen($file, "r") or die("Could not locate the specified
file! Please check if the file is valid.");
//---Determining the size of data1.dat
$file_length = filesize($file);
echo "\n";
echo "The size of the file is: $file_length.", "\n";
//---Moving the file pointer to 22nd byte in the file
$fs = fseek($fo, 22, SEEK_CUR);
//---Reading five characters from the current position of the
file pointer
$current_char = fread($fo, 6);
echo "Currently, the file pointer is at $current_char in the
file.", "\n";
?>
```

In the preceding code, the file data1.dat is opened. If the file-open operation was unsuccessful, the message Could not locate the specified file! Please check if the file is valid. is displayed. On the other hand, if the data1.dat is opened successfully, the total size of the file is calculated with the help of file-size() function and displayed on the screen. Remember that because of the fopen() function that was used to open the file, the file pointer is located in the beginning of the file. The fseek() function is then used to move the file pointer $fo to the 22nd byte relative to the beginning of the file with the help of the argument SEEK_CUR. The fread() function is then used to read six characters from the new position of the file pointer. Finally, the six characters, e star, that have been extracted from data.dat are displayed.

Figure 11-3 shows the output of the preceding code.

Now that you know how to read data from a file and various functions that help you to manipulate the read-related file operations, the following section discusses how you can write to a file.

FIGURE 11-3 *Content of the* `fseek()` *function in the preceding code*

Writing to a File

PHP provides the `fwrite()` function to write to an external file. This function takes three arguments. The syntax of the `fwrite()` function is given below.

```
int fwrite(int file_pointer, string string, int length)
```

The first argument, `file_pointer`, is the integer-type file pointer that references the file where you need to write. The second argument, `string`, is the information that needs to be written to the file. Finally, the third argument, `length`, is an optional argument. If it is specified, the write operation continues until the number of bytes specified by `length` have been written or the end of the string being written is reached, whichever is achieved first.

To better understand the `fwrite()` function, consider the following segment of a code.

```
$dataformat="A20A200A50A6A10A2A4A1A1A1A1A1A20A20A20A20A20A20A1";
            $line =
            pack($dataformat,$name,$address,$email,$gender,$birth_month,
            $birth_day,$birth_year,$fiction,$action,$horror,$thrillers,
            $comedy,$hobbies[0],hobbies[1],$hobbies[2],$hobbies[3],
            $hobbies[4],$hobbies[5],"\n");
```

```
                    echo $line,"<br>",strlen($line);
                    $fp = @fopen("data.dat","w+") or die("Could not open the file.
Please check if the
                     file exists.");
                    //----Writing to the file
                    $result = @fwrite($fp,$line) or die("Data could not be written
to the file.");

                    fclose($fp);
```

In the above code, the file data.dat is opened in w+ mode, which enables the file
to be read as well as written to. If for any reason the data.dat cannot be opened,
the message Could not open the file. Please check if the file exists.
will be displayed. After the file is opened successfully, the string stored in the
$line variable is written into the file. However, if the write operation was not suc-
cessful, the message Data could not be written to the file. is displayed. The
open file is then closed with the help of the fclose() function.

 NOTE

Note that since data.dat is opened in the w+ mode, if it contained some data, the
data will be deleted and the new data (stored in the $line variable) will be written to
the file.

The function fputs() works very much like the fwrite() function in PHP. In
fact, fputs() is an alias of fwrite(). Therefore, the syntax of fputs() is also iden-
tical to fwrite().

```
int fputs(int file_pointer, string string, int length)
```

Confused by the statement $dataformat="A20A200A50A6A10A2A4A1A1A1A1A1
A20A20A20A20A20A20A1";? The next section explains what this is.

Formatting the Data While Accepting Input

Consider the following statement:

```
$dataformat="A20A200A50A6A10A2A4A1A1A1A1A1A20A20A20A20A20A20A1";
```

The preceding statement causes the input accepted from the HTML form that you designed in Chapter 8 for Project 1 ("Creating a User Registration Form for an Online Shopping Site") into the variable $dataformat in a predefined format. The $dataformat variable stores the data related to a record in a single line, where each field entry is separated by fixed spaces reserved for them. The character A preceding a number (20, 200, 50, 6, 10, 2, 4, 1) represents a variable, such as $name, $address, $email, and so on, in the order they were accepted from the HTML form. Therefore:

◆ **A20.** Reserves 20 spaces for the value of the corresponding variable. These include $name, $hobbies[0], $hobbies[1], $hobbies[2], $hobbies[3], $hobbies[4], and $hobbies[5].

◆ **A200.** Reserves 200 spaces for the value of the corresponding variable. This single variable is $address.

◆ **A4.** Reserves 4 spaces for the value of the corresponding variable. This single variable is $birth_year.

◆ **A50.** Reserves 50 spaces for the value of the corresponding variable. This variable is $email.

◆ **A6.** Reserves 6 spaces for the value of the corresponding variable. This variable is $gender.

◆ **A10.** Reserves 10 spaces for the value of the corresponding variable. This single variable is $birth_month.

◆ **A2.** Reserves 2 spaces for the value of the corresponding variable. This variable is $birth_day.

◆ **A1.** Reserves 1 space each for the value of the corresponding variable. For each checkbox—$fiction, $action, $horror, $thrillers, $comedy— only one space has been reserved.

 NOTE

The spaces reserved for each variable-value is fixed. If, for example, a user enters a name whose length is greater than 20, the characters from the 21st position will be truncated. Similarly, if a name entry is shorter than the stipulated 20 characters, extra spaces will be appended to the name until the name is 20 characters long.

You also saw the use of the pack() function in the preceding code. You'll learn more about the pack() and unpack() functions in the next section.

The *pack()* and *unpack()* Functions

You can use the pack() function to "pack" data in a string. The concept of this function was taken from Perl. The syntax of the pack() function is specified below:

```
string pack(string format, argument 1, argument 2,  ... ... , argument n)
```

The pack() function formats the specified arguments—argument 1, argument 2, ... , argument n—as a string according to the format argument and returns the resultant string. To better understand the working of this function, consider the following code:

```
        $line =

pack($dataformat,$name,$address,$email,$gender,$birth_month,$birth_day,$birth_year,
            $fiction,$action,$horror,$thrillers,$comedy,$hobbies[0],$hob-
bies[1],$hobbies[2],
            $hobbies[3],$hobbies[4],$hobbies[5],"\n");
        echo $line,"<br>",strlen($line);
```

In the above code, the variables from $name to $hobbies[5] are formatted as specified by $dataformat. This implies that the registration information of a user, which was accepted from the registration form (index.htm), is presented in a single line, separated by spaces. The formatted string is then stored in the $line variable, which is then displayed on the screen with the help of the echo $line,"<br>",strlen($line); statement.

The unpack() function "unpacks" the data that you "packed" using the pack() function. In other words, the unpack() function extracts the data that was formatted using the pack() function and stores the extracted data of the unpacked string element-wise and transfers it to an associative array.

The syntax of the unpack() function is:

```
array unpack(string format, string data);
```

As you can see in the above syntax, the unpack() function takes two arguments—format and data. The format argument specifies the format according to which the string contained by the data argument will be formatted. Consider the following statement:

```
$dataformat =
"A20name/A200address/A50email/A6gender/A10birth_month/A2birth_day/A4birth_year/
A1fiction/A1action/A1horror/A1thriller/A1comedy/A20outdoorsports/A20adventuresports/
A20popmusic/A20rockmusic/A20aggressivemusic/A20photography";
$data= unpack($dataformat, $line);
```

In the above statement (from reader.php), the formatted string contained by the $line variable is unpacked in the manner denoted by $dataformat in first statement of the above code.

To understand what is going on here, you'll have to understand the first statement thoroughly. This statement consists of a list of format codes separated by /. Consider the first format code—A20name/—in the statement. Here A represents the corresponding (string) value passed by the variable earlier while packing the string. Similarly, 20 represents the space reserved for the string, and name represents the first element of the associative array, $data. Similarly, each format code in the first statement of the above example represents a particular variable, space reserved for it, and the element of the associative array, $data.

Now that you understand how the string contained by the $line variable will be de-formatted, understanding the working of the unpack() function should not be difficult anymore. The function reads the first 20 bytes of the string and assigns it to $data["name"]. Then it reads the next 200 bytes of the string and assigns it to $data["address"]. This continues until the last format code is unpacked and stored in the array.

You have gathered sufficient information to put what you learned earlier in this chapter into practice. Now it's time to do just that!

Putting Theory into Practice

In the previous project, you created a registration form (index.htm) that accepted input from the new user. Then you verified whether the entries were valid. Now you will store the validated user information to a file and read the recorded data from the file. For this, two PHP scripts have been created—output.php and reader.php.

In the next section, you'll learn to write the information accepted from index.htm to a file called data.dat.

output.php

The following script searches for a file called data.dat. If the file does not exist, it is created. If the file data.dat is located successfully, the file mode will be set to w+. This implies that if the file already contains data, the data will be deleted and new data, if any, will be written to the file.

In an HTML form, if a checkbox is checked, then a variable of the name of the checkbox control is created in PHP—for example, if a checkbox was defined in HTML as:

```
<INPUT type=checkbox name=fiction>
```

In this case, if the user has checked this checkbox, a variable called $fiction will be created when the form is submitted. This variable will then be made available in the main scope of the PHP program and the value of $fiction will be set as 1. However, if the checkbox was not checked, then the value of the checkbox will be set to null. This is why, on encountering variables whose value is null, the PHP compiler issues a warning. The following code snippet from output.php takes care of the matter.

```
if (empty($fiction)){ $fiction = "0";}
if (empty($action)){ $action = "0";}
if (empty($horror)){ $horror = "0";}
if (empty($thrillers)){ $thrillers = "0";}
if (empty($comedy)){ $comedy = "0";}

for($i=0;$i<5;$i++)
{
if (empty($hobbies[$i])){ $hobbies[$i] = "0";}
}
```

In the above code snippet, each checkbox in index.htm is first tested for existence. If the user checked the checkbox, no extra pains need to be taken. But if the checkbox was not checked, set its value as 0. This will help you avoid PHP compiler warnings and, at the same time, allow you to print and store the values of individual checkboxes in the registration form.

You might recall from the outlay of the registration form, index.htm, that Hobbies is a multiple selection box. This means that the user can select more than one value (more than one hobby) in the box. The values selected by the user will be stored in an enumerated array, hobbies[]. However, if no hobby was selected, the value of the corresponding hobby that will be transferred to hobbies[] will be null once again, which will again prompt the PHP compiler to issue a warning. To avoid this situation and ensure the smooth execution of the script, the following code snippet sets the value of any unselected hobby in the enumerated array as 0.

```
for($i=0;$i<5;$i++)
{
if (empty($hobbies[$i])){ $hobbies[$i] = "0";}
}
```

After the checkboxes in index.htm related to topics of interest have been evaluated, and selected hobbies have been transferred to an enumerated array, the entire data accepted from the registration form is "packed," or formatted as a string, and displayed in the browser window.

```
$dataformat="A20A200A50A6A10A2A4A1A1A1A1A20A20A20A20A20A20A1";


            //--------Packing the accepted Information Into a string------
               $line =

pack($dataformat,$name,$address,$email,$gender,$birth_month,$birth_day,$birth_year,
                $fiction,$action,$horror,$thrillers,$comedy,$hobbies[0],$hob-
bies[1],$hobbies[2],
                $hobbies[3],$hobbies[4],$hobbies[5],"\n");
               echo $line,"<br>",strlen($line);
```

The following code snippet finally writes the accepted (and formatted) data to data.dat. After the data is written to the file, data.dat is then closed.

NOTE

In the output of this script (`output.php`), if you don't like the first line in the browser window, comment out the statement echo `$line,"<br>",strlen($line);` as `//echo $line,"<br>",strlen($line);`.

```
$result = fputs($fp,$line) or die("Data could not be written to the file.");
                    fclose($fp);
```

The rest of the HTML script, which is a part of `output.php`, is used only to present the accepted data in a tabular format in the browser window.

Following is the complete code of `output.php`.

```
<html>
<head>
<title>Display Output </title>
</head>
<body>
<br><br><br>
<center>
<?php
```

```
//----Creating the file data.dat, if it doesn't exist, and opening it in the write
mode------
if (!(file_exists("data.dat")))
                    {
                     $fp = fopen("data.dat","w+");
                    }
                    else
                    {
                //-----------Otherwise, if file exists, then opening it in the
append mode--------
                     $fp = fopen("data.dat","a");
                    }
```

```php
//-----------Testing the checkboxes for existence. If the
checkbox is not checked, the value of the
                //-----------checkbox is set to 0----
                if (empty($fiction)){ $fiction = "0";}
                if (empty($action)){ $action = "0";}
                if (empty($horror)){ $horror = "0";}
                if (empty($thrillers)){ $thrillers = "0";}
                if (empty($comedy)){ $comedy = "0";}

                //---------Accepting the selected hobbies in an enumerated
array-------
                for($i=0;$i<5;$i++)
                {
                if (empty($hobbies[$i])){ $hobbies[$i] = "0";}
                }

                //---------Formatting all the information for a record in a
single line separated by spaces-------

$dataformat="A20A200A50A6A10A2A4A1A1A1A1A1A20A20A20A20A20A20A1";

                //---------Packing the accepted Information Into a string-------
                  $line =

pack($dataformat,$name,$address,$email,$gender,$birth_month,$birth_day,$birth_year,
                $fiction,$action,$horror,$thrillers,$comedy,$hobbies[0],$hob-
bies[1],$hobbies[2],
                $hobbies[3],$hobbies[4],$hobbies[5],"\n");
                  echo $line,"<br>",strlen($line);


                //----Writing the formatted string to the file data.dat
$result = fputs($fp,$line) or die("Data could not be written to the file.");
                    fclose($fp);
                ?>

                //---------Displaying the Information written to the file in the
browser window for verification-------
```

```
<h2> The following information was entered and accepted.</h2>
</center>
<table width="300" border="1" bgcolor="#EEFFEE" align="center"
cellspacing=2 cellpadding=5>
        <tr>
         <td>Full Name </td>
         <td>
           <h3><?php echo $name; ?> </h3>
         </td>
        </tr>

//---------First row of the displayed Information-------
         <tr>
          <td>e-mail </td>
          <td>
            <h3><?php echo $email; ?> </h3>
          </td>
         </tr>
         <tr>
           <td>Address </td>
           <td>
            <h3><?php echo $address; ?> </h3>
           </td>
         </tr>
         <tr>
           <td>Gender </td>
           <td>
            <h3><?php echo $gender; ?> </h3>
           </td>
         </tr>

//---------Second row of the displayed Information-------
         <tr>
           <td>Date of Birth</td>
           <td>
            <h3> <?php echo $birth_month," ",$birth_day,"
",$birth_year; ?> </h3>
                 </td>
```

```
    </tr>

//---------Third row of the displayed Information-------
  <tr>
    <td>
        You prefer these books
    </td>
    <td>
    <h3>
<?php
 if ($fiction)
 {
  echo "fiction <br>";
 }
 if ($action)
 {
  echo "action <br>";
 }
 if ($thrillers)
 {
  echo "thrillers <br>";
 }
 if ($horror)
 {
  echo "horror <br>";
 }
 if ($comedy)
 {
  echo "comedy ";
 }
?>
</h3>
</td>
    </tr>

//---------Fourth row of the displayed Information-------
  <tr>
    <td>
```

```
        Your hobbies are :
        </td>
        <td>
        <?php
        for ($i=0;$i<6;$i++)
        {
         if(!($hobbies[$i]=="0"))
         {
           echo "<h3>",$hobbies[$i],"</h3><br>";
         }
        }
        ?>
        </td>
</table>
</body>
</html>
```

To view the output of the above code:

1. Open the browser window and display index.htm.
2. Enter the information as shown in Figure 11-4.

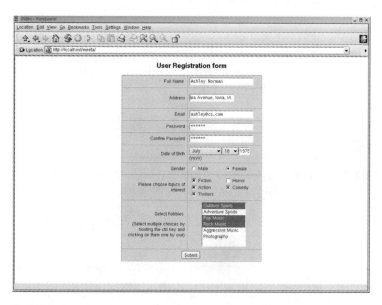

FIGURE 11-4 *Information filled into the user-registration form* index.htm

3. Click on the Submit button for the validation of data.

4. The information filled in by you will be validated and errors, if any, will be displayed. The displayed information is shown in Figure 11-5.

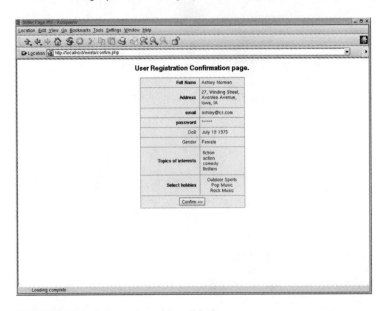

FIGURE 11-5 *Information after validation*

5. Click on the Confirm button to confirm registration. Next, ouput.php will be called. The information displayed currently will be written to the file data.dat. The information written to the file will be formatted and displayed, as shown in Figure 11-6.

NOTE

Note that the information that is displayed in Figure 11-6 is *not* yet written to data.dat. You will learn to read the data written in an external file, data.dat in this case, in the next section.

In the next section, you'll learn how to read the information written in data.dat and display it in the browser window.

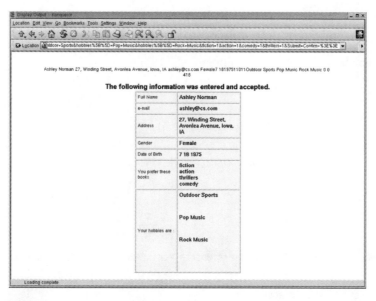

FIGURE 11-6 *Screen displaying the output of* output.php *written to* data.dat

reader.php

After you've worked your way through the code in output.php, the code in reader.php should not give you too much trouble. Let me explain this code, in case you missed out on something.

The information that you'll read from data.dat will be presented as a table. The HTML part of the code deals with the formatting issue. The PHP part of the code deals with making the information readable from data.dat. Consider the following code snippet:

```
if (!(file_exists("data.dat")))
{
 die("<tr><td>File does not exist</td></tr>");
}
else
{
 $fp=fopen("data.dat","r");
}
```

The above code tests data.dat for existence. If the file was not located, the message File does not exist is displayed. Otherwise, if data.dat was found successfully, it is opened in read mode. Because of the fopen() function, remember that the file pointer, by default, is located in the beginning of the file.

Now consider the following code snippet:

```
while (!(feof($fp)))
   {
   if(!($line =fgets($fp,419)))
   {
    die("</table></body></html>");
   }


   $dataformat =
```
"A20name/A200address/A50email/A6gender/A10birth_month/A2birth_day/A4birth_year/
```
                A1fiction/A1action/A1horror/A1thriller/A1comedy/
```
A20outdoorsports/A20adventuresports/
```
                A20popmusic/A20rockmusic/A20aggressivemusic/A20photography";
                $data= unpack($dataformat, $line);
```

Here data.dat is read until the end of file (EOF) of the file is reached. Note that when the EOF is reached, the HTML tags—table, body, and html—are closed. This means that all of the information has been read and there is nothing more to display. Meanwhile, while the data is still being read, the individual elements are "unpacked" as specified by $dataformat into an associative array called $data.

These individual elements are later picked up by the following code and are formatted (into a table, as mentioned earlier) so that the information can be displayed in the browser window.

```
echo "<tr>";
                echo "<td><b>". $data["name"]."
         </b>
           </td>
        \n";
           echo "<td><b>". $data["address"]."
         </b>
           </td>
        \n";
           echo "<td><b>". $data["email"]."
```

```
          </b>
            </td>
        \n";
            echo "<td><b>". $data["gender"]."
        </b>
            </td>
        \n";
            echo "<td><b>". $data["birth_month"] ."-".$data["birth_day"]
. "-". $data["birth_year"
            ]." </b>
            </td>
        \n";
            echo "<td><b>";

            if (!empty($data["fiction"]))
              {
                  echo "fiction",  "<BR>\n";
               }
            if (!empty($data["action"]))
               {
                  echo "action",   "<BR>\n";
               }
            if (!empty($data["horror"]))
               {
                  echo "horror",   "<BR>\n";
               }
            if (!empty($data["thriller"]))
               {
                  echo "thriller", "<BR>\n";
               }
            if (!empty($data["comedy"]))
               {
                  echo "comedy",   "<BR>\n";
               }

            echo  "
        </b>
            </td>
```

```php
    \n";
echo "<td><b>";

  if (!empty($data["outdoorsports"]))
  {
    echo $data["outdoorsports"],"<br>";
  }

  if (!empty($data["adventuresports"]))
  {
    echo $data["adventuresports"],"<br>";
  }

  if (!empty($data["popmusic"]))
  {
    echo $data["popmusic"],"<br>";
  }

  if (!empty($data["rockmusic"]))
  {
    echo $data["rockmusic"],"<br>";
  }

  if (!empty($data["aggressivemusic"]))
  {
    echo $data["aggressivemusic"],"<br>";
  }

  if (!empty($data["photography"]))
  {
    echo $data["photography"],"<br>";
  }

  echo "</b></td></tr>";
  }
fclose($fp);
```

Following is the complete code of reader.php.

```
<html>
<head>
<title>Display Output </title>
</head>
<body>
<br><br><br>
<center>
<h2> The following information was retrieved from the file.</h2>
//----Formatting the Information (to be) retrieved from data.dat
as a table------
</center>
<table width="800" border="1" bgcolor="#EEFFEE" align="center"
cellspacing=2 cellpadding=5>
//----The first row of the table------
  <tr>
    <td>Full Name </td>
  <td>Address </td>
  <td>e-mail </td>
  <td>DoB </td>
  <td>Gender</td><td>Interests </td>
    <td>Hobbies </td>
  </tr>

<?php

//----Testing the file, data.dat, for existence and opening it in read mode------
if (!(file_exists("data.dat")))
{
 die("<tr><td>File is does not exist</td></tr>");
}
else
{
 $fp=fopen("data.dat","r");
}

/*    if (filesize($fp) == 0)
```

```
                                {
                                die("<td>File is empty !!</td></tr>");
                                }
                                */
                        //----------Displaying all records in the browser window until
            the EOF of data.dat is reached-------

                        while (!(feof($fp)))
                            {
                            if(!($line =fgets($fp,419)))
                                {
                                die("</table></body></html>");
                                }

                        //    echo "<tr><td>",$line,"<br>", strlen($line),"</td></tr>";
                        //----------Unpacking the information in data.dat into the
            associative array, $data-------
                            $dataformat =

"A20name/A200address/A50email/A6gender/A10birth_month/A2birth_day/A4birth_year/
                        A1fiction/A1action/A1horror/A1thriller/A1comedy/
A20outdoorsports/A20adventuresports/
                        A20popmusic/A20rockmusic/A20aggressivemusic/A20photography";
                            $data= unpack($dataformat, $line);

                        //----------Displaying individual elements of the file into the
            table created earlier-------
                            echo "<tr>";
echo "<td><b>". $data["name"]."
                    </b>
                    </td>
                \n";
                    echo "<td><b>". $data["address"]."
                </b>
                    </td>
                \n";
                    echo "<td><b>". $data["email"]."
                </b>
                    </td>
```

```
                    \n";
                        echo "<td><b>". $data["gender"]."
                    </b>
                        </td>
                    \n";
                        echo "<td><b>". $data["birth_month"] ."-".$data["birth_day"]
    . "-". $data["birth_year"
                        ]." </b>
                        </td>
                    \n";
                        echo "<td><b>";

                        if (!empty($data["fiction"]))
                            {
                                echo "fiction",  "<BR>\n";
                            }
                        if (!empty($data["action"]))
                            {
                                echo "action",   "<BR>\n";
                            }
                        if (!empty($data["horror"]))
                            {
                                echo "horror",   "<BR>\n";
                            }
                        if (!empty($data["thriller"]))
                            {
                                echo "thriller", "<BR>\n";
                            }
                        if (!empty($data["comedy"]))
                            {
                                echo "comedy",   "<BR>\n";
                            }

                        echo   "
                    </b>
                        </td>
                        \n";
                    echo "<td><b>";
```

```php
        if (!empty($data["outdoorsports"]))
        {
          echo $data["outdoorsports"],"<br>";
        }

        if (!empty($data["adventuresports"]))
        {
          echo $data["adventuresports"],"<br>";
        }

        if (!empty($data["popmusic"]))
        {
          echo $data["popmusic"],"<br>";
        }

        if (!empty($data["rockmusic"]))
        {
          echo $data["rockmusic"],"<br>";
        }

        if (!empty($data["aggressivemusic"]))
        {
          echo $data["aggressivemusic"],"<br>";
        }

        if (!empty($data["photography"]))
        {
          echo $data["photography"],"<br>";
        }

      echo "</b></td></tr>";
      }
    fclose($fp);
?>

</table>
</body>
</html>
```

After saving the above script as `reader.php`, call it in the browser window by typing the address of the file. You'll view the output of the above code, as shown in Figure 11-7.

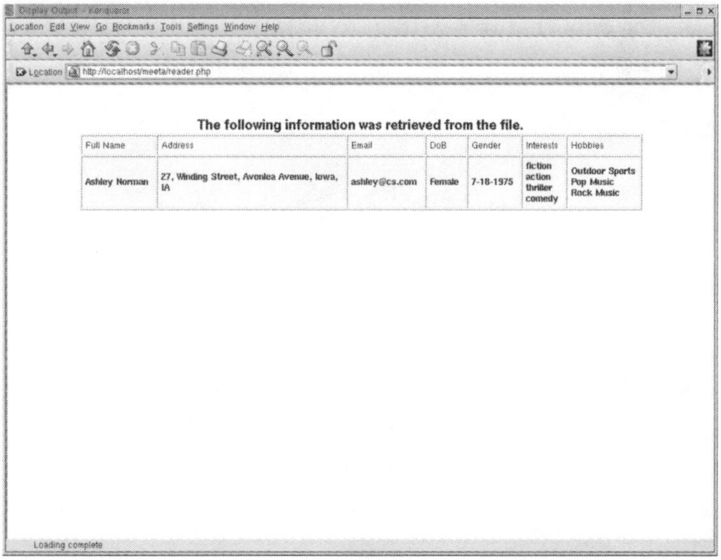

FIGURE 11-7 *Output of* `reader.php`

Summary

In this chapter, you learned the basics of file handling and put this knowledge into practice. First you learned to test the existence of a file with the help of the `file_exists()` function. Then you learned to open a file by using the `fopen()` function and close it by using the `fclose()` function. Next you learned to read from a file with the help of the `fread()` function. While reading a file, you learned to determine the file size by using the `filesize()` function and to determine whether the EOF of the file has been reached with the help of the `feof()` function. Here you also learned about the `fgetc()` and `fgets()` functions, which help you read strings in the specified file. You also learned about the `fseek()` function, which helps you to manipulate the placement of the file pointer. Next you learned to write data to a file by using the `fwrite()` and `fputs()` functions. Here you learned to format the data while accepting input from an HTML form. You also learned the use of the `pack()` and `unpack()` functions, which help you to format a string in a specified format and unpack the formatted data as per another format into an associative array. Finally, you created two PHP scripts—output.php and reader.php. The output.php script accepts the data input from the registration form, index.htm, and writes it to another file, data.dat. The reader.php script then reads the data that was written to data.dat and displays it as a table in the browser window.

PART IV

IV

Professional Project 3

Project 3

Project 3 Overview

A Personal Finance Manager is an accounting application like Quicken or Microsoft Money that enables you to maintain bank accounts, cash, credit cards, and investment accounts. You record all your deposits and expenses and the system generates many reports that help you to monitor your financial health.

An accounting application is composed of many modules, each performing certain specific tasks. A Personal Finance Manager handles cash, bank accounts, credit cards, and other financial transactions. An Inventory module records movement of inventory items, an Accounts Receivable module records customer transactions, and an Accounts Payable module records supplier transactions. These modules need to talk to each other. For example, when a customer buys some goods, the Financial Accounting module needs to reflect the monetary value of the purchase, and the Inventory module needs to be updated with the physical movement of the inventory items.

Traditionally, accounting applications have been developed around the client/server model. The modules share a central database and are connected to each other with some sort of a network protocol.

The Internet brings some very exciting possibilities to the traditional way of designing applications. The various modules of an accounting application need no longer be connected with wire. Using ASP.NET and web services, we can design applications that can send and receive data using the Internet and HTTP.

In this Project, I want to show you how to build a Web-Enabled Personal Finance Manager using ASP.NET web forms (we will extend this to incorporate web services later in the book). Its design is steeped in the double entry system of accounting. You can easily extend the concepts developed in this chapter to build other accounting modules. In fact, each new module is actually a new web form that will be very similar to the one that we design here.

Chapter 12

Handling Data
Storage

In the previous projects, you learned to create a Web page using HTML and to accept information from a user in this Web-based form. This information was then stored in a text file. You also learned to retrieve information from this text file.

In this project, you will learn to store the user information in a database. In this chapter, you will learn about the basics of databases. In particular, you will discuss MySQL because it is the most commonly used database in PHP. This chapter will cover concepts like creating databases and tables. You will also learn to add, modify, and delete records in a database. In the next chapter, you will learn to store the user information accepted from an HTML form in a database instead of in a simple text file.

Before you learn how to create a database and link it to a Web page, let us discuss what is a database.

An Introduction to Database Concepts

Since the dawn of time, man has felt the need to store information. For example, the ancient Egyptians used logs to keep an account of the grain in their granaries. These logs are now considered to be the first form of flat files. In the previous chapter, you learned how to save the entered user information in a text file, which, in database jargon, is called a *flat file*.

A flat file stores all the information in a single file and you cannot connect one piece of information with the other. A flat file is mostly created in the form of a simple text file. All the text in a text file is stored without any formatting and as single lines of information of equal length.

Another way of storing text in a flat file is by separating each piece of information by using a comma. All the information relating to a specific type is grouped together in a single line. An advantage of using a flat file is that it takes less amount of space as compared to a database.

A flat file is a compromise between cost and features. It provides adequate efficiency and is easy to write. This is why programmers prefer using a flat file when the data only needs to be stored and cost is a major constraint. However, if you want to store data efficiently and retrieve it quickly in the manner you prefer, a database is the answer!

A *database* is used to store a large quantity of information. Unlike a flat files, a database stores information in a structured format and you can easily retrieve specific information from it. This information can be in the form of text, date, or graphics. An advantage of a database over a flat file is that you can extract specific information from it, which is not possible in case of a flat file.

A simple example of a database is a telephone directory. All the information in a directory, such as the names, addresses, and telephone numbers, are stored in a structured format. For example, you might have noticed that all the names in a directory are stored alphabetically. This helps in searching for specific information. If you need to search for the telephone number of a person called Hanks, Adrian, you can directly begin searching under the section that contains names beginning with H instead of starting from the beginning.

The information in a database is stored in the form of tables, fields, and records that play an important role in structuring the information as well as making searches fast and efficient. In the next section, you will learn about the concept of tables and their constituents in detail.

Tables

Most of you would have seen filing cabinets in offices. These cabinets are used to store paper files. Each cabinet, or at least each shelf of a cabinet, contains files of a similar type or category. For example, all the files related to sales might be stored in one cabinet and those related to production might be stored in another cabinet. Similarly, a database contains many tables and each table maintains data about a specific object or entity. For example, an Employee table would contain personal information about all the employees of a company. Similarly, a Customer table would contain details about customers, and a table called Sales would contain the company's sales information. Just as each cabinet has a label that helps you to identify the content of the cabinet or shelf without actually opening the cabinet, similarly, each table has a unique name that helps you to identify the table's content.

Let's take the example of a library database. The database contains three tables— Books, Members, and Transactions. The Books table contains information regarding all the books available in the library. The Members table contains information regarding every member who has registered as a member of the library. Finally, the Transactions table contains information regarding every book that has been issued.

All the data in the database is stored in a specific format. Every table stores data in the form of rows and columns. A *row* stores data in a horizontal format, while a column stores data in a vertical format. The columns in a table are known as *fields*, and the rows are referred to as *records*. Figure 12-1 shows all the three tables in the database.

The following sections discuss the various constituents of a table in detail.

Fields

As explained earlier, fields are a collection of information of the same type or category. As you might recall, the library database consists of three tables – Books, Members, and Transactions. The Books table would contain fields like a unique identification of a book, the book's title, the category, and the price of the book. The Members table would contain details like a unique identification of a member, the member's name, the address, and the phone number. Finally, the Transactions table would contain a unique transaction number, the date on which a book was issued, the book's identification, the identification of the member to whom the book was issued, and the date the book is due for return.

Therefore, the fields of a table are nothing but the attributes that best explain the characteristics specific to the table. All this data is stored in separate columns and can contain both text as well as numeric data. However, depending on your requirement, you can even restrict the type of data that can be stored in each field. For example, you can restrict the content of the field containing the members' phone number to only accept numeric values or the Return date field of the Transactions table to only contain dates. Just as in the case of a table, a field of a table also has a unique name called the *field name*, which you can use to reference each field separately.

You can also classify the fields in a table as either *required* or *optional*. As the name suggests, if the field is classified as required, a user will need to enter a value for the field. The user cannot leave it blank! For example, a field for a member's name cannot be left blank. However, if the field is optional, the user has the choice

Books

Book _id	Name	Category	Price
B001	Let's talk about Computers	Business	100
B002	50 Mouthwatering Recipes	Cookery	125
B003	Living Life Without Fear	Psychology	150
B004	Chinese Cuisine, Anyone?	Cookery	200
B005	Stars Shine Down	Fiction	220

Members

Member_id	Name	Address	Phone_no
M001	Julie Andrews	4630 College Ave.	415834-2919
M002	Joan Allen	36 Broadway Ave.	415836-7128
M003	Anthony Willis	8 Sliver Ct.	415986-7020
M004	Linda Lawrenze	674 Darwin Ln.	415848-2089
M005	Peter Holloway	36 Upland Hts.	301946-8854

Transactions

Tran_no	Issue Date	Return Date	Book_id	Member_id
T001	01/15/2002	02/15/2002	B001	M003
T002	01/16/2002	02/16/2002	B002	M002
T003	02/22/2002	02/22/2002	B003	M001
T004	02/22/2002	02/22/2002	B004	M002
T005	02/27/2002	02/27/2002	B005	M005

FIGURE 12-1 *Tables in the Database*

NOTE

An *attribute* is a characteristic of an entity. For example, a name is a characteristic of an author and, therefore, it is an attribute of the author entity.

whether or not to enter a value for the field. For example, a member might not have a phone number. Figure 12-2 shows the Members table with the field names and values.

	Members ←		Table Name
Field Name ← **Name**		**Address**	**Phone_no**
M001	Julie Andrews	4630 College Ave.	415834-2919
M002	Joan Allen	36 Broadway Ave.	415836-7128
M003	Anthony Willis	8 Sliver Ct.	415986-7020
M004	Linda Lawrenze	674 Darwin Ln.	415848-2089
M005	Peter Holloway	36 Upland Hts.	301946-8854

FIGURE 12-2 *Fields in the Members Table*

NOTE

An *entity* is something that you can identify easily. For example, an entity can be defined as a person, an object, a place, an activity, or a concept about which you can store information. To reflect the real-world relationships, an entity can either be dependent on another entity or can be independent. You will learn about relationships and dependent entities in a later section called Relational Database Management Systems (RDBMS's).

You must have heard several times about records. No! We are not talking about musical or championship records. We are talking about the records in a database. Let's see what a record in a database is.

Records

Records are separate pieces of information about an entity. This information is grouped together and stored in a table. Each piece of information is stored in a separate field. For example, if the book, Living Life Without Fear, has been issued, then a corresponding record should be created in the Transactions table. Similarly, the details about the book would be a record in the Books table, and the details about the member would be a separate record in the Members table.

Figure 12-3 shows the records of the Members table.

Members			Table Name
Field Name	Name	Address	Phone_no
M001	Julie Andrews	4630 College Ave.	415834-2919
M002	Joan Allen	36 Broadway Ave.	415836-7128
M003	Anthony Willis	8 Sliver Ct.	415986-7020
M004	Linda Lawrenze	674 Darwin Ln.	415848-2089
M005	Peter Holloway	36 Upland Hts.	301946-8854

Record

FIGURE 12-3 *Records in the Members Table*

You have just learned about databases. Next, you will look at the advantages of using databases.

Advantages of Using Databases

Using a database to store the information obtained by using a Web page has certain advantages. Some of these advantages are given below:

- ◆ Automation of the repetitive tasks performed while managing data
- ◆ Timely updating of data
- ◆ Provision of easy access to the data stored in various tables of a database

◆ Storage of a large volume of data in a systematic manner

◆ Quick and efficient search for and retrieval of specific data from a large volume of data

Database Management System

A *database management system* (DBMS) is a system by which all the data in a database is organized, stored, retrieved, and manipulated. A database contains a large quantity of information, which has to be stored in a central location, indexed, and stored in a sequential manner. A DBMS performs all these tasks. It also takes care of securing and maintaining the integrity of the data stored in the database. You can send instructions to the DBMS about the specific data you require and it retrieves the data and returns it back to you.

The concept of database management provides connectivity with software based on programming languages as old as C and COBOL. A DBMS provides as much flexibility as you require. For example, you can add new tables, fields, and records without disturbing the existing content of the database or the database structure.

A DBMS provides certain advantages such as:

◆ **Maintaining data integrity.** The use of a DBMS helps to maintain data integrity by not allowing the duplication of records where required or by ensuring that only one user has access to the data at one time.

◆ **Ensuring security of data.** A DBMS also ensures the security of data by allowing only authorized users to access or modify the database. Authorized users are provided passwords that they can use to access the database. A DBMS can also restrict the access of users to specific tables and fields in the database. For example, only an administrator might have the right to enter data about new books in the database and only the librarian might have the rights to issue books.

◆ **Querying for data.** A DBMS provides users the facility to search for specific information in a database. For example, you could search for all the books issued to a particular member or the total number of books issued on a particular day. Most DBMS's provide certain report writers to create these search strings, which are also known as queries.

◆ **Ensuring the independence of data.** While using a DBMS, you do not need to remember the structure of all the tables in the database every time you search for certain data. For example, while searching for a book issued to a particular member, you only need to send to the DBMS, the code equivalent of "give me the details of the member whose Member_id is this and who has been issued a book with this Book_id on the specified date." The DBMS searches for the record that matches the specified search criteria and sends it back to the calling program or the user.

◆ **Entering and updating data in the database.** Most DBMS's have a system that you can use to add or modify the data stored in a database. However, in this case, data entry is done in a specific format that you cannot change. If you need to enter data in a particular format or need to put certain restrictions on the type of the accepted data, it is advisable to create a program using a commonly used programming language such as C or Visual Basic for managing the data. You can then link the program to the database.

Relational Database Management System

As explained previously, a database has multiple tables and each table contains information of a specific type. Maintaining different tables helps in ensuring clarity in data storage and a faster retrieval of information from the database. You can retrieve different types of information from the tables by ensuring a relationship between them. For example, when retrieving the details of a book that is issued to a member, you could also retrieve information about the member who has issued the book and the transaction details. This is possible only if a relationship exists between the three tables: Books, Members, and Transactions. Adding fields from the other tables to a main table ensures a relationship between the different tables. For example, the Transactions table would contain the Book_id and Member_id fields. These fields form a link to the specific records in the Books and Members tables. In this manner, flexibility and speed in data retrieval is ensured.

You can have three types of relationships between the different tables in a database.

◆ **One-to-One.** In this case, exactly one record in both the tables map to each other. This type of relationship is not very common. It is used, for example, if a member is restricted to borrowing only one book at a time. However, this is an unrealistic scenario and, therefore, this type of relationship is not common.

♦ **One to Many.** This relationship implies that a reference to one record in a table is used multiple times in the other table. For example, in case of the Books and the Transactions tables, if a book can be rented out multiple times, you would have a single Book_id from the Books table being repeated multiple times in the Transactions table.

♦ **Many to Many.** This is the most common type of relationship, in which multiple records of a table map to multiple records of the other table. For example, it exists when a book can be borrowed by n number of members and a member can borrow n number of books.

You have just learned about the records in a table. However, you may wonder how you can decide which fields to include or not to include in a table. The answer is – through Normalization. Normalization is the process of determining what should be included in a table.

Database Normalization

Normalization is a process that is followed in a relational database management system to categorize data into smaller groups for easier and more efficient management. Although there are six stages in normalization, by the third stage, all the data in a table is dependent on only one key field. A key field is similar to a primary key that enforces the condition that only unique values can be stored in the field. This is what normalization is all about.

 NOTE

You can create a relational database by using an RDBMS. Each table in a relational database is linked to another table by using a common attribute or attributes. For example, the Books table is linked to the Transactions table by using the common Book_id field. By linked, we mean that every Book_id that is inserted in the Transactions table should already exist in the Books tables.

Why We Need Normalization

The question that still comes to our mind is, "Why do we require normalization?" The answer is simple. Normalization helps us in reducing redundancy. If we have the same data repeated n number of times in our database, not only does the size of the database increase unnecessarily, there is also a problem with the storage and retrieval of data. Due to the large amount of data, a search for specific information not only takes a long time but also requires extra effort. This redundancy forces the following issues:

♦ **Inconsistencies.** Since data is entered repeatedly, there is bound to be inconsistency and, subsequently, the occurrence of errors.

♦ **Updating errors.** While inserting new records or modifying old ones, data can become inconsistent because you might update the information in one record and not in the others. Since the same information is repeated, the data will become inconsistent.

♦ **Linking errors.** If a relation exists between two tables, changing the values in one table can cause inconsistency in the data of the other table.

Normalization helps in changing the structure of tables so that they are easy to use, understand, and manage. In a normalized table, each record has a *primary key* and a group of attributes that can be defined as the characteristics of an entity.

Normalizing Forms

We mostly use the first four forms of normalization. These include the following:

♦ First normal form
♦ Second normal Form
♦ Third normal Form
♦ Boyce-Codd normal Form

The First Normal Form

A table is in the *first normal form* if each cell of the table contains only one value. In the first normal form, all the extra information has to be arranged properly. The first normal form is not found in relational databases since a relational database cannot contain an unnormalized table. Therefore, in a relational database, all the tables are already in the first normal form. For example, in Table 12-1, the data is not normalized because the Projcode field for the employee named Jill contains three values. After normalizing the table, the data would appear as shown in Table 12-2.

Table 12-1

Emp_id	Name	Projcode	Department
E001	Jack	P002	Acc
E002	Jim	P564	Mkt
E003	Mary	P888	Acc
E004	Jill	P564	Mgt
		P888	
		P002	
E005	Jones	P002	Mkt

Table 12-2

Emp_id	Name	Projcode	Department
E001	Jack	P002	Acc
E002	Jim	P564	Mkt
E003	Mary	P888	Acc
E004	Jill	P564	Mgt
E004	Jill	P888	Mgt
E004	Jill	P002	Mgt
E005	Jones	P002	Mkt

The Second Normal Form

In the *second normal form*, all the redundant information is removed and the information is stored in a separated table. For example, in the above code, since the Projcode and Department columns have redundant information (repetition of information about E004), you can create a separate table for it. Therefore, Table 12-2a is normalized to arrive at Table 12-3.

Table 12-2a

Emp_id	Name	Projcode
E001	Jack	P002
E002	Jim	P564
E003	Mary	P888
E004	Jill	P564
E004	Jill	P888
E004	Jill	P002
E005	Jones	P002

Table 12-3

Emp_id	Department
E001	Acc
E002	Mkt
E003	Acc
E004	Mgt
E005	Mkt

A table is in the second normal form if it is in the first normal form and all the attributes in the table are dependent on the main key or the primary key. In the above tables, the primary key is the Emp_id. In the above example, Table 12-3 is in second normal form because the records in the table are dependent on Emp_id and not just a part of the primary key. For example, Department is in no way related to the employee's name and project code.

You normalize a form to the second normal form by removing the attributes that are not fully related to the main key. You then group the removed information in another table. A common field connects both the tables to each other.

Third Normal Form

In the *third normal form*, the table must be in the second normal form and all the non-key fields (secondary fields, such as Department) are only dependent on the primary key, the Emp_id. In the above example, the project code is not dependent on the employee's name. Therefore, Table 12-2 can be further normalized into Table 12-4.

Table 12-4

Emp_id	Projcode
E001	P002
E002	P564
E003	P888
E004	P564
E004	P888
E004	P002
E005	P002

Boyce-Codd Normal Form

A table is in a *Boyce-Codd normal form* if all the other keys are potential primary keys. Mostly, all the tables are considered to be normalized by the time you reach the third normal form. However, in certain cases, even if a table is in the third normal form, the table may not be fully normalized. A table is not normalized if:

◆ The values of two fields can be used together to get a unique value

◆ The values in two fields overlap and have at least one common attribute

If neither of the above conditions applies, then a table can be considered to be normalized in the third normal form.

Now that you know about the process of normalization, let's discuss the concept of denormalization in databases.

Denormalization

You just learned about normalization and how after normalizing, you obtain a set of tables that are related to each other and form a database. However, sometimes it is necessary to introduce redundancy in your tables. You must be puzzled! After trying to convince you of the virtues of having a normalized table where there is no redundancy, now I am telling you to introduce redundancy. No! This is not a mistake. Sometimes you need to sacrifice having a normalized database in favor of a database that provides faster query resolution. Having redundant data in tables helps in reducing the CPU time and disk I/O operation. Therefore, denormalization is the deliberate entering of redundant data in a table to improve performance.

Now that you know about databases, let's talk about the various databases supported by PHP.

PHP Support to Various Databases

You can use PHP to connect to different types of databases. PHP has been tested successfully on various types of databases and operating systems. Some database servers that PHP supports are listed below:

◆ **MySQL.** This is a powerful relational database management system containing modifiable source code. It is the most preferable option for Linux users due to its robust, swift, and reliable structure. You can obtain more information about MySQL from the link, `http://www.mysql.com`.

◆ **mSQL.** This is also a very fast and reliable database management system. More information about this database is available at the Web site, `http://www.huges.com.au`.

◆ **Microsoft SQL Server 2000.** The vendor of this database is Microsoft, and the database provides fast access to developers who are working on a Windows platform. Additional information about this database is available at `http://www.microsoft.com/sql`.

◆ **Oracle.** Another popular database management system that is used by thousands of users all over the world is Oracle. You can obtain more information regarding the database management system from the link, `http://www.oracle.com`.

◆ **PostgreSQL.** This is another popular relational database management system. The source code of PostgreSQL is shared and it is compatible with most of the other types of databases. Additional information about PostgreSQL is available at **http://wwwpostgresql.com**.

 NOTE

MySQL is the most commonly used database in PHP. So we will only use MySQL in this book.

In the following section, we'll discuss the Web database architecture. This information will help you when you will link the registration form that you created in Chapter 8 to the MySQL database in Chapter 12.

Web Database Architecture

The time for static Web pages is long gone. Nowadays, more and more customers are asking for dynamic Web pages. The use of Web databases in Web page development requires developers to have an in-depth knowledge of both databases and the Web, since Web database application development is a synthesis of the two technologies.

The increased demand for Web-based databases can be attributed to an increase in the use of the Internet and intranet by the corporate world. This is fundamentally due to an increase in the use of the Client/Server technology in business applications. This technology is used by large organizations to provide all its employees simultaneous access to a database. This has introduced the concept of online databases in which a change made by one user is automatically reflected to the rest of the users. Previously, this technology used large data servers and client applications that connected to the main database. With advancement in technology, the industry has progressed to the use of Web technologies to ensure Client/Server connectivity. Since a browser is readily available, it is not necessary to create a separate application to provide a user interface. This technology is fast developing into the most efficient source of simultaneous database access.

There are many tools available in the market to create Web databases that not only provide methods for entering and modifying the data in databases but also methods for managing and delivering data to Web pages. It is important for developers who create Web databases and design queries to understand the fundamentals behind the designing of databases. An application that uses a Web database to store and retrieve data is known as a *Web Database application.*

A basic Web database application required the following components to function.

◆ **Database server.** The database server is used to store all the information entered by users and to display information on a Web page.

◆ **Web server.** The second component, the Web Server, contains the CGI and PHP scripts that are used to establish a connection with the database server.

◆ **Web browser.** The Web browser serves as the client interface. It is used to transfer information between a client and the Web server.

The HTTP protocol is used to transfer information from a Web browser to a Web server and vice versa. Similarly, ODBC and JDBC are some Application Programming Interfaces (API's) that are used to establish a connection between the Web server and the database. The above information is shown graphically in Figure 12-4.

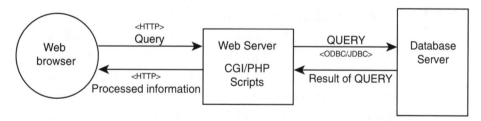

FIGURE 12-4 *Web Database Application Architecture*

Advantages and Disadvantages of Using Web Databases

The use of databases on the Web provides certain advantages and disadvantages. Listed below are some advantages of having a database-driven Web site.

◆ **Attractive and customized information.** You can customize the way information is available on your Web site. You can also make use of Web elements to make the data appear attractive.

◆ **Easier maintenance of content.** It is easier to maintain data on a Web site.

◆ **Freshness of data.** It is easier to update data in databases than in Web pages. In the case of dynamically generated Web pages, only the content or information needs to be changed, whereas manually changing a Web page requires adding addition content as well as maintaining the design of the Web site in relation with other Web pages.

◆ **Ready availability of data.** Most organizations already have the necessary data available with them. They only need to put this data on the Web.

◆ **Easy visibility.** It is easier to view data on a Web page instead of in a database.

However, the use of databases on the Web also has certain disadvantages. These disadvantages are listed below.

◆ **Investment in development time.** The Web page has to be developed, which involves the investment of time and effort.

◆ **Web skill set requirements.** You need developers with a skill set that maps to both Web application development and database proficiency. They should be able to build and maintain Web sites on a regular basis as well as work with and maintain the database. The former skill is not required when you use databases.

◆ **Investment in hardware, software, and employees.** You need to invest in additional employees to create and maintain a database-driven Web site. This is an added expense because the employees need to process the required skills to manage databases.

◆ **Scope of the user.** The data that you display on your Web page might not fulfill the requirement of the users who access your Web site. The users might use complex queries and get irrelevant records or no records at all.

You will now learn to create databases and tables in MySQL. You will also learn to insert, modify, and delete records in a table within a database.

MySQL Database Programming

There are many commands available in MySQL that you can use to perform database administration tasks such as creating databases and tables and viewing their structure. MySQL also provides commands for inserting, modifying, and deleting records from a database. Let's begin by understanding how to perform administrative tasks on a database.

Using the *mysqladmin* Command

Administering databases involves numerous tasks such as:

◆ Creating databases

◆ Deleting databases

◆ Checking the status of a database

◆ Resetting the values of the variables in a database

You use the mysqladmin command available in MySQL to perform these tasks. The syntax of the command is as follows:

```
# mysqladmin [options] Command1, Command2...
```

Table 12-5 lists the different tasks that you can perform by using mysqladmin.

Table 12-5 Commands in MySQL

Command	Task
create <database name>	To create a database with the specified name
drop <database name>	To delete the specific database along with all its tables
extended-status	To display the extended status information from the server
flush-tables	To clear all the table information
flush-host	To clear all the cached information
flush-threads	To clear all the stored thread information
flush-logs	To clear all the logged information about the server
refresh	To clear all the table information and to refresh all the logs
ping	To check and monitor connectivity with the mysql daemon

continues

Table 12-5 _(continued)_

Command	Task
variables	To print all the information about variables
status	To display the status information at the command prompt
version	To display the version information from the server
shutdown	To shut down the server
password	To change the password

In the next section, you will learn to use the MySQL monitor. You can use the MySQL monitor to perform many tasks such as creating databases and tables.

Using the MySQL Monitor

MySQL is an effective database server developed by MySQL AB. The source code of MySQL is freely available and can be downloaded for free from the site, `http://www.mysql.com`. The software is compatible with both Windows and Linux platforms.

MySQL is a relational database management system that provides the facility to manage databases. You can also modify the source code to meet your requirements. MySQL also provides the following features:

◆ Support for languages such as Perl, Python, and PHP

◆ Support for a thread-based memory allocation system (Therefore, it is quite fast)

◆ Support for fixed as well as variable length records

◆ Support for a host-based verification system that provides security through verifying passwords that are encrypted during transit

◆ Support for large databases

◆ Support for different types of field datatypes

◆ Support for UNIX sockets, TCP/IP sockets, and Named Pipes for providing connectivity

Although MySQL is installed along with Linux, you can also install it separately. The recommended method for novice users is by using the RPM (Red Hat Package Manager) file. You can test if MySQL has been installed properly by executing some basic commands. We will begin by invoking the MySQL monitor from the command prompt. For detailed information on installing MySQL with PHP, refer to Chapter 2, "Installing and Configuring PHP."

To start MySQL, enter the following command at the command prompt:

```
[root@localhost root] # mysql
```

Figure 12-5 shows the output of the above command.

```
[root@localhost root]# mysql
Welcome to the MySQL monitor.  Commands end with ; or \g.
Your MySQL connection id is 10 to server version: 3.23.41

Type 'help;' or '\h' for help. Type '\c' to clear the buffer.

mysql>
```

FIGURE 12-5 *Using the MySQL monitor*

Now that you have used the MySQL monitor, you can execute the MySQL commands for creating database and tables and for adding, modifying, and deleting records from the tables.

Creating Databases

In the previous section, you learned that you can create a database by using the create <database> command at the command prompt. However, you do not need to always execute this command from outside MySQL. You can also use the create command from inside MySQL. The syntax of the command is as follows:

```
mysql> create database if not exists Books;
```

CAUTION

It is necessary to end all the MySQL commands with a semicolon (;) to indicate the conclusion of the command. Otherwise, MySQL keeps on waiting for a semicolon or returns an error.

The output of the above command is shown in Figure 12-6.

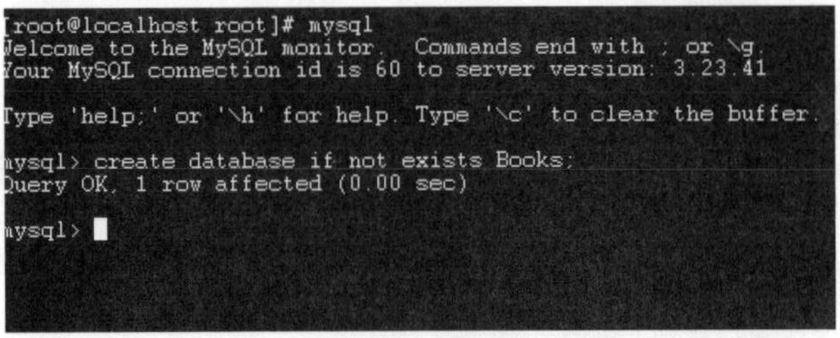

FIGURE 12-6 *Creating a Database in MySQL*

After a database has served its purpose and is no longer required, you should delete or drop it. This is important because if you do not delete the database, it occupies unnecessary disk space and is a burden on the system's memory. The syntax for dropping a database is given below.

```
mysql> drop database if exists Manuscript;
```

The above command will search for a database named `Books` and delete it. Another way of deleting a database is by using the `mysqladmin` command. The syntax of the command is given below.

```
mysql> exit;
    [root@localhost root] # mysqladmin drop Manuscript;
```

● **CAUTION**

The above commands assume that you have already created the `Manuscript` database.

While deleting or dropping a database, you will notice that you are asked to confirm whether you want to delete it. This ensures that you do not accidentally delete a database. You need to type y to complete the deletion. A message then appears confirming that the database has been deleted. The output of a sample deletion is shown in Figure 12-7.

In the next section, you'll learn to create tables in a database using MySQL.

```
Welcome to the MySQL monitor.  Commands end with ; or \g.
Your MySQL connection id is 65 to server version: 3.23.41

Type 'help;' or '\h' for help. Type '\c' to clear the buffer.

mysql> create database if not exists Books;
Query OK, 1 row affected (0.00 sec)

mysql> exit
Bye
[root@localhost root]# mysqladmin drop Manuscript;
Dropping the database is potentially a very bad thing to do.
Any data stored in the database will be destroyed.

Do you really want to drop the 'Manuscript' database [y/N] y
Database "Manuscript" dropped
[root@localhost root]#
```

FIGURE 12-7 *Deleting a Database in MySQL*

CAUTION

You must be cautious while deleting or dropping a database because once a database is deleted, its content cannot be retrieved.

Creating Tables

In the previous section, you learned to create and delete a database. In this section, you will learn to create a table and store data in it. You can create different tables to store different types of data. For example, you can create a Books table to store information about books and an Authors table to store information about authors.

The first step while creating a table is to obtain access to the database. Obtaining access implies gaining control of a database so that you can make modifications to it or create tables in it. The MySQL command is used to gain access to a database. After you have gained access to a database, you can use the different commands available in it to create tables and to view their structure.

Now, we will look at how we can perform these tasks.

Using a Database

As explained earlier, the first step in creating a table is to obtain access to the database in which you want to insert the table. You use the syntax given below to access a database. At the MySQL prompt, enter the code given below.

```
mysql> use Books
```

CAUTION

You must ensure that the Books database already exists before you try the above command.

On the successful execution of the above code, you will be able to access the database and the following message appears: "Database changed". This message implies that the database named Books exists and is ready for use. The output of the above command is shown in Figure 12-8.

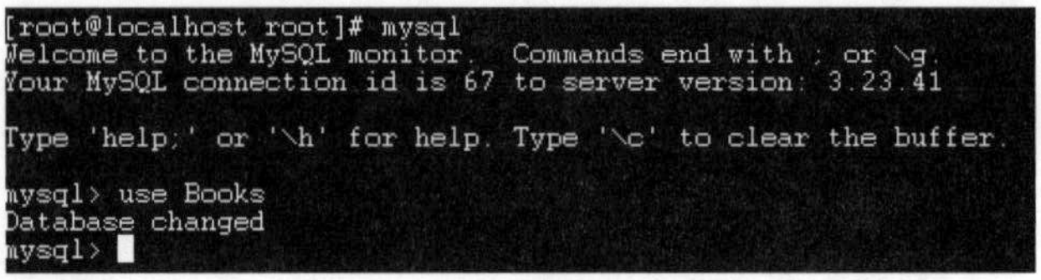

```
[root@localhost root]# mysql
Welcome to the MySQL monitor.  Commands end with ; or \g.
Your MySQL connection id is 67 to server version: 3.23.41

Type 'help;' or '\h' for help. Type '\c' to clear the buffer.

mysql> use Books
Database changed
mysql>
```

FIGURE 12-8 *Accessing a Database*

Now that you have gained access to the database, you can begin to construct tables for the database. However, before you go on to the actual creation of a table, you need to know about the different field types available in MySQL. Each field in a table needs to belong to a specific datatype. You will learn about these datatypes in the next section.

Field Datatypes in MySQL

As you already know, tables contain a set of fields that you can use to store values. The field types are the datatypes that determine the type of data that can be stored in each field. These field types and their description are listed in Table 12-6.

Table 12-6 Field Datatypes in MySQL

Type	Description
char	Used to store the string type data.
varchar	Used to store string values but of a larger size than a char datatype.

Type	Description
blob/text	Used to store strings of characters. The fields can store a maximum of 65535 characters.
int	Used to store integer type data. The maximum size of the datatype is 2147483646 numeric values.
bigint	Used to store integer values. This is similar to int, the only difference is that you can store a maximum of 9223372036854775806 numeric values.
smallint	Used to store small integer values. A smallint field can store a maximum of 32766 numeric values.
tinyint	Used to store integer values. This is the smallest of the integer datatypes and can store a maximum of 126 numeric values.
float	Used to store decimal values.
date	Used to store date values. The values are stored in the yyyy-mm-dd format and range from 1000-01-01 to 9999-12-31.
datetime	Used to store the time along with the date.
year	Used to store the year value.

Using the create Command to Construct Tables

You have already obtained access to the database named Books. Now you will learn to create new tables in the database. The syntax for creating a table is given below.

```
mysql> create tablename (first_fieldname fieldtype, second_fieldname
fieldtype,...,n_fieldname fieldtype);
```

You will now use the above syntax to create a table named Products, which has five fields. The fields and their datatypes are shown in the code given below.

```
create table Products (
                Productid bigint(20) NOT NULL auto_incre-
ment,

                Name varchar(40) NOT NULL default '',
                Description varchar(200) NOT NULL default
'',

                Price varchar(20) NOT NULL default '',
```

```
                                    Category varchar(20) NOT NULL default '',
                                    PRIMARY KEY (Productid)
                              );
```

The preceding code creates a table named `Products`, which contains fields with the following characteristics.

- ◆ The table contains five fields: `Productid`, `Name`, `Description`, `Price`, and `Category`.

- ◆ The `Productid` field is of the *bigint* datatype and can contain a numeric value, with a maximum size of `20` characters. It also cannot contain a `NULL` value and the value is auto incremental in nature. This means that every new record takes the previous record's `Productid` and adds one to it, to create the current record's `Productid` value.

- ◆ The `name` field is also of the *varchar* datatype and contains a string with a maximum of `40` characters. The content of the filed cannot be `NULL`.

- ◆ The `Description` field is of the *varchar* datatype and has a maximum size of `200` characters. This field also cannot contain a `NULL` value.

- ◆ The `Price` field is of the *varchar* datatype and can contain a maximum of `20` characters.

- ◆ The `Category` field will contain the category to which the product belongs. This field also belongs to the *varchar* datatype and can contain a maximum of `20` characters.

- ◆ The primary key for the table is `Productid`. This means that this field will have unique values and the records in the table are indexed based on these values.

The output of the above code is given in Figure 12-9. The figure shows the confirmation message that the table has been created.

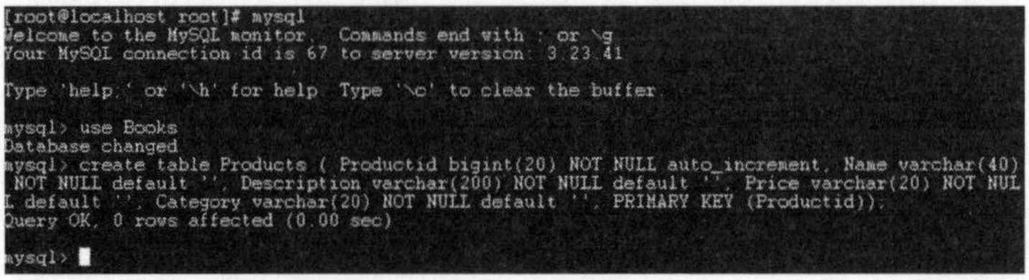

FIGURE 12-9 *Table Created in MySQL*

Now that you have learnt to create a table, you will learn to review the contents of a database and lists the tables that it contains.

Viewing the Table in a Database

While you are working with a database, you might not remember the different tables you have created in it. You might also not remember the name of a specific table in the database. MySQL provides a command that you can use to list the various tables in the database. In the current example, you will display the table you just created in Books.

MySQL provides the show tables command to display all the tables available in the currently open database. The syntax of the command is given below.

```
mysql> show tables;
```

The output of the above command is shown in Figure 12-10.

FIGURE 12-10 *Previewing Tables in MySQL*

Suppose you are working with multiple tables. How will you keep track of which table contains which fields? In the next section, you will learn how you can review the structure of a table.

Viewing the Table Structure

You might also want to find out the fields that are available in a table. MySQL provides a command to view the structure of a table. The command to view the fields available in a table is given below.

```
mysql> explain Products;
```

You can use this command to find out the fields of a table (Products, in the above case) and their datatypes. This information is important while designing queries because unless you know the fields that are available in a table, you cannot create effective queries. The output of the above command is shown in Figure 12-11.

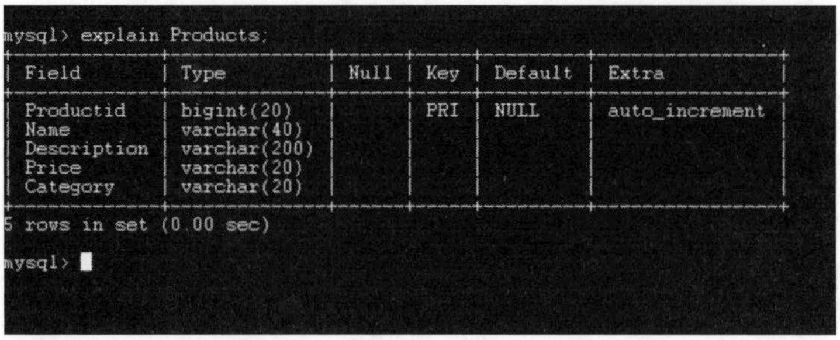

FIGURE 12-11 *Viewing the Table Structure*

As you can see, the output contains six columns. The names of these columns and their explanations are given below.

- ◆ **Field.** This column contains the names of the fields that were specified while creating the table.

- ◆ **Type.** This column contains the datatypes for each field. As explained previously, the datatype can be *text*, *char*, *integer*, *varchar*, *float*, or any one of the datatypes listed in Table 12-2. These datatypes are specified at the time of creating the table. Once a datatype has been specified, the field can only contain data that belongs to the specific datatype. For example, if a field is of the *char* datatype, it will store text as characters or strings even if the text contains numbers. The maximum size of data that the field can store also appears within parentheses along with the datatype.

- ◆ **NULL.** This column determines if a field can contain a blank value. If a field is blank, it will contain a NULL value.

- ◆ **Key.** This column specifies which field is the primary key. A field that contains the primary key can contain only unique values, which means that you cannot repeat the same value for any other record. This also helps in indexing the values in the field. There can be a maximum of one primary key in each table and none of the values in the field can be NULL.

◆ **Default.** The column specifies a default value for a field. You can set a default value for a field to be used in case the field is left blank at the time of data insertion. This column is critical for fields that have been set to Not NULL.

◆ **Extra.** This column specifies any extra information about the field that MySQL can use while executing queries.

Now that you know how to create a table, you will now learn to can add, modify, and delete records in the table.

Entering Data into a Table

Now that you have successfully created a table, let's discuss how you can enter data into the table. You can use the insert command to enter data. The syntax of the insert command is given below.

```
mysql> insert into <tablename> values
('value_for_fieldone', 'value_for_fieldtwo',
                    ....'value_for_nthfield' );
```

Let's use the above syntax to insert new records in the table.

```
mysql> insert into Products values ('', 'Great
Expectations', 'Written by Charles
                    Dickens','200', 'Classic');
```

The output of the above command is given in Figure 12-12. 

FIGURE 12-12 *Entering Records in a Table*

You can similarly add other products to the Products table. Let's add another record to it.

```
mysql> insert into Products values ('', 'Last of
the Mohicans', 'Written by Charles
                    Dickens', '150', 'Classic');
```

Now that you have learned to insert records in a table, you will learn to view the data entered in the table.

Viewing the Data in a Table

Once all the data has been entered into a table, you might want to review it. You can use the `select` command for this purpose. The `select` command is used to retrieve the records from a table or tables based on certain conditions or criteria. The syntax of the command is shown below.

```
mysql> select [fieldname] from [tablename] where
[expression] order by [fieldname];
```

The code given below retrieves all the records from the specified table. The output of the code is shown in Figure 12-13.

```
mysql> select * from Products;
```

FIGURE 12-13 *Viewing the Data in a Table*

You can also restrict the output of the `select` command to specific fields by using the field names instead of an asterisk (`*`). For example, you can restrict the output to display only the `Productid`, `Name`, and `Price` of the product. The code to achieve this is given below, and the output appears as shown in Figure 12-14.

```
mysql> select Productid, Name, Price from
Products;
```

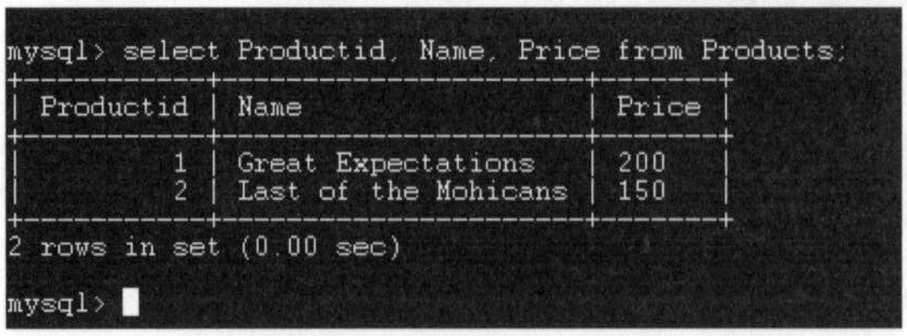

FIGURE 12-14 *Viewing Selective Fields*

You can also restrict the output of the select command by using the `where` condition. In the next section, you will learn to use complex select statements to retrieve data based on specific conditions.

Complex select *Statements*

Now that you know the basic format of the `select` command, you will see how to use the `select` statement to create complex queries. As explained previously, you use the `where` clause if you need to search for specific information in the database. An example is given below.

```
mysql > select * from Products where Price =200;
```

The above code will display all the records in the `Products` table whose price is equal to `200`. The output for the above code appears in Figure 12-15. You can further qualify the `where` statement by using the comparison operators that you learned about in a previous chapter. Some of these comparison operators are shown in Table 12-7.

```
mysql> select * from Products where Price =200;
| Productid | Name              | Description               | Price | Category |
|         1 | Great Expectations | Written by Charles Dickens | 200   | Classic  |
1 row in set (0.00 sec)

mysql>
```

FIGURE 12-15 *Viewing Selective Fields Based on a Condition*

NOTE

The `select` command is a very powerful tool. You can use it to create queries that search multiple tables based on a criterion and return a specific output.

Table 12-7 Comparison Operators

Operator	Purpose
==	Equal to
>	Greater than
<	Less than
>=	Greater than or equal to
<=	Less than or equal to
!=	Not equal to
like	Compares string text

You can also use the `all` and `distinct` keywords to select all or specific records from the database. The `distinct` keyword will return specific records from specific columns. It also ignores duplicate records retrieved from the columns specified in the `select` statement. An example is:

```
mysql >select distinct Category from Products;
```

The above code will return all the records containing unique categories from the `Products` table.

You can use the `And` and or operators to combine two or more conditions. The difference in the use of both the operators is their implementation. In case of the and operator, all the conditions need to be fulfilled for the record to be included in the output, whereas in the case of the or operator, even if one of the conditions returns True, the record is included in the output. In the example given below, the output will contain all the `Productid`'s whose `Category` is `Fiction` or whose `Price` ranges between `100` and `150`.

```
mysql > select Productid from Products where Category = 'Fiction'
OR Price >100 AND
          Price<150;
```

Another clause that can be used along with the `select` statement is the `group by` clause. You use this clause to group the records containing similar data in specific columns. Once the data is grouped, you can use aggregate functions such as `sum` and `max` to perform calculations on this data. For example, in the code given below, all the records are grouped together based on the `Category` field and the maximum price in each `Category` is displayed.

```
mysql > max(Price), Product_id, Name from Products GROUP BY
Category;
```

Having learned about inserting records, in the next section, you will learn to modify the existing records in a table.

Modifying the Data in a Table

You can use the `update` command to make changes to the data stored in a table. You can make changes to a single record or to multiple records in a database. A point that you need to remember is that the `update` command does not return a set of records, it only makes changes to the data in the database. The syntax of the `update` command is given below.

```
mysql> update <tablename> set <fieldname> = '<New value>' ;
```

For example, you can change the value for the `Category` field of all the records to `Fiction`. The code to perform the task is given below and the output is shown in Figure 12-16.

```
mysql> update Products set Category = 'Fiction';
mysql> select * from Products;
```

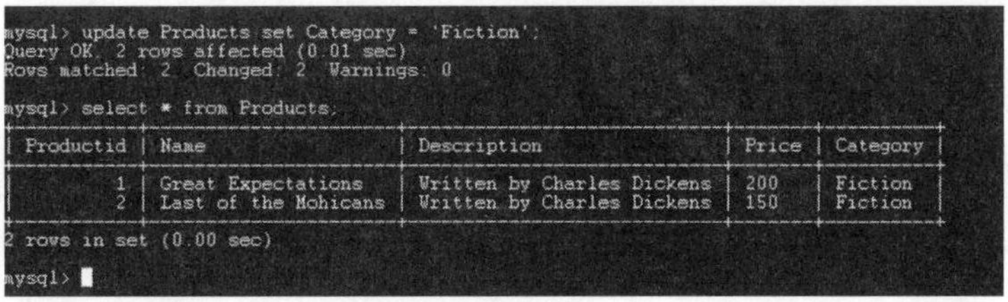

```
mysql> update Products set Category = 'Fiction';
Query OK, 2 rows affected (0.01 sec)
Rows matched: 2  Changed: 2  Warnings: 0

mysql> select * from Products;
+-----------+----------------------+---------------------------+-------+----------+
| Productid | Name                 | Description               | Price | Category |
+-----------+----------------------+---------------------------+-------+----------+
|         1 | Great Expectations   | Written by Charles Dickens | 200   | Fiction  |
|         2 | Last of the Mohicans | Written by Charles Dickens | 150   | Fiction  |
+-----------+----------------------+---------------------------+-------+----------+
2 rows in set (0.00 sec)

mysql>
```

FIGURE 12-16 *Modifying the Data of a Specific Field*

You can also use the `where` clause to narrow down the update based on a specific condition. For example, you may want to increase the price of the products whose value is more than `150` to `200`. The code to do so is given below.

```
mysql> update Products set Price = '200' where Price > 150;
```

You can also use the `update` statement to modify records in multiple tables based on a condition. This type of updating is called `cascade updation` since the changes made in one table are reflected in all the related tables.

After having learned how to insert and modify the records in a table, you must be curious about to delete records from a table. The next section covers this aspect.

Deleting Data from a Table

You can delete information from a table by using the `delete` command. You can delete single or multiple records from a table by using this command. You can also use the `where` clause with the `delete` command to delete records based on certain conditions.

CAUTION

Just as you need to be cautious while deleting a database, you also need to be cautious while deleting records. This is because once a record is deleted, it cannot be recovered.

The syntax of the command for deleting a record is given below.

```
mysql> delete <fieldname> from <tablename> [where
expression];
```

You can use the code given below to delete the records of all the products whose price is below `200`.

```
mysql> delete from Products where Price<200;
```

The output of the above code is shown in Figure 12-17.

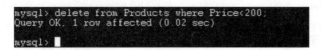

FIGURE 12-17 *Deleting a Record Based on a Specific Condition*

CAUTION

If you do not specify a field name, then all the records in the table will be deleted.

You must now be confident about adding, modifying, and deleting records from a table. However, suppose you need to modify the structure of a table. The next section explains this concept in detail.

Modifying the Table Structure

You can modify the structure of a table by using the `alter` command. You can perform the following tasks by using the `alter` command.

◆ Adding a column to a table

```
mysql> alter table <tablename> add <new-
field> <definition> ;
```

◆ Changing the datatype of a table

```
mysql> alter table <tablename> change
<columnname> <newdefinition>;
```

◆ Indexing a table

```
mysql> alter table <tablename> add index
<columnname> (<columnname>) ;
```

◆ Adding a unique column to a table

```
mysql> alter table <tablename> add unique
<columnname> (<columnname>) ;
```

◆ Deleting a column from a table

```
mysql> alter table <tablename> drop
<columnname>;
```

By now, you must be comfortable with using databases and tables. In the next chapter, we will look at how we can link a Web page to a database and store information in the database.

Summary

In this chapter, you learned about databases. You learned that you can use databases to store information. You learned about the tables, fields, and records that form a part of a database. You also learned about Database Management Systems (DBMS's) and Relational Database Management Systems (RDBMS's). Next, you learned about normalization. You learned about the four forms of normalization. Then, you learned about the various databases supported by PHP, especially about MySQL. Next, you learned about Web database architecture. Then, you learned to use the mysqladmin command administer databases, and to create users, databases, and tables in MySQL. You also learned to add, modify, and delete records from a database. Finally, you learned to retrieve records by using the select command and to modify the structure of a table.

Chapter 13

**Using PHP with
SQL Databases
(MySQL)**

In the previous chapter you learned about the basic concepts of MySQL. You learned about databases and how to create them. You also learned about tables, fields, and records that form the basics of databases. In this chapter, you will learn to link the code written in PHP with a database. You will also learn to insert the records in the database and retrieve the records. In the previous chapter you learned to perform the above actions in MySQL; now you will perform them in programs written in PHP. However, in PHP's case, you will use an HTML form to accept the information from the user and send the query to the MySQL database.

Working with MySQL

Nowadays, the success or failure of a Web site does not depend entirely on the attractiveness of the Web page. The content or information that your Web page provides also determines the success or failure of your site. This is the reason why a majority of organizations want dynamic Web pages. The use of Java and DHTML may facilitate the creation of dynamic Web pages, but using dynamic content in these Web pages is a different issue. With the rapid growth of the Internet, more and more users are visiting Web sites. These users expect the Web sites to always have the latest information. If the users do not find the latest information on a site, they normally do not return to the site. Therefore, constant updating of the Web site is required. The question that arises is who is responsible for changing the content of the Web site. The responsibility can rest neither with the people who provide the content for the Web site nor with the developers who create the HTML Web page. In addition, content providers may have absolutely no knowledge of HTML. Their responsibility is limited to providing content for the Web page. The Web page developers, on the other hand, are preoccupied with creating the Web page and are not expected to periodically transfer data between Word documents and the Web page.

The periodic maintenance of the Web site poses another problem. Most organizations prefer to continue with only one design because changing the design may mean investing in creating a new Web page. This involves both time and money.

A solution to these problems is using data-driven Web sites. In data-driven Web sites, the storage of content and the hosting of the Web site are done at separate locations. You have a simple HTML Web page that acts like a template for different types of content. The content management system integrates both the content and the Web pages. In this case, no separate HTML coding is required to update the content each time the content is changed.

As explained earlier, there are two components in use, the PHP script that accepts the query, and the database, which in this case is MySQL. You have already learned how you can embed a PHP script in an HTML Web page. In this chapter, you will learn how to combine the simple HTML Web page you learned to create in Chapter 9 with the database you learned to create in the previous chapter. You will also learn how you can insert records in a database by using Web pages. You will also learn to query the database from the Web pages and display the result.

You will now learn how to connect to the MySQL database server.

Connecting to a Database

The basic idea behind a database-driven Web site is that the information to be displayed on the Web site is stored on the database server. This information is then extracted dynamically from the database and displayed on the Web page. These dynamic Web pages can then be viewed in any ordinary Web browser. The process of connecting your Web site to a database is explained below.

The users enter the address of the Web page in their Web browsers. This information is sent to the Web server that passes the information to the database server in the form of a query. The database server then returns the result back to the Web server that formats the information into an HTML format and displays it in the browser.

However, before you can establish a connection between the MySQL database and the Web page, you must learn to connect to MySQL. PHP provides a built-in function to make this connection. This function is called the `mysql_connect()` function.

You use the `mysql_connect()` function to establish a connection with the MySQL database. This function also accepts certain parameters that determine who can connect to the database and where to connect. The function returns a value that confirms that the connection has been established. This value is stored in a variable known as the connection identifier. This identifier is used internally by PHP to verify that the connection has been established. If multiple connections are made to the same database by using the `mysql_connect()` function, only the first instance of the function actually establishes the connection. All the subsequent connections use the connection identifier returned by the first command. The syntax of the `mysql_connect()` function is given below.

```
$connect = mysql_connect(<address>, <user id>, <password>);
```

The command can contain three parameters. The explanations about these parameters and the connection identifier are as follow.

- ◆ **Address.** The `address` parameter contains the IP address or the host name of the computer where the MySQL server is installed. You can specify the address as `localhost` if MySQL is running on the same computer as the Web server.

- ◆ **User id.** The `user id` parameter contains the user ID of a user who has rights to access the database. This user ID should exist on the MySQL server and should have been assigned the appropriate level of rights.

- ◆ **Password.** The `password` parameter provides the corresponding password to the ID specified in the user ID parameter. A password is used to ensure that only an authorized person is given access to the database. When this parameter is not provided, the password is assumed to be blank.

- ◆ **$Connect.** The `$connect` variable is the connection identifier. This variable contains the value True if the connection is established. It contains the value False if the connection is not established. You can use the variable in your code to refer to the connection or connect to the database.

```php
<?php
    $connection= mysql_connect("localhost","root","")
or die("A connection to the Server could not be established !");

echo "Root user login in MySQL server  @ localhost successful.";
?>
```

In the code specified above, a connection is established with the MySQL server by using the user ID root. The address is `localhost` because both the Web server and the MySQL server are running on the same machine. The confirmation of whether the connection is successfully established is stored in the variable $con-nection. If the connection fails, the program execution ends after displaying an error message. You use the die() function to display this message. The die() function is one of the error handlers available in PHP. You can also use the @ symbol to suppress the default errors displayed by the system and instead display customized messages created by you. You will learn about error handlers and how to create customized error handlers later in this chapter. The output of the code given above appears in Figure 13-1.

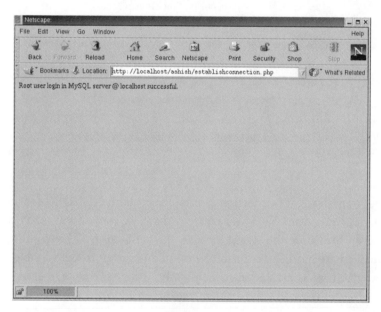

FIGURE 13-1 *Connecting to MySQL*

Now that you have established a connection with the MySQL server, you need to select the database in which you want to insert or modify data. Suppose you do not have a database. In such a case, you first need to create the database. The following section covers this procedure.

Creating a Database in MySQL

The mysql_create_db() function is used to create databases in MySQL. The following is the syntax for the command.

```
$createtable = mysql_create_db($dbname);
```

The $dbname variable contains the name of the database to be created, and the $createtable variable contains the result of the attempt to establish the connection. The result can be either True or False depending on whether the connection is successful. The code given below establishes a connection with a database named Mytestdb.

```
<?php

$connect = mysql_connect("localhost","root","")
                                        or
die("A connection to the server could not be established !");

$createdb =mysql_create_db("Mytestdb")
    or die("database could not be created !");

echo "Database Mytestdb was created successfully.";

?>
```

In the code given above, a connection is established with MySQL by using the mysql_connect() function. Next you create a database named Mytestdb on the MySQL server by using the mysql_create_db() function. The confirmation whether the database has been successfully created is stored in the variable $cre-atedb. If the database is created successfully, the value is True. Otherwise, it is False. The output of the code given above appears in Figure 13-2.

You will now select the database in which you want to insert or modify information.

Selecting a Database

Once you have created a database through PHP, or if the database already exists in MySQL, you can add tables and insert records in the database. Select a database before you begin to work with it. PHP provides the mysql_select_db() function to select a database in MySQL. Following is the syntax of the function.

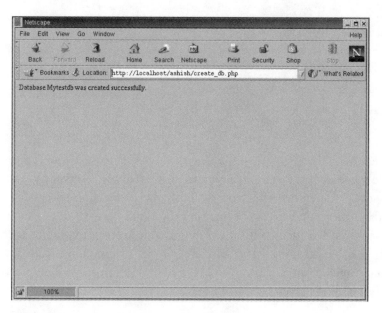

FIGURE 13-2 *Creating a database in MySQL*

```
$connect = mysql_select_db($dbname)
```

In the syntax given above, the database name is passed as an argument to the function. The function passes a value to the $connect variable, confirming that the database has been successfully selected. If the value is True, then the database has been successfully selected. Some of the reasons why the variable could contain False are:

◆ The database does not exist on the MySQL server.

◆ The database is locked for exclusive use by another developer. If multiple users try to access the same database simultaneously and if one user exclusively locks the database, then the other users will get an error message.

```
<?php

$connect= mysql_connect("local-
host","root","")

                    or die("A connection to the
server could not be established !");
```

```
                              $result=mysql_select_db("Mytestdb")
                              or die("Database could not be
selected");

                              echo "Database Mytestdb was success-
fully selected.";

                         ?>
```

In the code given above, you are connecting to the MySQL server by using the mysql_connect() function. After you establish the connection successfully, you select the database named Mytestdb by using the mysql_select_db() function. If the database is selected successfully, then the variable $connect contains the value True. If the variable contains the value False, the die() function is called, which displays a customized error message and closes the Web page. The output of the code specified above is given below in Figure 13-3.

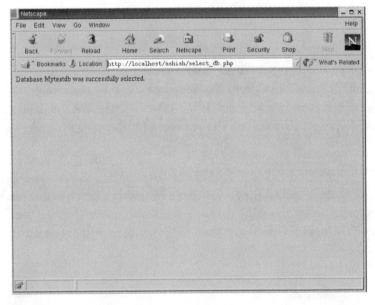

FIGURE 13-3 *Selecting a database in MySQL*

In the next section, you will learn how to create a new table in the database. You need to create a table before you can begin to insert information in the database.

Creating a Table in a Database

In Chapter 9, you learned to save in a simple text file the information entered by a user. You did not use any tables; you saved the information directly into the text file. In the case of databases, this is not possible. You need to create tables before you can store information in the databases. In the code given below, you will create a table named Maildata. Later you will store records in this table. In Chapter 11, "Handling Files," you learned about tables, fields, and records.

```php
<?php

$connection=
mysql_connect("localhost","root","")
                                    or die("Could not connect to MySQL in
localhost !");


$selectdb=mysql_select_db("Mailinglist")
                                    or die("Could not select Mailinglist
Database!");


$sqlquery = "create table if not exists
Maildata (Name varchar(50) Not
                                    Null, Email varchar(50) Not Null,
Secondaryemail varchar(50) Not Null Primary
                                    Key)";


$queryresult = mysql_query($sqlquery)
                                    or die(" Query could not be executed.");


echo " Table Maildata successfully created
in the Mailinglist database.";
            ?>
```

After the connection with MySQL has been established and access to the Mailinglist database secured in the code given above, you create a table named Maildata by using the `create table()` function. The table has three fields: Name, Email, and Secondaryemail. The datatypes of all the fields are varchar and you can store a maximum of 50 characters in each of the fields. Neither of the fields accepts a NULL value, and the primary field in the table is Email. This means that the fields will contain unique values. Therefore, two people sharing the same e-mail ID cannot log on to the database simultaneously. The output of whether the `select` statement is successful is returned to the `$queryresult` variable. If the query returns records, the variable will contain the value True, and if the variable contains the value False, an error message is displayed. The output of the code specified above is given in Figure 13-4.

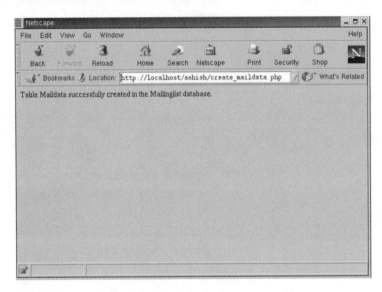

FIGURE 13-4 *Creating a table in the database*

Figure 13-5 exhibits the error message that is displayed if you are unable to select the database where you want to create the table.

You now know how to create a table in MySQL. In the next section, you will learn how to insert records in the table.

Inserting Records in a Table

So far, you have learned how to connect to MySQL and gain access to the database. You have also learned to create a database and a table in the database. Now you will learn how to insert information into the table. The information that is to be stored in the databases is accepted through the HTML Web page. You must save this file in the /var/www/html directory. Following is the code that you will use to create the HTML file to accept the information. You will name the HTML file as `add_row.html`.

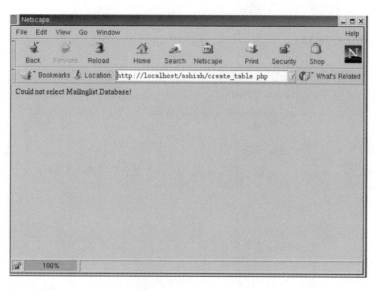

FIGURE 13-5 *Error displayed when creating a table in the database*

```
<html>
<head>
<title>Newsmail registration form</title>
<meta http-equiv="Content-Type" content="text/html;
charset=iso-8859-1">
</head>

<body bgcolor="#FFFFFF" text="#000000">
<p> </p>
<form name="Mailinglist" method="post" action="addrow.php">
<table width="287" border="0" align="center" cellpadding="3">
<tr bgcolor="#FFFFFF">
<td colspan="2">
<div align="center"><b>Enter mailing list information</b></div>
</td>
</tr>
<tr bgcolor="#FFFFFF">
<td width="107">
<div align="right">Name </div>
</td>
<td width="162">
```

```
                                             <input type="text" name="name" size="25">
                      </td>
                      </tr>
                      <tr bgcolor="#FFFFFF">
                      <td width="107">
                      <div align="right">e-mail</div>
                      </td>
                      <td width="162">
                                        <input type="text" name="E-mail"
size="25">
                      </td>
                      </tr>
                      <tr bgcolor="#FFFFFF">
                      <td width="107">
                      <div align="right">Secondary e-mail</div>
                      </td>
                      <td width="162">
                                        <input type="text" name="Secondaryemail"
size="25">
                      </td>
                      </tr>
                      <tr bgcolor="#FFFFFF">
                      <td colspan="2">
                      <div align="center">
                                        <input type="submit" name="Submit"
value="Submit">
                      </div>
                      </td>
                      </tr>
                      </table>
                      </form>
                      </body>
                      </html>
```

In the code given above, the created Web page accepts the name, the e-mail ID, and the alternative e-mail ID of a user. After the user has finished entering the required information, the user clicks on the Submit button. When the button is clicked on, all the entered information is transmitted to the MySQL server. As you may notice in the code, the information is transmitted to the PHP script by using the POST method. The Web page appears as shown in Figure 13-6.

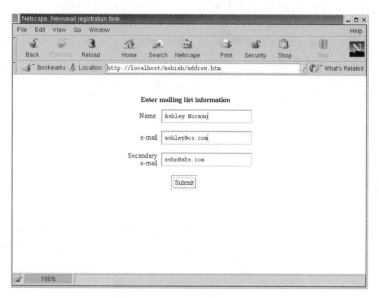

FIGURE 13-6 *Accepting information from users*

Now the information is sent to the MySQL server for inserting the information in the Mailinglist table in the form of records. The following steps have to be performed to insert the information into the table. You will

◆ Use the `mysql_connect()` command to establish a connection with MySQL.

◆ Use the `mysql_select()` function to select the `Mailinglist` database.

◆ Use the `mysql_query()` function to send the information to the MySQL server database. The information is passed in the form of a `select` query that is stored in a variable in the form of a string. This variable is passed as a parameter in the `mysql_query()` function. The variable will contain the values True or False based on whether the information is successfully inserted into the table. If the variable contains the value False, an appropriate error message is displayed. You will now create the actual PHP script that will handle the task of inserting the information in the table. The script will be saved as addrow.php.

```
<html>
<head>
<title>Add a new row in  mail data table</title>
</head>
<body bgcolor="#FFFFFF" text="#000000">
<p> </p>


<?php

$connect=
mysql_connect("localhost","root","")
        or die("Could not connect to database
in localhost !");


$result=mysql_select_db("Mailinglist")
        or die("Could not select Mailinglist
database !");


$sqlquery = "INSERT INTO Maildata VAL-
UES('". $Name ."','". $Email . "','".
$Secondaryemail."')";


$queryresult = mysql_query($sqlquery) or
die(" Could not execute mysql
query !");


echo "<table border=1 align=center
width=500>";
echo " <tr> ";
echo "   <td> ";
echo "    Name";
echo "   </td>";
echo "   <td>".$name. "</td>";
echo " </tr>";
echo " <tr> ";
echo "   <td > ";
echo "    Email";
echo "   </td>";
```

```
echo "    <td >".$Email. "</td>";
echo "  </tr>";
echo "  <tr> ";
echo "    <td > ";
echo "       Secondary e-mail";
echo "    </td>";
echo "    <td>".$Secondaryemail. "</td>";
echo "  </tr>";
echo "</table>";
```

```
?>
</body>
</html>
```

In the code given above, a connection is established with MySQL by using the `mysql_connect()` function. Next you gain access to the database Mailinglist. The database contains a table named Maildata. You will insert the record in this table. You created the select query and stored it in the variable $sqlquery. The string contains the name, e-mail address, and secondary e-mail address of the user. This information will be used later in the book to create a mailing list and send information to a group of registered users. In the select statement, you may observe that each piece of information is linked with the specific field in the table where the information should be saved. You must specify the information in the same sequence in which the fields are created in the table. If the select query is executed successfully and the information is inserted into the table, the variable $queryresult will contain the value True. If the variable contains the value True, then the output is displayed as shown in Figure 13-7. However, if the variable contains the value False, an error message is displayed and the user exits the Web page. The variable will contain the value False in the situations given below.

◆ The e-mail address already exists.

◆ Another user has exclusively locked the table.

◆ The MySQL server may be overloaded and may be unable to handle any more queries.

◆ The user does not have the required write permission to insert information in the table.

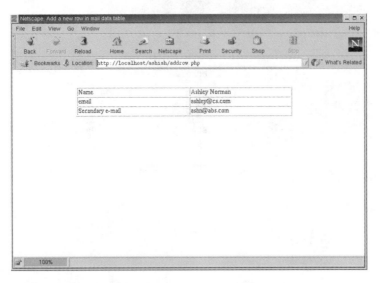

FIGURE 13-7 *Displaying accepted information*

After inserting information into the database, you may want to view specific information from a table. The next section covers this topic.

Retrieving Information from a Table

Now that you have established a connection with the database and stored some information, you may want to retrieve information from the database. However, you cannot directly extract information from the database. To get the necessary information, you need to create queries written in *Structured Query Language* (SQL). These queries extract the necessary information from the database and return the information as records.

MySQL provides the `mysql_query()` function to transmit the query to the server and return the result to the calling program. The function takes the query as an argument and passes it to the MySQL server. The server then processes the query and returns the requested information. The syntax of the `mysql_query()` function is given below.

```
$queryres = mysql_query($query_string);
```

In the preceding code, the mysql_query() function takes the variable $query_
string as a parameter and stores the result in $queryres. The variable
$query_string should contain the formatted query written in SQL. The
variable $queryres contains the value True if the select query is executed success-
fully. The variable can contain the value False only in the following conditions:

◆ Users may not have the necessary permission to access the queried
information.

◆ There may be a syntax error in the select query.

◆ The queried information may not be available.

 NOTE

You do not need to add a semicolon to the select query while assigning it to the
variable.

You need to perform the following steps to extract information from a table in
MySQL.

1. You must first connect to MySQL by using the mysql_connect() function.

2. Next you have to select the database in which the information exists by
using the mysql_select_db() function.

3. Next you need to create a select query to insert or retrieve the necessary
information from a table in the database. In Chapter 11, "Handling
Files," you learned about creating queries by using the select statement.
The string is passed as a parameter to the mysql_query() function,
which then sends the query to the MySQL server.

4. Finally the query is executed on the MySQL sever and a value is
returned and stored in a variable. The variable contains the value True if
the select query has been successfully executed, and the value False if it
has not executed successfully. In case of failure, an error message is displayed.

The code given next contains a select query that retrieves all the records stored in
Maildata. The output of the code is shown in Figure 13-8.

```
<html>
<head>
<title> Displaying Records Retrieved From A Table </title>
</head>
<?php

                                $connect=
mysql_connect("localhost","root","")
                                or die("Could not connect to MySQL server
in localhost !");

                                $result=mysql_select_db("Mailinglist")
                                    or die("Could not select Mailinglist
Database");

                                echo "Database Mailinglist was
successfully selected.", "\n";

                                echo "<BR>";
                                $sqlquery = "SELECT * from Maildata";
                                $queryresult = mysql_query($sqlquery)or
die("Query Failed");

                                echo "<BR>";
                                echo "All the records from the table
Maildata retrieved successfully.", "\n";

                                ?>


            </html>
```

The code connects to MySQL by using the `mysql_connect()` function and accesses the Mytestdb database by using the `mysql_select_db()` function. After the connection has been established, an SQL query is created, which is stored in the `$query_string` variable. This string is then passed to the MySQL server by using the `mysql_query()` function. If the query is executed successfully, the variable `$query_result` contains the value True.

PHP provides many functions to retrieve the information if the query executes successfully. These functions process each row of information separately. There-

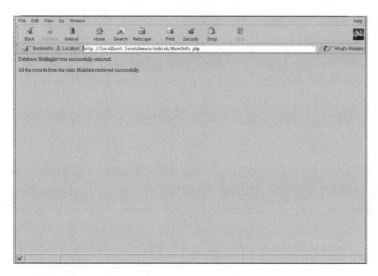

FIGURE 13-8 *Querying in a database in MySQL*

fore, you need to call the function as many times as the number of rows in the result. For example, if the query returns 20 rows of data, you will call the function 20 times. Instead of writing the statement 20 times, you can use the `mysql_affected_rows()` function to retrieve the number of affected rows and store the information in a variable. You can then use the variable to keep track of the number of rows returned and the number of rows processed. You will learn more about this function later in the chapter. You can then use a `while` loop, which will run until all the records in the result are traversed and displayed on the Web page. The following two functions are used by PHP to retrieve the information from the result.

◆ **The mysql_fetch_row() function.** This function returns the result as an enumerated array. While using an enumerated array, the information is fetched from the result in the form of an indexed array. The array stores the first field from the result at `index1`, the next field at `index2`, and so on.

◆ **The mysql_fetch_array() function.** This function returns the result as an associative array. In the case of associative arrays, the fields are indexed based on their field names. If an error is encountered and no value is retrieved, the function returns the value NULL.

Now consider these functions in detail.

The mysql_fetch_row() *function*

The `mysql_fetch_row()` function processes the information from the result one record at a time. The information is stored in the format of an enumerated array and each field of the record is stored as an element of the array. The syntax of the function is given below.

```
$Resrow = mysql_fetch_row($result);
```

As explained earlier, the `$Resrow` variable indicates whether the select query has executed successfully. The variable `$Resrow` stores the values in the same order in which the information is received. Therefore, the value stored in the first field of the result is assigned to the first element of the array `$Resrow` and the second field is stored in the second element. Similarly, all the other values retrieved in the result are assigned to their respective fields. The number of rows in the array is the same as the number of rows in the result.

When you use the `mysql_fetch_row()` function to retrieve information, the following steps are performed:

1. You will connect to the database by using the `mysql_connect()` function.
2. Next you will select the database named Mailinglist by using the `mysql_select_db()` function.
3. Next you create the SQL query to retrieve the information from the database. This query is stored in the variable `$MyQuery`.
4. When this query is executed, all the records from the Mailinglist table in the Mailinglist database are retrieved.
5. The `$Result` variable contains the value that indicates whether the query has been executed successfully. The variable contains the value True to indicate that the execution has been successful. The variable will contain the value False in any of the following circumstances:
   - ◆ A user gains exclusive access to the table by using an exclusive lock.
   - ◆ The MySQL server is unable to execute any more SQL queries.
   - ◆ The table used in the query statement does not exist.
   - ◆ The user who is requesting the information does not have the required read permission.
6. Create a variable named `$Resrow` and store the number of records returned in the result by executing the `mysql_effect_rows()` function.

7. Use a `while` loop to execute the loop until `$Resrow` does not return zero.

8. The variable `$Resrow` is a one-dimensional array and its first element stores the value of the first field of the `Mailinglist` table.

9. The `while` loop retrieves each row from the `Mailinglist` table and displays the information on the Web page.

In the next section, you will learn to perform the same action by using the `mysql_fetch_array()` function.

The `mysql_fetch_array()` function

In the previous section, you learned to retrieve the information from the result by using the `mysql_fetch_row()` function. In this section, you will use the `mysql_fetch_array()` function to retrieve information from the resultset one record at a time. However, in the case of the `mysql_fetch_array()` function, the records are retrieved in the form of an associated array. In the case of an associated array, each element of the array contains a field from a row of the resultset. Each element of the array is named by its corresponding field name in the resultset. The syntax of the `mysql_fetch_array()` function is given below.

```
$Resrow = mysql_fetch_array($result);
```

In the syntax given above,

- ◆ The `$result`, which is also known as the result identifier, contains the resultset returned by the `mysql_query()` function.

- ◆ The `$Resrow` variable is an associated array that will contain a row from the result returned by the `mysql_fetch_array()` function.

- ◆ The first element of the `$Resrow` variable contains the value in the first field of the resultset. The label of the element is the same as the field name. Similarly, all the other elements of the variable also contain their corresponding field values and names.

The advantage that the `mysql_fetch_array()` function has over the `mysql_fetch_row()` function is that in the case of the `mysql_fetch_array()` function, you do not need to remember the actual order in which the fields are placed in the table.

You need to perform the following steps if you use the `mysql_fetch_array()` function to retrieve information:

1. A connection is established with MySQL by using the `mysql_connect()` function.

2. Next you connect to the `Mailinglist` database by using the `mysql_select_db()` function.

3. Then the select statement is created that will extract the required information from the table `Mailinglist`, which is in the `Mailinglist` database.

4. The query is stored in the `$MySQLQuery` variable.

5. The `$MySQLQuery` variable is passed as a parameter to the `mysql_query()` function, which executes the query and returns and stores the result in the `$result` variable.

6. If the query is successful, the variable `$result` contains the value True. The variable can contain the value False for any of the following reasons:

   ◆ Another user has locked the table.

   ◆ The table does not exist.

   ◆ The MySQL server is unable to handle any more select queries.

   ◆ The user doesn't have the necessary read permission for the accessed table.

7. Create a variable named `$Resrow` and store the number of records returned in the result by executing the `mysql_effect_rows()` function.

8. Use a `while` loop to execute the loop until `$Resrow` does not return zero.

9. The variable `$Resrow` is a one-dimensional array and its first element stores the value of first field of the Mailinglist table. The field name is assigned as the label for the element.

10. The `while` loop retrieves all the information from the Mailinglist table by using the `mysql_fetch_array()` function and displays it on the Web page.

You will now learn how you can update information that already exists in a database.

Updating Information in a Table

You have learned how to insert information into a table. In the same way, you can also update information stored in a table. You use the update command to perform updating in a table in MySQL. While updating information in a table, it is a good idea to first display the existing information before changing it. The following steps are performed while updating information in a table.

1. You must first accept the information in an HTML page based on which information needs to be updated in the table. This information should be from a field in the table that has unique records, which is mostly the primary key.

2. When the user clicks on Submit, a PHP script is executed.

3. This script establishes a connection with the MySQL database server and selects the database by using the mysql_select_db() function.

4. The query is then sent to the MySQL database server by using the mysql_query() function. The query is further qualified by using the where clause. The condition used in the where clause ensures that only a single record is stored in the result identifier.

5. The information is then stored in the result identifier and returned to the browser.

6. The information is then displayed in the HTML form created by the PHP script.

7. The form control on the HTML page displays the values from the returned result. The value is stored in a field linked to one form control. The form is displayed in the browser.

8. The user makes the necessary changes in the information and clicks on the Submit button to indicate that the information should now be updated.

9. Another PHP script is now called that establishes a new connection with the database and updates the information in the required table by using the update command in the select query. The query is executed by using the mysql_query function.

10. The result identifier indicates whether the information has been successfully updated. If the information is successfully updated, then the successfully updated message appears, otherwise an error message is displayed.

The code given below creates an HTML form that displays all the records available in the Maildata table. Each record will contain an Edit hyperlink. The user clicks on the hyperlink to make changes in the record. When the hyperlink is clicked on, the value stored in the Email field of corresponding records is passed to the next HTML page. The new HTML page will display the record for editing. Save this code in a file named db_browser3.php.

```
<html>
<head>
<title>Maildata record browser</title>
</head>

<body bgcolor="#FFFFFF" text="#000000">

<?php

$connect=
mysql_connect("localhost","root","")
or die("Could not connect to MySQL server
in localhost !");

$selectdb=mysql_select_db("Mailinglist")
or die("Could not select mail data data-
base !");

$sqlquery = "SELECT * from Maildata";

$queryresult = mysql_query($sqlquery);

echo "<table width=700 border=1 align=cen-
ter>";

echo " <tr>";
echo "   <td width=200> <center><b>Name
</b></center></td>\n";

echo "   <td width=200> <center><b>e-
mail</b></center></td>\n";

echo "   <td width=200>
<center><b>Secondary e-
```

```
                                        mail</b></center></td>\n";
                          echo "   <td width=100>
<center><b>Action</b></center></td>\n";

                          echo "   </tr>\n";
                          while ($row=mysql_fetch_array($queryre-
sult))
                          {
                                        echo "   <tr>\n";
                                        echo "
<td>".$row["Name"]."</td>\n";

                                        echo "
<td>".$row["Email"]."</td>\n";

                                        echo "
<td>".$row["Secondaryemail"]."</td>\n";

                                        echo "      <td><A
href=\"displayform.php?Email=".$row["Email"]."\">edit</a></td>\n";
                                        echo "   </tr>\n";
                          }
                          echo "</table>\n";
             ?>
             </body>
             </html>
```

The output of the code given above appears in Figure 13-9.

The Web page created by using the above will display the record's information for editing. Once the user has made the necessary changes, they click on the Submit button. When the Submit button is clicked on, this information is sent to the MySQL server where the information is updated in the database. You will save the code in a file named display.php. The output of the code given below is shown in Figure 13-10.

```
             <html>
             <head>
             <title>Mail record update form</title>
             </head>

             <body bgcolor="#FFFFFF" text="#000000">
```

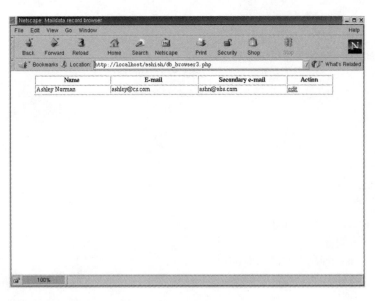

FIGURE 13-9 *Displaying all the available records for editing*

```php
<form name="maildata" method="post" action="update.php">
<table width="250" border="1" align="center">

<?php

$connect=
mysql_connect("localhost","root","")

or die("Could not connect to MySQL server
in localhost !");

$result=mysql_select_db("Mailinglist")
or die("Could not select Mailinglist
Database");

$sqlquery = "SELECT * from Maildata where
Email='" .$Email ."'";

$queryresult = mysql_query($sqlquery);

if($row=mysql_fetch_array($queryresult))
    {
```

```php
echo "<tr> ";
echo " <td> Name </td>";
echo " <td width=\"150\"> ". $row["Name"] . " </td>";
echo "</tr>";
echo "<tr> ";
echo " <td> e-mail </td>";
echo " <td>". $row["Email"]."</td>";
echo " <td> <input type=\"hidden\" Name=\"Email\" value=\"".$row["Secondaryemail"]."\" ></td>";
echo "</tr>";
echo " <tr> ";
echo " <td> secondary e-mail </td>";
echo " <td> ";
echo "   <input type=\"text\" Name=\"Secondaryemail\" value=\"".$row["Secondaryemail"]."\" >";
echo " </td>";
echo "</tr>";
echo "<tr> ";
echo " <td> ";
echo "  <center> ";
echo "  <input type=\"submit\" name=\"Submit\" value=\"Submit\">";
echo "  </center>";
echo " </td>";
echo "</tr>";
}
?>
</table>
```

```
</form>
</body>
</html>
```

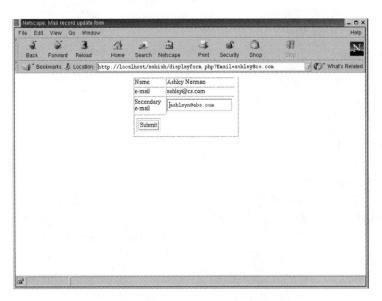

FIGURE 13-10 *Displays the record selected for modification*

The updated information is then retrieved from the MySQL database and displayed on a new HTML page. You will save this code in a file named changes.php. The code is given below, and the output of the final HTML page appears in Figure 13-11.

```
<html>
<head>
<title>New record In Newsmail table</title>
<meta http-equiv="Content-Type" content="text/html;
charset=iso-8859-1">
</head>
<body bgcolor="#FFFFFF" text="#000000">
<p> </p>

<?php
```

```
                                        $connect=
mysql_connect("localhost","root","")
                                            or die("Could not connect to
Database !");

                                        $result=mysql_select_db("Mailinglist")
                                                    or die("Could not select
Maildata database");

                                        $sqlquery = "UPDATE Maildata SET
Secondaryemail=\"".

                                         $secondaryemail."\" where
Email=\"".$Email."\"";

                                        echo $sqlquery;
                                        $result = mysql_query($sqlquery)
                                        or die("Could not execute SQL query");

                                        echo " Record was successfully updated.";

                ?>
```

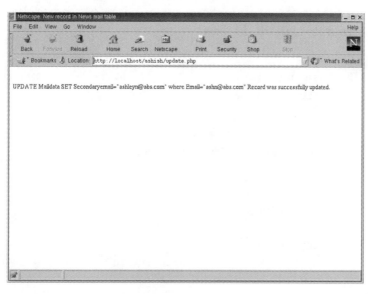

FIGURE 13-11 *Updating the changed user information*

```
</body>
</html>
```

In the code given earlier, you learned how to connect to a single database and how to display information stored in a table that exists in the database. Suppose you need to display information available in multiple databases. PHP provides a function to establish connections with multiple databases. You will now consider this procedure in detail.

Using Multiple Databases Simultaneously

Earlier in this chapter, you learned how to connect to a database and retrieve information from it. Sometimes you need to display information that may not be available in a single database. In such a case, you may need to establish connections with multiple databases simultaneously and retrieve specific information from them. This information is then formatted and displayed in the Web browser. For the user who has queried the information, the result of the query appears to originate from a single location. However, you need to write a code separately for establishing connection to each database.

The following code establishes connections with two databases and displays information retrieved from both the databases.

```
<html>
<head>
<title>Maildata record browser</title>
</head>

<body bgcolor="#FFFFFF" text="#000000">

<?php

                          $connect=
mysql_connect("localhost","root","")
                          or die("Could not connect to MySQL
server in localhost !");
```

```php
$db="Mailinglist";
$db2="Seconddb";

$sqlquery = "SELECT * from Maildata";
$queryresult = mysql_db_query($db, $sqlquery) or die("query failed");

echo "<table width=600 border=1 align=center>";
echo "  <tr>";
echo "    <td width=200> <center><b>Name </b></center></td>\n";
echo "    <td width=200> <center><b>e-mail</b></center></td>\n";
echo "    <td width=200> <center><b>Secondary e-mail</b></center></td>\n";
echo "   </tr>\n";
while ($row=mysql_fetch_array($queryresult))
    {
                echo "  <tr>\n";
                echo "    <td>".$row["Name"]."</td>\n";
                echo "    <td>".$row["Email"]."</td>\n";

                $sqlquery2 = "SELECT address from secondtable where Email='".$row["Email"]."'";
                $queryresult2 = mysql_db_query($db2,$sqlquery2);
                if ($row2=mysql_fetch_array($queryresult2))
                    {
echo "      <td>".$row2["address"]."</td>\n";
```

```
                                                                        }
                                                        else
                                                        {

                                                        }
echo "    <td>  </td>\n";

                                                        echo "  </tr>\n";
                                        }
                                        echo "</table>\n";
                        ?>
                        </body>
                        </html>
```

In the code given above, you established connections with the MySQL server. You may remember that while connecting to a single database you used the `mysql_select_db()` function to connect to the database. While connecting to multiple databases, the use of this function is not required. After establishing connection successfully, you connect to the two databases, Mailinglist and Seconddb, by using the `mysql_db_query()` function. You may remember that while connecting to a single database, you used the `mysql_query()` function to perform the same task. All the records from the Maildata table that exist in the Mailinglist database are retrieved and displayed in the form of a table. The corresponding addresses are also retrieved from the Secondtable table, which is available in the Seconddb database. The connection between both the tables is established based on the common field `Email`. Therefore, the value stored in the `Email` field in the Maildata table is searched for in Secondtable and the record found is displayed.

The output of the above code is shown in Figure 13-12.

Now consider some of the other MySQL functions that you can use in your PHP scripts.

Important PHP-MySQL Functions

In addition to the above functions, a few more MySQL functions are given below.

♦ `mysql_affected_rows()` **function.** This function returns the total number of rows that a query inserts or updates in a table. You can use this

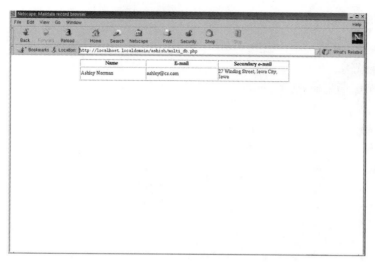

FIGURE 13-12 *Displaying information retrieved from multiple databases*

function to keep track of the number of records modified due to the execution of the query on the MySQL server. The use of this function is common when your result contains multiple rows.

◆ **mysql_num_fields() function.** This function contains the total number of fields returned after the execution of the query in the mysql_query() function. You can use the information stored in this variable if you need to manipulate the returned records based on their field position in the result.

◆ **mysql_num_rows() function.** This function is similar to the mysql_num_rows() function and returns the number of rows affected by the last select statement. If the value is zero, then it can be assumed that the query has not returned any record.

Next consider how you can handle errors in MySQL.

Error Handling in MySQL

You probably have written a large amount of code in PHP by now. You surely must have faced error messages. These error messages may be the ones returned by the system or the ones created by you. Most users would be unable to make head or tail of an error that consisted of a string of incomprehensible information. Consider the error given in Figure 13-13.

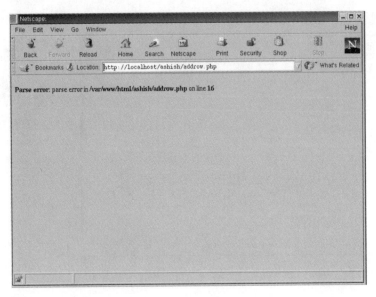

FIGURE 13-13 *A sample error*

Users would surely be at a loss if they confronted the error given above. Generally, a standard error handler in PHP will return the following information to the calling program:

♦ Information about where the errors occurred, such as file name, line in the program where the error occurred, and general information about the error

♦ Additional information about why the error may have occurred

As all this information is unformatted and is directly sent to the Web browser, the information may appear in an arbitrary manner and may puzzle a novice user. In the case of system-defined error handlers, another problem can be that the information may not appear at all. This is possible in cases where the HTML Web page contains a Java script. The Java script may retrieve an error while executing but may not display any information to the user. Therefore, it is the responsibility of developers to create customized error handlers. These error handlers display error information in a user-friendly format that a user can easily understand.

You have already used a couple of error handlers in the code at the beginning of the chapter. These error handlers were the @ symbol and the die() function. You used these functions to display customized error messages when the errors were encountered. In addition to displaying error messages, these error handlers can be configured to perform actions such as sending e-mail messages to the administrator that contain information about where the error had occurred. You will learn how to create customized error handlers later in this section. However, you will first learn about the different types of errors found in PHP.

Error Types in PHP

All errors fall mostly under two categories, standard errors and custom errors. The standard error type contains eight type of errors while the custom error type contains three types of errors. You will now consider both of these error types in detail.

Standard Error Types

Most of the errors that are encountered in scripts occur at the time when the scripts are compiled or executed. Some of these errors are of a critical nature and may cause the script to stop executing altogether. However, there are other others that are of a not-so-critical nature and that only serve as warnings. These errors do not stop the execution of the script. Most of these errors, which are of similar kinds, are handled in a similar manner. As mentioned earlier, standard error types are of eight kinds. Now consider these types in detail.

- ◆ **E_ERROR.** This is a critical error. If a script encounters this error, it is unable to recover and the execution is terminated. This error is mostly encountered at runtime. Its error number is 1.

- ◆ **E_WARNING.** This is not a critical error because the execution of the script does not stop if this error is encountered. This error is encountered at runtime and mostly the script can handle this kind of error. An instance where this error can occur is at the time of datatype mismatch. Although this is not a critical error, an error message is displayed to the user. Therefore, you need to create an error handler for this error. The error number is 2.

- ◆ **E_NOTICE.** This error type is also not critical, and the execution of the code does not stop if this error is encountered. This error occurs at the time of execution of the script and as it is not critical in nature, no message is displayed. This error may be encountered in cases where a variable may not be defined. The error number for this error is 8.

◆ **E_CORE_WARNING.** This error type is similar to the E_WARN-
ING error type and therefore both the error types are treated in the
same way. The error may appear as warning of errors encountered during
startup. The error number is 32.

◆ **E_CORE_ERROR.** This error type is similar to the E_ERROR error
type. However, the E_ERROR error type is raised by a function from
inside PHP while E_CORE_ERROR error type is raised by the core
code of PHP. Nevertheless, both the errors are handled in the same
manner. E_CORE_ERROR error type is caused due to errors encountered during startup. The error number for this error is 16.

◆ **E_PARSE.** The error type is raised by the parser and is mostly caused
by syntactical errors. This error is critical in nature and causes the script
to exit execution prematurely. The error is raised at compile time by the
parser and contains error number 4.

◆ **E_COMPILE_WARNING.** This error type is similar to the E_COM-
PILE_ERROR error type. As the name suggests, the error is a warning that
is displayed when a non-critical error is encountered at compile time.
The error type has corresponding items in the E_WARNING and
E_CORE_WARNING error types. All the three error types are treated
similarly. The error number is 128.

◆ **E_COMPILE_ERROR.** This error is similar to the E_ERROR and
E_CORE_ERROR error types and is raised at compile time. This is a
critical error and has the error number 64.

 NOTE

You will learn the importance of the error number later in this chapter.

In the next section, you will learn about custom error types.

Custom Error Types

Just as you have system-defined error types, so PHP provides three custom error
types. You can use these error types to raise errors in PHP. These are the only error

types that you can use to raise errors from inside scripts. Below, you will learn about these error types in detail.

◆ **E_USER_ERROR.** This is the most critical of the user-defined error types in PHP. It contains information similar to that in the system-defined error type E_ERROR. The script raises this error in the event that the error is encountered and the script stops execution. For example, this error will be raised if the script tries to divide a number by zero. The error number of this error type is 256.

◆ **E_USER_WARNING.** This error type is similar to the system-defined E_ERROR error type. The difference is that in this case, you can create your own customized warnings. This error type is used to provide warnings for errors that may not allow your script to function properly. The error number for this error type is 512.

◆ **E_USER_NOTICE.** This error type is also similar to the system defined E_NOTICE error type and performs the same function. With this error type, you have the advantage of specifying your customized error messages. You can use this error type to inform users of the problems that they may encounter. This error type is not critical in nature and has the error number 1024.

You will now learn to create customized error handlers.

Creating Customized Error Handlers

The process of creating error handlers in PHP is relatively simple. The process involves creating a standard function that will be called every time an error is raised. This function is defined in the PHP script and accepts five parameters: error number, description, file name, line number, and context. Two of the parameters, error number and description, are compulsory while the other three are optional. The syntax of the function is given below.

```
Function Errhandler($err_number, $err_string [, $errfile_name, $errline_num-
ber, $err_context])
        {
                [Code to handle the error]
        }
```

The parameters used in the function and their meanings are listed below.

◆ **$err_number.** (Compulsory.) This parameter contains an integer value. This unique value is assigned to each error number and each error is identified based on this value.

◆ **$err_string.** (Compulsory.) This parameter contains information about the error in the form of a string. This string contains information specific to the error, such as the possible reasons why the error occurred.

◆ **$errfile_name.** (Optional.) This parameter contains the name of the file in which this error was raised.

◆ **$errline_number.** (Optional.) This parameter contains the specific line number in which the error was encountered.

◆ **$err_context.** (Optional.) This variable maintains a list of all the variables that were being used in the script at the time the error occurred. It also contains the values of the variables at that time. All the information is saved in the form of an array.

Now you will be able to appreciate the simplicity of error handling in PHP. You only need to know the error number of the error that has occurred and, based on the number, you can execute the appropriate code.

Next you will learn about the default error-handling functions available in PHP.

Error-Handling Functions

PHP offers a set of error-handling functions that prevail over the default error-handling functions of PHP. These functions take priority over the default error-handling functions and can also be used to trigger the errors. Consider these functions in detail.

◆ **Err_log.** This function is used to log errors that occur in PHP. The information is stored in a simple log file. This file can the be e-mailed to any user, such as the administrator. This information is also useful for debugging.

◆ **Set_error_handler.** This function is used for registering other user-created functions to act as error handlers in PHP. These functions then override the default error-handling functions in PHP.

♦ **Reset_error_handler.** This function is used to list or register the
default error handlers in PHP that are used for handling errors. This
function is used after the `set_error_handler()` function is called and
changes the current error handler from the system handlers to customized error handlers or vice versa. Therefore, the currently registered
error handler could be either the system-defined error handler or the
user-defined error handler.

♦ **Error_reporting.** This function maintains a list of errors that are handled by the error-handling mechanism. This function is called if the
user-defined error handler is being used. The device requires the use of
this function to determine the errors that need to be handled.

♦ **Trigger_error.** This function is used to trigger an error so that the
error handler sends an error message. This function raises an error only
if the error type is a custom error type such as E_USER. You cannot
raise errors for system-defined error types such as E_ERROR or
E_NOTICE.

Now you will learn how to create custom error handlers in PHP. The first step is
to initialize all the necessary variables and flags.

Creating Custom Error Handlers

Before you begin to create an error handler for your script, you need to initialize
certain variables and set certain flags. These variables are later used to store information in the error log. Consider the code given below.

```php
<?php
        Function Errhandler($err_number, $err_string, $errfile_name, $errline_num-
ber, $err_context])
                        {
                            var $errmsg = "The error : $err_string occurred in the file
: $errfile_name at the line :
                            $errline_number);

                            var $halt_script = True;
                            var $notify = False;

                            var $remote = False;
```

```
var $display = True;
ver $email = False;
var $stdlog = True;

var $log_file = "";
var $email_addr = admin@comp.com;
var $remote_dbg = "localhost";
[Rest of the code]
}
```

The variables mentioned above store the error information. Three of these variables are the parameters that are passed to the error_log() function. Consider each of these variables in detail.

- ◆ **$remote_dbg.** This variable stores the address of the remote system that will debug the errors. This information is passed to PHP.
- ◆ **$errmsg.** This variable will contain a standard format in which all the customized error messages will be displayed.
- ◆ **$log_file.** This variable contains the name and location of the log file where the error information is stored. You do not need to specify a value for this variable if you want the information to be stored in the default logger of the system.
- ◆ **$email_addr.** This variable contains the e-mail address of the user to whom the error information needs to be e-mailed. This user is mostly the administrator.

CAUTION

Remote debugging is a facility that was available in PHP3 and is no longer available in PHP4.

You may also notice that certain flags have been set in the code given above. Now you will learn about these flags and their use.

- ◆ **$stdlog.** This flag is used to log errors in the default system log file or the one specified in the variable $log_file.

◆ **$email.** This flag is used to report errors by using e-mail.

◆ **$display.** This flag is used to display the errors encountered during the debugging process to the user. This error is displayed in the Web page by using an echo command.

◆ **$remote.** This flag is used to log errors encountered during the debugging process.

There are two other flags that are used in the program given above, the $notify flag and the $halt_script flag. These flags are used internally by the system to track whether a user needs to be informed if an error is encountered and whether the system should be halted at critical errors.

◆ **$halt_script.** If the value of this flag is set to True, the script stops execution when a critical error is encountered. The default value of this flag is True.

◆ **$notify.** This flag is used to determine that a user should be informed if an error is encountered. The initial value of the flag is False.

Now you need to know the type of errors that have occurred.

Creating Handlers for Specific Errors

You have learned to create error handlers. However, unless you are able to identify the type of errors that have occurred, you cannot create error handlers. In addition to this information, you need to set the $halt_script and $notify flags. You need to set the $halt_script irrespective of whether you want the script to stop executing the moment the error is encountered or want it to continue executing by ignoring the error. If you decide to process the error, the system assigns a category to the error based on its severity. The $notify variable is set to True, and the information about the error is logged into the error log file. Now you will write the code to implement these error handlers.

```php
<?php
    <! Initialized variables and set flags -->
    switch($err_number)
        {
                                    case E_COMPILE_ERROR :
                                    case E_CORE_ERROR :
                                    case E_ERROR :
```

```
                                    $type = "Critical Error";
                                    break;
                                    case E_USER_ERROR :
                                    case E_PARSE :
                                    $type = "Parse Error";
                                    break;

                                    case E_NOTICE :
                                    $type = "Notice";
                                    $halt_script = False;
                                    break;
                                    case E_USER_NOTICE :

                                    case E_CORE_WARNING :
                                    case E_WARNING :
                                    $type = "Warning";
                                    $halt_script = False;
                                    break;
                                    case E_COMPILE_WARNING :
                                    case E_USER_WARNING :


                                    default:
                                    $type = "Unknown Error";
                                    break;

                }
            [Rest of the code]

        }
```

After creating the handlers for specific error types, you will learn how to notify users that the error has occurred.

Informing Users about Errors

The final step in creating error handlers is to inform the users that an error has occurred. This is important because users expect the output of their queries or a message specifying why these queries failed to work. As explained earlier, a novice user may not understand the error if faced with a system error. Therefore, you need to display the error in a user-friendly format.

After the database has returned the error, either the program's execution is halted or the execution continues. The error handler makes this decision based on the severity level of the error. All the error information stored in the error log is displayed in the browser. The final code is given below.

```php
<?php
Function Errhandler($err_number, $err_string, $errfile_name, $errline_number, $err_context])
        {
            var $errmsg = "The error : $err_string occurred in the file
: $errfile_name at the line :
            $errline_number);

            var $halt_script = True;
            var $notify = False;

            var $remote = False;
            var $display = True;
            ver $email = False;
            var $stdlog = True;

            var $log_file = "";
            var $email_addr = admin@comp.com;
            var $remote_dbg = "localhost";
            switch($err_number)
                {
                                    case E_COMPILE_ERROR :
                                    case E_CORE_ERROR :
                                    case E_ERROR :
                                    $type = "Critical Error";
                                    break;
                                    case E_USER_ERROR :
                                    case E_PARSE :
                                    $type = "Parse Error";
                                    break;
```

```
                                                case E_NOTICE :
                                                $type = "Notice";
                                                $halt_script = False;
                                                break;
                                                case E_USER_NOTICE :

                                                case E_CORE_WARNING :
                                                case E_WARNING :
                                                $type = "Warning";
                                                $halt_script = False;
                                                break;
                                                case E_COMPILE_WARNING :
                                                case E_USER_WARNING :


                                                default:
                                                $type = "Unknown Error";
                                                break;

                    }
                If($notify)
                    {

                                                $errmsg = $type . $errmsg;
                                                If($email)
                                                {

        error_log($errmsg, 1, $email_addr);

                                                }
                                                If($remote)
                                                {

        error_log($errmsg, 2, $remote_dbg);

                                                }
                                                If($display)
                                                {
                                                                echo
        $errmsg;

                                                }
                                                If($stdlog)
```

```
                                                    {

If($log_file = "")

{

error_log($errmsg, o);

}
                                                                        else

{

error_log($errmsg, 2, $remote_dbg);

}
                                                    }
                              }
                         If($halt_script) exit -1;
                    }
          ?>
```

Next you will learn how you can use the error handler you just created to handle errors in your script.

Using the Error Handlers

After you have created a handler, you should test it by calling the function in your script. The error handler can process all the errors raised by PHP during execution and raise errors if the scripts do not execute as expected. You can raise errors by using the trigger_error() function. You learned about the trigger_error() function when you considered error handling functions earlier in the chapter. The syntax of the function is given below.

```
trigger_error(<errstring>, [errtype]);
```

In the preceding code, errstring contains a string of information describing the error and errtype contains the error type. By default, errtype contains the value E_USER_NOTICE.

 CAUTION

You can only use a custom error type (E_USER_ERROR, E_USER_WARNING, and E_USER_NOTICE) in the `trigger_error()` function. There is no function available in PHP that you can use to trigger internal PHP errors.

You may remember that I mentioned earlier that scripting languages sometimes may suppress the errors returned by the database and the users may be unable to determine why their search for specific information failed. You may now realize that this problem is solved when you use customized error handlers. This is because the display of error messages depends on you instead of on the system. Therefore, you can display all the error messages that you want the users to see.

```
<br><br>Lets try to select a Database that does not
exist.<br><br>

<?php
$connect=
mysql_connect("localhost","root","");
mysql_select_db("somewrongdatabase");
echo " Error   Number : ". mysql_errno().
" \n<br>Error Message :".
mysql_error(). "\n<br>";
?>

<br><br>Lets extract rows from a Table that does not
exist.<br><br>
<?php
$sqlquery = mysql_query("SELECT * FROM
somewrongtable");
echo " Error   Number :
".mysql_errno()."\n<BR>";
echo " Error Message :
```

```
".mysql_error()."\n<BR>";
                    ?>


                    <br><br>Lets select a database first and then try to extract
rows from a Table that
                    does not exist.<br><br>

                    <?php
                                mysql_select_db("books")
                                or die("even this database does not
exist");
                                $sqlquery = mysql_query("SELECT * FROM
somewrongtable");
                                echo " Error  Number : ". mysql_errno().
"\n<br>";
                                echo " Error Message : ". mysql_error().
"\n<br>";
                    ?>
```

The output of the above code appears in Figure 13-14. The output displays the error number and a brief description about the error encountered.

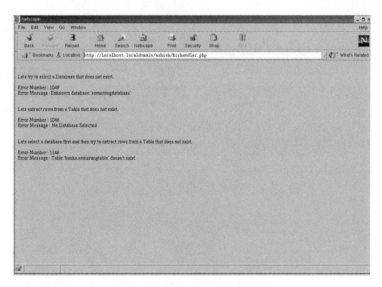

FIGURE 13-14 *The errors encountered and their description*

Summary

In this chapter, you learned how to integrate MySQL with PHP. First you learned how to connect to the MySQL server by using the `mysql_connect()` function. Then you learned how to create a database in the MySQL server by using the `mysql_create_db()` function to create the database. Next you learned how to connect to the database. Then you learned how to format a query by using the `mysql_query()` function and how to send it to the MySQL server. The information about whether the query executed properly was stored in another variable. Then you learned how to create a table in the database and insert records in the table. You then learned how to retrieve records from the table, both as separate records and as an array. Next you learned how to update the information stored in the table. In addition, you learned how to connect to multiple databases simultaneously and display information from both the databases together. You also learned about some of the other functions available in PHP. In addition, you learned about the different types of error handlers available in PHP. Finally, you learned how to create your own error handlers to display customized error messages.

PART V

Professional Project 4

Project 4

**Creating a Product
Catalog and
Shopping Cart and
Sending an E-mail**

Project 4 Overview

In this project, I'll teach you how to create a complete a product catalog and a shopping cart. You will also learn to implement an e-mail application in the product catalog. You will begin by learning about the basics of a product catalog. After you have created the product catalog, you will then learn how to create your own shopping cart.

In Chapter 14 you will learn to create and manage a product catalog. You will also learn various aspects of working with and managing a product catalog from the client side as well as the administrator side. The Bukbuz, Inc. online product catalog can be broken down into the following components:

◆ **Categories section:** The product catalog displays all the categories of books that are available at the Bukbuz, Inc. bookstore.

◆ **Search:** The search component of the product catalog allows customers to search for the books that they wish to buy.

◆ **Links to other pages:** The product catalog also contains links to several other pages on the Web site, such as viewing the shopping cart or personal settings.

◆ **Administrative component:** Only the system administrator can add new categories and books to the product catalog.

In Chapter 15 you will learn how to create a shopping cart. You will also learn to add and remove products from your shopping cart. You can also view your shopping cart and detailed information about the products that you have added to your shopping cart.

In Chapter 16 you will learn to create an HTML form that can accept user input. When the customers fill in the form and click on the Submit button, the feedback is sent as an e-mail message to the site administrator. You will also learn about the mail () function and the different arguments that it has.

Chapter 14

*Creating a
Product Catalog*

To attract and retain customers, a Web site needs to have a comprehensive yet flexible product catalog. Creating and managing a catalog can prove to be quite a complex process if it involves information sharing from a number of sources. A catalog should also provide certain value-added features, such as analyzing and understanding the interests of customers based on their buying patterns, order tracking, and so on.

In this chapter you will learn to create and manage a product catalog. You will also learn various aspects of working with and managing a product catalog from the client side as well as the administrator side.

Overview of a Product Catalog

The product catalog can be considered as the soul of the Bukbuz, Inc. Web site. All activities in the Bukbuz, Inc. Web site revolve around the product catalog. The product catalog contains information about all books that are available in the Bukbuz, Inc. bookstore. In addition, the product catalog allows you to view your shopping cart or your personal information.

Structure of the Product Catalog

The structure of the Bukbuz, Inc. product catalog can be compared to a tree structure. A tree structure is an algorithm that searches for records in a database. Each element of this algorithm is known as a node. A node can be divided into a number of branches known as children. All records in a tree structure are stored at locations known as leaves. There does not exist any structure beyond records. This is quite comparable to an actual tree, where there is a main trunk, followed by branches and finally leaves. The point from which leaves originate is known as the root.

Let me now compare this tree structure to the product catalog structure of Bukbuz, Inc. In case of Bukbuz, Inc. there exist several categories and subcategories of books and each book is stored according to its category. Each category, except for the parent category, exists under one category or the other. On this basis,

books can be considered as leaves of the tree structure, and categories as children. For example, books relating to the Internet are categorized under the category Internet. The Internet category is itself under the parent category, Computer.

These categories are stored in the category table in the database. When customers search for a specific category of books, they can use the search option of the product catalog. The search results are to a great extent affected by the design of the database. One of the main factors that determine the efficiency and effectiveness of a database is the ease and speed of searching data in the database. The structure of the database should be such that your search results are obtained in a fast and easy manner.

In our case, the product catalog shares information with a number of tables in the database, such as products, customerinfo, and category. As a result, we need to have such a database design, which can provide a solid support to various processes that are associated with the product catalog.

Various Components of the Bukbuz, Inc. Product Catalog

To understand the functioning of the Bukbuz, Inc. online product catalog, let us break down the product catalog into various components that make up the complete product catalog. Figure 14-1 displays the complete online product catalog of Bukbuz, Inc.

The Bukbuz, Inc. online product catalog can be broken down into the following components:

- ◆ **Categories section:** The product catalog displays all the categories of books that are available at the Bukbuz, Inc. bookstore. Modifications to categories in the product catalog, such as addition, deletion, and updating of categories can only be made by the system administrator. You will learn how to add or remove categories from the product catalog in the later topics of this chapter.

- ◆ **Search:** The search component of the product catalog allows customers to search for the books that they wish to buy. Customers can base their search either on the author of the book or the name of the book.

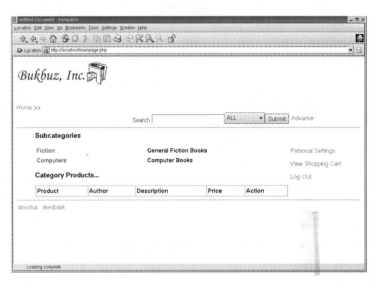

FIGURE 14-1 *The Bukbuz, Inc. online product catalog*

◆ **Links to other pages:** The product catalog also contains links to several other pages on the Web site, such as viewing the shopping cart or personal settings.

◆ **Administrative component:** Only the system administrator can add new categories and books to the product catalog. I will be dealing in detail about the administration of the Bukbuz, Inc. Web site later in the chapter.

We will be discussing each of these components in detail a little later in the chapter. Before we move further, let us first look at the source code of the product catalog.

```html
<html>
<head>
<title>Untitled Document</title>
<meta http-equiv="Content-Type" content="text/html; charset=iso-8859-1">
</head>
<body bgcolor="#FFFFFF" text="#000000">
<p><img src = "Logo.jpg" width = "264" height = "63"></p>
<p> </p>
```

```php
<?php
```

```
$host="";
$dbusername="root";
$dbpassword="";
$database="books";
$x=mysql_connect($host,$dbusername,$dbpassword);
$x2=mysql_select_db($database);
if (empty($category))
{
$category=1;
}
$childval=$category;
//$catline[]=" ";
$query = "select categoryid, name from category where categoryid=\"" .
$childval ."\"";
$result=mysql_query($query);
if ($row=mysql_fetch_array($result))
{
$catid[1]=$row["categoryid"];
$catname[1]=$row["name"];
}
while (!($childval==0))
{
$query="select parentcategoryid from category where
categoryid=\"".$childval."\"";
$result=mysql_query($query);
if ($row=mysql_fetch_array($result))
{
$childval= $row["parentcategoryid"];
$query = "select categoryid,name from category where categoryid=\"" .
$childval ."\"";
$result=mysql_query($query);
if ($row=mysql_fetch_array($result))
{
$catid[]=$row["categoryid"];
$catname[]=$row["name"];
}
}
}
```

```
        for ($i=count($catname); $i>0;$i--)
        {
        //$categoryid=$catid[count($catname)];
        echo "<A href=mainpage.php?category=".$catid[$i]."&customerid=".$cus-
tomerid.">".$catname[$i] . "</a> >> ";
        }
    ?>


        <table width="900" border="0" cellpadding="3" cellspacing="1">
        <tr>
        <td> </td>
        <td> </td>
        <td> </td>
        <td>
        <form name="form1" method="post" action="searchcustomer.php">
        <div align="right">Search
        <input type="text" name="search" size="20">
        <select name="searchfor">
        <option value="ALL">ALL</option>
        <option value="titles">Book Titles</option>
        <option value="author">Authors</option>
        </select>

    <?php
  echo "<input type=\"hidden\" name=\"category\" value=\"".$category."\">";
    ?>


    <?php
        echo "<input type=\"hidden\" name=\"customerid\" value=\"".$cus-
tomerid."\">";
    ?>


        <input type="submit" name="Submit" value="Submit">
        </div>
        </form>
        </td>
        <td><a href="advancesearch.htm">advance</a></td>
        </tr>
```

```
          </table>
          <hr>
          <table width="90%" border="0" align="center" cellspacing="1" cell-
padding="3">
          <tr>
          <td>
          <h2> Subcategories </h2>
          <table width="100%" border="0"  cellspacing="1" cellpadding="3">

      <?
          $query="select categoryid,name,description from category where parentcat-
egoryid=\"".$category."\"";
          $result=mysql_query($query);
          while ($row = mysql_fetch_array($result))
          {
          echo " <tr> ";
          echo "    <td   height=\"5\"> ";
          echo "       <p><b><a href=\"mainpage.php?category=".$row["catego-
ryid"]."&customerid=".$customerid."\">".$row["name"]."</a></b></p>";
          echo "
          </td>";
          echo "    <td width=\"400\"  height=\"5\"> ";
          echo "       <p><b>". $row["description"]."</b></p>";
          echo "    </td>";
          echo " </tr>";
          }
          >
          </table>
          <h2>Category Products...</h2>
          <table width="100%" border="1" align="center" cellspacing="1" cell-
padding="3">
          <tr>
          <td><b> Product </b></td>
          <td><b> Author  </b></td>
          <td><b> Description </b></td>
          <td><b> Price </b></td>
          <td colspan=2><b> Action </b></td>
          </tr>
```

```php
<?
        $query="select productid,name, author, description,price from products
where category=\"".$category."\"
        ";
        $result=mysql_query($query);
        while ($row = mysql_fetch_array($result))
        {
        echo " <tr>
        ";
        echo "    <td>
        ";
        echo "        <p><b>".$row["name"]."</b></p>
        ";
        echo "    </td>";
        echo "    <td> ";
        echo "        <p><b>".$row["author"]."</b></p>";
        echo "    </td>";
        echo "    <td> ";
        echo "        <p>". $row["description"]."</p>";
        echo "    </td>";

        echo "    <td> ";
        echo "        <p>". $row["price"]."</p>";
        echo "    </td>";

        echo "    <td width=\"120\"> ";
        echo "        <A target=\"_blank\" href=\"addtocart.php?customerid=".$cus-
tomerid."&productid=".$row["productid"]."\">Add to cart</a>";
        echo "    </td>";
        echo "    <td width=\"120\"> ";
        echo "        <A target=\"_blank\" href=\"removefromcart.php?cus-
tomerid=".$customerid."&productid=".$row["productid"]."\">Remove from cart</a>";
        echo "    </td>";
        echo " </tr>";
        }

    ?>
        </table>
```

```
        </td>
        <td width="17%">


    <?php
        echo " <p><a href=\"personalsettings.php?customerid=".$customerid."&cate-
gory=".$category ."\">Personal Settings</a></p> ";
        echo "         <p><a href=\"viewshoppingcart.php?customerid=".$cus-
tomerid."&category=".$category ."\">View shopping cart</a></p>";
    ?>


        <p><a href="login.htm">log out</a></p>
        </td>
        </tr>
        </table>
        <hr>
        <table align = \"center\">
        <tr>
        <td><a href = "aboutus.htm" target = "_blank"> aboutus </a></td>
        <td><a href = "feedback.htm" target = "_blank"> feedback </a></td>
        </tr>
        </table>
        <p> </p>
        <p> </p>
        </body>
        </html>
```

The output of this code is the Bukbuz, Inc. product catalog.

Let us now discuss the process of user registration in the Bukbuz, Inc. Web site.

User Registration

As you already know, any customer who is not registered at the Bukbuz, Inc. Web site cannot place an order to purchase a book. Registration of a customer is important not only from the security point of view but also for maintaining a database of the customers of the Bukbuz, Inc. bookstore. After customers get registered, they can then log in to the Web site by using their login name and can then place an order for the selected books.

A customer can get registered at the Bukbuz, Inc. Web site in the following two ways:

◆ Using the Bukbuz, Inc. Web site home page
◆ Clicking on the Add to Cart link in the Product Catalog page

User Registration through the Bukbuz, Inc. Home Page

To register at the Bukbuz, Inc. Web site, a customer needs to first click on the link, which is provided just below the Password text box. Figure 14-2 displays the Bukbuz, Inc. home page.

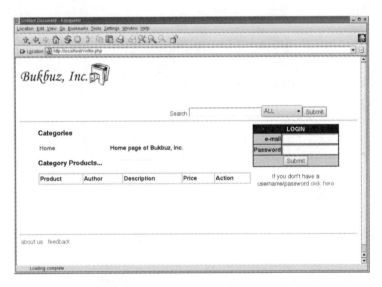

FIGURE 14-2 *The Bukbuz, Inc. home page*

In the Bukbuz, Inc. home page, notice that below the login section there exists a link for those customers who are not already registered with the Bukbuz, Inc. Web site. When the customer clicks on this link, the User Registration form appears, as shown in Figure 14-3.

In the User Registration form, customers enter their details, such as full name, address, date of birth, and e-mail address. The e-mail value is used by the customers as the login name. Let us now discuss the source code for the User Registration form.

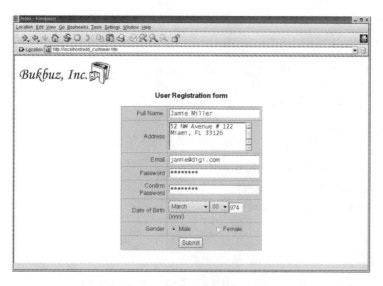

FIGURE 14-3 *The User Registration form*

The User Registration Form

The User Registration form is a simple HTML file, named add_customer.htm. The User Registration form only accepts the user input and displays it on the screen. This form does not store any user-accepted value in the books database. Following is the source code for the User Registration form.

```
<html>
<head>
<title>Index</title>
</head>
<body>
<p><img src = "Logo.jpg" width = "264" height = "63"></p>
<h2 align="center">User Registration form</h2>
<form name="registration" method="post" action="confirm.php"
enctype="multipart/form-data">
<table width="400" border="1" align="center" cellpadding="5"
cellspacing="0" bgcolor="#CCCCCC">
<tr>
<td width="47%">
<div align="right">Full Name </div>
</td>
```

```
<td colspan="2">
<div align="left">
<input type="text" name="name" size="25"

maxlength="25">
</div>
</td>
</tr>
<tr>
<td width="47%" height="57">
<div align="right">Address</div>
</td>

<td height="57" colspan="2">
<textarea name="address" cols="21" rows="4"></textarea>
</td>
</tr>
<tr>
<td width="47%">
<div align="right">Email</div>
</td>
<td height="2" colspan="2">
<input type="text" name="email" size="25" maxlength="50">
<td>
</tr>

<tr>
<td width="47%">
<div align="right">Password</div>
</td>
<td height="2" >
<input type="password" name="password" size="25"

maxlength="15">
</td>
</tr>

<tr>
```

```
<td width="47%">
<div align="right">Confirm Password</div>
</td>
<td height="2" >
<input type="password" name="cpassword" size="25"
maxlength="15">
</td>
</tr>

<tr>
<td width="47%">
<div align="right">Date of Birth</div>
</td>
<td height="2" >
<select name=birth_month>
<option selected
value=1>January
<option value=2>February
<option
value=3>March
<option value=4>April
<option value=5>May
<option value=6>June
<option value=7>July
<option value=8>August
<option value=9>September
<option value=10>October
<option value=11>November
<option value=12>December</option>
</select>
<select
=birth_day>
<option selected value=1>01
<option value=2>02
<option value=3>03
<option value=4>04
<option value=5>05
<option value=6>06
```

```
<option value=7>07
<option value=8>08
<option value=9>09
<option value=10>10
<option value=11>11
<option value=12>12
<option value=13>13
<option value=14>14
<option value=15>15
<option value=16>16
<option value=17>17
<option value=18>18
<option value=19>19
<option value=20>20
<option value=21>21
<option value=22>22
<option value=23>23
<option value=24>24
<option value=25>25
<option value=26>26
<option value=27>27
<option value=28>28
<option value=29>29
<option value=30>30
<option value=31>31</option>
</select>
<input maxlength=4 name=birth_year size=4>
(yyyy) </td>
</tr>
<tr>

<td width="47%">
<div align="right">Gender</div>
</td>
<td>
<table border=0 width="100%">
<tr>
<td height="2" width="26%">
```

```
<input type="radio" name="gender" value="Male">
Male </td>
<td height="2" width="27%">
<input type="radio" name="gender" value="Female">
Female</td>
</tr>
</table>
</td>
</tr>

<tr>
<td colspan="3">
<div align="center">
<input type="submit" name="Submit" value="Submit">
</div>
</td>
</tr>
</table>
</form>
</body>
</html>
```

In the preceding code, when the customer clicks on the Submit button, all the input information is forwarded to the file confirm.php.

The confirm.php File

When the customer clicks on the Submit button, the User Registration Confirmation page appears, as shown in Figure 14-4. The User Registration Confirmation page is a PHP file, called confirm.php.

The confirm .php file parses all information received from the add_customer.htm file. In addition, this file validates all the information that is entered by the customer. Following is the source code for the confirm.php file.

```
<html>
<head>
<title>Index</title>
</head>
<body>
```

FIGURE 14-4 *The User Registration Confirmation form*

```html
<h2 align="center">User Registration Confirmation page.</h2>

<table width="300" border="1" align="center" cellpadding="5" cellspac-
ing="0" bgcolor="#EEEEFF">
<tr>
<td width="47%" align="right"> <B> Full Name </B> </td>
<td >
```

```
// --- Validation for name.
```

```php
<?php
if(empty($name))
{
die(" No Name submitted");
}
elseif ( (strlen($name) < 5) || (strlen($name) > 50))
{
die("Invalid name");
}
else
{
echo $name;
```

```
        }
    ?>

        </td>
        </tr>
        <tr>
        <td width="47%" height="57" align="right"><B> Address </B></td>
        <td height="57">
```

`// --- Validation for Address.`

```php
    <?php
        if(empty($address))
        {
        die(" No address submitted");
        }
        elseif ( (strlen($address) < 5) || (strlen($address) > 200))
        {
        die("Invalid address");
        }
        else
        {
        echo $address;
        }
    ?>

        </td>
        </tr>
        <tr>
        <td width="47%" align="right"> <B>Email</B> </td>
        <td height="2">
```

`// --- Validation for e-mail.`

```php
    <?php
        if(empty($email))
        {
        die(" No email address submitted");
```

```php
        }
        elseif ( (strlen($email) < 5) || (strlen($email) > 100))
        {
        die("Invalid email address, email address too long or too short.");
        }
        elseif(!ereg("@",$email))
        {
        die("Invalid email address, no @ symbol found");
        }
        else
        {
        echo $email;
        }
    ?>


        </td>
        </tr>
        <tr>
        <td width="47%" align="right"> <B>Password </B></td>
        <td height="2">

// --- Validation for password.
    <?php
        if(empty($password) || empty($cpassword))
        {
        die(" No password submitted");
        }
        elseif ( ((strlen($password) < 5) || (strlen($password) > 15)))
        {
        die("Invalid password length address");
        }
        elseif ( !(strlen($password) == strlen($cpassword))
        {
        die(" Passwords do not match! ");
        }
    }
        elseif( !($password === $cpassword))
        {
        die(" Passwords do not match! ");
```

```
        }
        else
        {
        for ($i=0;$i<strlen($password);$i++)
        {
        echo "*";
        }
        }
    ?>


        </td>
        </tr>
        <tr>
        <td width="47%" align="right"> Date of Birth </B></td>
        <td height="2">

// --- Validation for Date of birth.

    <?php
        if (empty($birth_month) ¦¦ empty($birth_day) ¦¦ empty($birth_year) )
        {
        die(" Date of birth not submitted or incomplete.");
        }
        switch($birth_month)
        {
        case 1: print "January "; break;
        case 2: print "February "; break;
        case 3: print "March ";break;
        case4: print "April ";break;
        case 5: print "May "; break;
        case 6: print "June "; break;
        case 7: print "July "; break;
        case 8: print "August "; break;
        case 9: print "September "; break;
        case 10: print "October "; break;
        case 11: print "November "; break;
        case 12: print "December "; break;
        default: die("Invalid birth month !!");
```

```php
        }
        if (($birth_day < 1) || ($birth_day > 31))
        {
        die(" Invalid date !");
        }
        else
        {
        echo $birth_day, " ";
        }
        if (($birth_year < 1900) || ($birth_year >1999))
        {
        die("Invalid birth year");
        }
        else
        {
        echo $birth_year;
        }
    ?>


        </td>
        </tr>
        <tr>
        <td width="47%" align="right">
        Gender
        </td>
        <td height="2" width="26%">


// --- Validation for Gender.

    <?php
        if (empty($gender))
        {
        die(" Gender not specified");
        }
        elseif (!(($gender=="Male") || ($gender=="Female")))
        {
        die("Invalid value for gender");
        }
```

```
        else
        {
        echo $gender;
        }
    ?>


        </td>
        </tr>
        <tr>
        <td colspan="3">


// --- Passes the Information to the add_customer.php file.


        <FORM Name=confirm action="add_customer.php">


    <?php
        echo "<input type=hidden name=\"name\" value=\"".$name."\" >\n";
        echo "<input type=hidden name=\"address\" value=\"".$address."\" >\n";
        echo "<input type=hidden name=\"email\" value=\"".$email."\" >\n";
        echo "<input type=hidden name=\"password\" value=\"".$password."\" >\n";
        echo "<input type=hidden name=\"gender\" value=\"".$gender."\" >\n";
        echo "<input type=hidden name=\"birth_month\" value=\"".$birth_month."\"
>\n";

        echo "<input type=hidden name=\"birth_day\" value=\"".$birth_day."\"
>\n";

        echo "<input type=hidden name=\"birth_year\" value=\"".$birth_year."\"
>\n";
    ?>


        <center>
        <input type="submit" name="Submit" value="Confirm >>">
        </center>
        </form>
        </td>
        </tr>
        </table>
        </body>
        </html>
```

After validating the information, the confirm.php file forwards all the information to add_customer.php. You have already learned about input validations in Chapter 10, "Form Parsing in PHP," under the topic "Form Validations."

Till now all the information that the customer has entered has not been stored in the database. It is the add_customer.php file that stores all the information entered by the customer in the database.

The add_customer.php File

The add_customer.php file parses the information it receives from the confirm.php file and then updates the "books" database with this information.

In addition to this, the add_customer.php file also performs some minor validations, such as validating whether all the fields have been filled or not and validating whether the same information is already present in the database.

Consider the following piece of code that validates information.

```php
<?php

// --- Checks whether the fields are empty or not.

        if ( empty($name) )
        {
        die("name left blank");
        }
        if ( empty($email) )
        die("email left blank");
        }
        if ( empty($address) )
        {
        die("address left blank");
        }
        if ( empty($birth_day) )
        {
        die("birth day left blank");
        }
        if ( empty($birth_month))
        {
```

```
        die("birth month left blank");
        }
        if ( empty($birth_year) )
        {
        die("birth year left blank");
        }
        if ( empty($gender))
        {
        die("gender left blank");
        }
        if (empty($password))
        {
        die ("Password empty.");
        }
```

// --- Checks whether or not the e-mail address specified by the new customer already exists in the database.

```
        $host="";
        $database="books";
        $dbusername="root";
        $dbpassword="";
        $x=mysql_connect($host,$dbusername,$dbpassword);
        $x1=mysql_select_db($database);
        $query="select email from newsmail where email='".$email."'";
        $result=mysql_query($query);
        if($row=mysql_fetch_array($result))
        {
        die(" Sorry that user " .$email. " already exists !  <br>");
        }
```
// --- Rest of the code here.

The first part of the preceding code first validates whether all the fields have been appropriately entered or not. If any of the fields have not been entered, then a message appears on the screen stating that the concerned field is empty.

The second part of the code validates data by querying the database. For example, in the preceding code, first a check is performed in the "books" database for the e-mail field. If the customer enters the e-mail value that already exists in the database, then the customer receives a message stating that the e-mail value already exists.

After performing these minor validations, the add_customer.php file then inserts the received information into the database. Consider the following piece of code.

```
// --- Initial part of the code here.


// --- Customer entered values are inserted into different tables of the database.


        $query="INSERT into customerinfo
VALUES('".$customerid."','".$name."','".$address."','".$dob."','".$gender."')";
        $result=mysql_query($query);
        if (!($result))
        {
        die(" User personal information could not be stored");
        }
        $query ="INSERT into newsmail VALUES('".$name."','".$email."','".$cus-
tomerid."')";
        $result=mysql_query($query);
        if (!($result))
        {
        die("User e-mail information could not be stored ");
        }
        $query ="INSERT into login
VALUES('".$customerid."','".$email."','".md5($password)."')";
        $result=mysql_query($query);
        if (!($result))
        {
        die(" User authentication information could not be stored");
        }
// --- Remaining part of the code.
```

In this code snippet the customer-entered values are inserted into different tables of the database. The customer name, address, age, and date of birth values are inserted into the customerinfo table. A unique customer ID is also assigned to the customer. The value of customer ID is inserted in the customerid field of the customerinfo table. Similarly, the customerid, e-mail, and customer name values are inserted in the newsmail table and the customerid, e-mail, and password values are stored in the login table. However, in the login table it is only the hashed value of password that is stored and not the clear text value.

After having discussed the various functions and working of the add_customer.php file, let us now look at the complete source code of the add_customer.php file.

```
// --- Checks whether the fields are empty or not.
```

```php
<?php
    if ( empty($name) )
    {
    die("name left blank");
    }
    if ( empty($email) )
    {
    die("email left blank");
    }
    if ( empty($address) )
    {
    die("address left blank");
    }
    if ( empty($birth_day) )
    {
    die("birth day left blank");
    }
    if ( empty($birth_month))
    {
    die("birth month left blank");
    }
    if ( empty($birth_year) )
    {
    die("birth year left blank");
    }
    if ( empty($gender))
    {
    die("gender left blank");
    }
```

```
if (empty($password))
{
die ("Password empty.");
}
```

// --- Checks whether or not the values specified by the new customer already exists in the database.

```
$host="";
$database="books";
$dbusername="root";
$dbpassword="";
$x=mysql_connect($host,$dbusername,$dbpassword);
$x1=mysql_select_db($database);
$query="select email from newsmail where email='".$email."'";
$result=mysql_query($query);
if($row=mysql_fetch_array($result))
{
die(" Sorry that user " .$email. " already exists !  <br>");
}
```

// --- Increments the value of the Customer ID by one from the last maximum value assigned.

```
$query="select MAX(customerid) as customerid from customerinfo";
$result=mysql_query($query);
if($row=mysql_fetch_array($result))
{
$customerid = ++$row["customerid"];
}
else
{
die("something wrong with the customerinfo table!");
 }
```

// --- Customer entered values are inserted into different tables of the database.

```
$dob = $birth_year . "-" . $birth_month . "-" . $birth_day;
```

```
            $query="INSERT into customerinfo
VALUES('".$customerid."','".$name."','".$address."','".$dob."','".$gender."')";
            $result=mysql_query($query);
            if (!($result))
            {
            die(" User personal information could not be stored");
            }
            $query ="INSERT into newsmail VALUES('".$name."','".$email."','".$cus-
tomerid."')";
            $result=mysql_query($query);
            if (!($result))
            {
            die("User e-mail information could not be stored ");
            }
            $query ="INSERT into login
VALUES('".$customerid."','".$email."','".md5($password)."')";
            $result=mysql_query($query);
            if (!($result))
            {
            die(" User authentication information could not be stored");
            }

// --- Displays the Customer ID, name, gender, e-mail, and address values.

            echo " <center>New User added successfully </center><br>";
            echo "   <hr><br><br>";
            echo "   Customerid/Login ID : <b>".$customerid."</b><br>";
            if ($gender=="M")
            {
            echo "Name : Mr. ";
            }
            else
            {
            echo "Name : Ms. ";
            }
            echo $name,"<br>";
            echo "   E-mail : ",$email,"<br>";
            echo "   Password : ";
```

```
for ($i=0;$i<strlen($password);$i++)  {echo "*";}
echo "<br>\n";
echo "  Address : ",$address,"<br>";
?>
<A href="login.htm">Proceed to login page</a>
```

Figure 14-5 displays the output of the add_customer.php file.

FIGURE 14-5 *The New User Added Successfully screen*

To log in to the Bukbuz, Inc. Web site, you need to click the link that appears below the customer information in the output screen of the add_customer.php file. When the customer clicks on this link, a login screen appears, as shown in Figure 14-6. The Customer Login page is a simple HTML file. In the username text box customers need to enter their e-mail address as the username and the password that was specified in the User Registration form.

Following is the source code for the Customer Login page.

```
<html>
<head>
<title>Untitled Document</title>
<meta http-equiv="Content-Type" content="text/html; charset=iso-8859-1">
```

```
        </head>
        <body bgcolor="#FFFFFF" text="#000000">
        <p><img src = "Logo.jpg" width = "264" height = "63"></p>
        <p> </p>
        <p> </p>
        <p> </p>
        <form name="form1" method="post" action="login.php">

        <table width="38%" border="0" align="center" cellspacing="0" cell-
padding="2">
        <tr>
        <td colspan="2" bgcolor="#000000">
        <div align="center"><font color="#FFFFFF"><b>LOGIN</b></font></div>
        </td>
        </tr>
        <tr bgcolor="#CCCCCC">
        <td width="44%"> </td>
        <td width="56%"> </td>
        </tr>
        <tr bgcolor="#CCCCCC">
        <td width="44%">
```

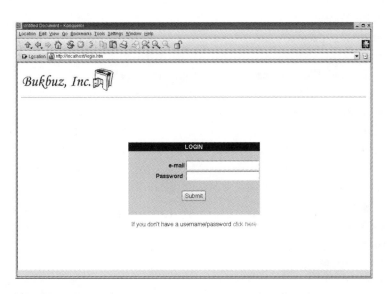

FIGURE 14-6 *Customer Login page*

```
<div align="right"><b>e-mail</b></div>
</td>
<td width="56%">
<div align="center">
<input type="text" name="email" size="20" maxlength="100">
</div>
</td>
</tr>
<tr bgcolor="#CCCCCC">
<td width="44%">
<div align="right"><b>Password </b></div>
</td>
<td width="56%">
<div align="center">
<input type="password" name="password" maxlength="15" size="20">
</div>
</td>
</tr>
<tr bgcolor="#CCCCCC">
<td colspan="2"> </td>
</tr>
<tr bgcolor="#CCCCCC">
<td colspan="2">
<div align="center">
<p>
<input type="submit" name="Submit" value="Submit">
</p>
<p> </p>
</div>
</td>
</tr>
</table>
</form>
<p align="center">If you don't have a username/password <a
href="add_customer.htm">click
here</a></p>
</body>
</html>
```

After entering their e-mail address in the username field and a password, customers need to click on the Submit button. When the Submit button is clicked, the product catalog screen appears.

This is the complete user registration process through the Bukbuz, Inc. home page. Let us now discuss the process of user registration when an unregistered customer clicks on the Add to Cart link in the Product Catalog page.

Process of User Registration When a Customer Clicks on the Add to Cart Link in the Product Catalog Page

Consider a situation when a customer does not register at the Bukbuz, Inc. Web site through the Bukbuz, Inc. home page and clicks on the Home link to go to the product catalog directly. In the product catalog, the customer can browse through different categories and books. However, when the customer selects a book and clicks on the Add to Cart link, the customer is directed to the login screen. In the login screen, the unregistered customer needs to click on the link below the login box. When the customer clicks on the link to get registered at the Bukbuz, Inc. Web site, the User Registration form appears.

After learning about the complete user registration process, let us now discuss the working of the Bukbuz, Inc. product catalog.

Working of the Bukbuz, Inc. Product Catalog

When customers visit the Bukbuz, Inc. Web site, the first page that they come across is the Bukbuz, Inc. home page. Customers who are registered users can log in to the Web site by entering their e-mail address and password in the login section provided on the Bukbuz, Inc. home page. After entering the e-mail and password, the customer then needs to click on the Submit button to view the Bukbuz, Inc. product catalog.

Selecting and Browsing the Product Catalog

As discussed previously, there are many categories and subcategories of books in the Bukbuz, Inc. product catalog. The basic or the root category is Home. Hence, all the categories of books are under one main category, Home. The product catalog displays all the parent categories under the root category, Home. Figure 14-7 displays the categories that are under Home.

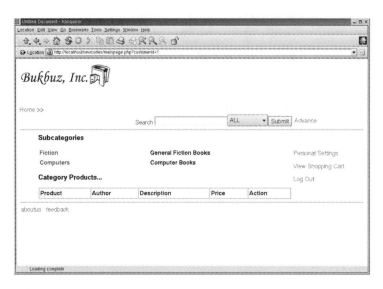

FIGURE 14-7 *Bukbuz, Inc. product catalog displaying all categories under the Home category*

Observe that on the upper-left side of the home page, just below the Bukbuz, Inc. logo, there is a link for Home. In the Product Catalog page, the customer selects the category of book to purchase. Suppose the customer has selected Fiction. In the Product Catalog page, observe that Fiction has now moved to the right of the Home link. Under the subcategories section you can now see Science instead of Fiction. Science is a subcategory under the parent category Fiction. When customers click on Science, they can view all the books that are under the Science category. Figure 14-8 displays all books that are under the category of Science.

Also, notice in the figure that now Science appears on the right-hand side of the Fiction category. Of the books that are available, suppose the customer wants to purchase the book *"Gama Protocol"*. Then the customer needs to add this book to the shopping cart. To do so, the customer needs to click the Add to Cart link adjacent to the selected book. When the customer clicks the link, a screen appears saying that the book has been added to the shopping cart. Figure 14-9 displays the screen confirming that the book has been added to the shopping cart of the customer.

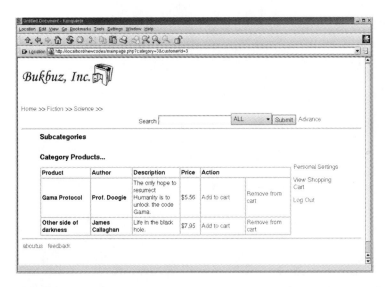

FIGURE 14-8 *Bukbuz, Inc. product catalog displaying all books that are under the Science category*

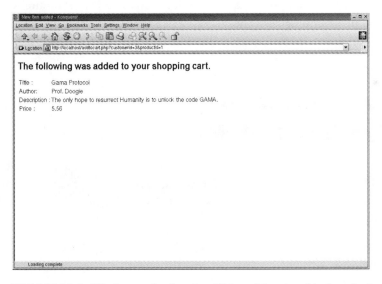

FIGURE 14-9 *Window confirming the addition of the selected book to the shopping cart*

To confirm that the book has been added to the shopping cart, customers can click on the View shopping cart link. When customers click on the View shopping cart link, they can view their shopping cart. Figure 14-10 displays the shopping cart of the customer with the selected books.

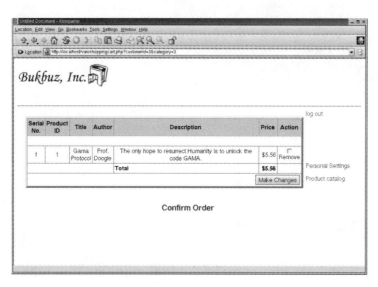

FIGURE 14-10 *Viewing the shopping cart*

I'll be dealing with the shopping cart in detail in Chapter 15, "Shopping Carts." After viewing the shopping cart, the customer can then come back to the product catalog by clicking on the Product Catalog link in the shopping cart.

The Search Function of the Product Catalog

The product catalog allows the customers to search for books that they wish to purchase. On the upper-left corner of the Bukbuz, Inc. product catalog, you can view the search section. Figure 14-11 displays the search section on the Bukbuz, Inc. home page.

Customers can base their search for books in the Bukbuz, Inc. product catalog on the following criteria:

◆ **The author of the book:** Customers can search the books of any particular author by specifying the name of the author in the search text box and then choosing By Author in the drop-down list.

◆ **The title of the book:** Customers can also search for books on the basis of the titles of the books. To do so, they can specify the title of the book in the search text box and then choose By Title in the drop-down list.

FIGURE 14-11 *The search section on the Bukbuz, Inc. home page*

◆ **By specifying a search word:** The Bukbuz, Inc. product catalog allows
customers to search for the books by specifying a search word in the
search text box and then choosing All in the drop-down list. When the
search is based on All, the word specified in the search text box is
matched with any words in the description field of the book, the title
field of the book, and the author field.

A customer can search for books both from the Bukbuz, Inc. home page as well
as the Bukbuz, Inc. product catalog. The search feature on the home page of Bukbuz, Inc. is enabled by using the searchvisitor.php file, while the search feature on
the product catalog is enabled by using the searchcustomer.php file. Let us now
discuss each of these files in detail.

The searchvisitor.php File

The searchvisitor.php file enables the search feature on the Bukbuz, Inc. home
page. Following is the complete code for searchvisitor.php.

```
        <html>
        <head>
        <title>Search Page</title>
        </head>
        <body bgcolor="#FFFFFF" text="#000000">
    <?php

// --- Checks whether or not the $search variable exists.

        if(!isset($search))
        {
```

```
            die("Search data not submitted!");
            }


// --- Checks whether or not the $search variable is empty.


        if(empty($search))
        {
        die("Search data empty!");
        }


// --- Checks whether or not the $searchfor variable exists.


        if(!isset($searchfor))
        {
        die("Search criteria not submitted!");
        }


// --- Checks whether or not the $searchfor variable is empty.


        if(empty($searchfor))
        {
        die("Search criteria empty!");
        }


// --- Checks in the MySQL database. All the results are queried from the products
table

        $connect= mysql_connect("localhost","root","")
        or die("Could not connect to MySQL server in localhost !");
        $selectdb=mysql_select_db("books")
        or die("Could not select books data database !");
        echo "<table width=700 border=1 align=center>";
        echo " <tr>";
        echo "  <td width=200> <center><b>Productid  </b></center></td>\n";
        echo "  <td width=200> <center><b>Title</b></center></td>\n";
        echo "  <td width=200> <center><b>Author</b></center></td>\n";
        echo "  <td width=200> <center><b>Description</b></center></td>\n";
        echo "  <td width=200> <center><b>Price</b></center></td>\n";
```

```
echo "   <td width=100> <center><b>Category</b></center></td>\n";
echo "  </tr>\n";
$sqlquery = "SELECT * from products";
$queryresult = mysql_query($sqlquery);
while ($row=mysql_fetch_array($queryresult))
{

// --- Search by using the title of the book.

if ($searchfor="title")
{
if (stristr($row["name"],$search))
{
echo "  <tr>\n";

echo "    <td>".$row["productid"]."</td>\n";

echo "    <td>".$row["name"]."</td>\n";
echo "    <td>".$row["author"]."</td>\n";
echo "    <td>".$row["description"]."</td>\n";

echo "    <td>".$row["price"]."</td>\n";
$sqlquery2 = "SELECT name
from category where categoryid='".$row["category"]."'";
$queryresult2 = mysql_query($sqlquery2);
if ($row2=mysql_fetch_array($queryresult2))
{
echo "    <td><a
href=\"visitor.php?category=".$row["category"]."\">".$row2["name"]."</td>\n";
}
else
{
echo " <td> Category missing !!</td>";
}
echo "  </tr>\n";
}
}
```

```
// Search by using the author of the book.

        elseif ($searchfor="author")
        {
        if (stristr($row["author"],$search))
        {
        echo "    <tr>\n";

        echo "        <td>".$row["productid"]."</td>\n";

        echo "        <td>".$row["name"]."</td>\n";
        echo "        <td>".$row["author"]."</td>\n";
        echo "        <td>".$row["description"]."</td>\n";

        echo "        <td>".$row["price"]."</td>\n";

        $sqlquery2 = "SELECT name from category where categoryid='".$row["cate-
gory"]."'";
        $queryresult2 = mysql_query($sqlquery2);
        if ($row2=mysql_fetch_array($queryresult2))
        {
        echo "        <td><a
href=\"visitor.php?category=".$row["category"]."\">".$row2["name"]."</td>\n";
        }
        else
        {
        echo " <td> Category missing !!</td>";
        }
        echo "    </tr>\n";
        }
        }

// --- If search criteria is All.

        else
        {
        if ( (stristr($row["name"],$search)) ||
```

```
(stristr($row["description"],$search)) ||
(stristr($row["author"],$search))
)
{
echo "   <tr>\n";

echo "      <td>".$row["productid"]."</td>\n";
echo "      <td>".$row["name"]."</td>\n";
echo "      <td>".$row["author"]."</td>\n";
echo "      <td>".$row["description"]."</td>\n";
echo "      <td>".$row["price"]."</td>\n";
$sqlquery2 = "SELECT name from category where categoryid='".$row["cate-
gory"]."'";
$queryresult2 = mysql_query($sqlquery2);
if ($row2=mysql_fetch_array($queryresult2))
{
echo "      <td><a
href=\"visitor.php?category=".$row["category"]."\">".$row2["name"]."</td>\n";

}
else
{
echo " <td> Category missing !!</td>";
}
echo "   </tr>\n";
}
}
}
echo "</table>\n";
?>
   </body>
   </html>
```

Let me now break this code down and explain what each part of the code does.

Verifying the $search *and* $searchfor *Variables*

Consider the following code snippet taken from the preceding code.

```php
<?php

// --- Checks whether or not the $search variable exists.

        if(!isset($search))
        {
        die("Search data not submitted!");
        }

// --- Checks whether or not the $search variable is empty.

        if(empty($search))
        {
        die("Search data empty!");
        }

// --- Checks whether or not the $searchfor variable exists.

        if(!isset($searchfor))
        {
        die("Search criteria not submitted!");
        }

// --- Checks whether or not the $searchfor variable is empty.

        if(empty($searchfor))
        {
        die("Search criteria empty!");
        }
```

Observe that in this code, first the code searches for whether the $search variable exists or not. The value of this variable is the text that the customer wants to search. For example, if the customer wants to search for the word gama in the products catalog, then the value that is assigned to the $search variable is gama. After searching for the existence of the $search variable, the code then searches whether the $search variable is empty or not. If the customer does not enter any value in the search text box and clicks on the Search button, then this message appears: "Search data not submitted".

After verifying the $search variable, the code then verifies the $searchfor variable. The value of the $searchfor variable is the search criteria that is selected by the customer. The value of the $searchfor variable can be Title, Author, or All.

Connecting to the MySQL Database and Retrieving the Results

Consider the following code snippet.

```
$connect= mysql_connect("localhost","root","")
or die("Could not connect to MySQL server in localhost !");
$selectdb=mysql_select_db("books")
or die("Could not select books data database !");
echo "<table width=700 border=1 align=center>";
echo " <tr>";
echo "  <td width=200> <center><b>Productid  </b></center></td>\n";
echo "  <td width=200> <center><b>Title</b></center></td>\n";
echo "  <td width=200> <center><b>Author</b></center></td>\n";
echo "  <td width=200> <center><b>Description</b></center></td>\n";
echo "  <td width=200> <center><b>Price</b></center></td>\n";
echo "  <td width=100> <center><b>Category</b></center></td>\n";
echo "  </tr>\n";
$sqlquery = "SELECT * from products";
$queryresult = mysql_query($sqlquery);
while ($row=mysql_fetch_array($queryresult))
{
// --- remaining part of the code here.
```

In this code snippet the code first connects to the MySQL server and selects the "books" database. From the "books" database the code then queries the products table to retrieve records that match with the search criteria.

Now that you have learned about the searchvisitor.php file, it is time to learn about the searchcustomer.php file.

Search Based on Criteria

Consider the following code snippet.

```php
// Search by using the title of the book.

        if ($searchfor="title")
        {
        if (stristr($row["name"],$search))
        {
        echo "  <tr>\n";

        echo "    <td>".$row["productid"]."</td>\n";

        echo "    <td>".$row["name"]."</td>\n";
        echo "    <td>".$row["author"]."</td>\n";
        echo "    <td>".$row["description"]."</td>\n";

        echo "    <td>".$row["price"]."</td>\n";
        $sqlquery2 = "SELECT name
        from category where categoryid='".$row["category"]."'";
        $queryresult2 = mysql_query($sqlquery2);
        if ($row2=mysql_fetch_array($queryresult2))
        {
        echo "    <td><a
href=\"visitor.php?category=".$row["category"]."\">".$row2["name"]."</td>\n";
}
        else
        {
        echo " <td> Category missing !!</td>";
        }
        echo "  </tr>\n";
        }
        }

// Search by using the author of the book.

        elseif ($searchfor="author")
        {
        if (stristr($row["author"],$search))
        {
        echo "  <tr>\n";
```

```
        echo "    <td>".$row["productid"]."</td>\n";


        echo "    <td>".$row["name"]."</td>\n";
        echo "    <td>".$row["author"]."</td>\n";
        echo "    <td>".$row["description"]."</td>\n";


        echo "    <td>".$row["price"]."</td>\n";


        $sqlquery2 = "SELECT name from category where categoryid='".$row["cate-
gory"]."'";
        $queryresult2 = mysql_query($sqlquery2);
        if ($row2=mysql_fetch_array($queryresult2))
        {
        echo "    <td><a
href=\"visitor.php?category=".$row["category"]."\">".$row2["name"]."</td>\n";
        }
        else
        {
        echo " <td> Category missing !!</td>";
        }
        echo "  </tr>\n";
        }
        }

// --- If search criteria is All.


        else
        {
        if ( (stristr($row["name"],$search)) ||
        (stristr($row["description"],$search)) ||
        (stristr($row["author"],$search))
        )
        {
        echo "  <tr>\n";


        echo "    <td>".$row["productid"]."</td>\n";
        echo "    <td>".$row["name"]."</td>\n";
        echo "    <td>".$row["author"]."</td>\n";
```

```
echo "    <td>".$row["description"]."</td>\n";
echo "    <td>".$row["price"]."</td>\n";
$sqlquery2 = "SELECT name from category where categoryid='".$row["cate-
gory"]."'";
$queryresult2 = mysql_query($sqlquery2);
if ($row2=mysql_fetch_array($queryresult2))
{
echo "    <td><a
href=\"visitor.php?category=".$row["category"]."\">".$row2["name"]."</td>\n";


}
else
{
echo " <td> Category missing !!</td>";
}
echo "   </tr>\n";
}
}
}
echo "</table>\n";
?>
    </body>
    </html>
```

In the preceding code snippet, if the search criteria ($searchfor) is Title, then the Title column returned by the products table is searched for a substring $search. The substring $search contains the value that is to be searched. If the substring is found, then the entire record is printed in the form of a table. The table row includes five columns from the products table, and the sixth column contains a link to the visitor.php file. This link is the category to which the book belongs.

The searchcustomer.php File

Just like you learned about the searchvisitor.php file, let us first look at the source code for the searchcustomer.php file.

```
<html>
<head>
<title>Search Page</title>
```

```
        </head>
        <body bgcolor="#FFFFFF" text="#000000">
    <?php

// --- Checks whether or not the $search variable exists.

        if(!isset($search))
        {
        die("Search data not submitted!");
        }

// --- Checks whether or not the $search variable is empty.

        if(empty($search))
        {
        die("Search data empty!");
        }

// --- Checks whether or not the $searchfor variable exists.

        if(!isset($searchfor))
        {
        die("Search criteria not submitted!");
        }

// --- Checks whether or not the $searchfor variable is empty.

        if(empty($searchfor))
        {
        die("Search criteria empty!");
        }

// --- Checks in the MySQL database. All the results are queried from the products
table

        $connect= mysql_connect("localhost","root","")
        or die("Could not connect to MySQL server in localhost !");
        $selectdb=mysql_select_db("books")
```

```php
        or die("Could not select books data database !");
        echo "<table width=700 border=1 align=center>";
        echo " <tr>";
        echo "  <td width=200> <center><b>Productid   </b></center></td>\n";
        echo "  <td width=200> <center><b>Title</b></center></td>\n";
        echo "  <td width=200> <center><b>Author</b></center></td>\n";
        echo "  <td width=200> <center><b>Description</b></center></td>\n";
        echo "  <td width=200> <center><b>Price</b></center></td>\n";
        echo "  <td width=100> <center><b>Category</b></center></td>\n";
        echo "  </tr>\n";
        $sqlquery = "SELECT * from products";
        $queryresult = mysql_query($sqlquery);
        while ($row=mysql_fetch_array($queryresult))
        {

// Search by using the title of the book.

        if ($searchfor="title")
        {
        if (stristr($row["name"],$search))
        {
        echo "  <tr>\n";

        echo "     <td>".$row["productid"]."</td>\n";

        echo "     <td>".$row["name"]."</td>\n";
        echo "     <td>".$row["author"]."</td>\n";
        echo "     <td>".$row["description"]."</td>\n";

        echo "     <td>".$row["price"]."</td>\n";
        $sqlquery2 = "SELECT name
        from category where categoryid='".$row["category"]."'";
        $queryresult2 = mysql_query($sqlquery2);
        if ($row2=mysql_fetch_array($queryresult2))
        {
        echo "     <td><a href=\"mainpage.php?customerid=" $customerid. "&catego-
ry=".$row["category"]."\">".$row2["name"]."</td>\n";
        }
```

```php
         else
         {
         echo " <td> Category missing !!</td>";
         }
         echo "   </tr>\n";
         }
         }


// Search by using the author of the book.

         elseif ($searchfor="author")
         {
         if (stristr($row["author"],$search))
         {
         echo "   <tr>\n";

         echo "      <td>".$row["productid"]."</td>\n";

         echo "      <td>".$row["name"]."</td>\n";
         echo "      <td>".$row["author"]."</td>\n";
         echo "      <td>".$row["description"]."</td>\n";

         echo "      <td>".$row["price"]."</td>\n";

         $sqlquery2 = "SELECT name from category where categoryid='".$row["cate-
gory"]."'";
         $queryresult2 = mysql_query($sqlquery2);
         if ($row2=mysql_fetch_array($queryresult2))
         {
         echo "      <td><a
href=\"visitor.php?category=".$row["category"]."\">".$row2["name"]."</td>\n";
         }
         else
         {
         echo " <td> Category missing !!</td>";
         }
         echo "   </tr>\n";
         }
```

```php
    }

// --- If search criteria is All.

    else
    {
    if ( (stristr($row["name"],$search)) ||
    (stristr($row["description"],$search)) ||
    (stristr($row["author"],$search))
    )
    {
    echo "   <tr>\n";

    echo "      <td>".$row["productid"]."</td>\n";
    echo "      <td>".$row["name"]."</td>\n";
    echo "      <td>".$row["author"]."</td>\n";
    echo "      <td>".$row["description"]."</td>\n";
    echo "      <td>".$row["price"]."</td>\n";
    $sqlquery2 = "SELECT name from category where categoryid='".$row["cate-
gory"]."'";
    $queryresult2 = mysql_query($sqlquery2);
    if ($row2=mysql_fetch_array($queryresult2))
    {
    echo "      <td><a href=\"mainpage.php?customerid=" $customerid. "&catego-
ry=".$row["category"]."\">".$row2["name"]."</td>\n";

    }
    else
    {
    echo " <td> Category missing !!</td>";
    }
    echo "   </tr>\n";
    }
    }
    }
    echo "</table>\n";
?>
    </body>
    </html>
```

Observe that the searchcustomer.php is quite similar to the searchvisitor.php file. However, there are two differences:

- ◆ The searchvisitor.php file has a link to the visitor.php file (Bukbuz, Inc. home page), while the searchcustomer.php file has a link to the main-page.php file (Product Catalog page).
- ◆ The searchvisitor.php includes only the category value, while the search-customer.php in addition to including the category value also includes the customerid value.

Links to Other Pages on the Product Catalog

You can access other pages of the Bukbuz, Inc. Web site from the Bukbuz, Inc. product catalog. There are several links in the Product Catalog page that direct you to other pages of the Bukbuz, Inc. Web site.

On the lower-left corner of the product catalog, there are two links: About Us and Feedback. When you click on the About Us link, a new window appears, as shown in Figure 14-12.

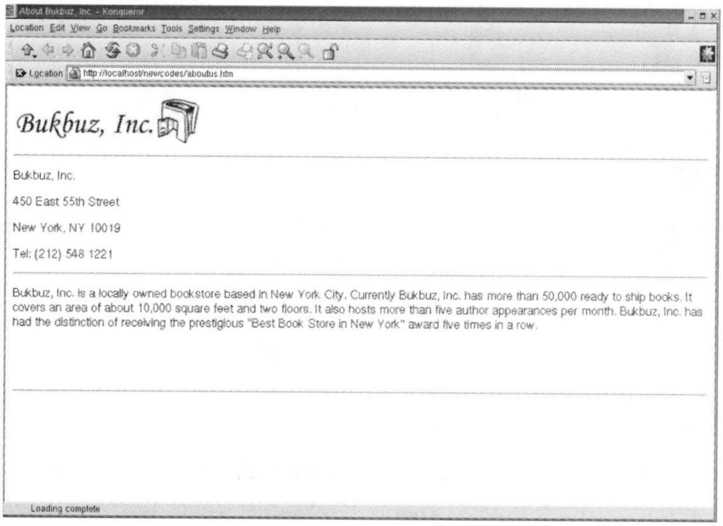

FIGURE 14-12   *The About Us page*

The About Us page displays information about Bukbuz, Inc. Following is the source code for the About Us page.

```
            <html>
            <head>
            <title>About Bukbuz, Inc.</title>
<meta http-equiv="Content-Type" content="text/html;
            charset=iso-8859-1">
            </head>
            <body bgcolor="#FFFFFF" text="#000000">
            <p><img src="Logo.jpg" width="264" height="63"></p>
            <hr>
            <p>About Bukbuz, Inc.!</p>
            <p>Bukbuz, Inc. is a locally owned book store located in New
            York City. Currently Bukbuz, Inc. has more than 50,000 ready-to-
            ship books. It covers an area of about 10,000 square feet and two
            floors. It also hosts more than five author appearances per month
            and has had the distinction of receiving the prestigious "Best
            Book Store in New York" award five times in a row.</p>
            <p> </p>
            <p></p>
            <p> </p>
            <hr>
            <p> </p>
            <p> </p>
            </body>
            </html>
```

The Feedback link, adjacent to the About Us link, opens the feedback form in a new window. The Feedback form contains two sections, one containing feedback questions and the other containing a suggestion box. Figure 14-13 displays the Feedback Web page.

The Personal Settings Link

There might be situations when customers would like to change their personal details. The Bukbuz, Inc. product catalog allows customers to update their personal information. For example, in case of a change of address, customers need to update their personal information on the site too. This is because books ordered on the Bukbuz, Inc. Web site are delivered to the address that is mentioned in the User Registration form. To do so, they need to click on the Personal Settings link on the right side of the product catalog. When a customer clicks on the Personal Settings link, a new window appears, as shown in Figure 14-14.

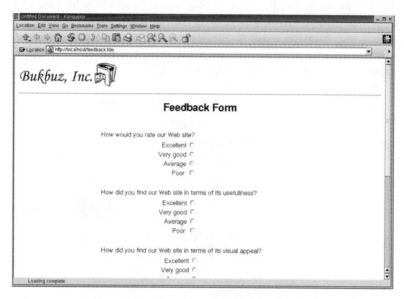

FIGURE 14-13 *The Feedback page*

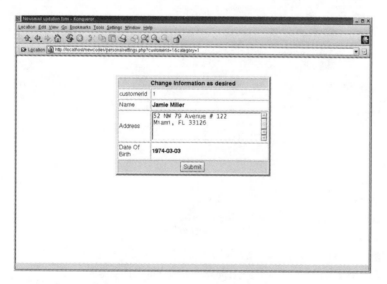

FIGURE 14-14 *Update Personal Settings window*

Notice that in this case the only field that can undergo a change is the address field. The e-mail field cannot be changed because it is also used as the login name for the site. In case users need to change their e-mail address field, then they need to notify the site administrator. They can do so by sending a mail to the administrator by using the feedback link on the Bukbuz, Inc. home page.

Following is the code for the personalsettings.php file.

```
<html>
<head>
<title>Newsmail updating form</title>
<meta http-equiv="Content-Type" content="text/html;

charset=iso-8859-1">
</head>

<body bgcolor="#FFFFFF" text="#000000">
<p> </p><form name="newsmailform" method="post"

action="update_customerinfo.php">
  <table width="250" border="5" align="center" cellpadding="3">
    <tr>
      <td colspan="2" bgcolor="#dddddd">
        <div align="center"><b>Change Information as

desired</b></div>
      </td>
    </tr>

<?php

$host="";
$uname="root";
$pass="";
$database="books";
$connection= mysql_connect($host,$uname,$pass)
   or die("Database connection failed ! <br>");

$result=mysql_select_db($database)
   or die("Database could not be selected");
```

```
$query = "SELECT * from customerinfo where customerid='"
.$customerid ."'";

$result = mysql_query($query);

if($row=mysql_fetch_array($result))
{
echo " <tr> ";
echo " <td> ";
echo " customerid";
echo " </td>\n";
echo " <td > ";
echo $row["customerid"];
echo "        </td>\n";
echo "     </tr>\n";
echo "<tr> \n";
echo " <td> ";
echo "   Name";
echo " </td>\n";
echo " <td><b> ";
echo  $row["name"];
echo " </b></td>\n";
echo " </tr>\n";
echo " <tr > ";
echo " <td > ";
echo "   Address";
echo " </td>\n";
echo " <td> ";
echo " <textarea name=\"address\" cols=30 rows=4>

".$row["address"]."</textarea>";
echo " </td>\n";
echo " </tr>\n";
echo "<tr > \n";
echo " <td> ";
echo "   Date Of Birth";
echo " </td>\n";
echo " <td><b> ";
```

```
        echo  $row["dob"];
        echo " <b></td>\n";
        echo " </tr>\n";
        echo "    <tr> ";
        echo "      <td colspan=\"2\" bgcolor=\"#dddddd\">\n ";
        echo "        <div align=\"center\"> \n";
        echo "          <input type=\"hidden\" name=\"customerid\"

    value=\"".$customerid."\">\n";
        echo "          <input type=\"submit\" name=\"Submit\"

    value=\"Submit\">\n";
        echo "          </div>\n";
        echo "        </td>";
        echo "</tr>\n";
        }
    ?>


        </table>
      </form>
    </body>
  </html>
```

This code allows the customers to update or modify their personal settings. However, as mentioned earlier, in the User Registration form, the only field that is most likely to undergo a change is the address field.

After making the required changes, the customer then needs to click on the Submit button to confirm the changes. When the Submit button is clicked, a window appears stating, "Address updated successfully," as shown in Figure 14-15.

After the address is successfully updated, the customer can click on the Back to website link to return to the Bukbuz, Inc. product catalog.

Let us now look at the administrative component of the Bukbuz, Inc. product catalog.

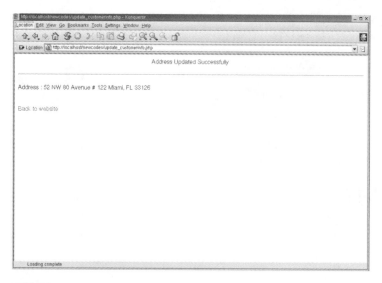

FIGURE 14-15 *Successfully updated address field*

The Administrative Component of the Bukbuz, Inc. Product Catalog

A proper administration and management of the product catalog determines its effectiveness and efficiency. The administrative component of the product catalog deals with sharing of information from various sources, maintaining and updating the databases, and adding or removing products from a product catalog.

Figure 14-16 displays the Administrator Page of the Bukbuz, Inc. Web site.

Observe that in the Administrator Page there are three categories, namely Products, Categories, and Customers. Under each category there are several links for the administrator. Using these links, the administrator can perform various functions on the product catalog.

Under the Products category, observe that there are three categories, namely:

◆ **Add Products:** Used to add products to the product catalog.

◆ **Remove Products:** Used to remove products from the product catalog.

◆ **Product Browser:** Used to browse products in the product catalog.

FIGURE 14-16 *Administrator Page*

Under Categories, the links are:

- ◆ **Add Categories:** Used to add categories to the product catalog.
- ◆ **Remove Categories:** Used to remove categories from the product catalog.
- ◆ **Category Browser:** Used to browse categories in the product catalog.

Under Customers, the links are:

- ◆ **Add Customers:** Used to add customers to the Bukbuz, Inc. database.
- ◆ **Remove Customers:** Used to remove customers from the Bukbuz, Inc. database.
- ◆ **Customer Browser:** Used to search for customers in the Bukbuz, Inc. database.

The Administrator Page is a simple HTML file, index.htm, which contains links for managing the complete product catalog. Before discussing each of these links in detail, let us first look at the source code for the Administrator Page.

```
<html>
<head>
<title>Administrator Page</title>
<meta http-equiv="Content-Type" content="text/html; charset=iso-8859-1">
```

```
          </head>
          <body bgcolor="#FFFFFF" text="#000000">
          <h1 align="center"><b>Administrator Page</b></h1>
          <table width="54%" border="0" align="center">
          <tr>
          <td><b>PRODUCTS</b></td>
          </tr>

// --- Link for adding products.

          <tr>
          <td><a href="addproducts.php">Add Products</a>, <a
href="removeproducts.php">Remove
          Products</a>, <a href="productbrowser.php">Product Browser</a></td>
          </tr>
          <tr>
          <td> </td>
          </tr>
          <tr>

// --- Link for adding Categories

          <td><b>CATEGORIES</b></td>
          </tr>
          <tr>
          <td><a href="addcat.php">Add Categories</a>, <a
href="removecat.php">Remove
          Categories</a>, <a href="categorybrowser.php">Category Browser</a></td>
          </tr>
          <tr>
          <td> </td>
          </tr>

// --- Link for adding Customers.

          <tr>
          <td><b>CUSTOMERS</b></td>
          </tr>
```

```
        <tr>
        <td><a href="../add_customer.htm" target="_blank">Add Customers</a>, <a
href="removecust.htm">Remove
        Customers</a>, <a href="browsecust.php">Customer Browser</a></td>
        </tr>
        <tr>
        <td> </td>
        </tr>


// --- Link for Pending orders.

        <tr>
        <td>
        <div align="center"><a href="pendingorders.php">Pending Orders</a></div>
        </td>
        </tr>
        <tr>
        <td> </td>
        </tr>


// --- Link to log out

        <tr>
        <td>
        <div align="center"><a href="logout.php"><b>Logout</b></a></div>
        </td>
        </tr>
        <table>
        </body>
        </html>
```

This code contains links to various files that the system administrator uses to manage the Bukbuz, Inc. product catalog. In this code the first link points to the file addproducts.php. The administrator will use this file to add products to the Bukbuz, Inc. product catalog.

Adding Products

In the Bukbuz, Inc. product catalog only the system administrator can add products to the product catalog. To do so, the administrator needs to use the Administrator Page. In the Administrator Page, under Products, there is a link Add Products. When the administrator clicks on the Add Products link, the Add Product form appears, as shown in Figure 14-17.

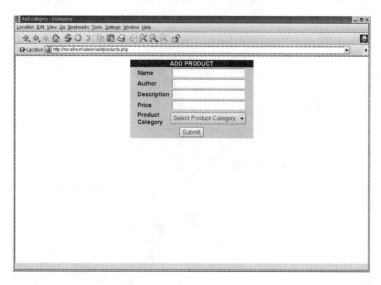

FIGURE 14-17 *Add Product form*

The Add Product form is a simple HTML form. Following is the source code for the Add Products form.

```
        <html>
        <head>
        <title>Add category</title>
<meta http-equiv="Content-Type" content="text/html; charset=iso-8859-1">
        </head>

        <body bgcolor="#FFFFFF" text="#000000">
        <table width="350" border="0" align="center" cellpadding="0" cellspac-
ing="0" height="70">
        <tr>
        <td bgcolor="#000000" height="14">
```

```
<div align="center"><b><font color="#FFFFFF">ADD PRODUCT</font></b></div>
</td>
</tr>
<tr>
<td width="48%" height="82" bgcolor="#CCCCCC">
<form name="form2" method="post" action="add.php">
<table width="75%" border="0" align="center">
<tr>
<input type="hidden" name="type" value="product" size="20">

<td width="36%"><b> Name</b></td>
<td width="64%">
<div align="center">
<input type="text" name="proname" size="20">
</div>
</td>
</tr>
<tr>
<td width="36%"><b> Author</b></td>
<td width="64%">
<div align="center">
<input type="text" name="proauthor" size="20">
</div>
</td>
<tr>

<tr>
<td width="36%"><b>Description</b></td>
<td width="64%">
<div align="center">
<input type="text" name="prodescription" size="20">
</div>
</td>
</tr>
<tr>
<td width="36%"><b>Price</b></td>
<td width="64%">
<div align="center">
```

```
                    <input type="text" name="proprice" size="20">
                    </div>
                    </td>
                    </tr>
                    <tr>
<td width="36%"><b>Product Category</b></td>
                    <td width="64%">
                    <div align="center">
                    <?php
                    $host="";
                    $username="root";
                    $password="";
                    $database="books";

                    $x=mysql_connect($host,$username,$password);
                    $x1=mysql_select_db($database);
                    $query="select categoryid,name from category";
                    $result=mysql_query($query);

                    echo "                    <select name=\"parentcategory\">";
                    echo "                     <option>Select Product Category</option>";
                    while($row=mysql_fetch_array($result))
                    {
                    echo "                     <option value=\"". $row["categoryid"]."\">" .
$row["name"] ."</option>";
                    }

                    ?>
                    </div>
                    </td>
                    </tr>
                    <tr>
                    <td colspan="2" height="2">
                    <div align="center">
                    <input type="submit" name="Submit2" value="Submit">
                    </div>
                    </td>
                    <tr>
```

```
</table>
</form>
</td>
</tr>
<table>
</body>
</html>
```

In the Add Product form, the administrator needs to fill in the information about the new product that will be added, as shown in Figure 14-18.

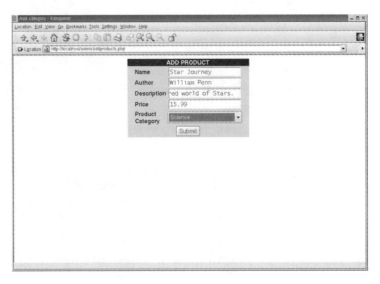

FIGURE 14-18 *Adding a new product*

After filling in all the details about the new book, the administrator needs to click the Submit button. When the administrator clicks on the Submit button, the details of the new book appear on the screen, as shown in Figure 14-19.

The add.php file parses all details of the new book that are entered by the administrator in the Add Products HTML form. The source code for the add.php file is given below.

```php
<?php
    $host="";
    $database="books";
    $dbusername="root";
```

```
$dbpassword="";

$x=mysql_connect($host,$dbusername,$dbpassword);
$x1=mysql_select_db($database);

if ($type=="category")
{
  echo"<table align=\"center\" border=1>";
  echo"<tr><td>Parent Category </td><td>".$parentcategory."</td></tr>";
  echo"<tr><td>Name </td><td>".$catname."</td></tr>";
  echo"<tr><td>Description </td><td>".$catdescription."</td></tr>";
  echo"</table><br><br>";

    $query="select categoryid from category where categoryid='".$parent-
category."'";
    $result=mysql_query($query);
    if($row=mysql_fetch_array($result))
    {
      $query2="INSERT into category
VALUES('','".$parentcategory."','".$catname."','".$catdescription."')";
      $result2=mysql_query($query2);
```

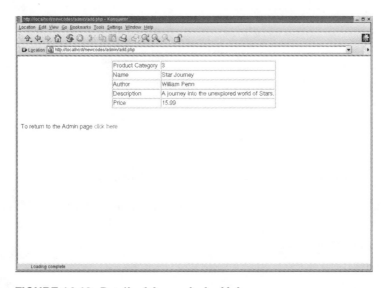

FIGURE 14-19 *Details of the new book added*

```
//     echo "Category added as <b>".$query."</b>\n";
      }
     else
     {
      echo "Parentcategory Does Not EXIST !!!";
     }
   }
   elseif($type=="product")
   {

     echo"<table align=\"center\" border=1>";
     echo"<tr><td>Product Category </td><td>".$parentcategory."</td></tr>";
     echo"<tr><td>Name </td><td>".$proname."</td></tr>";
     echo"<tr><td>Author </td><td>".$proauthor."</td></tr>";
     echo"<tr><td>Description </td><td>".$prodescription."</td></tr>";
     echo"<tr><td>Price </td><td>".$proprice."</td></tr>";
     echo"</table><br><br>";

     $query="INSERT into products VALUES('','".$proname."','".$proau-
thor."','".$prodescription."','".$proprice."','".$parentcategory."')";

     $result=mysql_query($query);
     //echo "Product added as<b> ".$query."</b>\n";
     }
     else
     {
      echo "type should be product/category. But it was ".$type. " !!!";
     }

   ?>
     <br>
     To return to the Admin page <A href="index.htm">click here</a>
```

This code adds the details of the new books to the products table in the "books" database.

Removing Products

In the same way an administrator can add products to the product catalog, an administrator can also remove products from it. To remove products from the product catalog, the administrator needs to click on the Remove Products link in the Administrator Page. The Remove Products link opens two HTML forms in the same window, as shown in Figure 14-20.

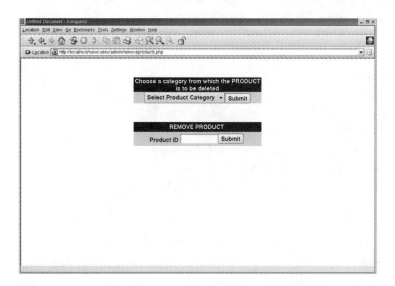

FIGURE 14-20 *Remove products from the product catalog*

Following is the source code for the removeproducts.php file.

```
<html>
<head>
<title>Untitled Document</title>
<meta http-equiv="Content-Type" content="text/html; charset=iso-8859-1">
</head>

<body bgcolor="#FFFFFF" text="#000000">
<p> </p>
<table width="37%" border="0" align="center" cellpadding="0" cellspac-
ing="0" height="66">
<tr>
<td bgcolor="#000000" height="10">
```

```
<div align="center"><b><font color="#FFFFFF">Choose a category from which
the PRODUCT is to be deleted</font></b></div>
</td>
</tr>
<tr>
<td bgcolor="#CCCCCC" height="17">
<form name="form3" method="post" action="catprobrowser.php">
<p align="center"><b>

<?php
$database="books";
$host="";
$username="root";
$password="";
 $x=mysql_connect($host,$username,$password);
 $x1=mysql_select_db($database);
 $query="select categoryid,name from category";
 $result=mysql_query($query);

 echo " <select name=\"categoryid\">\n";
 echo "  <option value=\"0\">Select Product Category</option>\n";
 while($row=mysql_fetch_array($result))
 {
  echo " <option value=\"". $row["categoryid"]."\">".$row["name"]
."</option>\n";
 }
 echo " </select>";
?>
<input type="submit" name="Submit32" value="Submit">
</b></p>
</form>
</td>
</tr>
</table>
<p> </p>
<table width="37%" border="0" align="center" cellpadding="0" cellspac-
ing="0" height="66">
    <tr>
```

```
        <td bgcolor="#000000" height="10">
        <div align="center"><b><font color="#FFFFFF">REMOVE PRODUCT
</font></b></div>
        </td>
        </tr>
        <tr>
        <td bgcolor="#CCCCCC" height="17">
<form name="form3" method="post" action="deleteproduct.php">
        <p align="center"><b>Product ID
<input type="text" name="productid" size="10">
        <input type="submit" name="Submit3" value="Submit">
        </b></p>
        </form>
        </td>
          </tr>
</table>
        <p> </p>
        <p> </p>
        </body>
        </html>
```

This code generates the two Remove Products forms. The administrator can choose either of these two forms for removing products from the product catalog.

In the first form, the administrator chooses a category from which the product has to be deleted. After choosing a category from the category drop-down list, the administrator then needs to click on the Submit button. When the Submit button is clicked, the form submits the requested information to the catprobrowser.php file. The catprobrowser.php displays all the products of the submitted category, as shown in Figure 14-21.

As can be seen, the catprobrowser.php file displays all products that fall in the category that is selected by the administrator, in this case Science, in the table. The last column of the table contains the delete option against each row. To delete the specified book, the administrator needs to click the corresponding delete option.

Following is the source code of the catprobrowser.php file.

```
        <html>
        <head>
        <title>maildata record browser</title>
```

```
</head>

<body bgcolor="#FFFFFF" text="#000000">

<?php

$connect= mysql_connect("localhost","root","")
    or die("Could not connect to MySQL server in localhost !");

$selectdb=mysql_select_db("books")
    or die("Could not select books data database !");

$sqlquery = "SELECT * from products where category='".$categoryid ."'";

$queryresult = mysql_query($sqlquery);

echo "<table width=700 border=1 align=center>";
echo " <tr>";
echo "  <td width=200> <center><b>Product ID </b></center></td>\n";
echo "  <td width=200> <center><b>Name </b></center></td>\n";
echo "  <td width=200> <center><b>Description</b></center></td>\n";
echo "  <td width=100> <center><b>Price</b></center></td>\n";
```

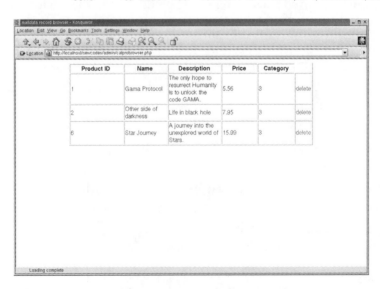

FIGURE 14-21 *Products under the selected category*

```
        echo "   <td width=100> <center><b>Category</b></center></td>\n";

        echo "   </tr>\n";
        while ($row=mysql_fetch_array($queryresult))
        {
        echo "   <tr>\n";
        echo "      <td>".$row["productid"]."</td>\n";
        echo "      <td>".$row["name"]."</td>\n";
        echo "      <td>".$row["description"]."</td>\n";
        echo "      <td>".$row["price"]."</td>\n";

        $sqlquery2 = "SELECT name from category where categoryid='".$categoryid
."'";

$queryresult2 = mysql_query($sqlquery);
        if($row2=mysql_fetch_array($queryresult2))
        {
        echo "      <td>".$row["category"]."</td>\n";
        }
        else
        {
        echo " Category name not found !!";
        }
        echo "      <td><A href=\"deleteproduct.php?productid=".$row["produc-
tid"]."\">delete</a></td>\n";
        echo "   </tr>\n";
        }
        echo "</table>\n";
        ?>
        </body>
        </html>
```

In this way the administrator can remove products from the product catalog. However, suppose the administrator does not remember the category to which the book belongs but has a list that tells about the product ID of the book. In such a case, the administrator can use the second form on the same page.

The second form accepts the product ID values. To remove a product, the administrator enters the product ID of the book and clicks on the Submit button. When the Submit button is clicked, the form is submitted to the deleteproduct.php file. The deleteproduct.php file removes data from the database and updates the tables, as shown in Figure 14-22.

FIGURE 14-22 *Updating of tables after the products are removed*

Following is the source code for the deleteproduct.php file.

```
<html>
<head>
<title>Delete Product        </title>
<meta http-equiv="Content-Type" content="text/html; charset=iso-8859-1">
</head>

<body bgcolor="#FFFFFF" text="#000000">

<?php
if(!isset($productid))
{
die("Product ID not submitted !");
}


if(empty($productid))
{
```

```php
  die("Product ID empty !");
}

$host="";
$username="root";
$password="";
$database="books";

$x=mysql_connect($host,$username,$password);
$x1=mysql_select_db($database);

$query="delete from products where productid ='".$productid."'";
$result=mysql_query($query);
if($result)
{
  echo "Product record deleted from Products table.<br>\n";
}
else
{
  echo "Product record not found in Products table !<br>\n";
}

echo " Product record in Orders table left Intact !<br>";

?>

<br><br>

To return to Admin page <A href="index.htm"> Click here! </a>
<br><br>

</body>
</html>
```

In this way the administrator can remove a product from a product catalog. Let us now look at the product browser.

Product Browser

The product browser is used by the administrator to view products in a product catalog. When the administrator clicks on the Product Browser link on the Administrator Page, a window appears displaying a list of all books that are available, as shown in Figure 14-23.

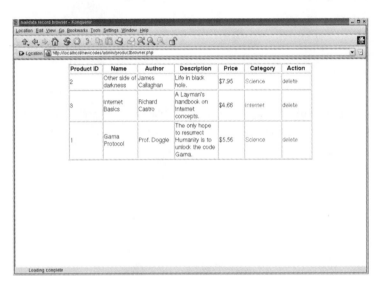

FIGURE 14-23 *Product browser window*

The Product Browser link on the Administrator Page points to the product-browser.php file. This file reads all records from the products table and displays them in the browser window. Following is the source code for the product-browser.php file.

```
<html>
<head>
<title>maildata record browser</title>
</head>
<body bgcolor="#FFFFFF" text="#000000">

<?php

$connect= mysql_connect("localhost","root","")
    or die("Could not connect to MySQL server in localhost !");
```

```php
$selectdb=mysql_select_db("books")
    or die("Could not select books data database !");
$sqlquery = "SELECT * from products";
$queryresult = mysql_query($sqlquery);

echo "<table width=700 border=1 align=center>";
echo " <tr>";
echo "   <td width=200> <center><b>Product ID </b></center></td>\n";
echo "   <td width=200> <center><b>Name </b></center></td>\n";
echo "   <td width=200> <center><b>Author </b></center></td>\n";
echo "   <td width=200> <center><b>Description</b></center></td>\n";
echo "   <td width=100> <center><b>Price</b></center></td>\n";
echo "   <td width=100> <center><b>Category</b></center></td>\n";
echo "   <td width=100> <center><b>Action</b></center></td>\n";

echo "  </tr>\n";
while ($row=mysql_fetch_array($queryresult))
    {

    echo "  <tr>\n";
    echo "     <td>".$row["productid"]."</td>\n";
    echo "     <td>".$row["name"]."</td>\n";
    echo "     <td>".$row["author"]."</td>\n";
    echo "     <td>".$row["description"]."</td>\n";
    echo "     <td>".$row["price"]."</td>\n";

    $sqlquery2 = "SELECT name from category where categoryid='".$row["cate-
gory"]."'";
    $queryresult2 = mysql_query($sqlquery2);
    if ($row2=mysql_fetch_array($queryresult2))
    {
    echo "     <td><A href=\"catprobrowser.php?categoryid=".$row["catego-
ry"]."\">".$row2["name"]."</a></td>\n";
    }
    echo "     <td><A href=\"deleteproduct.php?productid=".$row["produc-
tid"]."\">delete</a></td>\n";
    echo "  </tr>\n";
    }
```

```
        echo "</table>\n";
    ?>
        </body>
        </html>
```

The productbrowser.php file also contains two links. The first link is the Category ID to which the product belongs. By using this link, the administrator can view all books that fall under that category. The second link is the Delete link, which points to the deleteproduct.php file. This link carries the product ID of its corresponding product by using the GET method and submits it to the deleteproduct.php file.

Let us now discuss how an administrator can add, remove, or browse categories.

Adding Categories

To add a category to the product catalog, the system administrator clicks on the Add Category link. When the Add Category link is clicked, the addcat.php file displays the Add Category form, as shown in Figure 14-24.

FIGURE 14-24 *The Add Category form*

The administrator can choose a category under the root category, which is home, or can choose a parent category to place the category in it. If the newly created category ID is placed in an already existing category, then it is known as a subcategory.

Following is the source code for the addcat.php file.

```
<html>
<head>
<title>Add category</title>
<meta http-equiv="Content-Type" content="text/html; charset=iso-8859-1">
</head>
<body bgcolor="#FFFFFF" text="#000000">
<table width="350" border="0" align="center" cellpadding="0" cellspac-
ing="0" height="277">
<tr>
<td bgcolor="#000000" height="2">
<div align="center"><b><font color="#FFFFFF">ADD
CATEGORY</font></b></div>
</td>
</tr>

<tr>
<td width="48%" height="121" bgcolor="#CCCCCC">
<form name="form1" method="post" action="add.php?type=category">
<table width="75%" border="0" align="center">
<tr>
<td width="36%"><b> Name</b></td>
<td width="64%">
<div align="center">
<input type="text" name="catname" size="20">
</div>
</td>
</tr>

<tr>
<td width="36%"><b>Description</b></td>
<td width="64%">
<div align="center">
<input type="text" name="catdescription" size="20">
</div>
```

```
        </td>
      </tr>

      <tr>
      <td width="36%"><b> Parent Category</b></td>
      <td width="64%">
      <div align="center">

<?php
      $host="";
      $username="root";
      $password="";
      $database="books";
      $x=mysql_connect($host,$username,$password);
      $x1=mysql_select_db($database);
      $query="select name,categoryid from category";
      $result=mysql_query($query);
      echo "                 <select name=\"parentcategory\">";
      echo "                  <option>Select Product Category</option>";
      while($row=mysql_fetch_array($result))
      {
      echo "                  <option value=\"".
$row["categoryid"]."\">".$row["name"] ." </option>";
      }
   ?>
      </div>
      <td>
      </tr>
      <tr>
      <td colspan="2">
      <div align="center">
      <input type="submit" name="Submit22" value="Submit">
      </div>
      </td>
      </tr>
      </table>
      </form>
      </td>
```

```
        </tr>
        </table>
        </body>
        </html>
```

Removing Categories

Removing categories from a product catalog is quite similar to removing products from a product catalog. To remove a category, the administrator clicks on the Remove Category link in the Administrator Page. When the Remove Category link is clicked, the removecat.php file displays two forms in the browser window.

Let me first discuss the source code of the removecat.php file.

```
        <html>
        <head>
        <title>Untitled Document</title>
        <meta http-equiv="Content-Type" content="text/html; charset=iso-8859-1">
        </head>

        <body bgcolor="#FFFFFF" text="#000000">
        <p> </p>
        <table width="37%" border="0" align="center" cellpadding="0" cellspac-
ing="0" height="66">
        <tr>
        <td bgcolor="#000000" height="2">
        <div align="center"><b><font color="#FFFFFF">Choose a category to
REMOVE!</font></b></div>
        </td>
        </tr>
        <tr>
        <td bgcolor="#CCCCCC" height="17">
        <form name="form3" method="post" action="deletecategory.php">
        <p align="center"><b>
        <?php
         $host="";
         $username="root";
         $password="";
         $database="books";
```

```php
$x=mysql_connect($host,$username,$password);
$x1=mysql_select_db($database);
$query="select categoryid,name from category";
$result=mysql_query($query);

echo " <select name=\"categoryid\">\n";
echo "  <option value=\"0\">Choose a category to delete</option>\n";
while($row=mysql_fetch_array($result))
{
 echo " <option value=\"". $row["categoryid"]."\">".$row["name"]
."</option>\n";
}
echo " </select>";
?>
<input type="submit" name="Submit32" value="Submit">
</b></p>
</form>
</td>
</tr>
</table>
<p> </p>
<table width="37%" border="0" align="center" cellpadding="0" cellspac-
ing="0" height="66">
<tr>
<td bgcolor="#000000" height="10">
<div align="center"><b><font color="#FFFFFF">REMOVE CATEGORY
</font></b></div>
</td>
</tr>

<tr>
<td bgcolor="#CCCCCC" height="17">
<form name="form3" method="post" action="deletecategory.php">
<p align="center"><b>Product ID
<input type="text" name="categoryid" size="10">
<input type="submit" name="Submit3" value="Submit">
</b></p>
</form>
```

```
</td>
</tr>
table>

p> </p>
p> </p>
body>
<html>
```

As mentioned above, the removecat.php displays two forms, in the same window, for removing categories from the product catalog. By using the first form, the administrator can remove categories by selecting the name of the category from the drop-down list. When using the second form, the administrator can remove the categories by entering the category ID. However, both these forms submit the requested information to the deletecategory.php file.

The deletecategory.php File

The deletecategory.php file performs the following functions:

◆ It checks for the existence of the $categoryID variable. If the variable is not found, then the program exists.

◆ It checks if $categoryID is an empty variable or not. If the variable is found empty, the program terminates.

◆ It checks if $categoryID is less than 2. If categoryid is less than 2, then the program terminates. This check prevents the deletion of the home directory.

◆ It establishes a connection with the database and passes a query that returns the parent category ID of the category to be deleted. This parent category is stored in a variable called $parentcategoryID. If the database does not return a parent category for the category to be deleted, the program quits.

◆ After retrieving the $parentcategoryID values, it queries again for the subcategories of this category. For each subcategory retrieved, the file updates the parent category from the original $categoryID to $parentcategoryID. If the file is unable to update the parent category for any of the records, the program quits.

◆ The program searches for a record in the category table, where the category ID is the one that was submitted to deletecategory.php using the POST or GET method.

Following is the source code for the deletecategory.php.

```
<html>
<head>
<title>    Delete Category    </title>
<meta http-equiv="Content-Type" content="text/html; charset=iso-8859-1">
</head>

<body bgcolor="#FFFFFF" text="#000000">
<?php
 if(!isset($categoryid))
 {
  die("category ID not submitted !");
 }

 if(empty($categoryid))
 {
  die("category ID empty !");
 }
 if($categoryid<2)
 {
  die("Sorry this category can't be deleted !");
 }
 $host="";
 $username="root";
 $password="";
 $database="books";

 $x=mysql_connect($host,$username,$password);
 $x1=mysql_select_db($database);

 $query="select parentcategoryid from category where categoryid
='".$categoryid."'";
 $result=mysql_query($query);
 {
```

```php
        if($row=mysql_fetch_array($result))
          {
$parentcategoryid=$row["parentcategoryid"];
}
else
{
die("Parent Not Found!!!");
}
}
    $query="select * from category where parentcategoryid ='".$catego-
ryid."'";

    $result=mysql_query($query);
    while($row=mysql_fetch_row($result))
{
$query2="Update category SET parentcategoryid='".$parentcategoryid."'
where parentcategoryid='".$categoryid."'";
$result2=mysql_query($query2);
if(!$result2)
{
die("Tree shift failed !! <br>");
}
else
{
echo "Successfully shifted tree<br>";
}
}
$query="delete from category where categoryid ='".$categoryid."'";
 $result=mysql_query($query);
 if($result)
 {
echo "category record deleted from category table.<br>\n";
}
 else
 {
echo "category record not found in category table !<br>\n";
}
?>
```

```
<br><br>
To return to Admin page <A href="index.htm"> Click here! </a>
<br><br>
</body>
</html>
```

Category Browser

The administrator uses the Category Browser link in the administrator table to browse through all categories of the product catalog. When the administrator clicks on the Category Browser link, the categorybrowser.php file displays all the records from the category table, as shown in Figure 14-25.

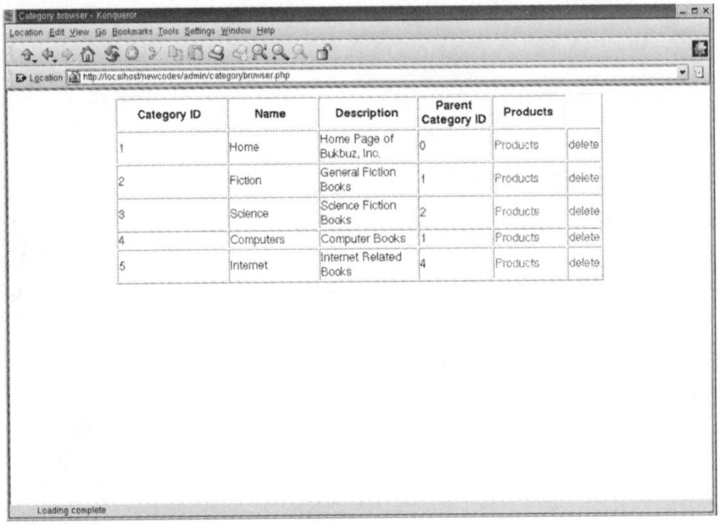

FIGURE 14-25 *Category Browser*

In addition, it also contains the links for products under the different categories. When the administrator clicks on the product link corresponding to a category, all the products that are placed under this category are displayed.

Following is the source code for the categorybrowser.php file.

```
<html>
<head>
<title>Category browser</title>
```

```
        </head>

        <body bgcolor="#FFFFFF" text="#000000">

        <?php

        $connect= mysql_connect("localhost","root","")
            or die("Could not connect to MySQL server in localhost !");

        $selectdb=mysql_select_db("books")
            or die("Could not select books data database !");

        $sqlquery = "SELECT * from category";

        $queryresult = mysql_query($sqlquery);

        echo "<table width=700 border=1 align=center>";
        echo " <tr>";
        echo "  <td width=200> <center><b>category ID </b></center></td>\n";
        echo "  <td width=200> <center><b>Name </b></center></td>\n";
        echo "  <td width=200> <center><b>Description</b></center></td>\n";
        echo "  <td width=100> <center><b>Parent</b></center></td>\n";
        echo "  <td width=100> <center><b>Products</b></center></td>\n";
        echo " </tr>\n";
        while ($row=mysql_fetch_array($queryresult))
        {
        echo " <tr>\n";
        echo "    <td>".$row["categoryid"]."</td>\n";
        echo "    <td>".$row["name"]."</td>\n";
        echo "    <td>".$row["description"]."</td>\n";
        echo "    <td>".$row["parentcategoryid"]."</td>\n";
        $sqlquery2 = "SELECT name,categoryid from category where catego-
ryid='".$row["categoryid"]."'";
        $queryresult2 = mysql_query($sqlquery2);
        if ($row2=mysql_fetch_array($queryresult2))
        {
        echo "    <td><A href=\"catprobrowser.php?categoryid=".$row["catego-
ryid"]."\">Products</a></td>\n";
```

```
            }
            echo "    <td><A href=\"deletecategory.php?categoryid=".$row["catego-
ryid"]."\">delete</a></td>\n";
            echo "  </tr>\n";
            }
            echo "</table>\n";
        ?>


        </body>
        </html>
```

Adding Customers

You have already seen the process of user registration in the earlier topics. An administrator can also register customers for the Bukbuz, Inc. Web site by clicking on the Add Customers link on the Administrator Page. This link points to the add_customer.php file. Thus when the administrator clicks on the Add Customers link, the User Registration form appears. The administrator can then fill in all the details and register a user.

Removing Customers

To remove a customer, the administrator needs to simply click on the Remove Customers link on the Administrator Page. When the Remove Customers link is clicked, the removecust.htm file displays the Remove Customer form, as shown in Figure 14-26.

The source code for the removecust.htm file is given below.

```
        <html>
        <head>
        <title>Remove Customer</title>
        <meta http-equiv="Content-Type" content="text/html; charset=iso-8859-1">
        </head>

        <body bgcolor="#FFFFFF" text="#000000">
        <p> </p>
        <p> </p>
        <table width="37%" border="0" align="center" cellpadding="0" cellspac-
```

```
ing="0" height="66">
            <tr>
        <td bgcolor="#000000" height="10">
        <div align="center"><b><font color="#FFFFFF">Remove a customer from cus-
tomerinfo/login</font></b></div>
        </td>
        </tr>
        <tr>
        <td bgcolor="#CCCCCC" height="17">
        <form name="form3" method="post" action="deletecustomer.php">
        <p align="center"><b>customer ID
        <input type="text" name="customerid" size="10">
        <input type="submit" name="Submit3" value="Submit">
        </b></p>
        </form>
        </td>
        </tr>
        </table>
        <p> </p>
        <p> </p>
        </body>
        </html>
```

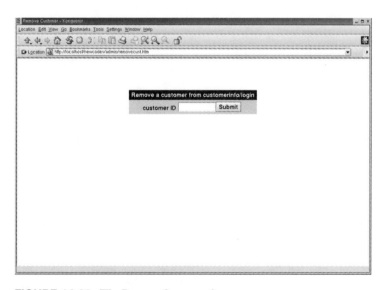

FIGURE 14-26 *The Remove Customer form*

When the administrator enters the customer ID and clicks on the Submit button, the customer ID value goes to the deletecustomer.php file. The deletecustomer.php file performs the following functions:

◆ Checks for the existence of the $customerid value by using the ISSET method. If the $customerid is not found, the program terminates.

◆ Checks whether the $customerid variable is empty or not. If the variable is empty, the program quits.

◆ Queries the "books" database and deletes all records from the customerinfo table that contain the customer ID, which is to be deleted. The program displays an error message or a success message on failure or success of this query.

◆ Queries to delete all the authentication information. The SQL query deletes that record from the login table, which contains this customer ID.

◆ Queries to delete all mail information for this customer ID. The SQL query removes records from the newsmail table containing the customer ID.

◆ Deletes the current shipping cart of this customer ID. All records for this customer ID are deleted in the neworders table.

Figure 14-27 displays the output of the deletecustomer.php file.

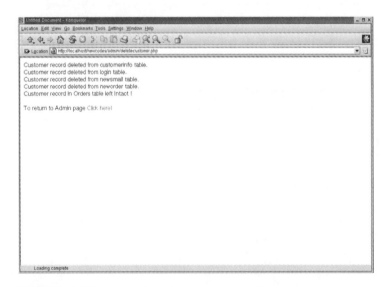

FIGURE 14-27 *Output of the deletecustomer.php file*

Following is the source code of the deletecustomer.php file.

```
<html>
<head>
<title>Untitled Document</title>
<meta http-equiv="Content-Type" content="text/html; charset=iso-8859-1">
</head>
<body bgcolor="#FFFFFF" text="#000000">

<?php
if(!isset($customerid))
{
die("Customer ID not submitted !");
}
if(empty($customerid))
{
die("Customer ID empty !");
}
$host="";
$username="root";
$password="";
$database="books";
$x=mysql_connect($host,$username,$password);
$x1=mysql_select_db($database);
$query="delete from customerinfo where customerid ='".$customerid."'";
$result=mysql_query($query);
if($result)
{
echo "Customer record deleted from customerinfo table.<br>\n";
}
else
{
echo "Customer record not found in customerinfo !<br>\n";
}
$query="delete from login where customerid ='".$customerid."'";
$result=mysql_query($query);
if($result)
{
```

```
echo "Customer record deleted from login table.<br>\n";
}
else
{
echo "Customer record not found in login table !<br>\n";
}
$query="delete from newsmail where customerid ='".$customerid."'";
$result=mysql_query($query);
if($result)
{
echo "Customer record deleted from newsmail table.<br>\n";
}
else
{
echo "Customer record not found in newsmail table !<br>\n";
}
$query="delete from neworder where customerid ='".$customerid."'";
 $result=mysql_query($query);
if($result)
{
echo "Customer record deleted from neworder table.<br>\n";
}
else
{
echo "Customer record not found in neworder table !<br>\n";
}
echo "Customer record in Orders table left Intact !<br>";
?>

<br><br>
To return to Admin page <A href="index.htm"> Click here! </a>
<br><br>
</body>
</html>
```

In addition to the management of products and categories, the administrator can also find out the status of the orders that the customers have placed. For this the administrator needs to click on the Pending Orders link.

Pending Orders

The task of managing customer orders at Bukbuz, Inc. lies with the administrator of the Bukbuz, Inc. Web site. Knowing the status of orders helps in clearing off the backlogs and in the timely delivery of products.

To know all the orders that are pending, the administrator needs to click on the Pending Orders link in the Administrator Page. When the administrator clicks on the Pending Orders link, the pendingorders.php file opens the Pending Orders page, as shown in Figure 14-28.

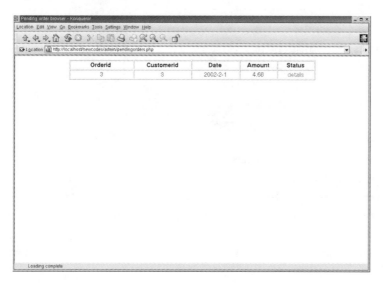

FIGURE 14-28 *Pending Orders information page*

Following is the source code for the pendingorders.php file.

```
<head>
<title>Pending order browser</title>
</head>
<body bgcolor="#FFFFFF" text="#000000">

<?php
$connect= mysql_connect("localhost","root","")
or die("Could not connect to MySQL server in localhost !");
$selectdb=mysql_select_db("books")
or die("Could not select books data database !");
```

```
$sqlquery = "SELECT * from orders";
        $queryresult = mysql_query($sqlquery);

        echo "<table width=700 border=1 align=center>";
        echo " <tr>";
        echo "  <td width=200> <center><b>Orderid   </b></center></td>\n";
        echo "  <td width=200> <center><b>Customerid</b></center></td>\n";
        echo "  <td width=200> <center><b>Date</b></center></td>\n";
        echo "  <td width=100> <center><b>Amount</b></center></td>\n";
        echo "  <td width=100> <center><b>Status</b></center></td>\n";
        echo " </tr>\n";
        while ($row=mysql_fetch_array($queryresult))

        {
        if ($row["status"]=="Pending")
        {
        echo " <tr>\n";
        echo "    <td><center>".$row["orderid"]   ."</center></td>\n";
        echo "    <td><center>".$row["customerid"]."</center></td>\n";
        echo "    <td><center>".$row["orderdate"] ."</center></td>\n";
        echo "    <td><center>".$row["price"]     ."</center></td>\n";
        echo "    <td><center><A
href=\"orderdetails.php?orderid=".$row["orderid"]."\">details</a></center></td>\n";
        echo " </tr>\n";
        }
        }
        echo "</table>\n";
    ?>
        </body>
        </html>
```

The preceding code gives information about various pending orders that have been placed by customers. Observe that in the Status column there exists a link, named details. When you click on this link, the order ID from the pending-order.php file is passed to the orderdetails.php file. Figure 14-29 displays the product invoice generated from the orderdetails.php file.

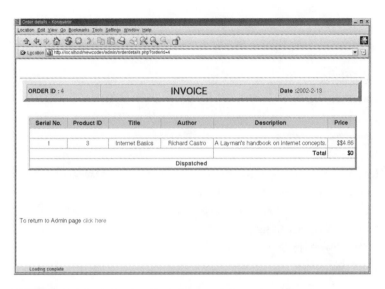

FIGURE 14-29 *Order Details and Status Information page*

The orderdetails.php File

The orderdetails.php file performs the following functions:

◆ Accepts the orderid value from the pendingorders.php file.

◆ Queries the orders table to extract all columns for this order ID record.

◆ Queries the products_ordered table to retrieve all product IDs with this order ID.

◆ Queries the products table to retrieve all columns, except the Category column, for each product ID retrieved.

◆ Calculates the total price from the Price column.

Following is the complete source code for orderdetails.php.

```
<html>
<head>
<title>Order details</title>
<meta http-equiv="Content-Type" content="text/html; charset=iso-8859-1">
</head>
<body bgcolor="#FFFFFF" text="#000000">
<p> </p>
<hr>
```

```
<table width="950" border="10" align="center" cellspacing="1" cell-
padding="3">

    <?php
    $database="books";
    $hostname="";
    $dbusername="root";
    $dbpassword="";
    $connect=mysql_connect($hostname,$dbusername,$dbpassword);
    $dbselect=mysql_select_db($database);
    $query="select * from orders where orderid='".$orderid."'";
    $result=mysql_query($query);
    if($row=mysql_fetch_array($result))

     echo "<tr bgcolor=\"#dddddd\">";
     echo "<td><b>ORDER ID  :</b> ".$orderid." </td>";
     echo "<td width=500><center><h1> INVOICE</h1></center> </td>";
     echo "<td><b>Date :</b>".$row["orderdate"]."</td>";
     echo "</tr>";
    }
   ?>

    </table>


    <table width="950" border="0" align="center" cellspacing="1" cell-
padding="3">
      <tr>
        <td width="85%" height="229">
           <table width="100%" border="5" align="center" cellspacing="0"
cellpadding="3">
      <tr bgcolor=#cccccc>
      <td ><center><b>Serial No.</b></center></td>
      <td ><center><b>Product ID</b></center></td>
      <td ><center><b>Title</b></center>   </td>
      <td ><center><b>Author</b></center> </td>
      <td width="200">
      <center><b>Description</b></center>
      </td>
```

```
<td>
<center><b>Price</b></center>
</td>
</tr>
<tr>
<td colspan="6"> </td>
</tr>
<?php

//--display detailed product listing for all products in the shopping cart.

$query="select productid from products_ordered where
orderid='".$orderid."'";
$result=mysql_query($query);
while($row=mysql_fetch_array($result))
{
$proquery="select productid,name,author,price,description from products
where productid='".$row["productid"]."'";
$proresult=mysql_query($proquery);
if($pro=mysql_fetch_array($proresult))
{

echo " <tr> ";
echo "     <td > ";
echo "      <center>" .  ++$serialcount . "</center>";
echo "     </td>";
echo "     <td><center>".$pro["productid"]."</center></td>";
echo "     <td><center>".$pro["name"]."</center></td>";
echo "     <td><center>".$pro["author"]."</center></td>";
echo "     <td> ";
echo "      <center>".$pro["description"] . "</center>";
echo "     </td>";
echo "     <td> ";
echo "       <div align=\"right\"> $".$pro["price"]."</div>";
echo "     </td>";
echo " </tr>";

$carttotal+=$pro["price"];
```

```php
        }
        }

        echo "     <tr> ";
        echo "        <td colspan=\"4\"> </td>";
        echo "        <td align=\"right\" ><b>Total</b></td>";
        echo "        <td > ";
        echo "           <div align=\"right\"><b>$".$carttotal."</b></div>";
        echo "        </td>";
        echo "  </tr>";
?>


        <tr>
          <td colspan="7" >
        <center>

<?php
        echo "    <A href=\"updateorderstatus.php?orderid=".$orderid."&status=dis-
patched\">";
        ?>


        <b>Dispatched</b></a>
        </center>
        </td>
        </tr>
        </table>
        </form>
        </td>
        </tr>
        </table>
        <p> </p>
        <p> </p>
        To return to Admin page <A href="index.htm"> click here</a>
        </body>
        </html>
        <html>
```

Summary

In this chapter you learned how to create an online shopping cart. You learned that to attract and retain customers, a Web site needs to have a comprehensive yet flexible product catalog. You also learned about the components of the Bukbuz, Inc. product catalog, namely the following:

◆ Categories section

◆ Search

◆ Links to other pages

◆ Administrative component

Then you learned how to enable the search feature and perform searches on different criteria. Next you learned to view other pages of the Web site by using links. Finally, you learned about the administrative component of the product catalog, which includes adding, removing, and browsing through products, categories, and customers.

Chapter 15

Shopping Carts

The Internet has completely redefined the meaning of shopping. Nowadays, you do not need to physically go to a department store to make your purchases. All you need to do is log on to the Internet, browse through a Web site, add selected products to your shopping cart, and place your order. The shopping cart is one of the most popular applications on the Internet today, due to its widespread use. It is helpful not only to customers but also to vendors. It allows vendors to display their products to users worldwide instead of just to the local population—and to do that without incurring any additional costs.

In the previous project, you learned to create a product catalog. In this chapter I will discuss how to create a shopping cart and add or remove selected products from it.

Shopping Carts: An Overview

Let me begin by taking you on a tour of a department store. While shopping in a department store, the first thing you do is look around in the store to search for products that you need to buy. You select the products and keep adding them to your shopping cart. After you have placed all of the products your want in your shopping cart, you approach the billing counter where you have to stand in the checkout line, make your payment, and collect your stuff. By now you must be wondering why I am stating the obvious. Compare this to placing an order on the Internet, where you can select, order, and receive the products without physically having to go to the department store.

Shopping on the Internet is quite similar to physical shopping. It involves browsing through the products and adding selected products to your shopping cart. However, the meaning of "shopping cart" is quite different in the context of Internet shopping. With respect to the Internet, a shopping cart is a file that temporarily stores all the products that you wish to buy. In technical terms, a shopping cart is an online transaction processing system that establishes a link between a customer and several database items that are stored in a server. The shopping cart helps you keep track of the purchases that are made by customers.

The structure of a shopping cart is discussed below.

Structure of a Shopping Cart

The structure of a shopping cart can be simple or complex, depending on the information that needs to be extracted from it. It might contain only the product ID if there is just one customer. However, if you have to maintain the shopping carts of many customers simultaneously, then the shopping cart should also contain the Customer ID. In addition, you can add products to your shopping cart from different pages of the Web site. It's just like selecting different products from different departments of a department store. In such a situation, a customer might want to check out only once after he or she has selected all the products, rather than checking out again and again each time another product is selected. Here your shopping cart application should be able to differentiate between the information of any two customers as they add items to their shopping cart from different Web pages of a Web site. The structure of a shopping cart should be such that it clearly distinguishes between different customers and the products selected by them.

Now consider the structure of a shopping cart you are going to create. In this example, you need to know which customer has ordered which book. This information will be stored in your database in a table called neworder. This table stores all products that have been selected by different customers.

To create the neworder table, you need to give the following SQL command:

```
CREATE TABLE neworder (
id bigint(20) NOT NULL auto_increment,
customerid varchar(20) NOT NULL default '',
productid varchar(20) NOT NULL default '',
PRIMARY KEY  (id))
```

In the preceding code you noticed that the neworder table consists of three fields, namely:

1. **id**: This is the primary key of the neworder table. The id field is an auto increment field.

2. **customerid**: Each customer is assigned a unique customer ID, which uniquely identifies a customer in the customerinfo table. However, in

the `neworder` table the value of the `customerid` field appears a number of times, as a customer can buy more than one product. As a result, `customerid` will appear as many times in this table as the number of products in his/her cart.

3. **productid**: Each product is assigned a unique product ID, which uniquely identifies a product in the `products` table. Just like the `customerid` field, the `productid` field can also appear more than once in the `neworder` table, since more than one customer can order the same product.

After having learned the structure of the shopping cart, you'll now start working with the shopping cart.

How a Shopping Cart Works

In the previous chapter, you created a product catalog. Recall that on the product catalog page, next to each product there was a link named `Add to Cart`. When you click on this link, it adds the selected product to your shopping cart. The following section discusses how you can add products to your shopping cart.

Adding Products to a Shopping Cart

When you click on the `Add to Cart` link in the Product Catalog page, the product that you have selected is added to your shopping cart. In the mainpage.php file, the source code for the `Add to Cart` link is:

```
addtocart.php?customerid=$customerid&producid=$productid
```

In the preceding code, the `Add to Cart` link passes two values to the addtocart.php file by using the GET method. These two values are:

◆ The customer ID of the customer who has clicked on the link

◆ The product ID of the product corresponding to the link

The addtocart.php file will now be discussed in detail.

The addtocart.php file

The addtocart.php file accepts the `customerid` values and the `productid` values from the mainpage.php file. After accepting these values, the code performs a search in the neworder table to verify whether a customer might not have selected the same product again. To do so, the addtocart.php file matches the customerid and the productid values in the existing neworder table with the customerid and productid values that it has just accepted from the mainpage.php file. If any matching records are found, a message stating "This product is already in your shopping cart!!" appears. However, if no matching records are found, then the addtocart.php file adds the customerid and productid values in the neworder table and displays a message stating "The following book was added to your shopping cart:", as shown in Figure 15-1.

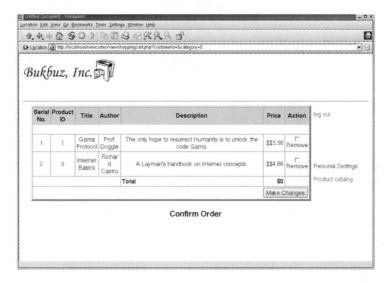

FIGURE 15-1 *Adding products to a shopping cart*

Following is the code for the addtocart.php file.

```
<html>
<head>
<title> New Item added</title>
</head>
<body>
<?php
        $host="";
        $database="books";
        $dbusername="root";
        $dbpassword="";
```

```php
            $x=mysql_connect($host,$dbusername,$dbpassword);
            $x1=mysql_select_db($database);
// --- Searches If any records with the same data exist In the neworder
table.
            $query = "Select customerid,productid from neworder where
customerid='".$customerid."' and productid='".$productid."'";
            $result=mysql_query($query);
            if ($row=mysql_fetch_array($result))
            {
             die ("<h2>This product is already in your shopping cart
!!</h2>");

            }
// ---- Adds new records In the neworder table.
            $query="INSERT into neworder
VALUES('','".$customerid."','".$productid."')";
            $result=mysql_query($query);
?>
            <h1>The following book was added to your shopping cart:</h1>
            <table border=0>
<?php
            $query="select name, author, description, price from products
where productid='".$productid."'";
            $result=mysql_query($query);
            if ($row=mysql_fetch_array($result))
            {
            echo "<tr><td>Title :</td><td>"        .$row["name"]   ."
</td></tr>";

            echo "<tr><td>Author:</td><td>"        .$row["author"]   ."
</td></tr>";

            echo "<tr><td>Description :</td><td>".$row["description"]   ."
</td></tr>";

            echo "<tr><td>Price :</td><td>"        .$row["price"]   ."
</td></tr>";

            }
?>
            </table>
            </body>
            </html>
```

After you have added products to your shopping cart, you might want to view your shopping cart. Recall that in the product catalog, you were provided with a link `View Shopping Cart`. By clicking on this link you can view your shopping cart.

Viewing a Shopping Cart

To view the products that your have added to your shopping cart, you need to click on the `View Shopping Cart` link on the product catalog page. In the mainpage.php file, the source code for the `View Shopping Cart` link is:

```
viewshoppingcart.php?customerid=$thiscustomerid
```

According to the preceding code, when you click on the `View Shopping Cart` link, the `customerid` value is passed to the viewshoppingcart.php file by using the GET method.

The viewshoppingcart.php File

The viewshoppingcart.php file allows you to view and work with your shopping cart. By using the viewshoppingcart.php file, you can remove the products that you do not wish to purchase, confirm your order, view personal information, and even view the details of the products that you have selected.

First look at the code for the viewshoppingcart.php file.

```
<html>
<head>
<title>Untitled Document</title>
<meta http-equiv="Content-Type" content="text/html; charset=iso-8859-1">
</head>
          <body bgcolor="#FFFFFF" text="#000000">
          <p> </p>
          <hr>
          <table width="950" border="0" align="center" cellspacing="1"
cellpadding="3">
          <tr>
          <td width="85%" height="229">
          <form name="form2" method="post"
action="viewshoppingcart.php">
```

```html
<table width="100%" border="5" align="center" cellspacing="0"
cellpadding="3">
<tr bgcolor=#cccccc>
<td ><center><b>Serial No.</b></center></td>
<td ><center><b>Product ID</b></center></td>
<td ><center><b>Title</b></center>   </td>
<td ><center><b>Author</b></center> </td>
<td width="200">
<center><b>Description</b></center>
</td>
<td>
<center><b>Price</b></center>
</td>
<td>
<center><b>Action</b></center>
</td>
</tr>
<tr>
<td colspan="7"> </td>
</tr>
<?php
$database="books";
$hostname="";
$dbusername="root";
$dbpassword="";
$connect=mysql_connect($hostname,$dbusername,$dbpassword);
$dbselect=mysql_select_db($database);
$serialcount=0;
$query="select productid from neworder where
customerid='".$customerid."'";
$result=mysql_query($query);
while($row=mysql_fetch_array($result))
{
//--check for any changes to the cart.
if (isset($$row["productid"]))
{
  if ($$row["productid"]==1)
{
```

```
                        $deletequery="delete from neworder where
productid=".$row["productid"];
                        $deleteresult= mysql_query($deletequery);
                        }
                        }
                        }
        // --- Display detailed product listing for all products in the shopping
cart.
                        $query="select productid from neworder where
customerid='".$customerid."'";
                        $result=mysql_query($query);
                        while($row=mysql_fetch_array($result))
                        {
                        $proquery="select productid,name,author,price,description from
products where productid='".$row["productid"]."'";
                        $proresult=mysql_query($proquery);
                        if($pro=mysql_fetch_array($proresult))
                        {
                        echo " <tr>
                        ";
                        echo "    <td >
                        ";
                        echo "     <center>" .  ++$serialcount . "</center>
                        ";
                        echo "    </td>
                        ";
                        echo "    <td><center>".$pro["productid"]."</center></td>
                        ";
                        echo "    <td><center>".$pro["name"]."</center></td>
                        ";
                        echo "    <td><center>".$pro["author"]."</center></td>
                        ";
                        echo "    <td> ";
                        echo "     <center>".$pro["description"] . "</center>
                        ";
                        echo "    </td>
                        ";
                        echo "    <td>
```

```
                           ";
                    echo "           <div align=\"right\"> $".$pro["price"]."</div>
                           ";
                       echo "        </td>
                           ";
                    echo "      <td>
                           ";
                    echo "          <center>
                           ";
                    echo "             <input type=\"checkbox\" name=\"".$pro["produc-
tid"]."\" value=\"1\">Remove ";
                    echo "          </center>
                           ";
                    echo "      </td>";
                    echo " </tr>
                           ";
                    $carttotal+=$pro["price"];
                    }
                    }
                    echo "       <tr>
                           ";
                    echo "       <td colspan=\"4\"> </td>";
                    echo "       <td ><b>Total</b></td>
                           ";
                    echo "       <td >
                           ";
                    echo "            <div
align=\"right\"><b>$".$carttotal."</b></div>
                           ";
                    echo "       </td>
                           ";
                    echo "       <td>
                     </td>";
                    echo "   </tr>
                           ";
        ?>
        <tr>
        <td colspan="7" >
```

```
        <div align="right">
        <input type="submit" name="Submit" value="Make Changes">
        </div>
        </td>
        </tr>
        </table>
        </form>
        </td>
        <td width="15%" height="229">
        <p><a href="login.htm">log out</a></p>
        <p> </p>
        <p> </p>
        <p> </p>
        <?php
                echo  " <p><a href=\"personalsettings.php?customerid=".$cus-
tomerid."&category=".$category."\">Personal Settings</a></p> ";
        ?>
        <?php
                echo "<p><a href=\"mainpage.php?category=".$category."&cus-
tomerid=".$customerid."\">Product catalog</a></p>";
        ?>
                <p> </p>
                </td>
        </tr>
        </table>
        <?php
                echo "      <center><a
href=\"confirmorder.php?customerid=".$customerid."&category=".$category."\"><h2>Conf
irm Order</a></h2></center>
                        ";
        ?>
        <p> </p>
        <p> </p>
    </body>
        </html>
```

In the preceding code, viewshoppingcart.php accepts the customerid and the last visited category values from the mainpage.php file. As a result, when you return to the Product Catalog page from your shopping cart, the Product Catalog page displays the category of book that you added last to your shopping cart. After accepting the customerid value from the mainpage.php file, the viewshoppingcart.php file performs a search in the neworder table. It selects those productids from the neworder table whose corresponding customerid values match with the customerid value that is forwarded by the mainpage.php file. The shopping cart then needs to show the details of the products that you have selected. In this example, the product details will include the author of the book, price of the book, and the description of the book. To show these details, the viewshoppingcart.php file performs another search in the products table of the database. The results of the search are displayed in a tabular format, as shown in Figure 15-2.

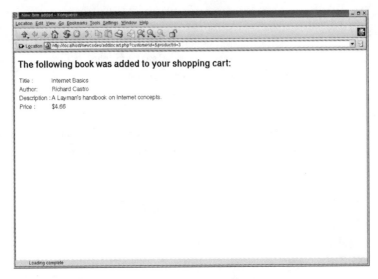

FIGURE 15-2 *A shopping cart*

In Figure 15-2 you'll notice that next to each product there is a check box named Remove. This check box allows you to remove any selected product from your shopping cart. Now you'll learn how you can remove products from a shopping cart.

Removing Products from a Shopping Cart

Your shopping cart displays unconfirmed orders. This allows you to remove a particular product from your shopping cart if you do not want to purchase it. As discussed earlier, all information about the shopping cart is stored in the `neworder` table in the database. When you view your shopping cart, the viewshopping-cart.php file places a check box named Remove next to each product. The name attribute of the check box is the `productid` of the product against which the check box is placed. In this example, the `productid` of the book `Gama Protocol` is `1`. Therefore, the name attribute of the check box corresponding to the book `Gama Protocol` is also `1`.

As a result, when you check the `Remove` check box to remove a particular book from your shopping cart, a variable with the same name as the `productid` is created. After you have checked the `Remove` check box, you need to click on the "`Make Changes`" button. When you click on the "`Make Changes`" button, the viewshop-pingcart.php file checks for the existence of variables whose names correspond with the productids that exist in the `neworder` table. If there are any variables by the name of selected productids, those records are deleted from the `neworder` table and are no longer displayed in your shopping cart.

After you have created your shopping cart, you can confirm your order by clicking on the Confirm Order button. When you click on the Confirm Order button, information relating to your selected products is passed to the confirmorder.php file. You will learn about the confirmorder.php file in the next chapter.

Summary

In this chapter you learned to create a shopping cart. You learned to add and remove products from your shopping cart. You also learned to view your shopping cart and how you can view detailed information on the products that you have added to your shopping cart.

Chapter 16

By now you're likely to be quite comfortable with the Bukbuz, Inc. Web site. You have learned not only about the various aspects of creating and managing a product catalog, but also about creating and managing a shopping cart. Based on the experience that you have had while working with the Bukbuz, Inc. Web site, you need to give Bukbuz, Inc. some feedback. For this purpose, you will use the feedback form, whose link is located on both the Bukbuz, Inc. home page and the Bukbuz, Inc. product catalog.

In this chapter you will learn to send an e-mail by using the `mail ()` function of PHP.

The Bukbuz, Inc. Feedback Form

The Bukbuz, Inc. home page and product catalog both contain two links at the bottom of their pages that are commonly seen in all Web sites. These links are "About us" and "feedback." The "About us" page is a simple HTML page, which you have already studied in Chapter 14, "Creating a Product Catalog," in the section "Overview of the Product Catalog."

The "feedback" form is an HTML form that accepts user input and then sends the user input to Bukbuz, Inc. Figure 16-1 displays the Bukbuz, Inc. Feedback Form.

To create this feedback form you need to run the following code.

```
<html>
<head>
<title>Untitled Document</title>
<meta http-equiv="Content-Type" content="text/html; charset=iso-8859-1">
</head>
<body bgcolor="#FFFFFF" text="#000000">
<p><img src="Logo.jpg" width="264" height="63"></p>
<hr>
<h1 align="center">Feedback Form</h1>
```

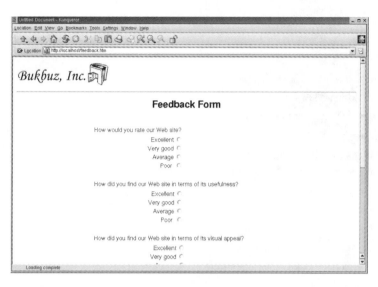

FIGURE 16-1 *The Bukbuz, Inc. Feedback Form*

```
// --- Submits the information to feedback.php.


        <form name="form2" method="post" action="feedback.php">
        <table width="426" border="0" align="center">
        <tr>
        <td> </td>
        </tr>


// --- Feedback questions.


        <tr>
        <td>How would you rate our Web site?</td>
        </tr>
        <tr>
        <td>
        <table width="50%" border="0">
        <tr>
        <td width="88%">
        <div align="right">Excellent</div>
        </td>
        <td width="12%">
```

```
<input type="radio" name="q1" value="1">
</td>
</tr>
<tr>
<td width="88%">
<div align="right">Very good</div>
</td>
<td width="12%">
<input type="radio" name="q1" value="2">
</td>
</tr>
<tr>
<td width="88%">
<div align="right">Average</div>
</td>
<td width="12%">
<input type="radio" name="q1" value="3">
</td>
</tr>
<tr>
<td width="88%">
<div align="right">Poor </div>
</td>
<td width="12%">
<input type="radio" name="q1" value="4">
</td>
</tr>
</table>
</td>
</tr>
<tr>
<td>  </td>
</tr>
<tr>
<td>How did you find our Web site in terms of its usefulness?<br>
</td>
</tr>
<tr>
```

```
<td>
<table width="49%" border="0">
<tr>
<td width="93%">
<div align="right">Excellent</div>
</td>
<td width="7%">
<input type="radio" name="q2" value="1">
</td>
</tr>
<tr>
<td width="93%">
<div align="right">Very good</div>
</td>
<td width="7%">
<input type="radio" name="q2" value="2">
</td>
</tr>
<tr>
<td width="93%">
<div align="right">Average</div>
</td>
<td width="7%">
<input type="radio" name="q2" value="3">
</td>
</tr>
<tr>
<td width="93%">
<div align="right">Poor </div>
</td>
<td width="7%">
<input type="radio" name="q2" value="4">
</td>
</tr>
</table>
</td>
</tr>
<tr>
```

```
<td>  </td>
</tr>
<tr>
<td>How did you find our Web site in terms of its visual appeal?</td>
</tr>
<tr>
<td>
<table width="50%" border="0">
<tr>
<td width="93%">
<div align="right">Excellent</div>
</td>
<td width="7%">
<input type="radio" name="q3" value="1">
</td>
</tr>
<tr>
<td width="93%">
<div align="right">Very good</div>
</td>
<td width="7%">
<input type="radio" name="q3" value="2">
</td>
</tr>
<tr>
<td width="93%">
<div align="right">Average</div>
</td>
<td width="7%">
<input type="radio" name="q3" value="3">
</td>
</tr>
<tr>
<td width="93%">
<div align="right">Poor </div>
</td>
<td width="7%">
<input type="radio" name="q3" value="4">
```

```
</td>
</tr>
</table>
</td>
</tr>
<tr>
<td>  </td>
</tr>
<tr>
<td>How would you rate the ease of navigation of our Web site?
<p></p>
</td>
</tr>
<tr>
<td>
<table width="50%" border="0">
<tr>
<td width="93%">
<div align="right">Excellent</div>
</td>
<td width="7%">
<input type="radio" name="q4" value="1">
</td>
</tr>
<tr>
<td width="93%">
<div align="right">Very good</div>
</td>
<td width="7%">
<input type="radio" name="q4" value="2">
</td>
</tr>
<tr>
<td width="93%">
<div align="right">Average</div>
</td>
<td width="7%">
<input type="radio" name="q4" value="3">
```

```
</td>
</tr>
<tr>
<td width="93%">
<div align="right">Poor </div>
</td>
<td width="7%">
<input type="radio" name="q4" value="4">
</td>
</tr>
</table>
</td>
</tr>
<tr>
<td> </td>
</tr>
<tr>
<td>Your Suggestions :</td>
</tr>
<tr>
<td>
<div align="center">
<textarea name="textfield" cols="50" rows="7"></textarea>
</div>
</td>
</tr>
<tr>
<td>
<div align="center">
<input type="submit" name="Submit" value="Submit">
</div>
</td>
</tr>
</table>
<form>
<p> </p>
</body>
</html>
```

This code performs the following functions:

◆ Creates an HTML form, which accepts user input.

◆ Provides users with choices for answering the questions that have been asked.

◆ Submits the user input to a PHP file. This PHP file will ultimately process all the information and send it to Bukbuz, Inc.

When a customer visits the Bukbuz, Inc. Web site and clicks on the feedback link, the feedback form appears. After giving his/her feedback, the customer then clicks on the Submit button. When the Submit button is clicked, all the customer-input information is passed on to a php file called feedback.php.

The *mail ()* function

The feedback.php file uses the built-in `mail ()` function to send e-mail. The `mail ()` function uses the Simple Mail Transfer Protocol (SMTP) server for mailing. On the Internet it is the SMTP server that is used to exchange e-mail.

 NOTE

The `mail ()` function of PHP assumes that the computer on which the application is running already has an SMTP server set up.

Let me now discuss the `mail ()` function in detail.

The `mail ()` function is a built-in function in PHP that is used to send e-mail. The `mail ()` function has the following syntax:

```
$result = mail($recipient, $subject, $message, $ additional_headers );
```

In this syntax:

◆ **$recipient:** The `$recipient` argument takes the e-mail address of the receiver. You can specify more than one e-mail address under this argument. However, in cases of multiple e-mail addresses, each address should be separated by a comma. For example,

```
// --- Only one e-mail address
$result = mail ( "bookworm@bukbuz.com");
```

```
                    // --- More than one e-mail address
                    $result = mail ( "bookworm@bukbuz.com, bookfreak@bukbuz.com, ");
```

◆ **$subject:** The $subject argument takes the subject of the message. This
   argument accepts a string value.

◆ **$message:** The $message takes the content or the body of the mail message. This argument also accepts a string value. To specify more than one
   line, you need to separate each line by \r\n. For example,

```
                    $result = mail ( "Dear Customer, \r\nThere are a lot more books
       that will be added soon.\r\happy reading");
```

◆ **$additional_headers:** The $additional_headers argument is used only
   when you have to attach some text at the end of the e-mail header. This
   argument also accepts string values.

Now that you know the syntax of the mail () function, you will now create a program that will send an e-mail by using the mail () function.

```php
    <?php
        if (empty($mailto))
        {
        die("No Recipient name found!");
        }
if (empty($mailsubject))
            {
        $mailsubject="";
                }
        if(empty($mailbody))
{
        $mailbody="";
        }
        $result = mail($mailto,$mailsubject,$mailbody);
        if ($result)
        {
        echo "<h1><center>E-mail sent successfully!!</center></h1>";
        }
        else
        {
        echo "<h1><center>E-mail could not be sent.</center></h1>";
```

```
          }
    ?>
```

This code:

- Checks whether there is some value in the recipients field. If no value is found, the program terminates, displaying a message "No Recipient name found!"

- Checks for the subject field value. If no value is found, the mail is sent without any subject.

- Performs a similar search for the message field value.

- Stores the outcome of the mail () function in the variable $result.

- Returns True if mail is sent successfully and False if mail is not sent.

Taking a cue from the preceding code, now create the code that sends an e-mail to Bukbuz, Inc.

The feedback.php File

When the customer fills in the feedback form and submits it, the feedback.php file sends an e-mail to the Bukbuz, Inc. administrator. Following is the source code for the feedback.php file.

```
<html>
        <head>
        <title>Feedback Page</title>
        </head>
        <body bgcolor="#FFFFFF" text="#000000">

    <?php
        $message="";

// --- Subject of the mail.

        $mailsubject ="Feedback From Customer";

// --- Body of the mail.

        $mailbody = "The user entered the following rating: \n";
```

```php
        if (isset($q1))
        {
         $mailbody.="The user rated the Web site as ".$q1 ."\n";
         }

        if (isset($q2))
         {
         $mailbody.= "The user rated the usefulness as ".$q2."\n";
         }

        if (isset($q3))
        {
         $mailbody.= "The user rated the visual appearance as ".$q3."\n";
         }

        if (isset($q4))
         {
         $mailbody.="The user rated ease of navigation as". $q4."\n";
         }

        $mailbody.="Have a nice day";

// --- A mail is sent to the Bukbuz, Inc. administrator.

        $email="admin@bukbuz.com";

// --- Result stored in the $result variable.

        $result = mail($email,$mailsubject,$mailbody);
        if ($result)
        {

// --- If mail is delivered successfully.

        echo "<p><h1><center>E-mail sent to site
administrator.</center></h1></p>";
        }
        else
```

```
        {

// --- If the e-mail is not sent.

        echo "<p><b>E-mail could not be sent.</b></p>";
        }
   ?>

        <h1><center>Thank you for your time ! </center></h1>
        </body>
        </html>
```

In this code:

- ◆ The subject of the mail is "Feedback From Customer."

- ◆ The body of the mail gives the customer rating about the site. The first line of the message body is "The user entered the following rating." Then the user rating appears along with the questions, and the last line of the message is "Have a nice day!"

- ◆ The `$result` variable stores the output generated by the `mail ()` function.

- ◆ If the mail is delivered successfully, True is returned and a message stating "E-mail sent to site administrator" appears. Figure 16-2 displays a message that the mail has been sent successfully.

- ◆ If mail is not delivered, then False is returned and a message stating "E-mail could not be sent" is displayed.

FIGURE 16-2 *Mail delivery confirmation message*

Summary

In this chapter you learned to create an HTML form that can accept user input. You created a feedback form for Bukbuz, Inc. When the customers fill in the form and click on the Submit button, the feedback is sent as an e-mail message to the site administrator.

You also learned about the mail () function and the different arguments that it has.

PART VI

Professional Project 5

Project 5

**User
Authentication
and Tracking**

Project 5 Overview

In this project, I'll teach you how to ensure security of your Web site and keep track of the users who visit your Web site. Today user authentication is the most widely used tool for providing security. It ensures that only authenticated users are allowed to access the resources.

Keeping track of all the users who visit your Web site helps you to determine the general trends and preferences. Session tracking, which helps you trap all the relevant information about the users accessing your Web site, is the most popular method in use today.

In Chapter 17 you will learn to secure sensitive information, such as user passwords, using encryption and hashing. You will learn to create user-specific accounts or profiles in the Web site, which would only be accessible to individual users. To implement this restricted access to personal or private information, you will learn to create a PHP script that will authenticate users before they can access their profiles (accounts). You will also learn to hash sensitive information, such as passwords. Hashing allows you to further secure the passwords and other sensitive information stored in the database beyond simple encryption.

In Chapter 18 you'll learn about session tracking and how to implement the session tracking functionality offered by PHP to your advantage. You will learn about various built-in session tracking functions that you need to use to implement session tracking in your Web site. These functions include `session_register()`, `session_unregister()`, `session_start()`, `session_name()`, `session_destroy()`, `session_encode()`, and `session_decode()`.

Chapter 17

*User
Authentication
Scripts*

Today, most Web sites offer personalized service to their customers. This means that users need to register to a site before they can buy a product from the site. This is important because the registration helps both the user and the vendor to keep track of a transaction. Also, most sites offer some discount to registered users on their purchases.

These transactions are carried out over the Internet, which is a "truly democratic" medium. Everyone with connectivity to the Internet is free to access whatever data they like or need. It is all out there. But this freedom comes at a very high cost—the threat to security to a site or an e-transaction. Organizations all over the globe are implementing measures to ensure the security of transactions over the Internet. However, as the developer of a commercial site, it is your responsibility to ensure that your Web site and your customers are safe from prying eyes.

There are all kinds of people out there who can access your Web site. Most of them are harmless visitors who will simply surf through your Web site looking for information or a product. However, there is another category of users who get their thrills from tampering with, stealing, and possibly destroying the sensitive data that can be accessed from a Web site. This sensitive data might include the status of orders that were placed through your site or the membership information. Imagine the loss an e-business might suffer by losing the current status of orders that were placed through its Web site or if their membership information were lost. For successful Web portals, the loss incurred could be well in the millions!

In earlier chapters (13, 14, and 15) you learned to create a functional Web site that catered to the book orders from the users of Bukbuz.com. In this chapter, you will learn to create user-specific accounts or profiles in the Web site, which would be accessible only to individual users. An account or a profile is a private page where user-specific information (details) and settings are stored. This private page is accessible only to the user, after they log into the page. To implement this restricted access to personal or private information, you will learn to create a PHP script that will authenticate a user before they can access their profile (account). You will then learn to secure the passwords stored in the database by using encryption and/or hashing.

Authentication: The Basics

Authentication is the process of establishing the legitimacy or the valid identity of a user before allowing access to the requested information. Besides the integrity of the supplied information, authentication also assures the recipient-end (the Web site, in this case) of the integrity of the source (the client, who originated the request) of the information.

In its economical, simplest, and most predominantly used form, the authentication process uses a unique user name (or a similar unique ID) and password to gain access to a resource or an account. Several complex authentication protocols and algorithms, such as digital certificates, MD5, DES, and RSA, are also used for authentication purposes.

Password-based authentication, as mentioned earlier, is the most commonly implemented authentication method that is used in Web sites across the globe. The following section discusses password-based authentication method in detail.

Password-Based Authentication

In password-based authentication, a user must specify a valid and unique user identity and the corresponding password to gain access to the account. However, before the password-based authentication is possible, each user must register on the given Web site. During registration, the user needs to supply the intended user identity (which should be unique), a password, and individual details for authorization. After the details—user id, and password—are verified and accepted by the Web server, the user details might be stored in either a database or a file. The user is then allocated an account, which is only accessible to the specified user.

Each time a user needs to access their private account on a Web site, they must specify the allocated user ID and the corresponding password. This is where PHP comes into the picture. PHP scripts are used to validate the login attempts by site users to verify the supplied user ID and password.

To understand how PHP scripts are used to implement authentication, consider a simple example. In this example, you'll create the following:

◆ A very simple HTML form, test.html, which will accept a password from the user. This password should be easypassword.

◆ A simple PHP script, verify.php, which will verify the password supplied by the user and, if the correct password was supplied, display the next page in the browser window.

NOTE

Since a password is the key to gaining access to a user account, you might add a warning to the account set-up Web page warning that the password a user uses should be difficult to guess. Suggest the users not to use their nickname, date of birth, name of a loved one, telephone number, or such easily identifiable passwords. You might also suggest that the chosen password is not too short! It makes guessing the password comparatively easy. However, you might also warn them that the password should not be so long that they find it difficult to remember it. As the experts recommend, passwords should have 8 to 10 characters and should be a mix of numbers and letters. Never divulge your password to anybody, not even your closest friends. If in case you had to tell your password to someone for a (valid) reason, change the password as soon as possible. Also, periodically changing passwords is a very good practice and helps you secure your account to a considerable extent.

The code that should be included in test.html is as follows:

```html
<html>
<head>
<title>Basic Authentication Script</title>
<meta http-equiv="Content-Type" content="text/html;
charset=iso-8859-1">
</head>
<body bgcolor="pink" text="#000000">
<p> </p>
<p> </p>
<p> </p>
<form name="form1" method="post" action="verify.php">
  <table width="500" border="5" align="center" cell-
padding="10" cellspacing="2">

      <tr bgcolor="#eeeeee">
        <td height="1"> Password
          <input type="password" name="password">
          <input type="submit" name="Submit" value="Login">
        </td>
      </tr>
      <tr>
```

```
                    <td bgcolor="#dddddd">
                        <div align="center"><b>Enter the password to see the
next page.</b></div>
                        </td>
                    </tr>
                </table>
            </form>

            </body>
            </html>
```

The above code is used to create an HTML form with two basic elements—a text box that accepts the password and the Login button. Figure 17-1 shows the HTML form that you have created by using the above code.

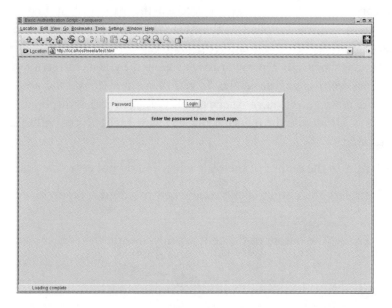

FIGURE 17-1 *HTML form, test.html, for basic authentication*

In the HTML form, after entering the password in the Password box when you click on the Login button, the PHP script—verify.php—is called. This script, as the name suggests, verifies the supplied password. The PHP script, verify.php, contains the following code:

```
<?php
if (empty($password))
{
die ("You did not specify the password!");
}
if (!($password== "easypassword"))
{
die("You did not specify the valid password.");
}
echo " You have successfully logged in !";
?>
```

When you click on the Login button in the HTML form, verify.php is called. The password supplied by you in the HTML form is accepted in the variable called `password`. After the above script receives the password, it first checks whether the password was supplied. If the `Password` field in test.html was found empty (that is, if no password was entered), you receive the message `You did not specify the password!`. If a password was supplied by you, the script checks whether the password is `easypassword`. If yes, then the user-specific account is opened and the message `You have successfully logged in!` is displayed in the browser window. Otherwise the message `You did not specify the valid password.` is displayed.

Figure 17-2 displays the output of the code when you do not enter the password.

Figure 17-3 displays the output of the code when you do not supply the correct password.

Figure 17-4 displays the output of the code when you enter the correct password.

 NOTE

Password-based authentication in a real-life situation is not as simple as the above example. There is much more to it. You will learn to write real-life authentication code a bit later in this chapter.

The next section familiarizes you with the advantages as well the disadvantages of password-based authentication

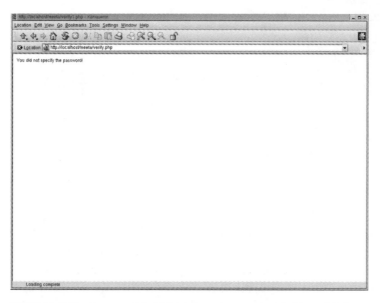

FIGURE 17-2 *Output of the PHP script when no password is specified*

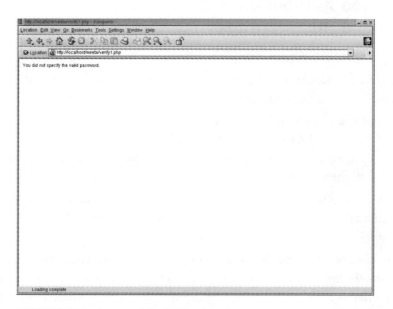

FIGURE 17-3 *Output of the PHP script when the correct password is not specified*

FIGURE 17-4 *Output of the PHP script when you enter the correct password*

Password-based Authentication: Advantages and Disadvantages

Password-based authentication has the following advantages to offer:

- ◆ **Easy implementation.** Password-based authentication is very easy to implement and does not require any extra hardware equipment.

- ◆ **Separate accounts for individual users.** Use of password-based authentication allows the administrator(s) to allocate an individual account to each user. Personal information, settings, and preferences of users can be stored in these accounts. This allows personalized service for each user.

- ◆ **Relative safety.** If passwords are safeguarded and measures to implement additional security are used, this is a relatively safe method of ensuring security.

- ◆ **Creation of multi-tier Web sites.** Use of password-based authentication allows the creation of multi-tiered Web sites. For example, a single site can offer as many as three tiers—administrators, group moderators, and users or administrators, resellers, users. The information in one tier is not accessible to others (except the administrators), which ensures increased security to sensitive information.

Despite the advantages mentioned above, password-based authentication also poses a few disadvantages. These include the following:

♦ **Easy to forget passwords.** Most of the users face a common problem in password-based authentication—that of forgetting passwords. This causes a lot of trouble not only to them, since they are temporarily locked out of their accounts, but also to the administrators who either end up retrieving forgotten passwords or creating new accounts if the passwords can't be retrieved.

♦ **Security risk.** A password is secret information, meant only for the user who owns the given account. However, sometimes users divulge their password to another user or write the password somewhere in case they forget it. This leads to enhanced security risk because in both cases, another user (or maybe an unwanted element) gains access to the password and can use the knowledge to their advantage, causing a lot of loss to the user.

♦ **Need to change the passwords frequently.** To prevent others from guessing a password, users must change their passwords frequently. This might lead to the problem of forgetting passwords.

Now that you know the basic mechanism of password-based authentication, in the following section I'll take you through a quick tour of how passwords are stored and safeguarded from unauthorized access.

Storing Passwords

You can use the following to store the user passwords:

♦ Flat files
♦ Databases

You'll learn more about these methods of storing passwords in the following two sections.

Storing Passwords in Flat Files

Storing passwords in files, such as .htaccess, is the most primitive and hassle-free method of storing passwords. However, passwords stored in a flat file are most vulnerable to hackers and other malicious accesses. This is because information is stored in non-encrypted format in these files. Therefore, even accidental access to the password file can expose the entire set of user names and the corresponding passwords to the attacker.

Even if you restrict the access to the password files or apply other security measures, hackers generally use sophisticated mechanisms to break into a system and can easily access the password file. The security implications of the compromise of a password file by a hacker are tremendous and can lead to heavy losses. This is the reason why passwords are no longer stored in flat files.

Moreover, password files should only be used if the number of registered users is low. If a large number of users are registered on the Web site, the file and the information stored in it might become unmanageable.

 NOTE

PHP (or any other scripting language for that matter) does not play any role in file-based password authentication. The authentication is done by the operating system running on the Web server.

Storing Passwords in Databases

Using databases to store passwords is the most convenient and reasonably safe method of storing passwords. This is because, where flat files make use of various access mechanisms offered by the operating systems, databases offer much stronger access resistance to unauthorized access than simple flat files. This doubly secures the passwords, because even if an attacker gains access to the database, an extremely sophisticated decryption mechanism to decrypt the information can be used to further secure the sensitive information.

Besides ensuring increased security to stored passwords, databases can store a large number of user details and passwords. However, you might recall from your earlier brush with database systems in Chapters 12 and 13 ("Handling Data Storage" and "Using PHP with SQL Databases (MySQL)") that databases, unlike flat files, are easier to administer and manage.

You need to store passwords in such a manner that they are safe from security breaches, intrusions, and unauthorized or malicious access. If compromised, the

NOTE

Passwords are vulnerable not only when they are stored. Passwords can also be eavesdropped upon and hacked while being exchanged between the user machine and the Web server during the authentication process. The use of strong external password encryption mechanisms, such as Kerberos and Public Key Infrastructure (PKI), can ensure the security of passwords while in transit. Developed by MIT, Kerberos is a key-based authentication mechanism used to assign a unique key called a *ticket*, issued by Kerberos Authentication Server (AS) to each user that logs on to the Web site. This key is then used throughout the session. PKI, on the other hand, uses digital certificates issued by a third party called a *Certificate Authority* (CA). These digital certificates are used to establish the identity of the sender and the authenticity of the request. Both Kerberos and PKI can be embedded in software applications, or offered as a service or a product. Since these external measures offer highly secure transactions, more and more authentication mechanisms are adopting them.

hacker gains unlimited access to all accounts and can misuse the knowledge extensively and thus harm the users of the Web site.

In the next section, you'll learn about encryption and hashing mechanisms that help in securing the authentication process so that the security loopholes in password-based authentication are closed up.

Data Encryption and Hashing

You must be wondering how the question of encrypting data arose when I was talking about password-based authentication and high level of security that databases offer while storing data. Databases are secure, but one cannot depend on a single security step. To understand my point, consider the following example.

Suppose an intruder somehow gains access to your password database just for a few hours. This intruder can download the entire password list and then use this information later on. In this case, you can only try to patch the database security breach. You can either request every user of your Web site to change their passwords immediately or block all the users!

Neither option suggested above is very good. These actions would generate negative feedback for your site and users will not be happy with your service. Therefore, apart from database security, another step to encrypt each and every password becomes important. But how can encrypting or hashing passwords be more secure?

To understand this, recall the above example again. An intruder has gained access to the password table in the database and was able to access the entire password list. Now, if the passwords are stored in an incomprehensible format, the database and all his efforts will prove to be almost useless, as this intruder cannot use any of that information to gain access into the various accounts on your Web site. The intruder will have to attack each and every password separately to gain access.

You'll learn more about encryption in the following section.

Encrypting Data

Encryption (or *cryptography*) is the science of protecting data from unauthorized and malicious access. Encryption is the method of hiding actual information by applying some algorithm, so that the encrypted text looks nothing like the original text, and no one else can read it. However, encryption techniques also ensure that you should be able to retrieve the original information anytime you want.

 NOTE

Encryption technology is not an invention of modern man. The science of cryptography dates back to ancient Egyptians, who encrypted messages by simply replacing the original picture in the hieroglyphics with another symbol. This encryption technique is now referred to as *substitution cipher*.

Data is encrypted on the basis of two components—a *key* and an *encryption algorithm*. The key might be an agreed-upon number, word, or a passphrase that is used to encrypt plain text. The next component of encryption is the encryption algorithm, which is also referred to as a *hash algorithm*. The encryption algorithm is a logical series of steps that are used to convert original text into an unreadable format.

The next logical question is: how is data encrypted? The entire encryption process can be broken down into the following steps:

1. Plain text, such as passwords, needs to be encrypted.

2. A key and an algorithm are used to convert the chunk(s) of this plain text into random bits. In encryption terminology, the plain text that needs to be encrypted is referred to as *cleartext*. The resultant text that you get after encrypting cleartext is known as *ciphertext*.

NOTE

On the basis of the value of the key, the algorithm being used may generate different output each time it is used.

3. Depending on the requirements, the ciphertext then can either be stored (in a database) or transmitted to the recipient across a transmission medium.

4. When the ciphertext needs to be converted back to the original cleartext, the same algorithm and key that were used to encrypt the text are used to decrypt the information.

Figure 17-5 depicts the encryption model described above.

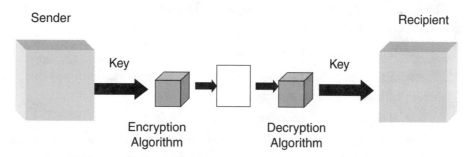

FIGURE 17-5 *Traditional encryption model*

Two encryption techniques exist on the basis of number of keys used. These include:

◆ Single key encryption
◆ Public key encryption

You'll learn about these two cryptography techniques in the following two sections.

Single Key Encryption

In this technique, a single key is used to encrypt as well as decrypt data. In other words, the same key that was used to encrypt data is also used to decrypt data. As a result, a party that has access to the encrypted data but not the key cannot reconstruct the message.

 NOTE

The single key that is used for single key encryption is also referred to as *secret key*. As a result, this encryption technique is also known as *secret key cryptography* or *symmetric key cryptography*.

Although simple, this technique has some problems associated with it. If the secret key becomes known to to the intruder, all the data that was encrypted using this key is compromised. Also, if a lot of secret communication is carried out, a large number of secret keys are required. To ensure that single key cryptography works successfully, you'll need to ensure the following:

- The key should be generated easily.
- The key should be long and must be generated randomly, so that it is difficult to guess the key.
- The maximum safety and secrecy of the key must be ensured.
- The encryption algorithm must encrypt the data thoroughly, so that the original data cannot be recovered without the key, even if part of the original message is known.

Besides the key, the success of the single key encryption technique depends a lot on the encryption algorithm. Some of the commonly used algorithms in secret key cryptography are listed below:

- **Data Encryption Standard (DES).** This is a 56-bit private-key algorithm that breaks data into fixed-size blocks; each of these blocks is encrypted independently of the other blocks. However, the output from one block affects the way the next is encrypted.

◆ **Triple-DES (3DES).** This is an advanced and more secure version of DES, where each block is encrypted three times using at least two different keys.

◆ **International Data Encryption Algorithm (IDEA).** This is a symmetric block cipher mechanism that uses a 128-bit key to encrypt data in blocks of 64 bits. Since the length of the key used in this algorithm is large enough, even comprehensive key searches can fail. In addition, IDEA masks the statistics of how the ciphertext is dependent on the cleartext. These facts make IDEA a highly secure algorithm.

◆ **Ron's Code 4 (RC4).** This is a block cipher algorithm whose key size can be up to 2048 bits. This is a fast, strong, and secure algorithm.

◆ **CAST-128.** This is a block cipher algorithm that uses a variable key length and generates 64-bit-long blocks. The key length can vary from 40 bits to 128 bits in increments of 8 bits.

 NOTE

The term "CAST" is derived from the initials of the two creators of this algorithm, Carlisle Adams (CA) and Stafford Tavares (ST).

◆ **Advanced Encryption Standard (AES).** This algorithm has successfully replaced DES and its various versions. This is a secret key block cipher algorithm that allows the use of variable key length, ranging from 128, 192, and 256 bits. It is also a very fast encryption method that can encrypt 8.8 MB/sec on a 200 MHz Pentium Pro machine.

Single key encryption is subject to various attacks, which can still access the original data despite the encryption. These attacks include the following:

◆ **Brute force attacks.** In a brute force attack, the ciphertext is intercepted. Keys are then randomly generated and applied to the ciphertext until the legitimate key is achieved. This key is then used to decrypt the scrambled data into its original form. As a result, this attack is dependent on the length of the key. The longer the length of the key, the more difficult to decipher the encrypted data.

- ◆ **Differential cryptanalysis attacks.** In a differential cryptanalysis attack, a probable key is worked out by comparing pairs of ciphertexts whose corresponding cleartexts contain known differences. The difference in resulting ciphertext is then compared and determined.

- ◆ **Linear cryptanalysis attacks.** In this attack, ciphertext bits are XORed together and the known cleartext bits are XORed together. Again, when the result of the two operations is XORed together, a single bit is achieved that is the XOR of some of the bits of the key that was used for encryption. If a large number of these cleartext and ciphertext pairs are XORed, a clear picture of the key emerges.

 NOTE

XOR stands for eXclusive OR. This is a Boolean operation and return True, if only one of the two strings contains a 1 at a particular bit position, and a False if both strings contain 0's or 1's at the given positions. Therefore, it is similar to the OR operation, except for the fact that it returns False when both bits are positive (1's). For example, 0 XOR 0 returns 0, 0 XOR 1 returns 1, 1 XOR 0 returns 1, and 1 XOR 1 returns 0.

Public key encryption addresses the common problems and threats faced by the single key encryption method. You'll learn more about public key encryption in the following section.

Public Key Encryption

This is an advanced encryption technique and uses a set of two keys instead of the single key used in single key encryption. One of the keys in the key pair is freely distributable and is shared between the communicating entities. This key is referred to as the *public key*. The other key in the pair is a secret key, which is not distributable and is privately owned by the communicating entity. This key is obviously known as the *private key*. Data is encrypted with the help of the public key. On the other hand, the private key is used to decrypt the data.

Public key encryption is implemented with the help of the RSA algorithm named after its creators—Rivest, Shamir, and Adelman. This algorithm states that each communicating party must own a key that is publicly accessible to all other par-

NOTE

The data that is encrypted using a public key can only be decrypted by using the corresponding private key. Similarly, the data encrypted with a private key can only be decrypted using the corresponding public key. As a result of this asymmetry, public key encryption is also referred to as *asymmetric encryption.*

ties. A private key must also be implemented that remains secret to all the other parties except for the one that owns it. As a result, *2n* keys are required for global communication. Here *n* represents the number of users. The procedure for public key encryption is given below.

1. Plain text, such as passwords, needs to be encrypted.
2. The sender obtains the public key of the destination party from a trusted and publicly accessible third party, such as a Certification Authority (CA).

 NOTE

VeriSign is one of the well-known CAs.

3. The sender encrypts the data using the recipient's public key it just obtained.
4. On receiving the encrypted data, the recipient decrypts the ciphertext using the private key they own.

Public key encryption provides enhanced security. This is because the keys need not be shared between the sender and the receiver. All communications feature only the public key, and the private key remains hidden from prying eyes, as no private key is ever shared or transmitted with the data being accessed or exchanged.

Despite being a strong encryption mechanism, public key encryption is subject to the *cycle* attack, where ciphertext is decrypted repeatedly in this attack until the original cleartext is achieved. However, this is an extremely slow and weak attack, since it requires large number of attack cycles. Moreover, it fails if the length of the key is large.

 NOTE

The attack that is most often considered for RSA encryption is the factoring of the public key. Although difficult and extremely time-consuming, if this attack can be realized, messages encrypted using a public key can be decoded.

PHP supports various encryption mechanisms by providing an interface to the popular Mcrypt library. Similarly, MySQL also provides encryption functions, such as `encode()` and `decode()`, for encryption purposes. In the next section, you'll learn to implement encryption in PHP using these functions.

Implementing Encryption in PHP

Since you have been learning about working with MySQL in this book, in this section I will tell you how to implement the encryption functions provided by MySQL in your PHP scripts. You'll learn about the Mcrypt library in Appendix B.

One of the easiest methods of implementing encryption in PHP is using `encode()` and `decode()` functions provided by MySQL. These functions are used to respectively encrypt and decrypt cleartext data, such as passwords.

The syntax of the `encode()` function is specified below:

```
string encode(string string, string password)
```

The `encode()` function takes two arguments. The first argument represents the string that needs to be encrypted as the password supplied by the second argument, `password`.

The syntax of the `decode()` function is specified below:

```
string decode(string password, string string)
```

Like its counterpart, the `decode()` function takes two arguments. The first argument represents the string that needs to be decrypted using the second argument. The first argument should be a string returned by the `encode()` function.

Consider the following code snippet to understand the use of these encryption functions.

```
/ MySQL's encode function to store encrypted passwords.) */

$mingle= "encode('".$password."','".$password."')";

$sqlquery = "INSERT INTO login VALUES('". $customerid
."','".$mingle.")";
```

In the above code, the encode() function is being used to encrypt the supplied password. This encrypted password is then being stored into the database that holds the login IDs of registered users and passwords.

 NOTE

The above code snippet is a part of the code I'll discuss a bit later in this chapter.

In this section you learned how passwords can be stored in an encrypted form with the help of the encode() function and how passwords are decrypted back using the decode() function and matched with the passwords entered by a user. I also talked about the added security that encryption provides over plain text storage. Hashing is another widely stored method to store passwords that adds a security wall apart from the normal database security. In the next section, you'll learn why hashing is emerging as the darling of the Web community and experts alike.

Hashing

Although encryption secures your data extensively, hashing ensures the maximum security for your data, especially in case of passwords. In *hashing*, a hash message, known as a *hash function*, is generated for the data that needs to be secured. The data is then encrypted and the hash function is stored (or sent to the recipient during a transaction) along with the encrypted data. When the data needs to be restored to its original format, both the data as well as the hash function need to be decrypted. In addition, another hash function is generated and the two hashes are compared. If the two match, it implies that the data is intact and has not been tampered with.

 NOTE

A hash function is a value generated from the input text such that under no circumstances can the original text be revealed from the hash value. You need a formula to convert plain text into hashes.

Hashing is considered stronger than encryption. This is because encrypted text can be decrypted back, if somehow the encryption key is revealed. However, hashing is a one-way process. Consider the following example to understand how hashing is different from encryption and how it ensures maximum security to your data.

Consider the statement "A mod B = C." In this case, you obtain C as a remainder value when A is divided by B. If you were simply supplied with the value C, you would not be able to guess the original values of B or A because so many combinations of A and B can produce the same result!

Consider another example. Suppose you have a string "SECRET" that you need to hash (that is, you need to generate a hash value). You decide that you'd make use of corresponding ASCII values of the characters used in the string.

$$
\begin{array}{rcl}
S &=& 83 \\
E &=& 69 \\
C &=& 67 \\
R &=& 82 \\
E &=& 69 \\
T &=& 84 \\
\hline
&& 454
\end{array}
$$

Upon adding, you have a number 454, which is a hash value. If you are given the number 454, you cannot find out the original text from this number, even if you were told that the number was achieved by adding the ASCII values (meaning that the "key/algorithm" is known to you). However, many other input strings can also produce the same hash. For example, TECRES, CESTER, or any such permutation and combination can produce the hash value of 454. You can see that even though you are changing the sequence of occurrence of the characters, the hash remains the same. To prevent this confusion, multiply the ASCII value of each character with the position at which it is appearing in the original text. In this case the positions of each character in the string are shown below:

```
Position   123456
Text        SECRET
```

Now multiply the position of each character in the string with its ASCII value, as shown below:

$$(83 * 1) + (69 * 2) + (67 * 3) + (82 * 4) + (69 * 5) + (84 * 6)$$

Now add the values again to form a new hash. You'll get the following result:

```
83
138
201
328
345
504
— — — —
1599
```

Now the new hash is 1599, and difficult for anyone to guess where it came from!

Let me next explain how hashes are useful in storing passwords. Say you generate a hash for each password that is stored in the database. Even if a hacker was somehow able to gain access to the database and download the password hashes, there is no way they can find the original password from this hash!

But how will you retrieve the original password from a hash, if necessary, or how are users authenticated on the basis of the hashed passwords stored in a database? Simple: you match the hashes. Hashing works differently than encryption, where the password stored in the database needs to be explicitly decrypted and matched with the corresponding password entered by a user. In hashing, first the hash stored in the database is read and the new hash is calculated for the password entered by the user. Then, if the hashes match, the user has entered the correct password.

In the example related to the "SECRET" string that I quoted earlier, a new, difficult-to-guess hash value, 1599, was achieved. But again, this value can be common for a lot of other words. It is very difficult to find algorithms that generate unique values—or at least values that are very rare—to match with another value and that can't be reverted back! Such an algorithm is the Message Digest algorithm MD5.

You'll learn about MD5 and how to implement MD5 in the following section.

Implementing MD5 Hashing in PHP

Developed by RSA Data Security, Inc., *Message Digest 5* (*MD5*) is a hashing algorithm which produces a 128-bit unique digest of data. MD5 also ensures that a piece of data that will produce the same message digest is extremely hard to produce mathematically. When you use MD5, passwords are stored as hashes. The formula is applied to each piece of text to return a unique value.

 NOTE

You can learn more about MD5 hashing at the site **www.faqs.org/rfcs/rfc1321.html**.

You can use the md5() function to implement hashing in your PHP scripts. The syntax of the function is:

```
string md5(string str)
```

As you can see, the function takes a single argument in the form of the string, str, whose equivalent MD5 hash needs to be calculated.

Since encryption and hashing offer security at different levels, it is a common practice among Web developers to implement encryption as well as hashing to ensure a higher level of password-security. You'll learn to practically implement the use of encryption as well as hashing in the next section.

Creating PHP Authentication Scripts

Consider the following code to understand the implementation of MD5 hashing and encryption. The developers at the Bukbuz site have used the codes discussed in this section as a prototype for implementing authentication and ensuring that the passwords stored in their databases are safe and secure from unauthorized access. Since the site developers wanted to ensure maximum security, they have implemented encryption as well as hashing of the passwords stored in their database.

Following is the code of a simple HTML form. This form accepts a customer ID and a password. When you click on the Submit button, a PHP script, createuser_php_md5.php, is called.

```html
<html>
<head>
<title>add user</title>
</head>
<body bgcolor="#FFFFFF">
<form name="form1" method="post"
action="createuser_php_md5.php">
    <table width="330">
      <tr>
        <td colspan="2" >
          <div align="center"><b>Enter customerid and pass-
word</b></div>
        </td>
      </tr>
      <tr>
        <td>
          <div align="right">Customer ID</div>
        </td>
        <td>
          <input type="text" name="customerid">
        </td>
      </tr>
      <tr>
        <td>
          <div align="right">Password</div>
```

```
            </td>
            <td>
              <input type="text" name="password" maxlength="15">
            </td>
          </tr>
          <tr>
            <td colspan="2">
              <center>
                <input type="submit" name="Submit" value="Submit">
              </center>
            </td>
          </tr>
        </table>
      </form>


      </body>
      </html>
```

Figure 17-6 shows the HTML form that authenticates an existing user or is used to create a new user.

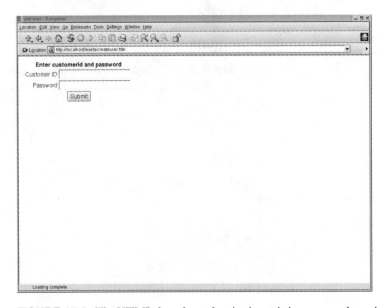

FIGURE 17-6 *The HTML form for authenticating existing users and creating new users*

As mentioned earlier, when you click on the Submit button in the form, a PHP script is called. This script is createuser_php_md5.php. The code in this script is as follows:

```
<html>
<head>
<title>Password Result</title>
</head>

<body bgcolor="#FFFFFF" text="#000000">
<p> </p>

<?php

/Setting the environmental variables of the MySQL database
$host="";
$uname="root";
$pass="";
$database="books";
$tablename="login";

/Connecting to the database
$connect= mysql_connect($host,$uname,$pass)
   or die("Database connection failed ! <br>");

/Selecting a particular database from the set of available
databases
$selectdb=mysql_select_db($database)
   or die("Database could not be selected");

/Querying the database
$sqlquery = "select customerid from testlogin where
customerid='".$customerid."'";
echo $sqlquery . "\n<br>";
$queryresult = mysql_query($sqlquery);

/Fetching the result of the query into a variable
if($row=mysql_fetch_array($queryresult))
```

```
                    {
                     die ("User already exists, please choose another name or
customerid
                    was not a number.");
                    }


                    /MySQL's encode function.(to store encrypted passwords.)

                    $mingle= "encode('".$password."','".$password."')";

                    $sqlquery = "INSERT INTO testlogin VALUES('". $customerid
                    ."',".$mingle.")";


                    /PHP built-in MD5 function to store password hashes

                    $sqlquery = "INSERT INTO login VALUES('". $customerid ."',
  '".
                    md5($password) . "')";


                    $queryresult = mysql_query($sqlquery);
                    if (!$queryresult)
                    {
                      die(" Query could not be executed.<br>");
                    }
                    ?>

                    /Displaying the result in the browser window
                    <table width="330" border="0" align="center" cellpadding="5"
                    cellspacing="2">
                      <tr>
                        <td colspan="2" bgcolor="#dddddd">
                          <div align="center"><b>New password entered for
                            <?php echo $customerid;
                              ?>
```

```
        as </b></div>
    </td>
  </tr>
  <tr bgcolor="#eeeeee">
    <td width="50%">
      <div align="right">Customer ID</div>
    </td>
    <td>
      <center>
        <?php echo $customerid; ?>
      </center>
    </td>
  </tr>
  <tr bgcolor="#eeeeee">
    <td>
      <div align="right">Password</div>
    </td>
    <td>
      <center>
        <?php echo $password; ?>
      </center>
    </td>
  </tr>
  <tr bgcolor="#eeeeee">
    <td colspan="2"><center>Try your new password in the <a
href="login.htm">login page</a></center></td>
  </tr>
</table>

<p> </p>
</body>
</html>
```

In the above code, database variables, host (host), user name (uname), password (pass), database name (database), and the table (tablename) with which this script will interact are set. A connection is then established with the specified database. If the connection was not successful, the message Database connection failed! is displayed. However, if the connection was established successfully, you can then try to access the database (login, in this case) where the desired table (testlogin) is located. In case of failure while executing either of these two activities, corresponding messages are displayed.

After you have established a connection to the desired database and table in it, the script checks whether the customer ID (customerid) that you entered in the HTML form already exists in the database. If the supplied customer ID already exists in the database, the message User already exists, please choose another name or customerid was not a number is displayed the supplied password is then encrypted and hashed. After the customer ID is created successfully in the database, the corresponding password is also stored in the database. The encode() function is used for encrypting the password, whereas the md5() function hashes the stored password.

Figure 17-7 depicts the output of the above code, when you log into the site with a new customer ID.

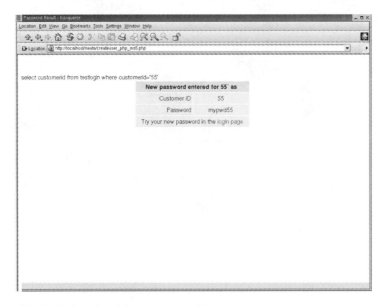

FIGURE 17-7 *Supplying a new user ID*

Figure 17-8 depicts the output of the above code when you log into the site with an existing customer ID (that is, when the user is already registered with the Bukbuz site).

FIGURE 17-8 *Supplying an existing user ID*

With the model worked out by developers at Bukbuz Inc., the new user can now log into the Bukbuz Website by clicking on the login page hyperlink. Figure 17-9 shows the page that appears.

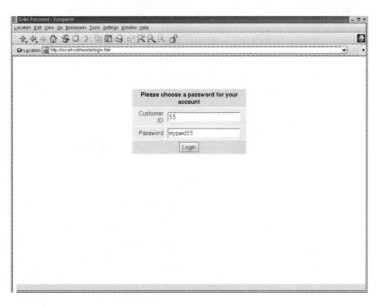

FIGURE 17-9 *Logging in as a registered user*

If the login was successful, the user finds himself (or herself) logged into their private account (or home page). Figure 17-10 shows the home page of the user.

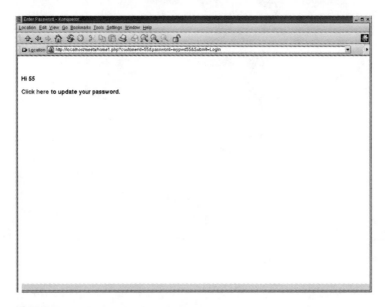

FIGURE 17-10 *Logging into the home page*

The code for the home page is given below:

```
<html>
<head>
<title>Enter Password</title>
<meta http-equiv="Content-Type" content="text/html;
charset=iso-8859-1">

</head>
<body bgcolor="#FFFFFF" text="#000000">
<p> </p>
<?php
if (empty($password)) { die("No Password specified");}
if ((strlen($password) < 5) || (strlen($password) > 15))
{ die("Password too long/short");}

?>
<?php
```

```php
$host="";
$uname="root";
$pass="";
$database="books";

$connect= mysql_connect($host,$uname,$pass)
    or die("Database connection failed ! <br>");

$selectdb=mysql_select_db($database)
    or die("Database could not be selected");

/* To verify passwords based on MD5 hashes */

$sqlquery = "SELECT password from testlogin where
customerid='" .$customerid ."'";
$queryresult = mysql_query($sqlquery);

if($row=mysql_fetch_array($queryresult))
 {

   if(!(md5($password) == $row["password"]))
    {
         die(" Invalid Password.");
    }
 }
else
 {

       die(" User not found.");

 }


/* To verify passwords based on MySQL's encode/decode */
/*
$mingle= "decode(password,'".$password."')";
$sqlquery = "SELECT " .$mingle. " as pass  from test-
login where customerid='" .$customerid
```

```
                    ."'";
                    $queryresult = mysql_query($sqlquery);

                    if($row=mysql_fetch_array($queryresult))
                    {

                      echo "Password : ".$password."<br>";
                      echo "MySQL Pwd: ".$row["pass"]."<br>";

                      if(!($password == $row["pass"])
                    )
                      {
                            die(" Invalid Password.");
                      }
                    }
                    else
                    {

                            die(" User not found.");

                    }
                    */

                    ?>
                    <p><b>Hi
                      <?php echo $customerid; ?>
                      </b></p>
                    <?php
                      echo " <p><b><a

href=\"updatepassword.php?customerid=".$customerid."&password=".$password."\">Click
                    here</a>";
                    ?>
                        to update
                    your password.</b> </p>
                    <p> </p>
                    </body>
                    </html>
```

The preceding code mostly resembles the code in createuser_php_md5.php. Therefore, I will not bore you by repeating the same explanation as above. The new password that you chose to log in is permanent. However, it has not been recorded into the database. You now need to click on the Click here link in the home page to update your password. Figure 17-11 shows the next screen that appears. Here you need to enter the customer ID and the password that you chose to log in.

FIGURE 17-11 *Updating the password*

When you click on the Login button now, update.php is invoked. This script initiates the process of updating your password. The code in update.php is as follows.

```
<html>
<head>
<title>Password Result</title>
</head>

<body bgcolor="#FFFFFF" text="#000000">
<p> </p>
<?php

$host="";
$uname="root";
```

```
$pass="";
$database="books";
$tablename="testlogin";

$connect= mysql_connect($host,$uname,$pass)
    or die("Database connection failed ! <br>");

$selectdb=mysql_select_db($database)
    or die("Database could not be selected");

$sqlquery = "select customerid from testlogin where cus-
tomerid='".$customerid."'";
echo $sqlquery . "\n<br>";
$queryresult = mysql_query($sqlquery);

if(!($row=mysql_fetch_array($queryresult)))
{
 die("Customer ID not found in database ! record cant be
updated!");
}

/* MySQL's encode function.(to store encrypted pass-
words.) */

/*
$mingle= "encode('".$password."','".$password."')";

$sqlquery = "UPDATE testlogin SET password=".$mingle;
*/

/* PHP builtin  MD5 function.(to store password hashes.)
*/

$sqlquery = "UPDATE testlogin SET password='".
md5($password) . "'";
```

```php
$queryresult = mysql_query($sqlquery);
if (!$queryresult)
{
   die(" Query could not be executed.<br>");
}


?>


<table width="330" border="0" align="center" cell-
padding="5" cellspacing="2">
   <tr>
     <td colspan="2" bgcolor="#dddddd">
       <div align="center"><b>New password entered for
         <?php echo $customerid;
            ?>


         as </b></div>
     </td>
   </tr>
   <tr bgcolor="#eeeeee">
     <td width="50%">
       <div align="right">Customer ID</div>
     </td>
     <td>
       <center>
         <?php echo $customerid; ?>
       </center>
     </td>
   </tr>
                                 <tr bgcolor="#eeeeee">
     <td>
       <div align="right">Password</div>
     </td>
     <td>
       <center>
         <?php echo $password; ?>
       </center>
     </td>
```

```
                                    </tr>
                                    <tr bgcolor="#eeeeee">
                                      <td colspan="2"><center>Try your new password in the
<a href="login.htm">login
                                    page</a></center></td>
                                      </tr>
                                    </table>

                                    <p> </p>
                                    </body>
                                    </html>
```

Now when you click on the Submit button, updatepassword.php is called, which does a final update of the password. Figure 17-12 depicts the new screen.

FIGURE 17-12 *Final updating of the password*

The code for updatepassword.php is as follows:

```
                                    <html>
                                    <head>
                                    <title>Update Password form</title>
                                    </head>
```

```
<body bgcolor="#FFFFFF" text="#000000">
<br><br><br>
<form name="maildata" method="post" action="update.php">
  <table width="250" border="1" align="center">

<?php

echo "<tr> ";
echo " <td> Customerid   </td>";
echo " <td width=\"150\">".$customerid."</td>";
echo "  <input type=\"hidden\" name=\"customerid\"
value=\"".$customerid."\">";
echo "</tr>";
echo " <tr> ";
echo " <td> New Password </td>";
echo " <td> ";
echo "  <input type=\"text\" name=\"password\">";
echo " </td>";
echo "</tr>";
echo "<tr> ";
echo " <td> ";
echo "  <center> ";
echo "  <input type=\"submit\" name=\"Submit\"
value=\"Submit\">";
echo "  </center>";
echo " </td>";
echo "</tr>";

?>
  </table>
</form>
</body>
</html>
```

The output of the above code is shown in Figure 17-13.

FIGURE 17-13 *Output of final updating of the password*

You can also browse through the customer IDs and corresponding passwords stored in the database. The code to do so is:

```
<html>
<head>
<title>maildata record browser</title>
</head>

<body bgcolor="#FFFFFF" text="#000000">

<?php

$connect= mysql_connect("localhost","root","")
    or die("Could not connect to MySQL server in
localhost !");

$selectdb=mysql_select_db("books")
    or die("Could not select mail data database !");

$sqlquery = "SELECT * from testlogin";
```

```
$queryresult = mysql_query($sqlquery);

echo "<table width=700 border=1 align=center>";
echo " <tr>";
echo "  <td width=200> <center><b>Customerid </b></cen-
ter></td>\n";
echo "  <td width=200> <center><b>Password</b></cen-
ter></td>\n";
echo "  <td width=100>
<center><b>Action</b></center></td>\n";
echo "  </tr>\n";
while ($row=mysql_fetch_array($queryresult))
{
  echo "  <tr>\n";
  echo "    <td>".$row["customerid"]."</td>\n";
  echo "    <td>".$row["password"]."</td>\n";
  echo "    <td><A
href=\"displayform.php?email=".$row["email"]."\">edit</a></td>\n";
  echo "  </tr>\n";
}
echo "</table>\n";
?>
</body>
</html>
```

The preceding code browses the database where the customer IDs and their encrypted and hashed passwords are stored. The output of this code is shown in Figure 17-14.

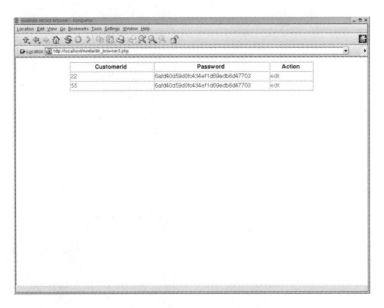

FIGURE 17-14 *Viewing the database that stores the customer IDs and passwords*

Summary

In this chapter, you learned to secure sensitive information, such as user pass-words, using encryption and hashing. You learned to create user-specific accounts or profiles in the Web site, which would be accessible only to individual users. An account or a profile is a private page where user-specific information (details) and settings are stored. This private page is accessible only to the user, after they log into the page. To implement this restricted access to personal or private informa-tion, you will learn to create a PHP script that will authenticate a user before they can access their profile (account).

You then learned about implementation of security in your Web site. You learned that passwords are among the most sensitive information that might be stored in a Web database. You learned about encryption and hashing of information, such as passwords, that allow you to secure the passwords and other sensitive informa-tion stored in the database.

Chapter 18

After you have put up a functional Web site, visitors will come flocking to your site. Some will visit your site out of need, while others will simply visit your site out of curiosity. If somehow you could gather, analyze, and implement information about your visitors and their preferences, it may prove very useful in determining the general preferences and trends. For example, you could use this information to offer personalized service to your clients. By offering this personalized service to your users, you can easily gain an edge over your competitors.

There are two ways you can trap relevant information about the users accessing your Web site. One method is the use of cookies; the other, more popular method is the implementation of session tracking in your Web site.

In this chapter, you'll learn about session tracking and how to implement the session-tracking functionality offered by PHP to your advantage. You'll learn about cookies in detail in Chapter 24, "Cookies."

An Overview of Sessions

In layman's terminology, a *session* is the time duration for which a user remains connected to a Web site. However, in programming terminology, a session is defined a little differently. In the Web development community, a session is referred to as a block of information that stores all types of variables and values that provide information about users and their visits to your Web site.

 NOTE

Introduced in the 4.0 release, PHP's session-handling features are built in. As a result, no additional packages other than the PHP distribution are required for your scripts to be able to support session-handling functionality.

A session contains an identification string that is used to uniquely identify a user who accesses your site. This identification string is commonly known as the *ses-*

sion ID (SID). Each session is associated with a unique session ID, which can track a user in two ways:

◆ **By storing and retrieving the session ID in a cookie.** This is the easiest and widely preferred method of tracking sessions. When a user visits the site, a SID is generated and stored within the cookie that is automatically sent by the Web server to every client that accesses it. However, this might not be an entirely foolproof method, because some users distrust the use of cookies and disable cookies in their browser settings. Also, you might end up with inconsistent data, in case the user refuses to accept one of the cookies. In addition, this method also poses a security threat because someone can fake the cookies and get access to virtually any other user's account.

◆ **By embedding the session ID into the URL.** This is a comparatively difficult method of tracking sessions. However, this method allows you to track sessions in every situation, including those where the cookies are disabled. In this method, the SID is appended (manually or automatically) to the current URL, as shown in the Address bar of the browser window. In order to manually append the SID to the URL, you'll need to add the following statement in your PHP script:

```
                <a href="test.php?<?=SID?>">Click here to visit the
next page.</a>
```

You can also set the session ID to be automatically appended to the URL. By doing so, you wouldn't have to write the preceding statement in every PHP script of yours! To achieve this objective, you'll need to compile PHP with the following option:

```
                enable-trans-id
```

When a user accesses your site, the session ID is sent to the user's computer during the login process, after which a user session is initiated. If the use of cookies is enabled at the client-end, the session ID is sent to the user in a cookie. This cookie is called PHPSESSID. At the same time, the session ID is also stored in the server as a temporary file.

From previous chapters, you might have gathered that PHP supports two types of variables, local and global. There is a third category of variables available in PHP. These are known as the session variables. You'll learn about session variables in detail in the following section.

Session Variables

A *session variable* is a global variable that, if registered as a session variable, retains its value on all pages that use PHP4 sessions. In other words, a session variable continues to exist if it is not deleted explicitly. As mentioned earlier, the session variable and its value are stored as a temporary file at the server end. A sample format in which a session variable is stored at the server side is shown below:

```
Welcome ¦ s:5: "78"
```

In the above statement, the name of the session variable is Welcome. The corresponding value of the variable is 78.

A session variable can store the following values:

◆ Integer values

◆ String values

◆ Arrays

◆ Objects

Before you can access a session variable programmatically (that is, extract the value stored in a session variable), you'll need to register the session variable. You'll learn more about registering session variables in the next section.

Registering a Session Variable

You need to register a variable before you can access it. Registering a session variable also helps it retain its value on all the pages that use PHP4 sessions. The procedure to register a session variable is as follows:

1. The PHP parser receives the cookie.
2. The PHP parser retrieves the value of PHPSESSID from this cookie.
3. The PHP parser then searches for a matching session file.
4. The PHP parser then searches for a matching session ID stored in a temporary session file.
5. The PHP parser then searches for the specified session variable in this session file.
6. After successfully locating the variable, the parser extracts the value stored in the session variable.

In order to register a session variable, first assign a value to the variable (that will act as a session variable) and call the `session_register()` function. The syntax of the function is as follows:

```
bool session_register(mixed arg1, mixed arg2,  ...., argn);
```

This function takes one or more variables that need to be registered with the current session. The function returns True if the variable(s) was set successfully. Otherwise, it returns False.

After a variable has been registered as a session variable, `variable_name` will have the value assigned to it before it was registered as a session variable on all subsequent pages that use sessions. Changes to the variable value will be automatically registered in the session and saved for further reference. Consider the following example to understand this concept.

```php
<?php
$vb1 = "This variable is to be registered!";
session_register('vb1');
echo $vb1;
?>
```

In the preceding code, a variable called `vb1` is defined and is assigned the value `This variable is to be registered!` The `session_register()` function is then used to register the variable.

CAUTION

Make sure that there are no whitespaces or newline characters in your script before the <?php tag. You will end up with an error!

The output of the preceding code is shown in Figure 18-1.

In the preceding Figure, `68e94706737416c5246c39f7f1ed885a` represents the session ID that has been generated as a result of registering `vb1` as a session variable.

In the next section, you'll learn to unregister a session variable that you registered with the help of `session_register()` function.

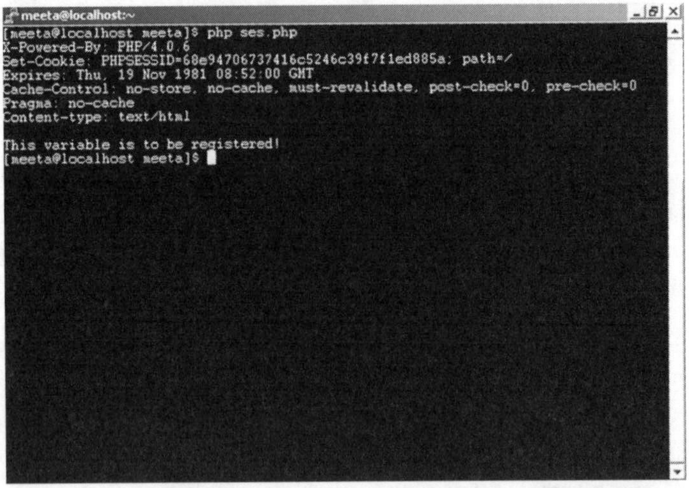

FIGURE 18-1 *Registering a session variable*

Unregistering a Session Variable

You can also unregister a session variable (that is, remove the session variable from the memory) from the current session, when you don't need it anymore. The function to use for the purpose is session_unregister().

The syntax of the session_unregister() is specified below:

```
bool session_unregister(string name);
```

As you can see in the above syntax, the session_unregister() function takes a single argument in the form of the name of the session variable that needs to be unregistered. The function returns True if the session variable was unregistered successfully. Otherwise, it returns False.

Consider the following code snippet:

```php
<?php
session_register(vbl);
if (session_is_registered(vbl))
{
session_unregister(vbl)
echo "The session has been unregistered successfully!";
}
```

```
else
{
echo "The session could not be unregistered.";
}
?>
```

In the preceding code, the session vbl is registered. The function session_is_registered(vbl) checks whether the variable is registered or not. (The function returns True if the specified variable is registered. Otherwise, it returns False.) A corresponding message is displayed depending on the fact whether the variable was unregistered or not.

The output of the preceding code is shown in Figure 18-2.

FIGURE 18-2 *Unregistering a registered session variable*

In the next section, you'll learn to start a session with the help of the corresponding function provided by PHP.

Initiating a Session

You can use the session_start() function to initiate a session. This is a built-in PHP function that is used to create a new session or resume the current session on the basis of the session ID passed to it via a GET variable or a cookie. The syntax of the function is as follows:

```
bool session_start();
```

The function always returns True.

NOTE

Since the session_start() function is used to perform several tasks that include checking whether a user is currently logged on, it is advisable to use the session_start() function at the beginning of the PHP script.

Consider the following code:

```php
<?php
session_start();
$vbl = "This variable is registered!";
session_register('vbl');
echo $vbl;
?>
<html>
<head>
<title>Starting a Session</title>
</head>
</body>
</html>
```

In the preceding code, a session is initiated with the help of the session_start() function. A session variable is then registered and its value is displayed in the browser window.

NOTE

A dialog box may appear asking for your confirmation to set cookies. This message will appear only when you have configured your browser to warn you before setting cookies. If you encounter this message, click on the OK button to allow the cookies to set.

Figure 18-3 shows the output of the preceding code snippet.

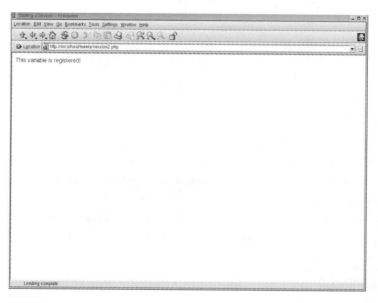

FIGURE 18-3 *Starting a session*

You can also modify a session variable after starting a session. Consider the following code snippet to understand this concept.

```php
<?php
session_start();
session_register('counter');
$counter++;
if ($count==1)
{
echo "<h1><center>Welcome! You are a first-time visitor
<center></h1>";
}
else
{
$disp="<h1><center>You have visited this page $counter times.
Thanks for your visit!</center></h1>";
}
?>
<html>
```

```
<head>
<title>Modifying Session Variable</title>
</head>
<body>
<?php
echo "$disp";
?>
</body>
</html>
```

In the preceding code, a session is initiated with the help of the session_start()
function. A session variable is then registered by using the session_register()
function and its value is displayed in the browser window. Another variable,
counter, is incremented each time you visit the page (or press the Refresh button
in the browser window) and a corresponding message is displayed in the browser
window.

Figure 18-4 shows the output of the above code, if you have visited the page for
the first time.

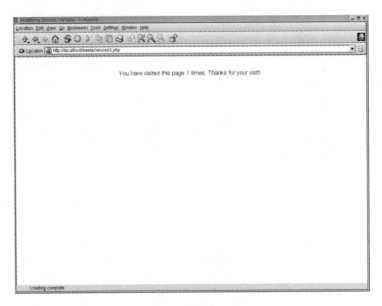

FIGURE 18-4 *Viewing the page for the first time*

Figure 18-5 shows the output of the preceding code if you have visited the page a few times.

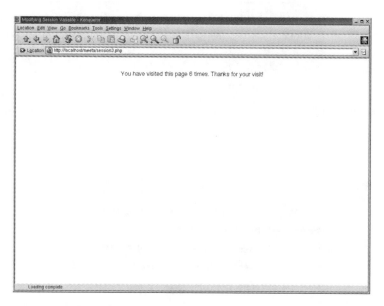

FIGURE 18-5 *Output of the above code after viewing the page a few times*

In the next section, you'll learn to set a session name.

Assigning a Name to a Session

You can use the session_name() function to get or set the name of the current session. The session name references the session ID stored in a cookie or a URL. As a result, it can contain only alphanumeric characters. Also, special characters, such as tildes (~) and question marks (?) cannot be used in a session name.

The syntax of the function is specified below:

```
string session_name(string name);
```

The session_name() function accepts a single argument in the form of the name of the session cookie. When no name is specified, the function returns the current name of the session.

> **CAUTION**
>
> The session_name() function should be called before the session_start() and session_register() functions. If you fail to do so, you will end up with an error message.

Consider the following code snippet to understand the use of the session_name() function.

```php
<?php
$old = session_name('Old-Session');
$new = session_name('New-Session');
$current = session_name('Current-Session');
session_register('New-Session');
echo "The old session name was $old.", "\n";
echo "The new session name is $new!", "\n";
echo "The current session name is $current!!";
?>
```

In the preceding code, session names have been assigned to three variables, old, new, and current. The value New-Session has been registered and the session names currently held in the three variables are displayed.

Figure 18-6 shows the output of the above code. Note that when the session variable is registered, the session names shift to the older value. For example, variable old reverts to its older value, PHPSESSID. Similarly, new now holds the value Old-Session and current holds New-Session.

In the next section, you'll learn to delete a session.

Deleting a Session

You can use the session_destroy() function to delete a session. This function deletes (or destroys) all the data registered to the current session. The syntax of the function is specified below:

```
bool session_destroy();
```

FIGURE 18-6 *Modifying the value of the session variable*

Consider the following code snippet:

```php
<?php
session_start();
session_register("vbl");

$result_delete = session_destroy();
if ($result_delete=1)
{
echo "The session is destroyed!", "\n";
}
else
{
echo "The session could not be destroyed.", "\n";
}
echo $pop;
?>
```

In the above code, the session is initiated and a variable called vbl is registered. The variable is then deleted with the help of the session_destroy() function. A corresponding message is also displayed.

Figure 18-7 shows the output of the above code.

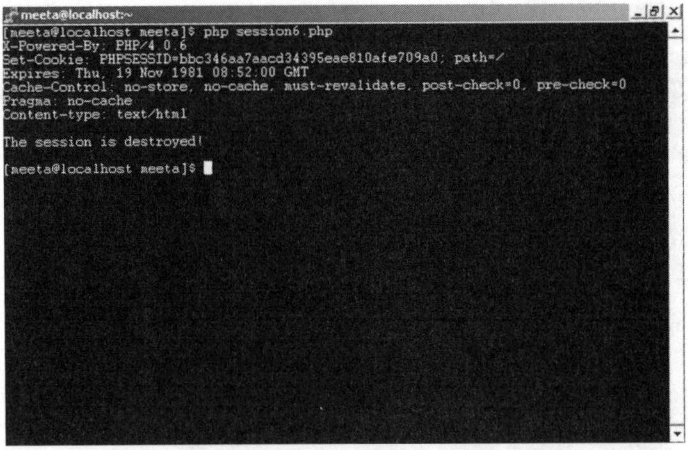

FIGURE 18-7 *Deleting a session variable*

NOTE

Though the `session_destroy()` function destroys the current session, the value of the session variable is still retained.

In the next section, you'll learn to store sessions in the form of strings.

Encrypting/Decrypting Session Data

In PHP, you can store all the session variables in the string format. PHP also allows you to extract these strings back to the original variables. This is referred to as *encoding and decoding* of data.

PHP provides the `session_encode()` function to encode the current session information into a string. This string can then be decoded to the original variables by using the counterpart `session_decode()` function.

The syntax of the `session_encode()` function is:

```
string session_encode();
```

The session_encode() function is used to encode the session information of the current session into a data string.

The syntax of the session_encode() function is:

```
string session_decode(string data);
```

The session_decode() function, on the other hand, decodes the session information encoded by the session_encode() function back to its original form.

Consider the following code snippet:

```
session_name();
session_start();
session_register("customerid");
session_encode();
$url= "Location: mypage.php?PHPSESSID=".$PHPSESSID;
header($url);
```

In the preceding code snippet, the current session is assigned a name and started. The variable, customerid, is registered as a session variable. The session_encode() function is then used to encode the data. You'll learn more about encoding and decoding session information in the next section.

Tracking Sessions

In order to track user information, the development team at Bukbuz has decided to use sessions. This will also help them enhance password security, as the user password need not be transmitted through the URL. Instead, a session ID will be generated and used for the purpose.

Consider Figure 18-8. This is the login form that you used in Chapter 17, "User Authentication Scripts."

When you click on the Enter! button, the login.php script is called. Login.php validates the supplied customer ID and matches the password. If you supply a wrong password, the message Password wasn't submitted is displayed in the browser window. Similarly, if no password was supplied, the message Empty password!! is displayed. If you enter a password whose length is less than 5, the message Invalid password length! is displayed.

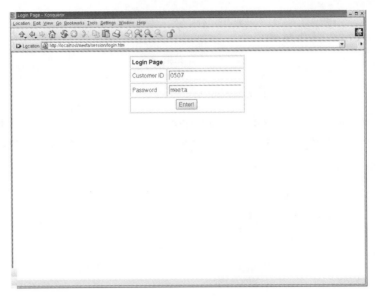

FIGURE 18-8 *The main Login page*

The code contained in login.php is as follows:

```php
<?php

//Authenticating the password
if (!isset($password))
{
 die("Password wasn't submitted !");
}

if (empty($password))
{
 die("Empty password !!");
}

if ((strlen($password) < 5) || (strlen($password) > 15))
{
die("Invalid password length!");
}

//Setting database environmental variables
```

```
$host="";
$uname="root";
$pass="";
$database="books";
$connect= mysql_connect($host,$uname,$pass)
    or die("Database connection failed ! <br>");

//Selecting a database
$selectresult=mysql_select_db($database)
    or die("Database could not be selected");

//Querying the database for specified customer ID and extracting
the corresponding password
$sqlquery = "SELECT password from login where customerid='"
.$customerid ."'";

$sqlresult = mysql_query($sqlquery);

if($row=mysql_fetch_array($sqlresult))
{
/*
echo $password."<br>";
echo md5($password)."<br>";
echo $row["password"]."<br>";
*/
 if(!(md5($password) == $row["password"]))
 {
die(" Password doesn't match !");
 }

}
else
{
 die(" No such user !!");
}

//Implementing session encoding
session_name();
session_start();
```

```
session_register("customerid");

//session_encode();

$url= "Location: mypage.php?PHPSESSID=".$PHPSESSID;

header($url);


?>
```

When a user logs in successfully to their personalized account (home page), as shown in Figure 18-9, login.php also creates a session by customer ID.

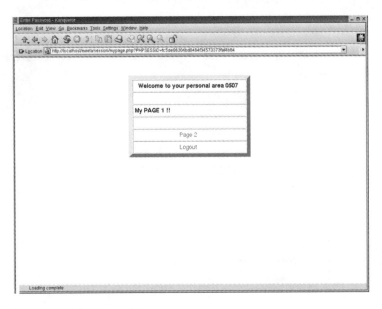

FIGURE 18-9 *The user's home page*

When your customer ID and corresponding password are authenticated, you can log into your personalized home page. Then mypage.php takes over the control. Besides displaying the user's home page, this PHP script verifies whether a session exists. If a session does not exist, this script redefines the session. The code in mypage.php is as follows:

```
<?php


session_name();

session_start("customerid");


if (!(session_is_registered("customerid")))
```

```
                                    {
                                    session_unset();
                                    session_destroy();
                                    die("Please <a href=\"login.htm\"> Login</a> First!<br>") ;
                                    }

                                    ?>
                                    <html>
                                    <head>
                                    <title>Enter Password</title>
                                    <meta http-equiv="Content-Type" content="text/html;
charset=iso-8859-1">
                                    </head>
                                    <body bgcolor="#FFFFFF" text="#000000">
                                    <p> </p>

                                    <table width="330" border="10" align="center" cellpadding="5"
cellspacing="2">
                                      <tr>
                                        <td>
                                          <div align="center"><b>Welcome to your personal area
                                            <?php echo $customerid; ?>
                                            </b></div>
                                        </td>
                                      </tr>
                                      <tr>
            <td> </td>
                                      </tr>
                                      <tr>
                                        <td>
                                          <b>My PAGE 1 !!</b>
                                        </td>
                                      </tr>
                                      <tr>
                                        <td> </td>
                                      </tr>
                                      <tr>
                                        <td>
```

```
                               <center>

                       <?php
                           echo "  <a href=\"mypage2.php?PHPSESSID=".
$PHPSESSID."\">Page 2</a>";
                       ?>
                               </center>
                           </td>
                           </tr>
                               <tr>
                           <td>
                               <center>
                                   <a href="logout.php">Logout</a>
                               </center>
                           </td>
                         </tr>
                       </table>
                       <p> </p>
                       </body>
                       </html>
```

The home page defined by mypage2.php is shown in Figure 18-10.

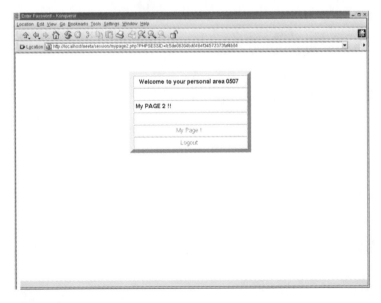

FIGURE 18-10 *The user's home page–2*

The code for mypage2.php is as given below:

```php
<?php

session_name();
session_start("customerid");

if (!(session_is_registered("customerid")))
{
session_unset();
session_destroy();
die("Please <a href=\"login.htm\"> Login</a> First!<br>");
}

?>
<html>
<head>
<title>Enter Password</title>
<meta http-equiv="Content-Type" content="text/html;
charset=iso-8859-1">
</head>
<body bgcolor="#FFFFFF" text="#000000">
<p> </p>

<table width="330" border="10" align="center" cellpadding="5"
cellspacing="2">
   <tr>
     <td>
       <div align="center"><b>Welcome to your personal area
         <?php echo $customerid; ?>
         </b></div>
     </td>
   </tr>
   <tr>
     <td> </td>
   </tr>
   <tr>
     <td>
```

```
          <b>My PAGE 2 !!</b>
        </td>
      </tr>
      <tr>
        <td> </td>
      </tr>
      <tr>
        <td>
          <center>


<?php          echo "  <a href=\"mypage.php?PHPSESSID=".
$PHPSESSID."\">My Page !</a>";
          ?>
          </center>
        </td>
      </tr>
            <tr>
        <td>
          <center>
            <a href="logout.php">Logout</a>
          </center>
        </td>
      </tr>
    </table>
    <p> </p>
    </body>
    </html>
```

When you click on the Logout hyperlink, the Login screen is displayed once again. This page is shown in Figure 18-11.

The code for the logout.php is given below:

```php
<?php
session_name();
session_start("customerid");
if (session_is_registered("customerid"))
{
session_unset();
```

```
session_destroy();
$url = "Location: login.htm";
header($url);
}
else
{
 die ("Only logged in users can be thrown out ! ");
}
?>
```

FIGURE 18-11 *The Logout screen*

NOTE

If you would like to implement session tracking feature in every page of your Web site, you can add the following statements in the beginning of every code.

```
session_name();
session_start();
session_register("customerid");
session_encode();
$url= "Location: mypage.php?PHPSESSID=".$PHPSESSID;
header($url);
```

Summary

In this chapter, you learned about session tracking and how to implement the session-tracking functionality offered by PHP to your advantage. You learned about various session tracking built-in functions that you need to use to implement session tracking in your Web site. These functions include: session_register(), session_unregister(), session_start(), session_name(), session_destroy(), session_encode(), and session_decode().

PART VII

Professional Project 6

Project 6

Beyond the Lab

Project 6 Overview

In this project, I'll teach you about some of the advanced concepts of PHP.

In Chapter 19, you will learn how to create and use images in PHP. You'll learn about the different image formats that are used on the Web, the basic image creation functions available in PHP, and how to manipulate pixels and set colors. Finally, you'll learn how to create graphs and bar charts in PHP.

In Chapter 20, you'll learn about the different input validators available in PHP. You will also learn how to validate an e-mail address.

Chapter 21 covers some of the most commonly used environment variables and command options that are used in CVS.

In Chapter 22, you'll learn to create code for PEAR, the PHP Extension and Application Repository.

In Chapter 23, you will learn about the Web portal system called PHP-Nuke that is slowly but steadily gaining a following among Web developers.

In Chapter 24, you'll learn how cookies are a simple yet powerful feature of PHP. They can help you enhance your Web site by tracking visitors, including how long they stay, how many times they return, which things they follow with interest on your site, and a lot more. You will learn to set a cookie, access it, and delete it after you are through using it.

Chapter 19

Graphics in PHP

Until now you have learned to create databases in MySQL and create HTML Web pages that contain PHP scripts for entering, retrieving, and displaying information. In this chapter, you will learn that the use of PHP is not limited to only uninteresting things, such as accepting and processing information. If you are interested in adding graphics and other animations in your Web site, you positively should read this chapter.

Graphics on the Web

Have you ever tried to create a Web page for yourself? I have, and believe me it is not a very easy task. I am not talking about the actual creation of the Web page, because anyone with good knowledge of HTML and a little R&D can create a nice Web page. No, I am talking about the actual content that you can put in the Web page. When I was creating a Web page for myself, I had no dearth of information. I had loads of information that I wanted to share with everyone. Finally, when I hosted my Web site and got feedback, I was shocked. Everyone had only one thing to say regarding my Web site: It was boring!

Yes, you guessed right. I made the fundamental mistake of putting only text on the site and no graphics. Everyone agreed that the content that I provided was good, but no one wanted to read paragraphs of text when all that was needed was a single photograph. I realized the truth in the saying "One good picture is worth a thousand words." This is especially true in the case of Web pages, which not only have to be informative but also light. One of the ways of reducing the file size is the judicious use of graphics. When I replaced text with images, not only did my Web site become informative but it also became visually appealing. In this chapter, I will share with you some of the things I have learned since I started to use graphics in my Web page.

You can use graphics in your Web page either by using already available images or by creating them from scratch.

Using Scanned Images

As mentioned previously, you can either reuse already existing images or you can create fresh images. Since using existing images is easier, we will discuss that first. Numerous sites on the Web offer images that you can use in your Web site. Some of these images are available without any obligation, while other sites demand that their images should only be used if you provide a link to their site from your Web page. You can also use images available in print, such as books, magazines, and other photographs. You can use these images by first scanning them and then storing them on your computer.

CAUTION

Some Web sites protect the graphics used on their site by declaring copyright for them. This means that you cannot use these images unless you have explicit permission from the owner or administrator of the site. The permission should be in writing and should explicitly mention that the bearer has the right to reuse the images or other graphics. A similar copyright also exists for images found in books and other written media. You therefore should make sure that the graphics you use are not covered by copyright.

Scanning is the conversion of a printed image or a photograph into a graphic image. This image can then be stored on a computer. When you scan an image, its content is not recognized by a computer. All text and graphics elements are converted into dots and stored on a computer in the same format. We will discuss the different formats of graphic images later in this chapter.

You can also use a digital camera to take photographs of images and store them on your computer. A digital camera is similar to a normal camera, the only difference being that in the case of a digital camera, the image is stored in the camera itself. When you have taken your photographs, all you need to do is attach the camera to your computer and save the images directly on your computer. This saves the trouble of getting the photographs developed and processed.

Even after you get the image that you want to place in your Web page, you might not be able to use it as is. You may need to resize the image or crop the areas of the image that you do not want to appear on your Web page. If the image is too dark or the objects appear blurred, you can use one of the available graphics packages to increase the brightness or to modify the image. Most graphics software have certain tools that you can use to easily perform these tasks and add effects to the image.

Sometimes you may not get a specific image that you want to place on your Web page. In this case you might need to create an image from scratch.

Creating New Images

In addition to using an already existing image, you can also create an image from scratch. This is an excellent option if you want a specific image to appear on your Web page. (Most artists would enjoy doing this as a way of unleashing their creativity.) You can use any of the currently available graphics packages—such as Flash, Freehand, CorelDraw, or Photoshop, to name a few—to create these graphic images.

Not only can you create images but you can also insert text in your graphics. Most of the graphics that require text are the logos, banners, and other images that are used to announce or give information. While using text in graphics, you should to keep the following points in mind:

- **Use colors that are browser-friendly.** Browser-friendly colors belong to the palette of 256 base colors. You can use these colors without any problem in your Web site. It is advisable to only use these colors because a unique color combination might not appear properly in all the Web browsers or operating systems.

- **Use a variety of fonts but only use the standard fonts.** Although it sounds a little strange, this statement implies that you can use different types of fonts in your graphics to highlight different pieces of text. However, a unique font like a unique color might appear distorted or in an unexpected manner in different browsers. This is because a browser might not support the font that you specified. Some of the standard fonts are Times New Roman, Arial, and Courier New.

- **Use anti-aliasing in graphics containing text.** You need to ensure that you use anti-aliasing to make sure that the edge of the text in your graphic merges with the background. This ensures that the graphic and Web page appear as one. A disadvantage in using anti-aliasing is that sometimes if the text used in the graphic is too small the final image will appear blurred.

CAUTION

You must be eager to start using text in the images you place on your Web page, but a word of caution: You must restrict the use of text in graphics on your Web page. This is because the use of text in the graphics increases the file size of the graphic images. This in turn increases the size of the Web page. A heavy image or an image of a large size increases the download time of the Web page. Therefore, the graphic elements will take a long time to download, and in the meantime, the user might lose interest in your Web site. Now you will not want that to happen.

After creating the graphics, you will want to save them. The next section discusses the different formats in which you can save graphics for future use on your Web site.

Formats of Web Graphics

Graphics used on the Web can be broadly divided into two types, bitmaps and vector graphics.

Bitmaps

Bitmaps are images that are stored in the form of pixels or dots. Each picture can comprise millions of such pixels. In case of bitmaps, each pixel can be manipulated separately. You can manipulate pixels by changing their colors or deleting them. Some of the supported formats for Web graphics are BMP, PSD, TIFF, JPG, GIF, and PNG.

Vector Graphics

Vector graphics are complex images in which pixel level manipulation is not possible. Mostly these types of graphics are used for creating line art and illustrations. A major disadvantage in using vector graphics is that you cannot use these images directly on the Web. You need to first convert them to bitmap format and then use them. Some of the commonly supported vector graphic formats are EPS, WMF, and AI.

Commonly Used Graphic Formats

From all the bitmap formats mentioned previously, there are only three formats that are most commonly used to store graphics that you can use in your Web page. These formats are GIF, JPG, and PNG. PNG is the most recent addition to the list due to the compact and light files. Let's discuss each of these formats separately.

- **Graphic Interchange Format (GIF):** The GIF format is the most commonly used format for graphic images used in Web pages. The format supports a maximum of 256 colors and an 8-bit compression. Mostly all images that are used as logos and banners on the Web are stored in GIF format. Most of the images stored in GIF format use solid colors. You can also save animated images, integrated images, and transparencies in GIF format. Animated images are multiple images that run in a sequence and are browser-independent. Therefore, the image appears to be in continuous movement. Integrated images are a boon for people with slow Internet access, because in this case the image appears in layers. You can also create a GIF image that has one color as the background and is set as transparent. Since most graphics comprise basic shapes such as ellipses, squares, and rectangles, the use of transparencies offers an excellent opportunity for creating complex images.

- **Joint Photographic Experts Group (JPEG):** This is another commonly used format, which is used for saving images of very high quality. JPEG images use 24-bit compression and support 16 million colors. Generally, all complex images such as photographs and drawings are saved in JPEG format. The earlier JPG formats did not support transparency. However, new versions are being developed that support transparency. Although these versions might support transparency, these graphic images would not be compatible with the earlier versions of Web browsers.

- **Portable Network Graphics (PNG):** The PNG format is the latest addition to the list of acceptable graphic image formats. The popularity of this format can be attributed to its support of all the bit formats, such as 8-bit, 24-bit, and 32-bit. Currently, a major drawback in using PNG format graphic files is that these images are not supported by the earlier versions of Web browsers.

Now that you know about the different types of formats in which you can save Web graphics, let's discuss how images can be used in PHP.

Creating Images in PHP

Graphics form an integral part of any Web site. Graphics can be used right from navigation to supplementing written text. PHP provides many functions that you can use to create and utilize graphics in your Web page. The use of graphics offers numerous possibilities (such as improving the popularity of your Web page—remember what I told you about my personal Web site). You may use simple images on your Web page. You might have dynamic images that change when users place their cursor on the image, or you can use animations to improve the appearance of your Web page. Although this is possible by using HTML, you can do these actions and more by using PHP.

The thought of using dynamic graphics might bring to your mind numerous instances where you can use this feature. Some of the ideas that come to my mind are given below:

◆ Illustrating information in foreign languages and certain formulae that cannot appear in normal fonts

◆ Displaying sensitive information such as a newly registered user's user ID and password in an image file so that the information cannot be intercepted during transfer

◆ Dynamically creating headlines and captions for information retrieved from a central database when the Web page opens

◆ Dynamically creating graphs and reports based on the user's input or query

◆ Dynamically displaying banners and links to information and customizing these links based on user requirements

PHP provides numerous ways that you can provide the above functionalities. The process is simple. You will use the same IMG tag that you generally use in HTML to insert a graphic. In this case, instead of using a static image, you will provide a link to a PHP script. The image is created whenever the program is executed.

The format of images that you can change is dependent on the version of the GD library installed on your machine. Besides the GD library, you need to install a few other libraries before you can create images in PHP. Let's learn how you can install GD and the other libraries on your machine.

Installing Required Graphics Libraries

The GD library is the most critical component that you need to install before you can create an image in PHP. If you have already installed the GD library on your computer, then you can move to the next section.

You can check if the library is installed on your computer by opening the phpinfo.php file in your browser and checking if the gd section exists. If the section appears in the Web page, then rest assured that the GD library is already installed on your system. However, if it's not installed, you can download the library from the PHP Web site. Detailed instructions on how to install this package are also available at the site.

The installation procedure of the GD library is simple. You need to execute the following commands once you have downloaded the file from the Web. Remember that you need to be logged in as the root to install the package.

```
./configure
make
make install
```

 CAUTION

The versions of GD earlier than 1.6 provide support for both GIF and JPEG formats, while the versions after 1.6 provide support for JPEG and PNG. You need to install the version of GD based on your requirement.

The GD library provides a number of functions that you can use in PHP to create different shapes, to change colors, and to create shapes filled with colors. Other libraries that you need to install are the zlib library and the PNG library. The zlib library is available at and the PNG library is available at a PHP Web site, and the FreeType font is available at **http://freetype.sourceforge.net**.

Let's now look at some of the functions provided by PHP that you could use while writing codes for creating dynamic images in PHP.

Providing Header Information

By default, each code written in PHP would contain a header file that provides information about the type of image that will be stored by using the code. The header files contain the Content-type header that stores this information. You can also direct the image information into the HTML Web page by specifying this in the header. The following code specifies that the output should be displayed in the Web page.

```
header ("Content type: text/html");
```

You can also use the header() function to specify that the output file should be JPG, GIF, or PNG, depending on your requirement. Therefore, you can use the header information to specify the different types of image files that you want to create in your program. The following code displays how you can specify these instructions in your code.

```
Header ("Content type: text/html");
Header ("Content type: text/html");
```

You'll learn to create images in PHP in the next section.

Steps for Creating an Image

Before you actually begin the process of creating an image, you should understand the steps involved in creating an image in PHP and displaying it in the browser. Creating an image involves first designing the image in the computer's memory before displaying the final output in the browser.

Following is a list of all the steps you need to perform while creating an image.

1. First you need to create an image canvas where you will create the actual image. An image canvas is an area allocated in the computer's memory where the image is drawn virtually before the final image is displayed in the browser or saved to a file.

2. The next step is to create the actual image on the canvas. You can create this image by using the various functions available in PHP. You will learn about these functions shortly.

3. After constructing the entire image, you then send this image to the browser and display it to the user.

4. The final action is the cleanup. You do not require the image stored on the canvas after sending it to the browser. This is why you need to release the memory by cleaning the canvas.

Declaring the Coordinates for the Image

Most of us might remember how we learned to draw. We learned that all drawings consist of shapes. Each shape contains a certain number of lines. A line is created between two points or coordinates. Just as this is the foundation of creating a drawing, you can use the same theory to learn to create an image. You might have learned about coordinates while working with graphs. A coordinate is a combination of two values, X and Y. The X value is calculated horizontally, and the value Y is used vertically. In graphs these values progress from the bottom-left corner moving outward. However, in case of PHP these coordinates are calculated from the top-left corner of the canvas. Figure 19-1 displays how coordinates map to the image canvas.

Now that you have created the image canvas and decided upon the colors you want to use in the image, the next logical step is to learn about functions that will help you in creating the proper environment to create the images that you want.

Using Basic Functions for Image Creation

As explained earlier, PHP provides numerous functions for creating images in PHP. These functions primarily require details regarding the image identifier or the canvas and the coordinates where the image is created. Let's look at some of the basic functions that you need to understand before you can create an image.

Creating the Image Canvas

As mentioned previously, the first step in creating an image is to create a blank canvas for creating the image. You can create a canvas by using the `ImageCreate()`

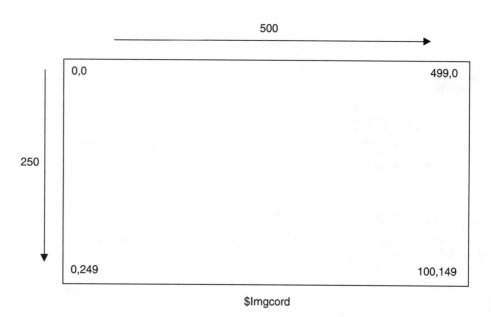

FIGURE 19-1 *Image canvas created based on coordinates*

function. The ImageCreate() function accepts two parameters: the height and the width for the image. The function returns a value known as the image identifier, which you can use in the rest of the code to reference the area in the memory allocated for the image. The command would look like the code given below.

```
$imgcord = ImageCreate(250,500);
```

The above code will create a canvas in the memory that can contain an image of 250 pixels in width and 500 pixels in height. The image identifier returned by the function is stored in the variable $imgcord.

You can either display an image in a browser or save this information to an image file. Let's learn how you can do the latter.

Saving an Image to a File

The only information that you require to save an image to a disk is the image identifier. This is because this identifier contains the location of the canvas in the memory that stores the entire image. You can either use the ImageJPEG(), ImageGIF(), or ImagePNG() function, which you learned about earlier, depending on your choice of output format. You can specify two other parameters along with the function. The first is a file name for the image file. The third option is a value to specify the level of quality you want to provide for the image. This value can range between −1 and 100. The value 0 would produce a low image quality file but of a relatively small size. On the other hand, a file created by using the value 100 would be of excellent quality but not feasible for use on the Web due to its heavy size. Therefore, determining the quality of your image file is a balance between file size and quality. Neither of these can be compromised. Let's look at each of the functions separately.

The *ImageGIF()* Function

This function can display the image in the browser or save it in a GIF file. The syntax of the function is as given below.

```
$intvar = ImageGIF(int img [, string filename])
```

The above code creates a GIF image from the image stored in the image identifier img, which was returned from ImageCreate(). The function saves the image using the name provided in the optional parameter filename. If the filename parameter is not provided, the GIF image is directly displayed in the browser.

The default format of the image is GIF87a, unless you make the image transparent by using the ImageColorTransparent() function, in which case the image format will change to GIF89a.

The *ImagePNG()* Function

This function can display the image in the browser or save it in a PNG file. Nowadays, this is the most common image format used on the Web. The syntax of the function is as shown below.

```
$intvar = ImagePNG(int img [, string filename])
```

Similar to the ImageGIF() function, the above code creates a PNG image from the image stored in the image identifier img, which was returned from ImageCreate(). The function saves the image using the name provided in the optional parameter filename. If the filename parameter is not provided, the PNG image is directly displayed in the browser.

The *ImageJPG()* Function

This function can display the image in the browser or save it in a JPEG file. The syntax of the function is given below.

```
$intvar = ImageJPEG(int img [, string filename])
```

This function is used if you want to save the image as a JPG image file. The above code creates a JPEG image from the image stored in the image identifier img, which was returned from ImageCreate(). The function saves the image using the name provided in the optional parameter filename. If the filename parameter is not provided, the PNG image is directly displayed in the browser.

Once you have displayed the image in the browser or saved it to an image file, you need to release the memory used to store the image information. In this way, the image canvas is cleared of all information. You use the ImageDestroy() function to clear the canvas.

Destroying the Image

After you have finished working with an image and saved it to a file or displayed it in the browser, you can now destroy the image. The ImageDestroy() function clears the image canvas and removes all information about the image from the memory. The syntax of the function is given below.

```
$intvar = ImageDestroy (int img)
```

The value in img is the image identifier that was returned by the ImageCreate() function.

The ImageCopy() *Function*

You use this function to copy a part of the image. The syntax of the function is given below.

```
intvar = ImageCopy(resource destn_img,
          resource source_img, int destn_x, int destn_y,
     int source_x, int source_y, int source_w, int source_h)
```

A number of parameters have been given above. The first parameter, source_img, specifies the original image; the next two parameters, source_x and source_y, are the coordinates from where you need to start copying the image. This image is copied to the destination image in destn_img at the coordinates destn_x and destn_y. You can specify the width and the height of the new image by using the parameter's source_w and source_h.

The GetImageSize() Function

You can use this function to determine the size of the image file. The function also returns the file type, which can be JPEG, GIF, SWF, or PNG format. You can also retrieve the height and width of the image that can be used later in the HTML IMG tag. The syntax of the function is given below.

```
$arrvariable = getimagesize(string filename [, array imginformation])
```

The function returns the information in the form of an array containing four elements. The elements contain information in the following sequence: width of the image, height of the image, flag containing the image type, and a text string. The height and width of the image is calculated in pixels. The flag contains a separate number for each format—for example, 1 for GIF, 2 for JPG, 3 for PNG, and 4 for SWF. The text string contains the height and width in a formatted string. You can use this string in the IMG tag. You can also pass the URL of the image location to the GetImageSize() function.

NOTE

SWF format is used for Flash files.

In the above section, you learned how to create a canvas on which you can create shapes and finally save the information as an image file. In the next section, you will learn how to create the shapes. Let's begin manipulating a pixel, which is the smallest unit of an image that can be manipulated.

Working with a Pixel

A pixel is a unit of measurement and is used for measuring the resolution of an image. It is also the smallest piece of an image that can be manipulated. You can change the color of a specific pixel based on your requirement.

The ImageSetPixel() *Function*

This function is used to set the color of a single pixel. The function takes four parameters. The img parameter, which is the first parameter, is the image identifier. The next two parameters are the X and Y coordinates, which specify the precise location of the pixel whose color needs to be changed. The final parameter (colr) is the actual color to which the pixel needs to be changed.

```
$intvar = ImageSetPixel(int img, int X, int Y, int colr)
```

Let's create a script and use the above function to manipulate a single pixel. The output of the above code appears as shown in Figure 19-2.

```
<html>
<head>
</head>
<body>

<?php
            $img=ImageCreate(200,200);

            $bgcolor=ImageColorAllocate($img,200,200,200);
            $pixelcolor=ImagecolorAllocate($img,255,0,0);

    /*
            RGB Red = 0..255 , Green = 0..255 , Blue = 0..255.
    */

            ImageSetPixel($img,50,50,$pixelcolor);
            ImagePNG($img,"pic.png");
                ImageDestroy($img);
    ?>

            <img src="pic.png" border=0>
```

```
                    </body>
                    </html>
```

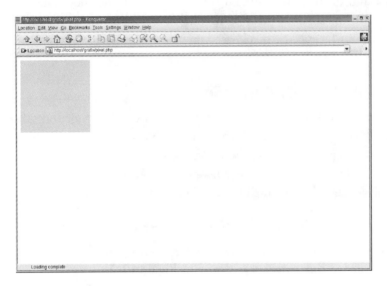

FIGURE 19-2 *Manipulating a pixel*

The ImageColorAt() *Function*

This function is used to get the index of the color of a pixel. The syntax is as follows.

```
$intvar = ImageColorAt(int img, int X, int Y)
```

You should use the ImageColorAt() function if you want to know the index of color of a pixel at the coordinates X and Y on the image represented by the image identifier img.

Before you begin to create the actual image, you need to specify the color for the image.

Setting Colors for Images

You can create images of different types of colors in PHP. However, these colors do not exist by default in PHP. What I mean is that these colors are not predefined; instead you need to create the color before you can use it. You use the ImageColorAllocate() function to create a color. The following commands display how you can create the basic colors red, green, and blue. These colors together are called RGB color mode, and all other colors are combinations of these basic colors. You can experiment with the various combinations to create the color you want.

```
$red = imagecolorallocate($imgcord, 255,0,0);
                    //Creates the color Red
$green = imagecolorallocate($imgcord, 0,255,0);
                    //Creates the color Green
$blue = imagecolorallocate($imgcord, 0,0,255)
                    //Creates the color Blue
$white = imagecolorallocate($imgcord, 0,0,0);
                    //Creates the color White
$black = imagecolorallocate($imgcord, 255,255,255);
//Creates the color Black
```

 NOTE

The RGB color mode is a standard based on which all other colors are created. A color contains a combination of all three basic colors, red, green, and blue. Each of these colors holds a value that ranges between 0 and 255. Another term related to the RGB colors are the Web safe colors. These colors are the same combinations of RGB colors but only contain the colors that are easily accepted by all browsers.

The first parameter used contains the image identifier. This is the same value that was returned by the ImageCreate() function. The next three parameters are the color combination. The above code creates a color based on the combination used. If all the three parameters are 255, you create the color black, and if all of them are 0, you create the color white. As you can see, the output for each color is stored in a separate variable. You can use these variables to create an image of the specific color.

The ImageFill() *Function*

Until now you used the basic shapes as empty images without any color. However, you can also fill images with colors by using the ImageFill() command. This function takes four parameters: the image context, the two coordinates from where it needs to start filling color, and the actual color. The syntax of the function is given below.

```
$intvar = ImageFill(int img, int X, int Y, int colr)
```

The above code will fill the image img with a specific color colr starting from the coordinates X to Y. For example, if the coordinates are 0,0, the fill will start from the top-left corner of the canvas. Given below is an example of how you can fill color in an image.

```
<?php

$imgcord = imagecreate(250,500);
$blue = imagecolorallocate($imgcord, 0,0,255);    //Creates the color Blue
$red = imagecolorallocate($imgcord, 255,0,0);    //Creates the color Red

ImageRectangle(($imgcord, 175,165, 200,225, $blue);

ImageFill($imgcord, 0,0, $red);
ImageString($imgcord, 3,170, 220,"Welcome to the World of PHP", $blue);

ImagePNG($imgcord);
ImageDestroy($imgcord);

?>
```

The ImageColorDeAllocate() Function

You can use this function to cancel the allocation of or to de-allocate a color for an image. The syntax of the function is as given below.

```
$intvar = ImageColorDeallocate(int img, int index)
```

You should use ImageColorDeAllocate() function if you want to de-allocate the color of a previously allocated color of the image.

The ImageColorSet() Function

You can use this function to set the color for the specified palette index. The syntax of the function is as follows.

$boolvar = ImageColorSet (int img, int index,
int red, int green, int blue)

You can use the `ImageColorSet()` function if you want to set the specified index in the palette to the specified color.

The ImageColorsForIndex() *Function*

You can use this function to get the color for an index. The syntax of the function is as given below.

$arrvar = ImageColorsForIndex (int img, int
index)

You can use the `ImageColorsForIndex()` function if you want to get an associative array of the RGB color combinations for the specified color index.

The ImageFillToBorder() *Function*

You use `ImageFillToBorder()` function to change the color of a border with a particular color. The syntax of the function is given below.

$intvar = ImageFillToBorder(int img, int X, int Y, int
border, int colr)

The above code fills the image `img` with the color `colr` from the coordinates `X` and `Y`.

By now you have learned to create a canvas and to allocate colors for shapes in PHP. You can also include text along with your graphics. The next section explains this concept.

Drawing Text

PHP does not just provide the function to create a image—you can also display text along with the image. You can use the `ImageString()` function to display text at a specific location in the image. The function requires six parameters. The first parameter is the image contest, after that the font number, next the coordinates where the text should appear on the canvas, then the actual text, and finally the color in which the text should appear. The font that you use in your string can belong to any of the five predefined fonts available in PHP. Let's create a script that used the ImageString() function.

```
<html>
<head>
</head>
<body>

<?php

$img=ImageCreate(300,300);

$bgcolor=ImageColorAllocate($img,200,200,200);

$red=ImagecolorAllocate($img,255,0,0);

$green=ImagecolorAllocate($img,0,255,0);

$blue=ImagecolorAllocate($img,0,0,255);

$grey=ImagecolorAllocate($img,50,50,50);

$black=ImagecolorAllocate($img,0,0,0);



ImageString($img,0,20,20,"Line 1",$red);

ImageString($img,1,20,40,"Line 2",$green);

ImageString($img,2,20,60,"Line 3",$blue);

ImageString($img,3,20,80,"Line 4",$grey);

ImageString($img,4,20,100,"Line 5",$black);

ImageString($img,5,20,120,"Line 6",$red);
```

```
ImageStringUp($img,0,50,200,"Line 1",$red);

ImageStringUp($img,1,100,200,"Line 2",$green);

ImageStringUp($img,2,150,200,"Line 3",$blue);

ImageStringUp($img,3,200,200,"Line 4",$grey);

ImageStringUp($img,4,250,200,"Line 5",$black);

ImageStringUp($img,5,300,200,"Line 6",$red);


ImageSetPixel($img,50,50,$pixelcolor);

ImagePNG($img,"pic.png");

ImageDestroy($img);
                                    ?>
                                    <img src="pic.png" border=0>
                                    </body>
                                    </html>
```

The output of the above code appears in Figure 19-3.

Let's now learn how to manipulate characters in your code.

The ImageChar() *Function*

You use this function to draw a character horizontally. The function takes five parameters. The first is the image identifier img. The next two parameters are the coordinates from where the text should begin. The next parameter is the actual string, and the final parameter is the color in which the string should appear.

The syntax of the function is given below.

```
                $intvar = ImageChar(Int img, int font, int X, int Y, string
c, int color)
```

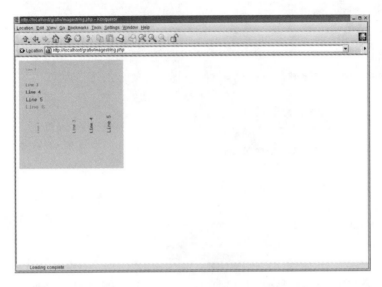

FIGURE 19-3 *Displaying text in an image*

The ImageLoadFont() *Function*

This function is used to load a new font. The function only takes a single parameter, which is the name of the bitmap file where the font is stored. The syntax
of the function is given below.

```
$intvar = ImageLoadFont (string file)
```

If you want to load a user-defined bitmap font, you need to use the ImageLoad-
Font() function. The function returns a unique identifier, which is used to utilize
the font in the rest of the program. This identifier should be more than 5, since
the numbers 1 to 5 are restricted to the built-in system fonts.

The ImageFontHeight() *Function*

You can use this function to retrieve the height of a font. You can then manipulate the height in your program. The height is calculated in pixels. The syntax of
the function is given below.

```
$intvar = ImageFontHeight(int font)
```

The ImageFontWidth() *Function*

This function retrieves the width of the font. You can use this function to manipulate the width of the font. The function only takes a single parameter, which is the font name. The syntax of the function is given below.

$$\text{\$intvar = ImageFontWidth(int font)}$$

Let's use the ImageFontHeight() and the ImageFontWidth() functions to write a program that retrieves their values and displays them.

```php
<html>
<head>
</head>
<body>

<?php

$img=ImageCreate(300,300);

$bgcolor=ImageColorAllocate($img,200,200,200);

$red=ImagecolorAllocate($img,255,0,0);

$green=ImagecolorAllocate($img,0,255,0);

$blue=ImagecolorAllocate($img,0,0,255);

$grey=ImagecolorAllocate($img,50,50,50);

$black=ImagecolorAllocate($img,0,0,0);


for
($i=0;$i<6;$i++)
{

ImageChar($img,$i,20,20+($i*20),"S",$red);

$height[]=Imagefontheight($i);
```

```php
$width[]=Imagefontwidth($i);

                                                                  }

                                                                  /*
                                                                  RGB Red = 0..255 ,
Green = 0..255 , Blue = 0..255.

                                                                  */



ImageSetPixel($img,50,50,$pixelcolor);

ImagePNG($img,"pic.png");

ImageDestroy($img);
                                                                  for
($i=0;$i<6;$i++)
                                                                      {

echo "font ".$i." height=".$height[$i]."<br>";
                                                                      }


                                    ?>
                                    <img src="pic.png" border=0>
                                    </body>
                                    </html>
```

The output of the above code appears in Figure 19-4.

The ImageCharUp() Function

You can use this function if you want to vertically display text in an image on the canvas. This function, which is similar to the ImageChar() function, accepts six parameters. The first parameter is the image identifier followed by the font in which the character should appear. The next two parameters are the coordinates from where the image should begin, followed by the actual string, and finally the color in which the string should appear.

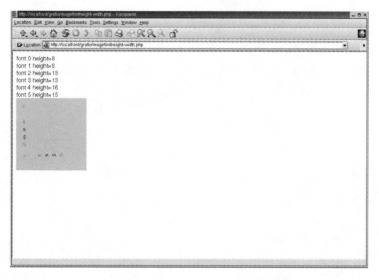

FIGURE 19-4 *Manipulating text in an image*

```
$intvar = imagecharup(int img, int font, int X, int Y,
string c, int color)
```

Let's create a program by using the text manipulation functions you have learned up to this point.

```
<html>
<head>
</head>
<body>

<?php

$img=ImageCreate(200,200);

$bgcolor=ImageColorAllocate($img,200,200,200);

$red=ImagecolorAllocate($img,255,0,0);

$green=ImagecolorAllocate($img,0,255,0);

$blue=ImagecolorAllocate($img,0,0,255);
```

```
$grey=ImagecolorAllocate($img,50,50,50);

$black=ImagecolorAllocate($img,0,0,0);


ImageChar($img,0,20,20,"S",$red);

ImageChar($img,1,20,40,"S",$green);

ImageChar($img,2,20,60,"S",$blue);

ImageChar($img,3,20,80,"S",$grey);

ImageChar($img,4,20,100,"S",$black);

ImageChar($img,5,20,120,"S",$red);


ImageCharUp($img,0, 20,160,"S",$red);

ImageCharUp($img,1, 40,160,"S",$green);

ImageCharUp($img,2, 60,160,"S",$blue);

ImageCharUp($img,3, 80,160,"S",$grey);

ImageCharUp($img,4,100,160,"S",$black);

ImageCharUp($img,5,120,160,"S",$red);
```

```
                                               /*
                                               RGB Red = 0..255 ,
    Green = 0..255 , Blue = 0..255.
                                               */
```

```
ImageSetPixel($img,50,50,$pixelcolor);

ImagePNG($img,"pic.png");

ImageDestroy($img);
                    ?>
                    <img src="pic.png" border=0>
                    </body>
                    </html>
```

The output of the above code appears in Figure 19-5.

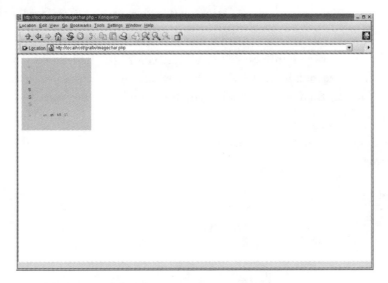

FIGURE 19-5 *Manipulating characters in an image*

In the above section, you learned how to manipulate text by using PHP code. In the same way, you can also create simple shapes and display these shapes in a Web browser. You'll learn more about the same in the following sections.

Drawing Basic Objects

As I explained earlier, an image is created of shapes and a shape is made up of a number of lines. Therefore, if you want to create a shape, you need to learn how to create lines. Some of the simple shapes that you can create using lines are the rectangle and the circle. You can also create arcs. Arcs are nothing but parts of an entire circle. However, first things first—let's learn to create a line.

Drawing a Line

You can use the ImageLine() functions to create a line. The function takes six parameters. The first one is the image identifier. The next four are the X Y coordinates, the first two coordinates being the point from where the line should begin and the next two coordinates the point where the line should end. The final parameter is the color. Let's create a line.

```
Imageline($imgcord, 5,5, 125,50, $red);
```

By using the above code you can create a line that starts from the coordinates 5,5 and continues until the coordinates 125,50. The color specified is red, and the image identifier $imgcord indicates the canvas where the information should be transferred. You can then display this information in a browser or saved in a file by using the image identifier.

Let's write a code that uses the ImageLine() function to create a line and save it as a PNG image file.

```
<html>
<head>
</head>
<body>

<?php

$img=ImageCreate(200,200);

$bgcolor=ImageColorAllocate($img,200,200,200);

$red=ImagecolorAllocate($img,255,0,0);


ImageLine($img,50,50,150,150,$red);

ImagePNG($img,"pic.png");
```

```
ImageDestroy($img);

?>
<img src="pic.png" border=0>
</body>
</html>
```

The output of the above code appears in Figure 19-6.

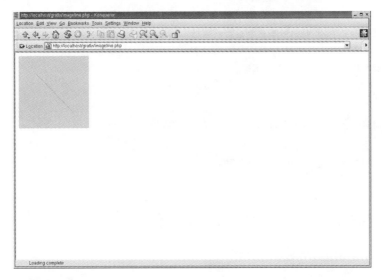

FIGURE 19-6 *Drawing a line in an image*

Drawing an Ellipse

You use this function to create an ellipse. The function takes five parameters. The first parameter is the image identifier, followed by the coordinates where the circle should be centered (C1 and C2). The next parameters are the height and the width of the ellipse (H and W) and finally the color of the image border. In this case, the ellipse will not be filled with any color.

The syntax of the function is given below.

```
intvar = ImageEllipse(resource img, int C1, int C2, int W,
int H, int colm)
```

Let's now write a script that creates an ellipse and saves it to a PNG file.

```php
                              <html>
                              <head>
                              </head>
                              <body>

                              <?php

$img=ImageCreate(300,300);

$bgcolor=ImageColorAllocate($img,200,200,200);

$red=ImagecolorAllocate($img,255,0,0);


Imageellipse($img,50,50,100,50,$red);

Imagefilledellipse($img,50,150,50,100,$red);


Imagefilledellipse($img,50,150,50,50,$red);

Imageellipse($img,50,50,50,50,$red);


ImagePNG($img,"pic.png");

ImageDestroy($img);
                              ?>
                              <img src="pic.png" border=0>
                              </body>
                              </html>
```

You have just learned how to create an empty ellipse. You can also create an ellipse filled with a specific color by using the filled ellipse function.

Drawing a Filled Ellipse

You use this function to create a filled ellipse. The function takes five parameters. The first parameter is the image identifier, followed by the coordinates where the ellipse should be centered (C1 and C2). The next parameters are the height and the width of the ellipse (H and W) and finally the color with which the image should be filled.

The syntax of the function is given below.

```
                    $intvar = ImageFilledEllipse(resource img, int C1, int C2,
int W, int H, int colm )
```

Let's now create a rectangle and then create another rectangle that has a specific color filled in it.

Drawing a Rectangle

You learned about the `ImageRectangle()` function when you learned the graphic functions available in PHP. As you would know by now, you can use this function to create a rectangle in PHP. The function takes six parameters. The first one is the image identifier, then the coordinates of the point where the rectangle should begin, next the coordinates of the point where the rectangle should end, and finally the color that you want to use to create the rectangle. The code is given below.

```
                                        ImageRectangle($imgcord, 175,165,
200,225, $blue);
```

In the above code, a rectangle is created on the canvas from the location 175,165 to the location 200,225. The color specified is blue.

Drawing a Filled Rectangle

You can also create a filled rectangle instead of creating an empty one with only an outline. The `ImageFilledRectangle()` function is used for this purpose. The function takes six parameters. The first one, as always, is the image identifier. Next are the coordinates from where you need to start filling the color, followed by the coordinates where the fill must end. The last parameter is the color that you want to use to fill in the rectangle. The final code will appear as follows.

```
                    <html>
                    <body>
```

```php
<?php

$img=ImageCreate(300,300);

$bgcolor=ImageColorAllocate($img,255,100,100);

$red=ImagecolorAllocate($img,255,0,0);


Imagefilledrectangle($img,50,170,150,270,$red);


ImagePNG($img,"pic.png");
ImageDestroy($img);
?>
<img src="pic.png" border=0>
</body>
</html>
```

The output of the preceding code appears in Figure 19-7.

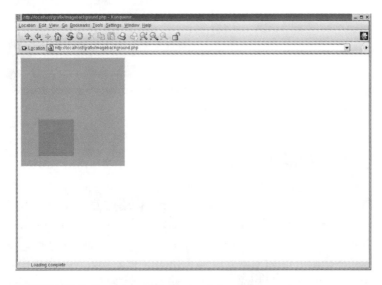

FIGURE 19-7 *Drawing a filled rectangle in an image*

Let's write a code that creates two rectangles, one filled and one empty. You will then save the image to a PNG image file.

```
                          <html>
                          <head>
                          </head>
                          <body>

                          <?php

$img=ImageCreate(300,300);

$bgcolor=ImageColorAllocate($img,200,200,200);

$red=ImagecolorAllocate($img,255,0,0);


Imagerectangle($img,50,50,150,150,$red);

Imagefilledrectangle($img,50,170,150,270,$red);


ImagePNG($img,"pic.png");

ImageDestroy($img);
                          ?>
                          <img src="pic.png" border=0>
                          </body>
                          </html>
```

The output of the preceding code appears in Figure 19-8.

Now that you have learned how to create the basic images, you can use combinations of these to create complex images. There are certain advanced shapes such as arcs and polygons that you can create in PHP.

Drawing Advanced Objects

As you can create basic images, you can similarly create a circle or an arc in PHP. I explained earlier that an arc is a part of a circle. To create a circle or an arc you should use the ImageArc() function. The function takes eight parameters. The

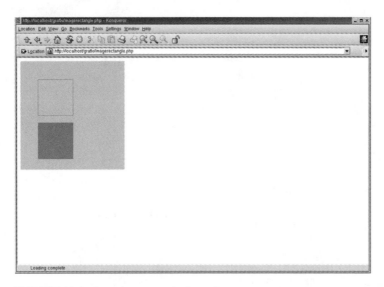

FIGURE 19-8 *Drawing rectangles in an image*

first is the image identifier, then the next two parameters are the X and Y coordinates that specify the location that forms the center of the circle. The next two parameters specify the height and width of the circle. The begin and end parameters used while creating an arc specify the points on a circle where the arc should begin and end. The begin and end points are calculated clockwise based on the degree from the right-hand location. (Remember your trigonometry class in school. The 0 degree starts from the rightmost location, and if you move clockwise in degrees, an arc created on a perpendicular line would be 45 degrees while a full arc or half circle would form 180 degrees.) You will now create an arc and line and save the file as a PNG image. The final parameter colm is the color in which the arc should be created.

```php
<?php
$imgcord = imagecreate(250,500);
$red = imagecolorallocate($imgcord,
255,0,0);        //Creates the color Red

$green = imagecolorallocate($imgcord,
0,255,0);        //Creates the color Green

$blue = imagecolorallocate($imgcord,
0,0,255);        //Creates the color Blue

imageline($imgcord, 5,5, 125,50,
$red);
```

```
                                    imagearc($imgcord, 100,25, 120,125,
0, 180, $green);

                                    ImagePNG($imgcord);
                                    ImageDestroy($imgcord);

                      ?>
```

In the above code, you first create the canvas 250 pixels in width and 500 pixels in height. Then you create three colors—red, green, and blue—and assign them to three variables. After this you create a line that starts from the coordinates 5,5 and continues to the coordinates 125,150. Finally, you created a half circle that connected both the ends of the line. The center point of this arc is specified at the coordinates 100,25. The width and height of the arc are declared as 120 and 125, respectively. The arc begins at 0 degrees and ends at 180 degrees.

 CAUTION

You can create advanced shapes only if you have GD 2.0 or later installed on your computer.

The ImageFilledArc() *Function*

You can use this function if you want to create a partial ellipse and fill it with any color. The syntax is as shown below.

```
            $intvar = ImageFilledArc (int img, int C1, int C2, int W, int H,
int S, int E, int color, int style)
```

The image is centered at the C1, C2 coordinates (e.g., 0,0 is the top-left corner of a Web page). The img parameter is the image identifier. The W and H parameters specify the width and height of the image, whereas the starting and ending coordinates are specified in the S and E parameters. The style parameter can be specified as bit-wise or by any of the following options:

◆ IMG_ARC_PIE

◆ IMG_ARC_CHORD

◆ IMG_ARC_NOFILL

◆ IMG_ARC_EDGED

The `IMG_ARC_PIE` and `IMG_ARC_CHORD` are used for different purposes. `IMG_ARC_CHORD` is used to connect the starting and ending angles with a straight line, whereas `IMG_ARC_PIE` creates the rounded edge for the image. If you just want to outline the arc and not fill it with color, then you should use the `IMG_ARC_NOFILL` option. Lastly, the `IMG_ARC_EDGED` option is used along with the `IMG_ARC_NOFILL` option to connect the beginning and ending angles to the center. This creates an image of a pie with just an outline and no filled-in color.

Let's now write a code that will create arcs, save the output in an image file of PNG format, and display the image in a browser.

```
                       <html>
                       <head>
                       </head>
                       <body>

                       <?php

$img=ImageCreate(500,500);

$bgcolor=ImageColorAllocate($img,200,200,200);

$red=ImagecolorAllocate($img,255,0,0);


for($i=0;$i<20;$i++)
                                                 {

Imagearc($img,50,50,20 + ($i*5),50,180,270,$red);


                                                 }

for($i=0;$i<20;$i++)
                                                 {

Imagefilledarc($img,50,200,50,50,$i*2,$i*2+40,$red);
                                                 }

Imagefilledarc($img,50,250,50,50,180,270,$red,IMG_PIE);
```

```
Imagefilledarc($img,100,300,50,50,180,270,$red,IMG_NOFILL);

Imagefilledarc($img,150,350,50,50,180,270,$red,IMG_CHORD);

Imagefilledarc($img,200,400,50,50,180,270,$red,IMG_EDGED);



ImagePNG($img,"pic.png");

ImageDestroy($img);
                            ?>
                            <img src="pic.png" border=0>
                            </body>
                            </html>
```

Similarly, you can also create polygons and fill them with a specific color.

The ImagePolygon() Function

This function is used to draw a polygon. The syntax is as follows.

```
            $intvar = ImagePolygon(int img, array points, int
num_points, int color)
```

This function is also similar to the `ImageRectangle()` function. The above code creates a polygon by using the image img, and the points array contains the polygon's vertices. For example, the element point[0] will contain the value x0, point[1] = y0, point[2] = x1, point[3] = y1, and so on. The total number of vertices of the polygon is specified in the parameter num_points.

The ImageFilledPolygon() Function

You can use this function to draw a filled polygon. The syntax of the function is given below.

```
            $intvar = ImageFilledPolygon(int img, array points, int
num_points, int color)
```

The preceding code creates a filled polygon image by using the image identifier img with a specific color color. The value stored in points is a PHP array that contains the polygon's vertices. For example, the element points[0] will contain the value x0, points[1] = y0, points[2] = x1, points[3] = y1, and so on.

In the previous sections, you learned to create some basic and advanced images in PHP. In the next section, you will learn how you can create new images by adding new shapes to existing JPG, GIF, or PNG images.

Drawing Images on Other Existing Images

You can also create new images by using certain functions to modify existing images. These functions are used in cases where certain images are available in files or at certain URLs. You can create copies of these images and use them elsewhere. You can make copies of existing images of both JPG or PNG image formats and use them.

The ImageCreateFromJPEG() Function

This function is similar to the ImageCreateFromGIF() function. You use this function to create a new image from a JPEG file or URL. The syntax of the function is given below.

```
$intvar = ImageCreateFromJPEG(string filename)
```

In the above code, the ImageCreateFromJPEG() function creates a JPEG image from the image provided in the filename parameter.

The ImageCreateFromPNG() Function

You use this function to create a new image from a PNG file or URL. The syntax of the function is given below.

```
$intvar = ImageCreateFromPNG(string filename)
```

In the above code, the ImageCreateFromPNG() function creates a PNG image from the file provided in the filename parameter. Let's now write a code that will create rectangles and save the image as a PNG file.

```
<html>
<head>
</head>
<body>

<?php

$pic=ImageCreate(600,600);

$col1=ImageColorAllocate($pic,200,200,200);

$col2=ImageColorAllocate($pic,0,0,255);

ImageFilledRectangle($pic,1,1,100,100,$col2);

ImagePNG($pic,"pic.png");

ImageDestroy($pic);
?>
                                    <img src="pic.png"
border=0>
                                    </body>
</html>
```

The output of the above code is shown in Figure 19-9.

The ImageCreateFromString() Function

You use this function to create a new image from the image stream, which is stored in a string. The syntax of the function is given below.

```
$intvar = ImageCreateFromString(string filename)
```

The `ImageCreateFromString()` function is used to obtain an image from the given string.

Now that you know how to create basic and advanced shapes, you can use these shapes to create images dynamically at runtime. These images are based on user input or based on information stored in a database. From the multitude of uses

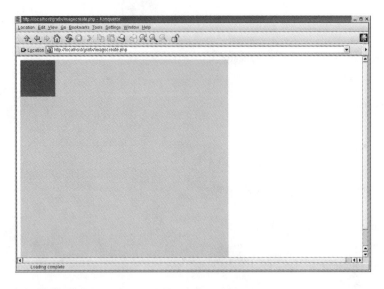

FIGURE 19-9 *Displaying a PNG image in a browser*

that dynamic image generation has, two of the uses are creating graphs and bar charts dynamically.

By now you know how to create and display images dynamically in a PHP Web page. Let's take one step further and create complex images such as bar charts by using these shapes.

Dynamically Creating Charts in PHP

You might have created graphs in school or seen them on the Web. These graphs are created against an X and a Y axis. On one side you have the base objects, and the values are plotted against these base values. You can also create these graphs or bar charts dynamically in PHP.

In the example that follows, you will accept the number of objects that a user wants to plot on the graph. After entering the value, the user will be prompted for the names of these objects and their corresponding values. After the values have been entered, the graph is created based on these values. The graph will change every time based on the user's input.

In the code given below, the user is prompted to enter the number of bars to display in the chart. Once the value has been entered, the user clicks the Submit button. The output of the code given below is displayed in Figure 19-10.

```html
<html>
<head>
<title>Graphics</title>
<meta http-equiv="Content-Type" content="text/html; charset=iso-8859-1">
</head>

<body bgcolor="#FFFFFF" text="#000000">
<p> </p>
<form name="form1" method="post" action="barformgenerator.php">
  <table width="26%" border="1" align="center" cellpadding="5">
    <tr>
      <td colspan="2">
        <div align="center"><b>Enter bar chart details</b></div>
      </td>
    </tr>
    <tr>
      <td width="51%">Enter the number of stats (bars)</td>
      <td width="49%">
        <input type="text" name="datacount" size="2">
      </td>
    </tr>
    <tr>
      <td colspan="2">
        <div align="center">
          <input type="submit" name="Submit" value="Submit">
        </div>
      </td>
    </tr>
  </table>
</form>
<p> </p>
</body>
</html>
```

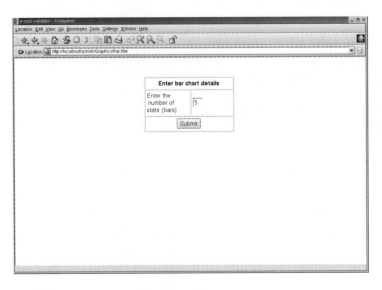

FIGURE 19-10 *Accepting input from the user*

After clicking the Submit button, the user is prompted to enter the names and the corresponding values for the objects. The number of prompts depends on the number specified by the user in the previous Web page. The Web page appears as shown in Figure 19-11.

```html
<html>
<head>
<title>Graphics</title>
<meta http-equiv="Content-Type" content="text/html; charset=iso-8859-1">
</head>

<body bgcolor="#FFFFFF" text="#000000">
<p> </p>
<form name="form1" method="get" action="barchart.php">
  <table width="26%" border="1" align="center" cellpadding="5">
    <tr>
      <td colspan="3">
        <div align="center"><b>Enter bar chart details</b></div>
      </td>
    </tr>
    <tr>
      <td width="25%"><center>Serial Number</center></td>
```

```
        <td width="26%"><center>Bar title text</center></td>
        <td width="49%"><center>Value</center></td>
    </tr>
<?php

for ($i=0;$i<$datacount;$i++)
{
 echo "    <tr>   ";
 echo "        <td width=\"25%\"><center>",$i+1,"</center></td>";
 echo "        <td width=\"26%\">";
 echo "          <input type=\"text\" name=\"title[]\" size=\"10\">";
 echo "        </td>";
 echo "        <td width=\"49%\"> ";
 echo "          <input type=\"text\" name=\"arr[]\" size=\"4\">";
 echo "        </td>";
 echo "    </tr>";
}
?>
    <tr>
      <td colspan="3">
        <div align="center">
<?php
    echo "<input type=\"hidden\" name=\"datacount\" value=\"".$datacount."\" >
";
?>
          <input type="submit" name="Submit" value="Submit">
        </div>
      </td>
    </tr>
  </table>
</form>
<p> </p>
</body>
</html>
```

The user enters the value as shown in Figure 19-11. After entering the names for the objects and their corresponding values, the user clicks the Submit button. The chart is created based on the entered values. The final chart appears as shown in Figure 19-12.

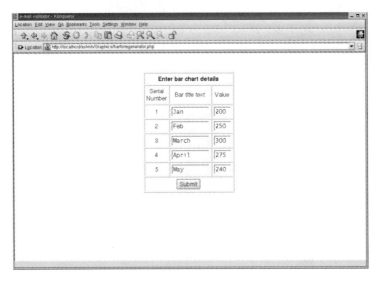

FIGURE 19-11 *Accepting legends from the user*

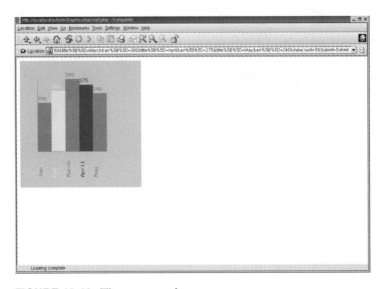

FIGURE 19-12 *The output graph*

```php
<head>
</head>
<body>

<?php
/*
$arr[0] = 15;
$arr[1] = 120;
$arr[2] = 131;

$title[0] = "Line 1";
$title[1] = "Line 2";
$title[2] = "Line 3";
*/

  $xcanvas=350;
  $ycanvas=350;
  $chartwidth=200;
//  $datacount=3;

  $pic=ImageCreate($xcanvas,$ycanvas);
  $bgcolor=ImageColorAllocate($pic,200,200,200);

  $color[]=ImageColorAllocate($pic,0,0,255);
  $color[]=ImageColorAllocate($pic,0,150,0);
  $color[]=ImageColorAllocate($pic,235,235,0);
  $color[]=ImageColorAllocate($pic,255,0,0);

$max_array_value = 0;

for($i=0;$i<$datacount;$i++)
{
 if($arr[$i] > $max_array_value)
  {
   $max_array_value = $arr[$i];
  }
}
```

```php
if($max_array_value==0)
{
die("max stat value is 0 !");
}


$resize_ratio= $chartwidth/$max_array_value;
$barwidth =round( 200/$datacount) ;

for($i=0;$i<$datacount;$i++)
{
 if (!($j<3))
 {
  $j=0;
 }
 else
 {
  $j++;
 }

 $startx =  50+($i*$barwidth);
 $endx    = 50 +( $i * $barwidth) + $barwidth;
 $starty = 250-$arr[$i]*$resize_ratio;
 $endy    = 250;

 ImageFilledRectangle($pic,$startx,$starty,$endx,$endy,$color[$j]);
 Imagestring($pic,5,$startx,$starty-20,$arr[$i],$color[$j]);
 Imagestringup($pic,5,$endx-$barwidth,$endy+70,$title[$i],$color[$j]);


}
 ImageLine($pic,50,50,50,250,$color[3]);
 ImageLine($pic,50,250,250,250,$color[3]);



 ImagePNG($pic,"pic.png");
 ImageDestroy($pic);
?>
<img src="pic.png" border=0>
</body>
</html>
```

Besides the functions discussed up to this point, you can use some other functions in your programs for manipulating images. These functions can retrieve a specific color or return the color index number of a specific color. You can also retrieve the index number of a color that is closest to the color you want.

Other Useful Functions

There are certain other functions that you can use in PHP to manipulate images. Let's look at each one of them in detail.

The ImageInterlace() Function

You can use this function to enable or disable interlace. Interlace implies that the image blends into the background. The syntax is as follows.

```
$intvar = ImageInterlace (int img [, int interlace])
```

If you want to turn the interlace bit on or off, you need to use the `interlace` parameter. The use of this parameter is optional. If the value of `interlace` is 1, then the image `img` will be interlaced; otherwise the image will not be interlaced. This function is generally used to determine if the interlace bit is set for the image and return the value.

The ImageColorClosest() Function

This function is used to get the index of the closest color to the specified color. The syntax of the function is given below.

```
$intvar = ImageColorClosest( int img, int red, int
green, int blue)
```

You can use this function if you want to know the index of the closest color to the specified color combination. This value is calculated by taking into account the distance between the color you want and the specified combination.

The ImageColorClosestAlpha() Function

This function is used to get the index of the specified color including alpha or its closest possible alternative.

The ImageColorExact() Function

This function is used to get the exact index of the specified color.

The ImageColorExactAlpha() Function

This function is used to get the index of the specified color including alpha. The syntax is as follows.

```
$intvar = ImageColorExactAlpha (resource img, int
red, int green, int blue, int alpha)
```

You can use this function if you want to know the index of the specified color combination including alpha in the palette of the image img. The value -1 is returned in case the color does not exist.

The ImageColorResolve() Function

You can use this function to get the index of the specified color or its closest possible alternative. The syntax of the function is as follows.

```
$intvar = ImageColorResolve(int img, int red, int
green, int blue)
```

If you want a definite result of a color index for the requested color combination, you need to use ImageColorResolve() function. This function will return either the exact color or the closest possible alternate.

The ImageColorResolveAlpha() Function

You can use this function to get the index of the specified color including alpha or its closest possible alternative. The syntax of the function is as shown below.

```
$intvar = ImageColorResolveAlpha (resource img, int red, int
green, int blue, int alpha)
```

If you want a definite result of a color index for the requested color combination, you need to use the ImageColorResolveAlpha() function. This function will return either the exact color including alpha or the closest possible alternate.

Summary

In this chapter, you learned how to create and use images in PHP. You learned about the need for using images in Web pages. Then you learned that you can use two types of images in your Web sites—you can either use scanned images or create new images from scratch. Next you learned about the different formats of images that are used on the Web. You learned about the GIF, JPG, and PNG image formats. Then you learned about the steps involved in creating images. You learned about the different libraries that need to be installed on your system before you can create and use images in PHP.

Next you learned about the basic image creation functions available in PHP. You learned how to create an image canvas, how to save the image once it is created, and how to delete the information stored on the canvas. You then learned how to manipulate pixels and set colors. Next you learned how to manipulate text and characters and then how to create basic shapes, such as lines, ellipses, and rectangles. You also learned how to fill color in these shapes. Then you learned how to create advanced objects, like arcs and polygons. Next you learned how you can create images on existing images. Finally, you learned how to create graphs and bar charts in PHP.

Chapter 20

In the earlier projects, you learned how to create an HTML page to accept user input. You can create the form and code how the information entered by the user should be processed. However, how can you ensure that the user enters information only in a specific format or enters information at all? This is where input validation is required.

In this chapter, you will learn about the need for validating input and the methods that are available for validating the data entered by the user. This is vital data that has to be validated before it is sent to the Web server. You will also learn how you can ensure a user enters all the required information in the Web page before submitting the page to the Web server.

Validation Basics

You might create an excellent Web page that accepts information from the user and processes it. However, you can never predict how a user might enter the information. You might provide detailed instructions as to how the information should be entered. Still a user might enter the information incorrectly, either intentionally or unintentionally. For example, the phone number might only accept numeric values and no spaces or special characters. Now if users enter their phone number and add a space to distinguish between the area code and the actual number, the information will not be saved and the database will return an error. All this can be avoided if you create an input validator that checks the entered information before it is sent to the database.

At the basic level, you can control the information entered by the user by using controls such as list boxes, check boxes, and radio buttons where the user only needs to select the information instead of entering it. The area where the problem arises is when the user needs to enter information in a text box. Since there is a very limited scope of control on what the user can enter, it is this information that needs to be validated foremost. In this chapter, you will look at some methods that you can use in your code to validate the information before it is sent to the database server. However, before you learn about these methods you should understand the requirement or the need for validating the user input.

Requirement for Validation

Unless users enter valid or proper information, they cannot get proper values or output. Another reason why users need to provide proper information is because every database has certain rules based on which it stores information. Unless the information is provided in the required format, the database will return an error.

Nobody wants to enter incorrect data intentionally (unless they get pleasure out of getting error messages when they submit the form). Most users make an honest mistake when they enter incorrect information. This mistake can either be due to the nonavailability of the data with them, because they were unable to comprehend what information was required, or simply a little bit of carelessness. Therefore, it becomes your responsibility as a Web designer and developer to ensure that the users are provided proper guidance on how to enter the data completely and accurately. Let's now learn about what needs to be validated.

What Should Be Validated

Now the question that arises is what should you validate. Users might enter data that could be invalid in many ways. Some of the common ones are that the string is empty or doesn't conform to the length of the value that is acceptable on the database. Let's now look at some of the commonly performed validation checks.

◆ **Length:** A check is required to verify that a user doesn't enter a value that is more than or less than the specified string length. For example, if the Name field in the database at the back end only accepts a maximum of 20 characters, you need to ensure that the value entered by the user should also be a maximum of 20 characters.

◆ **Datatype:** A check is required to verify that the datatype of the entered information conforms to the required datatype. A database stores information based on datatypes such as char, varchar, int, or boolean. The database will return an error if the information entered by the user doesn't belong to the same datatype as specified in the database. For example, if the Zip code field in the database only accepts numeric characters, you need to verify that the user enters only numbers and no alphabets or special characters. An exception to this rule is the varchar datatype, which accepts any kind of information, both numeric and alphanumeric.

◆ **Mandatory:** A check is required to verify that the information is entered for all mandatory or essential fields. Some fields are essential for saving a record in the database, or some other information might be necessary for the transaction to be completed successfully. For example, in an online shopping mart if the address of the customer is not entered in the proper format, the transaction should fail. Or if all the numbers of the credit card are not entered, the form should return an error before the information is sent to the database.

◆ **Range:** A check is required to verify that the information supplied by the user exists in the range of acceptable values, if such a range is specified. For example, if you require users to enter their salary details, you can provide them with a list box containing the ranges of salaries.

◆ **Listing:** A check is required to verify that the entered information exists in the list of acceptable values. For example, if you require users to specify their gender, you must provide them with a list of values from which they can select. You need to ensure that the users only select a value that already exists in the list.

◆ **Dependence:** A check is required to verify that a value is entered in a field that is dependent on another field. This is critical in cases where certain values are calculated based on the information that users enter in a particular field. For example, if an online shopping mart offers discounts based on the amount for which the customer places the order, the value cannot be calculated correctly unless the customer correctly enters the number of required items. Therefore, the discount field is dependent on the amount of the total order, which in turn depends on the number and price of amount orders. If any of these values is missing, the discount cannot be calculated.

Validation can be performed either at the server side or at the client side. At the server side validation is handled by PHP, while at the client side the validation is handled at the HTML page. Let's first look at how we can validate information at the HTML level.

Performing Validations in an HTML Web Page

Your first line of defense in the world of the Internet is your HTML page. You can use controls that assist the user not only in entering information but also in entering it in the correct format. For example, you can use HTML elements like list boxes and radio buttons to provide the user with a limited range of options to choose from. Although using HTML-based Web pages is not an effective method for performing complex validations, you can perform simple validations. Some of these validations and their solutions are listed below:

- Restricting the value that a user can enter to a group of values by using radio buttons
- Restricting the size of the information that a user can enter by using the SIZE attribute
- Restricting the value that a user can enter to a group of values by using radio buttons
- Restricting the size of the value that a user can enter in a text box by using the MAXLENGTH attribute
- Restricting the values that a user can enter to a range of values by using a list box

However, there are certain actions or validations that are beyond the control of HTML. For example, you might want the user to only enter numeric values in a particular field or want the date to appear in a particular format. You might want a user to enter information from a specific range of values only. None of these validations is possible by using HTML. To perform these validations you need to write a code in a scripting language, such as VBScript, JavaScript, or PHP, to name a few. Let's learn how you can make these validations possible in PHP.

Performing Validations in PHP

You have learned to validate the user's input at the basic level in HTML. There you learned how to check the size of the input and set the maximum number of characters the field will accept. However, you still need to ensure that the data that has been entered by the user conforms to specified standards.

Something that you need to remember here is that users should get the opportunity to correct any mistakes they make in the form instead of receiving an error message when the database is unable to process the query. For this reason you need to check the content before the information is passed to the database server.

PHP provides numerous functions to validate information entered in an input field. These functions can be generally divided into three categories based on the types of information that a user mostly enters. These validation categories include:

◆ Validating string information

◆ Validating date information

◆ Validating integer information

Let me first explain how you can validate string information.

Validating String Information

The most common validation requirement is for checking string information. You can use string functions to validate string information. You learned about a few of these functions in Chapter 9, "HTML Basics." These functions were isempty(), strlen(), and strcmp(). As you might recall, the isempty() function is used to check whether a string variable doesn't contain any value, while strlen() and the strcmp() functions are used to check if the length of the string is more than or less than the required length or if the content of two strings is similar to each other.

Let's now look at these and some of the other functions that are available in PHP.

The count_chars() Function

This function is used to retrieve information about the characters that are used in the string:

```
$intvar = count_chars(string strvar [, mode])
```

The function returns a mixed variable and is used to count the number of occurrences of a character in a string.

The ltrim() *Function*

This function is used to remove the whitespaces from the beginning of a string. You can use this function to determine if a user has entered spaces instead of valid information. The syntax of the function is as given below.

```
$strval = ltrim(string strvar [, string charlist])
```

The second parameter is optional. If the second parameter is not specified, the above code will remove all the whitespaces, tabs, line feed characters, NULL value, and a carriage return from the entered information. (These characters appear as shown in Table 20-1.) You can include these characters in the second parameter to keep these values. You can use the . character to specify multiple values.

Table 20-1 Characters and Their Values

Value	Character
Tab character	"\t"
Whitespace	" "
Carriage return	"\r"
Line feed	"\n"
Vertical tab	"\xOB"
NULL	"\0"

The rtrim() *Function*

This function is similar to the trim() function. However, it removes whitespaces from the end of a string. The syntax of the function is as given below.

```
$strval = rtrim(string strvar [, string charlist])
```

The second parameter is optional and can contain any of the values specified in Table 20-1.

The trim() *Function*

This function is used to extract all the empty spaces from the beginning and end of a string, storing the result into another string. The syntax of the function is as given below.

```
$Intval = strspn (string strvar1, string $strvar2)
```

The second parameter is optional, and you can use it to specify characters that the function should not exclude from the result. If this parameter is not specified, the function will remove all spaces and these special characters. The list of these characters appears in Table 20-1.

The chop() *Function*

This function is similar to the rtrim() function and is used to extract whitespaces and special characters from the right of the string.

The similar_text() *Function*

You use this function to compare two string values and retrieve similar characters between them. The syntax of the function is as given below.

```
$Intval = similar_text(string firststr, string secondstr [, float percent])
```

In the above code, firststr is compared to secondstr and returns the number of common characters in both the strings. If the third parameter is specified, the return value contains the amount of similarity in percentage.

The strcasecmp() *Function*

This function is used to perform a binary comparison of two strings and return the number of similar characters, storing it in an integer variable. The casing of the two strings will not be taken into account when the strings are compared. The syntax of the function is as given below.

```
$Intval = strcasecmp (string strvar1, string strvar2, int charlen)
```

If $Intval contains a value <0, this means that $strvar1 is less than $strvar2; however, if the value of $Intval is >0, then $strvar1 is more than $strvar2. In case the value is 0, this means that both the strings are equal.

The strncasecmp() *Function*

This function is used to perform a binary comparison of two strings for the first x number of characters. The function returns the number of similar characters and stores it in an integer variable. This function is similar to the strcasecmp function. However, in this case you can specify the maximum number of characters that should be compared from both the strings.

In case the size of the string is less than the specified number of characters, then only the number of characters in the string are used for comparison. The casing is not taken into account when the strings are compared. The syntax of the function is as given below.

```
$Intval = strncasecmp (string strvar1, string strvar2, int charlen)
```

If $Intval contains a value <0, this means that $strvar1 is less than $strvar2; however, if the value of $Intval is >0, then $strvar1 is more than $strvar2. In case the value is 0, this means that both the strings are equal.

The strcmp() *Function*

This function compares the binary values of two strings and returns an integer value indicating which string's binary value is greater. The syntax of the function is as given below.

```
$Intval = strcmp (string strvar1, string
strvar2)
```

If $Intval contains a value <0, this means that $strvar1 is less than $strvar2. However, if the value of $Intval is >0, then $strvar1 is more than $strvar2. In case the value is 0, this means that both the strings are equal.

The strcspn() *Function*

This function is used to calculate the length of a string that doesn't match the string declared in a second string. The syntax of the function is as given below.

```
$Intval = strcspn (string strvar1, string
strvar2)
```

This function returns an integer value. In the above code, $strvar1 is compared to $strvar2, and $Intvar contains the number of characters in $strvar2 that are not there in $strvar1.

The strlen() *Function*

This function is used to calculate the length of the specified string. The syntax of the function is as given below.

$$\text{\$Intval = strlen (string strvar1)}$$

The above code returns the length of $strvar1 and stores it in the variable $Intval.

The strnatcmp() *Function*

This function is used for comparing two strings based on their natural ordering. The term *natural ordering* means that items in a list are ordered following the same rationale that a normal human being would follow to order the items. For example, a person counting items numbered from 1 to 20 would place the number 10 after the number 9. However, a computer would analyze the same list of items and place 10 immediately after 1. The syntax of the function is as given below.

$$\text{\$Intval = strcmp (string strvar1, string}$$
strvar2)

If $Intval contains a value <0, this means that $strvar1 is less than $strvar2; however, if the value of $Intval is >0, then $strvar1 is more than $strvar2. In case the value is 0, this means that both the strings are equal.

The strnatcasecmp() *Function*

The strnatcasecmp() function is also similar to the strnatcmp() function. The difference is that the strnatcasecmp() function performs a case-insensitive comparison between two strings.

$$\text{\$Intval = strcasecmp (string strvar1, string}$$
strvar2)

If $Intval contains a value <0, this means that $strvar1 is less than $strvar2; however, if the value of $Intval is >0, then $strvar1 is more than $strvar2. In case the value is 0, this means that both the strings are equal.

The strncmp() *Function*

The function performs a binary comparison of the first x number of characters. This function is similar to strcmp(), but in the case of the strncmp() function you can also stipulate the maximum number of characters that you can use from each string while performing the comparison. The comparison is, however, case sensitive. The syntax of the function is as given below.

```
                    $Intval = strncmp (string strvar1, string
strvar2, int strlen)
```

If $Intval contains a value <0, this means that $strvar1 is less than $strvar2; however, if the value of $Intval is >0, then $strvar1 is more than $strvar2. In case the value is 0, this means that both the strings are equal.

The str_pad() *Function*

This function is used for padding a specified string with another specified string. The function accepts two parameters of the string and the number of characters that need to be padded both sides of the string. If you provide the optional parameter of the string or characters that should be used to pad, they will be used. Otherwise, default spaces are used to pad the string. You also have the option to specify the pad type. The pad type can contain any of the following options: str_pad_left, str_pad_right, or str_pad_both.

As the names suggest, you can pad the string on the left side, on the right side, or on both sides. The string is not padded in case a negative value or a value less than the size of the specified string is used. The syntax of the function is as given below.

```
        $strval = str_pad(string strvar1, int pad_length,
        [, string pad_str, int pad_type])
```

The strpos() *Function*

The function is used to search for the first time a specified string appears in another string. For example, you might want to search where a certain word appears for the first time. The function returns a numeric value of the position where the string occurs for the first time. In the example given below, $strvar2 is searched for in $strval1, and the position where the string is first displayed is sent back and stored in the variable $Intval. The syntax of the function is as given below.

```
$Intval = strpos (string strvar1, string strvar2 [, int $offset])
```

The variable $Intval contains the value False if the string $strvar2 is not found in $strvar1; otherwise, it contains True. If $strvar2 contains an integer value, then the value is treated as the ordinal position of the character. The difference between the strpos() and strrpos() function is that in the strpos() function $strvar2 can be a string. If you specify the optional parameter $offset, the search begins after $offset number of characters in the string.

The strrchar() *Function*

This function is used to search for the last time a character appears in a string. The function returns the rest of the string from the point onward from where the character is found. If you don't find the variable $strvar, the function will return the value False. However, if the string contains several characters, then only the first character will be used in the search. The syntax of the function is as given below.

```
$strval = strrchar(string strvar1, string strvar2)
```

If $strvar2 is not found, then the variable contains the value False, and if $strvar2 contains an integer value, then the value is treated as the ordinal position of the character. If $strvar2 contains an integer value, then the value is treated as the ordinal position of the character.

The strrpos() *Function*

This function is used to search for the last instance of a specified string that appears in another string. For example, you might want to search where a certain word appears for the last time in another string. The function returns a numeric value of the position where the string occurs for the last time. In the example given below, $strvar2 is searched for in $strval1 and the position where the string last appears is sent back and stored in the variable $Intval. The syntax of the function is as given below.

```
$Intval = strrpos (string strvar1, char
$searchchar)
```

$searchchar can only contain a single character, and even if a string is specified, only the first character of the string will be used for the search. If $strvar2 contains an integer value, then the value is treated as the ordinal position of the character.

The strspn() *Function*

You can use this function to find the number of characters in a string that match another specified string. The function returns an integer value. The syntax of the function is as given below.

```
$Intval = strspn (string strvar1, string
$strvar2)
```

In the code given above, the function searches for $strvar1 in the string $strvar2 and returns the part of the string $strvar1 that contains the characters.

Now that you know how to validate string information, it's time to learn how you can validate dates entered by the user.

Validating Date Information

The date() function is used to determine if a user has entered a valid date. The function takes three integer parameters: the day, the number, and the year. If the date is valid the function returns True; otherwise, the function returns False. A month is valid if its value is between 1 and 12; the validity of the date depends on the specified month, and the year value should range between 1 and 32767. A leap year is taken into account while determining the number of valid dates in the month of February. The syntax of the function is as given below.

```
$strval = date(string format [, int timestamp])
```

Validating Integer Information

You also have certain mathematical functions that you can use to validate the integer values entered by a user. Let's look at a few of these functions.

The max() *Function*

This function is used to find the highest value from a range of values. The function returns an integer value, which is stored in a variable. The syntax of the function is given below.

```
$val = max (mixed var1, mixed var2, mixed var3)
```

The max() function can process integer, string, float, or array variables. In the above code, if var1 is an array, the function will retrieve the highest element from the array. However, if var1 is a string, a float, or an integer, you need to pass at least two more values to determine the largest value from the range. You can specify any number of elements in the range that you want to compare. The datatype of the returned value depends on the datatypes of the passed arguments.

The min() *Function*

The min() function is similar to the max() function; the only difference is that in this case the lowest value from a range of values is returned. Just as in the case of the max() function, even here you can specify any number of elements in the range that you want to compare. The datatype of the returned value depends on the datatypes of the passed arguments. The syntax of the function is given below.

```
$val = max (mixed var1, mixed var2, mixed var3)
```

In the above code, if the values passed as parameters are of the float datatype, then the function will return a float; however, if the variables are integers, then the function will return an integer value.

Functions for Validating User Input

Before you use the string, mathematical, and date functions, you need to determine the datatype of the entered information. Based on this information you can use the appropriate function. Some of these functions are given as follows.

The gettype() *Function*

This function can be used to retrieve the datatype of a specified variable. You can check if a variable is integer, string, boolean, double, object, array, resource, or NULL. Nowadays, instead of using this function, programmers prefer to use the functions `function_exists()` and `method_exists()`. The syntax of the function is as given below.

```
$strval = gettype(mixed variable)
```

You can use the `settype()` function to specify the datatype a variable should use.

The settype() *Function*

This function is used to specify the datatype a variable should belong to. The function accepts two parameters: the variable name and the datatype that the variable should be set to. The possible datatypes that you can use or set a variable to are integer, string, boolean, double, object, array, resource, or NULL. The syntax of the function is as given below.

```
$strval = settype(mixed variable, string
specified_datatype)
```

The is_array() *Function*

This function is used to determine if the specified variable is an array. The function will return the value True if the variable is an array and False if it is not an array. The syntax of the function is as given below.

```
$boolval = is_array(mixed variable)
```

The is_bool() *Function*

This function is used to determine if a variable contains a boolean value. The function will return the value True if the variable contains a bool value and False if it does not contain a bool value. The syntax of the function is as given below.

```
$boolval = is_bool(mixed variable)
```

The is_double() *Function*

This function is the same as the is_float() function and provides the same functionality.

The is_float() *Function*

This function is used to determine if a variable contains a float value. The function accepts a single parameter of mixed datatype and returns True if the variable contains a float value; otherwise, it returns False.

The is_int() *Function*

The is_int() function confirms that a variable contains an integer value. The function will return the value True if the variable contains an integer; otherwise, it will return False. The syntax of the function is as given below.

```
$boolval = is_int(mixed variable)
```

The is_integer() *Function*

This function is the same as the is_int() function and provides the same functionality.

The is_long() *Function*

This function is the same as the is_int() function and provides the same functionality.

The is_null() *Function*

This function determines if a variable contains a NULL value. If the variable contains a NULL value, the function will return the value True. In case the variable doesn't contain NULL, then the function will return the value False. The syntax of the function is as given below.

```
$boolval = is_null(mixed variable)
```

The is_numeric() *Function*

This function is used to determine if the information entered by a user is a numeric string or an integer value. The function returns the value True if the entered information is either a numeric value or a numeric string; otherwise, it returns False.

The is_object() *Function*

This function is used to determine if a variable contains an object. The function returns True if the variable has an object; otherwise, it returns False. The syntax of the function is as given below.

```
$boolval = is_object(mixed variable)
```

The is_real() *Function*

This function is the same as the is_float() function and provides the same functionality.

The is_resource() *Function*

This function is used to determine if a variable is a resource. The function returns True if the variable is a resource; otherwise, it returns False. The syntax of the function is as given below.

```
$boolval = is_resource(mixed variable)
```

The is_scalar() *Function*

This function is used to determine whether a variable is scalar in nature. The function returns True if it is; otherwise, it returns False. You have already learned that scalar datatypes are string, integer, boolean, and float. The syntax of the function is as given below.

```
$boolval = is_scalar(mixed variable)
```

CAUTION

Resources are not considered to belong to the scalar datatypes.

The is_string() Function

This function is used to determine if a variable contains a string value. If it does the function will return the value True; otherwise, it will return False. The syntax of the function is as given below.

```
$boolval = is_string(mixed variable)
```

The isset() Function

This function is used to determine if a variable is set or not. If the variable is set or exists, the function returns True; otherwise, False. If the variable contains the value NULL, the isset() function will still return the value False. The syntax of the function is as given below.

```
$boolval = isset (mixed variable)
```

The strval() Function

This function is used to retrieve the string value stored in a variable. The function returns the string value of the variable supplied as a parameter. The variable can be of any scalar datatype. The syntax of the function is as given below.

```
$strval = strval(mixed variable)
```

 CAUTION

You cannot use this function to evaluate or change arrays or objects.

Besides user input, other information that needs to be validated is the e-mail address. The next section discusses this concept.

Validating E-Mail Addresses

Many Web sites nowadays offer casual visitors the option of being registered with the site. These sites provide registered users with certain facilities, such as receiving the following:

- ◆ Articles
- ◆ Announcements of the release of new products
- ◆ Event information
- ◆ Offers to receive gifts

While providing these services, the administrator of the Web site needs to ensure that the e-mail address entered by the user is not empty and conforms to certain standards. The administrator also has to ensure that the e-mail address entered by the user is valid. There are three methods by which an e-mail address can be validated. Let's look at each one in detail.

Simple Validation

In simple validation a check is made to see if the symbols @ and . appear in the e-mail address. At a more advanced level, you can also check for malformed IP addresses. This type of validation is known as syntax checking. This means that every e-mail address that is entered on the Web site is at the minimum checked for a valid IP address. This check is besides the normal check for the @ symbol and the . symbol.

Let's use the following code and see how you can validate the e-mail address entered by a user. The script will check for the @ symbol to determine if the e-mail address is valid or not. The output of the code given below appears in Figure 20-1.

```
<html>
<head>
<title>e-mail validator</title>
        <meta http-equiv="Content-Type"
content="text/html; charset=iso-8859-1">
</head>

<body bgcolor="#FFFFFF" text="#000000">
```

```
<p> </p>
<form name="form1" method="post" action="e-mail.php">
<table width="26%" border="1"
align="center" cellpadding="5">
<tr>
<td colspan="2">
<div align="center"><b>Enter an
e-mail address to test</b></div>
</td>
</tr>
<tr>
<td width="25%">E-mail</td>
<td width="75%">
<input type="text" name="email"
size="30">
</td>
</tr>
<tr>
<td colspan="2">
<div align="center">
<input type="submit"
name="Submit" value="Submit">
</div>
</td>
</tr>
</table>
</form>
<p> </p>
</body>
</html>
```

The above Web page accepts the user's e-mail address. When the user presses the
Submit button, the control goes to email.php. The script first checks whether the
variable $email is set or not. If the variable is not set, the script returns an error
and exits the Web page. Next the variable is checked to see if it is empty or not.
If the field was left blank and the variable contains no value, the script returns an
error message and exits the Web page. Then the value is checked for its size. If the

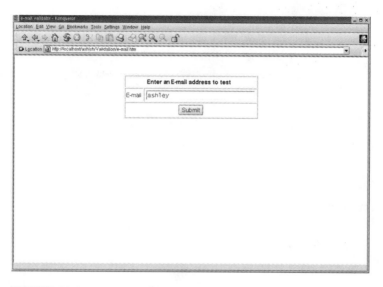

FIGURE 20-1 *Accepting e-mail from a user*

number of characters is less than 3 or more than 200, the e-mail address is declared invalid and the Web page closes.

Next the value is checked for the @ symbol. If this symbol doesn't exist in the entered e-mail address, the e-mail address is declared invalid. If the symbol exists, then the message that the e-mail is in the correct format appears.

Now the username and the host name sections are evaluated. To assist you in evaluating these sections, the entered information is broken up and the specific values are stored in each of the variables. The first check is to determine if either the host name or the username is empty. If either of these values is empty, the script returns an error message and exits the Web page.

Next the host name is checked and it is determined if the host name exists on the Internet. If the host name exists, a message appears that the address has been validated; otherwise, the message appears that the host name does not exist. Finally, you have a link through which you can test another e-mail address. When you click on this link, you will return to the original Web page.

The code for the script is given below.

```html
<html>
<head>
<title> E-mail validator </title>
```

```
                                 <meta http-equiv="Content-Type"
content="text/html; charset=iso-8859-1">
                         </head>
                         <body bgcolor="#FFFFFF" text="#000000">

                 <?php

                                         if (!isset($email))
                                         {
                                                 die("Host name
value wasn't properly submitted.Retry.");
                                         }

                                         if(empty($email))
                                         {
                                             die("Hostname field
was left blank ! Retry.");
                                         }

                                         if ( (strlen($email) <
3) ¦¦ (strlen($email) > 200))

                                             {
                                 die("Invalid E-mail address, E-
mail address too long or too short.");
                                         }
                                         elseif(!ereg("@",$email))
                                         {
                                           die("Invalid E-mail
address, no @ symbol found");

                                         }
                                         else
                                         {
                                           echo "<b>".$email."</b>
is correct in format.<br>";

                                         }

                                         list($username,$hostname)
= split("@",$email);
```

```
                                              if ( (empty($username))
or (empty($hostname)) )

                                              {
                                                die("username or host-
name section is not valid.");

                                              }


                                              if(checkdnsrr($hostname))
                                              {
                                                echo "<b>". $email
."</b>'s hostname has a valid MX record !<br>";

                                              }
                                              else
                                              {
                                                die("<b>". $email
."</b>'s hostname does not exist");

                                              }



                        ?>


                        <br>
            To test another host name<A href="e-mail.htm"> click here
</a>
                        <br>
                        </body>
                        </html>
```

You would have noticed in Figure 20-1 that the user only entered a first name. This is a common practice with novice e-mail users, or it could be an oversight. In either case, the page returns an error message as shown in Figure 20-2.

As you can see, the message indicates that the @ symbol is missing. This is the first level of check to determine if the e-mail address is valid. Next the user enters an e-mail address with the @ symbol as shown in Figure 20-3.

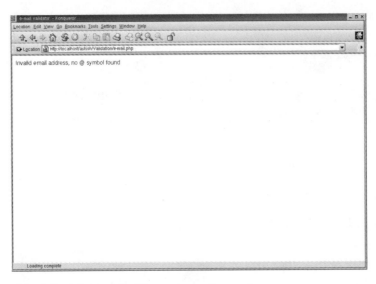

FIGURE 20-2 *E-mail address not entered correctly*

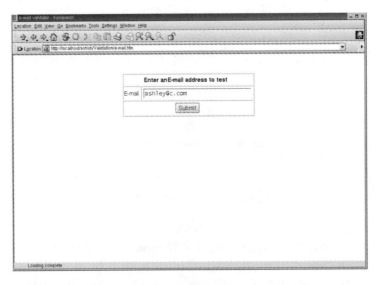

FIGURE 20-3 *Entering the e-mail address with the @ symbol*

In the preceding code, the user enters the e-mail address which includes the @ symbol. Now a check is made to see if the username and host name are valid. Since both the username and the hostname are entered, the script now checks if the domain name exists. The output appears in Figure 20-4.

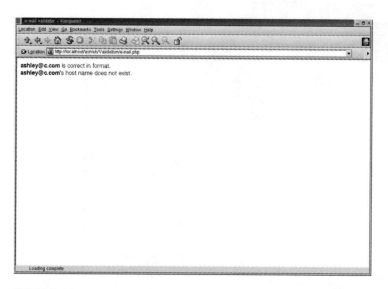

FIGURE 20-4 *Error message indicating that the host name does not exist*

As you can see in the above error message, although the e-mail address is entered in the correct format, the host name does not exist. This could be because the host name actually might not exist or because it may be a private e-mail address. A private e-mail address that exists on a private network can only be used by the members of the internal network, and cannot be accessed from outside. In such a scenario the above error message would appear. The user now enters the e-mail address as shown in Figure 20-5.

The above e-mail address is entered in the correct format and the host name is valid. When the user clicks the Submit button, the entered information is validated and the successful message appears as shown in Figure 20-6.

However, you can easily trick the Web server by entering any e-mail address and by using the @ symbol in the address. Therefore, you need a more secure level of validating the e-mail address.

DNS Validation

The next level of security that you can implement to ensure that users enter a valid e-mail address is to use the Domain Name System, or DNS, validation. The DNS server checks that the domain name entered in the e-mail address actually exists.

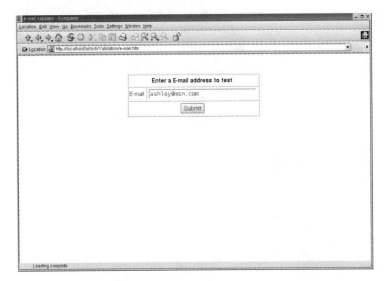

FIGURE 20-5 *Entering the correct e-mail address*

FIGURE 20-6 *Message indicating that the e-mail address is successfully validated*

A valid domain name will have an A or an MX entry in the DNS. Let's try to see how this works.

You will check for the @ symbol to determine if the e-mail address is valid or not.

In the code given below, the user enters the host name to be validated. When the host name has been entered, the user clicks the Submit button to forward the information to the Web server. The script on the Web server then validates the information. The output of the code given below appears in Figure 20-7.

```
<html>
<head>
<title>Hostname Validator</title>
        <meta http-equiv="Content-Type" con-
tent="text/html; charset=iso-8859-1">
</head>

<body bgcolor="#FFFFFF" text="#000000">
<p> </p>
<form name="form1" method="post"
action="hostname.php">
    <table width="400" border="1" align="center" cell-
padding="5">
      <tr>
        <td colspan="2">
          <div align="center"><b>Enter a host name to
test</b></div>
        </td>
      </tr>
      <tr>
        <td width="23%">Host name </td>
        <td width="77%">
          <p>http://
            <input type="text" name="hostname"
size="30">
          </p>
          <p>example : ( www.google.com )</p>
        </td>
      </tr>
      <tr>
        <td colspan="2">
          <div align="center">
            <input type="submit" name="Submit"
```

```
value="Submit">
                                    </div>
                                 </td>
                              </tr>
                           </table>
                        </form>
                        <p> </p>
                        </body>
                        </html>
```

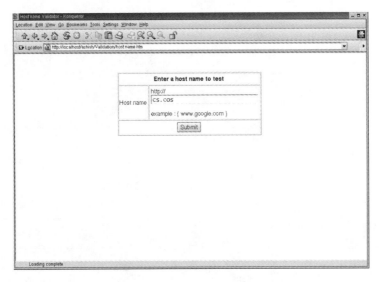

FIGURE 20-7 *Entering the host name for validation*

As you can see in the preceding code, the user enters the value cs.cos. This host name needs to be validated. In the script, the first thing that is validated is that the variable $hostname is set. Next a check is made to see if the host name field has been left blank. If the field has been left blank and the value is empty, the script returns an error and exits the Web page. If the variable is not blank, it is then checked by using the checkdnsrr() function to determine if the host name is valid. If the function returns the value True, a successful message is displayed; otherwise, a message is displayed indicating that the host name does not exist. The code for the script is as follows.

```
<html>
<head>
```

```
<title> hostname validator </title>
<meta http-equiv="Content-Type" content="text/html;
charset=iso-8859-1">

</head>
<body bgcolor="#FFFFFF" text="#000000">

<?php

if (!isset($hostname))
{
  die("Hostname value wasn't properly submitted.
Retry.");
}

if(empty($hostname))
{
  die("Hostname field was left blank ! Retry.");
}
echo "<b>". $hostname ."</b> ";

if(checkdnsrr($hostname))
{
  echo "has a valid MX record !<br>";
}
else
{
  die("does not exist");
}


?>

<br>
To test another hostname<A href="hostname.htm"> click
here </a>

<br>
</body>
</html>
```

When the user submits the host name entered in Figure 20-7, the script validates the host name and enters an error message since the host name `cs.cos` does not exist. This error message appears as shown in Figure 20-8.

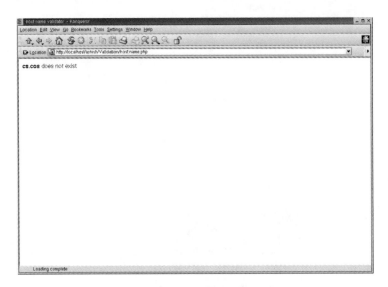

FIGURE 20-8 *Error showing invalid host name*

Now the user enters the host name as shown in Figure 20-9.

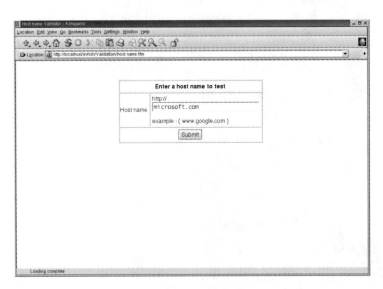

FIGURE 20-9 *Hostname reentered*

After the uses enters the host name given in Figure 20-9 and presses the Submit button, the host name is validated and the host name found information is displayed as shown in Figure 20-10.

FIGURE 20-10 *Message indicating that the host name is successfully validated*

Although DNS validation is enough, you can also implement an additional check based on IP address.

SMTP Validation or IP Address Validation

In most cases, a DNS check is enough to ensure that the user has entered a valid e-mail address. However, sometimes you might need to introduce another level of security by validating the user's identity based on the IP address of the user's machine. Since every IP address is unique on the Internet, it becomes easy to determine if a user who is trying to access the system is valid or not. This is true in cases where the user enters a valid e-mail address but from different locations. Therefore, it becomes difficult to validate that a valid user has entered the e-mail address.

A solution to this problem is to use Simple Mail Transfer Protocol (SMTP) to authenticate the user directly on the domain mail server. This ensures that the user is genuine and the e-mail address is valid.

However, there is a problem associated with this approach. The problem is that many mail servers do not support this function. This is because a mail server tries to accommodate as many e-mails as possible. The server, therefore, might accept the e-mail address.

Let's try to implement this theory into practice. The code given below creates the HTML page that will accept the user's name and display the user's IP address. The output of the code given below appears in Figure 20-11.

```html
<html>
<head>
<title>IP finder !</title>
<meta http-equiv="Content-Type" content="text/html;
charset=iso-8859-1">

</head>


<body bgcolor="#FFFFFF" text="#000000">
<p> </p>
<form name="form1" method="post" action="ip.php">
  <table width="26%" border="1" align="center" cell-
padding="5">

    <tr>
      <td colspan="2" height="2">
        <div align="center"><b>Enter your
name</b></div>

      </td>
    </tr>
    <tr>
      <td width="25%">Name </td>
      <td width="75%">
        <input type="text" name="name" size="30">
      </td>
    </tr>
    <tr>
      <td colspan="2">
        <div align="center">
          <input type="submit" name="Submit"
value="Submit">
        </div>
```

```
            </td>
          </tr>
        </table>
      </form>
      <p> </p>
    </body>
  </html>
```

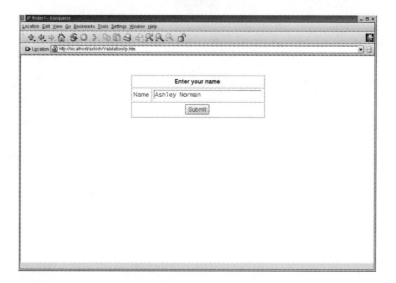

FIGURE 20-11 *Accepting the user's name*

When the user presses the Submit button, the user's IP address is also sent to the Web server. The server then validates the IP address and displays the message as shown in Figure 20-12. The variable is first checked for being empty, otherwise the IP address of the user's machine is retrieved from the environment variable $REMOTE_ADDR. This information is then displayed in the Web browser. You can also manipulate this information depending on your requirement.

CAUTION

Sometimes the code might not work behind a firewall. This is because the
$REMOTE_ADDR variable might not be able to store the IP address of a machine that
exists behind a firewall. In such a case you can use the following code to solve this
problem:

```
If(getenv(HTTP_X_FORWARDED_FOR))
$ip=getenv(HTTP_X_FORWARDED_FOR)
```

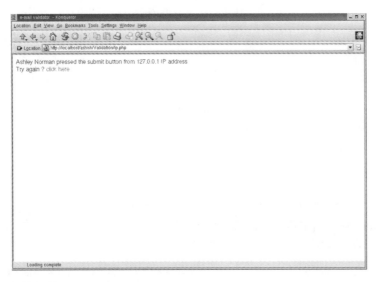

FIGURE 20-12 *Displaying the IP address*

Summary

In this chapter, you learned about the different input validators available in PHP.
You learned about the basic concepts regarding validation. Then you learned
about the need for validation. You then learned about the different functions
available in PHP. In particular, you learned about the string, mathematic, dates,
and variable functions. Finally, you learned how to validate e-mail addresses in
PHP. You learned that you can validate the information in three ways. The simplest way is to check for the @ and the . symbol. You can then validate the e-mail
on the DNS server. Finally, you can validate the address based on the machine's
IP address.

Chapter 21

Synchronization between team members is a must for the smooth execution of a project. This synchronization assumes higher proportions when many people in a team are working on the same code. In such a situation, you need to keep the following points in mind:

◆ One team member should not be able to overwrite or modify the code that is being worked on by another member of the team.

◆ Changes made to the code are tracked and are made known to all members of the team.

◆ In case a bug affects the code, you should be able to retrieve the earlier unaffected version of the code.

◆ There exists a common storehouse for keeping the source code, which is accessible by all members of the team, irrespective of their location.

◆ All versions of the code are maintained and can be referred to anytime in the future.

An application that can effortlessly accomplish all these tasks seems too good to be true! This is where Concurrent Versions System (CVS) steps in and befits a doctor's prescription.

In this chapter you will learn how CVS maintains the different versions of files and directories. You will also learn to obtain PHP from CVS. I will also discuss some of the most commonly used environment variables and command options that are used in CVS.

CVS: An Overview

CVS is a version control system that:

◆ Allows more than one person to work simultaneously on a common set of files and directories

◆ Maintains a complete history of all your files, including the latest version and the earlier versions

◆ Allows you to access your files from any Internet connection

◆ Supports most of the common operating systems

CVS was first written as a set of shell scripts by Dick Grune. He published these shell scripts in Volume 6 of a newsgroup page on the Internet, **comp.sources.unix**, in December 1986. However, the CVS in use today is a result of the work done by Brian Berliner. He coded and designed CVS in April 1989.

 NOTE

CVS is freely available for download from various Web sites, such as **www.cyclic.com** and **www.cvshome.com**.

PHP and CVS

As you already know, PHP is an open-source language and is constantly undergoing changes and upgrades. Innumerable people are involved with the development of PHP all around the world. As a result, all these people (commonly referred to as the PHP development team) need to be in sync with each other all the time. They need to ensure that no major changes are introduced in the source code without any prior notification, no bugs are introduced in the source code, and all changes are first reviewed thoroughly and then only these changes are incorporated. This is why all development of the PHP language is managed by CVS.

CVS helps in tracking down all changes and modifications that are proposed. In addition, it also helps in bringing together the people from different parts of the world to make their contributions to the development of PHP.

The PHP development team, and other people who are involved with the development of the PHP language and maintenance of the **www.php.net** Web site, need to have a CVS account. CVS account members can:

◆ Modify those parts of the PHP CVS tree for which he/she has been given the permissions. You will learn more about the PHP CVS tree later in the chapter.

◆ Rectify bugs in the PHP bug database.

◆ Modify PHP documentation in the annotated PHP manual.

According to PHP's official documentation, the following do not require a CVS account:

♦ Those who are learning PHP

♦ Those who are working with PHP codes

♦ Those who are creating Web pages using PHP

♦ Those who are working with PHP extensions or are creating PHP extensions on an experimental basis

♦ Those who are submitting a patch to PHP

♦ Those who are studying the PHP source

♦ Those who are adding comments and notes to the PHP documentation

On the other hand, the following should have a CVS account:

♦ Those who are involved with the actual development of the PHP language, such as the PHP development team

♦ Those who are maintaining an official, bundled PHP extension

♦ Those who are maintaining the official PHP site, **www.php.net**, and the PHP documentation

♦ Those who are translating the PHP documentation

 NOTE

To obtain a CVS account you need to fill out the CVS account requisition form at the Web site **http://www.php.net/cvs-php.php**.

At the core of CVS is a central repository, where all updated files and directories—whose versions have to be controlled—are stored. You will now learn about the CVS repository in detail.

The CVS Repository

The CVS repository is a central storehouse that contains the earlier and the most recent versions of files and directories. While working with CVS it is a common practice not to work directly with any files stored in the repository. You should first check the selected file out into some other directory, usually known as a working directory. Only after you have checked out your file from the repository into a working directory should you make any changes to that file.

After you have made the necessary changes you can then check in to commit the updated files back into the repository. In this way the repository is able to:

◆ Maintain the most recent and updated files.

◆ Record when and what changes were made to the file and who made them.

◆ Secure updated files from any unauthorized access. This is accomplished by giving file-access permissions and allowing only authorized users to check out or commit files into the repository.

You can create your CVS repository at any location either on your local computer or on a remote location. To access a repository you need to first mention the access method at the CVS command prompt and then the location of the repository. However, if your repository is stored locally, then providing the access method is optional and it is assumed to be :local:. For example, if your repository is stored locally at the location /usr/local/RepCVS, you can either use :local:/usr/local/RepCVS or simply use /usr/local/RepCVS.

 NOTE

In the Windows environment, you need to provide the access method. For example, if your repository is located at the location C:\usr\local\RepCVS, then you use :local:C:\usr\local\RepCVS.

When your repository is stored on a remote location, the repository name is in the following format:

```
                :access method: [[user][:password:]@] hostname [[:[port]]/path
where repository Is stored
```

CAUTION

When you are checking out your files from a remote repository, you should not specify your password in the repository name. This is because the password gets stored as clear text in each directory that you create.

Accessing the CVS Repository

You can access your CVS repository by:

◆ Using $CVSROOT environment variable

◆ Using command options

Accessing the CVS Repository by Using the Environment Variable

When you are using the $CVSROOT environment variable, you must set the $CVSROOT environment variable with the entire path to the root of the repository. In the example used above, the CVS repository is situated at the location /usr/local/ RepCVS.

As a result, in this example we need to set the $CVSROOT environment variable equal to /usr/local/RepCVS. However, methods of accessing the CVS repository are different for the users who are using csh and tcsh shell scripts and for the users who are using sh and bash shell scripts. The csh and tcsh users need to have setenv CVSROOT /usr/local/RepCVS in their respective .cshrc and .tcsh files. On the other hand, the sh and bash users need to have

```
CVSROOT = /usr/local/RepCVS
export CVSROOT
```

in their .bashrc file.

You will learn about other environment variables under the topic "Environment Variables."

Accessing the CVS Repository by Using the Command Line

To access a CVS repository by using the command line, you use the -d (where d stands for directory) command option. In this example, the CVS repository is

RepCVS. Therefore, to access this repository using the command line, you need to use the following command:

```
cvs -d /usr/local/RepCVS checkout Bookbuzz/Books
```

You will learn about other command options under the topic "CVS Command Options."

The CVS Repository Structure

A CVS repository consists of the following two components:

- CVSROOT directory ($CVSROOT/CVSROOT), which contains all files that are required for administering CVS.
- Other non-CVSROOT directories, which contain all files that are created by users.

All of these components are stored in the form of a directory-tree-like structure in the CVS repository. In this example, the repository is

```
/usr/local/RepCVS
```

Figure 21-1 illustrates the structure of the CVS repository and how files and directories are stored in the repository.

As you can see in the figure, the RepCVS repository includes the following three directories:

- **CVSROOT:** As discussed, the CVSROOT directory comprises all CVS administrative files and directories.
  - **gnu:** The gnu directory contains the following three files:
  - **diff:** the source code for GNU diff file
  - **rcs:** the source code for RCS
  - **cvs:** the source code for CVS
- **Bookbuzz:** This directory comprises directories and files that you have committed into your CVS repository. This directory name can be any user-defined name.

After having discussed the directory tree structure of a CVS repository structure, you will next learn how you can obtain the latest PHP source tree through anonymous CVS.

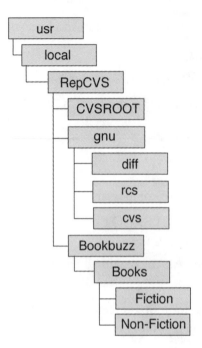

FIGURE 21-1 *The CVS repository structure*

Obtaining the PHP Source Tree through CVS

To obtain PHP from CVS you need to perform the following steps:

 NOTE

CVS does not support pre-generated parser and scanner files. Therefore, to compile PHP you should have bison 1.28 or later and flex 2.54 or later installed on your computer. In addition, ensure that you have autoconf 2.13 or later, automake 1.4 or later, and libtool 1.4 or later for configuring CVS.

1. To configure CVS, add the following in your ~/. cvsrc file:

```
cvs -z3
update -d -P
checkout -P
diff -u
```

2. To log in to the PHP anonymous CVS server, type

```
cvs -d :pserver:cvsread@cvs.php.net:/repository login
```

To log in to the CVS server, you need to use `phpfi` as the password.

3. To obtain the PHP 4.0 CVS source tree, type

```
cvs -d :pserver:cvsread@cvs.php.net:/repository co
```
php4

4. To move to the PHP 4.0 directory, type

```
cd php4
```

5. To log in to the Zend CVS repository, type

```
cvs -d :pserver:cvsread@cvs.zend.com:/repository login
```

To log in to the Zend CVS server, you need to use `zend` as the password.

6. To access the Zend and Thread Safe Resource Manager (TSRM) CVS tree, type

```
cvs -d :pserver:cvsread@cvs.zend.com:/repository co
```
Zend TSRM

7. To generate the configuration script, you need to run

```
./buildconfig
```

After you have performed all of these steps, you can install PHP in the same way as you learned in Chapter 2, "Installing and Configuring PHP."

It is recommended that you use CVS for obtaining PHP only when you want to obtain the latest updates and fixes. It is not recommended to obtain PHP from CVS. This is because CVS is a development version and can be unstable or can lead to compilation problems in PHP.

After having learned about obtaining PHP from CVS, you will learn to create a CVS repository.

Creating a CVS Repository

You have already learned that you can choose any location to create a CVS repository. However, before creating a CVS repository, keep the following points in mind:

◆ Have enough memory and disk space where you want to create your CVS repository. It is recommended that you use a machine with at least 32 MB RAM.

◆ All machines that are using CVS should be able to access CVS either locally or through a network.

◆ The configuration should allow client machines to access the CVS repository via the CVS protocol.

If you want to create a CVS repository, you need to execute the CVS init command. This command creates an empty repository at the specified location. For example, if you want to create a repository in usr/local/RepCVS, you need to give the following command:

```
cvs -d /usr/local/RepCVS init
```

NOTE

If you create a new repository in an already existing repository, then the new repository does not overwrite any of your existing files in the repository.

Now you will learn about the different environment variables that are recognized by various CVS commands.

Environment Variables in CVS

Environment variables play an important role in the functioning of CVS. The following environment variables are recognized by CVS commands:

◆ $CVSREAD

◆ $CVSUNMASK

◆ $CVSROOT

◆ $CVSIGNORE

◆ $CVSWRAPPERS

◆ $CVSEDITOR

◆ $VISUAL

- ◆ $CVS_RSH
- ◆ $CVS_PASSFILE
- ◆ $CVS_SERVER
- ◆ $HOME or $HOMEDRIVE
- ◆ $PATH
- ◆ $CVS_CLIENT_PORT
- ◆ $CVS_RCMD_PORT
- ◆ $CVS_SERVER_SLEEP
- ◆ $CVS_CLIENT_LOG
- ◆ $CVS_IGNORE_REMOTE_ROOT
- ◆ $COMPSEC
- ◆ $TMP

Each of these environment variables is now explained in detail.

$CVSREAD: Makes files in the working directory read-only.

$CVSUNMASK: Manages file permissions in a repository.

$CVSROOT: Contains the full path name to the root of the CVS source repository. You can overwrite the $CVSROOT environment variable by specifying the -d option with the repository.

$CVSIGNORE: Specifies a list of files that should be ignored by CVS.

$CVSWRAPPERS: Specifies a list of files that should be treated by CVS as wrappers.

$CVSEDITOR: Initiates the editor to enter log messages. If $CVSEDITOR is not set, $EDITOR can be used in its place. You can override $EDITOR by $CVSEDITOR.

$VISUAL: Can be used if both $CVSEDITOR and $EDITOR are not set.

$CVS_RSH: Determines an external program with which CVS connects when you specify the :ext: access method.

$CVS_PASSFILE: By default the value of this variable is $HOME/ .cvspass. You use this variable in the client-server mode when you want to access the CVS login server.

$CVS_SERVER: By default the value of this variable is cvs. Specifies the program that should be started on the server side when you want to access a remote repository using RSH. You use this variable in the client-server mode.

$HOME or **$HOMEDRIVE**: Searches for the directory where the .cvsrc file is located. You use $HOMEDRIVE when you are working on a Windows NT platform and $HOME in case you are working on a Unix platform. In Windows NT you also need to set $HOMEPATH in addition to $HOMEDRIVE.

$PATH: Specifies all programs that CVS will use. However, you use $PATH only when the $RCSBIN is not set.

$CVS_CLIENT_PORT: You use this variable in the client-server mode, if you have not specified any port in $CVSROOT and want to access the server by using CVS's password authentication, Kerberos, or GSSAPI.

$CVS_RCMD_PORT: Specifies the port number that you will use to access the RCMD demon on the server.

$CVS_SERVER_SLEEP: By using this variable, you can specify the time (in seconds) by which initiation of a child process will be delayed in the server.

$CVS_CLIENT_LOG: Also debugs the server when you are working in the client-server mode. When you set this variable, it logs all information that you send to the server into CVS_CLIENT_LOG.in and all information from the server into $CVS_CLIENT_LOG.out.

$CVS_IGNORE_REMOTE_ROOT: Precludes CVS from overwriting the CVS/ROOT file when you specify the -d command option. This option works only for CVS 1.0 or older.

$COMPSEC: By default, this variable is set to CMD.EXE. You can use this variable in OS/2 only, and use it to specify the name of the command interpreter.

$TMP: Includes the directory that stores temporary files.

After having learned about environment variables in CVS, you will now learn about various command-options in CVS.

CVS Command Options

CVS is a Character User Interface (CUI) tool. There are several CVS commands that you can use to carry out various functions in CVS. As discussed in the previous topic, these commands are used with various environment variables. Before learning about these commands, you will first learn about the structure of a CVS command.

Structure of a CVS Command

All CVS commands that you use have a definite syntax. The following is the syntax for a CVS command:

```
            cvs [ cvs global options ] cvs command [cvs command specific
options] [ command arguments]
```

In this syntax:

cvs: Stands for the name of the CVS application.

cvs global options: You specify those CVS options here that have an effect on all subcommands of CVS.

cvs command: You specify a CVS subcommand here.

cvs command specific options: You specify those options here that are specific to the cvs command that you have given.

command arguments: You specify command arguments here that indicate what action is to be performed.

After having learned the generic structure of CVS commands, you will now learn about various CVS commands and command options.

Types of CVS Command Options

CVS command options can be divided into two categories:

◆ CVS global options
◆ CVS command-specific options

CVS global options are those options that affect all CVS subcommands, while CVS command-specific options affect only those commands with which they are given.

CVS Global Command Options

CVS global command options, as the name suggests, are not specific to any particular CVS command. Global command options affect all CVS subcommands. Following is a list of global options that are available in CVS:

◆ `– allow-root = rootdir`: Specifies a root CVSROOT directory.

◆ `-a`: Authenticates communication when using a GSSAPI connection.

◆ `-b bindir`: No longer in use in the current versions of CVS.

◆ `-d <repository name>`: Specifies the name of the repository that is to be used. By using this command option, you can override the $CVSROOT environment variable.

◆ `-e <editor>`: Specifies the editor to enter log messages. You can use this option to override $CVSEDITOR and $EDITOR environment variables.

◆ `-f`: Specifies CVS to ignore and not read the ~/ .cvsrc file.

◆ `-H or – help`: Displays CVS help. If you specify this option with a specific command, it displays help for that specific command.

◆ `-l`: Specifies CVS to only execute the command and not log it in the command history.

◆ `-n`: Does not allow any CVS command to remove, update, merge, or create any files.

◆ `-r`: Sets files in the working directory as read-only.

◆ `-s <variable = value>`: Initiates a user variable.

◆ `-t`: Displays the details about all CVS actions that occur while executing a program.

◆ `-v or – version`: Displays the CVS version and other copyright information about CVS.

◆ `-w`: Sets files in the working directory as read-write.

◆ `-z <level>`: Compresses the data that is being transmitted.

After having studied the CVS global command options, you will now learn the CVS command-specific options.

Command-Specific Options

In contrast to global options, the CVS command-specific options affect only some CVS commands. Following is a list of some of the most commonly used command-specific options that are available in CVS:

- **-k:** Works with `add`, `diff`, `checkout`, `import`, and `update` commands. Alters default keyword processing.

- **-l:** This is different from the global `cvs -l` option. It works only in the current working directory and not other directories. Works with the `checkout`, `commit`, `log`, `editors`, `rdiff`, `remove`, `tag`, `unedit`, `update`, `edit`, `annotate`, and `watch` commands.

- **-m <message>:** In the message part, the log information is stored. You can use this command in place of an editor. Works with `import`, `add`, and `commit` commands.

- **-P:** Prunes all directories that are empty.

- **-R:** This option is set by default and recursively processes directories. It works with the `checkout`, `commit`, `diff`, `rdiff`, `remove`, `status`, `unedit`, `update`, `watch`, and `annotate` commands.

- **-W:** Specifies those file names that should be filtered.

All these command options work only with specific CVS commands and not all CVS commands. You can learn about other CVS command options at the Web site **http://www.loria.fr/~molli/cvs/doc/cvs_1.html**.

Summary

In this chapter you learned about Concurrent Versions System (CVS) and how you can effectively use it to manage all your files and directories when you are working in a team environment. You learned that at the core of the CVS is a central CVS repository, where updated versions of files and directories are stored. Then you learned about the structure of a CVS repository and how you can obtain a PHP source tree from the anonymous CVS. Next you learned about environment variables in CVS. Finally, you learned about various CVS command options.

Chapter 22

Suppose you have created a PHP application and want to share the application code with other developers on the Internet. You may wonder what sort of header information should be provided while distributing a code. You may even wonder about the standards that you need to follow while writing professional PHP codes or while naming a function. What guidelines need to be followed while creating a class or how do you name constants and global variables?

If you are looking for answers for these questions in PHP, you need to know that PEAR has all the answers. What is PEAR?

Introduction to PEAR

PEAR is the short form of PHP Extension and Application Repository. As the name suggests, PEAR consists of a set of PHP extensions and a PHP code library. The Web applications are created based on numerous classes that form the foundation of PEAR. These classes provide support for handling errors and for passing variables and constants to the classes that have been derived from them.

PEAR provides a standard set of classes for error handling and destructors. These destructors can be further extended so that all the child classes can use them. Since classes in PHP do not contain support for destructors, you can use classes derived from PEAR to provide this functionality. This is critical in cases where certain functions need to be run when objects are destroyed or removed from memory.

In addition, PEAR also supplies standards and guidelines that you should follow while creating Web applications or PHP applications for the purpose of distribution.

PEAR provides the following features:

- ◆ A detailed set of standards that developers can use to write code
- ◆ A defined library of functions that a user can use to write code
- ◆ A set of tools for sharing and updating code
- ◆ Means by which developers can share their code with one another

Let's look at the standards that developers need to follow while writing code for PEAR.

Coding Standards in PEAR

As mentioned earlier, PEAR contains a set of standards that developers use to write their code. This provides consistency across developers, who can then share the code with one another and store it in the code repository or library. Developers who want their code to become a part of PEAR can be made to follow the coding standards. The code could be either shipped along with PHP or available on the Internet. The developers who need this code can download it along with the PHP install tool and then use it.

Indentation of Code

You should remember the following indentation guidelines:

♦ All codes created for PEAR should be indented with four spaces.

♦ Tabs should not be used to indent the codes.

If the editor used to modify the PEAR code is Emacs, you need to ensure that the indent-tabs-mode is set to NIL.

You need to follow certain standards while using control structures in PEAR.

Using Control Structures

Just as you have control structures in PHP, so you have the same control structures in PEAR. The control structures include the `if` conditional statement, the `switch` conditional statement, the `for`, `while`, `do ... while`, and `foreach` conditional loops. For detailed information regarding conditional structures, refer to Chapter 4, "Control Structures." Given below are the syntaxes for the `if` conditional statement and the `foreach` conditional loop.

```
if (expression)
    {
                statement1;

    }
```

```
elseif (expression)
    {
                    statement2;
    }
else
    {
                    statement3;
    }

foreach(arrexpression as $array)
    {
                statements;
    }
```

 NOTE

It is preferable to use the curly braces because they improve the readability of the code.

Naming Functions and Methods

You use the "'-bumpy case style-'" for naming functions and methods. This style specifies that the words of the name should be capitalized. You also need to add the package name in front of the function name to ensure that there is no clash between product names. Given below are some examples of acceptable functions and method names.

◆ setValue()

◆ assignData()

◆ CalculateRevenueData()

Although PHP usually does not support class variables that are private, you can still declare them for minor use. You can only access a private variable inside the class in which it is declared. To declare a variable as private you need to add an underscore in front of the variable name, for example, `_Intdata`, `_getResult()`, or `_$this->value`.

Let's now look at the standards you need to follow while using constants.

Naming Constants

You should keep the following facts in mind while naming constants:

◆ The standard that needs to be followed while naming a constant is that the name of the constant should always be in uppercase and should have an underscore separating each word.

◆ You need to append the name of the class or package where these constants are used to the name of the constant.

◆ The name of the class or package should be in uppercase.

Suppose you are using constants in the package XY:: package. In this case, the name of the constants should always begin with "XY_".

Naming Global Variables

A standard similar to the constant-naming standard needs to be followed when naming global variables. In addition, the name of the global variables specified in the package should begin with an underscore followed by the package name and an underscore. For example, in the case of a package declared in PEAR, you will declare a global variable as `$_Package_for_PEAR`.

 NOTE

Refer to Chapter 3, "Variables, Operators, and Constants," for more information about global variables.

Using Functions in PEAR

The other standard related to functions declared in PEAR specifies that you should not have a space between the name of the function, the opening bracket, and the first parameter or argument passed to the function. This is completely different from conditional statements, where you need to add a space between the name of a conditional statement and the first bracket. This is considered as the biggest difference between conditional statements and functions. In addition, there should be a space between the commas and each parameter provided in the function, and there should not be any space between the last parameter and the closing bracket. For example,

```
$Result = Calculator($Num1, $Num2);
echo $Result;
```

In the example given above, the minimum number of spaces between the variable, the equal to sign, and the function should be one. You can also increase the amount of space to align multiple functions as in the case of a block of functions. For example,

```
$Result                = Calculator ($Num1, $Num2);
$Interest_Amt          = InterestCal($Result);
$Installment_Amount = InstCal(Prin_amt, $Interest_Amt);
```

Defining Functions

Another standard that you need to follow while defining functions is to include braces with the functions.

Consider the following code.

```
function IntCompare($Num)
  {
      if (($Num>9) && ($Num<100))
        {
              echo  $ Num, " is a 2 digit number";
        }
      elseif (($Num>99) && ($Num<1000))
        {
              echo $ Num, " is a 3 digit number";
        }
      elseif (($Num>999) && ($Num<10000))
        {
              echo $ Num, " is a 4 digit number";
        }
      elseif ($Num>=10000)
```

```
                {

                        echo $ Num, " is a 5 digit number or more";

                }

        else

                {

                        echo $ Num, " is a single digit number";

                }

        }
```

You should not forget to put the argument containing the default values at the end of the list. This ensures that arguments with variable values are evaluated first. The function should also return a value, when it is necessary to do so. The code given above has been modified to return a value as shown below.

Dealing with Comments

When you create documentation for classes, you need to keep in mind the standards mentioned in PHPDoc. PHPDoc is documentation for PHP, which contains standards that are similar to the conventions followed in JavaDoc, which is a documentation for Java. You can get more information about these standards from the PHP Web site.

As a rule, you must comment on everything that you feel should be remembered while going through the code or for later reference. These comments could also include information that is general in nature.

To add comments, you can use either the C style (/*   */) or the C++ style (//) of commenting information. However, you should avoid the use of the Perl-style of commenting, where the # symbol is used to add comments. This is because statements beginning with # may not be interpreted correctly by the PHP compiler.

Including Class Files

The use of the require_once () function is necessary whenever you need to include class files unconditionally. However, if you need to use class files based on certain conditions, you need to use the include_once() function. The use of either of these two functions will ensure that you include the class only once, thus making your code less bulky and more readable. Both the functions share the same file list. After using one function included in a file, you do not have to include it by using the other.

 NOTE

A point that you need to remember is that both `require_once ()` and `include_once()` are not functions but statements. The difference between them is that you do not have to use parentheses while including the file name.

Working with PHP Tags

You have learned that you can use two types of tags while writing code in PHP. You can use either <?...?> tags or <?php...?> tags. However, you should always use <php...?> tags while writing code for PEAR. This makes your code conform to PEAR-standards and allows you to port your application to different operating systems, while ensuring that the code will still work in the same way.

Attaching Header Information

You need to attach the following piece of information in the header of the codes you create for PEAR before you distribute the code.

```
/* vim: set expandtab tabstop=4 shiftwidth=4: */
// +----------------------------------------------------------------------+
// | PHP version 4.0
:
// +----------------------------------------------------------------------+
// | Copyright (c) 1997, 1998, 1999, 2000, 2001, 2002 The PHP Group       :
// +----------------------------------------------------------------------+
// | This source file is subject to version 2.0 of the PHP license,       :
// | that is bundled with this package in the file LICENSE, and is        :
// | available through the world-wide-web at                              :
// | http://www.php.net/license/2_02.txt.                                 :
// | If you did not receive a copy of the PHP license and are unable to   :
```

```
// ¦ obtain it through the world-wide-web, please send a note to          ¦
// ¦ license@php.net so we can mail you a copy immediately.               ¦
// +--------------------------------------------------------------------+
// ¦ Authors: Original Author <author@example.com>                        ¦
// ¦ Your Name <you@example.com>
  ¦
// +--------------------------------------------------------------------+
//
// $Id$
```

The code given above resolves the copyright issue and provides your contact information to the user.

For your name to be added to the list of known authors, you should make a substantial change or modification to the base code. Mostly the amount of change that you should make should not be less than 10 to 20 percent of the code. Any small change or modification to the code cannot qualify you to be added as one of the authors of the code. An exception to this rule can be made if you have rewritten a function or provided a new logic that enhances the code or provides new functionality for future developers.

If the code is not added to the PEAR library of code, the code should include licensing information, author information, and specific copyright information. You need to provide explicit comments along with every code to ensure consistency across all codes.

PEAR and CVS

In Chapter 21, you learned about CVS. The following information applies only to packages that use CVS. These packages connect to CVS from `cvs.php.net`.

You need to include the `$Id$` CVS keyword in all the files that do not already contain this tag. Another option is to remove forms like `Last Modified`.

You use various CVS tags to specify the versioning of the code before releasing it. Table 22-1 shows a list of CVS tags that you can use.

Table 22-1 CVS Tags and Their Use

Tag Name	Purpose
QA_n_n	This is an optional tag and is used if you need to release a trial version before releasing the actual code. This is similar to the release candidate that Microsoft releases for its products.
MAINT_n_n	This is also an optional tag and is used if you need to release a modified version of an existing version of code. There is no need for releasing a new version because there is no major change in the code.
RELEASE_n_n	This is a required tag and is specified along with the final release of the code. If you do not specify the tag, you cannot retrieve the code from the CVS server in the same state it was at the time of the release.

The code given in the following example tags the 2.2 version of PageArchitect.

```
$ cd pear/ PageArchitect
$ cvs tag RELEASE_2_2
T Construct.php
T README
T arcpackage.xml
```

Contributing Codes to PEAR

As explained earlier, PEAR is a repository of code that you can reuse to create new classes and write code. In addition to reusing the existing code in PEAR, you can also

◆ Contribute and maintain new classes in PEAR

◆ Alter existing code to meet PEAR coding standards

◆ Create and post patches for existing PEAR classes

You can mail any new changes you make to the existing code to the PEAR mailing list at pear-dev@lists.php.net. These changes should be based on the latest CVS version. You should send only the changes that you have made to the code and not the complete code. You can extract any changes made by using the diff command available in CVS. Next you attach the difference to a mail and send it to the mailing list. You can also send the changes or patches directly to the original author or authors of the code. In this case, the author is not always the one responsible for maintaining the latest copy of the code or might not be available. Given below are the steps you need to perform to send the patches to the mailing list.

1. Navigate to the location where the code should be stored.

```
# cd / cvs/php.net/pear/Code_changes
```

2. Get the latest version of the code.

```
# cvs update
```

3. Perform any necessary changes.

```
# editor add_resources.php
```

4. Check whether any updating has happened to the original code during the time you were making changes in the code. If any modifications have been done, incorporate the changes in your modified code. This will ensure that the copy of the code that you place back in the repository is the latest code.

```
# cvs update
```

5. Generate the patch by using the latest version from CVS.

```
# cvs diff -u add_resources.php > code_diff.txt
```

6. The text file code_diff.txt contains any modification made to the original code. This file is then mailed to the mailing list.

 CAUTION

The PEAR mailing lists only accept attachments of the content type `text/plain`. Check the end of the file to determine the content type. Therefore, it is important that the output file should belong to a specific application such as Notepad. You can also rename the output file if it currently does not open in a text editor.

You can also submit certain code that you want other developers to test and experiment with before creating the final version. This ensures that the code is tested in real-life scenarios and that possible errors are handled. However, when submitting this code to the mailing list you need to attach documentation stating all assumptions and information regarding the code. The optimum place to store this information is in the <status> tab of the package.xml file. The following list provides some of the values that can be specified in the tag.

- ◆ **Alpha:** This value specifies that the code is one of the first versions and contains many bugs. This code is unstable because it is changed many times.

- ◆ **Beta:** This is more stable as compared to an alpha version and can be used cautiously. However, even in this version of the code, bugs may exist.

- ◆ **Devel:** This code is meant for developers who like to test the code, report any bugs, or suggest any changes. This code can be anywhere between an alpha version of the code to a relatively stable one.

- ◆ **Stable:** This version of the code derived after extensively testing the code and fixing any known bug is considered stable. Separate documentation of this code is created for both users and production.

- ◆ **Snapshot:** This is the final version of the code that can be posted at the site. The code is posted along with the date on which it is published.

You can also store sample codes along with the documentation. This is very helpful when the code is of a complex nature. However, you need to remember that the sample codes should be a supplement to the documentation and not a replacement for the documentation. Both the documentation and the examples are stored in a subdirectory called docs in the package directory.

You can also store experimental scripts along with your code. This is suggested in cases where the code has to be compiled by the developer before using it. These scripts require certain programs or supplement files such as templates and graphics to work properly. These scripts are stored in another directory, named tests.

Requirement to Make Changes in PEAR

We have learned about the changes that we can make in the PEAR code and the ways of making the changes. However, another question that we need to answer is "Why do we need to make changes in the existing code?" Your answer might be "to get my code into PEAR" (even if it provides redundant information) or that "the existing code is not clear." Both these reasons are not valid enough to suggest changing an existing PEAR code. This is because these reasons are personal in nature. You should make changes to the code only if the existing code does not have a specific function or functionality or if it is very slow. All these reasons validate modifying the code to provide these functionalities. Either you can make changes to the existing class or, if this is not possible, you can create a new class that provides these functionalities.

While writing a new code, you need to remember that the APIs that the code contains should be compatible with the APIs in the original code. If it is not possible to write a code that is compatible with the original code, you need to create a wrapper class. The wrapper class will provide compatibility between the classes in the original code and the classes in the new code.

Help in PEAR

If you have any problems related to PEAR, such as problems relating to writing codes on certain topics or problems encountered while debugging a code, you can post these problems on the PEAR mailing lists to receive answers from other developers. Generally, these queries can be divided into two types, general queries and technical queries. General queries contain questions about the use of PEAR components and other basic concepts used in PEAR. These questions are posted at **pear-general@lists.php.net**. Technical questions are generally discussions between developers who are actually developing code to be put in PEAR. These discussions are generally in the form of question and answers and are posted at **pear-dev@lists.php.net**.

Summary

In this chapter, you learned about PEAR. You learned that PEAR contains a repository of code that developers can reuse. You also learned about the coding standards that you should follow to create code for PEAR. You learned about standards that you need to follow for indenting, using control structures, declaring functions, defining functions, using comments, and including class files. You learned about the naming conventions that you can follow while naming functions, methods, constants, and global variables. You also learned to use PHP code tags and to add header information to the code. In addition, you then learned about standards that you should follow while using CVS. You also learned about the RELEASE_n_n, QA_n_n, and MAINT_n_n tags. You also learned why you need to make changes in an existing code and how you can contribute code for PEAR. Finally, you learned about the mailing lists where you can send any queries related to PEAR.

Chapter 23

PHP-Nuke

While surfing the net, you definitely must have come across a Web site that offers news and other articles that need to be updated frequently, personalized user accounts, online polls, frequently asked questions (FAQs), search engines, and links to related Web sites. A lot of Web sites on the Internet also offer an open publishing system. An open publishing system means that anyone can register to the Web site and post news articles and comments to it. These sites also offer a number of discussion forums.

Have you ever wanted to add this dynamism to your Web site? Have you wanted to give the users of your Web site the opportunity to participate in a friendly community where they can post their own views and articles or maybe participate in an online forum or newsgroup? One thing is for sure, if you add this feature to your Web site, you can definitely increase the popularity of your site!

However, programming all these features into your site means huge codes and equally huge effort! If you have ever wondered about a tool that you can use to create a Web site that is dynamic, interactive, open, and at the same time easy to create, then read on. This chapter is for you.

To make your sites dynamic and open to users, you need a software application generally referred to as a Web portal system or a content management system. A Web portal system is defined as a software system that allows individuals with no Web development skills to update and manage their Web sites locally or across a network. In this category of Web portal systems, PHP-Nuke has emerged as the current buzzword in the field of PHP.

In this chapter, you will learn to install and configure PHP-Nuke on your Apache server. After you successfully install and configure PHP-Nuke, you will learn to tailor, administer, and manage your site using PHP-Nuke.

What Is PHP-Nuke?

So what is PHP-Nuke? Purely written in PHP, PHP-Nuke is a powerful and easy-to-use content management system that enables you, as a Web site administrator, to build an automated Web site to distribute news and articles with users of the system, conduct online polls and surveys, offer fast and efficient search options, and personalize the interface of users on the basis of their individual requirements. PHP-Nuke also allows your users to submit comments, discuss articles, and participate in online forums.

Other features of PHP-Nuke include the following:

◆ Web-based administration

◆ Access statistics that depict user access to the Web site with the help of a counter

◆ Personalized and customizable interface for registered users

◆ Various managers, such as Themes Manager, Ephemerids Manager, Download Manager, FAQ Manager, and File Manager for managing resources (for example, Theme Manager allows you to avail more than 43 themes for your Web site interfaces)

◆ GUI-based administration with graphic Topics Manager

◆ Option to edit or delete articles, comments, news stories, and forums

◆ Easy tracking of the users with the help of HTTP Referers' page

◆ Integrated banners advertisement system

◆ Search engine whose functionality resembles the functionality of Yahoo's search engine

◆ Support to various database systems, such as MySQL, mSQL, PostgreSQL, ODBC, ODBC_Adabas, Sybase, and Interbase

◆ Support for 22 languages from all over the world

◆ Comments option in polls

◆ Categorized articles, headlines, newsletters, and review systems

Now that you know what PHP-Nuke is, you'll learn to install and configure PHP-Nuke in the next section.

Installing and Configuring PHP-Nuke

Various versions of PHP-Nuke are available today. Some of the most used are PHP-Nuke-4.4.1a and PHP-Nuke-5.0. However, the latest version available at the time of writing this book is PHP-Nuke-5.4. This section deals with the installation of PHP-Nuke-5.4.

This section will serve as a generalized guide for the installation and configuration of all other versions. This is because the instructions for the installation of all versions of PHP-Nuke are basically the same.

 NOTE

As I just stated, the steps for the installation of all the versions are basically the same. However, it is recommended that you go through the documentation available with the version that you are installing.

To install PHP-Nuke, you'll need to download the PHP-Nuke source file from the Web. The source file can be downloaded free of cost from various sites on the Internet. One of them is **http://www.phpnuke.org/**.

 NOTE

You must have the basic knowledge to install and configure PHP4, Apache, and MySQL to be able to breeze through the rest of this section. You can refer to Chapter 2, "Installing and Configuring PHP," for detailed information on the process of installation of PHP and MySQL.

The prerequisites to install PHP-Nuke on your system are listed below:

◆ A Web server running PHP

◆ A MySQL database server

◆ Windows or Linux operating system

After you have downloaded the source file of PHP-Nuke-5.4, the following steps will guide you through the installation and configuration of PHP-Nuke-5.4.

1. Unzip or untar the source file in the installation directory (such as /nuke) on the local drive of your machine. The command to untar the source file is:

```
tar -zxvf PHP-Nuke 5.4.tar.gz
```

Two subdirectories, html/ and sql/, will be extracted and created in the installation directory (/nuke). The html/ directory contains all the PHP files required for working of PHP-Nuke, and the sql/ directory contains the script instructions for configuring the MySQL database, if it is not already configured.

NOTE

Make sure that the files Install and Readme have been downloaded correctly. These are the most important files for the installation of PHP-Nuke.

CAUTION

Do not unpack the source files into the root directory of your Web server. If for some reason the installation is not successful, it might affect the functioning of your Web server.

2. Copy or move the files from the current html/ directory to the home directory /var/www/html. The command to copy files is:

```
cp * /var/www/html
```

The command to move files from the html/ directory to /var/www/html is:

```
mv * /var/www/html
```

NOTE

You can skip this step if you create a folder—say nuke—in /var/www/html, set it as the home directory, and modify the Apache server to point to this new home directory. Refer to Apache help documentation if you face any problems.

3. Now you need to configure the MySQL database for PHP-Nuke. The database that will be used to hold PHP-Nuke-related information needs to be created. The information of the user who will control this database

and therefore PHP-Nuke also needs to be added to the database. To create the MySQL database called nuke, the command is as follows:

```
create database nuke
```

4. After creating the database, you need to import the default database schema from the file nuke.sql, which exists in the installation directory /nuke/sql/. The command to import the default database schema is:

```
mysql -D nuke -u root -p < nuke.sql
```

You will be prompted for a password. Press the Enter key. This is because you specified the password as blank (" ") in the above command (-p). Figure 23-1 shows the command and its result.

FIGURE 23-1 *MySQL command to create the PHP-Nuke database called nuke and its output*

5. Now you need to set the database name, username, and password and update the system configuration. To do so, open the config.php file in the /var/www/html directory. Change the settings to the following parameters, if necessary:

```
$dbhost = "localhost";
$dbuname = "root";
$dbpass = "password"
$dbname = "nuke"
```

NOTE

The password that you supply for $dbpass is the password that you use for your root account. Here I have specified the password as password for the sake of easy understanding.

6. You can also change the default theme (NukeNews) for PHP-Nuke. The themes are available in the themes/ directory. To change the default theme, change the $Default_Theme parameter in the config.php file, as follows:

```
$Default_Theme = "Odyssey";
```

You may skip this step if you don't want to set a default theme of your choice. You'll learn to set a theme, other than the default theme for your site, using the GUI interface of PHP-Nuke a bit later in this chapter.

7. After making the changes to the configuration file, save the changes and close it.

8. Now you'll need to set the user-id, group-id, and modes for the files in the installation directory. If you fail to do so, despite the installation of PHP-Nuke, you will not be able to run it. The command to set rights to nuke/ directory is:

```
chown -R www:www;
                           chown 770 nuke/;
                           chown 660 nuke/*;
```

9. Open your favorite browser and in the Address bar, specify the location where your PHP-Nuke (http://localhost/nuke) is installed. Figure 23-2 depicts the default PHP-Nuke layout.

Now you are ready to work with PHP-Nuke. Don't be disheartened by the layout you see right now. PHP-Nuke offers wide-ranging options for customizing the look and feel of the current layout. You will learn to change it later in this chapter.

FIGURE 23-2 *The default configuration and layout of the site using PHP-Nuke*

Administering and Managing the Site

After you have installed and configured PHP-Nuke on your Web server, you are ready to go! There are various aspects of administration and management of your Web site other than creating the site.

Some of the most common administration-related tasks include changing the default administrator password, creating another administrator account, and adding a user to the site. Common site management-related tasks include the modification of the default site settings, changing the look and feel of the site by modifying various blocks, modifying, adding, or deleting topics, managing forums, creating Ephemerids, and managing advertisement banners on the site.

PHP-Nuke can help you in the administration as well as the efficient management of the site. In the next sections you will learn about the various aspects of administration and management of your Web site.

Administering the Site

Now that your PHP-Nuke server is all installed and configured, to customize the interface, you'll need to start from the administration section. Let me now tell you how you can administer the site and change it to your liking.

PHP-Nuke offers graphical administration. In order to view the administration section, you need to follow the steps specified below:

1. In the browser window, specify the address of admin.php as http://local-host/admin.php.

2. Login page appears (as shown in Figure 23-3) and you will be asked to log in to the section.

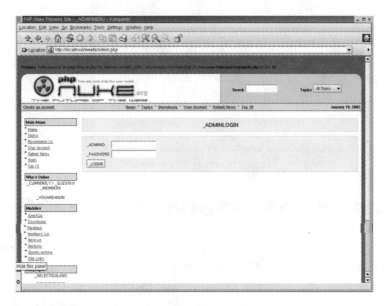

FIGURE 23-3 *Logging in to the Administration page*

3. Specify the Admin ID as God and the password as Password.

 NOTE

When the PHP-Nuke server is launched for the first time, you will need to log in as a super user whose login ID is God and password is Password. To ensure the security of the site, it is extremely important that you change this default login ID and password.

After you have successfully logged in as an administrator, the Administration page will be visible in the browser window, as shown in Figure 23-4.

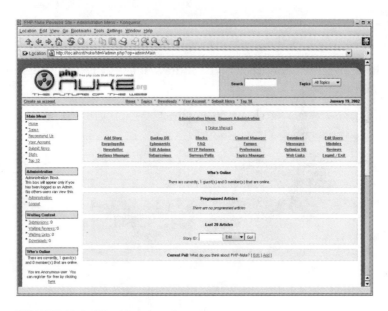

FIGURE 23-4 *The Administration page*

Changing the Administrator (Super User) Password

As mentioned earlier, the first thing you should preferably do after logging in is to change the administrator password, so that besides the administrator (that is you) no one else can log in to the administration section as a super user (God). This is because if someone else logs in as the super user, that person might remove your privileges as the administrator or render the entire site (and your hard work of so many days) inaccessible and useless!

To change the administrator password, follow the steps specified below:

1. In the Administration page, click Edit Admins. The Author's Administration page appears.

2. In the Modify Info section, set Nickname as Admin.

3. In the Email box, type your e-mail address. This is where you will receive the e-mail related to the administration of the site.

4. Make sure that the Super User permission is checked. If not, check Super User. By setting this one permission you grant yourself full access to all the aspects of the site, such as Articles, Topics, Users, Surveys, Sections, Web Links, Ephemerids, FAQ, Download, Reviews, Newsletter, Forum, Content, and Encyclopedia.

5. Set the password that you prefer for the account. Needless to say, your password must be kept a secret known only to you.

6. Reenter the password in the Retype Password box and click on the Save button to save the changes. You will return to the Author's Administration page.

Figure 23-5 depicts the details of the Administrator (God) account being modified.

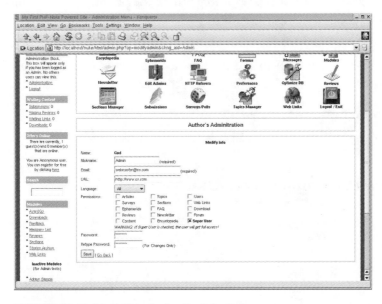

FIGURE 23-5 *Modifying the details of the God account*

Adding a Privileged User

A privileged user is one who has more rights than the normal user. You might want to add a privileged user for the site in case you want someone trusted and responsible to handle your site in your absence. Also, if you expect a great deal of activity on your site, you can allocate administration of specific sections, such as news, articles, topics, and forums, to different individuals.

To add another administrator (or privileged user), follow the steps given below:

1. In the Add a New Administrator section, type the name of the new administrator in the Name box.

2. In the Nickname box, type the nickname of the new administrator. (The nickname is Admin1 in our case.)

3. In the E-mail box, type the e-mail address of the new administrator.

4. Check Articles, Topics, Users, Surveys, Sections, Web Links, Ephemerids, FAQ, Download, Reviews, Newsletter, Forum, Content, and Encyclopedia. If you do not want the new administrator to be as powerful as you, make sure that the Super User permission is not checked. However, if you want to grant all the permissions including full access, check the Super User box.

5. Set the password for the account.

6. Click on Add Author to add the new administrator account. Figure 23-6 shows the result of adding the privileged user.

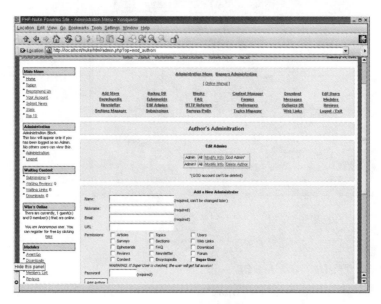

FIGURE 23-6 *The Author's Administration page depicting the new privileged user*

Adding (or Registering) a User

In order to register a new user to your site, you need to follow the steps specified below:

1. In the Administration page, click Edit Users.

2. In the Add a New User section, add the details of the user you intend to register to the site. Figure 23-7 shows the sample details of a fictitious user.

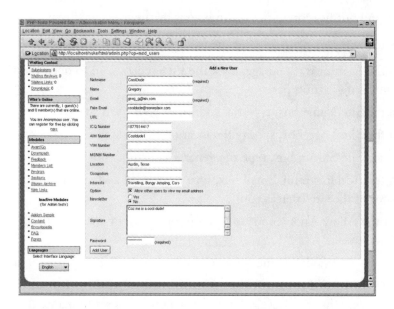

FIGURE 23-7 *Adding a new user*

3. Click on Add User to add the details of the new user to your site.

Let me now tell you how you can manage the various aspects of the site to tailor them to your liking and requirements.

Managing the Site

Management of a site that offers a wide range of services—such as downloading, search, ability to participate in forums, articles, news, online polls, advertisements, and so forth—is a complex task. In this section you'll learn to manage your Web site efficiently, using the services offered by PHP-Nuke.

Let me first tell you about how to change the general look and feel of your Web site by configuring the general features of the site.

Configuring the General Features of the Site

General features of a site include the site name in the title bar of the browser window, URL, logo, and slogan of the site, theme of the site, time format, language(s) supported, and notification of new submissions by the users of the site.

The steps to configure some or all of the features of the site are as follows:

1. In the Administration page, click the Preferences icon to open the Web Site Configuration page.

2. In the Site Name box, type the address of your Web site.

3. In the Site Logo box, specify the location of the logo of your site.

4. In the Site Slogan box, type the general slogan of your Web site.

5. In the Administrator Email box, type the e-mail address of the administrator of the site (that is you).

6. Set the Allow Anonymous to Post option to No by selecting the No radio button.

7. From the Default Theme for your site list box, select Odyssey (or any other theme of your preference).

8. Make sure that the Locale Time Format option is set to match that of your location.

9. In the Multilingual Options section, set the Activate Multilingual Features option to Yes if you want the user to view the content of the site in more than one language.

10. In the Mail New Stories to Administrator section, set the Notify New Submission by Email option to Yes if you want the administrator to be notified of every new submission made by users to the site. The default settings in this section (Mail New Stories to Administrator) generally serve well. However, you can change them to your liking.

11. In the Comments Moderation section, select Moderation by Admin from the Type of Moderation drop-down list. This implies that the comments on the Web site posted by the users can only be moderated (or changed) by the administrator of the site.

12. Until now, the administration interface is non-GUI. If you want the interface of the Administration page to be GUI, set the Graphics in Administration Menu radio button in the Graphic Options section to Yes. Figure 23-8 depicts the main Administration page after it has been changed to GUI.

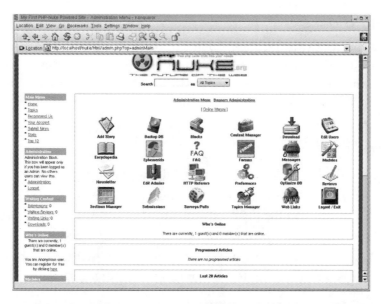

FIGURE 23-8 *The GUI-based Administration page*

13. Click on the Save button to save any changes that you made and return to the main Administration page.

Figure 23-9 shows a sample Web Site Configuration page.

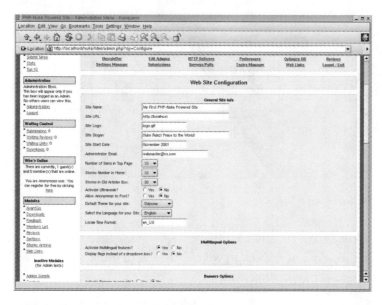

FIGURE 23-9 *A Sample Web Site Configuration page*

Modifying Blocks

A block is a chunk of your Web page. Some of the visible blocks used in a Web site based on PHP-Nuke include advertisement banners, Surveys, News, Stories, Articles, Downloads, Links, and Login. In this section, you'll learn to activate a block and add a new block of your own to the Web site.

By default, the Search block is deactivated. The steps for activating the Search block are listed below:

1. Click on the Blocks icon in the main Administration page.

2. In the Blocks Administration table, against the Search option, click on the Activate link in the Functions column. The Block Activation page appears.

3. As shown in Figure 23-10, under "Do you want to Activate this block?" click on Yes. You'll return to the main Administration page.

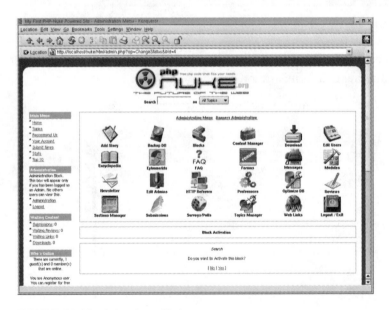

FIGURE 23-10 *Activating a block*

You can similarly deactivate a block, change (edit) it, or delete it entirely. If you want, you can also add a new block in your Web site. In order to add a block, you need to follow the steps specified next:

1. In the Add a New Block section, as shown in Figure 23-11, type the name of the block in the Title section.

FIGURE 23-11   *The Add a New Block section*

2. In the Content box, type the content that should be part of the block.
3. Set the position of the block as Right from the Position drop-down list.
4. Click the Create Block button to create the block.

Many sites feature a block called Quote of the Day. Figure 23-12 shows a sample block called Quote of the Day, which features a quote and will be placed at the right side of the site.

Figure 23-13 shows the Blocks Administration table before a new block has been created.

When the new block is created successfully, it is added to the table, as shown in Figure 23-14.

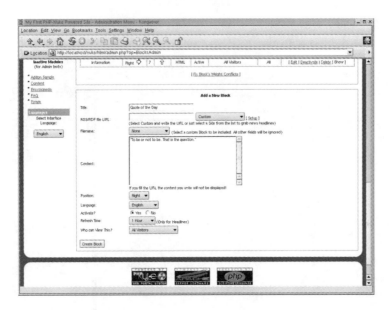

FIGURE 23-12 *Adding a block called Quote of the Day*

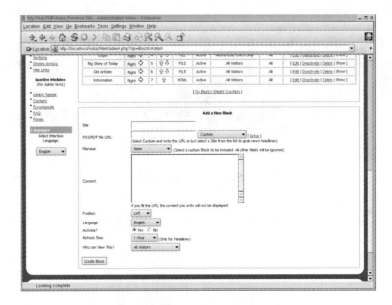

FIGURE 23-13 *Blocks Administration table before adding a block*

FIGURE 23-14 *Blocks Administration table after adding the new block*

Modifying Topics

Topics are a fundamental feature of a PHP-Nuke-based Web site. The use of Topics can help you in the categorization of the content posted on the site. Topics being a very important feature, PHP-Nuke offers a Topics Manager that helps you in adding or deleting a topic or editing an existing topic.

The steps to add a new topic by using Topics Manager are as follows:

1. To open the Topics Manager page, click on the Topics Manager icon in the main Administration page. The Topics Manager page is shown in Figure 23-15.

2. In the Add a New Topic section, type the name of the topic in the Topic Name box.

3. Click on Add Topic to add the topic to the list of existing topics. As shown in Figure 23-16, the new topic is added to the Current Active Topics section.

Managing Forums

Forums are the online discussion boards on your Web site. These facilitate the active participation of registered users (or nonregistered users, if you allow) in an

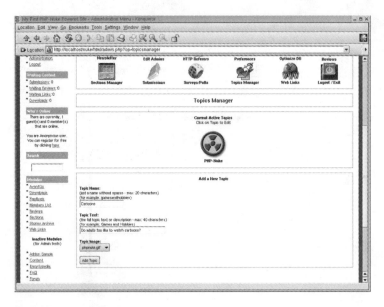

FIGURE 23-15 *The Topics Manager page*

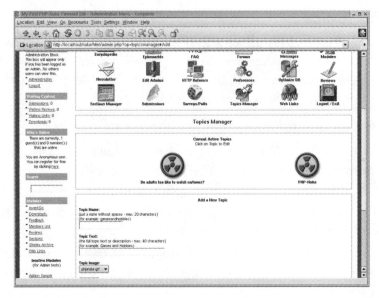

FIGURE 23-16 *The Current Active Topics section after adding a new topic*

online discussion. The Forums section allows you to add, delete, or moderate a forum. You can also ban offensive words in discussions or offensive users from accessing your site permanently or temporarily.

The steps for adding a new forum to your site are:

1. Click on the Forums icon in the main Administration page. The Forum Main Menu page appears, as shown in Figure 23-17.

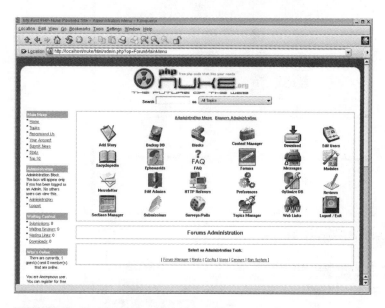

FIGURE 23-17 *The Forum Main Menu page*

2. Click on the Forum Manager link in the Forums Administration section to open the Forums Administration page.

3. In the Add Categories section, type the name of the forum that you want to create in the Categories box. For example, to create a forum called Unix and Linux, you'll need to type Unix and Linux, as shown in Figure 23-18.

4. Click on Add to create the forum. The new forum is added to the Forum Categories, as shown in Figure 23-19.

Now that you have created a forum successfully and added it to the list of existing forums, you'll learn to censor an offensive word. For this you need to return to the Forum Main Menu page. The steps to censor a word are:

1. In the Forum Main Menu page, click on the Censure link. The Forum Censor page is opened.

2. In the Add New censor word section, type the word in the Word box that you want to be censored from all the forums on your Web site.

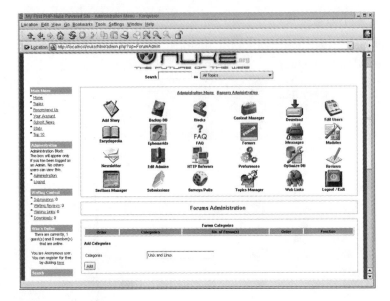

FIGURE 23-18 *Adding a forum*

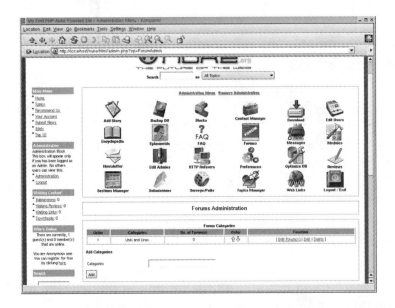

FIGURE 23-19 *The new forum*

3. Type the replacement word in the Replacement box. This word, as the name suggests, will replace any instance of the censored word on your Web site. For example, Figure 23-20 shows that the word Damn is being censored and is to be replaced by Darn.

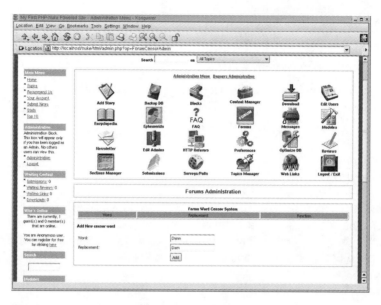

FIGURE 23-20 *Censoring a word*

4. Click on Add to add the word to the list of censored words. Figure 23-21 shows the result of censoring the word Damn.

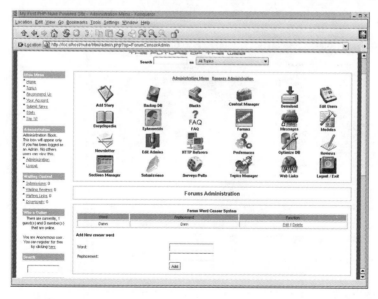

FIGURE 23-21 *The result of censoring a word*

You will now ban an offensive user from accessing your Web site. Return to the Forum Main Menu page and follow the steps given below to do so.

1. Click on the Ban System link.

2. In the Add new banned rules section, type the IP address or the user-name in the IP/Username box. You can ban users that are not registered on your site by using their IP addresses.

CAUTION

Make sure that you have selected Username from the drop-down list in the right of the IP/Username text box if you want to ban a user by using their corresponding username. Similarly, ensure that IP address is selected from this drop-down list if you choose to ban a user using the IP address of their computer.

3. Type in the time duration in the Durations box. This time-duration could be seconds, minutes, hours, days, months, or years, which can be selected from the drop-down list and specifies the time interval for which you want to ban the user from accessing your site. Figure 23-22 shows a user called Cooldude from being banned from your site.

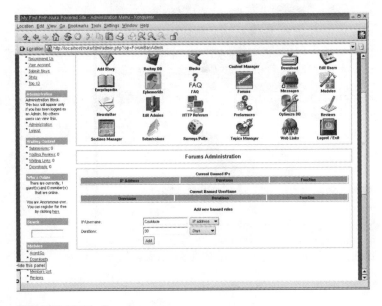

FIGURE 23-22 *Banning a user*

4. Click on Add to add the user to the list of banned users, as shown in Figure 23-23.

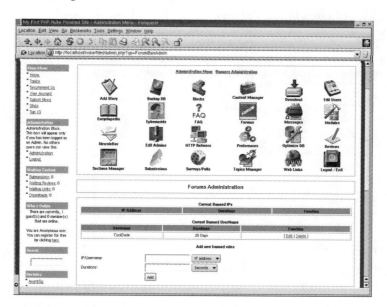

FIGURE 23-23 *The result of banning a user*

Managing Ephemerids

Ephemerids are an interesting feature of PHP-Nuke. You can use Ephemerids to remind all your registered users of specific events, such as the Fourth of July, Christmas, and so on. The steps in order to create an Ephemerid are as follows:

1. In the main Administration page, click on the Ephemerids icon to open the Ephemerids Administration page.

2. In the Add a New Ephemerid section, set the date that you want to remind as Day, Month, and Year.

NOTE

In case of monthly reminders, you can omit the year or the month.

3. In the Ephemerid Description text area, type the message that you want to display to your users.

4. Click on Ok to add the Ephemerid.

Figure 23-24 depicts an Ephemerid set for Christmas Day.

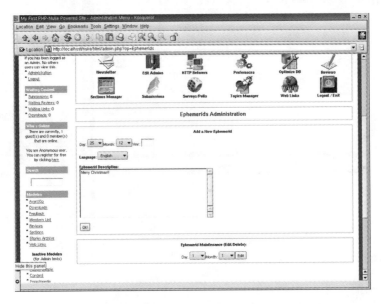

FIGURE 23-24 *An Ephemerid set for Christmas Day*

Managing Banners

Most Web sites also sport commercial advertisements from commercial organizations. PHP-Nuke offers a built-in banner-based advertising system to support this feature. This banner system allows the administrator to create a separate account for each advertiser. This banner system also allows the advertisers to add multiple banners, which are routinely rotated by PHP-Nuke itself.

You need to follow the steps below in order to create a commercial banner for a client:

1. In the main Administration page, click on the Banners Administration link (above the administration icons).

2. In the Banners Administration section, specify the name of the client who wants to advertise through your site.

3. Set the Contact Name and Contact Email.

4. In the Client Login and Client Password boxes, specify the login name and the password with which the client can log in to the banner system.

5. In the Extra Info text area, specify any additional information, if necessary. Figure 23-25 depicts the details of a fictitious client.

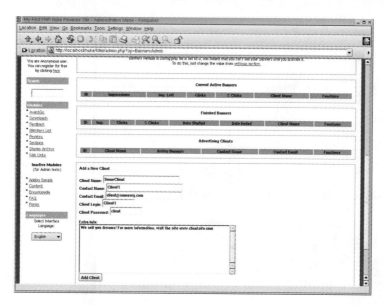

FIGURE 23-25 *Details of a client who wants to advertise through your Web site*

6. Click on Add Client to add the client to the clientele list. The client details are added to the list of Advertising Clients.

7. As shown in Figure 23-26, in the Add a New Banner section, you can add further details (Client Name, Image URL, and Click URL) of the client.

8. Click on Add Banner to add the banner to the list of Current Active Banners. The banner is created, as shown in Figure 23-27.

9. Now you'll need to activate the banner since a banner is not visible until it is activated. Return to the main Administration page to do so.

10. In the main Administration page, click the Preferences icon. The Web Site Configuration page appears.

11. Under the Banners Options section, activate the banner by selecting the Yes radio button for the "Activate Banners in your site?" option.

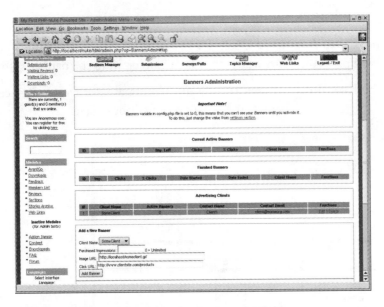

FIGURE 23-26 *Creating the banner for the specified client*

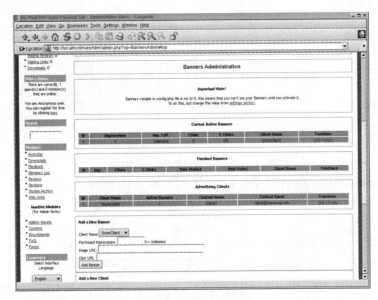

FIGURE 23-27 *Result of banner creation*

12. Now you'll need to activate the banner since, as stated above, a banner is not visible until it is activated.

13. Click Save Changes to save the changes and return to the main Administration page.

Now the banner of your client is ready. The Finished Banners table helps you view the statistics per banner. These include the number of times the banner is clicked, the percentage of views converted into clicks, and so on. You can easily attract more clients with this simple yet powerful banner facility.

There is much more to PHP-Nuke. However, I have pretty much covered the basics that will get you interested in PHP-Nuke. Explore much more into the depths of PHP-Nuke and make your site more interactive and interesting and your life easier. So what are you waiting for?

Summary

In this chapter, you learned about the Web portal system called PHP-Nuke that is slowly but surely gaining a steady following among Web developers. PHP-Nuke is a tool for fast and efficient development of a Web site. It offers a number of advantages. It is easy to install and configure. In addition, it is a GUI-based development tool, which is very simple to use.

In this chapter, you learned to install and configure PHP-Nuke on your Apache server. After you successfully installed and configured PHP-Nuke, you learned to tailor, administer, and manage your site using PHP-Nuke. You learned to change the default administrator password, create a new administrator, add a new user to your site, change the general settings, such as themes, of your site, modify various blocks that are displayed on your site, modify topics, create, edit, and manage forums, create Ephemerids for your users, and create commercial banners for your advertisers.

Chapter 24

Cookies

ave you tried accessing Yahoo Mail or any other Web-based mail? Most of these sites prompt you to remember your login ID, so that next time when you log in to the site you are only prompted for the password. Have you ever wondered how a site remembers your login ID and other details? The answer is cookies (not the ones you eat, by the way!).

In this chapter, you will learn about cookies and the role they play in maintaining the state between your subsequent visits to a Web page. You will learn to implement cookies in your Web site by setting and creating them. You'll also learn to access and delete cookies. And you'll learn why there is such furor around the use of cookies among the Web community and how you can prevent loss of sensitive data.

What Is a Cookie?

You already know that the Internet is based on Hypertext Transfer Protocol (HTTP), which is a stateless protocol. This implies that once a transaction between the client machine and the Web server is finished, the Web server loses all the memory regarding the transaction.

Let me try to explain this concept in simple English. Suppose a user visits a commercial site, adds three books to the shopping cart, and before making the payment for the books, moves on to another site. After a while the user returns to the same site. Will the user need to add the three books chosen earlier again to the shopping cart? The answer is yes because as I said earlier, HTTP is stateless and therefore loses any memory of the earlier actions. This means the user will have to search for the same books again and add them to the shopping cart and pay for the books before moving on to the next site. However, the answer to the same question can be no, the user would not have to add the books again, if the site uses cookies. So what is a cookie?

A cookie is a small piece of information (or a message, if you like) that a Web server can store through your Web browser on to your hard disk when you visit the corresponding site. The Web server can also retrieve this information later when you visit the same site next time.

When you visit a cookie-enabled Web site, you might need to log in to the site or register using a password and other relevant information. This information is stored into a small text file whose maximum size is 4 KB. This file is referred to as a cookie and contains the relevant user-related information, such as User ID, password, list of pages that the user visited, and the date the user last visited a page.

For example, say you searched for some book on the well-known online book store Amazon, at **http://www.amazon.com/**. This is a cookie-enabled site, and Figure 24-1 depicts the cookie that was created on your local hard disk.

```
ubid-main
058-3955710-9452444
amazon.com/
0
2916341376
31961269
1377043424
29456181
*
x-main
hQFiIxHUFj8mCscT@Yb5Z7xsVsOFQjBf
amazon.com/
0
2916341376
31961269
1377143424
29456181
*
session-id
058-3442978-4900108
amazon.com/
0
1257717760
29466815
2871432720
29465430
*
session-id-time
1011427200
amazon.com/
0
1257717760
29466815
2871432720
29465430
*
```

FIGURE 24-1 *A sample cookie*

In Figure 24-1, `058-3955710-9452444` is the unique ID that will be assigned to you when you visit the Amazon site for the first time. The site also stores a session ID, in this case `058-3442978-4900108`, that uniquely identifies the given session along with the time when the given session started. As shown in Figure 24-1, the session ID time is `1011427200`. A main ID, `hQFiIxHUFj8mCscT@Yb5Z7xsV-sOFQjBf`, is also stored for the internal processing by the site. The rest of the information in the cookie is considered the housekeeping information for your browser.

As you saw in Figure 24-1, the information that is stored in a cookie is in the format of name and value. Consider the following name-value pair:

`ubid-main 058-3955710-9452444`

In the above example, `ubid-main` is the name and `058-3955710-9452444` is the corresponding value.

Now that you have the basic idea what a cookie is, let me explain what role it has to play and how it helps while you browse the Internet. Continuing the same example I cited above, suppose you visit an online bookstore and add three books to your shopping cart. The list of all the items that you picked up is stored in the cookie that was created automatically. You might continue browsing the site after adding books to your shopping cart. When you are through browsing the site, you would now like to pay for all the items that you picked. When you return to the shopping cart, all the items that you added to it are very much there. Make the payment and the transaction is over! Simple, isn't it? Cookies can make your life this easy.

Most of the sites that are created nowadays feature cookies. The use of cookies is popular among the Web community for the following reasons:

◆ To determine how many users visit the given Web site and how often. These statistics are especially helpful if the site uses proxy servers that make keeping a tab on visitors a problem.

◆ For storing details of the users who visit the site or register on the Web site. However, since the cookie stores the details at the client's hard disk, extra details need not be stored in a database.

◆ For helping a site store individual user preferences at the client end, thus allowing users to customize the interface (such as layout and colors) as per their liking.

◆ To prevent repetitive logins, thus making the login process faster. In addition, since the cookie is stored at the client end, the Web server need not be burdened each time a user needs to log in to the site. The server only needs to authenticate the first-time users.

◆ For tracking a user's path and activities on a given Web site. In addition to determining the general preferences of users, this feature allows the Web administrators to track miscreants.

◆ For generating individual user profiles. For example, some sites display personalized messages to their users when they log in to the site.

◆ For storing the items selected by the site users in their respective shopping carts.

Now that you have the basic idea of what a cookie is and the reason why it is used, let me discuss how a cookie works.

How Does a Cookie Work?

A cookie works in the following manner:

1. When you type the URL of the destination Web site in the Address bar of your browser, the address is located and if found successfully, a request is sent to the Web server that hosts the site.

2. If the Web server accepts the request, the Web browser at the client end checks for an existing cookie from the given site.

3. If the cookie is found, the browser sends all the name-value pairs in the cookie to the server as the HTTP header. In addition, the expiration date of the cookie, if any, and a path is also sent to the server along with the name-value pairs. The expiration date indicates the date and time when the cookie will be considered invalid. The path helps the Web server to associate various values in the cookie to different pages of the site that is being accessed. This information (name-value pairs, expiration date, and path), when received by the server, is then used by the server for internal use and other activities, such as validating the user.

4. If the corresponding cookie is not found on the local hard disk, the server is notified about the absence of a cookie. In this case, the server generates a new ID for the client who requested a connection and sends the cookie containing the name-value pair(s) to the requester's Web

browser. The browser then stores this cookie on the hard disk of your machine.

The communication between the client and server using cookies is depicted in Figure 24-2.

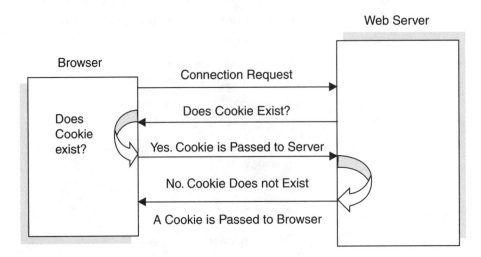

FIGURE 24-2 *Communication between server and browser using cookies*

In the next section, you will learn about the parameters that determine the validity and the longevity of a cookie.

The Scope of a Cookie

As you already know, a cookie is a name-value pair. In addition to the name and value parameters, several other parameters are used, which allow you more control over your cookies. For example, you can control the time span for which a cookie will be considered valid. Similarly, you can also control the type of information it will provide and the security parameters it will support. In other words, these parameters define the scope of a cookie.

The parameters that are used to determine the scope of a cookie are:

◆ **Expiration parameter:** This parameter defines the validity, life span, and longevity of a cookie. It determines the date and time of expiration of a cookie, where the time is specified in the GMT format. After a cookie reaches its expiration date and time, it can no longer be sent to a client.

NOTE

The default value used for this parameter is `Until the browser is closed.` This implies that the cookie survives only until the Web page in the browser window is open. The moment you close the browser window on the client machine, the cookie is discarded and becomes unavailable next time you run the browser.

◆ **Path parameter:** This parameter is used to limit the scope of a cookie to a certain part of the document tree within the Web server. In simpler terms, this parameter specifies the path to all files and directories on a Web server for which the cookie is considered valid. By setting the path scope within a document hierarchy, the cookie is sent to the Web server only if the client requests a page that exists in the specified path.

 NOTE

The default value of this parameter is `/`, which implies that the given cookie will be available by default to any pages in the same directory as the page that created it or in pages lower down in the hierarchy.

◆ **Domain parameter:** This parameter is used to specify the domain for which the cookie is valid. The cookie can be limited to a particular host by specifying the name of the host as `singlehost.com`. Similarly, a cookie can also be made valid for an entire domain by specifying the value of this (domain) parameter as `.domainname.com`. The `.` in the domain value implies that the cookie is not limited to a specific host within the domain.

 NOTE

The default value of the domain parameter is the domain name of the server that generated and set the cookie on the client's hard disk. This value is generated automatically.

◆ **Security parameter:** This parameter ensures that the confidential data stored in the cookie is safe from unauthorized access while it travels from the Web server to the client machine. By enabling this parameter a secure channel, such as Secure Hypertext Transfer Protocol (HTTPS), is used for exchanging cookies between the server and the client. If the value of this parameter is not specified, the cookie is sent through an unsecured channel.

 NOTE

The default value of the secure parameter is `disabled`. As a result, all the data and cookies are exchanged between the two communicating ends regardless of the fact whether the transmission channel is secure or not.

You must remember that the cookie name and value parameters are mandatory for the definition of a cookie. The rest of the parameters—expiration, domain, security, and path—are optional.

Figure 24-3 depicts a cookie that contains all the parameters, mandatory as well as optional, that a cookie can take.

```
MyCOOKIE=Figure_18;
expires=Fri, 1-Feb-2001 24:00:00 GMT;
path=/;
domain=.niit.com;
secure
```

FIGURE 24-3 *A cookie with all parameters*

The next section throws light on the restrictions that you might face while using cookies.

Restrictions While Using Cookies

Since a cookie might contain confidential information, such as login ID and password, there are various restrictions on the use of cookies to prevent their abuse. These restrictions include:

◆ The maximum allowed size of a cookie is 4 KB. This is because cookies are stored on the user's hard disk. If the size of a cookie is large, it is possible that cookies from various Web sites a user visits in a day might fill up the client's hard disk.

◆ A Web server cannot store more than 20 cookies on a user's computer. This again ensures that one Web server does not fill up the client's hard disk.

◆ A browser at the client end can store a maximum of 300 cookies.

◆ Only the Web server that issued a cookie to a client can read the data stored in the cookie. Although all cookies are stored in the same folder, a Web server cannot access or read cookies that have been created by other Web servers or domains.

Now that you know how a cookie does its work and you know about its scope, you will learn about the implementation of cookies in PHP.

Implementing Cookies in PHP

Implementation of cookies in PHP is very simple. This is because cookie support is fully integrated in PHP. For example, cookies are automatically considered as global variables and can be accessed from anywhere in the PHP script. Also, they are accessed and read as normal variables. In this section you'll learn to deal with various aspects of cookies in PHP. These include:

◆ Creating a cookie

◆ Accessing a set cookie

◆ Using multiple-value cookies

◆ Deleting a cookie

Creating Cookies

You need three basic functions to create a cookie. These include:

- ◆ setcookie()
- ◆ time()
- ◆ mktime()

Let us now learn how to create a simple cookie using the above functions.

The setcookie() *Function*

You can create a cookie in PHP by using the setcookie() function. The Web server uses this function to set a cookie and send it to the client when the client requests a connection.

CAUTION

If you have used the setcookie() function to set a cookie, you will need to call this function before any <html> or <head> tag. Otherwise, you will encounter an error message. This is because cookies must be sent before any HTTP headers during a connection. The logic behind this fact is that a cookie is set as part of the HTTP header. As a result, it can't be set after the header has already been sent!

Another important thing that you need to remember while using the setcookie() function is that even a single whitespace or a newline character before the PHP tag in your script can cause your script to malfunction.

The syntax of the setcookie() function is specified below:

```
setcookie (string name, string value, int expiry, string path, string domain, int
secure);
```

As the above syntax specifies, the setcookie() function takes six arguments. These include:

- ◆ **name:** This argument specifies the name of the variable that will hold the corresponding value in the name-value pair. This is a global variable. As a result, this variable is accessible in the subsequent PHP scripts.

NOTE

If you set a cookie with an invalid name (a name value that contains invalid characters), the Web server automatically changes the name of the cookie. For example, if you happen to set the name of a cookie as My%Cookie, the name will be automatically converted to My_Cookie.

◆ **value:** This argument holds the value of the variable specified by the name argument.

◆ **expiry:** This argument specifies the time after which the cookie will be considered invalid and thus rendered unusable. The value of this argument is specified in Greenwich Mean Time (GMT). As mentioned earlier, if you do not specify the value of this argument, the cookie is considered to be valid as long as the browser window at the client side remains open. With the closing of the browser window, the cookie expires.

 NOTE

The value of the expiry argument is specified by two functions, time() and mktime(), about which you'll learn a bit later in this chapter.

◆ **path:** This argument, as you learned earlier, specifies the hierarchy of files and directories on the Web server for which the cookie is considered to be valid. The default value of this argument is /. As a result, if you do not specify the value of the path argument in the setcookie() function, the cookie will be considered valid for the entire files and directories on the Web server. However, if you specify the path, the cookie will be valid only for the files and subdirectories located in the specified directory.

◆ **domain:** This argument is used to specify the host or domain name for which the cookie is considered to be valid. If no value is specified for this argument, the host (Web server) that issued the cookie is considered to be the default value of this argument.

◆ **secure:** This argument determines whether the cookie must be transferred through a secure channel. If no value is specified for the argument, an insecure channel is used to transfer the cookie. However, if the value of this argument is 1, the cookie is transmitted using the HTTPS protocol that ensures secure transactions over the Internet.

All arguments except the name argument in the setcookie() function are considered to be optional. Except for expiry and secure, which are integer values, all the other arguments can be bypassed by specifying " " (empty string). In order to skip the expiry and secure arguments, you'll need to use 0.

You'll need two more functions, time() and mktime(), to create a cookie. You'll learn about these two in the following section.

The time() and mktime() Functions

You can use the time() and mktime() functions to set the life span of a cookie to avoid the expiry of the cookie when the browser window closes.

The time() function is used to determine the current time. It returns time in seconds. The syntax of the time() function is specified below.

```
int time();
```

The mktime() function, on the other hand, accepts units of time, such as hours, minutes, seconds, months, and years, as parameters and is used to convert this information into a time stamp. Just like the time() function, the time stamp returned by the mktime() function is in seconds. The syntax of the mktime() function is specified below.

```
int mktime(int hour, int minute, int second, int month, int year, int
isDaylightSavingsTime);
```

In the above syntax, as the respective names of the variables suggest, hour accepts an integer value and is used to specify the number of hours. Similarly, minute and second specify the number of minutes and seconds, respectively. The month argument is used to return the specified month, and the year argument is used to denote the specified year.

The last argument of the mktime() function is interesting. It is used to set the daylight saving according to the time zone you specify while installing PHP on your computer. The default value of this argument is -1, which implies that the value of this argument is unknown. If this argument is set to 1, the returned time includes the daylight saving settings, and if the value is set to 0—no points for guessing!—the daylight saving option is off.

Now that you have basic knowledge of all the functions that are used to set a cookie, consider the following code.

```php
<?php
$name = "MyCookie";
$value = "This is my first Cookie!";
$expiry = mktime(0, 0, 0, 7, 1, 2002);
$domain = "localhost.localdomain";
$setcookie($name, $value, $expiry, /, $domain, 0);
?>
<html>
 <head>
 <title> Testing the Cookie </title>
 </head>
  <body>
  <br> <br> <br>
  <h1 align = center> This appears when the cookie is created
successfully! </h1>
 </body>
 </html>
```

In the above code snippet, a cookie called MyCookie is created. Since the value of the value variable is This is my first Cookie!, this will be the text that is stored in the cookie. The expiry information defined by the expiry variable is mktime(0, 0, 0, 7, 1, 2002), which implies that the given cookie will expire at midnight on July 1, 2002. The cookie can access the entire hierarchy of files and folders on the Web server (denoted by the domain variable) because the path variable is set to / in the setcookie() function.

NOTE

Note that in the above code, I have used the default values of the `path` and `security` variables. Therefore, the `setcookie()` function in the above code can simply be rewritten as `setcookie(($name, $value, $expiry, $domain)`. It will work just fine!

Figure 24-4 shows the result of the previous code snippet.

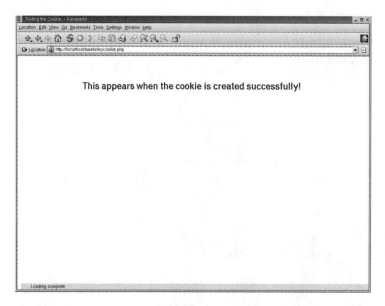

FIGURE 24-4 *Creating a simple cookie*

If you would like to see the use of the `time()` function, set the value of the `expiry` variable as `$expiry = time() + 86400;` in the above code. This will cause the cookie to be rendered invalid in 24 hours after it was first created. The `time()` function is used to determine the time (in seconds) the cookie was first created. `86400` (60x60x24 = 86400) is used to specify the number of seconds after which the cookie will expire.

In the next section, I discuss how to access a cookie.

CAUTION

Before you execute the above code, you must ensure that your browser is set to accept cookies. Otherwise, you will end up with an error message. You can configure your browser to accept cookies in the security settings of your browser. For example, to enable Microsoft Internet Explorer to accept cookies, you need to choose the Internet Options option in the Tools menu of the browser window. Then click on the Security tab in the Internet Options dialog box and click the Custom Level button. Here you need to set the two cookie options—Allow cookies that are stored on your computer" and "Allow per-session cookies (not stored)"—to enable cookies.

Accessing Cookies

While working with cookies in PHP, after you have successfully set a cookie, the most important fact that you need to remember is that you cannot set and access a cookie in the same request. After you set a cookie, you'll need to reload the Web page before you can use it.

Consider the code given below.

```php
<?php

if (!(isset($kookie)))
{
 $pagecount=0;
 setcookie("kookie",$pagecount);
 echo "<center> This is the first time you have accessed this
page in this session.</center>";
 echo "<center> A cookie was sent to you and stored in your
computer.</center>";
}
else
{
 $pagecount=++$kookie;
 setcookie("kookie",$pagecount, time() - 10 );
 setcookie("kookie",$pagecount);
 echo "<center>View Count :<b> " .$kookie.
"</b></center>\n<br>";
}
```

```
?>
<html>
<head>
<title>Page title</title>
</head>
<body>

<center><b> Refresh button will refresh the page and the page
count! :-) </b></center>

</body>
</html>
```

In the above code, the function isset() is used to determine whether a cookie called kookie has been set or not. If the cookie has not been set, a variable page-count is set to 0. The same variable is also used to set the value of the cookie in the name-value pair to 0. Also, the messages This is the first time you have accessed this page in this session. and A cookie was sent to you and stored in your computer. are displayed. On the other hand, if this is not the first time the page has been accessed, the variable pagecount is incremented with the help of the statement $pagecount=++$kookie;. The cookie is then reset and a message depicting the number of times the page has been viewed is displayed on the screen. Every time you refresh the page (by clicking the Refresh button in the browser window), the view count is incremented by 1.

 NOTE

The function isset() takes a variable as an argument and determines if the variable has been set or not. If the variable passed to the isset() function as the parameter is set, it returns True. Otherwise, it returns False.

Figure 24-5 shows the result when you execute the above code. Since the cookie has just been set, you'll not be able to access the cookie.

FIGURE 24-5 *Viewing the Web page for the first time*

Figure 24-6 shows the result of the preceding code after you have refreshed the Web page once. Now that the cookie was set when you first saw the page, this time you will be able to access the cookie.

FIGURE 24-6 *Viewing the Web page after refreshing it once*

Figure 24-7 shows the result of the preceding code after you have refreshed the Web page a few times.

FIGURE 24-7 *Accessing the cookie after refreshing the page content a few times*

You can use built-in PHP functions such as header() to reduce the burden of programming. Consider the following code snippet. This snippet is used to set a cookie and reload the same page that was used to set the cookie.

```php
<?php

if (!(isset($kookie_new)))
setcookie("kookie_new", "A Short Cut");
header("Location: $PHP_SELF?kookie_new = 1");
exit;

?>
```

In the above code, the header() function is used to send a raw HTTP header string as a part of the HTTP header. The Location string that has been used above redirects the browser to an HTML page. By setting the corresponding URL for the Location string as PHP_SELF, the current page open in the browser window will be reopened automatically.

You can also use the header() function and Location string to redirect the browser to a different HTML page. Consider the code below to understand this.

```php
<?php

if (!(isset($kookie_new)))
setcookie("kookie_new", "A Short Cut");
header("Location: test.html");
exit;


?>
```

Figure 24-8 shows the results of the above code snippet that opens test.html.

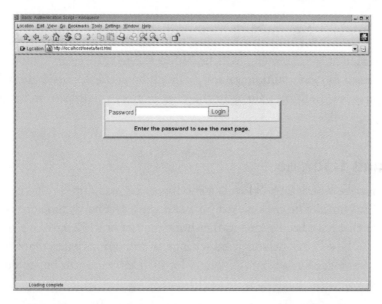

FIGURE 24-8 *Redirecting the Web browser to another page using a cookie*

After you have successfully set a cookie, you can access it by using one of the two methods specified below:

◆ **Using the name of the cookie as a variable.** When you try to access a cookie in PHP, a variable with the same name as the cookie is created. This variable name, then, can be used by your scripts. As a result, you can either reload the page that was used to create the cookie or load another page that uses the cookie. Suppose you created a cookie called

My_Cookie. You can use the name of the cookie as a variable in your script as specified below:

```
echo "My_Cookie";
```

◆ **Using $HTTP_COOKIE_VARS ["cookie_name"].** Again, the variable that is created by default in PHP by using the cookie name is also stored in the global array as $HTTP_COOKIE_VARS ["cookie_name"]. An additional advantage of using this global array is that it helps in distinguishing between different cookie names on the basis of their data sources, even if they happen to have the same name. You can use this global array in your PHP scripts as given below:

```
echo "$HTTP_COOKIE_VARS ["My_Cookie"]"
```

Until now you have learned about single-value cookies. This implies that the cookies you have created until now have just held one value, such as page count or the Web page that your browser will be redirected to. However, sometimes a cookie may need to store multiple values. A shopping cart is a classic example of a cookie that stores multiple values. In the next section, you'll learn more about multiple-value cookies.

Multiple-Value Cookies

Now you must be wondering, "How is a shopping cart a multiple-value cookie?" The answer is simple! The cookie used for a shopping cart needs to keep track of various items that have been added to the shopping cart or the length of a session besides maybe the user ID, personalized settings, or the various pages that the user has visited in the current session. A whole lot of information to be stored in a small cookie, whew!

As the name suggests, the cookies that can store more than one value are referred to as multiple-value cookies. These cookies may prove to be very useful to you as a Web developer. As you might recall, the number of cookies that can be stored by a Web server on a single computer is restricted to 20! Therefore, instead of creating a bevy of cookies when a customer goes on a shopping spree and unnecessarily populating the user's hard disk, you can make wonderful use of multiple-value cookies.

To make use of multiple-value cookies, you need to specify a cookie as an array. As a result, every bit of information that you'll need to store as a part of one single cookie will be stored as an element of this array. Consider the code specified below that deals with multiple-value cookies.

```php
<?php

$gmtseconds = time();
if (isset($kookie))
 {
  $pagecount=++$kookie[0];
  setcookie("kookie[0]", $pagecount,$gmtseconds + 60);
  setcookie("kookie",$kookie,$gmtseconds + 60);
  setcookie("kookie",$gmtseconds,$gmtseconds + 60);


  echo "Hi " . $kookie .  " !!<br>\n";
  if ($kookie==1)
   {
    echo "You have seen this page for the first time !<br>\n";

   }
  else
   {
    echo "You have seen this page " .$kookie[0]  . " times.<br>\n";
    echo "I remember U last saw this page ".($gmtseconds - $kookie)." seconds ago";
}
  exit;
 }
else
 {
  if (isset($name))
   {
    $pagecount=0;
    setcookie("kookie[0]", $pagecount ,$gmtseconds + 60);
    setcookie("kookie", $name,$gmtseconds + 60);
    setcookie("kookie", $gmtseconds,$gmtseconds + 60);
    echo " The cookie is set ! Please press the Refresh button to see what happens next.";
```

```
                              exit;
                          }
                    }


              ?>
```

In the preceding code, the cookie called `kookie` is a multiple-value cookie. The first element of this cookie, `kookie[0]`, contains the latest page count (the number of times you have visited the page) with the help of the variable `pagecount`. The next element of this cookie, `kookie`, contains the name of the user. Similarly, the third element, `kookie`, contains the time you last visited the site.

When you visit the page, the script checks if the cookie is set. Since you are visiting the page for the first time, the cookie will not be set. As a result, the script will set the cookie (`kookie[0]`) and record your name in `kookie` and the time (in seconds) when you visit the Web page in `kookie`. Also, a message will be displayed stating `The cookie is set! Please press the Refresh button to see what happens next.`

After you refresh the Web page, the script is executed again. The count is incremented with the help of the statement `$pagecount = ++kookie[0]` and new values—latest count and access time—are recorded in the array. Since now the value of the variable `pagecount` is `1`, the message `You have seen this page for the first time.` is displayed.

In case you have visited the page a couple of times (that is, refreshed the page a few times), the message `You have seen this page <number> of times.` is displayed, where `<number>` represents the value stored in `kookie[0]`. Another message, `I remember U last saw this page <time> seconds ago.`, is displayed. Here, `<time>` represents the value stored in `kookie`.

Figure 24-9 shows the output of the cookie when you log in to the page for the very first time.

Figure 24-10 shows the output of the execution of the cookie when you refresh the page for the first time.

Figure 24-11 depicts the output of the preceding code when you refresh the Web page three times.

FIGURE 24-9 *Output of the cookie when you log in to the page for the very first time*

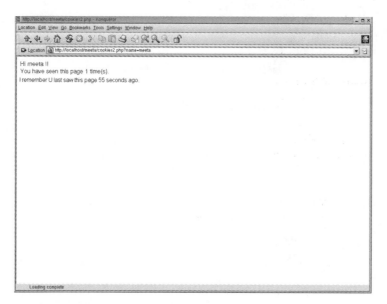

FIGURE 24-10 *Output of the cookie when you refresh the page for the first time*

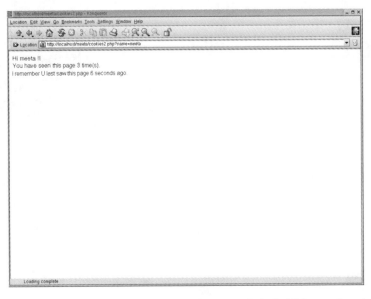

FIGURE 24-11 *Output of the cookie when you refresh the Web page three times*

The corresponding HTML part of the code that calls the PHP script (cookies2.php) specified earlier is as follows.

```
<html>
<head>
<title>Testing a Multiple Value Cookie</title>
</head>
<body bgcolor="blue" text="white">
<p>   </p>
<p>   </p>
<p>   </p>
<p>   </p>
<p>   </p>
<form name="nameform" method="GET" action="cookies2.php">
<center>
  <table>
    <tr>
      <td>
<b> Name </b>
</td>
      <td>
```

```
<input type="text" name="name">

        </td>
        <td>
          <input type="submit" name="Submit" value="Login">
        </td>
      </tr>
    </table>
  </center>
</form>


</body>
</html>
```

The above HTML code generates a very simple HTML form that contains three elements: the Name label, a text box that accepts the corresponding name, and the Login button. When you enter a name in the Name text box and press the Login button, the PHP script cookies2.php is called. This script, as explained earlier, then handles the further execution of the form.

Figure 24-12 shows the HTML form that is created using the above HTML code.

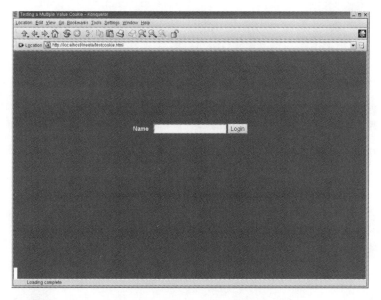

FIGURE 24-12 *The HTML form that calls the cookie*

This brings us to the final frontier of working with cookies, which is deleting cookies. In the next section, you'll learn about the same.

Deleting Cookies

After a cookie has served its purpose and you don't need it any longer, you might want to delete it. No use unnecessarily storing unwanted cookies! PHP does not boast of an exclusive function for this purpose. In fact, the good old setcookie() function once again comes to the rescue! Call the setcookie() function with only the name parameter when you want to delete a cookie. The syntax to delete a cookie is:

```
setcookie("cookie_name");
```

Therefore, if you would like to delete a cookie called kookie, you can delete it by using the following statement in your script:

```
setcookie("kookie");
```

 CAUTION

There is one very important fact about deleting cookies in PHP that you must know and remember when you delete one. If you would like to create a cookie with a name that already exists, you will first need to create it with a new value and only then delete the old cookie. This means if you need to create a cookie called kookie that already exists, you'll first write the following statement in your script:

```
setcookie("kookie", "New Cookie");
```

Only after you have reset the value of the existing cookie will you have the statement pertaining to the deletion of the cookie in your PHP script, which is:

```
setcookie("kookie");.
```

Baffling, isn't it? Let me explain why it is so. The reason behind this "anti-logic" rule is that all the cookies in a PHP script are sent to the Web server in a reverse order. This is the reason why you'll need a delete statement after the reset statement. If you forget to remember this simple fact, you might end up with so many errors and so frustrated that you'll never want to work with cookies in PHP anymore!

The common phobia among frequent Internet users and even some Web developers is that the use of cookies is dangerous! Is that so? Look for the answers in the next section.

Are Cookies Harmful?

Many of us who have been using the Internet for some time now may come across a lot of myths concerning cookies. The popular versions of these include:

- **Myth #1: A cookie file is a secret way for a Web server to find out everything that you store on your hard disk.** This is the most common myth. However, it is just a myth. The cookie is simply a small text file that contains only the information that *you* supplied to a Web server. Moreover, it does not possess any capability of scanning your hard disk! Therefore, rest assured, there is absolutely no way a Web server can get into your system with the help of an innocent cookie.

- **Myth #2: A cookie file is used to spread viruses.** A cookie is a small text file whose size cannot exceed 4 KB. Viruses are usually large files that contain executable code or macros. So rest assured, a cookie *cannot* be used to spread viruses, even if someone wanted to do so.

- **Myth #3: Other Web servers that you visit can read the information stored in other cookies.** This again is utterly incorrect. A Web server can only access the cookies that were generated by it.

Although harmless to a large extent, cookies can serve as a powerful weapon in the hands of greed. The recent uproar with an infrastructure provider called DoubleClick was such an example. DoubleClick provided the cookie-enabled advertising capability in many sites and tracked user movement within a given site as well as across sites. With this, they created a huge database with user preferences and other sensitive information. They then threatened to sell this information. Laws are being worked out globally to prevent this misuse of cookies. Most individual sites do not possess this capability since cookies are site specific.

As I stated earlier, there are more myths to cookies than harm. However, prevention is always better than cure. To protect yourself from any potential danger, you can take a few steps that will reduce your vulnerability in case a site decides to misuse sensitive information provided by you.

◆ **As a user:** As a user, you can either force your browser to refuse all cookies or generate a warning if you access a site that uses cookies. You can set your Netscape Navigator 4.x to warn if you are visiting a cookie-enabled site by selecting the Edit menu and choosing Preferences. In the Preferences dialog box, click Advanced for cookie-related options. In Microsoft's Internet Explorer 5.x and above, choose Tools, Internet Options to open the Internet Options dialog box. Click the Security tab, select a particular zone (Internet, Local intranet, Trusted sites, or Untrusted sites), and then click the Custom Level button. Scroll down the options screen to Cookies and select the Prompt radio button to be prompted for all persistent and session cookies. You can similarly select Disable to refuse any cookies. Another option to combat cookie problems as a user is to log in as an anonymous user wherever possible.

◆ **As a Web site developer:** As a developer, you are free to use cookies. However, since some users might not trust the use of cookies, make sure that the use of cookies is optional in your site. If you really want to use cookies in your site, make sure that sensitive information is stored in an encrypted format in the cookie. This would prevent theft of account names, login IDs, and passwords to a considerable extent. If you have decided to use cookies in your site, provide a way, such as a message box, to inform your user that your site uses cookies and that they would need to enable cookies if they want to use your site.

Now you know that cookies can be an extremely useful and effective method of marketing if handled properly. However, they can also as easily be the weapons of theft of sensitive user-related information. Therefore, it is very important that you use cookies intelligently, both as a user and as a Web developer.

Summary

Cookies are a very simple yet powerful feature of PHP. They can really help you as a Web developer to enhance your Web site by tracking who visits your site, how long they visit, how many times they return, the things they follow with interest on your site, and a lot more. You can use this information for targeting users of different choices and preferences for various marketing schemes and ensuring that users are not unnecessarily clobbered with advertisements that hold no interest for the particular user.

Besides helping you customize your Web site according to the individual preference of a user, you can also make a user's life easier by eliminating the need to log in repetitively in a specified time period. This is something your frequent visitors will really appreciate!

In this chapter, you learned more about cookies. In addition to the basic information regarding a cookie, which includes the working of a cookie, scope of a cookie, and restrictions related to a cookie, you learned to implement cookies in your Web site. You learned to set a cookie, access it, and delete it after you are through with its use.

Finally, you learned about the various reasons that have caused an unjustified cloud of suspicion hanging over cookies, which has resulted in many users disabling the use of cookies in their browsers. Therefore, you learned that to ensure the proper functioning of your site, either you must make cookies optional or inform the user to enable the use of cookies if they would like to visit your site.

PART VIII

Appendixes

Appendix A

Working with Directories

Directories play a crucial role in the organization of related data. You can use directories and subdirectories to further categorize the data that is stored on your system. In fact, directories are a very important and eminent feature of today's popular operating systems and platforms, which include Microsoft Windows, Unix, Linux, and Mac OS.

You learned to work with files in PHP in Chapter 11, "Handling Files." Besides the basic file manipulation, you might also need to use, control, and manipulate directories while working with PHP. In this appendix, you will learn to work with directories. You'll learn to read and process the contents of a directory, copy files, move files, delete files, and delete a directory.

Common Directory Operations

The most common operations that you might need to perform while working with directories include the following:

- ◆ Reading files in a directory
- ◆ Copying files from one location to another
- ◆ Moving files from one location to another
- ◆ Deleting files
- ◆ Deleting directories

You will learn about each of these operations in the following sections.

Reading Files

You need to use the `opendir()`, `readdir()`, and `closedir()` functions to access a directory, read its contents, and close the directory, respectively. Let us consider these basic functions and their working individually.

The syntax of the opendir() function is specified below:

```
resource opendir (string path);
```

The opendir() function returns a directory handle that can be used in subsequent directory calls. This function takes a single argument, which specifies the path to the intended directory. The opendir() function returns True if the path specified is valid and the destination directory is opened successfully. On the other hand, if the path specified is invalid or the directory cannot be opened due to lack of permissions, the function returns False.

 NOTE

The keyword resource is used for directory handles.

The closedir() function is used to close the specified directory. If the function is able to close the directory, it returns True. Otherwise, False is returned. The syntax of the closedir() function is:

 CAUTION

For the closedir() function to work successfully, the directory specified by the directory handle must have been opened by the opendir() function.

```
void closedir (resource dir_handle);
```

The readdir() function is used to read the content of the specified directory. The syntax of this function is:

```
string readdir (resource dir_handle);
```

The readdir() function takes a single argument in the form of a directory handle whose content needs to be read and returns the name of the next file in the specified directory. However, the names are returned in a random manner.

Consider the following code to understand the use of the three functions discussed just now.

```php
<?php
$dir = opendir('/home/meeta/new');

while ($read_file = readdir($dir))
{
echo "$read_file", "\n";
}

closedir($dir);

?>
```

In the above code, a directory called new is being opened, which is located in /home/meeta/. After each file in the directory is read successfully, the directory is then closed.

Figure A-1 shows the output of the preceding code snippet.

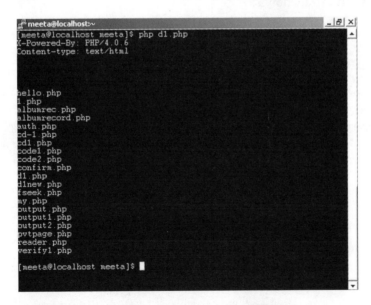

FIGURE A-1 *Output of reading the contents of a directory*

In the next section, you'll learn how to copy files using a simple PHP scriptlet.

Copying Files

You use the copy() function to copy a file from its original location to the new location. The syntax of the copy() function is specified below:

```
int copy(string source, string destination);
```

As you can see, copy() takes two arguments. The first argument denotes the source file that is being copied, and the second argument represents the destination file. The function returns True if the copy operation is successful. Otherwise, it returns False.

NOTE

If the destination file specified in the function already exists, the source file is copied to the destination file. However, if the destination file does not exist, a new file with the specified name is created and the source file is then copied to it.

Consider the following code to understand the use of the copy() function.

```php
<?php
$source = '/home/meeta/hello.php';
$destination = '/home/meeta/new/h1.php';

if(copy($source, $destination))
{
echo "File copied successfully.", "\n";
}

else
{
echo "The specified file could not be copied. Please try
again.", "\n";
```

```
        }

    ?>
```

In the preceding code, a file called `hello.php`, which is located in `/home/meeta`, is being copied to a new location, `/home/meeta/new`, with the new name `h1.php`. If the file is copied successfully, the message `File copied successfully.` is displayed. On the other hand, if the copy operation is unsuccessful, the message `The specified file could not be copied. Please try again.` is displayed.

 CAUTION

You might end up with an error message while copying a file from one directory to another if you do not have proper rights to do so. Therefore, before copying files make sure that you have the corresponding rights.

Figure A-2 shows the output of the preceding code snippet.

FIGURE A-2 *Output of copying a file to another directory*

In the next section, you'll learn to move files from one directory to another.

Moving Files

In order to move a file from one location to another, PHP offers the use of the rename() function.

NOTE

As you might recall from your previous Unix experience, the rename() function, as the name suggests, serves to rename the specified file. However, specifying the source and destination paths instead of file names will serve to move the file.

The syntax of the function is:

```
int rename(string source_path, string destination_path);
```

Like the copy() function, the rename() function also takes two arguments. The first argument denotes the source file that is being moved, and the second argument represents the destination path. The function returns True if the move operation is successful. Otherwise, it returns False.

CAUTION

Just like while copying files, you might again end up with an error message while moving a file from one directory to another if you do not have proper rights to do so. Therefore, before moving files make sure that you have the proper rights to do so.

Consider the following code snippet to better understand the use of the rename() function for moving files.

```php
<?php
$source = '/home/meeta/hello.php';
$destination = '/home/meeta/figures';

if (rename($source, $destination))
{
```

```
echo "The file was moved successfully.", "\n";
}


else
{
echo "The specified file could not be moved. Please try again.",
"\n";

}

?>
```

In the above example, an attempt is made to move the file `hello.php` from `/home/meeta` to the new location, `/home/meeta/figures`. If the file is moved successfully, the message `The file was moved successfully.` is displayed. However, if the move operation ends up in failure, the message `The specified file could not be moved. Please try again.` is used to warn the user.

Figure A-3 shows the output of the preceding code snippet, if you do not have sufficient rights to move the file from the old location to the new.

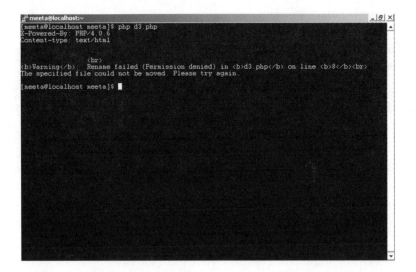

FIGURE A-3 *Output of moving a file to another directory when the requisite rights have not been applied*

NOTE

The use of the `rename()` function slows down the execution of your program considerably because the `rename()` function needs to place a system call to a program called `rename`. Therefore, it is recommended that you create your own script to move files from one location to another.

Now we know that a typical moving operation is a set of two independent operations: copying the source file to the specified destination and then deleting the original file from the source path. Following is a sample function that you can use for moving files.

```
Function move($source, $destination)
{
copy($source, $destination)
or die ("Could not copy the specified file.");
//The unlink() function is used to delete files.
unlink($source)
or die ("Could not delete the original file.");
}
```

In the next section, you'll learn to delete one or more files within a directory using the `unlink()` function.

Deleting Files

Extra and useless files are a burden on your system. To ease this burden on your system, you must delete unwanted and unnecessary files periodically. PHP offers you the `unlink()` function to delete files in a directory.

The syntax of the `unlink()` function is:

```
int unlink(string file_name);
```

The `unlink()` function takes a single argument in the form of the name of the file that needs to be deleted. The function returns 1 if the delete operation is carried out successfully. In case of encountering a failure, the function returns 0.

Consider the following script.

```php
<?php

$file_delete = '/home/meeta/my.php';

If (unlink($file_delete))
{
echo "The file was deleted successfully.", "\n";
}

else
{
echo "The specified file could not be deleted. Please try
again.", "\n";
}

?>
```

In the above code, the file `my.php` is deleted from the `/home/meeta/` directory. If the deletion is successful, the message `The file was deleted successfully.` is displayed. In case of failure, the message `The specified file could not be deleted. Please try again.` is displayed to the user.

 NOTE

Like other operations, proper access rights also play an important role in the file deletion operation. If you face trouble in deleting a file (in Unix and Linux platforms), make sure that you have the *write* right to the directory. This right is required because according to Unix and Linux, you modify the specified directory while deleting a file (or subdirectory) from it.

Figure A-4 shows the output of the preceding code snippet.

Until now, I have used examples that explain to you how you can work with individual content, such as files of a directory. This can prove to be extremely tedious

FIGURE A-4 *Output of deleting a file*

and monotonous. In the next section, I show you how to manipulate multiple files and subdirectories in the specified directory.

 NOTE

The unlink() function is meant for Unix and Linux platforms and may not work if you are using the Microsoft Windows platform.

Working with Multiple Files in a Directory

In the previous section, you learned to delete individual files. Now suppose you would like to delete all the files in a directory that contains, say, 245 files and subdirectories. Instead of deleting individual contents of a directory, you would like to delete all the files and subdirectories in a go. PHP does not offer a built-in function for this purpose. However, you can use two methods: mapdir() and maptree() in PEAR's File_Find class.

In the next two sections, you'll learn about the mapdir() and maptree() functions and how to use them in your PHP scripts.

NOTE

PEAR stands for PHP Extension and Application Repository. Refer to Chapter 22, "PEAR," for detailed information on PEAR.

The mapdir() Function

Since the mapdir() function is a method in the File_Find class of PEAR, you'll need to include the class in your script. In order to do so, you'll need to add the following statement before you use the mapdir() function.

```
include_once 'File/Find.php';
```

The syntax of the mapdir() function is specified below:

```
resource mapdir(resource dir_handle);
```

The mapdir() method returns an array containing all the subdirectories in the specified directory along with the list of all the files in the specified directory and its subdirectories.

Consider the following code to display the names of all the files in a specified directory.

```
<?php

include_once 'File/Find.php';

$file_read = File_Find::mapdir('/home/meeta/new');

foreach ($file_read as $fr)
{
echo "$fr", "\n";
}

?>
```

In the preceding code, all the files in the /home/meeta/new directory are being read and printed with the help of the mapdir() method. Figure A-5 shows the output of the preceding code.

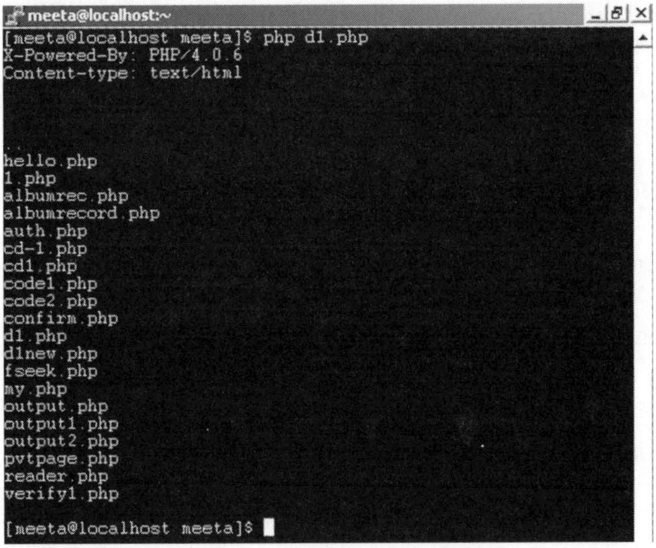

FIGURE A-5 *Output of using the* mapdir() *method*

The next section throws more light on the maptree() method.

The maptree() *Function*

You can use the maptree() method to manipulate all the files and subdirectories in the specified directory. Also a method of PEAR's File_Find class, the map-tree() method is more powerful than the mapdir() method. This is because the maptree() method can load an entire directory tree into an array. The syntax of this method is specified below:

```
resource maptree(resource dir_handle);
```

The maptree() method returns an array. The resultant array, in fact, consists of two different arrays. The first array contains all the subdirectories in the directory specified by the directory handle that the method takes as an argument. The second array, on the other hand, contains all the files in the specified directory and its subdirectories. The following statement depicts this concept.

```
dir_tree($dirs, $files) = File_Find::maptree('/var/www/html/meeta');
```

The `maptree()` function, as you can see from the above code, returns an array `dir_tree`, which in turn consists of two separate arrays: `$dirs` and `$files`. The `$dirs` array contains the constituent subdirectories, and the `$files` array contains all the files in the specified directory and its subdirectories.

Consider the following code snippet to understand how you can use the `maptree()` function to delete multiple files in the specified directory.

```php
<?php

include_once 'File/Find.php';

dir_tree($dir_delete, $file_delete) =
File_Find::maptree('/home/meeta/figures2');

foreach ($file_delete as $fd)
{
    if (!(unlink($fd)))

    {
        echo "Could not delete the file.", "\n";
    }
    else
    {
        echo "The file was deleted successfully.", "\n";
    }
}

?>
```

In the above code, all the content of the specified directory (/home/meeta/figures2) is accepted in a single array, `dir_tree`. This array, in turn, contains all the subdirectories in an array called `dir_delete` and files in a separate array called `file_delete`. All the files stored in the `file_delete` array are then deleted with the help of the `foreach` loop.

Figure A-6 shows the output of the preceding code.

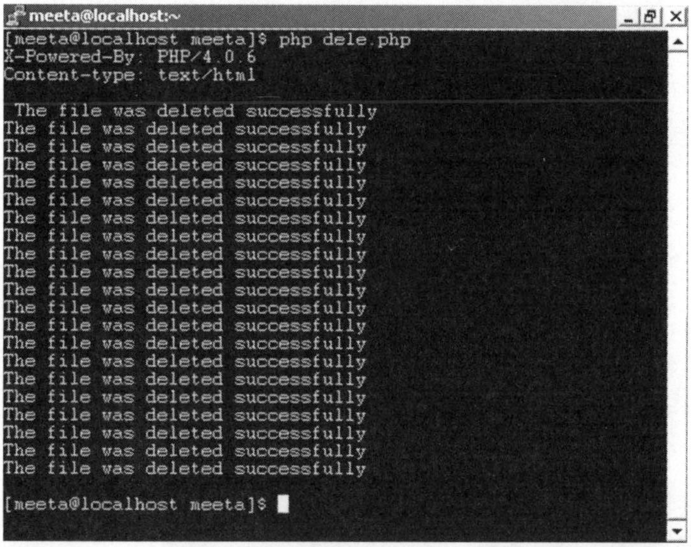

FIGURE A-6 *Deleting files in a directory using the* maptree() *method*

In the next section, you'll learn to delete directories.

Deleting Directories

You can use the rmdir() function to delete directories. In order to delete a directory, you should have proper rights to the specified directory. Another very important fact that you need to remember while deleting a directory is that the directory must be empty. If the directory is not empty, you will not be able to delete the specified directory.

The syntax of the rmdir() function is specified below:

```
int rmdir(string dir_name);
```

As shown in the above syntax, the function takes a single argument, the name or the path of the directory that needs to be deleted.

Consider the following simple code snippet that is used to delete an empty directory called dir1.

```
<?php
```

```php
$dir_delete = '/home/meeta/dir1';

if (rmdir ($dir_delete))
{
    echo "Directory deleted successfully.", "\n";
}
 else
   {
    echo "Could not delete the directory.", "\n";
?>
```

The output of the above code is shown in Figure A-7.

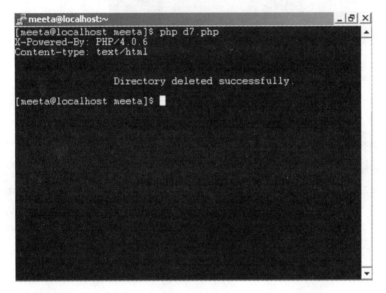

FIGURE A-7 *Deleting an empty directory*

The preceding code is very basic and unrealistic. Consider the following code snippet that deletes a directory and its contents.

```php
<?php

include_once 'File/Find.php';

dir_tree($dir_delete, $file_delete) =
File_Find::maptree('/home/meeta/Dir3);
```

```
foreach ($file_delete as $fd)
{
    if (!(unlink($fd)))

    {
        echo "Could not delete the file.", "\n";
    }
    else
    {
        echo "The file was deleted successfully.", "\n";
    }
}


foreach ($dir_delete as $dd)
{
    if (!(rmdir($dd)))

    {
        echo "Could not delete the directory.", "\n";
    }
    else
    {
        echo "The directory was deleted successfully.", "\n";
    }
}

?>
```

In the above code, all the constituent files are stored in the array file_delete, and all the subdirectories of the specified directory are stored in the array called dir_delete. The first foreach loop is used to delete the files with the help of the unlink() method, which was discussed earlier. The second foreach loop is used to delete the subdirectories.

The output of the preceding code snippet is shown in Figure A-8.

Let me now briefly discuss other frequently used directory-related functions in PHP in the next section.

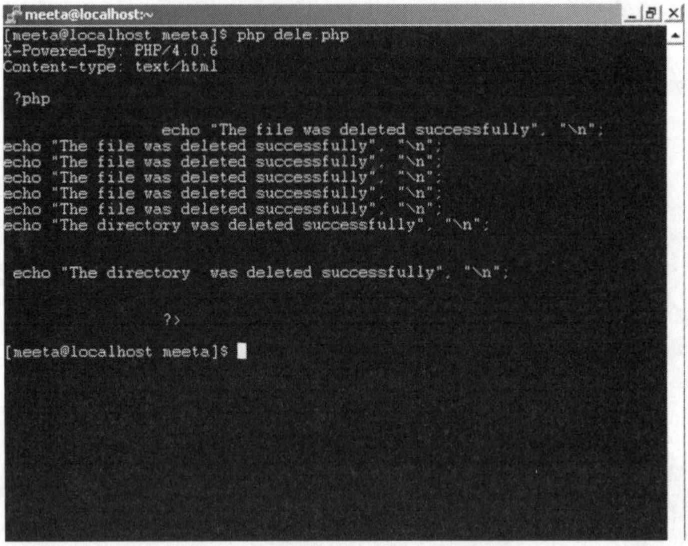

FIGURE A-8 *Deleting the entire content of a directory*

Other Directory Functions

Some of the other commonly used directory functions include:

- getcwd()
- chroot()
- chdir()
- dirname()
- mkdir()

Let us consider each of these functions in the following sections.

The getcwd() Function

This directory function is used to determine the current working directory. The syntax of the function is:

```
string getcwd();
```

Consider the following code snippet.

```
<?php
```

```
$working_dir = getcwd();
 echo "The current working directory is: $working_dir ", "\n";


?>
```

The output of this code is shown in Figure A-9.

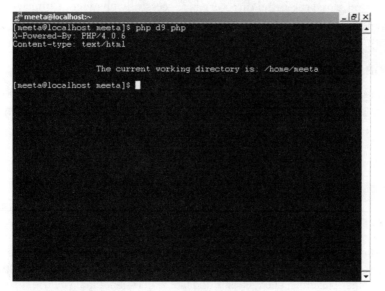

FIGURE A-9 *Determining the current working directory*

The chroot() *Function*

The chroot() function is used to change the root directory for the current process to the directory specified as the argument. The syntax of the function is:

```
bool chroot(string dir_name);
```

If the function changes the specified directory to the root directory for the given session, it returns True. Otherwise, it returns False.

 NOTE

It is not recommended to use this function on a Web server. This is because once the root directory has been changed for the given process, it cannot be reverted back. This can cause serious problems!

The chdir() *Function*

The chdir() function is used to change the current directory to the directory specified as the argument. The syntax of the function is:

```
bool chdir(string dir_name);
```

The function returns True if the directory is successfully changed. Otherwise, the function returns False.

The dirname() *Function*

The dirname() function is used to determine the directory-name component within the path (to a file) specified as the function argument. The syntax of the dirname() function is:

```
string dirname(string dir_path);
```

CAUTION

If you use the dirname() function on the Microsoft Windows platform, make sure that the correct slash ("/" or "\") is used since Windows uses both the slashes to specify paths. In other platforms, such as Unix and Linux, make sure that you use the correct slash ("/"). Otherwise, you might end up with an error message.

The mkdir() *Function*

The mkdir() function is used to create a directory in the location specified by the path argument. The syntax of this function is:

```
int mkdir(string dir_path, int mode);
```

The second argument of the function, mode, sets the access right to the newly created directory. The function returns True if the directory is created successfully. Otherwise, the function returns False.

Consider the following statement as an example of the implementation of the mkdir() function:

```
mkdir('/home/meeta/newdir', 0700);
```

Appendix B

As you learned in Chapter 17, "User Authentication Scripts," PHP along with MySQL offers powerful encryption and hashing functions. However, implementation of encryption and hashing can be simple and efficient as well as powerful if you make use of the functions included in the Mcrypt library. The Mcrypt library offers a number of key-based encryption functions to use with PHP.

The Mcrypt library supports a wide variety of block algorithms, which include the following:

- ◆ DES and Triple-DES
- ◆ Blowfish
- ◆ TWOFISH
- ◆ SAFER-SK64
- ◆ 3-WAY
- ◆ RC2
- ◆ GOST
- ◆ RC6
- ◆ RC4
- ◆ CAST
- ◆ IDEA
- ◆ AES

 NOTE

You can learn more about DES, Triple-DES, RC2, RC4, CAST, IDEA, and AES in Chapter 17.

The following section discusses the steps to install and configure the Mcrypt library to make it work with PHP.

Installing Mcrypt

The steps to install, configure, and build the Mcrypt library extension into your PHP distribution are listed below:

1. Download `libmcrypt-x.x.tar.gz` from the FTP site **ftp://mcrypt. hellug.gr/pub/mcrypt/libmcrypt/**. Another good site from which you can download the file is **ftp://argeas.cs-net.gr/pub/unix/mcrypt/**.

2. Gunzip the file in `/mcrypt` using the following command:

   ```
   gunzip libmcrypt-x.x.tar.gz.tar
   ```

3. Untar the file in `/mcrypt` using the following command:

   ```
   tar -xvf libmcrypt-x.x.tar.gz.tar
   ```

4. Type the following command:

   ```
   ./configure —disable-nls —disable-posix-threads
   ```

 NOTE

By setting the above configuration flags, `—disable-nls —disable-posix-threads`, you can make the Mcrypt library work with PHP in an Apache environment without any problems.

5. Type the following command:

   ```
   make
   ```

6. Type the following command:

   ```
   make install
   ```

 NOTE

If you have any problems with the installation process, refer to the documentation. You can also refer to the mailing list archive at **http://marc.theaimsgroup.com/**. This archive offers you detailed information to troubleshoot the installation and configuration process.

Mcrypt operates in four block cipher modes. If linked with the latest Mcrypt library, it can also operate in more secure block mode and in Stream mode. You'll learn about these modes in the next section.

Mcrypt Modes

The four block cipher modes of Mcrypt are:

◆ **Electronic CodeBook (ECB):** This mode is used for encrypting short and random data, such as keys.

◆ **Cipher Block Chaining (CBC):** This mode offers enhanced security over the ECB mode.

◆ **Cipher FeedBack (CFB):** This mode is used for byte-wise encryption in byte streams.

◆ **Output FeedBack (OFB):** This mode is comparable to CFB. However, it can also be used in applications where error propagation cannot be tolerated. This mode is phasing out because it has proved to be insecure, as it operates in 8-bit mode.

When linked with the latest Mcrypt library version, Mcrypt can also operate in more secure block mode and in Stream mode, which include:

◆ **nOutput FeedBack (nOFB):** This mode is comparable to OFB. However, it offers more security because it operates on an entire block (n bits) rather than one single bit.

◆ **Stream Mode:** This is an extra mode, which supports stream algorithms, such as WAKE and RC4.

 NOTE

Currently, PHP does not support the encryption or decryption of bit streams. The present version of PHP, which is PHP4, only supports handling of strings.

Consider the simple code snippet given below to understand the implementation of functions in the Mcrypt library.

```
<?

$key  = "this is my key";
$info = "Welcome to the world of Mcrypt encryption.";

$crypted_msg = mcrypt_cbc(MCRYPT_LOKI97, $key, $info,
MCRYPT_ENCRYPT);

$ crypted_msg = bin2hex($crypted_msg);
echo "$ crypted_msg ";

?>
```

You need a key to encrypt a message. The key variable, as the name suggests, will be used as the key to encrypt the information that needs to be encrypted. This information is stored in the info variable. In the above code, I have used the CBC mode of encryption. Therefore, the function mcrypt_cbc() has been used. The syntax of this function is specified below:

```
string mcrypt_cbc(string cipher, string key, string data, int mode)
```

This function takes four arguments. The first argument, cipher, denotes the encryption algorithm that will be used to encrypt the data. The second argument, key, is the key supplied to the algorithm. This key must be kept secret. The next argument, data, represents the information that will be encrypted. The final argument, mode, is the most important. It defines whether the data will be encrypted or decrypted.

In the preceding code, the result of encryption will be stored in crypted_msg in binary format. To convert this data from binary format to hexadecimal, the function bin2hex() has been used. The result of conversion will be stored back in crypted_msg. This encrypted information will finally be displayed on the screen.

Appendix C

Working with PostgreSQL in PHP

In Project 3 (Chapters 12 and 13), you learned to accept information from a user in an HTML-based Web form. You then learned to store the user information in a database. You also learned to retrieve information from this database based on user queries. In the same project, you used the MySQL database to store and manage the information.

Although MySQL is a popular database package, developers working in the Linux-Apache environment also use PostgreSQL. In this appendix, you will learn to use the PostgreSQL database to store information and manage data. You will also learn to use PostgreSQL to store information. You will also refresh your knowledge about database concepts, such as databases, tables, fields, and records. In addition, you will learn to add, modify, and delete records in a PostgreSQL database.

Before you learn how to create a database and link it to the specified Web page, let me discuss what PostgreSQL is.

Introduction to PostgreSQL

You already know that a Relational Database Management System (RDBMS) has the advantage of using simple data structures and nonprocedural query language for the purpose of querying and retrieving information from the database. On the other hand, a simple Database Management System (DBMS) has the advantage of using user-defined datatypes, direct object references, and methods.

Compared to an RDBMS and a DBMS, PostgreSQL is an ORDBMS, or an Object Relational Database Management System. An ORDBMS is a synthesis of the best features of an RDBMS and a DBMS. An ORDBMS is generally used in applications that require speedy retrieval of information from a database. This is possible by the use of indexes and direct object references, such as those used in Web server database applications.

The original version of Postgre was developed at the University of California at the Berkeley Computer Science Department. The project was headed by Professor Michael Stonebraker and received sponsorship from the Army Research

NOTE

The terms PostgreSQL and Postgre are used interchangeably. So do not start wondering if the two terms refer to two different entities.

Office (ARO), the well-known (especially in the Internet community) Defense Advanced Research Projects Agency (DARPA), the National Science Foundation (NSF), and ESL Inc. The current version of PostgreSQL is a successor of the original code. This code is constantly evolving because of its open source.

The majority of functions and features found in most present-day RDBMS databases were first tested in PostgreSQL. Conventionally, most relational databases provide support for data models that use named relations and contain attributes that belong to a specific datatype. However, the current RDBMS model has certain inadequacies due to which it might be unable to support applications involving data processing in the future.

Postgre overcomes these limitations by providing support for additional features such as datatypes, functions, and inheritance. It also provides support for using rules and for maintaining transaction integrity, constraints, and triggers. This is why PostgreSQL is known as an Object Relational Database Management System.

You have the basic knowledge of MySQL from the earlier projects in this book. The next section attempts to compare the features of MySQL and Postgre and find the areas where Postgre scores over MySQL.

Comparison between PostgreSQL and MySQL

Most developers who work with PHP are perpetually faced with the question of which database to use, Postgre or MySQL. Let me first tell you about the disadvantages of Postgre. These include:

◆ **The limit of 8 KB of data for each row:** This is a major drawback because sometimes your record might exceed the 8 KB limit. This is common in cases where the user has to enter information in a text area.

In case the limit is exceeded, the database returns an error to the user. Although attempts are on to remove this drawback, the process might take time.

◆ **The use of the serial datatype:** PostgreSQL allows the use of the *serial* datatype. This datatype provides the same functionality that the *auto_increment* datatype provides in MySQL. The drawback is that the variable is not dropped along with the table in which it exists. Therefore, when you attempt to re-create the table, you encounter a name conflict. Since the *auto_increment* datatype in MySQL does not have this drawback, developers prefer using MySQL as compared to PostgreSQL.

However, PostgreSQL also offers certain advantages. Let's discuss and compare the advantages and disadvantages of PostgreSQL with those of MySQL.

◆ **Transaction rollback:** This facility is not available in MySQL while it is available in Postgre, for example, if you are attempting to perform insertion and updation of multiple records simultaneously using a single transaction. In the case of MySQL, all the commands are executed until an error is encountered. In this case, the error is displayed; however, the currently executed commands are not rolled back. This is possible in the case of Postgre. In this case, all or none of the commands get executed. If an error is encountered, the database is set back to the position from where the transaction started to execute.

◆ **Subselects:** Subselects are not available in MySQL, whereas they are available in Postgre. These subselects not only save time but also increase processing speed since the records are retrieved based on multiple conditions.

◆ **Stability:** Postgre provides a more stable environment as compared to MySQL. A Postgre database server lasts longer and can handle more queries as compared to a MySQL server, which packs up the moment it is overloaded with a large number of queries.

◆ **Robustness:** Postgre databases offer a robust system that can withstand the severe load due to multiple simultaneous connections. Postgre can support approximately three times more simultaneous connections than the connections supported by MySQL. Similarly, MySQL doesn't provide a robust daemon, which is provided by PostgreSQL. This is highlighted due to its stable nature and its ability to handle more queries than MySQL without facing a problem.

◆ **Record-level locking:** Another advantage in using Postgre is that, while inserting records in the database, Postgre performs a record-level lock while MySQL locks the entire table. In this way, Postgre can handle multiple queries on the same table, while in the case of MySQL, the queries pile up and MySQL might crash.

◆ **Performance:** MySQL scores over PostgreSQL in the field of performance. This is because MySQL provides better performance because it supports a record of a size more than 8 KB. This is a size restriction in the case of PostgreSQL.

◆ **Database corruption:** This is a common problem in the case of Postgre, while in the case of MySQL, the database files are not corrupted as easily.

◆ **Load support:** MySQL can support an average number of transactions. However, if the number of simultaneous connections increases, the system may crash. This is not the case with PostgreSQL, which can support up to three times the number of connections supported by MySQL.

◆ **Display pages/second:** You can display a greater number of pages per second in the case of PostgreSQL. In the case of MySQL this number might be achieved but at the cost of wearing out the hardware.

◆ **Persistent connections:** Another advantage for Postgre is its use of the concept of persistent connections to its advantage. As an estimated figure, Postgre provides a 30 percent quicker query-resolving functionality due to its use of persistent connections. Therefore, Postgre saves time in repeatedly establishing connections and authentications. However, MySQL is not affected by this either way.

◆ **Triggers and views:** Postgre offers the facility of creating triggers and views to developers. This facility is not available in MySQL. A developer can store all the commands that need to be performed on a table or tables based on a condition. This trigger can then be executed whenever the condition becomes True. This saves not only time but also effort on the part of the processor in creating the same query repeatedly.

Looking at the above comparison carefully, you might conclude that both databases have their own advantages and disadvantages. Depending on your preference and requirements you can use either of these databases. For example, you might want to have scalability or you might want to implement transaction processing. Therefore, if you require the use of views, transactions, and subselects you might learn to use PostgreSQL, whereas if you just want the use of a simple Relational Database Management System you should stick with good old MySQL.

The PostgreSQL Architecture

PostgreSQL uses the each-user-separate-process client/server model to handle query resolving. PostgreSQL databases primarily contain three components. They are:

◆ A front-end application that resides at the client end

◆ A daemon process that receives queries from the client side, sends it to the appropriate database, and sends the output back to the client who issued the request

◆ Single or multiple databases at the back end that resolve the query

Applications attempt to establish a connection with a database by using a library. This request is sent to a daemon process known as the postmaster. The postmaster accepts requests from all the clients and redirects the requests to the appropriate database. A postmaster can administer a single database or multiple databases. If the connection is successfully established, a pointer to the database is returned back to the postmaster. The postmaster then sends this connection identifier back to the client application. The client application can then connect directly to the database server instead of connecting through the postmaster.

The library that is required to establish the connection between the application and the postmaster is the libpq library. The client application needs to use this library to establish multiple connections to various databases. However, the LIBPQ library is still a single threaded application and doesn't allow multiple connections to be executed simultaneously. This necessitates that both the databases as well as the postmaster run on the same machine. The process is shown in Figure C-1.

 NOTE

Another point to be remembered is that both the postmaster daemon and the Postgre servers run using the same user ID, superuser, that is available in Postgre. The Postgre superuser is in no way related to the root user available in Linux. As a result, all the file rights that are related to the database files should only be assigned to the Postgre superuser.

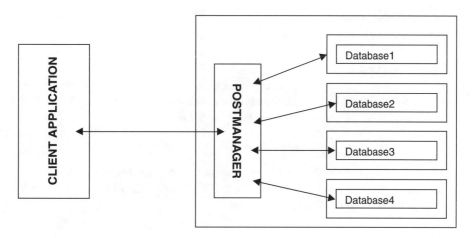

FIGURE C-1 *The PostgreSQL architecture*

In the next section, you'll learn to install and configure Postgre on your machine to make it work successfully with your PHP scripts.

Installing and Configuring PostgreSQL

Before you install Postgre, make sure that the following minimum prerequisites are met:

◆ A Unix-compatible platform to run PostgreSQL

◆ Pentium 166 MHz

◆ 16 MB RAM

◆ At least 110 MB disk space (50 MB to unpack the source, 60 MB to install and compile the source; if you are planning to run regression tests, you'll need an extra 20 MB disk space)

 NOTE

You can use the df command to determine the disk space available on your machine.

◆ GNU tools

 NOTE

If you are running Linux, the GNU tools will already be installed. You can test whether GNU tools have been installed by using the following command:

```
gmake --version
```

If the GNU version is displayed, you have GNU tools installed. If you need to install GNU, make sure that you install version 3.76.1 or later. You can download the latest GNU package at **ftp://ftp.gnu.org/gnu/**.

◆ ISO/ANSI C Complier

 NOTE

The latest version of GCC is recommended. However, PostgreSQL works with most of the C compilers available today.

Additional utilities might also be useful during installation. These include utilities such as GNU Readline Library (for increasing the readability and usability of the Postgre command-line console), OpenSSL (to make the connections between the Postgre client and the back end secure), and Ant/JDK (for supporting JDBC).

 CAUTION

The disk space requirements of Postgre, being a database system, will increase with time. Therefore, you need to carefully plan the amount of data you'll store on the Postgre database server.

Download the source file and save the file in /usr/src/pgsql, or move it to this location after it is finished downloading. Now that you have the source file and have met all the installation requirements, you can begin installing and configuring PostgreSQL by following the steps given below:

1. Create a separate user account to manage the Postgre databases and related system files.

CAUTION

Do not use the `root` account for management of Postgre databases and files because it can cause a security lapse to your Linux (or Unix) server.

2. Move into the `/usr/src/pgsql` directory and unpack the downloaded source file. Use the following command to do so:

```
tar -xzvf postgresql-7.1.3.tar.gz
```

NOTE

Verisign is one of the well-known Certificate Authorities (CAS).

3. Grant the ownership of the Postgre source directory to the user who will manage Postgre databases and files. The command to do so is:

```
chown -R postgres.<username> postgresql-7.1.3
```

Log out as `root` and log in as the user who will manage Postgre. (You created this user in step 1.)

4. Now you need to compile the Postgre source tree. Type the following command to do so:

```
./configure
```

The above command uses the default installation script, checks for software dependencies, and creates the necessary files for the working of Postgre.

5. Next you need to compile the Postgre source. Type the following command to do so:

```
gmake
```

NOTE

The source compilation may take some time.

6. Next you need to perform a regression test to verify that Postgre is functioning properly and commands are executing correctly. The command
   to do so is:

   ```
   gmake check
   ```

   This step is optional but recommended because it can point to possible
   problems that can hamper the performance of Postgre.

CAUTION

If you are still logged in as root, you'll not be able to execute this command. You
need to be logged in as Postgre superuser to run this command.

7. Now you need to install compiled programs and libraries. The command
   to do so is:

   ```
   su -c "gmake install"
   ```

   You will be prompted for the root password. The above command will
   compile the source and install it into the directory structure where you
   compiled the Postgre source tree (step 4).

CAUTION

Back up your database before you perform this step.

8. The next step is to set environmental variables. Add the following statement to the /etc/profiles file:

```
PATH=$PATH:/usr/local/pgsql/bin
MANPATH=$MANPATH:/usr/local/pgsql/man
export PATH MANPATH
```

This step is optional but recommended because environmental variables are helpful for the performance of Postgre and shutting down and starting the postmaster.

9. Log in to the system as root. This will allow your operating system to utilize the new setting of environmental variables.

10. Type the following command to restart and initialize PostgreSQL:

```
/usr/local/pgsql/bin/initdb -D /usr/local/pgsql/data
```

This command will also set the directory where Postgre data will be stored (/usr/local/pgsql/data in our case).

11. The last step in the installation process is to verify the working of PostgreSQL. Type the following command:

```
createdb mytest
```

If the message CREATE DATABASE is displayed on the screen, the command and the entire installation and configuration process were successful.

The next section briefly covers the basic Postgre concepts.

PostgreSQL Concepts

A PostgreSQL database consists of the following components (or entities):

◆ **Classes:** Better known as a table, a class is a systematic collection of information in a database. A database contains many tables and each table maintains data about a specific object or entity. For example, an Employee table would contain personal information about all the employees of a company. Similarly, a Customer table would contain details about customers, and a table called Sales would contain the company's sales information. Just as each cabinet has a label that helps you to identify the content of the cabinet or shelf without actually opening the cabinet, similarly, each table has a unique name that helps you to identify the table's content.

◆ **Object Instances (Records):** Also referred to as rows in everyday language, Records are separate pieces of information about an entity. This information is grouped together and stored in a table. Each piece of information is stored in a separate field. For example, if the book Living Life without Fear has been issued, then a corresponding record should be created in the Transactions table. Similarly, the details about the book would be a record in the Books table, and the details about the member would be a separate record in the Members table.

NOTE

Each record (or row) in a table has a permanent object identifier (OID) associated with it. This OID is unique for a given database cluster.

◆ **Attributes (Fields):** Also referred to as columns, the fields of a table are nothing but the attributes that best explain the characteristics specific to an entity whose details are stored in a table. All the data stored in separate columns can contain both text as well as numeric data. However, depending on your requirement, you can even restrict the type of data that can be stored in each field. For example, you can restrict the content of the field containing members' phone numbers to only accept numeric values or the Return date field of the Transactions table to only contain dates. Just as in the case of a table, a field of a table also has a unique name, called the field name, which you can use to reference each field separately.

◆ **Database Clusters:** A collection of databases that are managed by a single postmaster process is referred to as a database cluster.

I wouldn't bore you by repeating the database basics, as they mostly remain the same for all database systems. However, in the next section I discuss the database programming basics that are specific to Postgre.

NOTE

The terms classes, object instances, and attributes are a throwback to the object-relational aspect of PostgreSQL. However, I will continue to use the terms tables, rows, and columns in the rest of this appendix.

PostgreSQL Database Programming

There are many commands available in Postgre that you can use to perform database administration tasks, such as creating databases and tables and viewing their structure. Postgre also provides commands for the insertion, modification, and deletion of records from a database.

Let's begin by understanding how to perform administrative tasks on a database.

Using the *mysqladmin* Command

Like administering any other database system, administering Postgre databases involves numerous tasks. Some of the most common tasks include the following:

- Creating databases
- Deleting databases
- Checking the status of a database
- Resetting the values of the variables in a database

You use the `mysqladmin` command available in MySQL to perform these tasks. The syntax of the command is as follows:

```
# mysqladmin [options] Command1, Command2 ...
```

Table C-1 lists the different tasks that you can perform by using `mysqladmin`.

Table C-1 Commands in PostgreSQL

Command	Task
create <database name>	To create a database with the specified name.
drop <database name>	To delete the specific database along with all its tables.

continues

Table C-1 *(continued)*

Command	Task
extended-status	To display the extended status information from the server.
flush-tables	To clear all the table information.
flush-host	To clear all the cached information.
flush-threads	To clear all the stored thread information.
flush-logs	To clear all the logged information about the server.
password	To change the password.
ping	To check and monitor connectivity with the mysql daemon.
refresh	To clear all the table information and to refresh all the logs.
shutdown	To shut down the server.
status	To display the status information at the command prompt.
variables	To print all the information about variables.
version	To display the version information from the server.

In the next section, you will learn to use the PostgreSQL interactive monitor. You can use the PostgreSQL monitor to perform many tasks, such as creating databases and tables.

Using the PostgreSQL Interactive Monitor (*psql*)

MySQL is an effective database server developed by MySQL AB. The source code of MySQL is freely available and can be downloaded free of cost from the site **ftp://ftp.postgresql.org/pub/**. The software is compatible with both Windows and Linux platforms.

PostgreSQL is an open source Object Relational Database Management System that provides the facility to manage databases. Therefore, you can also modify its source code to meet your requirements. Postgre also provides the following features:

◆ Support for languages such as Perl, Python, and PHP

- ◆ Support for a thread-based memory allocation system (therefore, it is quite fast)
- ◆ Support for fixed as well as variable length records
- ◆ Support for a host-based verification system that provides security through verifying passwords that are encrypted during transit
- ◆ Support for large databases
- ◆ Support for different types of field datatypes
- ◆ Support for Unix sockets, TCP/IP sockets, and Named Pipes for providing connectivity

To start PostgreSQL, enter the following command at the command prompt:

```
psql template1
```

Now that you have used the PostgreSQL monitor, you can execute the Postgre commands for creating databases and tables and for adding, modifying, and deleting records from the tables.

Creating Databases

In the previous section, you learned that you can create a database by using the `create <database>` command at the command prompt. However, you do not need to always execute this command from outside the Postgre environment. You can also use the `create` command from inside Postgre. The syntax of the command is as follows:

```
createdb test
```

You should have proper privileges create the database. Otherwise, you will end up with an error message, as shown in Figure C-2.

```
% createdb test
NOTICE:user "your username" is not allowed to create/destroy databases
createdb: database creation failed on test
```

FIGURE C-2 *Output when you create a database with proper privilege*

CAUTION

Unlike MySQL, do not end any command in PostgreSQL with a semicolon (;). Ending a command with a semicolon generates an error.

The command to access a database that you have created is as follows:

```
psql test
```

The output of the above command is shown in Figure C-3.

```
Welcome to the POSTGRESQL interactive sql monitor:
  Please read the file COPYRIGHT for copyright terms of POSTGRESQL

    type \? for help on slash commands
    type \q to quit
    type \g or terminate with semicolon to execute query
 You are currently connected to the database: test
```

FIGURE C-3 *Accessing a database*

After a database has served its purpose and is no longer required, you should delete or drop it. This is important because if you do not delete the database, it occupies unnecessary disk space and is a burden on the system's memory. The syntax for dropping a database is given below:

```
dropdb test
```

The above command will search for a database named test and delete it.

CAUTION

This action will physically remove all the files associated with the database. However, this action is irreversible. Therefore, delete a database only when you are sure that there is no use for it.

In the next section, you'll learn to create tables in a database using PostgreSQL.

Creating Tables

In the previous section, you learned to create and delete a database. In this section, you will learn to create a table and store data in it. You can create different tables to store different types of data. For example, you can create a Books table to store information about books and an Authors table to store information about authors.

The first step while creating a table is to obtain access to the database. Obtaining access implies gaining control of a database so that you can make modifications to it or create tables in it. After you have gained access to a database, you can use the different commands available in it to create tables and to view their structure.

Now we will look at how we can perform these tasks.

Using a Database

As explained earlier, the first step in creating a table is to obtain access to the database in which you want to insert the table. You use the syntax given below to access a database. At the PostgreSQL prompt, enter the code given below:

```
psql dbname
```

CAUTION

You must ensure that the specified database already exists before you try the above command.

Now that you have gained access to the database, you can begin to construct tables for the database. However, before you go on to the actual creation of a table, you need to know about the different field types available in PostgreSQL. Each field in a table needs to belong to a specific datatype. You will learn about these datatypes in the next section.

Field Datatypes in PostgreSQL

As you already know, tables contain a set of fields that you can use to store values. The field types are the datatypes that determine the type of data that can be stored in each field. These field types and their descriptions are listed in Table C-2.

Table C-2 Field Datatypes in PostgreSQL

Type	Description
bigint	Used to store integer values. This is similar to int, the only difference being that you can store a maximum of 9,223,372,036,854,775,806 numeric values.
blob/text	Used to store strings of characters. The fields can store a maximum of 65,535 characters.
char	Used to store the string type data.
date	Used to store date values. The values are stored in the yyyy-mm-dd format and range from 1000-01-01 to 9999-12-31.
datetime	Used to store the time along with the date.
float	Used to store decimal values.
int	Used to store integer type data. The maximum size of the datatype is 2,147,483,646 numeric values.
smallint	Used to store small integer values. A smallint field can store a maximum of 32,766 numeric values.
tinyint	Used to store integer values. This is the smallest of the integer datatypes and can store a maximum of 126 numeric values.
varchar	Used to store string values but of a larger size than a char datatype.
year	Used to store the year value.

As you can see, Postgre supports the datatypes that are used in SQL and MySQL. Postgre also allows you to create your own customized datatypes.

Using the create *Command to Construct Tables*

You have already obtained access to the database named Books. Now you will learn to create new tables in the database. The syntax for creating a table is given below.

```
mysql> create tablename (first_fieldname fieldtype, second_fieldname fieldtype,
... ,n_fieldname fieldtype);
```

You will now use the preceding syntax to create a table named Products, which has five fields. The fields and their datatypes are shown in the code given below.

```
create table Products (
Productid   bigint(20)    NOT NULL   auto_increment
     primary key,
Name varchar(40)    NOT NULL   default '',
Description   varchar(200)   NOT NULL   default '',
Price   varchar(20)   NOT NULL   default '',
Category   varchar(20)   NOT NULL   default '',
)
```

The above code creates a table named Products, which contains fields with the following characteristics:

◆ The table contains five fields: Productid, Name, Description, Price, and Category.

◆ The Productid field is of the *bigint* datatype and can contain a numeric value, with a maximum size of 20 characters. It also cannot contain a NULL value, and the value is auto incremental in nature. This means that every new record takes the previous record's Productid and adds one to it to create the current record's Productid value.

◆ The name field is also of the *varchar* datatype and contains a string with a maximum of 40 characters. The content of the filed cannot be NULL.

◆ The Description field is of the *varchar* datatype and has the maximum size of 200 characters. This field also cannot contain a NULL value.

◆ The Price field is of the *varchar* datatype and can contain a maximum of 20 characters.

◆ The Category field will contain the category to which the product belongs. This field also belongs to the *varchar* datatype and can contain a maximum of 20 characters.

◆ The primary key for the table is Productid. This means that this field will have unique values and the records in the table are indexed based on these values.

The create statement resembles the statement used in traditional RDBMS. Now that you have learned to create a table, you will learn to review the contents of a database and list the tables that it contains.

Viewing the Table in a Database

While you are working with a database, you might not remember the different tables you have created in it. You might also not remember the name of a specific table in the database. PostgreSQL provides a command that you can use to list the various tables in the database. In the current example, you will display the table you just created in Books.

MySQL provides the show tables command to display all the tables available in the currently open database. The syntax of the command is given below:

```
show tables;
```

Suppose you are working with multiple tables. How will you keep track of which table contains which fields? In the next section, you will learn how you can review the structure of a table.

Viewing the Table Structure

You might also want to find out the fields that are available in a table. MySQL provides a command to view the structure of a table. The command to view the fields available in a table is given below:

```
explain Products;
```

You can use the above command to find out the fields of a table (Products, in the above case) and their datatypes. This information is important while designing queries because unless you know the fields that are available in a table, you cannot create effective queries.

As you can see, the output contains six columns. The names of these columns and their explanations are given below:

◆ **Field:** This column contains the names of the fields that were specified while creating the table.

◆ **Type:** This column contains the datatypes for each field. As explained previously, the datatype can be *text*, *char*, *integer*, *varchar*, *float*, or any one of the datatypes listed in Table C-2. These datatypes are specified at the time of creating the table. Once a datatype has been specified, the field can only contain data that belongs to the specific datatype. For example, if a field is of the *char* datatype, it will store text as characters or strings even if the text contains numbers. The maximum size of data that the field can store also appears within parentheses along with the datatype.

◆ **NULL:** This column determines if a field can contain a blank value. If a field is blank, it will contain a NULL value.

◆ **Key:** This column specifies which field is the primary key. A field that contains the primary key can contain only unique values, which means that you cannot repeat the same value for any other record. This also helps in indexing the values in the field. There can be a maximum of one primary key in each table, and none of the values in the field can be NULL.

◆ **Default:** This column specifies a default value for a field. You can set a default value for a field to be used in case the field is left blank at the time of data insertion. This column is critical for fields that have been set to Not NULL.

◆ **Extra:** This column specifies any extra information about the field that MySQL can use while executing queries.

Now that you know how to create a table, you will learn to add, modify, and delete records in the table.

Entering Data into a Table

Now that you have successfully created a table, let's discuss how you can enter data into the table. You can use the insert command to enter data. The syntax of the insert command is given below:

```
                    insert into <tablename> values ('value_for_field-
one', 'value_for_fieldtwo',

                'value_for_nthfield' );
```

Let's use the preceding syntax to insert new records in the table.

```
insert into Products values ('', 'Great
Expectations', 'Written by Charles
                    Dickens','200', 'Classic');
```

You can similarly add other products to the Products table. Let's add another record to it.

```
insert into Products values ('', 'Last of the
Mohicans', 'Written by James
                    Fenimore Cooper, '150', 'Classic');
```

Now that you have learned to insert records in a table, you will learn to view the data entered in the table.

Viewing the Data in a Table

Once all the data has been entered into a table, you might want to review it. You can use the select command for this purpose. The select command is used to retrieve the records from a table or tables based on certain conditions or criteria. The syntax of the command is shown below:

```
select [fieldname] from [tablename] where [expres-
sion] order by [fieldname];
```

The code given below retrieves all the records from the specified table:

```
select * from Products;
```

You can also restrict the output of the select command to specific fields by using the field names instead of an asterisk (*). For example, you can restrict the output to display only the Productid, Name, and Price of the product. The code to achieve this is given below:

```
select Productid, Name, Price from Products;
```

You can also restrict the output of the select command by using the where condition. In the next section, you will learn to use complex select statements to retrieve data based on specific conditions.

Complex select *Statements*

Now that you know the basic format of the select command, you will see how to use the select statement to create complex queries. As explained previously, you use the where clause if you need to search for specific information in the database. An example is given below:

```
select * from Products where Price =200;
```

The above code will display all the records in the Products table whose price is equal to 200. You can further qualify the where statement by using the comparison operators that you learned about in Chapter 4, "Control Structures." Table C-3 lists the comparison operators and their definitions.

 NOTE

The select command is a very powerful tool. You can use it to create queries that search multiple tables based on a criterion and return a specific output.

Table C-3 Comparison Operators

Operator	Purpose
==	Equal to
>	Greater than
<	Less than
>=	Greater than or equal to
<=	Less than or equal to
!=	Not equal to
like	Compares string text

You can also use the all and distinct keywords to select all or specific records from the database. The distinct keyword will return specific records from specific columns. It also ignores duplicate records retrieved from the columns specified in the select statement. An example is:

```
select distinct Category from Products;
```

The preceding code will return all the records containing unique categories from the `Products` table.

You can use the and and or operators to combine two or more conditions. The difference in the use of both the operators is their implementation. In case of the and operator, all the conditions need to be fulfilled for the record to be included in the output, whereas in the case of the or operator, even if one of the conditions returns True, the record is included in the output. In the example given below, the output will contain all the `Productids` whose `Category` is `Fiction` or whose `Price` ranges between `100` and `150`.

```
select Productid from Products where Category = 'Fiction' OR Price >100 AND
         Price<150;
```

Another clause that can be used along with the `select` statement is the `group by` clause. You use this clause to group the records containing similar data in specific columns. Once the data is grouped, you can use aggregate functions such as `sum` and `max` to perform calculations on this data. For example, in the code given below, all the records are grouped together based on the `Category` field, and the maximum price in each `Category` is displayed.

```
        max(Price), Product_id, Name from Products GROUP BY Category;
```

Having learned about inserting records, you will learn, in the next section, to modify the existing records in a table.

Modifying the Data in a Table

You can use the `update` command to make changes to the data stored in a table. You can make changes to a single record or to multiple records in a database. A point that you need to remember is that the `update` command does not return a set of records—it only makes changes to the data in the database. The syntax of the `update` command is given below:

```
                    update <tablename> set <fieldname> = '<New
value>' ;
```

For example, you can change the value for the `Category` field of all the records to `Fiction`.

```
update Products set Category = 'Fiction';
                    select * from Products;
```

You can also use the where clause to narrow down the update based on a specific condition. For example, you may want to increase the price of the products whose value is more than 150 to 200. The code to do so is given below:

```
update Products set Price = '200' where Price >
150;
```

You can also use the update statement to modify records in multiple tables based on a condition. This type of updating is called cascade updation since the changes made in one table are reflected in all the related tables.

After having learned how to insert and modify the records in a table, you must be curious about how to delete records from a table. The next section covers this aspect.

Deleting Data from a Table

You can delete information from a table by using the delete command. You can delete single or multiple records from a table by using this command. You can also use the where clause with the delete command to delete records based on certain conditions.

CAUTION

Just as you need to be cautious while deleting a database, you also need to be cautious while deleting records. This is because once a record is deleted, it cannot be recovered.

The syntax of the command for deleting a record is given below:

```
delete <fieldname> from <tablename> [where expres-
sion];
```

You can use the code given below to delete the records of all the products whose price is below 200.

```
delete from Products where Price<200;
```

CAUTION

If you do not specify a field name, then all the records in the table will be deleted.

You must now be confident about adding, modifying, and deleting records from a table. However, suppose you need to modify the structure of a table. The next section explains this concept in detail.

Modifying the Table Structure

You can modify the structure of a table by using the `alter` command. You can perform the following tasks by using the `alter` command.

◆ Adding a column to a table:

```
alter table <tablename> add <newfield>
<definition> ;
```

◆ Changing the datatype of a table:

```
alter table <tablename> change <column-
name> <newdefinition>;
```

◆ Indexing a table:

```
alter table <tablename> add index <column-
name> (<columnname>) ;
```

◆ Adding a unique column to a table:

```
alter table <tablename> add unique <column-
name> (<columnname>) ;
```

◆ Deleting a column from a table:

```
alter table <tablename> drop <columnname>;
```

By now, you must be comfortable with using databases and tables in PostgreSQL. However, this is just elementary information and you'll need to explore more to be conversant with PostgreSQL. Refer to the PostgreSQL manual for detailed information.

Appendix D

**A Ready Reckoner
to Basic HTML
Tags**

Table D-1 HTML Tags and Their Uses

Name	Tag	Description
HTML	<HTML> ... </HTML>	Is used to create an HTML document.
Head	<head> ... </head>	Is used to specify the title for the Web page and other hidden information about the Web page.
Body	<body> ... </body>	Is used to declare the body of the Web page. The body will contain all the elements that would actually appear on the Web page.
Heading	<h*i*>	Is used to format text headings. The heading tags range from h1 to h6. The h1 tag displays the heading in the smallest font, while the h6 heading displays the heading in the largest font.
Break Line	 	Is used to insert lines between text.
Paragraph	<p> ... </p>	Is used to insert lines amid paragraphs.
Comment	<!-- ... -->	Is used to insert comments along with the code.
Font	<font> ... </font>	Is used to specify the fonts for text.
Boldface	<b> ... </b>	Is used to make text bold.
Italics	<I> ... </I>	Is used to italicize text.
Subscript	_{...}	Is used to change the font of text to subscript.
Superscript	^{...}	Is used to change the font of text to superscript.
Underline	<u> ... </u>	Is used to underline text.

Name	Tag	Description
Code	<code> ... </code>	Is used to display code along with plain text.
Title	<title> ... </title>	Is used to specify the title for the Web page.
Pre	<pre> ... </pre>	Is used to create preformatted text. All the text included between the tags is displayed in the same format as it is specified in the code.
Citation	<cite> ... </cite>	Is used while creating a citation that is usually in italics.
Emphasis	<em> ... </em>	Is used to emphasize a word. The text generally appears as either bold or italic.
Strong	<strong> ... </strong>	Is used to emphasize a word. The text generally appears as either bold or italic.
Blockquote	<blockquotes> ... </blockquotes>	Is used to indent text from both sides.
Div	<div> ... </div>	Is used to format large blocks of HTML and is also used in style sheets.
Center	<center> ... </center>	Is used to center align graphics and text on the Web page.
Definition List	<dl> ... </dl>	Is used to create a definition list.
Definition Term	<dt>	Is used to specify a definition term.
Definition	<dd> ... </dd>	Is used to write a definition.
Numbered/Ordered	<ol> ... </ol>	Is used to create a numbered list.
List Numbering tag	<li>	Is used to add a number in front of each item in a numbered list.
Bulleted List	<ul> ... </ul>	Is used to create a bulleted list.

continues

Table D-1 *(continued)*

Name	Tag	Description
Bullets	<bl> [...] </bl>	Is used to add a bullet in front of each item in a bulleted list.
Table	<table> ... </table>	Is used to create a table list.
Row	<tr> ... </tr>	Is used to create a single row.
Cells	<td> ... </td>	Is used to create a single cell in a row.
Table Heading	<th> ... </th>	Is used to create a table header.
Table Border	<table border=i>	Is used to set the width of the border around the cells.
Cell Spacing	<table cellspacing=i>	Is used to set the amount of space that should appear between cells.
Cell Padding	<table cellpadding=i>	Is used to set the amount of space that should appear between the border of the cell and the content in the cell.
Table Width	<table width=i>	Is used to set the width of the table. This value can be set in pixels or as a percentage of the entire document.
Cell Alignment	<tr align = i>	Is used to set the horizontal alignment of (Horizontal) text within the cells. Text can be either top aligned, center aligned, or bottom aligned.
Cell Alignment	<tr valign = i>	Is used to set the vertical alignment of (Vertical) text within the cells. The text can be either top aligned, middle aligned, or bottom aligned.
Columnspan	<td colspan = i>	Is used to specify the number of columns a cell should span.
Rowspan	<td rowspan = i>	Is used to specify the number of rows a cell should span.

Name	Tag	Description
Textwrap	<td nowrap>	Is used to specify that the text should not wrap after it reaches the end of the line in a cell.
Adding Images	<img src= imgname>	Is used to add an image to the Web page.
Image Alignment	<img src= imgname align=i>	Is used to align an image in the Web page.
Image Border	<img src= imgname border=i>	Is used to create a border around an image in the Web page.
Line tag	<hr>	Is used to add a single line to the Web page.
Font Size	<font size = i> ... </font>	Is used to set the size of a font. The size ranges from 1 to 7.
Font Color	<font color= ?> ... </font>	Is used to set the color of a font. The value can either be a fixed hexadecimal value or the font name.
Hyperlink	<a href = "URL"> ... </a>	Is used to create a hyperlink.
Mailto	<a href= mailto:EMAIL> ... </a>	Is used to create a mailto hyperlink.
Target	<a name = 'linkname"> ... </a>	Creates a target link within a document.
Accessing Target	<a href = '#linkname'> ...	Is used to link to the target from a different </a> location of the Web page.

These are the common tags that are used in HTML scripts. You can search for other tags on the Internet.

Appendix E

A Ready Reckoner to PHP Functions

Table E-1 Mathematical Functions and Their Uses

Name	Syntax	Description
abs	mixed abs(mixed number)	Is used to return the absolute value of a specified number. The return type depends on the datatype of the parameter.
acos	float acos(float argm)	Is used to return the arc cosine of the specified argument in radians.
asin	float asin(float argm)	Is used to return the arc sine of arguments in radians.
atan	float atan(float argm)	Is used to return the arc tangent of arguments in radians.
atan2	float atan2(float X, float Y)	Is used to calculate the arc tangent between the two variables X and Y. The result is returned in the form of radians.
ceil	float ceil(float value)	Is used to return the highest integer value derived after rounding off the value in the parameter. Return type is also float.
cos	float cos(float argn)	Is used to return the cosine of the arguments passed.
decbin	string decbin(int number)	Is used to return the binary value of the number passed as the parameter. The return datatype is a string type.
dechex	string dechex(int number)	Is used to return the hexadecimal value of the passed numeric value.
decoct	string decoct(int number)	Is used to return a string of octal values derived from the passed numeric value.

Name	Syntax	Description
exp	float exp(float argm)	Is used to calculate the exponential value of the passed argument e to the power of a value.
floor	float floor(float value)	Is used to retrieve the lowest number after rounding off the passed parameter value. The return type is float.
getrandmax	int getrandmax()	Is used to retrieve the largest possible value returned by the rand() function.
hexdec	int hexdec(string hex_str)	Is used to return the decimal value derived from the passed hexadecimal string.
log	float log(float argm)	Is used to return the natural logarithm of the argument passed as the parameter.
log10	float log10(float argm)	Is used to return the base-10 logarithm of the value passed as the argument.
octdec	int octdec(string octal_str)	Is used to retrieve the decimal value of the passed octal number.
pi	float pi()	Is used to retrieve the approximate value of pi.
pow	number pow(number base, number exp)	Is used to calculate the value of the parameter base raised to the power of the value exp.
rand	int rand() or int rand(int minimum, int maximum)	Is used to return a random value between the minimum and maximum values. If no parameter is provided, then the function returns a value between 0 and the RAND_MAX value.

continues

Table E-1 *(continued)*

Name	Syntax	Description
round	float round(float val [, int digitnum)	Is used to round off a float value. The digitnum value defines where the decimal point should be placed.
sin	float sin(float argm)	Is used to return the sine value of the arguments passed as parameters.
sqrt	float sqrt(float argm)	Is used to return the square root of the float variable passed as an argument.
tan	float tan(float argn)	Is used to return the tangent value of the passed arguments in radians.

Table E-2 String Functions and Their Uses

Name	Syntax	Description
bin2hex	string bin2hex(string str)	Is used to return a string containing ASCII values. This string is the hexadecimal representation of the value passed in the parameter str.
chr	string chr(int ascii)	Is used to return a single character based on the ascii value (*i*) passed to the function.
echo	echo (string arg1, string [argn] ...)	Is used to display the string passed as the parameter.
explode	array explode(string separator, string str [, int limit])	Is used to return an array of strings derived from an originally large string.
get_meta_tags	array get_meta_tags(string filename [, int use_include_path])	Is used to remove all the tags from the file passed as a parameter.

Name	Syntax	Description
implode	string implode(string connect, array sections)	Is used to create a single string by combining all the elements in the sections array and include the connect string between each element.
join	string join(string connect, array sections)	Is used to joint the elements of the sections array. Identical to implode.
ltrim	string ltrim (string str [, string charlist])	Is used to remove all the whitespaces from the beginning of the string.
md5	string md5(string str)	Is used to calculate the md5 value of the string passed as a parameter.
metaphone	string metaphone(string str)	Is used to determine the derived metaphone value of the string passed as the parameter.

Table E-3 Array Functions and Their Uses

Name	Syntax	Description
array_count_values	array array_count_values (array input)	Is used to return an array using the values of the input array as keys and their frequency in input as values.
array_diff	array array_diff (array array1, array array2 [, array ...])	Is used to return an array containing all the values of array1 that are not present in any of the other arguments. Note that keys are preserved.
array_filter	array array_filter (array input [, mixed callback])	Is used to filter elements of an array using a callback function.

continues

Table E-3 *(continued)*

Name	Syntax	Description
array_flip	array array_flip (array trans)	Is used to flip all the values of an array.
array_intersect	array array_intersect (array array1, array array2 [, array …])	Is used to compute the intersection of arrays.
array_keys	array array_keys (array input, mixed [search_value])	Is used to return all the keys of an array.
array_map	array array_map (mixed callback, array arr1 [, array arr2 …])	Is used to apply the callback to the elements of the given arrays.
array_merge	array array_merge (array array1, array array2 [, array …])	Is used to merge two or more arrays.
array_merge_recursive	array array_merge_recursive (array array1, array array2 [,array …])	Is used to merge two or more arrays recursively.
array_push	int array_push (array array, mixed var [, mixed …])	Is used to push one or more elements onto the end of an array.
array_rand	mixed array_rand (array input [, int num_req])	Is used to pick one or more random entries out of an array.
array_reduce	mixed array_reduce (array input, mixed callback [, int initial])	Is used to iteratively reduce the array to a single value using a callback function.
array_reverse	array array_reverse (array array [, bool preserve_keys])	Is used to return an array with elements in reverse order.
array_search	mixed array_search (mixed needle, array haystack, bool strict)	Is used to search the array for a given value and return the corresponding key if successful.
array_shift	mixed array_shift (array array)	Is used to pop an element off the beginning of an array.
array_slice	array array_slice (array array, int offset, int [length])	Is used to extract a slice of the array.
array_splice	array array_splice (array input, int offset [, int length, array[replacement]])	Is used to remove a portion of the array and replace it with something else.

Name	Syntax	Description
array_sum	mixed array_sum (array arr)	Is used to calculate the sum of values in an array.
array_unique	array array_unique (array array)	Is used to remove duplicate values from an array.
array_unshift	int array_unshift (array array, mixed var, mixed ...)	Is used to push one or more elements onto the beginning of an array.
array_values	array array_values (array input)	Is used to return all the values of an array.
array_walk	int array_walk (array arr, string func [, mixed userdata])	Is used to apply a user function to every member of an array.
arsort	void arsort (array array [, int sort_flags])	Is used to sort an array in reverse order and maintain index association.
asort	void asort (array array [, int sort_flags])	Is used to sort an array and maintain index association.
compact	array compact (mixed varname [, mixed ...])	Is used to create an array containing variables and their values.
count	int count (mixed var)	Is used to count elements in a variable.
each	array each (array array)	Is used to return the current key and value pair from an array and advance the array cursor.
end	mixed end (array array)	Is used to set the internal pointer of an array to its last element.
extract	int extract (array var_array [, int extract_type [, string prefix]])	Is used to import variables into the symbol table from an array.
in_array	bool in_array (mixed needle, array haystack [, bool strict])	Is used to return TRUE if a value exists in an array.
key	mixed key (array array)	Is used to fetch a key from an associative array.

continues

Table E-3 (continued)

Name	Syntax	Description
ksort	int ksort (array array [, int sort_flags])	Is used to sort an array by key.
list	void list (...)	Is used to assign variables as if they were an array.
natsort	void natsort (array array)	Is used to sort an array using a natural order algorithm.
next	mixed next (array array)	Is used to advance the internal array pointer of an array.
pos	mixed pos (array array)	Is used to get the current element from an array.
prev	mixed prev (array array)	Is used to rewind the internal array pointer.
range	array range (mixed low, mixed high)	Is used to create an array containing a range of elements.
rsort	void rsort (array array [, int sort_flags])	Is used to sort an array in reverse order.
shuffle	void shuffle (array array)	Is used to shuffle an array.
sizeof	int sizeof (mixed var)	Is used to get the number of elements in a variable.
sort	void sort (array array [, int sort_flags])	Is used to sort an array.
uasort	void uasort (array array, function cmp_function)	Is used to sort an array with a user-defined comparison function and maintain index association.
uksort	void uksort (array array, function cmp_function)	Is used to sort an array by keys using a user-defined comparison function.
usort	void usort (array array, string cmp_function)	Is used to sort an array by values using a user-defined comparison function.

Table E-4 Date and Time Functions and Their Uses

Name	Syntax	Description
checkdate	int checkdate (int month, int day, int year)	Is used to validate a Gregorian date/time.
date	string date (string format, int [timestamp])	Is used to format a local time/date.
datetime		Is used to parse about any English textual description into a Unix timestamp.
getdate	array getdate ([int timestamp])	Is used to determine the date/time information.
gettimeofday	array gettimeofday ()	Is used to determine the current time.
gmdate	string gmdate (string format [, int timestamp])	Is used to format a GMT/CUT date/time.
localtime	array localtime (int [timestamp], bool [is_associative])	Is used to determine the local time.
mktime	int mktime (int hour, int minute, int second, int month, int day, int year [, int is_dst])	Is used to determine the Unix timestamp for a given date.
strftime	string strftime (string format, int [timestamp])	Is used to format a local time/date according to locale settings.
strtotime	int strtotime (string time [, int now])	Is used to sort the specified date and time.
time	int time ()	Is used to return the current Unix timestamp.

Table E-5 Directory Functions and Their Uses

Name	Syntax	Description
chdir	bool chdir (string directory)	Is used to change directory.
chroot	bool chroot (string directory)	Is used to change the root directory.
closedir	void closedir (resource dir_handle)	Is used to close directory handle.
getcwd	string getcwd ()	Is used to get the current working directory.
opendir	resource opendir (string path)	Is used to open directory handle.
readdir	string readdir (resource dir_handle)	Is used to read entry from directory handle.
rewinddir	void rewinddir (resource dir_handle)	Is used to rewind directory handle.

Table E-6 File Functions and Their Uses

Name	Syntax	Description
chgrp	int chgrp (string filename, mixed group)	Is used to change file group.
chmod	int chmod (string filename, int mode)	Is used to change file mode.
chown	int chown (string filename, mixed user)	Is used to change file owner.
copy	int copy (string source, string dest)	Is used to copy files.
dirname	string dirname (string path)	Is used to return directory name component of path.
diskfreespace	float diskfreespace (string directory)	Is used to return available space in directory.
fclose	bool fclose (int fp)	Is used to close an open file pointer.
feof	int feof (int fp)	Is used to test for end-of-file on a file pointer.
fflush	int fflush (int fp)	Is used to flush the output to a file.

Name	Syntax	Description
fgetc	string fgetc (int fp)	Is used to get character from file pointer.
fgets	string fgets (int fp, int length)	Is used to get line from file pointer.
file	array file (string filename [, int use_include_path])	Is used to read entire file into an array.
file_exists	bool file_exists (string filename)	Is used to check whether a file exists.
fileatime	int fileatime (string filename)	Is used to get last access time of file.
filectime	int filectime (string filename)	Is used to get inode change time of file.
filegroup	int filegroup (string filename)	Is used to get file group.
filemtime	int filemtime (string filename)	Is used to get file modification time.
fileowner	int fileowner (string filename)	Is used to get file owner.
fileperms	int fileperms (string filename)	Is used to get file permissions.
filetype	string filetype (string filename)	Is used to get file type.
flock	bool flock (int fp, int operation, int [wouldblock])	Is used to provide portable advisory file locking.
fopen	int fopen (string filename, string mode, int [use_include_path])	Is used to open file or URL.
fputs	int fputs (int fp, string str, int [length])	Is used to write to a file pointer.
fread	string fread (int fp, int length)	Is used to perform the binary-safe file read operation.
fscanf	mixed fscanf (int handle, string format [, string var1 ...])	Is used to parse input from a file according to a format.
fseek	int fseek (int fp, int offset [, int whence])	Is used to seek a file pointer.
fstat	array fstat (int fp)	Is used to get information about a file using an open file pointer.
ftell	int ftell (int fp)	Is used to tell file pointer read/write position.

continues

Table E-6 (continued)

Name	Syntax	Description
fwrite	int fwrite (int fp, string string, int [length])	Is used to perform the binary-safe file write operation.
is_dir	bool is_dir (string filename)	Is used to tell whether the file name is a directory.
is_executable	bool is_executable (string filename)	Is used to determine whether the file name is executable.
is_file	bool is_file (string filename)	Is used to tell whether the file name is a regular file or not.
is_readable	bool is_readable (string filename)	Is used to tell whether the file name is readable.
is_uploaded_file	bool is_uploaded_file (string filename)	Is used to tell whether the file was uploaded via HTTP POST.
is_writable	bool is_writable (string filename)	Is used to tell whether the file name is writable.
mkdir	int mkdir (string pathname, int mode)	Is used to make a directory.
pathinfo	array pathinfo (string path)	Is used to return information about a file path.
pclose	int pclose (int fp)	Is used to close process file pointer.
popen	int popen (string command, string mode)	Is used to open process file pointer.
Readfile	int readfile (string filename, int [use_include_path])	Is used to read a file and write it to standard output.
rename	int rename (string oldname, string newname)	Is used to rename a file.
rmdir	int rmdir (string dirname)	Is used to remove directory.
stat	array stat (string filename)	Is used to give information about a file.
umask	int umask (int mask)	Is used to change the current umask.
unlink	int unlink (string filename)	Is used to delete a file.

Table E-7 HTTP and Mail Functions and Their Uses

Name	Syntax	Description
domain [,int secure]]]]])		Is used to send a cookie.
ezmlm_hash	int ezmlm_hash (string addr)	Is used to calculate the hash value needed by EZMLM.
header	int header (string string [, bool replace])	Is used to send a raw HTTP header.
mail	bool mail (string to, string subject, string message [, string additional_headers, string[additional_parameters]])	Is used to send mail.
setcookie	int setcookie (string name [, string value [, int expire [, string path [, string	

Table E-8 Mcrypt and Mhash Functions and Their Uses

Name	Syntax	Description
mcrypt_cbc	string mcrypt_cbc (int cipher, string key, string data, int mode [, string iv])	Is used to encrypt or decrypt data in CBC mode.
mcrypt_cfb	string mcrypt_cfb (int cipher, string key, string data, int mode, string iv)	Is used to encrypt or decrypt data in CFB mode.
mcrypt_ecb	string mcrypt_ecb (int cipher, string key, string data, int mode)	Is used to encrypt or decrypt data in ECB mode.
mcrypt_encrypt	string mcrypt_encrypt (string cipher, string key, string data, string mode, string [iv])	Is used to encrypt plain text with given parameters.
mcrypt_ofb	string mcrypt_ofb (int cipher, string key, string data, int mode, string iv)	Is used to encrypt or decrypt data in OFB mode.
mcrypt_get_block_size	int mcrypt_get_block_size (int cipher)	Is used to get the block size of the specified cipher.

continues

Table E-8 *(continued)*

Name	Syntax	Description
mcrypt_get_cipher_name	string mcrypt_get_cipher_ name (int cipher)	Is used to get the name of the specified cipher.
mcrypt_get_key_size	int mcrypt_get_key_size (int cipher)	Is used to get the key size of the specified cipher.
mhash	string mhash (int hash, string data, string [key])	Is used to compute hash.
mhash_count	int mhash_count ()	Is used to get the highest available hash ID.
mhash_get_block_size	int mhash_get_block_size (int hash)	Is used to get the block size of the specified hash.
mhash_get_hash_name	string mhash_get_hash_ name (int hash)	Is used to get the name of the specified hash.

Table E-9 Miscellaneous Functions and Their Uses

Name	Syntax	Description
constant	mixed constant (string name)	Is used to return the value of a constant.
die	void die (string message)	Is used to give the output of a message and terminate the current script.
eval	mixed eval (string code_str)	Is used to evaluate a string as PHP code.
exit	void exit (mixed status)	Is used to terminate current script.
leak	void leak (int bytes)	Is used to leak memory.
pack	string pack (string format [, mixed args ...])	Is used to pack data into binary string.
sleep	void sleep (int seconds)	Is used to delay execution.
uniqid	int uniqid (string prefix [, bool lcg])	Is used to generate a unique ID.

Name	Syntax	Description
unpack	array unpack (string format, string data)	Is used to unpack data from binary string.
usleep	void usleep (int micro_seconds)	Is used to delay execution in microseconds.

Table E-10 MySQL Functions and Their Uses

Name	Syntax	Description
mysql_affected_rows	int mysql_affected_rows (resource [link_identifier])	Is used to get number of affected rows in the previous MySQL operation.
mysql_change_user	int mysql_change_user (string user, string password, string [database], resource[link_identifier])	Is used to change logged-in user of the active connection.
mysql_close	bool mysql_close (resource [link_identifier])	Is used to close MySQL connection.
mysql_connect	resource mysql_connect (string [hostname [:port] [:/path/to/ socket]], string [username], string [password])	Is used to open a connection to a MySQL server.
mysql_create_db	int mysql_create_db (string database name, resource [link_identifier])	Is used to create a MySQL database.
mysql_db_query	resource mysql_db_query (string database, string query, resource [link_identifier])	Is used to send a MySQL query.
mysql_drop_db	bool mysql_drop_db (string database_name, resource [link_identifier])	Is used to drop (delete) a MySQL database.
mysql_fetch_array	array mysql_fetch_array (resource result, int [result_type])	Is used to fetch a result row as an associative array, a numeric array, or both.

continues

Table E-10 (continued)

Name	Syntax	Description
mysql_fetch_field	object mysql_fetch_field (resource result, int [field_offset])	Is used to get column information from a result and return as an object.
mysql_fetch_lengths	array mysql_fetch_lengths (resource result)	Is used to get the length of each output in a result.
mysql_fetch_row	array mysql_fetch_row (resource result)	Is used to get a result row as an enumerated array.
mysql_field_len	int mysql_field_len (resource result, int field_offset)	Is used to return the length of the specified field.
mysql_field_name	string mysql_field_name (resource result, int field_index)	Is used to get the name of the specified field in a result.
mysql_get_server_info	int mysql_get_server_info ([resource link_identifier])	Is used to get MySQL server information.
mysql_pconnect	resource mysql_pconnect (string [hostname [:port] [:/path/to/socket]] [, string username [,string password]])	Is used to open a persistent connection to a MySQL server.
mysql_query	resource mysql_query (string query [, resource link_identifier])	Is used to send a MySQL query.
mysql_result	mixed mysql_result (resource result, int row, mixed [field])	Is used to get result data.
mysql_tablename	string mysql_tablename (resource result, int i)	Is used to get table name of field.

Table E-11 PostgreSQL Functions and Their Uses

Name	Syntax	Description
pg_close	bool bool pg_close (int connection) (int connection)	Is used to close a PostgreSQL connection.
pg_cmdtuples	int pg_cmdtuples (int result_id)	Is used to return number of affected tuples.

Name	Syntax	Description
pg_connect	int pg_connect (string host, string port, string options, string tty, string dbname)	Is used to open a PostgreSQL connection.
pg_dbname	string pg_dbname (int connection)	Is used to get the database name.
pg_exec	int pg_exec (int connection, string query)	Is used to execute a query.
pg_fetch_array	array pg_fetch_array (int result, int row [, int result_type])	Is used to fetch a row as an array.
pg_fetch_row	array pg_fetch_row (int result, int row)	Is used to get a row as an enumerated array.
pg_fieldisnull	int pg_fieldisnull (int result_id, int row, mixed field)	Is used to test if a field is NULL.
pg_options	string pg_options (int connection_id)	Is used to get the options associated with the connection.
pg_pconnect	int pg_pconnect (string conn_string)	Is used to open a persistent PostgreSQL connection.
pg_result	mixed pg_result (int result_id, int row_number, mixed fieldname)	Is used to return values from a result identifier.
pg_tty	string pg_tty (int connection_id)	Is used to return the tty name associated with the connection.
pg_untrace	bool pg_untrace ([int connection])	Is used to disable tracing of a PostgreSQL connection.

Appendix F

Web Site Design Best Practices

This appendix discusses the best practices that you should follow if you want to put up a professional Web site, liked and appreciated by everybody who visits the site. This appendix runs you through these best practices. You can access detailed information regarding this topic at **http://www.state.oh.us/bestpr/**.

Web design best practices have been grouped into the following categories:

- Design best practices
- Style guide
- Selecting external links
- Search engines
- Navigation
- Universal accessibility
- Backup plans
- Usage tracking
- Security
- Advertisements
- Trademarks

You will learn the best practices in each category in the following sections.

Design Best Practices

Recommended by experts, the Web site design-related best practices include the following:

- Thoroughly study and analyze all the policies and services of various Web-hosting organizations and then choose a facility that best matches your requirements.
- Write an effective mission statement that precisely conveys the reason you have created the Web site.

- Analyze and determine the profile and requirements of your target audience.

- Assemble an experienced and innovative Web team.

- The sky is the limit when you are to design your Web site. Be as creative as possible and do not limit your imagination.

- Assess your resources, including the budget that has been allocated to you and your staff.

- Plan the tiniest detail of the layout of your site. Do not leave anything for chance or for later.

- After your plans are in place, design a template and test it thoroughly before plunging head-on into the process of site development. This is important because you don't want to waste resources unnecessarily.

- Get your supervisor to approve the design and template.

- After everything is in place, get your site up. It is important that you follow a schedule while you are developing your site. Otherwise, you might end up wasting a lot of time in trivial things initially and would end up finishing things in unnecessary haste.

- It is very important that you publicize your site properly before you launch it. Also, to keep in circulation, you might need to publicize now and then.

- Once the site is up and running, your job is not over. You need to perform regular maintenance activities to ensure smooth working of the site.

Style Guide

It is highly important that you develop and maintain a proper style guide for your site. This style guide must take care of the following aspects:

- A clearly defined purpose of the style guide.

- A clearly defined plan for creating the Web page.

- A well-defined format section that provides detailed outlines and guidelines for the home page, menus, submenus, elements, sections, subsections, a navigation plan, links within the various pages in the site and to external sites, the size of graphics used and how graphics are going to be used, FAQ handling, and indexing.

◆ A detailed technical documentation that outlines the environment, hardware and software resources, and platforms used to support the site.

Selecting External Links

If you are providing a link to an external site, you must remember to specify the following very clearly:

◆ The purpose (why?) you are redirecting users to the specified location.

◆ The authenticity, credibility, and accuracy of the information you are referring your user to. Another point that you should keep in mind here is that the information that you are referring your user to should be updated frequently. It's no use redirecting a user to useless and outdated information.

◆ The security and sensitive information (such as credit card) of the user visiting the site is not compromised.

◆ The site is fast, effective, and user-friendly. The user should not be lost!

Making Your Site Visible to Search Engines

Search engines are one of the most widely used Internet tools. Besides, a search engine also offers you as a site administrator a chance to make your site popular. Therefore, you need to keep the following things in mind:

◆ Make sure that your search engine is located at a conspicuous position on your Web site. It must stand out and not be lost among the graphical or other elements of your site.

◆ Do not base your site solely on metadata. This is because some popular search engines do not use metadata as search criteria.

◆ Repeat the keyword as much as you can. This will make a search engine locate your site fast and often.

◆ Register your site to multiple search engines. This will increase the visibility of your site.

Page Design and Navigation

The points that you should remember in this area are:

◆ Make sure that your site has a consistent appearance throughout. You can use a template to ensure this.

◆ The header tag (`<head>`) should include metadata to provide information on the author(s) of the Web site. In addition, the header tag should also provide information (with the help of the `<doctype>` tag) about the version of HTML being used. The site should also have a `<title>` tag so that the title (main theme) of the page (or site) is displayed to the user.

◆ In the text avoid dark backgrounds and garish colors. Also, avoid underlining words, because a user might mistake them for hyperlinks.

◆ The hyperlinking within the site must be logical. Always ensure that you provide a link to the main page in every page of your site. This way, even if users get lost, they can reach the main page again. From the main page, the user can always follow links to the desired location on your site.

◆ Always provide a feedback link so that users can tell you what they think about your site. This feature will help you tremendously in the improvement of the site.

◆ It is preferable that you provide the latest date when the information on your site was updated. Also, specify the URL of your page. This information will be reflected in the printouts and will help the user remember the address of your site. And specify your contact information in case a user needs to contact you.

◆ Avoid heavy use of graphics in your site. These tend to slow down your site. Also, offer the users the option to turn off graphics if they want to.

Universal Accessibility

The points to keep in mind to make your site universally liked and accessible include:

◆ Choose the colors and background of your site carefully. Lavish use of color may sound nice, but not all users will appreciate it. Choose color combinations carefully so that reading is not a difficult task. Also, keep the use of red and green colors to a minimum to help users who might be color-blind.

◆ Provide users accessing your site with low-end and slow machines or slow connections the option to turn off heavy graphics.

◆ While developing your site, test its functioning with a large number of browsers. This way you'll ensure that users using a particular browser are not denied the chance to view your site. Also, do not use tags that are browser-specific.

◆ Avoid the use of frames. Some browsers do not support this feature.

◆ Check for spelling mistakes and grammatical errors carefully and thoroughly. These oversights can create a negative impression on the user.

◆ If you are offering files at your site, make sure that the files are not unnecessarily heavy. Users will appreciate this thoughtfulness on your part.

◆ Make sure that if a user would like to contact you, there are many ways to do so. These might include an e-mail address, a fax number, or a telephone number.

Backup Plans

Make sure to have a contingency plan ready in case your Web server goes down. This will prevent total shutdown of your site and prevent your company or organization from suffering a heavy loss because of halting of business during downtime of the site. You can have a backup Web server for this purpose. In addition, make sure that business-related data is not lost. For this, you need to perform regular backup of data. If the budget allows, experts recommend that you keep the data backup on two separate backup servers, one of the backup servers being located offsite. Though expensive, this measure will doubly ensure the safety of your company data.

Usage Tracking

By tracking the usage of your site, you can predict user preferences and likings. This data helps you to identify loopholes and to plan your future actions. You can use various logs, such as access logs, error logs, and transfer logs, to trap this data. You can also use cookies for the same. However, most users do not trust cookies. As a result, warn your users about the use of cookies if you are using them on your site.

Security

Organizations and commercial setups invest a lot of money to put up a site and keep it going. Therefore, ensuring the security of your site is a very important aspect of your work and responsibility.

You need to assess possible risks to your site and the cost of security even before you launch your site. You must also formulate a well-defined user policy that lists the responsibilities of the users. The basic steps to secure your Web site include:

◆ Placement of Web servers in a safe location, where the physical access to the servers is strictly controlled.

◆ Use of firewalls and other security measures to prevent unauthorized access to your Web servers and site.

◆ Regular use and analysis of log files. This will help you identify the security loopholes and take measures accordingly.

◆ A well-planned backup measure in case of Web server failure. If you mirror data on more than one server, the possibility of total shutdown of your site is minimum.

Advertisements

The recommended best practices in this field include the following:

◆ Make sure that you clearly refer to the company, organization, or individual who owns a product.

◆ Preferably, avoid commercial logos, as they can make your site slow. You can simply provide the company or product information in plain text and a hyperlink to the requisite site. Interested users will follow the link.

◆ Avoid preferences to a particular product, such as Microsoft Internet Explorer or Netscape Navigator.

Trademarks

The facts that you need to remember here include the following:

◆ Make sure that the user who accesses the information on your site is well informed about the copyrights. If users need to reuse the information from your site, provide for a mechanism, such as an e-mail facility, where they can seek your permission.

◆ If you have used logos or trademarks of other organizations, commercial setups, or individuals, make sure that you provide proper reference.

Index